Strategic Financial Management

Dr. G. Ramesh Babu
M.Com., Ph.D., MAIMA,
Department of Commerce,
S.S.R.J. College,
Khammam - 507003 (A.P.).

Himalaya Publishing House
ISO 9001:2015 CERTIFIED

First Edition : 2013
Edition : 2016
Edition : 2025

Published by : Mrs. Meena Pandey
for **HIMALAYA PUBLISHING HOUSE PVT. LTD.,**
"Ramdoot", Dr. Bhalerao Marg, Girgaon, Mumbai - 400 004.
Phone: 022-23860170, 23863863; **Fax:** 022-23877178
E-mail: himpub@bharatmail.co.in; **Website:** www.himpub.com

Branch Offices :

New Delhi : "Pooja Apartments", 4-B, Murari Lal Street, Ansari Road, Darya Ganj, New Delhi - 110 002. Phone: 011-23270392, 23278631; Fax: 011-23256286

Nagpur : Kundanlal Chandak Industrial Estate, Ghat Road, Nagpur - 440 018. Mobile: 09325409992, 09325908881

Bengaluru : Plot No. 91-33, 2nd Main Road, Seshadripuram, Behind Nataraja Theatre, Bengaluru - 560 020. Phone: 080-41138821; Mobile: 09379847017, 09379847005

Hyderabad : No. 3-4-184, Lingampally, Besides Raghavendra Swamy Matham, Kachiguda, Hyderabad - 500 027. Phone: 040-27560041, 27550139

Chennai : No. 34/44, Motilal Street, T. Nagar, Chennai - 600 017. Mobile: 09380460419

Pune : "Laksha" Apartment, First Floor, No. 527, Mehunpura, Shaniwarpeth (Near Prabhat Theatre), Pune - 411 030. Phone: 020-24496323, 24496333; Mobile: 09370579333

Cuttack : Plot No. 5F-755/4, Sector-9, CDA Markat Nagar, Cuttack - 753 014, Odisha. Mobile: 09338746007

Kolkata : 3, S.M. Bose Road, Near Gate No. 5, Agarpara Railway Station, North 24 Parganas, West Bengal - 700 109. Mobile: 09674536325

DTP by : HPH, Editorial Office, Bhandup (Sunanda)

Printed at : Geetanjali Press Pvt. Ltd., Nagpur. On behalf of HPH (P).

Dedicated to

In memory of my father

Late G. Laxminarayana

Ex-agriculture Officer,
Government of Andhra Pradesh,
Khammam, A.P.

Lord Shirdi Saibaba

The powerful source on earth

Preface

Strategic Financial Management is a growing subject in India. It occupies an important role in the present environment due to implication of privatisation, liberalisation and globalisation policies throughout the world. These policies forced the corporate sector to work efficiently and effectively to face the high degree of competition that exists in the market. It is one of the major subject for all finance professional courses in India. Every business management and finance professionals in India must know the intricacies of the financial aspects of management. This book is primarily intended to serve as a text and reference book for all management and commerce discipline of all universities and business schools in India. Since the book's synthesis, I am thankful to all authors who have contributed to the world of finance. I hope that I have interpreted their views accurately. I have made aknowledgements of every idea whose sources have been identified. It is my response to pay homage to late Sri. K. Ram Mohan Jyothi Education Society who has always inspired me towards achieving the goal. It is my pleasure to express my thanks to Smt. K. Meenakshi, President, JES, Hyderabad, K. Madhvi, Vice President, JES, Hyderabad; Smt. P. Indira, JES, Hyderabad; and Sri. P. Sithapathi Rao, Principal, SSRJ College, Khammam who always inspires talent and giving encouragement to completion of this academic assignment. I am thankful to my professors, Prof. P. Madhusudan Rao, Prof. A. Shankaraiah, Prof. Gangadhar, Prof. Krishna Reddy, Prof. Venkata Janardhan, Prof. Rajeshan, Prof. C. Bhavani Prasad, Prof. N. Hanumantha Rao, Prof. Krishnamachary, Prof. Indrasena Reddy, Prof. K. Sayulu, Prof. Subramanya Sharma, Prof. Venkataraman, Prof. Jogachary, Prof. Omprakash and Prof. K. Krishna Reddy of Kakatiya University, Dr. Supriya Dhillon, Director and Professor, KAIM, Charkhi Dadri, Haryana (MDU, Rohtak), Dr. Nandita Sen, Editor, International Journal of Economics, Hyderabad, Prof. A. Dhanalakshmi Acharya Bangalore, Business School, Bangalore, Prof. K. Pathania, Himachal Pradesh University, Shimla whose elderly advice has been of immense use to me.

I owe my gratitude to Sri. K.N. Pandey of Himalaya Publishing House Pvt. Ltd. for giving their personal attention in expediting the processing work of the book.

Dr. G. Ramesh Babu

Contents

1. Introduction 1 – 6
2. Project Planning and Capital Budgeting 7 – 79
3. Capital Market 80 – 188
4. Security Analysis 189 – 234
5. Portfolio Theory and Asset Pricing 235 – 249
6. Financial Services in India 250 – 284
7. Mutual Funds in India 285 – 331
8. Money Market Operations 332 – 388
9. Foreign Direct Investment in India 389 – 482
10. Foreign Exchange Exposure 483 – 499
11. Mergers, Acquisition and Restructuring 500 – 513

Detailed Contents

1. Introduction **1 – 6**

Financial Policy and Corporate Strategy • Financial Policy and Strategic Management • Strategic Financial Policy • Shareholders Value Creation • Economic Value Approach • Key Terms • Questions

2. Project Planning and Capital Budgeting **7 – 79**

Project Planning • Project Finance • Project Implementation • Project Monitoring • Project Evaluation • Capital Budgeting • Importance of Capital Budgeting Decisions • Importance of Capital Budgeting • Capital Budgeting Appraisal Methods • Practical Problems in Capital Budgeting • Summary • Key Terms • Questions

3. Capital Market **80 – 188**

Functions of Financial Markets • Efficiency • Primary Market • Secondary Market • The Bombay Stock Exchange • Settlements • National Stock Exchange • National Stock Exchange and London Stock Exchange Group Sign Letter of Intent Securities and Exchange Board of India Notification • Summary • Key Terms • Questions

4. Security Analysis **189 – 234**

Introduction • Technical Analysis • Summary • Key Terms • Questions

5. Portfolio Theory and Asset Pricing **235 – 249**

Precautions for Investment • Approaches in Portfolio Construction • Capital Asset Pricing Method (CAPM) • Summary • Questions

6. Financial Services in India **250 – 284**

Merchant Banking • Financial Institutions • Industrial Development Bank of India (IDBI) • Industrial Credit and Investment Corporation of India (ICICI) • Summary • Key Terms • Questions

7. Mutual Funds in India **285 – 331**

Summary • Key Terms • Questions

8. Money Market Operations **332 – 388**

Money Market • Section I • Section II • Section III • Section IV • Section II • Section III (Position Since 1990s) • Section IV • Summary • Key Terms • Questions • Annexure I • Annexure II

9. Foreign Direct Investment in India 389 – 482

Service Sector in India • Foreign Direct Investment Policy • Summary • Key Terms • Questions

10. Foreign Exchange Exposure 483 – 499

Foreign Exchange Exposure and Risk Management • Exchange Rate Determination and Forecasting • Foreign Exchange Market • Euro Forex Trading • Forex Margin • Currency Futures Trading • Summary • Key Terms • Questions

11. Mergers, Acquisition and Restructuring 500 – 513

Mergers • Valuation Related to Mergers and Acquisitions • Mergers and Acquisitions Laws: The Indian Scenario • Terms Relating to Mergers and Acquisitions • Case Study: NTPC • International Mergers and Acquisitions • Factors Affecting International Mergers and Acquisitions • Summary • Key Terms • Questions

1 Introduction

FINANCIAL POLICY AND CORPORATE STRATEGY

After the implementation of reforms in 1991, the entire global markets have changed drastically. The market has become a competitive environment to the corporate sector. The open economy or digital economy has created a challenging business environment to the corporate sector. The revolution in information technology has changed the situation dramatically. Before the information technology, every aspect has been INLINE but after the IT revolution everything has become ONLINE. The increased force of competition has made the companies to enhance their efficiency in all aspects of their activities. The cost cutting, cost reduction and other techniques are applied by the corporate sector in order to reduce the level of expenses to pass on to the customer as cheaper prices. The market became a battlefield and the business enterprises, which are providing high quality goods with lower price only, can survive.

The term strategy is derived from GREEK word *strategos*. The word strategy literally means the art of the general. It is often used to mean a number of things. Companies adopted a course of action which seemed to be appropriate to them. Such a course of action may be involving activities like expansion, diversification, focus, turnaround, stability or divestment. Strategy is one of the most significant concepts to emerge in the subject of management studies in the recent past. It emerged as a critical input to the organizational success. It has come in handy as a tool to deal with the uncertainties that organizations face. It has helped to reduce ambiguity and provide stability to conduct the business. The term strategy has been defined by several scientists in different ways.

"the determination of the basic long-term goals and objectives of an enterprise and the adoption of the courses of action and the allocation of resources necessary for carrying out these goals"

– Chandler (1962)

"the pattern of objectives, purpose, goals, and the major policies and plans for achieving these goals stated in such a way so as to define what business the company is in or is to be and the kind of company it is or is to be"

– Kenneth Andrews (1965)

"A unified, comprehensive and integrated plan designed to assure that the basic objectives of the enterprise are achieved"

– William F. Glueck (1972)

"A pattern in a stream of decisions and actions" **– *Henry Mintzberg (1987)***

"Developing and communicating the company's unique position, making trade-offs and forging fit among activities" **– *Michael E. Porter (1996)***

FINANCIAL POLICY AND STRATEGIC MANAGEMENT

The financial manager of any company has two important tasks: (1) allocation of funds (Investment decision) and (2) generation of funds (Financial decision). The objective of financial management is to maximize the wealth of shareholders and good access to the capital market for raising of sufficient funds whenever it wants. The financial manager will take into consideration of market imperfections such as transaction cost, bankruptcy costs, taxes, information gap, agency cost, etc. Strategic management considers all markets, including product, labour and capital as imperfect and changing. Strategies are developed to manage the business firm in uncertain and imperfect market conditions and environment. The market is a highly complex environment and it is continuously changing. The customer tastes are different; their desires are highly volatile, they need latest variety of products. The market is constantly changing and it is very dynamic. In a changing environment, it is highly impossible to catch the pulse of the customer. Therefore, the importance of strategic management cannot be ignored. It is an important task before the corporate sector, to analyze changing market conditions and environment to make forecasts and plan generation and allocation of resources. The shareholders' wealth is not the only criterion, but also there are many other influential constituents such as lenders, employees, customers, suppliers, competitors, government and society. Profitability and survival are most important objectives for the company employees. Survival independence, flexibility and self-sufficiency are the most important factors for the top level management of the company. The wealth maximization theory indicates that every firm should accumulate the wealth as far as possible. Strategic management is multidimensional; it focuses on growth, profitability and flow of funds.

STRATEGIC FINANCIAL POLICY

Financial goals are the quantitative expressions of a company's mission and strategy. Companies are not always governed by the maximum profit criteria. In practice, financial priorities change according to the change in economic and competitive environment. Financial goals put pressures on management for flow of fund. The goals are to be set as per the financial policy of the company. The strategic financial policy indicates two important factors, i.e., debt financing and internal financing. Debt financing is an important factor which cannot be ignored by finance specialist. The theory of capital structure indicates that financing decision is irrelevant. The financial experts argue that every firm should have optimum capital structure. There are two alternative theories which justify optimum capital structure, i.e., agency cost and information signaling. Agency costs are related to the cost of monitoring the performance of the managers. The agency cost is involved both in raising debt and equity. Some of the prominent academicians viewed that, if there is a tax benefit from debt, and then the debt should be used in the capital structure. In formulating the financing policy the company should not ignore the capital market considerations. The firms are following different kinds of debt policies. However, the conservative debt policy is an ideal one for a firm on the basis of the following factors:

- Minimizing the financial risk
- Greater financial flexibility
- Freedom from financial institutions

Debt can be used as a powerful weapon of competition especially when market is price sensitive.

Internal financing will show an impact on dividend policy. There are three contradictory views. The first view indicates that dividend policy does not matter for the company. The second view of the dividend policy is that there definitely exists low payout and high payout clientele because of differential personal taxes. The third view argues that there exists optimum dividend policies for each firm because of the information content or the agency cost. A firm may justify for a high retention policy for one or a combination of the following factors:

- Internal investment opportunities
- Stable earnings
- Growth
- Weak financial capability
- High leverage/external fund

A low retention policy may be followed because of the following factors:

- A strong commitment to pay dividends
- Dividend-oriented stockholders
- Informational value of dividend

In practice all firms want to pay dividends and they have long-term target payout ratio. In India firms on an average distribute more than 50% of their earnings. Therefore, the firms have growth opportunities to gain strategic product market positions. A low dividend payout also leads to high growth when the firm has high profitability.

$$G = Rb$$

G = growth, R = firms rate of return, b = retention rate.

Therefore, debt is a potential strategic weapon to gain dominance in a competitive market.

The financial goals of the majority group of companies are as follows:

- Maximizing the levels
- Book value of net worth
- Market value of per share
- Cash flow per share
- Operating profit before interest and tax
- Maximizing the ratio of price earnings, market rate of return, return on investment, net profit to net worth, net profit margin and market share
- Maximizing the growth: earning per share, total assets, sales
- Flow of funds without any interruption.

Growth is an important and influencing factor in the life of a business enterprise. A strong growth can be achieved through persuasion of the following factors.

- Growth potential of a single product company
- Growth potential of a multiple product company
- Shareholders value creation.

Growth occupies an important role in the survival of the firm's life. It can be ascertained through an interaction between four financial goals expressed as ratios-assets to sales and net profit to sales, and two financial policy ratios: retention and debt equity. A sustainable growth can be computed by the following formula.

$$Gs = PAT/S \times RE/PAT \times (1 + d/e)/na/s - (pat/s \times re/pat \times (1 + (d/e))$$

$$= \text{net margin} \times \text{retention} \times \text{leverage/asset turnover} - (\text{net margin} \times \text{retention} \times \text{leverage})$$

$$= p \times b \times 1/a \times (P \times b \times 1)$$

P = net margin = pat/sale

b = retention ratio = retained earnings (re)/net profit (pat)

1 = leverage = net assets or capital employed/equity = (1+d/e ratio) and

a = asset output ratio = net asset/sales.

Growth potential of a multi production organization:

The growth can be found by the following formulas

$$\text{Growth} = \frac{\text{Retained Earnings}\,(1 + \text{Debt/Equity Ratio})}{\text{Net Assets}}$$

$$GS = \frac{RE(1 + D/E)}{NA}$$

Growth = Asset Turnover × Profit Margin × Leverage Factor × Retention Ratio × (1 + D/E)

$$GS = b\,(r + (r - i)\,d/e)\,(1 - t)$$

B = Retention Ratio R = Rona I = Interest Rate

D/E = Debt Equity Ratio T = Corporate Tax

SHAREHOLDERS VALUE CREATION

Shareholders value creation may be defined, "as the excess of market value over book value per share". It is based on the notion of the present value of future cash flows using the cost of capital as the discount rate. The share value can be analyzed in the following manner.

- MV/BV approach
- EVA approach
- DCF approach

Market value to book value approach can be measured in the following situations.

If mv/bv > 1, the organization creating value of shareholders

If mv/bv = 1, the organization is not creating value of shareholders

If mv/bv < 1, the organization is destroying the value of shareholders.

$G = b \times ROE$

G = growth

b = retention rate

Ke = rf + (rm – rf) Beta e

Ke = cost of equity

RF= risk free rate of return

Rm = market rate of return

Beta e = beta e is the measure of variability of the company's equity returns

ECONOMIC VALUE APPROACH

EVA is a method to measure a company's true profitability and to steer the company correctly from the viewpoint of shareholders.

It helps the operating people to see how they can influence the true profitability. It improves profitability usually through the improved capital turnover.

Companies have usually done a lot in cutting costs but there is still much to do in improving the use of capital. It is best integrated in incentive system. Some economists view that, the earnings of the company in excess of charge for the capital employed. It is treated as excess of return on capital employed to the cost of capital employed. In this method a comparison will be made between ROCE AND COCE, i.e., return on capital employed and cost of capital employed. The economic value added to the shareholders.

Eva = trading result after tax – financial charge

EVA = net operating profit after tax – cost charges for capital employed.

It is net earnings in excess of the cost of capital supplied by lenders and shareholders. It represents the excess return to shareholders. It is the net value added to the shareholders.

The discounted cash flow technique is one of the approaches in shareholder value creation. The true economic value of a company depends upon the cash flows and discount rate. There are several methods to calculate the present or economic value of a firm. The following three methods are significant in study of shareholder value creation.

1. Weighted average cost of debt and equity
2. Estimation of firm's total value.
3. Valuation of equity and discount rate.

Economic value = PV of net operating cash flows + PV of terminal value.

A business enterprise or a commercial organization can use the following strategy to increase the shareholder value.

- Revenue enhancement
- Cost reduction
- Asset utilisation
- Cost of capital reduction.

Key Terms

1. **Financial condition:** The financial condition refers to the assets and liabilities of an accounting entity as per the balance sheet. It is said to be good if the total value of the assets is more than the total value of the liabilities.
2. **Financial gearing:** The use of debt capital by a firm. When a company has a debt capital, any change in its net profit (measured without deducting payments of interest on debt capital, payment of corporate income tax and payments of preference dividends) is magnified (or 'geared') and produced a larger change in the EPS of the company.
3. **Financial management:** Financial management can be defined as planning, organizing and controlling financial activities in an organization.
4. **Strategy:** A general method or policy for achieving specified objectives. In games theory a rule by which one player selects his choice. The rule may be a 'pure strategy' – i.e., a rule that he will definitely select a specified choice – or a 'mixed strategy' – i.e., a rule that gives the probabilities of his making each of a number of choices.
5. **Valuation:** A act or process of estimating the value of something. Also the estimation of value arrived at by this process.

Questions

1. What is finance?
2. What is policy?
3. What is financial policy?
4. What is strategy?
5. What is financial strategy?

2 Project Planning and Capital Budgeting

PROJECT PLANNING

Financial Goal

Every firm must have a goal. The financial goals of the firm should be to look after the welfare of shareholders. Shareholders are the real owners of the firm. It will be reflected in the market values of the shares. Every firm goal has two approaches: 1. Profit maximization and 2. Wealth maximization. Profit maximization means maximizing the income of firm. The business firm produces goods and services which will function in a market-oriented economy or in a government-controlled economy. Market economy operates in an operative environment. In this environment, every firm is expected to produce goods and services derived by society as efficiently as possible. Price is the most important factor in the market-oriented economy. Intensifying the competition in the market forces, the firms will have to provide goods and services at lower prices in order to satisfy the millions of customers. Prices are determined by demand and supply condition. They guide the allocation of the resources for various productive activities. The firm's efficiency is the barometer of the corporate sector. The profit maximization theory had been criticized in recent years. In the economy, profit maximization is regarded as unrealistic, difficult, inappropriate and immoral. It might lead to inequality of income and wealth. A high degree of competition would certainly ensure efficient production of goods and services desired by the society. This theory suffers from some limitations "it is vague, it ignores the timing of returns, and it ignores risk". Wealth maximization is another financial goal of the financial corporate sector. It is an appropriate and operationally terrible aspect to choose among the alternative financial actions. It means, maximizing the net present value of a course of action to shareholders. The net present value of the course of action is the difference between the present value of its benefits and the present value of its cost. The financial action which creates positive monetary benefits is wealth for shareholders. Hence, this situation is desirable and financial action which results in a negative NPV should be rejected and it will destroy the wealth of the shareholders. Hence, the firm should choose a project which yields highest NPV such that the shareholders wealth will be reflected in the market values of the company shares. Therefore, the market price of the firm's share serves as the company's performance indicator. In practice, there are innumerable factors which influence the price of a company share. It is usually agreed that the value of an asset depends upon its risk and return. The relation between risk and return is known as "risk-return – trade-off". The relationship between return and risk can be simply expressed as follows:

Return = Risk Free Rate + Risk Premium

In the business environment, firms will try to avoid risk and capture return. Risk is an intangible aspect. It can be handled by proper tools. Risk free rate is a compensation for time and a risk premium for risk. The desired rate of return will depend upon the accepted level of risk by the firms. A proper balance between return and risk should be maintained to maximize the return value of firm's shares. The company is a complex organization of various interested parties, like shareholders, creditors, suppliers, investors, financial institutions, debtors, employees and government agencies. There will be always conflict between interested groups. Hence, the management should reconcile the objectives of differences of vested interested parties. Resolving conflict is the efficiency of the management. A management will survive only when it manages the company in a good manner.

Project Management

Project management is an organized venture for managing projects. It involves scientific application of modern tools and techniques in management functions. It is a task to produce desirable outputs in consonance with pre-determined objectives. Project management has assured a great deal of significance in the corporate sector. It is a creation of rational choice among various alternatives. It facilitates optimum utilization of scarce resources for overall development. It has been practiced since beginning of civilization. It developed from several fields of application including civil, engineering, construction and heavy defence activity. The projects are of the varied types. The projects can be classified broadly into following categories:

(a) Development projects

(b) Labour intensive projects

(a) Development Projects

It is necessary for an individual or for a firm or for a country. The entire economic activity can be grouped into thirteen development programmes such as, "AGRICULTURE, ANIMAL HUSBANDRY, FORESTRY, FISHING, MINING, MANUFACTURING, CONSTRUCTION, ELECTRICITY, GAS AND WATER SUPPLY, TRANSPORT, STORAGE AND COMMUNICATION, TRADE, HOTELS AND RESTAURANTS, BANKING AND INSURANCES, REAL ESTATE, BUSINESS SERVICES, PUBLIC ADMINISTRATION, etc. Manufacturing, construction and electricity represents a host of industrial and commercial undertakings of the central government. These have been clubbed in different cognate groups keeping in view of their product and services.

(b) Labor Intensive Projects

Projects which are involving bulk amount of manpower and materials is known as "labour intensive projects". This project is grouped on the premise of availability of key inputs like workforce or raw materials. This project generates vast employment opportunities to the community. These projects are also categorized on the basis of demand and supply. From the financial dimensions, projects may be categorized as huge investments, medium and small investments respectively. There will be another classification, such as IMPORT SUBSTITUTION AND FOREGIN EARNINGS projects. Projects further classified as "COMMERCIAL AND NATIONAL PROFITABILITY" organizations. Commercial projects are concentrated by governments so that, returns could be ploughed back. This project includes expansion, reduce cost, compete the market, avoid stagnation, new technology, a new product. National projects are funded internally using indigenous technology or those using foreign technology or with the help of external and internal agencies.

Project Planning

Planning is a dynamic process. It aims at accelerating developments in all aspects. Plan requires projects and projects require planning. Planning with reference to projects is a means of organizing the work, deciding who does it, when, how and for whom, determining the resources required, allocating the resources on a time phased basis, defining and allocating responsibility, communication amongst all those involved on a project. It includes coordinating activities and people involved, controlling process, estimating time of completion and handling unexpected events and changes. Planning is a basis for the authority of project manager for the budgeting and financial control of a project. Project planning is a cyclic process. Project planning is a part of a project planning, which relates to the use of schedules and subsequently report progress within the project environment. In project management, a schedule consists a list of the project's terminal elements with intended start and finish dates. Terminal elements are the lowest elements in a schedule, which is not further, subdivided. Project schedule is clearly explained by a Gantt chart. A Gantt chart is a type of bar chart, which illustrate the date of completion of the project. It reveals about terminal and summary elements of a project. Charts can be used to show current schedule status using per cent complete shading. The chart was considered revolutionary when they were introduced. These charts have become a common technique for representing the phases and activities of a project work breakdown structure. Work break down structure is a tool used to define group projects', discrete work elements in a way that helps organize and define the total work scope of the project. It is a combination of product, data and service. It provides necessary framework for detailed cost estimating and control along with providing guidance for schedule development and control. The logical dependencies between tasks or defining using an activity network diagram that enables identification of the critical part. Project planning may be optimized to achieve the appropriate balance between resource usage and project duration to comply with objectives. The project duration is the most important factor in project management. The duration should not be extendable because cost escalation may spoil the objective of the business enterprise. The project plan becomes the base line. Progress will be measured against the base line throughout the life of the project. Analyzing progress compared to the base line is known as "EARNED VALUE MANAGEMENT". The project planning phases include "PROJECT CHART". "Project proposal" the output side include, "project requirements". "Project schedule" the project manager should always be cautious about cost overrun. Cost overrun is known as a cost increase or budget overrun. It is an unexpected cost incurred in excess of a budgeted account due to an under-estimation of the actual cost during budgeting. It should be distinguished from cost escalation. Cost escalation is used to express an anticipated growth in a budget cost due to factors such as inflation. Inflation is a universal problem cost overrun is common in infrastructure, building and technology projects.

Project planning takes the seats of a project from its inception and launches into the full blooming and steers it throughout its life. The real time benefits of planning may be available in the direction of project formulation. Project planning has the important aspects in the following manner:

(a) Project formulation
(b) Project financing
(c) Project implementation
(d) Project monitoring
(e) Project evaluation

(a) Project Formulation

Project formulation is a step in which ideas or aspirations will be converted into a feasible plan of action. It aims at a systematic analysis of project potential for arriving at an investment decision. It makes an objective assessment from all dimensions starting from identification of investment options up to its appraisal stage. It includes, "technical analysis, financial analysis, social profitability analysis and commercial analysis". It is a teamwork and should not be a single man show. Its efforts are drawn from several disciplines, "engineering, finance, economics, management" etc. It has an inbuilt warning program. Formulation is a complex and an intelligent task. Detailed project planning is the most important factor in project formulation. Project formulation process can further be divided into the following stages.

1. Project identification
2. Technical analysis
3. Economic analysis
4. Financial analysis
5. Project appraisal

1. Project identification

Project identification is the initial stage of the business enterprise. Projects will not exist by itself. The idea of project identification will come from different sources such as government organizations, financial institutions, non-governmental agencies and the public. The projects will emerge from the priorities and demands of the country. The surveys and an in-depth analysis will explore the birth of new desires, new priorities and new projects. Governments include legislature, planning commission, administrative ministries, research and development, government departments, public corporation, companies, boards, commissions, educational institutions etc. CSIR, ICMR, NCAER, NIRD, NIPF, ICAR, etc., are the best examples for their evaluation studies for different kind of projects. These institutes will develop a number of projects for import substitution, export possibilities, bringing out new products/new processes/technologies, controlling product prices, etc. Financial institutions exist for financing different kind of projects. IFCI, ICICI, IDBI, National small industries corporations are engaged in financing long and medium-term industries. These institutions have a wide variety of knowledge regarding identification of projects. They will provide the information regarding bankable investment opportunities, and the information regarding governmental organizations include political parties, pressure groups, chamber of commerce, technical consultancy, organizations, inter institutional groups are UNDP, UNIDO. These institutions always look out for opportunities in different kinds of projects. People also play an important role in generation of new projects. People's involvement in project formulation occupies a dominant role in materialization of the project. People have first-hand information about their areas, place, needs, desires, wants, demands, problems and opportunities. The modern governments are responsible for fulfillment of people's desires and their wishes. The modern government should work for the utmost satisfaction of the people; otherwise the political party will be thrown away from the power. Therefore, every political party will try to win the hearts of millions of the people by undertaking such mega projects. In India, at present, there are several demands for formulation of new projects. The interlinking of rivers is a long-standing demand to take up this project but the requirement of the financial resources are ₹ 15,00,000 crores and its completion will be ten years. If this project materializes, entire India will not face any water problem and cultivation may become very easy. There will be no death of farmers in India. India's mega project generates lakhs of cultivation and reduces the fear of food problem in the country. This situation will be helpful to boost up the manufacturing sector for GDP growth.

2. Technical analysis

It is the next process in the project formulation activity. If a project is found suitable in principle at initial stage, the top level management proceeds further. In technical analysis all aspects will be examined scientifically. It requires a closer observation of all aspects with feasible elements. The technical analysis is based on the following factors:

(a) Input analysis

(b) Demand and supply analysis

(a) Input analysis: For every business enterprise, input is necessary for delivery of finished product. The following input factors influence the investment decisions of the corporate sector.

1. Location
2. Raw material
3. Plant size
4. Utilities
5. Manpower
6. Environment
7. Climate
8. Technological aspects

Location occupies an important role in making strategic investment decision. It has to be decided judiciously and objectively without giving undue importance to the personal prejudices. A wrong selection of location may create several problems such as frequent flooding, sinking of heavy machines, non-availability of competent technical personnel etc. Therefore, selection of site should not be taken in hurried situations. The decision for locating a project should be taken collectively with the help of a team of professionals, technocrats, experts and representatives from the government, financial institutions and legal departments. The team of experts must give weightage to social, economic, national, regional and local considerations. The decision should be taken with proper justification based on factors such as decision making, cost benefit analysis, social cost benefit, discounted cost flow, etc. However, while taking the decision; the planning commission guidelines should be kept in mind in the following manner:

- Land cost and availability of land
- Quality of soil
- Abundant supply of water and power

- Availability of utility services
- Assurance of state government for any assistance
- Existing infrastructure
- Availability of trading network
- Availability of accessories' ancillary units
- Industrial peace
- Good labour relation

Raw material occupies an important factor in pricing strategy of initial product. It is assumed that 70% of expenses will be incurred towards cost of raw material. It occupies an important element in finished product cost. Hence, we cannot ignore the cost of raw material. Availability of raw material at the right time, in adequate quantity and quality at the right price is an important factor in selection of a project. The project should be established near raw material availability to reduce the cost and time substantially.

The size of plant is one of the influencing factors in determining the investment decision. The large industries require several technical aspects before making a decision. While selecting the plant location, it should also be kept in mind for expansion or diversification of the firm in future. There should be a provision for ancillary units. Ancillary units are necessary for large and heavy industries.

Utilities are necessary for any kind of plants. In the absence of utilities, it is highly impossible to run a plant. Utilities include supply of electricity, natural gas, water, sanitary and sewage service. Utilities are one of the prime considerations at the time of project selection. The utilities must be available at a regular interval and for concessional rates.

Manpower is one of the prominent factors in determining the project selection. Human resource cost also influence the production cost. Human resources are a host of "technical, managerial, professional, skilled, unskilled and semi-skilled". Therefore the availability of human resource in all categories at reasonable rates should be ensured by the company before making investment decision. The following factors occupy a dominant role in human resources department.

- No. of personnel required
- Category wise requirement
- Qualifications and experience
- Pay scales and perks
- Mode of recruitment
- Resignations and retirement

Man power planning is an important factor for smooth function of the project without interruption in production. The firm should think about placement cost, training expenses and administrative expenses for the viability of a project.

Environment is another important factor in making of strategic investment decision. The projects in India have to get compulsory clearance from the government of India for reducing the environmental pollution. At present, pollution is at dangerous levels in industrial cities and towns. The natural unbalance will create several problems in the atmosphere. Therefore, the central government separately established a ministry of environment for controlling and monitoring of these aspects. It engages to protect the nature and pollution free environment for Indian citizens.

Climate of the location of project is an important factor. Several projects require different kinds of climate. Some projects require cool and dry locations. Climate means, temperature, humidity in the air. Therefore project selection has to be made taking into consideration of the various factors.

Technology is playing an important role in selection of a project. In this modern world several technological methods are available to the entrepreneurs. They should select one of the next technologies from different alternative sources. The following aspect should be kept in mind while making a decision.

- Process of technology
- Size and cost of plant equipment
- Foreign exchange requirements
- Designing of layout
- Construction schedules

Choice of technology is one of the key instruments of development strategy. The relevancy of technology should be analyzed in different dimensions such as economy, profitability, quantity and quality, local conditions, competitiveness, obsolescence etc.

(b) Demand and supply analysis: Demand and supply is one of the most important factors for the corporate sector. The success of a project depends upon the several capabilities of the enterprise. It makes an attempt to determine whether the proposed project may be feasible in terms of time, price, place, quantity and quality or not? This situation ensures its profitability. The analysis explores about the existing and potential demand and supply position of goods in a systematic manner. The analysis must be made in mean to actual, but not in fantasy. Forecast is an element of estimation and it provides a proper guidance for taking up of several activities. The accurate forecast may reduce un-necessary huge amount of investment, labor and other factors in order to carry out analysis, a lot of information has to be gathered. Analyze, synchronize the data. The analysis should make an in-depth study of the following factors.

- Buyers
- Consumers
- Sellers

The desired information may be procured either through primary data or secondary data. The sources of data are available abundantly in the country through different forms. An in depth study of a literature available in the forms of

- Reports
- Surveys
- Periodicals
- Guides

The secondary data can be collected from the following sources.

- Plan documents
- Year books
- Economic surveys
- Sample surveys
- Statistical abstract
- Census
- Techno-economic surveys
- Stock exchange directories
- Guidelines for industries
- Reports of financial institutions
- RBI bulletins
- Annual reports
- Annual bulletins of exports and imports
- Souvenirs

The primary data can be collected through market surveys and personnel observation. The market surveys can be made an *ad hoc* basis or in regular nature. The surveys can be further classified as, "consumer panels and retail audit". The required information can be procured through a regular form of surveys. The data will be collected by the following methodology.

1. Sampling scheme
2. Size of samples
3. Time
4. Resources
5. Accuracy
6. Sampling system
7. Reliability
8. Quota sampling/random sampling/cluster sampling/systematic sampling/stratified strategy

After obtaining the data from either primary sources or secondary data, it has to be further processed, analyzed and interpreted with the help of a several statistical tools such as correlation, regression, and econometric methods, averages, frequencies, ratios with or without computer.

The data may be presented in the form of tables, charts, graphs, depicting various trends and highlights the data. The project selection mainly depends upon a big gap between supply and demand factors. Gap between these two factors will occupy a dominant role in finalization of the project. Savings of foreign exchange also plays a crucial role in making strategic investment decision.

3. Economic analysis

Economic analysis determines the ability of a project over a period of time. It closely observes the profit and loss elements in taking strategic decisions. Profit elements occupy a dominant role in making a final decision regarding the selection and implementation of the project. It is carried out by taking into consideration the following requirements.

(a) Cost of capital
(b) Working capital
(c) Operating cost
(d) Operating revenue
(e) Taxes
(f) Depreciation
(g) Profit

Financial management indicates that, every project involves a huge amount of investment and returns are available only after a certain period of time. The investment benefits will only realize after a specified period of time. The project involves several kinds of expenses such as "preliminary expenditure, land cost, plant and equipment cost, engineering and project management cost". The capital cost includes replacement and the modernizing expenditure.

Working capital occupies a dominant role in smooth functioning of the business activities. Once, the commencement of business activities is done, it should always be carried out without interruption in production of the goods. The requirement of working capital can be derived from the data relating to requirement of inventories, fuel, raw material, spare parts and other cash needs of the project in production and marketing. Accurate assessment of working capital requirement depends upon several factors.

Operating cost involves a repetitive nature. The cost will exist only after commencement of the production activities. They are recurring expenditure. They are classified as direct cost and indirect cost. Direct cost includes, "raw material, direct labor and overheads". Indirect cost includes, "salaries of supervisors, accounting staff, technical staff, stores operation, rentals, utility costs, consultancy fee, investment on working capital, transportation, sales promotion and advertising expenses". The operating requirements are a combination of estimation of cost on the basis of present prices and on the basis of prices that are likely to be incurred at the time of actual commission of a project.

Revenue is oxygen to the commercial enterprise without which no commercial enterprise will survive. The revenue is an intangible element. It depends upon the quantum of sales turnover. The operating revenues are estimated on the likely sales volume. In the high by competitive environment, a sale is the most important factor before any commercial enterprise. The sales depend upon several factors of the business environment. Selling price occupy a crucial role in reaching the targeted profit of the company. The customers at present desires at low cost with high quality of goods. The competition in the market put heavy pressures on company to become a market leader by achieving higher sales turnover. Every business enterprise wants to become a market leader by attracting the customers towards their brands. In order to attract the customers, the competition element will throw the companies to slash the prices of their products voluntarily. Hence, the organizations will take cost reduction programs in their company. Cost control, cost cutting activities will be taken up by the companies and apply the techniques, wastage of expenses, time and other elements be given due importance. Taxes, depreciation and profit, all these elements will be taken into considerations before making a decision. The viability of a project will be closely monitored by the top level management, financial institutions, bankers and government. Provision for depreciation and tax to be made while estimating the economic viability of a project. The economic viability of a project influenced by several factors such as "price, fluctuation, inflation, changes in government policy, availability of new technology."

4. Financial analysis

Analysis means, methodical classification of the data. Financial analysis is a study of the relationship among the various financial factors in a business. It is one of the ACID tests in the process of scientific management, investment policy and decision making. It can be classified into different categories.

(a) On the basis of data

(b) On the *modus operandi*

On the basis of data, the financial analysis can be categorized as external analysis and internal analysis. External analysis will be carried out by outsiders of the company. They include investors, credit agencies, government agencies, other creditors. These people will depend on the published financial statements. This kind of analysis serves only a limited purpose. Internal analyses are carried out by company executives and employees. Sometimes the officers carries out this analysis on instructions received from court or from a government. This analysis will be done with specific objectives.

On the basis of *modus operandi*, financial analysis can be of two types. A. horizontal analysis, B. vertical analysis.

A. **Horizontal analysis:** In case of this type of analysis, financial statement for a number of years are reviewed and analyzed. The current year's figures are compared with the standard or base year. The analysis statement usually contains figures for two or more years and the changes are shown regarding each item from the base year usually in the form of percentage. Such an analysis gives the management considerable insight into levels and areas of strength and weakness. Since this type of analysis is based on the data from year to year rather than on one data, it is also termed as 'dynamic analyses'.

B. **Vertical analysis:** In case of this type of analysis, a study is made of the quantitative relationship of the various items in the financial statements on a particular date. For example, the ratios of different items of cost for a particular period may be calculated with the sales as per that period. Such an analysis is useful in comparing the performance of several companies in the same group, or divisions or departments in the same company. Since this analysis depends on the data for one period, this is not very conducive to a proper analysis of the company's financial position. It is also called 'strategic analysis' as it is frequently used for referring to ratios developed on one date or for one accounting period.

Every business enterprise needs funds. The funds are procured by the companies through two major sources equity and debt. The long-term sources of finance met by equity shareholders. Equity shareholders are the owners of the company. The shares are held by the owners and public. The equity is a permanent fund in the company. It is the cheapest source of finance. It does not carry any repayment obligations. A proper planning fund deployment and a better utilization may enhance the value of share prices. A strong growth in company sales will be reflected in valuation of equity of the share of the company. A good financial performance shown by the company will be reflected in the wealth creation on stock markets. A high turnover in the stock markets is an indication of the better performance of the corporate sector. Debt is another source of finance to the corporate sector. The debt is financed by institutional agencies, banks and other financial institutions. The borrowings may be procured by issue of bonds, debentures, bank deposits. They are both secured and unsecured by nature. These financial instruments are carrying on obligation of repayment after a specified period of time. The corporate sector sometimes will get the financial assistance from the central government or state government. The assistance may be available in the form of grants are subsidies. The assistance is provided by the government to develop the specified projects in the specified areas to benefit the society. It is the social responsibility of the government to provide the assistance for the welfare of the society. It will lead to balanced regional development. After procurement of financial resources, the business enterprise will deploy the resources in the following manner.

1. Pre-investment phase
2. Construction phase
3. Implementation phase

The pre-investment phase does not require much financial resources. It requires little amount of financial resources for the purpose of conducting "surveys, feasibility studies, techno-economic surveys, consultancy, registration fee, cost of licences, trademarks, patents, etc. All of these expenses are known as preliminary expenses.

Construction phase is an important stage during the life cycle of project. It requires maximum amount of financial resources of the project. In this phase, the availability of financial resources must be mandatory and should not have any ambiguity. In this phase, the cost of land, buildings, civil works, machinery and equipment, ancillaries and contingencies. They involve capital expenditure and do not require any recurring expenses during this phase.

Implementation phase is last and final process for commencing activities of the project. It requires recurring expenditure on account of raw material, fuel, utilities, administrative and operating cost, recurring expenses, interest liability and depreciation, consumers and a lot of resources. However, the capital needs for a project should not be underestimated. The company should also give a due importance to foreign exchange resources. The project planning should know about the terms and conditions about foreign loans. A continuous evaluation of the project will clearly indicate the efficiency of the top level management.

After completion of all the three phases, the projections regarding annual sales, gross income, net income, will be made on the basis of market analyses which was already carried out. Further, the analysis of selling expenses, distribution expenses, manufacturing process, general expenses, administrative expenses have to be worked out separately for various products. All of the information regarding overall performance of a project is tabulated in three basic documents.

(a) The balance sheet
(b) Income statement
(c) Cash flow statement

Financial analysis will undertake a close study of the above three documents. The documents contain vast numerical information that explores many things about the affairs of the company. These documents will make it easier for evaluation regarding the operational strategy, financial strategy and investment strategy of a given project. Operational strategy means, good business strategies, plot changes in where a company is going. It finds new ways to structure your business operations and economics to create breakout results in top line growth, earnings and valuation as a competitive advantage. A shift in worldwide demographics, regulations, technologies and economics are transforming business operations management changing the game on competitors, sometimes permanently, is the outcome of a winning operations management strategy. It finds new ways to structure the business operations and economics to create breakout results in top line growth earnings and evaluation.

Financial Strategy

It is the important factor in achieving the success of a business enterprise. It is a practice a firm adopts to pursue its financial objectives. Middle and senior line managers meet a multiplicity of financial problems in their organization. Managers might be judged on their ability to achieve the financial objective of maximizing share value through internal accounting performance measures. Financial strategy issues will affect the organizations. It enables the organization to assess the financial risks that organizations face, in particular, credit, interest and foreign exchange risk and be able to adopt risk hedging strategies that suit the risk profile of the company. It provides a better understanding of how organizations are assured of financial performance internally and how their financial performance is assessed by stakeholders in a global scenario. The financial strategy needs the following factors.

- Future need for liquidity
- Future cash flow
- Relation between assets and liabilities
- Company's risk profile
- Time horizon
- Financing mode of business

Investment strategy is a set of rules, behaviours or procedures, designed to guide an investor's selection of an investment portfolio. The strategy will be designed around the investors risk return trade-off. Some kind of investors refer to maximize expected returns by investing in risky assets, others will prefer to minimize risk, but most will select a strategy somewhere in-between positive strategies, are often used to minimize transaction cost and active strategies such as market timing or an attempt to maximize returns.

Balance sheet is an important financial document. It explains about the financial status of a company. It contains assets and liabilities. Assets include fixed and current assets and investment. Liabilities consist of loans payable within a period of one year. An income statement exposes the information of actual operations of a business enterprise generally for a period of one year. It provides information about total sales, cost of goods sold, operating expenses, gross profit, net profit, depreciation and taxability. It also indicates about the growth and financial health of a business enterprise. It exposes about the surplus amount available for distribution as dividend or transfer to reserve to plough back reinvestment. The cash flow statement reveals about the changes occurred in cash position of the business enterprise over a period of one year. It is very useful to estimate about the financial resources, requirement to start the business enterprise, several techniques are available to evaluate profitability of the business enterprise. They are classified as follows:

(a) Commercial profitability

(b) Social cost benefit analysis

1. Commercial profitability

A project will be established for the purpose of profit. Profit is the oxygen to the business enterprise. Commercial profitability provides direct benefits which a project is likely to achieve at the prevailing market prices. It includes investment profitability analysis and financial analysis. Investment profitability analysis aims at assuring the earning capacity of the resources deployed for the project without hurdles for the sources of financing. Financial analysis takes into view the financial features for the smooth implementation and operation of the project. The following tools are available for appraising an investment:

(a) Simple rate of return

(b) Payback period

(c) Net present value

(d) Internal rate of return

(e) Financial ratios

Simple rate of return is the ratio of net profits to initial investment of the company in a normal year. The top level management will closely observe the rate of return. Capital budgeting is the best appraisal method for analyzing an investment project. The investment decisions termed as capital budgeting decisions. It requires a comparison of cost against benefits over a long period. Investment decision involve a careful consideration of various factors "profitability, safety, liquidity and solvency". There are several methods of evaluating and ranking the capital investment proposals. The basic approach is to compare the investment in the project with the benefits derived therefrom. The capital budgeting techniques, "payback period, NPV, IRR" have different methods of analysis of the various projects. Payback periods refer to the period in which the project will generate the necessary cash to recoup the initial investment. The payback period can be used as a criterion to accept or reject an investment proposal. A project whose actual payback period is more than what has been determined by the management will be directly rejected. It can also be used as a method of ranking in case of mutually exclusive projects. It is very useful in evaluation of those projects which involve high certainty. It discourages the projects which have long gestation period. This period reduces the possibility of loss on account of obsolescence. Net present value is considered to be the best method for evaluating the capital investment proposals. The NPV is the difference between the total present value of future cash inflows and the total present value of cash outflows. It can be used as accept or reject criterion. If the NPV is positive, the project should be accepted. If the NPV negative, the project should be rejected. IRR is that rate at which the sums of discounted cash inflows equal the sum of the discounted cash outflows. It is the rate which discounts the cash flows to zero. Internal rate of return is the maximum rate of interest which an organization can afford to pay on the capital invested in the project. A project which provides a stream of cash flows in uniformity can be calculated through the factor in "annuity table" aspects. If the project generates uneven cash flows the IRR is calculated making trial calculations in an attempt to compute the correct interest rate which equates the present value of cash inflows with the present value of cash outflows. In the process, cash inflows are to be discounted by a number of trial rates. Financial ratios are powerful tools for analysis. An accounting ratio shows the relationship in mathematical terms between two interrelated accounting figures. Ratios are used as a yardstick for evaluating the financial condition and performance of a firm. It is one of the techniques of financial condition. They can be expressed either in "times" or "percentage". Ratios can be classified in different manners. They could be classified as "profit and loss account ratio", "balance sheet ratio", "composite ratios". According to another classification, they are known as "profitability ratio, coverage ratio, turnover ratio and financial ratio". Profitability ratio indicates the efficiency of the business operations of the organization. The poor operational performances generate poor sales and lower profits. Generally bankers, financial institutions analyze the profitability of the enterprise for sanctioning financial assistance. Coverage ratio indicates the extent to which the interests of the persons entitled to get a fixed return or a scheduled repayment as per the agreed terms are safe. The higher the cover the better it is. Coverage ratios can be classified into three kinds. They are "fixed interest coverage ratio, fixed dividend coverage ratio, debt service coverage ratio". The turnover ratio indicates the efficiency with which the capital employed is rotated in the business. It provides information about the number of times which the capital has been rotated in the process of doing business. Financial ratios explore the information about the financial position of the company. It is a fundamental principle that, the requirement of short-term finance raised from sources of short-term finance. The long-term finance requirement should be made from long-term sources of finance. Financial ratios can be classified into two kinds "liquidity ratios and stability ratios". Liquidity ratios are also known as short-term solvency ratio. They explore about the utilization of working capital. Stability ratios help in providing the information about long-term solvency of the firm.

2. Social Cost Benefit Analysis

Social cost benefit analysis deals with the real contribution of an investment project towards the welfare of the society. The policymakers should think about not only for commercial viability of the project, but also see the associated cost and benefits to the society. The project should not undertake, which will result in heavy social cost to the society, though it may be financially viable. Now it has been gaining the momentum among the community. The planning commission has taken a decision; the feasibility study of the project for the public sector will include an analysis of social cost benefit to the community. As per the government guidelines, the private sector should also act as per the public sector project norms. The social cost benefit will be relevant while granting various licenses, approvals and sanctions. Therefore, social cost evaluation is beneficial as social cost benefit examines about how far the society will benefit, for commencing a project in terms of "employment opportunities, capital output ratio, value addition per unit of capital, savings in foreign exchange, cost benefit ratio". There is no legal obligation on companies to provide details of social costs and social benefits while preparing their financial statements. A project having higher employment potentiality has to be preferred. The capital output ratio measures the expected output in relation to the capital employed in the project. A project giving a higher output per unit of capital employed is to be preferred. The value addition refers to the cost incurred by an organization in converting materials into finished products. It considers the net contribution of the firm to the nation's economy. While evaluating different projects according to social cost benefit analysis, projects having "high value added" contents are to be valued high. Foreign exchange is an important criterion while making social cost benefit analysis. While evaluating the projects according to this analysis, projects can be ranked according to this analysis net contribution of the project are going to make to the foreign exchange reserves of the country. Projects having greater potentiality in terms of foreign exchange benefits will have priority over other projects. According to cost benefit ratio criteria the project are evaluated on the basis of total social revenue and cost associated with the projects. Social benefits include "all economic and non economic, internal and external benefits" of each, the society is likely to receive on account of the project. A project having the most favorable cost benefit ratio will be given highest preference. The financial analysis based on commercial and social profitability are two important tools in analyzing the investment project. The project will be accepted or rejected on the basis of financial analysis. The soundness of a project depends upon the following techniques:

(a) Break-even analysis
(b) Variable analysis
(c) Risk analysis

Break-even analysis is a technique to determine a level at which a project can operate without endangering the risk of making losses. It is that level of sales which equals the cost and expenses are at that level at which profit is zero. A low break-even point, have the maximum chances of showing dividends within the formative years itself. Variable analysis is related to study the impact on crucial variables such as raw materials, sales, volume, sales price, degree of capacity utilization, passing of capital expenditure, etc., over the economic viability of an enterprise. Risk is intangible element. It can be avoided, but not escapable. The risk analyses provide identifying the sources of risk such as rise in prices of raw materials, taxes and duties, product price as a rate impact and determine future returns for the project. It offers an opportunity to the entrepreneur to redesign his proposed project.

PROJECT FINANCE

Project finance is the most important factor in strategic investment decision. The funds required for a project can be obtained both through internal as well as external sources. The internal sources of fund include retained earnings and depreciation. The external sources of fund include raising of share capital, debentures and loans. Internal sources of financing are not possible in case of new enterprises. A new firm has to depend entirely on external sources of funds. Project finance is the long-term financing of infrastructure and industrial projects based upon the projected cash flows of the project rather than the balance sheets of the project sponsors. Infrastructure is the basic physical and organizational structures needed for the operation of a society or enterprise or the services and facilities necessary for an economy to function. The term infrastructure refers to the technical structure. That supports a society such as roads, water supply, sewers, power grids, telecommunications and so forth. As functionally, infrastructure facilitates the production of goods and services, it includes basic social services such as schools and hospitals. Infrastructure is a useful way to society as a group of investors, governments, and their citizens, ability to understand, advocate, and direct capital towards durable, with widespread, societal benefits. "The physical components of interrelated systems provided commodities and services essential to enable, sustain or enhance societal living condition".

A project financing structure involves a number of investors known as sponsors, as well as a syndicate of banks that provide loans for the operation. The loans are secured by the project assets and paid entirely from project cash flow, rather than from the general assets or credit worthiness of the sponsor's project, a decision in part supported by financial modeling. Financial modeling is the task of building an abstract representation of a financial decision making situation. It is a mathematical model designed to represent the performance of financial assets or a portfolio of a business, a project or any other investment. It is a general term usually related to accountant applications or to quantitative finance applications. In another dimension it is treated as a trade fact such as a welding or a science. The task of financial modeling is gaining momentum recently. Financial modeling is synonymous with cash flow forecasting. It involves the preparation of large, detailed models which are used for management decision making. Financial modeling include applications of business valuation, discounted cash flow valuation problem, capital budgeting, cost of capital or weighted average cost of financial statement analysis, project finance. They are almost always in discrete time and are usually deterministic. The financing will be made for the projects by taking revenue by producing contracts. Project lenders are having rights and control over a project, if the company has difficulties complying with the loan terms, for financing a project, a special purpose entity is created for each project, thereby shielding other assets owned by a project sponsor from the detrimental effects of a project failure. As a special purpose entity, the project company has no assets other than the project. Capital contribution commitments by the owners of the project company are sometimes necessary to ensure that the project is financially sound. Project finance is often more complicated than alternative financing methods. Project financing will be made in the sectors of mining, transportation, telecommunication and public utility services. At present project financing principles have been applied to public infrastructure under public private partnership or private financing initiative systems.

A project may be subject to a number of technical, environmental, economic and political risks especially in developing countries and emerging markets. Financial institutions and project sponsors will share the risk element in project development. The various patterns of implementations are sometime referred as, "project delivery methods". Financial institutions occupy a financing of project. Financial institution that provides financial services to its members will act as financial intermediaries. All financial institutions are highly regulated by the central government by different organs. Basically financial institutions can be classified into three kinds. They are

(a) Banking institutions

(b) Insurance companies

(c) Brokers, underwriters and investment funds

Banking institution involves in accepting deposits and sanctioning loans to the customers. A deposits account is a current account, savings account or other type of bank accounts. Banking institutions allow money to be deposited and withdrawn by the account holder. Banks are normally subject to prudential regulations which has the purpose of reducing the risk of failure of the bank. They facilitate the flow of money through the economy. A riskier or more expensive project may require limited resource financing secured by a surety from sponsors. Banking institutions can be broadly classified as "banks and development banks". Development banks are involved in promotion dimensions in the recent phenomenon. Development banks aim to perform a much wider role in the digital era. They play developmental and promotional role in industrial sector of the country. They undertake a variety of functions such as "finance promotion, technical skill, advices and economic planning". They are expected to act as catalyst in performing the developmental and promotional functions such as evolving projects idea, developing business skills, fostering a capital market as also to encourage new entrepreneurship. Development banks are spirit of finance. They are viewed as final intermediary supplying long and medium-term funds to bankable economic development projects and provide related services. They are expected to mobilize large capital from different sources. The task of transformation and exponential industrialization can be best handled only through development banks rather than normal process. A judicious blending of development and banking policies and its execution is the hallmark of the philosophy of the development banks. Development banks in India are known as all India development banks. They are presented below:

1. Industrial finance corporation of India
2. Industrial development banks of India
3. Industrial credit and investment corporation of India
4. Small industries development banks of India
5. Industrial re-construction bank of India
6. Shipping credit and investment company of India
7. State finance corporation
8. State industries development corporations

Insurance companies and pension funds also contribute towards development of industries. Insurance means, it is a form of risk management. It is primarily used to hedge against risk of a contingence, uncertainness. It involves pooling funds from many assured entities to pay for losses that somehow incur. The ensured entities are therefore protected from risk for a fee, with the fee being dependent upon the frequency and soverignity of the event occurring. Brokers, underwriters, investment funds actively participate for the development of industrial sector. They act as an intermediary to provide funds to the corporate sector.

PROJECT IMPLEMENTATION

Implementation means, to carry out, accomplish, fulfill or to give a practical effect to a desired project. Project implementation is the most crucial phase in project life cycle. Every project should be implemented by its project planning manager. Any deviation in project planning and implementation causes inconvenience to the shareholders top level management, banks, financial institutions and public. Implementation involves allocation of tasks to groups within the project organization. This phase occupies a crucial role and noticed by the planners and decision makers to derive intended objectives. The success of the plan depends upon/by its implementing capacity. There will be several problems in implementation such as slippages in schedules, cost overruns and poor performance. A reduction in project implementation delays through better management techniques. The implementation machinery should be strong and look after for timely completion of the project. The efficiency, capabilities and work culture will be helpful for easy completion of the project within specified period of time. The implementation of the project will have seven steps for completion in a time bound assignment.

(a) Initiative
(b) Time horizon
(c) Formal authority
(d) Procurement of resources
(e) Controlling
(f) Direction
(g) Completion

Project initiative is the first step in project implementation. It involves obtaining approval of the proposed strategies, project plan, relevant budget and selection of the project functionaries. Project manager occupies a prominent role in taking the initiative step. The project manager should be a dynamic person and result-oriented. He should be able to get things done quickly and effectively. He has to coordinate many activities of the project participant. He should have technical, administrative and managerial capabilities to coordinate several things. He should be able to communicate with superior, subordinate, customer and have good rapport with all departments. In this stage, several activities will be carried out by project manager, the several departments of the government. The project manager should have knowledge about preparing an interior budget and several tasks.

Time is the most important factor in completion of the specified project. The project should be completed and commenced the operations as per specified period. In this step, the finalization of technological parameters, selections of equipment, preparation of layout, identification of structure, preparation of specification of equipment buildings, auxiliaries, utilities, services, training of man-power, should be done by the project manager. The firm should adopt the latest management, modern techniques such as Gantt charts, milestone charts, bar charts, network analysis. These are described as "blueprints" for the management of a project.

Formal authority is the third stage of implementation of the project. All of the activities will be carried out by different persons by receiving formal instructions from their superiors. The key functionaries appointed for carrying out different tasks in order to execute the project within the scheduled period of time. The chief executive should follow the activities related to work schedule, placing of order for machinery and equipment, contracts for civil works. The project manager should assign duties to the project functionaries according to their experience and capabilities. He should assign all project staff members in fixing pin-pointed responsibility for any kind of negligence on the part of a personnel officer.

Procurement of resources is an important task in project implement process. The important resource for any project is presented in the following manner.

(a) Personnel
(b) Finance
(c) Materials and equipment

(a) Personnel

Personnel in any project or an organization are the most scarce and critical resource. The successful implementation of the plan/programmed project depends on the efficiency and effectiveness with which personnel engaged at various levels undertake their tasks and achieve results. Inevitably, manpower is required for use on some or all the activities of every project.

Major group generalized code:

Description of types of manpower

0. Professional, technical, related-workers
1. Administrative, executive and management workers
2. Clerical workers

3. Sales workers
4. Farmers, fishermen, hunters, loggers and related workers
5. Mines, quarry related workers
6. Workers in transport and communications
7, 8. Crafts men, production process workers and laborers not elsewhere classified
9. Service, sports and recreation workers
10. Workers not classifiable by occupation

(b) Finance

Finance is the most important element in smooth implementation of a project without any interruption in completion of a project. The flow of resources has to be planned, which of the activities of the project do not slow down or suffer a setback. The resource consumption will generally take place in three phases of the project cycle. The first phase (pre-investment), the second phase (construction), the third phase (normalization). In the first phase, resources are required for investigating various aspects of project ideas and for developing the project design. In the second phase, resources are required in providing basic finance of the project. In the last phase, project requires sufficient raw materials and other consumables. However, in the first phase, finance occupies a dominant role and consumes a lot more. In the second phase, the project requires maximum amount of funds are required which are usually of a non-recurring nature. However, the net result is that due to financial planning, the following consequences are inevitable:

- Increase in pre-operative expenses, mainly interest during construction,
- Enterprise's inability to repay principal and interest as per the amortisation schedule,
- Adverse impact on viability of the project,
- Loss on account of lost market opportunities, and
- Sickness at birth and a host of other unsavoury consequences associated with industrial sickness.

(c) Materials and Equipment

Project implementation is the most important stage in completion of a project within the stipulated time. A delay in project implementation can cost heavily to the business enterprise. A cost escalation is a normal phenomenon in these days because a high inflation is prevailing in the market. In implementation stage the project requires heavy machinery, plant equipment and other materials for smooth completion of project in a time schedule. For this purpose the purchase department of the project is made responsible to ensure procurement of supplies and equipment at the stipulated schedules in accordance with the drawing and specifications provided by the functional department. Management techniques like network analysis, scheduling and economic order quantity which are traditionally popular for operational situations are adopted.

Controlling stage aims at three parameters, i.e., time, cost and performance. Generally there are three main indicators "project proposal, project schedule and activity description". These three indicators are helpful to the respective managers to compare what actually takes place with what was expected. Once the indicators are selected for decision making process the control system will be designed specifying who reports what, to whom and when. The project manager will attend for "activity follow up, resource follow up, schedule follow up".

Planning of any type cannot be a foolproof system. Several changes have to be made according to the exigencies. Therefore, the project needs a thoughtful direction with a strong motivation. It must aim at avoiding any chances of hostility, resentment and apathy among the staff due to its coercive policies. It must rely on the established methods such as economic considerations, pride, work satisfaction, team spirit and social status of the project staff.

Completion is the important stage in termination of the project. It is a crucial stage. It spells out four dimensions "normal termination, non-termination, early termination and late termination". This stage is also continuous with the preparation of a balance sheet regarding the stresses and strains experienced right from the formulation of the project till its completion. The management at last will prepare a summary report which can serve as a guideline for future projects. Termination of project stage must not be neglected at any cost in the project cycle.

PROJECT MONITORING

Project monitoring occupies an important role in project management. This phase consists of several modern management techniques and administrative reforms. The importance and scope of management techniques cannot be ignored and avoided. Administrative improvements and reforms are necessary to reach the desired objectives of the project management. Reforms are useful for speedy and easy completion of the project. The welfare of the public is most important factor in large project management. In India, it is increasingly being felt that, administrative machinery has failed to deliver the goods and services. It has not also been able to handle the task of economic and social development. Every administrative system to be efficient, effective and responsible to the needs, desires, expectations and aspirations of the people, has to chalk out a detailed action plan well in advance. Several policies and strategies are necessary to bring about administrative improvements presented below.

- Systematic plan
- Continuous activity
- Long-term planning and development
- Evolution
- Responsibility management
- Deployment of professional staff
- Highly qualified staff with strong commitment
- Planning and organizing improvements in projects
- Socio-technical system with human and social factors
- Training and development of the staff
- Centralized and decentralized improvement programs

Management techniques play a great role in project monitoring phase. The techniques are of added significance for the cooperative sector which consists of industrial, agricultural production and distribution activities. Management techniques are a set of procedural steps which may be systematic procedures of investigating, planning controlling and supervising. The techniques have the following features:

(a) They are a set of procedural or formal steps.

(b) They have a multiple idea content

(c) They help in decision making

(d) They give the idea of efficiency (economy, speed, quality, stability, aesthetic approach)

Management techniques can be classified in several ways. For example marketing techniques, production techniques, purchasing techniques all of these techniques will be applied for achieving the goals of the firm. The management expert "Clay" gives a classification which is based on the objective of the techniques, they are:

(a) Detection (input and output analysis, attitude survey, production study, break-even analysis)

(b) Evaluation (job evaluation, work evaluation, cost benefit analysis)

(c) Improvement (method study, value analysis)

(d) Optimization (linear programming, operations research)

(e) Specification (strategic planning, plant layout)

(f) Control (cost control, labor control, production control)

(g) Communication (visual aids, report writing, Management Information System)

(h) Demonstration (MDP, learning, training)

The systematic applicability of management techniques are presented below:

1. Manpower planning
2. Organizational development
3. Organizational analysis
4. Organization and methods
5. Performance budgeting
6. Ratio analysis
7. Financial accounting
8. Cost benefit analysis
9. Cost effective analysis
10. Quantitative techniques
11. Electronic data processing
12. Management information system
13. Program evaluation and review technique
14. Critical path method
15. Gantt chart method
16. Work study
17. Method study
18. Work measurement

19. Economic order quantity
20. ABC analysis

PROJECT EVALUATION

Project evaluation is one of the most important factors in the process of project completion. A scientific approach to the assessment of the success of any project is the hallmark of any modern evaluation system based on two elements. Firstly, evaluation has come to be expected as a regular accomplishment to rational programs and secondly, there has been a strong move demanding a systematic rigorous and objective evidence of success. Evaluation means the value of a particular thing, idea or action. Evaluation is also termed as to examine and judge concerning the worth, quality, significance, amount, degree or conditions of any given thing. Evaluation is knowing about what is not known and also what is worth knowing. Evaluation is concerned with the progress of the project in meeting its principal objectives. Evaluation comes under two broad categories:

1. In terms of the project effects on the recipients
2. The objective or/goal of a project

The first category can be divided as "early evaluation, on-going evaluation and summary evaluation".

The second category can be described as objectives/goal of a project. The primary concern of project evaluation is ultimately concerned with bringing all about its goals. The evaluation aims at comparing the assessment of performance, *vis-à-vis* the total objectives. If any deviation found in evaluation of the project have to be highlighted, identified, analyzed and understood to find out the responsible executives for the various causes.

Methods

A variety of methodologies have been evolved by the academicians, professionals, practitioners for evaluating any project. Some of the important generally used practices are as follows:

(a) First-hand information
(b) Formal/Informal periodic information
(c) Graphic presentations
(d) Standing evaluation review committies
(e) Project profiles
(f) Control center

CAPITAL BUDGETING

The basic objective of the financial management is to look after the welfare of shareholders who may be satisfied with two elements. Dividend and capital appreciation. Dividend is a reward to the shareholder for his accepting level of risk. A business enterprise can satisfy the shareholders when it shows excellent performance in the business. Business is a game of return and risk. An intelligent business organization can reduce its risk levels and capture the profit. Profit is a jam and risk is ginger.

Every human being always wants jam. No one is interested in inviting risk. Risk can be escapable in some situations and not avoidable. Therefore, the management of a business enterprise depends upon several decisions. Decisions will definitely influence the profit levels. Investment decisions directly show an impact on the profitability of the organization. The day to day operations of the business enterprise requires several investment decisions. The correct decision of the investment may lead to growth of the organization exponentially. Investment means contribution to various securities. It refers to invest funds in various securities like shares, bonds, debentures and other financial assets. It is just like parking place of financial resources. The financial manager is concerned with the deployment of funds in various avenues of investments. He should take into consideration of the welfare of the shareholders of the company before making any investment decisions. He is related to financing and deployment of surplus resources for the achieving the desired goal of the firm. Financing decision is the most important aspect in the financial management area. It is related to the long-term financial requirement of the company and the sources, which the fund is to be raised. It also searches about the low cost funds. Therefore, the financial manager must design the optimum capital structure. The financial manager should always think about the low cost funds and risk. He should determine the amount of long-term finance requirement of the firm keeping in view of the company's policies. He has to decide the asset composition of the company. Generally, assets are broadly classified into two kinds, (a) fixed assets. (b) current assets. The financing aspects of fixed assets is known as capital budgeting.

Meaning of Capital Budgeting

A good financial planning is useful to reach the company's desired goals. Capital budgeting means planning for capital assets. Capital assets are also known as fixed assets. The financing decision of the fixed assets is called capital budgeting. The capital budgeting decision is related to take an investment decision whether to invest or not to invest in a project. The projects may be either setting up of a factory or purchasing sophisticated machinery or creating additional capacities to produce more goods. The financial manager should analyze various alternatives regarding their profitability and risk associated with them. He should evaluate various alternatives available to him and choose best alternative model in order to fulfill the goals of the firm. He should take into consideration of social responsibility of the business. Therefore, the capital budgeting decisions are important, crucial, and critical. It is a comparison process of cost against benefits over a long period. The investment decisions should consider several factors such as profitability, safety, liquidity and solvency.

Capital budgeting is an important function of the financial manager. He should evaluate different alternatives and expose the information to the board members for making a good decision.

IMPORTANCE OF CAPITAL BUDGETING DECISIONS

Capital is a scarce commodity. It is like precious metal. It should be utilized in a proper way otherwise; the lakhs of shareholders will burn their money in the company. The capital budgeting decision arises in the following situations

A. New technology

B. Sales

C. Diversification

D. Inventions

E. Legal formalities

A. New Technology

Technology is an important factor in the digital era. It occupies a dominant role in the production function of area of management. In this modern world, the market is highly competitive, and the customer always demands high quality and low price. As per the requirement of customers, the corporate sector should produce goods as per the trend in the market. The demanding nature of high quality goods and at low price has forced the corporate sector to sell the goods at reduced price levels. Therefore, the corporate sector followed the COST REDUCTION PROGRAMMES in order to meet the requirement of modern customers. The managements of the corporate sector have taken a decision to reduce the cost of production with latest technology. Technology is the most important tool in manufacturing process. It occupies a dominant role to reduce the production cost substantially. New technology enables the corporate sector to produce the goods at lower cost and with high quality of goods. It also enables the corporate sector to gain substantial savings in the form of time saving. Time is another important and influential factor in selection of best technology. The latest technology produces more goods in short period of time rather than traditional methods. The corporate sector noticed the importance of new technology and they adopted that by paying heavy amount of fees or royalty. For adopting new technology, it requires a capital budgeting decision. The series of consequences should be taken into consideration for making capital budgeting decisions. The replacement of existing machinery and importing of latest machinery and technology needs the deployment of heavy funds in the business. Hence, the importance of capital budgeting arises in this situation.

B. Sales

A high quality product enjoys good sales in the market. It will become market leader and enjoys the brand image. A good brand image and goodwill of the company will definitely boost the sales of the organization. Increased sales of goods may lead to the expansion of the business. An expansion of the business requires capital budgeting decision. Hence, the company should make investment decision regarding capital expenditure of additional plant capacity. The financial manager should estimate the financial requirement of the company when the company goes for expansion. He should take all precautions about the series of events occurring during the expansion process. It requires high efficiency to handle this situation

C. Diversification

Diversification is the important aspect in the life of the corporate sector. Risk always follows profit. A business organization can reduce its risk by entering into another field of operation of the business. It requires an additional amount of capital expenditure for purchase of new machinery and other establishment expenditure. The finance manager should draw the project planning and be able to execute the things as per schedule. Excellence in execution enables us to grow better than competition, produce at lower costs, meet customer expectations, and become consistently successful. Achieving superior performance is the key to competitive advantage. A speedy execution is the mother of good fortune. The financial manager should probe the cost of delay in project execution. A delay in execution is a costly affair. The delay in execution of project implementation in Air India and Indian Airlines has lost their market dominance. A delay in the National highway corridor plan conceived by the government at a cost of ₹ 11,000 crores have ended with ₹ 30,000 crores. Another example The

Bangalore International Airport has escalated the cost from ₹ 2000 crores to ₹ 6000 crores. In the private sector, there are other examples where one witnessed the fruits of execution excellence. Reliance Industries' Jamnagar refinery was completed in 24 months, making it a record of sorts in the petrochemical industry worldwide. It turned out to be a giant masterstroke that helped the company grow leaps and bounds in revenues and profits and emerge eventually as an undisputable leader in the private sector

D. Inventions

Research is the most important factor in the manufacturing process. Continuous research activities may lead to upgrade the present technology. An investment in upgrading technology is more useful to the corporate sector on long-term basis. Hence, the finance manager should take a good decision to allocate the funds towards R&D sector. A large amount of funds is required to establish laboratory and sponsoring the research project.

E. Legal Formalities

All business organizations are operating according to government policies. Government policies always influence the business environment. If the government issues a notification for installation of pollution control equipment in the factories require a high amount of funds. Therefore, the corporate sector needs to implement the legal formalities of the government as per the latest provisions and legislature in order to satisfy the rules and regulations.

Capital budgeting is a long-term planning for proposed capital outlays and the mode of financing. It requires a careful execution of the projects and is helpful to achieve the desired goals. The capital budgeting decisions can be classified as follows.

A. Mutually exclusive decisions.

B. Accept/Reject decisions.

C. Contingent decisions.

Mutually exclusive decision means, analysis of two or more business opportunities or alternative available to the company. A careful analysis of different alternatives provides various proposals. It indicates whether a project may be taken up or not to be taken by the company.

Accept or reject decisions means, exposing the information when the projects are independent and do not compete with each other. The financial manager will transmit the information whether to accept or reject the project based on minimum return on the required investment. He should make a comparison and select the best alternative, which provides more than desired return.

Contingent decisions are dependable proposals. The decision in investment in one project requires another additional capital outlays. For ex., if a company selected a project to establish a project in backward area needs to make additional investment capital outlays in roads, building of houses, hospitals, schools, etc.

Rationale of Capital Expenditure

Capital expenditure means investment of funds in new machinery and projects. The financial manager should be cautious about risk involved in new projects. He must be able to see the introduced capital must be utilized efficiently. Efficient utilization of funds is the basic objective of financial management. Generally, all business organizations have to continuously invest in business for replacement of machinery or expansion or improving its efficiency. The firm's basic objective is to maximize the return and minimize losses. This objective can be achieved by either increasing operational profit or cost reduction. Hence, the capital expenditure may occur in two situations (a) increase of profit related to expenses (b) introduction of cost reduction process. Capital expenditure increases the revenues of the firm by expanding its activities. If the company replaces the old machinery and old technology, will definitely reduce cost of production by introducing new technology and new machinery.

Capital investment decisions are more important in the corporate sector. The decisions may increase the profitability and achieve its desired goals. If firm works efficiently it can achieve its desired goals or otherwise there will be a chance of attack by risk. Risk is always a haunting factor behind profit. An increase in capital expenditure sometimes could not generate sufficient profits. Hence, by injecting an additional capital into the business may or may not generate adequate profits. However, the following factors will influence the capital investment decisions.

A. Size of fund

B. Return on investment

C. Targeted profit

D. Priority of projects.

E. Risk

A. Size of Fund

Fund is a scarce commodity. It should be utilized for achieving the desired goal of the firm. If a firm has vast financial resources, it can take a decision without verifying any other factors. It can accept all projects, which generate more profits. It will rationalize the decisions when funds are limited. Hence, the firm will make a decision according to the available financial resources only. The financial executive should be able to draw financial requirement of the company based on outflow and inflow of the cash. It is better to analyze the consequences of the inflow and outflow of cash during expansion or diversification stage. The financial manager should carefully take a decision on the following aspects.

A. New project cost

B. Preliminary expenses

C. Working capital

The financial manager should prepare the financial requirement of new project. Investment in new project may lead to introduction of additional capital. He should take a decision, by undertaking a new project but should not be disturb the existing project. He should take all precautions that a new project should not reduce the working capital of the company. He should adjust the amount of sale of the old assets to the new project. The financial manager of the company should also make tax adjustment on sale of the assets. He should also be required to assess the tax liability on the transactions occurred on sale of assets. He should also consider various investment allowances available under the tax provisions.

B. Return on Investment

The fundamental principle of financial management is to earn a minimum rate of return on every financial commitment of the firm. He will be responsible for monitoring of the funds. The fund should earn minimum return based on its cost of capital. The cost of capital is the most influencing and important factor in determining the capital expenditure decisions. For ex., if a firm raises financial resources at a cost of 12%, the company will not like to accept the proposal, which yields a rate of return less than 12%. The projects giving a yield below the desired rate of return will be rejected. Therefore, the financial manager should keep in mind about the cut-off rate of the investment.

C. Targeted Profit

Capital investment decisions are more important in commercial enterprises. The decision should increase revenues of the business enterprises. The financial manager should assess the future earnings of the company. The decision contains two elements, accounting profit and cash flows. Accounting profit is an income concept related to accounting process. In accounting process, gross revenue will be treated as cash flows. The cash flows of the business enterprise will not subtract depreciation charges and other amortization expenses. The cash flow approach is based on the following aspects, economic utility, accounting process, time factor. Economic value of the project is the basic factor in determining capital expenditure decisions. It is associated with cash inflows and outflows of the project. The financial manager will make a comparison that, the initial investment may warrant its cash inflows during lifetime of the project. Accounting profit is a controversial method to some extent. The ambiguities will arise due to different accounting policies and practices regarding assessment of inventory, depreciation, expenses etc. Hence, the account of profit may show differently due to different accounting policies and procedures followed by the business organizations. Time is one of the most important and influencing factor in case of new projects. Generally, profit is a paper figure. Not all payments may be settled at once. Therefore, the time taken in realizing or making payments is completely ignored. The cash flow approach undertakes the importance of the time factor while making capital expenditure decisions.

D. Priority of Projects

Financial manager is concerned with the evaluation of different alternative projects before company management. He will play an important role when a company is searching for a better project to make investment decision. If a number of projects are available to the company on an acceptable rate of profit, it should rank the projects according to their profitability. The company should rank all the projects according to their earning capabilities. The ranking of projects will rise when the capital is scarce. The objective of ranking is to look after the better utilization of monetary resources.

E. Risk

Risk is a general phenomenon in every business sector. It may be escapable and unavoidable. It is a fundamental principle that high return ventures attracts high risk, low return ventures create low risk. Therefore, different investment proposals have different degrees of risk and uncertainty. Risk may be defined as "the chance of future loss that can be foreseen." Risk comprises all elements, which cause for the variability in the return. It may arise by the factors such as wrong selection of investment, wrong timings, maturity, etc., it also may arise due to general economic conditions, competition, technological developments, consumer tastes and preferences, labor problems. The risk can be divided into the following major types: DEFAULT RISK, FINANCIAL RISK, BUSINESS RISK, LIQUIDITY RISK, MATURITY RISK, CALL RISK, INTEREST RATE RISK, INFLATION RISK, and CURRENCY RISK.

IMPORTANCE OF CAPITAL BUDGETING

Capital expenditure decisions will occupy an important role in the life of the business enterprise. It is the most crucial and critical business decision. The top-level management of the company should take a special care before making investment decisions. The following factors may influence the capital investment decisions.

(a) Large financial resources

(b) Long period

(c) Logical decisions

Capital expenditure decisions needs large amount of financial resources. It is not an easy task to raise finance from the capital market or other sources. The company should make a proper plan for the fulfillment of heavy investment programmed. At the same time, it should be observed that any wrong decision of investment decision might jeopardize the organization.

Capital expenditure decisions are involved to invest the money in long-term projects. Therefore, the entire investment made by the company will not be recouped in a short period. Hence, the company management shall wait to get the fruits of its investment results on long-term period. The deployment of heavy fund in business may not generate profits immediately

Capital expenditure decisions are based on logic. The company keeping in view of its earning capabilities will take the decisions. If a company takes a decision, it may not be irreversible. Therefore, the company should think twice before making final investment decision.

Capital expenditure decisions are related to top-level management of the company. It includes both planning for proposed capital outlays and their financing. Investment opportunities may be identified or created. At present, the market is full of competition and it is not easy to sell the product to the customers. In order to attract the customer, every company is going to influence the customer by offering goods at competitive prices. Competitive prices tend the companies to reduce the selling prices drastically. Hence, the corporate sector always try to incorporate cost reduction programs. Cost reduction programs include replacement of old machinery, improving the efficiency of installed capacity, adopting new technology methods, improving the manufacturing process, at plant levels. Sometimes the company may also add a new product to its portfolio due to demand from customers. The investment proposals may arise at different levels within a firm. Most of the investment idea generate from the plant level. In India, more than 50% of investment proposals from the corporate sector generates from plant levels. Marketing department of the company may also occupy a key position to make investment proposals. Idea generation is the most important factor in investment decision of various proposals. The corporate management of the Indian companies provides freedom to its human resources to expose new and innovative products to fulfill the needs of the modern Indian customer. The corporate sector generally adopts three methods for introduction of new products.

(a) Research studies.

(b) Suggestions from employees.

(c) Advices from consulting firms.

Research is the highly influential and important factor in discovery of a new products or services. Research means searching for new methods, new process and new technology. Technology is the dominant factor in the development of a nation. A sophisticated latest technology enhances the efficiency levels of the productivity. Improving the productivity levels stimulates the profitability of the corporate sector. Indian companies generally allow their employees to provide suggestions in finding of new investment proposals. The employees are encouraged to offer their suggestions to expose new initiatives. The companies will generally give top priorities when the suggestions come from workers. The important factor to get advices from consulting firms. Consultancy services are available in the market for new products. Goldman Sach, Abc consultants, Itcot, KPMG, ORG, MARG, IMRB, etc., are the best examples for providing the services required by the corporate sector. Therefore, the decision of capital investment lies with the top-level management of the company. The management should spend its time to make an investment decision and for its follow-up and execution of the new project. Capital budgeting decision lies with top-level management and it involves three levels.

(a) Operating

(b) Administrative

(c) Strategic.

Operating capital budget level is related with routine expenditure such as office automation. Junior level management may easily handle the office automation. Administrative capital budgeting handles the expansion programs of the company. Expansion is the most important factor in the corporate sector to accumulate profits continuously. A strong sales turnover in the market, brand loyalty in the market, tends to go for expansion. Brand image stimulates the profitability of the company. Goodwill of the company will definitely be useful to take investment decisions by the middle management. Middle management of the company is responsible for making capital budgeting decisions to medium range investments. Strategy is one of the important factors related to top-level management of the company. Strategic capital budgeting involves in acquisition of new units by the company. It requires a careful financial analysis of the series of consequences. Acquisition is the turning point to a commercial enterprise. It is an indication of stability in the business environment, which the company rotates. Strategy is a long-term planning of the company. Strategic planning is a top-down process.

CAPITAL BUDGETING APPRAISAL METHODS

Capital budgeting is related to provision of funds for specified investment decisions of the company. It undertakes all the aspects of financial consequences of the investment decisions. The top-level management will make project appraisal and evaluation before making a decision. There are several methods and techniques for evaluating different projects. The financial manager of the concern is to compare, different proposals, advantages and disadvantages in order to fulfill the desired goals of the firm. The capital budgeting appraisal methods are presented below;

1. Payback method
2. Discounted cash flow method
3. Accounting rate of return.

1. Payback Method

Payback is one of the methods in appraisal of capital budgeting techniques. It is oldest and commonly used method. It deals with the recoupment of investment made by a company in the business. It requires recovering its investment within a stipulated period. It represents the period in which the total investment in permanent assets pay back itself. In this method time factor will play a major role in taking decisions. The business concern wants its investment to recover as early as possible from its business operations. It gives top priority to the projects, which generates more cash inflows within short period. It selects the projects where the shorter period recovery is possible. The longer period project may get rejected and shorter period will be selected in this method. It analyses different alternatives available, compares all aspects, and make an investment decision for quick recovery of its capital invested in a project. In case of evaluation of a single project, it will be selected within period as desired by the board of directors. The top-level management will set broad guidelines for taking up a new investment proposals as a policy matter. If the project is unable to recover its investment within period, the company may not select the project. It gives priority to higher cash inflows and shorter time of recovery of investment. The business is involved with risk and uncertainty. The commercial enterprise always thinks about the safety of its principal, first and profit is next. Profit is an important factor for any kind of commercial enterprise, but safety of capital occupies a dominant role in making of investment decisions. However, profit is an inner element of the corporate sector but liquid is also important and influencing factor for making of investment decisions. It contains two elements, annual cash inflows and initial investment. In business environment cash inflows are most important factor. Sales occupy a dominant role in the cash inflow. Sales are the most important and dominating factor in all aspects of the corporate sector. A strong sales turnover will keep the company in a pleasant manner and it enhances the managerial capabilities. Initial investment is an important factor in the life of a business enterprise. The large and reputed organizations were built up with a low amount of capital in the history. Infosys was established with an initial investment of ₹ 25,000. The company approached various banks for a loan of ₹ 2,00,000 at the initial period. Therefore, a small investment will give a path to bigger opportunities. The appraisal method of the project should distinguish between acceptable and non-acceptable. It should be a convenient method to choose among several alternatives. The payback method fulfills desired goals of a business enterprise where they give top priority for shorter period projects. This method gives priority for bigger profits and quick recovery of investment as early as possible. The payback method has its advantages and disadvantages. The advantages are presented below;

A payback method is useful in high uncertainty, political instability, and rapid technological environment. It is a simple method to understand. It is useful to the newly established companies towards payment of dividend to shareholders, because after recovery of its initial investment, the firm will start paying rewards to owners. The disadvantages of the system will be as follows:

(a) The payback method ignores the firm after recovery of its investment from the project

(b) Long gestation period projects may not be taken up by this system

(c) It ignores the financial cost of the firm.

The payback method is suitable for projects less than 3 years. If a project, exceeding three years period seems to be quite hazy. It provides liquidity to the firm. It gives priority to liquidity rather than profitability. Liquidity is an important aspect in financial management. Therefore, some firms give top priority to the liquidity, then this method is more suitable for such type of organizations. It is suitable for short-term performance showing organizations

2. Discounted Cash Flow Method

Discounted cash flow method gives importance to profitability and time. This method is becoming popular day by day. It is an improvement of payback method. It gives priority to get the return after payback period. It depends upon cash inflow and outflow. It considers profit after tax only. It will be calculated with the help of discount factors. It recognizes that rupee of today is worth more than rupee one will receive at a future date. It will compare the cash inflows and outflows. This method can be classified as follows;

(a) The Net Present Value Method

(b) Present Value Index Method

(c) Internal Rate of Return

a. The Net Present Value Method

The net present value method takes into the consideration of the time value of money. It is a modern method of evaluating investment proposal. It gives priority for rupee received today. It undertakes into consideration of cash inflows during the life period of the project. It calculates each year cash inflows and outflows with discount factor. It will compare with the pre-determined rate of return framed by the management. This rate is known as "cut-off rate." The top-level management of the company will frame cut off rate based on cost of capital. The cost of capital is a highly influencing factor in financial aspects of the corporate sector. Finance is a scarce commodity. It is precious. Its availability depends upon many factors. The fund is the important factor for all decisions of the business enterprise. It is available in the market at fluctuating interest rates. The financial resources may be raised by the corporate sector in a good economic environment. The capital market is helpful to the corporate sector for raising of financial resources. The goodwill of the company is necessary to raise the resources from the market. This method will take into consideration of cash inflow and outflow. Cash inflow represent in the form of profit after tax. It includes depreciation. Cash outflow consist investments made by the firm in different stages in various projects. The working capital of the firm will be a part of cash outflow of the starting year. According to this method, a project will be accepted, if it is positive. The positive factor will be observed when the present value of cash inflows is more than present value of cash outflows. The dominant position of the cash inflows influences investment decisions. If the project generates negative results, it will be rejected. The dominant position of present value of cash outflow tends the company, not to accept the proposal. Therefore this method suggests whether a project can be undertaken or not with the help of discount factors and a combination of cash flows.

b. Present Value Index Method

Present value index provides a comparison of different investment proposals. It is a refinement of the net present value method. It can be computed by comparing the total of present value of future cash inflows and the total of the present value of future cash outflows. The present value index will be reflected in the form of percentage. It is known as benefit cost ratio. The high percentage of present value index project may be selected.

c. Internal Rate of Return

Internal rate of return is another method of computation of investment evaluation proposal. This method undertakes the consideration of time value of money. It considers all the cash inflows generated by the project during the life period of the asset. Internal rate of return is that rate at which the sum totals of cash inflows after discounting equals to the discounted cash outflows. The internal rate of return is the discount rate, which makes net present value of the project equal to zero. The internal rate of return represents rate of return on the uncovered investment balance in the project. It is also known as time adjusted rate of return. It was popularly known as trial and error method. This method selects a project, which provides a higher rate of return. It is useful for comparison of different project proposals. The calculation of internal rate of return is a laborious process. It is arrived after many calculations and it is not easy to understand.

3. Accounting Rate of Return Method

Accounting rate of return is known as average rate of return. It undertakes the importance of profitability of a project. The profitability of the project will be computed as per the accepted accounting principles. It undertakes the entire economic life of the project. This method will be calculated based on average yield. According to this method, the project will be accepted, if it generates more return than the expected rate of return of the company. Any project, which generate below the rate of return of the company's will be rejected. A series of number of project will be evaluated by this method and a decision will be taken, where the projects generate more than expected rate of return of the company. Accounting rate of return method is not popular in these days. This method does not take into account the time value of money. The accounting rate of return will be calculated in different ways. Each method provides different results. The reliability of this method is quite doubtful.

PRACTICAL PROBLEMS IN CAPITAL BUDGETING

Illustration No. 1:

Uma Industries Ltd. provides the following information. It manufactures goods by manual labor and is examining the proposals to introduce latest machinery. In the market, three alternative models are available. Prepare a statement of profitability showing the payback period method. As a financial manager of the company, how you are going to analyze the situation to the top-level management of the company.

Particulars	Machine a	Machine b	Machine c
Life of the machine	5yrs	6yrs	7yrs
Savings in scrap	1,000	1,500	2,000
Savings in wages	7,000	8,000	9,000
Additional maintenance cost	1,200	1,400	1,600
Additional supervision	800	3,100	2,000
Cost of machine	12,000	20,000	30,000

There are no corporate taxes.

Solution:

Statement showing annual cash inflows of machines.

Particulars	Machine a	Machine b	Machine c
Savings in scrap	1,000	1,500	2,000
Savings in wages	7,000	8,000	9,000
Total savings	8,000	9,500	11,000
Additional cost of maintenance	1,200	1,400	3,000
Additional cost of operation	800	3,100	2,000
Total addl. cost	2,000	4,500	5,000
Net Cash Inflow	6,000	5,000	6,000

Payback period

For machine a = original investment/average annual cash inflow

Payback period for machine a = 12,000/6,000 = 2 years

Payback period for machine b = 20,000/5,000 = 4 years

Payback period for machine c = 30,000/6,000 = 5 years

Machine A has shorter payback period.

This machine recovers its investment very quickly in 2 years. Therefore machine 'a' is better to select for buying.

Illustration No. 2:

M&N is an engineering company. The company intends to purchase a new machine for its factory purpose. In the market, four alternative models are available. You are required to examine the various alternative models and suggest to the management for buying of new machine from the market.

Particulars	Machine A	Machine B	Machine C	Machine D
Investment	4,00,000	5,00,000	6,00,000	7,00,000
Sales	6,00,000	7,00,000	8,00,000	8,50,000

Production expenses				
Raw material	80,000	90,000	95,000	95,000
Wages	70,000	50,000	55,000	60,000
Factory Overheads	75,000	65,000	60,000	70,000
Administrative cost	30,000	25,000	40,000	50,000
Selling and distribution expenses	15,000	20,000	25,000	30,000
Scrap value	40,000	40,000	30,000	80,000
Life of machine	3 yrs.	4 yrs.	3 yrs.	5 yrs.

Interest on capital 8% per annum
Income tax 50%

Solution:

Statement showing the net cash inflow of four machines.

Particulars	Machine A	Machine B	Machine C	Machine D
Total cost (2)	2,70,000	2,50,000	2,75,000	3,05,000
Investment	4,00,000	5, 00,000	6,00,000	7,00,000
Sales (1)	6,00,000	7,00,000	8,00,000	8,50,000
Depreciation(4)	1,20,000	1,15,000	1,90,000	1,24,000
Interest on capital (5)	32,000	40,000	48,000	56,000
Life of the machine	3 yrs	4 yrs	3 yrs	5 yrs
Profit before depreciation and interest. (1 – 2 = 3)	3,30,000	4,50,000	5,25,000	5,45,000
Depreciation and Interest (4 + 5 = 6)	1,52,000	1,55,000	2,38,000	1,80,000
Profit before tax (3 – 6 = 7)	178,000	2, 95,000	2, 87,000	3,65,000
Income tax 50%	89,000	1,47,500	1,43,500	1,82,500
Profit after tax	89,000	1,47,500	1,43,500	1,82,500
Add; depreciation	1,20,000	1,15,000	1,90,000	1,24,000
Net cash inflow	2,09,000	2,62,500	3,33,500	3,06,500
Payback period investment/ Net cash inflow	1.91 yrs	1.94 yrs	1.79 yrs	2.28 yrs

Recommendation: From the above analysis, it is better to select machine 'C' because it recovers the investment very quickly.

Note: the total cost is a combination of raw material, labor, factory overheads, administrative cost, selling and distribution cost.

Illustration No. 3:

The following information is available from the finance department of XYZ Ltd. You are required to select best project from the available data according to payback method.

Particulars	Project-X	Project-Y	Project-Z	Project-A	Project-B
Investment	8,00,000	9,00,000	7,00,000	6,00,000	5,00,000
Profit	2,00,000	2,50,000	1,50,000	1,75,000	2,50,000
Depreciation	10%	10%	10%	10%	10%
Income tax	50%	50%	50%	50%	50%

The depreciation of the project should be charged on straight-line method.

Solution:

Statement showing annual cash inflow of projects

Particulars	Project-X	Project-Y	Project-Z	Project-A	Project-B
PBT	2,00,000	2,50,000	1,50,000	1,75,000	2,50,000
(–) Tax	1,00,000	1,25,000	75,000	87,500	1,25,000
(+) Depr.	80,000	90,000	70,000	60,000	50,000
Total	1,80,000	2,15,000	1,45,000	1,47,500	1,75,000
Cash inflow					
Investment	8,00,000	9,00,000	7,00,000	6,00,000	5,00,000
Payback period	4.44yr	4.18yr	4.82yr	4.06yr	2.85yr

The above analysis shows that the project B should be selected because it provides immediate cash inflow of the investment. It recovers in shorter period of 2.85 years. (Corrected)

Illustration No. 4:

From the following particulars compute (a) payback period (b) post payback profitability (c) post back profitability index.

P/S investment annual cash inflow estimated life period scrap value

Project super	75,000	15,000	12 years	0
Project supreme	75,000	20,000	12 years	0
Project deluxe	75,000	18,000	10 years	0

Solution:

Computation of payback period of different projects

Payback period = Investment/annual cash inflow

For project super = 75,000/15,000 = 5 years

For project supreme = 75,000/20,000 = 3.75 years

For project deluxe = 75,000/18,000 = 4.16 years.

Post payback profitability = Annual cash inflow (estimated life-payback period)

For project super = 15,000 (12 – 5)

= 15,000 (7) = 1,05,000

For project supreme = 20,000 (12 – 3.75)

= 20,000 (8.25)

= 1,65,000

For project deluxe = 18,000 (10-4.16)

= 18,000 (5.84)

= 1,05,120

Post back profitability index for project super 1,05,000/75,000 × 100 = 140%

For project supreme 1,65,000/75,000 × 100 = 220%.

For project deluxe 1,05,120/75,000 × 100 = 140.16%

Illustration No. 5:

From the following information calculate payback period, post pay back profitability, post pay back profitability index of different projects.

P/s	Project-A	Project-B	Project-C	Project-D	Project-E	Project-F
Investment 60,000 each for all projects						
Cash inflows						
1st year	10,000	12,000	15,000	20,000	6,000	3,000
2nd year	10,000	12,000	15,000	20,000	6,000	3,000
3rd year	10,000	12,000	15,000	20,000	6,000	3,000
4th year	10,000	12,000	15,000	20,000	6,000	3,000
5th year	10,000	12,000	15,000	20,000	6,000	3,000
6th year	5,000	6,000	7,500	10,000	10,000	15,000
7th year	5,000	6,000	7,500	10,000	10,000	15,000
8th year	5,000	6,000	7,500	10,000	10,000	15,000
Life	8 years	8 years	8 years	8 years	8 years	8 years

Solution:

Calculation of payback period of different projects

Payback period = Investment/annual cash flows

For project A = 60,000 = (10,000 + 10,000 + 10,000 + 10,000 + 10,000 + 5,000 + 5,000)

= 7 years

For project B = 60,000 = 12,000 + 12,000 + 12,000 + 12,000 + 12,000 = 5 years

For project C = 60,000 = 15,000 + 15,000 + 15,000 + 15,000 = 4 years

For project D = 60,000 = 20,000 + 20,000 + 20,000 = 3 years

For project E = 60,000 = 6,000 + 6,000 + 6,000 + 6,000 + 6,000 + 10,000 + 10,000 + 10,000 = 8 years

For project F = 60,000 3,000 + 3,000 + 3,000 + 3,000 + 3,000 + 15,000 + 15,000 + 15,000 = 8 years

Calculation of post pay back profitability= Annual cash inflows X rest of payback period

For project-A = 5000 × 1 = 5000 for project-B = 6,000 × 3 = 18,000

For project-C = 37,500 for project-D = 70,000

For project-E = 0 for project F = 0

Post pay back profitability index for project A=

Post pays back profitability × 100/Investment

Project A = 5000 × 100/60,000 = 8.33%

Project B = 18,000 × 100/60,000 = 30%

Project C = 37,500 × 100/60,000 = 32.5%

Project D = 70,000 × 100/60,000 = 11.66%

Project E = 0 × 100/60,000 = 0

Project F = 0 × 100/60,000 = 0

Illustration No. 6:

The following information is available to you. You are required to calculate discounted payback period of the project.

Investment of the project ₹ 1,50,000 life of the project 6 years annual cash inflow of the project ₹ 50,000 discount factor 10%.

Solution:

Calculation of present value of cash inflows

Year	Inflow	PV factor at 10%	PV	Cumulative PV
1	50,000	.909	45,450	45,450
2	50,000	.826	41,300	86,750
3	50,000	.751	37,550	1,24,300
4	50,000	.683	34,150	1,58,450
5	50,000	.621	31,050	1,89,500
6	50,000	.564	28,200	2,17,700

The cumulative present value of cash inflows at the end of 3rd year is 1,24,300 and it is at the end of 4th year is 1,58,450

Hence, the payback period may be in between 3 and 4 years. It may be calculated as follows;

Discounted payback period = 3 years + 25,700/34150 = 3.75 years

Illustration No. 7:

From the following information, rank the projects as per payback period method.

PS.	Investment	Annual cash inflows estimated	Life of the project
Project M	1,00,000	25,000	6 years
Project N	80,000	16,000	7 years
Project O	40,000	8,000	8 years
Project P	1,50,000	30,000	7 years
Project Q	2,00,000	80,000	5 years
Project R	1,20,000	40,000	4 years
Project S	1,80,000	45,000	6 years
Project T	2,10,000	70,000	5 years
Project U	1,80,000	90,000	3 years

Solution:

Ranking of the projects according to payback period

Project	Investment	Annual cash inflows	Payback period	Rank
Project M	1,00,000	25,000	4 Years	4th
Project N	80,000	16,000	5 Years	5th
Project O	40,000	8,000	5 Years	5th
Project P	1,50,000	30,000	5 Years	5th
Project Q	2,00,000	80,000	2.5 Years	2nd
Project R	1,20,000	40,000	5 Years	5th
Project S	1,80,000	45,000	4 Years	4th
Project T	2,10,000	70,000	3 Years	3rd
Project U	1,80,000	90,000	2 Years	1st

Illustration No. 8:

RAKESH industries limited present the following information The Company examines two alternatives. Calculate (a) return on investment (b) payback period (c) discounted payback period (d) profitability index. The present value of ₹ 1 to be received at the end of each year, at 10% p.a. is given below.

Year	1	2	3	4	5
P.V.	.91	.83	.75	.68	.62

Particulars	Project A	Project B
Investment	1,00,000	1,40,000
Life of the project	5 years	5 years
Net income (after deprcn and tax)		
End of 2000	2,500	—
End of 2001	10,000	17,000
End of 2002	17,500	17,000
End of 2003	12,500	17,000
End of 2004	—	17,000

The project requires an additional amount of working capital of ₹ 10,000. The additional amount will be earned by the project after the expiry of the project. The company adopted straight-line method of depreciation.

Solution:

The project generates cash inflows for five years. The depreciation for project A is calculated as follows;

Depreciation for project A investment/life of the asset = 1,00,000/5 = 20,000

Depreciation for project B = investment/life of the asset. = 1,40,000/5 = 28,000

There is no scrap value for the projects.

Calculation of profit after tax;

Year	Project A			Project B		
	NI	deprcn.	Cash inflow	NI	deprcn.	Cash inflow
2000	2,500	20,000	22,500	—	28,000	—
2001	10,000	20,000	30,000	17,000	28,000	45,000
2002	17,500	20,000	37,500	17,000	28,000	45,000
2003	12,500	20,000	32,500	17,000	28,000	45,000
2004	—	—	—	17,000	28,000	45,000
Total	42,500	80,000	1,22,500	68,000	1,40,000	2,08,000

(a) Return on Investment

Calculation of ROI for project A = average investment/average return × 100

Average investment of project a = total net income/no. of years.

Average return on average investment = average investment/average return × 100

Calculation of return on investment of the project a and project b

Particulars	Project-A	Project-B
Investment	1,10,000	1,50,000
Life	5 years	5 years
Total net income	42,500	68,000

Average investment for project A = 42,500/4 = 10,625

Average investment for project B = 68,000/4 = 17,000

Average return for project A = 1,10,000 + 10,000 = 1,20,000/2 = 60,000

Average return for project B = 1,50,000 + 10,000 = 1,60,000/2 = 80,000

Average return on average investment = 10,625/60,000 × 100 = 17.70%

Average return on average investment for project B = 17,000/68,000 × 100 = 25%.

(b) Calculation of payback period for project A

Year	Cash in flow
2000	22,500
2001	30,000
2002	37,500
2003	10,000
	1,00,000

Average cash inflow 1,00,000/4 = 25,000

Payback period 1,10,000/25,000 = 4.4 years

Calculation of payback period for project B

Year	Cash inflow
2000	28,000
2001	45,000
2002	45,000
2003	22.000
	1,40,000

Payback period is 3.48

(c) Discounted payback period method

Year	PV factor	Project A	Project B	Cash inflow PV of cf	Cash inflow PV of cf
2000	.91	22,500	20,475	28,000	25,480
2001	.83	30,000	24,900	45,000	37,350
2002	.75	37,500	28,125	45,000	33,750
2003	.68	32,500	22,100	45,000	30,600
2004	.62	-----	-----	45,000	27,900

Total PV	95,600	1,55,080
Less; investment	80,000	1,40,000
	15,600	15,080

Discounted Payback

Year	Project A PV of Cash inflows	Project B PV of Cash inflows
2000	20.475	25,480
2001	24,900	37,350
2002	28,125	33,750
2003	22,100	30,600
2004	----	27,900

Payback period for project A   6500/22,100 = .29

Payback period for project B   12820/27,900 = .46

Therefore, project a payback period is 3.29 years and project b is 3.46 years.

(d) Profitability index method:

For project A = 15,600/80,000 × 100 = 19.5%

For project B = 15,080/1,40,00 × 100 = 10.77%

Illustration No. 9:

Hitech Engineering Company Limited is thinking to purchase a new machine. The company is considering two alternative models, which are available in the market. Two alternative machines X and Y have been suggested. The machines involve an investment of ₹ 6,00,000 and requiring ₹ 30,000 as additional working capital at the end of the 1st year. The earnings after taxation are expected to be as follows:

Year	Cash inflows	
	Machine X	Machine Y
1	60,000	1,80,000

2	1,80,000	2,40,000
3	2,40,000	3,00,000
4	3,60.000	1,80,000
5	2,40,000	3,60,000

The company requires a return on capital of 10%. You are required to compare the profitability of machines and state which alternative you consider financially preferable.

The present value of ₹ 1 due in n number of years

Year	1	2	3	4	5
Pave at 10%	0.91	0.83	0.75	0.68	0.62

Solution:

Hitech Engineering Company Ltd. statement showing the profitability of the two machines as per npv method:

Year	Discount	Machine - A		Machine - B	
		Cash inflow	Present value	Cash inflow	Present value
1	0.91	60,000	54,600	1,80,000	1,63,800
2	0.83	1,80,000	1,49,400	2,40,000	1,99,200
3	0.75	2,40,000	1,80,000	3,00,000	2,25,000
4	0.68	3,60,000	2,44,800	1,80,000	1,22,400
5	0.62	2,40,000	1,48,800	3,60,000	2,23,200

Total present value of Cash inflows	7,77,600	9,33,600
Total present value of Cash outflows	6,27,300	6,27,300
Net present value	50,300	3,06,300

Machine B is preferable. The cash inflow of Machine B is higher than Machine A. Machine B generates more cash inflows. Hence, it is suggested that the company should go for selection of project B as per capital budgeting technique.

Illustration No. 10:

Gowthami Traders is planning to install either of the two machines, which are mutually exclusive. The particulars of the following information reveal financial aspects. The machine A will recover salvage value of ₹ 3,000 and machine B will recover ₹ 2,000 in the 6th year. The cost of capital is 10%; the two machines will operate the same efficiency. Determine which machine is cheaper?

Year	Machine A	Machine B
Investment cost 0	20,000	16,000
Operating cost 1	4,000	5,000

Operating cost 2	4,000	5,000
Operating cost 3	4,000	5,000
Operating cost 4	5,000	7,500
Operating cost 5	5,000	7,500
Operating cost 6	5,000	7,500
Operating cost 7	6,000	
Operating cost 8	6,000	
Operating cost 9	6,000	
Operating cost 10	6,000	

Present value of 10%

Year 1 – .9091 Year 2 – .8264

Year 3 – .7513 Year 4 – .6830

Year 5 – .6209 Year 6 – .5645

Year 7 – .5132 Year 8 – .4665

Year 9 – .4241 Year 10 – .3855

Present value of an annuity of ₹ One per period at 10% discounting factor.

At the end of year 6 = 4.3553 at the end of year 10 = 6.1446

Capital recovery factor at 10% for 6 years = .2296 for 10 years = .1628

Solution:

Statement showing the computation of equivalent annual cost of two machines

Year	Machine A	P.V. factor 10%	Discounted cf
1	20,000	1.0000	20,000
2	4,000	.9091	3,636
3	4,000	.8264	3,305
4	4,000	.7513	3,005
5	5,000	.6830	3,415
6	5,000	.6209	3,104
7	5,000	.5645	2,822
8	6,000	.5132	3,079
9	6,000	.4665	2,799
10	6,000	.4241	2,544
11	6,000	.3885	2,331
			50,040

Cost after accounting for salvage value

50,040 – 3000 × .3885 = 50,040 – 1165 = 48,875

Equivalent annual cost = Total discounted cost × Capital recovery cost

50,040 × .1628 = 8146.51

Year	Machine B	P.V. factor 10%	Discounted cf
0	16,000	1.0000	16,000
1	5,000	.9091	4,545
2	5,000	.8264	4,132
3	5,000	.7513	3,756
4	7,500	.6830	5,122
5	7,500	.6209	4,656
6	7,500	0.5645	4,233
			42,444

Cost after accounting salvage 42,444 – 2000 × .5646

42,444 – 1129 = 41315

Equivalent annual cost = 42,444 × .2296 = 9745

Hence machine A is cheaper.

Illustration No. 11:

Nagarjuna Engineering Company is planning to make an investment decision regarding two alternative machines available in the market. From the following information, calculate the net present value of the two projects and suggest which of the following should be accepted at a discounted rate of 10%.

Particulars	Project M	Project N
Initial investment	40,000	60,000
Life of the asset	5 years	5 years
Scrap value	2,000	4,000

The profit before depreciation and after taxes (cash flows) is as follows

Year	Project M	Project N
Ist Year	10,000	40,000
IInd Year	20,000	20,000
IIIrd Year	20,000	10,000
IVth Year	6,000	6,000
Vth Year	4,000	4,000

Solution:

Calculation of present value of Project M

Year	Cash inflows	PV at 10%	PV of net cash flows
1	10,000	.9091	9091 = 00
2	20,000	.826	16,520 = 00
3	20,000	.751	15,020 = 00
4	6,000	.683	4,098 = 00
5	4,000	.621	3,726 = 00
5	Scrap: 2,000	.621	1,242 = 00
			49,697 = 00

Present value of all cash inflows	49,697 = 00
Less present value of initial investment	40,000 = 00
Net present value	9,697 = 00

Calculation of present value of Project N

Year	Cash inflows	PV factor	Present value of net cash
1	40,000 = 00	.909	36,360 = 00
2	20,000 = 00	.826	16,520 = 00
3	10,000 = 00	.751	7510 = 00
4	6,000 = 00	.683	4,098 = 00
5	4,000 = 00	.621	2,484 = 00
5	Scrap: 4,000 = 00	.621	2,484 = 00
	Total present value of inflows		69,456 = 00

Less; present value of initial investment	60,000 = 00
Net present value	9,456 = 00

The net present value of project M is higher than project N. Hence, the project M should be accepted as per the NPV approach.

Illustration No. 12:

A limited company is planning to make an investment decision for a project. It requires a capital outlay of ₹ 4,00,000. The following information is related to the proposed project. The annual income after depreciation but before tax is as follows:

Year	₹
1	2,00,000
2	2,00,000

3	1,60,000
4	1,60,000
5	80,000

Depreciation may be taken as 20% on original cost and taxation at 50% of net income

You are required to evaluate the project as per net present value method. The discounted factor is 10%.

Solution:

Statement of net cash inflow

Year	Profit after deprecn.	Income tax	Profit before deprecn. after tax
1	2,00,000	1,00,000	1,80,000
2	2,00,000	1,00,000	1,80,000
3	1,60,000	80,000	1,60,000
4	1,60,000	80,000	1,60,000
5	80,000	40,000	1,20,000

Calculation of discounted cash flows

Year	Net profit before deprcn. but after tax	PV 10%	Present value
1	1,80,000	0.909	1,63,620 = 00
2	1,80,000	0.826	1,48,680 = 00
3	1,60,000	0.751	1,20,160 = 00
4	1,60,000	0.683	1,09,280 = 00
5	1,20,000	0.621	74,520 = 00

PV of cash inflows	6,16,260 = 00
Less: initial investment	4,00,000 = 00
	2,16,260 = 00

Illustration No. 13:

Vamsi textiles are considering two mutually exclusive projects. These projects require an initial investment of ₹ 1,00,000 each and have a life of five years. The cost of capital is 10% and income tax rate is 50%. The company charges depreciation on strait line method. The estimated net cash inflows before depreciation and tax of the two projects as follows:

	Project X	Project Y
1.	40,000	60,000
2.	44,000	54,000
3.	56,000	44,000
4.	50,000	50,000
5.	60,000	40,000

Which project should be selected as per net present value method?

Solution:

Calculation of cash inflows of project X

Year	Cash inflow before Deprecia-tion in addition, tax.	Deprecia-tion	Profit after Deprecia-tion	Income Tax	Profit after Deprecia-tion and Tax	Profit before Depreia-tion and after Tax	Discount Factor @ 10%	Present value of Cash Inflows
1	2	3	4	5	6	7	8	9
1	40,000	20,000	20,000	10,000	10,000	30,000	0.91	27,300
2	44,000	20,000	24,000	12,000	12,000	32,000	0.83	26,560
3	56,000	20,000	36,000	18,000	18,000	38,000	0.75	28,500
4	50,000	20,000	30,000	15,000	15,000	35,000	0.67	23,800
5	60,000	20,000	40,000	20,000	20,000	40,000	0.62	24,800

Total present value of cash inflows:	1,30,960
Less: initial investment	1,00,000
Net present value	30,960

Calculation of cash inflows of project Y

Year	Cash inflow before Deprcn. in addition, tax.	Deprecia-tion	Profit after Deprecia-tion	Income Tax	Profit after Deprecia-tion and Tax	Profit before Deprecia-tion and after Tax	Discount Factor @ 10%	Present value of Cash Inflows
1	2	3	4	5	6	7	8	9
1	60,000	20,000	40,000	20,000	20,000	40,000	0.91	36,400
2	54,000	20,000	34,000	17,000	17,000	37,000	0.83	30,710
3	44,000	20,000	24,000	12,000	12,000	32,000	0.75	24,000
4	50,000	20,000	30,000	15,000	15,000	35,000	0.68	23,800
5	40,000	20,000	20,000	10,000	10,000	30,000	0.62	18,600
								1,33,510

Total net present value of cash inflows:	1,33,510 = 00
Less: initial investment	1,00,000 = 00
Net present value	33,510 = 00

From the above analysis, it is better to select project Y because it provides more present value of amount.

Illustration No. 14:

Gowtham engineering company is thinking to buy a machine, brand A for the manufacture of a new product at an investment of ₹ 2,00,000.

The annual operating costs are estimated at ₹ 75,000 excluding depreciation and these costs are estimated based on an annual production of 1,50,000 units. The fixed costs at this volume of production are an amount of ₹ 7,50,000 per annum. The selling price is ₹ 6 per unit of output. The machine has a five-year life and it provides no scrap value.

The company is now searching for another alternative model "DELUX". The model is capable of giving the same volume of production at estimated annual operating costs of ₹ 40,000 exclusive of depreciation. The fixed costs will however remain the same in value. This machine also will have a five-year life without scrap value. The investment of the machine is ₹ 1,75,000.

The management of the company has an offer for the sale of the brand A at ₹ 75,000 and the cost of removal thereof will amount to ₹ 15,000. Please ignore income tax.

Therefore, the company management found that the operating costs are low. In view of the lower operating costs, the company intends to dismantle the brand A model. It further thinks installation of deluxe brand. It is observed that the model has not yet started commercial production and that the time lags in the removal thereof. The project cost of capital is found 14% and the present value factors for five years are 0.88, 0.80, 0.68, 0.60, and 0.52.

As a financial manager of the company, state whether the company may replace model A machine by buying super model machine and provide your suggestion.

Solution:

Statement showing computation of net present value of super model machine.

Particulars	₹	
Cash outflow of super model machine		
Investment of the machine		1,75,000 = 00
Less: sale of brand A model of machine (75,000 – 15,000)		60,000 = 00
(I) Net cash outflow on deluxe model		1,15,000 = 00
Incremental cash inflow from deluxe brand		
Annual cash inflow from deluxe	1,33,750	
Annual cash inflow from brand A	75,000	

Net incremental cash inflow 58,750

(b) Present value of incremental cash inflows for five years at 14%

58,750 × 3.43 = 2,01,512.50

(c) Net present value of deluxe brand model 2,01,512 – 1,15,00 = 86,512 = 00

Therefore the net present value is positive

Particulars	Brand A	Deluxe model.
Cash outflow (Invest.)	2,00,000 = 00	1,75,000 = 00
Less; present value of cash		
Inflows for five years at 14%		
Brand A 75,000 (.88 + .77 + .66 + .60 + .52		
= 3.43 75,000 × 3.43 = 2,57,250		
Less: pvcf	2,57,250 = 00	3,08,750 = 00
	57,250 = 00	1,33,750 = 00
Inflows for five years at	1, 33,750=00	
14%. 3.43 × 90,000		

Computation of cash inflows of the two models

Particulars	Brand A	Delux model
Annual production	1,50,000	1,50,000
Selling price per unit	₹ 6	₹ 6
Sales	9,00,000	9,00,000
Less; operating costs	75,000	40,000
	8,25,000	8,60,000
Less: fixed cost	7,50,000	7,50,000
Annual cash inflow	75,000	90,000

Therefore it is better to buy delux model of the machine.

Illustration No. 15:

Ramesh engineering limited is specialized in electronic goods. They have recently developed technology to design a new product. They are quite confident of selling this product. They intended to produce 10,000 units. The investment for this project is ₹ 30,00,000. The project will have an economic life of four years and no significant terminal salvage value. In the first four years, the promotional expenses are planned as follows.

Year	Advertisement	Other expenses
1	1,05,000	60,000
2	85,000	80,000
3	75,000	90,000
4	45,000	1,20,000

The company incurred additional fixed operating cost for this new product which is estimated at ₹ 75,000 per year. The company requires 15% of profit after taxes on its investment. The corporate tax is on an average works to be 50%. The company follows depreciation of straight-line method. The variable cost of producing and selling the unit would be ₹ 300 per unit. The present value of annuity of ₹ One received or paid in a steady stream for four years at 15% is 3.0079. From the information available, you are required to work out a selling price per unit of the product keeping in view with the company-required rate of return.

Solution:

The company intends to produce a new product. The production of new product will be undertaken keeping in view of financial goal of the firm. Therefore, let us first calculate the annual cash outflow of the organization. The second step requires computing the net present value of cash inflows as per the financial values.

Annual Cash Outflow

Particulars	₹
Total variable cost per year 10,000 × 300	30, 00,000
Promotional expenditure per year	1,65,000
Fixed operating costs per year	75,000
	2,40,000
	32,40,000
Less; income tax at 50%:	16,20,000
	16,20,000
Tax advantage on depreciation	3,75,000
30,00,000 × 1/4 × 50/100 =	3,75,000
	12,45,000

Present Value of Cash Outflow

Present value factor for four years @ 15% 3.0079	
12,45,000 × 3.0079 =	38,33,355
Add; initial investment	30,00,000
Present value of cash outflow	68,33,355

Tax implications; the total cash outflow of the project ₹ 68,33,355 is divided by 3.0079. ₹ 22,71,802

Therefore the required annual revenue before tax 22,71,802 × 100/50 = 45,43,604

Hence the selling price per unit = 45,43,604/10,000 = 454

Illustration No. 16:

Karnataka Industries Ltd. intends to undertake a product in their factory. The following financial information is available to you, as a financial manager of the company; you are required to draw conclusions about the plans. A product is currently manufactured on a plant. The plant was bought for ₹ 1,50,000 six years ago. The plant is not depreciated fully for tax purpose and it has a book value of ₹ 70,000. The cost of the product is as follows:

Particulars	Unit cost
Direct material	28.00
Indirect labor	10.00
Other variable overheads.	18.00
Fixed overheads	20.00
	76.00

The company produces 12,000 units per annum. It intends to use the old machine in future and spending an amount of ₹ 50,000 towards repairs.

The company is searching for another suitable new machine that should be of latest technology. The latest equipment is available with an investment of ₹ 4,00,000. The old machine will be traded off for ₹ 55,000. The projected cost of the product will be as follows:

Particulars	Per unit ₹
Direct cost	18.00
Indirect labor	14.00
Other variable overheads	14.00
Fixed overheads	22.00
	68.00

The fixed overheads of the plant and machinery will be allocated from other departments including depreciation.

The company sold the old machine in the open market for ₹ 50,000. The new machine will have a life of 10 years and the scrap value is ₹ 25,000. The income tax rate of the corporate sector is 50%. The company-required rate of return on investment is 10%. The company charges depreciation on new and old machinery for 10 years. The company assumes the future sales will be stable. Ignore capital gains tax. As a financial manager of the company, please provide your suggestion regarding buying of new machine. The present values of ten years as follows; 0.91 .83 0.75 0.68 0.62 0.56 0.51 0.47 0.42 and 0.39 respectively. In addition, present value of annuity of ₹ 1 for 10 years at 10% discount rate is 6.1446.

Solution:

The data will be processed for arriving an accurate conclusion for buying a new machine by the company. The analysis will be done in four steps. In the first step, it requires the calculation of annual depreciation for new machine, in the second step old machine depreciation will be computed. In the third step computation of two machines annual cash outflows will be done. In the fourth step, the incremental effect will be studied.

First step: Computation of annual depreciation on new machine

Particulars	₹
Investment of the machine	4,00,000 = 00
Add; sale proceeds of the old plant	55,000 = 00
Total cost of the new machine	4,55,000 = 00
Less: salvage value	25,000 = 00
	4,30,000 = 00

Annual depreciation on new machine 4,30,000 × 10/100 = 43,000

Second step: Calculation of annual depreciation on old machine

Book value of old plant 70,000

Therefore, the depreciation of old machine is ₹ 7,000

Third step: Computation of net cash outflows of the two machines.

Particulars	old machine	new machine
Production of units per annum	12,000	12,000
Variable cost per unit	56	46
Cash outflow due to total variable		
Cost of the project.	6,72,000	5,52,000
Repairs per annum	50,000	—
Fixed overheads for depreciation	7,000	43,000
	7,29,000	5,95,000
Less: income tax savings	3,64,500	2,97.500
	3,64,500	2,97,500
Less: non cash outflows, i.e., deprcn	7,000	43,000
	3,57,500	2,54,500
Add: savings in annual cash		
Out flows due to purchase of		
New machine	----	1,03,000
	3,57,500	3,57,500

Step four: Computation of net present value of savings, if new machine is purchased.

Particulars	₹
Annual savings in cash outflows for life of the asset	1,03,000
Present value of total savings in cash inflows for ten years	—
1,03,000 × 6.1446	6,32,894
Add; present value of cash inflow at the end of 10th year	
On account of salvage value 25,000 × 0.386	9,650
	6,42,544
Less present value of cash outlay in the initial year	4,00,000
Net present value of saving	2, 42,544

Therefore, the above financial analysis reveals that the purchase of new machinery provides positive results. Hence the proposal may be accepted and if found financially viable the company can arrange for deploying the new machine.

Illustration No. 17:

Jyothy Engineering Limited is considering the purchase of new machinery. There are two alternative models available in the market. They are X and Y. They are involved with a cost of ₹ 1,25,000. The expected cash flows from the two machines are presented below. As a financial consultant, which project would you propose to select the new machine?

Year	Cash inflow	
	Investment A	Investment B
1	₹ 50,000	₹ 60,000
2	45,000	50,000
3	35,000	40,000
4	30,000	40,000

The company has a financial goal to earn 10% on investment. The risk premium rates are 2% and 8% respectively for investment A and B.

Solution:

The financial consultant shall examine various aspects in buying of a new machine. At the first instance, he should compare the profitability of the two investments based on net present value of cash inflows adjusted for risk premium.

Computation of present values of cash inflows of the two projects.

Year	Investment A			Investment B		
	DF 12%	Cash inflow	pvcf	DF 18%	Cash inflow	pvcf
1	0.89	50,000	44,500	0.847	60,000	50,820
2	0.80	45,000	36,000	0.717	50,000	35,850

3	0.71	35,000	24,850	0.609	40,000	24,360
4	0.64	30,000	19,200	0.516	40,000	20,640
			1,24,550			**1,31670**

The net present value of the two investments;

Project A 1,24,550 – 1,25,000 = –450

Project B 1,31,670 – 1,25,000 = 6,670

HENCE, the project b can be considered. Project A provides negative returns and project B yield positive return of ₹ 6,670.

Illustration No. 18:

ABC Engineering Company is searching for a better project. It provides financial data for two projects. As a financial manager of the firm, you are required to suggest the firm which project is more beneficial to the firm.

The investment of these two projects requires ₹ 35,000 each.

Year	Project A		Project B	
	Cash inflow	Coefficient	Cash inflow	Coefficient
1	30,000	0.7	25,000	0.8
2	25,000	0.6	35,000	0.7
3	25,000	0.9	25,000	0.6

The company is willing to take a decision for deployment of funds in a financially viable project. The risk free cut off rate is 10%.

Solution:

From the above financial information, it requires computations in two steps. In first instance, it needs to compute cash inflows with certainty. In second step, the cash inflows arrived from step I will be multiplied with discount factors of the cut off rate of the project.

Computation of cash inflows with certainty

Year	Project A			Project B		
	Cash inflow	Coefficient	Pvcf	Cash inflow	Coefficient	Pvcf
1	30,000	0.7	21,000	25,000	0.8	20,000
2	25,000	0.6	15,000	35,000	0.7	24,500
3	25,000	0.9	22,500	25,000	0.6	15,000

Computation of present values of cash inflows

Year	Discount factor @ 10%	Project A		Project B	
		Cash inflows	Present values	Cash inflows	Present values
1	0.90	21,000	18,900	20,000	18,000
2	0.83	15,000	12,450	24,500	20,335
3	0.75	22,500	16,875	15,000	11,250
			48,225		**49,585**

Net present value from project A = 48,225 – 35,000 = 13,225

Net present value from project B = 49,585 – 35,000 = 14,585

From the above financial information, it is better to select project B. It generates more cash inflows than project A.

Illustration No. 19:

Rajesh Engineering Limited is interested to know the more risky project from the available information. As a financial consultant, which project would you suggest? The degree of risk may be based on standard deviation.

Project A		Project B	
Cash inflow	Probability	Cash inflow	Probability
3,000	0.3	3,000	0.2
5,000	0.3	5,000	0.3
7,000	0.2	7,000	0.3
9,000	0.2	9,000	0.2

Solution:

The financial data will be processed further to know more risky project. It requires two steps. The first step involves computation of standard deviation of both projects.

Calculation of standard deviation project A

Cash inflows	Deviation from Mean 6000	Square of deviations	Probability	Weighted squ. deviations
1	2	3	4	5
3,000	–3000	90,00,000	0.3	27,00,000
5,000	–1000	10,00,000	0.3	3,00,000
7,000	+1000	10,00,000	0.2	2,00,000
9,000	+3000	90,00,000	0.2	18,00,000
			Standard deviation of the project A =	**50,00,000**

Square root of 50,00,000/1 = 2236.06

Calculation of standard deviation of project B

1	2	3	4	5
3,000	–3000	90,00,000	0.2	18,00,000
5,000	–1000	10,00,000	0.3	3,00,000
7,000	+1000	10,00,000	0.3	3,00,000
9,000	+3000	90,00,000	0.2	18,00,000
				42,00,000

Square root of 42,00,000/1= 2049.30

Therefore, the data explores the riskiness of the two projects. Project A is more risky than project B. Hence the company should select project B because it provides less risk.

Illustration No. 20:

Mahesh Engineering Limited has the following investment opportunities. As a financial consultant, which proposal would you select from various alternatives?

Proposals	Initial investment	Profitability index
1	2, 50,000	1.12
2	1, 75,000	1.10
3	2, 25,000	1.09
4	2, 00,000	0.07

The company has a surplus amount of funds as ₹ 3,50,000.

Solution:

The company is searching for better investment alternative. Therefore, it should be analyzed based on net present value of investment. The net present value of proposal 1 may be found as follows:

2,50,000 × (1.12 – 1) = 2,50,000 × 0.12 = ₹ 30,000

Net present value of proposal 2 and 3 is presented below.

Proposal 2 1,75,000 × (1.10 – 1.00) = 1,75,000 × 0.10 = 17,500

Proposal 3 2,25,000 × (1.09 – 1.00) = 2,25,000 × 0.09 = 20,250

37,750

The above numerical information reveals that the proposals 2 and 3 provide more benefits whereas proposal 1 generates ₹ 30,000 only.

Internal Rate of Return

Illustration No. 21:

Kasturi Industries Limited is interested to select a project. As a financial consultant of the company, you are requested to analyze two alternatives and select best one as per the principles of internal rate of return method.

Particulars	Project X	Project Y
Investment cash inflows	15,000	14,000
Year 1	7,000	2,000
Year 2	3,000	2,000
Year 3	2,000	3,000
Year 4	6,000	11,000

Solution:

From the above analysis, it is observed that the cash inflows are not uniform. Therefore, internal rate of return will have to be calculated by the Trial and error method. In this analysis at the first step factor should be found. The factor indicates the relationship between investment and cash inflows. The factor can be computed by the following formula.

$$F = I/C$$

Factor = factor to be located

I = Original investment

C= Average cash inflows per year

The factor in case of project x would be = F = I/C

Investment = 15,000

C = Average annual cash inflows

7,000 + 3,000 + 2,000 + 6,000 = 18,000/4 = 4,500

Therefore, f = 15,000/4,500 = 3.33

The factor in case of project Y would be as follows;

$$F = I/C$$

I = Initial Investment

C = Average annual cash inflows = 2,000 + 2,000 + 3,000 + 11000 = 18,000/4 = 4,500

$$F = 14000/4{,}500 = 3.11$$

The factor found in case of project X = 3.33

The factor found in case of project Y = 3.11

The factor should be verified in table of present value of ₹ 1 received annually for N years. The arrived digits should be verified on the line representing number of years corresponding to estimated useful life of the asset. Therefore the project x will have a useful life period of 4 years. The factor should be verified in line of 4 years in the said table.

In case of project 'X', it was found that 3.33 are available in the table at 8% column. Hence, it should be calculated at 8% and the result should be shown equal to investment amount. Otherwise, it should be calculated repeatedly unto tallying of investment amount of the project.

Calculation of present values of cash inflows of project X

Year	Cash inflows	Discounting factor at 8%	Present value of cash inflows
1	7,000	0.93	6510
2	3,000	0.86	2580
3	2,000	0.79	1580
4	6,000	0.73	4380
			15,050

Therefore, the project X internal rate of return is 8%. In the similar way project, Y factor was found as 3.11. It should be verified in the table on similar lines of 4 years of useful life period of the project. It was found as 12%. Therefore, the present values should be calculated as follows:

Year	Cash inflows	Discounting factor at 12%	Present value of cash inflows
1	2,000	0.89	1,780 = 00
2	2,000	0.79	1,580 = 00
3	3,000	0.71	2,130 = 00
4	11,000	0.64	7,040 = 00
			12,530 = 00

Therefore, the present value of cash inflows is less than the investment amount of the project at 12%. Hence, the arrived 12% is not correct and let us choose another rate in order to meet the investment amount of the project of ₹ 14,000. Let us assume as 10% as project cost.

Year	Cash inflows	Discounting factor at 10%	Present value of cash inflows
1	2,000	0.91	1,820 = 00
2	2,000	0.83	1,660 = 00
3	3,000	0.75	2,250 = 00
4	11,000	0.68	7,480 = 00
			13,210 = 00

The present value of cash inflows at 10% is less than the investment amount of the project. Hence, again let us select another rate in order to attain the investment amount of the project ₹ 14,000. It should be 8%; the following table will reveal the status of the project.

Year	Cash inflows	Discounting factor at 8%	Present value of cash inflows
1	2,000	0.93	1,860 = 00
2	2,000	0.86	1,720 = 00
3	3,000	0.79	2,370 = 00
4	11,000	0.73	8,030 = 00
			13,980 = 00

Therefore, the present value of cash inflows of the project 13,980 which nearly 14,000 of the investment amount of the project. Hence, the internal rate of return is 8%.

Illustration No. 22:

Sasank Traders are searching for best machinery to install in their factory. The machine is intended to produce a luxury article, which commands demand for five years only. The initial investment of the project is 2,90,000 and its working capital is ₹ 20,000. The working capital amount will be realized at the end year of the project. The scrap value is expected at the end of the project life period is ₹ 6,000 only. The earnings particulars of the company are as follows:

Year	Earnings (before depreciation and tax)	Tax payable
1	95,000	25,000
2	1,35,000	35,000
3	1,75,000	45,000
4	1,20,000	20,000
5	70,000	5,000

The present value factors at various rates of interest are given below. As a financial consultant, you are required to analyze the present value of cash inflows at various interest rates levels. Please indicate the internal rate of return of the project.

8%	10%	12%	14%	15%
0.93	0.91	0.89	0.88	0.87
0.86	0.83	0.80	0.77	0.76
0.79	0.75	0.71	0.67	0.66
0.73	0.68	0.63	0.59	0.57
0.68	0.62	0.57	0.52	0.50

Solution:

The calculation of internal rate of return involves two steps. In the first step, cash inflows should be adjusted as per the tax adjustments. The next step is to calculate present values of the cash inflows at various levels of interest rates. The earning can be modified as follows:

95,000 – 25,000 = 70,000

1,35,000 – 35,000 = 1,00,000

1,75,000 – 45,000 = 1,30,000

1,20,000 – 20,000 = 1,00,000

70,000 – 5,000 = 65,000

Year	Cash Inflows	8%	10%	12%	14%	15%
1	70,000	65,100	63,700	62,300	61,600	60,900
2	1,00,000	86,000	83,000	80,000	77,000	76,000
3	1,30,000	1,02,700	97,500	92,300	87,100	85,800
4	1,00,000	73,000	68,000	63,000	59,000	57,000
5	65,000	44,200	40,300	37,050	33,800	32,500
		3,71,000	3,52,500	3,34,650	3,18,500	3,12,200

At 15% of interest rate, the project generates ₹ 3,12,200 of cash inflows where the investment is equal; therefore, the internal rate of return of the project is 15%.

Illustration No. 23:

Janaki Industries Limited have an investment opportunity involving an amount of ₹ 50,000. The project generates the following estimated net cash flow after taxes and before depreciation.

Year	Cash inflow
1	8,000
2	8,000
3	8,000
4	8,000
5	8,000
6	9,000
7	11,000
8	16,000
9	11,000
10	5,000

Calculate the internal rate of return of the project using 10% and 15% of discount factor.

Solution:

Calculation of internal rate of return of the project at 10% and 15% discount factor.

Year (1)	Cash inflow (2)	10% factor (3)	Present value (2 × 3) = (4)	15% factor (5)	Present value (2 × 5) = (6)
1	8,000	0.91	7,280	0.87	6,960
2	8,000	0.83	6,640	0.76	6,080
3	8,000	0.75	6,000	0.66	5,280
4	8,000	0.68	5,440	0.57	4,560
5	8,000	0.62	4,960	0.50	4,000
6	9,000	0.56	5,040	0.43	3,870
7	11,000	0.51	5,610	0.38	4,180
8	16,000	0.47	7,520	0.33	5,280
9	11,000	0.42	4,620	0.28	3,080
10	5,000	0.39	1,950	0.25	1,250

Net present value at 10% = 50,000 – 55,060 = 5,060

Net present value at 15% = 50,000 – 44,540 = (–5460)

Therefore, the present value at 15% provides negative results and 10% generates positive returns. Therefore, the internal rate of return will be calculated as follows

The IRR of the project lies between 10% and 15%. Hence, the accurate internal rate of return can be computed as follows.

10% + positive npv @10% ------ X (15% – 10%)

Pv10percentage - pv15percentage

=10% + 5060

------- X 5%

= 55060 – 44540

= 10% + 5060

------ X 5%

= 10,520

= 10% + 0.481 × 5%

= 10% + 2.4% = 12.4%

Hence, the internal rate of return of the project is 12.4%.

Illustration No. 24:

Raj Industries Ltd. is searching for a project, which will yield the following, returns over a period.

Year	Cash inflows
1	85,000
2	85,000
3	95,000
4	95,000
5	80,000

The investment of the machinery involves ₹ 2,25,000 and the asset is to be depreciated at 20% per annum on written down value. Income tax rate is 50% the scrap value is zero. The cost of capital is 12%. As a financial manager of the company, draw your conclusions and how will you explain to the top-level management regarding undertaking of this project. The present value of the rupee at the rate of interest is as follows.

Year	1	2	3	4	5
At 10%	0.91	0.83	0.75	0.68	0.62
At 14%	0.88	0.77	0.67	0.59	0.52

Solution:

Calculation of internal rate of return

Year	Yield	Deprcn.	Net yield	Tax net	Cash Inflow	PV 10%	PV	PV 14%	PV
1	2	3	4	5	(3+5) = 6	7	8	9	10
1	85,000	45,000	40,000	20,000	65,000	.91	59,150	0.88	57,200
2	85,000	35,500	49,500	24,750	60,250	.83	50,007	0.77	46,393
3	95,000	28,900	66,100	33,050	61,950	.75	46,462	0.67	41,506
4	95,000	23,200	71,800	35,900	59,100	.68	40,188	0.59	34,869
5	80,000	92,400	(12,400)	(6200)	86,200	.62	53,444	0.52	44,824
	4,40,000	**2,25,000**			**3,32,500**		**2,49,251**		**2,24,792**

Note one. The scrap value of the asset is zero. Therefore, the last year entire amount is treated as depreciation

The investment is ₹ 2,25,000 the table reveals that the investment will earn 14% of internal rate of return.

Illustration No. 25:

ABC Industries limited involved in manufacturing goods on a machine that is not fully depreciated for income tax purpose. The firm has current book value of ₹ 1,50,000. The following financial information is presented for further analysis.

The variable cost per unit is ₹ 108.00 + fixed overheads ₹ 37 = 145 = 00

In the previous year the company produced 22,000 units and the firm paid expenses on repairs expected to average ₹ 13,000 per month, the repairs cost is not included in the above financial information.

The company made an arrangement with the supplier of the machine as trade in for new equipment. The new machine would cost ₹ 9,00,000 before allowing ₹ 2,50,000 for the old equipment. The projected costs associated with the new machine are as follows.

The variable costs per unit is ₹ 87.00 + fixed overhead 43 = 130

The fixed overheads are allocated from other departments and the depreciation of the equipment. The old machine can be sold at ₹ 1,25,000 in the market. The new machine has an expected life of 10 years and ₹ 45,000 salvage at that time.

The income tax is 50%. The cost of the new machine and book value of the old machine may be depreciated in 10 years. The rate is 14%.

The demand forecasting of the product is 25,000 units. As a finance expert, you are required to give a suggestion for making investment decision. The present value of annuity of ₹ 1 for 9 years @ 12% = 5.328. Present value of Re. 1 at the end of 10th year @ 12% = 0.319.

Solution:

Calculation of net present values of cash inflows accrued from the machine.

(I) Net cash outflow for new machine

		₹
Investment of the machine		9, 00,000
Trade in value of old machine		1, 25,000
	(a)	7, 75, 000

(II) (a) annual depreciation for new machine

(Straight-line method) $\dfrac{9,00,000-45,000}{10} = 85,500$

(b) Annual depreciation for old machine 1, 50,000/10,000 = 15,000

(III) Differential depreciation

Depreciation per annum for new machine	85,500
Depreciation per annum for old machine	15,000
(b)	70,500
Differential depreciation extra for new machine	70,500

(IV) Cash savings from operations per year

If new machine is acquired

Variable cost of production $87 \times 22,000 = 19,14,000 = 00$

Variable cost of production in case of old machine is

108 × 22,000 =	23,76,000
Repairs of old machine (13,000 × 12)	1,56,000
Old machine cost of operation	25,32,000
Therefore the differential cash savings on buyin	6,18,000
Per annum (c)	

(V) Differential cash flows after tax per annum

Because of new machine buying.

For first nine years

Differential cash savings from operations (c)	6,18,000
Less; differential depreciation (b)	70,500
Taxable savings	5,47,500
Less; tax at 55%	3,01,125
Net savings after tax	2,46,375
Add; differential depreciation	70,500
Annual cash inflow after tax	3,16,875 *

For 10th year

After tax cash inflow	3,16,875
Add scrap value of the new machine	45,000
	3,61,875

(VI) As per the financial numerical information, the old machine can presently be sold for ₹ 1, 25,000. Therefore, the company will lose the opportunity if the company retains the old machine or decides to replace it. Hence ₹ 1,25,000 financial resources are available under both alternatives.

Computation of net present value (NPV)

Particulars.	₹
The present value of cash inflows for 9 years at 12%	
3,16,875 × 5.328	16, 88,310
Cash inflow accruing at the end of 10th year	
3,61,875 × 0.319	1,15,438
Present value of total cash inflows	18,03,748
Less; present value of cash outflows	7,75,000
NPV	10, 28,748

The financial information reveals that the net present value of project is ₹ 10,28,748 and therefore it is better to select new machine and replace old machine.

Illustration No. 26:

XYZ Company is a newly floated company. It is setting up a project with an investment of ₹ 3.50 crores. The company is examining to decide the location of the project. The government of India rules indicates that a plant, which is located in backward area, provides a cash subsidy of ₹ 15,00,000. The rules further inform that tax concession is available for 10 years with 20% exemption. Therefore, the company is thinking about location of the project in either forward area or backward area. The company is going to mobilize financial resources from the market. It borrows the fund at 12% rate of interest from the lenders in forward area market. It has the capacity to borrow the funds from backward area at the rate of 10% interest cost. However, as per the other analysis, the backward area involves higher revenue costs. The borrowed fund should be refunded in four equal annual installments. The first installment of the borrowed capital starts from the 4th year of commencement of project. The company adopts straight-line method of depreciation. From these particulars, as a financial consultant, you are required to draw a conclusion for location of the project by using DCF techniques. The company needs your comment for making an investment decision.

It is assumed that the company will borrow from the market sum of ₹ 250 lacks.

Profit/loss before interest and depreciation (₹ in lakhs)

Year	Forward Area	Backward Area	PV Factor 15%
1	(5.5)	(55.00)	0.87
2	36.00	(25.00)	0.76
3	56, 00	10.00	0.66
4	76.00	22.00	0.57
5	110.00	47.00	0.50
6	144.00	102.00	0.43
7	158.00	156.00	0.38
8	232.00	192.00	0.33
9	332.00	232.00	0.28
10	432.00	332.00	0.25

Solution:

As per the financial information given in the problem, the solution will require two steps. Step I is to examine the surplus available if the project is located in backward area. The second step needs to study the consequences, if it is located in forward area. Hence, the beneficial to the company will be preferred to locate the factor.

Statement showing the net present value of the project at 15% forward area

1	2	3	4	5	6	7	8	9	10	11	12
0	-	-	-	-	-	-	-	100	-100	1.00	-100
1	–5.5	35	30	–70.5	-	–70.5	-	35	-35	0.87	–30.45
2	36	35	30	–29	-	–20	10	-	10	0.76	7.6
3	56	35	30	–9	-	-	35	-	35	0.66	23.1
4	76	35	30	11	-	+11	56	62.5	-	0.57	-
5	110	35	22.5	52.5	-	52.5	87.5	62.5	25	0.50	12.5
6	144	35	15.0	94	47	47	82	62.5	19.5	0.43	8.385
7	232	35	7.5	115.5	58	58	93	62.5	30.5	0.38	11.59
8	332	35	0	197	99	99	134	-	134	0.33	44.22
9	332	35	0	297	149	149	184	-	184	0.28	51.52
10	432	35	0	397	198	198	233	-	233	0.25	58.25

+ 217.165

– 130.450

Net Present Value + 86.7

Column 1 = year

Column 2 = profit/loss before interest and depreciation

Column 3 = depreciation

Column 4 = interest

Column 5 = profit/loss after depreciation

Column 6 = income tax @ 50%

Column 7 = profit after tax

Column 8 = cash inflows

Column 9 = net outflows (investment operating losses and loan repayment)

Column 10 = present cash flows

Column 11 = discounted value factor 15%

Column 12 = value of cash flows

Statement showing net present value of project located in backward area

1	2	3	4	5	6	7	8	9	10	11	12
0	-	-	-	-	-	-	-	85	–85	1.00	–85
1	–55	35	25	–115	-	–115	-	–80	–80	0.87	–69.6
2	–25	35	25	–85	-	-85	-	–50	–50	0.76	–38
3	10	35	25	–50	-	–50	-	–15	–15	0.66	–9.9
4	22	35	25	–38	-	–38	-	62.5	–62.5	0.57	–35.625

5	47	35	18.75	–6.75	-	–6.75	35	62.5	27.5	0.50	13.75
6	102	35	12.50	+55.5	-	+55.5	90.5	62.5	28	0.43	12.04
7	156	35	6.25	114.75	-	114.75	149.75	62.5	62.75	0.38	23.845
8	192	35	-	157	42.25	114.75	149.75	-	149.75	0.33	49.4175
9	232	35	-	197	82.25	114.75	149.75	-	149.75	0.28	41.93
10	332	35	-	297	182.25	114.75	149.75	-	149.75	0.25	37.4375

(+) 178.42 – 239.125 = –60.75

The net present value of project in forward area is +86.75 but the project in backward area shows a negative result of –60.75.hence project in forward area should be selected.

Illustration No. 27:

ABC Industries Limited provide the following information. The missing information related to the project should be calculated with the given data.

Particulars	₹
1. Life of the machine 4 years	
2. Annual cost saving	50,000
3. Scrap value	0
4. Internal rate of return	15%
5. Profitability index	1.075
6. Net present value	?
7. Investment of the project	?
8. Cost of capital	?
9. Payback period	?

The cumulative present values of the discount factor for 4 years is as follows

At 15% 2.855, at 14% 2.913, at 13% 2.974, at 12% 3.038

Solution:

As per the data given, the cost of capital, NPV, investment amount of the project and payback period should be calculated.

The project cost can be calculated as follows:

The savings per annum	₹ 50, 000
Life of the machine	4 years
Internal rate of return	15%

The project internal rate of return is 15% therefore the cash inflows for 4 years is 50,000

Considering cumulative discount factor is to be 2.855.

50,000 × 2.855 =1,42,750

The cost of the project is ₹ 1,42,750

The payback period of the project will be calculated as follows

Payback period = initial investment/annual savings

= 1,42,750/50,000 = 2.855

The cost of the capital can be calculated as follows:

With the help of profitability index, we can calculate cost of the capital of the project

Profitability index of the project is 1.075

If the profitability index were one, cash inflows and outflows would be equal. Therefore 1.075, the cash inflows would be more by 0.075 than outflow.

Profitability index PI = discounted cash inflows/cost of the project

1.075 = discounted cash inflows/1,42,750

Or 1.075 × 1,42,750 = 1,53,456

The annual cost saving is ₹ 50,000 hence the cumulative discount factor for 4 years

1,53,456/50,000 = 3.069

The discount factor at 12%, the cumulative discount factor for 4 years is 3.038; therefore, the cost of capital would be 12%.

The net present value of the project

NPV = total present value of cash inflows – cost of the project

= 1,53,456 – 1,42,750 = 10,706

Illustration No. 28:

Beta engineering limited is contemplating to purchase a new machine to replace the old machine from its factory. The following information is available for consideration.

The company has utilized the old machine since 5 years. The income tax rate is 50% and there is no interest cost.

Particulars	Old machine	New machine
Investment of the machine	50,000	65,000
Life of the machine	10 years	10 years
Selling price per unit	1.40	1.40
Material cost per unit	0.60	0.60
Machine running hours per annum	2,200	2,200
Units per hour	20	30
Power per annum	1,800	4,200

Stores per annum	6,200	7,300
Wages per running hour	2.75	5.00
All other charges per annum	7,500	8,500

The depreciation has to be charged on straight-line method. As per the data given, you are required to calculate the accounting rate of return of the project and suggest which machine is preferable.

Solution:

Valuation of old machine for computation of accounting rate of retrun.

(a) accounting rate of return = average net earnings/original investment × 100

(b) accounting rate of return = average net earnings/average investment × 100

(c) accounting rate of return = incremental earnings/incremental investment × 100

Accounting rate of return can be calculated through the above formulas for the given machine. For this purpose, profitability statement should be drawn to provide a meaning-full explanation.

Particulars	₹	
Investment of the machine	50,000	
Life of the machine	10 years	
Production 2,200 × 22	48,400	
Sales	60,500	
Less:		
Direct material 48,400 × 0.60	29,040	
Wages 2,200 × .2.75	6,050	
Power	1,800	
Stores	6,200	
Other charges	7,500	
Depreciation	5,000	55,590
Profit before tax	4910	
Income tax at 50%	2455	
Profit after tax	2455	

Accounting rate of return = 4,910/50.00 × 100 = 9.82%

Accounting rate of return = 4,910/25,000 × 100 = 19.64 %

Accounting rate of return = 7,650 – 2,455 = 5,195/6,5000 – 25,000 × 100

= 5,195/40,000 × 100 = 12.9%

Valuation of profitability statement of new machine

Particulars	₹	
Investment of the machine	65,000	
Life of the machine	10 years	
Production 2,200 × 30	66,000	
Sales 66,000 × 1.40 =	92,400	
Less: cost of sales		
Material 66,000 × 0.60 =	39,600	
Wages 2,200 × 5 =	11,000	
Power	4,200	
Stores	7,300	
Other charges	8,500	
Depreciation	6,500	77100
Profit before tax	15,300	
-tax	7.650	
Profit after tax	7.650	

Accounting rate of return = 7,650/65,000 × 100 = 11.76

Accounting rate of return = 7,650/32,500 × 100 = 23.57

Therefore, the following result is arrived for making a decision.

The old machine provides ARR-I, 9.82, ARR-ii, 19.64, ARR-iii 12.0% respectively

The new machine provides ARR I 11.76%, ARR. II 23.57%

Hence, it is better to replace the old machine because it provides more earnings inflow.

Illustration No. 29:

Sainadh Industries Ltd. provides the following information regarding two alternative machines X and Y. You are required to calculate the accounting rate of return.

Particulars	Machine X	Machine Y
Initial investment	65,000	65,000
Additional investment		
Working capital	6,000	7,000
Life of the machine	5 years	5 years
Scrap value	4,000	4,000
Income tax	55%	55%

Annual income after

Depreciation and tax

Year	Inflow	Inflow
1	3,500	7,500
2	4,500	6,500
3	5,500	5,500
4	6,500	4,500
5	7,500	3,500
	27,500	27,500

The company has adopted to charge the depreciation on straight-line basis.

Solution:

Calculation of accounting rate of return

ARR= Annual earnings/average investment × 100

Average income = total income/number of years.

Accounting rate of return for machine ×

Machine X = 27,500/5 = ₹ 5,500

Machine Y = 27,500/5 = ₹ 5,500

Average investment

$$\frac{\text{Original Investment} - \text{Scrap Value}}{2} + \text{Addl. net working capital} + \text{scrap value}$$

$$\text{Machine X} = \frac{65{,}000 - 4{,}000}{2} + 6000 + 4000$$

$$= 30{,}500 + 6000 + 4000 = 40{,}500$$

Machine Y = 30,500 + 7,000 + 4,000 = 41,500

Accounting rate of return machine X = 5,500/40,500 × 100 =13.5%

Accounting rate of return machine Y = 5,500/41,500 × 100 = 13.25%

Illustration No. 30:

Harish Engineering Limited is searching for a project. The following information provides two projects particulars. You are required to select a better project.

	Cash inflows	
Particulars	Project A	Project B
Year		
0	–15,000	–15,000
1	6,000	6,000
2	6,000	6,000
3	3,000	3,000

The risk less discount rate is 5%. Project A is less risky as compared to project B. The management of the company intends to consider risk premium rates at 5% AND 10% respectively.

Solution:

The risk-adjusted discount rate

Project A 5% + 5% = 10%

Project B 5% + 10% = 15%

Calculation of net present value of cash inflows of two projects

Year	PV	Project A (10%)	Discounted cash inflow	PV	Project B (15%)	Discounted cash inflow
0			–15,000			–15,000
1	0.91	6,000	5,460	0.87	6,000	5,220
2	0.83	6,000	4,980	0.76	6,000	4,560
3	0.75	3,000	2,250	0.66	3,000	1,980
			–2,310			–3,240

Both of these two projects generate negative results

SUMMARY

Every firm must have a goal. The financial goals of the firm should be to look after the welfare of shareholders. Shareholders are the real owners of the firm. It will be reflected in the market values of the shares. Every firm goal has two approaches: 1. Profit maximization and 2. Wealth maximization. Profit maximization means maximizing the income of firm. The business firm produces goods and services which will function in a market-oriented economy or in a government controlled economy. Market economy operates in an operative environment. In this environment, every firm is expected to produce goods and services desired by society as efficiently as possible. Price is the most important factor in the market-oriented economy. Intensifying the competition in the market forces, the firms to provide goods and services at lower prices in order to satisfy the millions of customers. Prices are determined by demand and supply condition. They guide the allocation of the resources for various productive activities. The firm's efficiency is the barometer of the corporate sector. The profit maximization theory had been criticized in recent years. In the economy, profit maximization is regarded as unrealistic, difficult, inappropriate and immoral. It might lead to inequality of income and wealth. A high degree of competition would certainly ensure efficient production of goods and services desired by the society.

Key Terms

1. **Investment:** An act or the activity of giving up a benefit presently enjoyed in order to gain a benefit in the future. Specifically purchasing securities; purchasing capital goods or fixed assets. Also the articles or cash acquired during this process. Also the value of the benefit given up.
2. **Regulating system:** A control system, the purpose of which is to hold constant the controlled conditions or to vary these under a predetermined program.
3. **Replacement investment:** The portion of gross investment which serves to replace the used up or worn out capital stock is known as replacement investment.
4. **Return on investment:** Ratio of net income after taxes have been paid to a firm or a division of a firm over a period to the average value during that period of the operating assets of the time. Synonym for rate of return.

Questions

1. What do you mean by project?
2. Explain how the projects are well implemented by the business houses?
3. What are the hurdles in project implementation?
4. Explain the importance of project monitoring function?
5. What is capital budgeting?
6. Explain the principles of disounted cash flow techniques?
7. What is the importance of payback period method?
8. How the corporate sector chooses their projects at present situation?

3 Capital Market

The development of a nation depends upon the activeness of the financial markets. Financial markets are dynamic and they occupy a prominent role in the modern economy. The financial markets act as a coordinator between the fund suppliers and borrowers. Financial markets mobilize financial resources from the sources of abundant supply and the resources will be converted into productive way of activities. They facilitate the smooth movement of funds from different sectors to productive sectors in the financial system. It facilitates mobilization and allocation of financial resources in the socially desirable and productive channels in the modern economy. A financial system comprises of four important elements, "FINANCIAL MARKETS, FINANCIAL INSTITUTIONS, FINANCIAL SERVICES and FINANCIAL INSTRUMENTS."

Market is where buyer and seller meet in a particular place in a specified time for exchange or to settle the transaction.

Financial markets are a particular geographical area of location where the fund savers and borrowers meet at a particular place in a particular time for settlement of their transaction. Financial transactions are under which financial assets are created and/or transferred. Financial markets exist whereever financial transactions, creation and transfer of financial assets or claims occur. A financial market may or may not have a particular physical existence. It facilitates buying and selling of financial claims, assets, services and securities. In financial markets funds are flown from abundant supply of sources to needy, dearth place of requirement. Fund is a scarce commodity; it is available for a price for a particular period of time. Fund suppliers in the market exist from individual savers, corporate entities, banking institutions, finance institutions and fund borrowers arises from firms, individuals, banks, commercial enterprises, government organisations etc., it is very important to know the meaning of Market closely. A market is a place which allows the purchaser and the seller to meet and gather information and lets them carry out exchange of various products and services. In other words the meaning of Market refers to a place where the trading of goods takes place. The place can be a market place or a street market.

FUNCTIONS OF FINANCIAL MARKETS

Financial markets occupy a dominant role in the emerging economy. The developing economies need a speedy, more dynamic, transparent, a high velocity activities for rapid growth. The speedy transaction settlement provides a high liquid fund to the economy. The dynamic economic system needs a speedy disposal of fund transfer. The velocity of fund transfer will make a speedy growth of industrial sector. A peace in the industrial sector stimulates the economic situation of a nation. A growth in economic activities leads to the increasing of "GROSS DOMESTIC PRODUCT (GDP)". A high GDP is the indication of wealth. A wealth is asset accumulation process. A wealth is the indication of prosperity. A strong asset formation creates richness of the economy. Therefore, capital formation is the most important factor for any kind of economy.

The market function is there so that the satisfaction of the buyers and sellers during a transaction can be ensured. The market generally depends on the adjustments of the price so that it can inform the participants involved in a transaction. This is done so that both the buyer and the seller are well informed and can bargain the right price out and satisfy themselves somewhat. The functions rendered by financial markets can be classified as follows:

A. Intermediary Functions

B. Financial Functions

A. Intermediary Functions

1. **Coordinator:** Financial markets provides easy transfer of real economic resources from lenders to ultimate borrowers.
2. **Income:** Financial markets provides income to the lenders through the form of interest/ dividend on their deployed financial resources. It leads to the enhancement of income levels of individuals and corporate savers.
3. **Productivity:** A financial market makes the nation to act in more productive way by diverting the funds from idleness to manufacturing activities.
4. **Capital formation:** Financial market always inspires the new savers through a better return/suitable interest a new flow of fund in the economy leads to strong capital formation in the country.
5. **Price:** The financial markets will know about the movement of fund supply and demand for financial resources.
6. **Marketability:** Financial market provides good marketability for the idle fund owners. If there is no financial market the fund owners are unable to find their parking place.

B. Financial Functions

The following function of a financial market includes:

- Borrowers are provided with to carry out their investment plans without any interruption in their routine activities.
- Lenders are provided with a suitable earning and deployment of resources in a productive way.
- Providing liquidity in the market for a continuous process.

Scope of the India Financial Market

The financial market in India at present is more advanced than many other sectors as it became organized as early as the 19th century with the securities exchanges in Mumbai, Ahmadabad and Kolkata. In the early 1960s, the number of securities exchanges in India became eight - including

Mumbai, Ahmadabad and Kolkata. Apart from these three exchanges, there was the Madras, Kanpur, Delhi, Bangalore and Pune exchanges as well. Today there are 23 regional securities exchanges in India.

The Indian stock markets till date have remained stagnant due to the rigid economic controls. It was only in 1991, after the liberalization process that the Indian securities market witnessed a flurry of IPOs serially. The market saw many new companies spanning across different industry segments and business began to flourish.

The launch of the NSE (National Stock Exchange) and the OTCEI (Over the Counter Exchange of India) in the mid-1990s, helped in regulating a smooth and transparent form of securities trading.

The regulatory body for the Indian capital markets was the SEBI (Securities and Exchange Board of India). The capital markets in India experienced turbulence after which the SEBI came into prominence. The market loopholes had to be plugged by taking drastic measures.

Potential of the India Financial Market

Indian Financial Market helps in promoting the savings of the economy - helping to adopt an effective channel to transmit various financial policies. The Indian financial sector is well-developed, competitive, efficient and integrated to face all shocks. In the Indian financial market there are various types of financial products whose prices are determined by the numerous buyers and sellers in the market. The other determinant factor of the prices of the financial products is the market forces of demand and supply. The various other types of Indian markets help in the functioning of the wide Indian financial sector.

Features of the Financial Market in India

Indian Financial Indices - BSE 30 Index, various sector indexes, stock quotes, Sensex charts, bond prices, foreign exchange, Rupee and Dollar Chart

- Indian Financial market news
- Stock News - Bombay Stock Exchange, BSE Sensex 30 index, S&P CNX-Nifty, company information, issues on market capitalization, corporate earnings statements
- Fixed Income - Corporate Bond Prices, Corporate Debt details, Debt trading activities, Interest Rates, Money Market, Government Securities, Public Sector Debt, External Debt Service
- Foreign Investment - Foreign Debt Database composed by BIS, IMF, OECD and World Bank, Investments in India and Abroad
- Global Equity Indexes - Dow Jones Global indexes, Morgan Stanley Equity Indexes
- Currency Indexes - FX & Gold Chart Plotter, J. P. Morgan Currency Indexes
- National and Global Market Relations
- Mutual Funds
- Insurance
- Loans
- Forex and Bullion

If an investor has a clear understanding of the Indian financial market, then formulating investing strategies and tips would be easier.

India ranks among the well known emerging markets in the global economic scenario. Since the economic liberalization policies were undertaken in the 1990s, emerging market India has really prospered which has helped to boost the Indian economy to a great extent.

Factors behind the favorable emerging market in India: In simple terms, emerging market is used to evaluate the socio economic scenario of the country in terms of the growth of the market and industrial development. According to the recent survey, there are around 28 emerging markets in the world out of which India ranks in the second place.

The main factors behind this booming emerging market are the economic liberalization and the perfect competition market, the high standard of living and per capita income, the development of medical facilities and infrastructure, the increase in foreign investments and so on. Over the few years, there has been a significant growth of the Indian market which has resulted in the high Gross Domestic Product (GDP). The average annual growth rate ranges between 6 to 7%. The growth rate of GDP was around 6.7% during the financial year 2008-09.

To boost the emerging market India, the government is also taking some positive steps. The main aim is to increase the growth rate to around 9%. Due to the favorable emerging market, more and more industries are being set up and the customer base is also increasing. Currently, India is the 4th largest economic system in the world in terms of the purchasing power parity.

The recent economic development has also put a positive impact on the various sectors. There has been a significant development in the agricultural, service and industrial sector in the country. Today, to complement the rapid pace of economic growth, the service sector contributes around 54% of the annual Gross Domestic Product.

Foreign Investment and Emerging Market India

The increase in foreign investment has also cast a favorable effect on the emerging market in India. Due to the increase in demand, well known global companies are investing in the Indian market. The foreign institutional investments (FII) amount has reached around US$ 10 billion mark. In case of the Foreign direct investments (FDI) there has been a significant increase of around 85.1% from US$ 25.1 billion to US$ 46.5 billion.

EFFICIENCY

A financial market or credit market is said to be efficient when it satisfies the following.

(a) The prices of financial assets are determined by the natural forces of demand and supply of funds.

(b) Financial resources must be allocated in a proper way and in the most socially productive purposes.

(c) The market should operate at the least cost level.

(d) The market should not waste the use of resources.

There are different forms of efficiency of the financial markets which are presented below.

(a) Intrinsic valuation efficiency
(b) Rationalization efficiency
(c) Allocation efficiency
(d) Arbitrage efficiency
(e) Insurance efficiency

Intrinsic value refers to the real value of financial asset. The valuation of a financial asset is an important element in the financial market efficiency. The intrinsic value of an asset is the present value of the future stream of cash flow associated with the investment in that asset. If the market price of a financial asset is equal to its intrinsic value, then it meets the requirement of valuation efficiency. If the markets are more perfect then the valuation efficiency can be achieved.

Rationalization efficiency refers to the operational efficiency. It can be achieved when the financial markets can minimize the administrative and transaction costs. It is possible when it provides maximum facilities and conveniences to the borrowers and lenders. The rationalization efficiency reflects a fair return to the financial intermediaries for their valuable services. Rationalization of all costs leads to the higher profitable position to the business community. It reduces the wasteful expenses while increasing the profitability of the business community.

The financial markets shall have allocation efficiency. They should be able to channelize their resources towards more profitable avenues. The earning is the efficiency of the market. It should allocate the resources where marginal efficiency of capital is the maximum.

Arbitrage means taking the advantage of price fluctuation in different markets at the same time. An intelligent investor can make gains by using commonly available information. If the financial market is said to be in efficient, there will be possible to gain from the use to commonly available information. If the markets are perfect such gains are not possible at all because the prices will reflect all the relevant and available information.

Financial Markets are essential for fund raising. Through Financial Market, borrowers can find suitable lenders. Banks also help in the process of financing by working as intermediaries. They use the money, which is saved and deposited by a group of people; for giving loans to another group of people who need it. Generally, banks provide financing in the form of loans and mortgages. Except banks other intermediaries in the Financial Market can be Insurance Companies and Mutual Funds. But more complicated transactions of Financial Market take place in stock exchange. In stock exchange, a company can buy other *company's* shares or can sell own shares to raise funds or they can buy their own shares existing in the market.

Basis of Financial Markets are the Borrowers and Lenders

Borrowers of the Financial Market can be individual persons, private companies, public corporations, government and other local authorities like municipalities. Individual persons generally take short or long-term mortgage loans from banks to buy any property. Private Companies take short or long-term loans for expansion of business or for improvement of the business infrastructure. Public Corporations like railway companies and postal services also borrow from Financial Market to collect required money. Government also borrows from Financial Market to bridge the gap between govt.

revenue and govt. spending. Local authorities like municipalities sometimes borrow in their own name and sometimes govt. borrows on behalf of them from the Financial Market.

Lenders in the Financial Market are actually the investors. Their invested money is used to finance the requirements of borrowers. So, there are various types of investments which generate lending activities. Some of these types of investments are depositing money in savings bank account, paying premiums to Insurance Companies, investing in shares of different companies, investing in govt. bonds and investing in pension funds and mutual funds.

Financial Market is nothing but a tool which is used to raise capital. Just like any other tool, it can be beneficial and can be harmful too. So, the ultimate outcome solely lies in the hands of the people who use it to serve their purpose.

The quantity of Market Demands in a competitive Free Market aggregates the individual demands with respect to a particular commodity. They are equalized with the quantity of Market Supplies through the fluctuations in the price of goods and services available in a market with a considerably large size. Price (of goods and services) therefore acts as an equalizer that works effectively in balancing the volume demanded by the consumers and the volume supplied by the suppliers so that equilibrium is maintained in the market.

An effective equilibrium between this and Market Supplies helps in keeping the prices of goods and services in the market more or less stable. This means that prospective customers do not have to shell out more money that will only increase the profits of the suppliers while simultaneously stretching their own resources to the limits or exceed it. At the same time a stable market also provides relief to the suppliers for they are then aware that they do not have to sell their products at subsidized prices by either reducing the margin of their profits or suffering losses.

So it is evident that the economy of the market including the price and quantity of things bought and sold is after all regulated by Market Demands and Market Supplies and does not change on its own. The size of the market is very important in this regard.

A market with a single producer and many consumers functions according to the wants of the producer who enjoys a monopoly. Such a producer, in the need to maximize the profits from the sales of his products, adjusts the prices and quantity accordingly. Such a market is not at equilibrium because the prices are higher and even the quality offered at those prices is usually lower in comparison to a competitive Free Market. A market with a lone consumer amidst numerous sellers is equally disbalanced, for here the consumer forces the sellers to lower their prices to meet the criteria of his demands. However, the economic theory of these Supplies cannot be applied in a small market with only a handful of producers (sellers) and consumers (buyers) as in such a case Market Supplies become directly proportional to Market Demands, that is, a change in any one, directly affects the other.

The Law of Demand refers to the consistent relationship between this and Market Supplies. According to this law, whenever there is a rise in the prices of goods and services, the demand of those same goods and services automatically fall considering the other factors remain the same, and *vice versa*.

An economy is bound to experience growth and recession at the same time. India Market Report is all about the rate at which the economy is growing and also the pace of recession. There are pros and cons attached with the entire Indian market — boasting with more than one billion plus population, emerging sectors full of untapped potential, opportunity for loads of investment to come in — this economy has the negative fallback with the inflationary rate and infrastructural weaknesses. The cons of the Indian economy have always played a deterrent factor to the economic growth.

A market report on India brings up the production and market trends, analyses the opportunities, gives projected figures of sales and marketing, formulates strategies for betterment. The report on Indian markets also reflects the market share, studies the segmentation, size, and growth of the domestic and global markets.

India Market Report studies the nature of a wide arena of industries in India — airlines, textiles, alcoholic drinks, analgesics, bakery and cereals, chemicals, cosmetics, deodorants, detergents, financial debit and credit cards, beverages, travel and tourism etc.

Statistics of the India market report are:

- GDP growth rate dipped from an average of over 9% in the previous three fiscal years to 6.7% during 2008-09.
- WPI registered a growth rate of nearly 13% in August 2008 and had an equally sharp fall to zero percent in March 2009.
- Fiscal accommodation led to an increase in fiscal deficit from 2.7% in 2007-08 to 6.2% of GDP in 2008-09.
- Industrial sector grew at 3.9% in 2008-09.

Figures in the India Market Report have always indicated that there was a steady progress on the infrastructure front. The six core industries of the India Market are electricity, coal, steel, crude oil, petroleum refinery products, and cement. The transport and communications, railways sector have all maintained a high growth rate steadily though there had been few downs at the same time.

It can easily be deciphered from the India Market Report that the market economy of India is highly sustainable but depends on balanced, equal and inclusive growth. It may also be noted from the India Market Report that infrastructure is highly essential for development and definitely it is the determining factor of an economy.

India Financial market is one of the oldest in the world and is considered to be the fastest growing and best among all the markets of the emerging economies. The history of Indian capital markets dates back 200 years toward the end of the 18th century when India was under the rule of the East India Company. The development of the capital market in India concentrated around Mumbai where no less than 200 to 250 securities brokers were active during the second half of the 19th century. The financial market in India today is more developed than many other sectors because it was organized long before, with the securities exchanges of Mumbai, Ahmadabad and Kolkata established as early as the 19th century.

By the early 1960s, the total number of securities exchanges in India rose to eight, including Mumbai, Ahmadabad and Kolkata apart from Chennai, Kanpur, Delhi, Bengaluru and Pune. Today there are 21 regional securities exchanges in India in addition to the centralized NSE (National Stock Exchange) and OTCEI (Over the Counter Exchange of India).

However, the stock markets in India remained stagnant due to stringent controls on the market economy that allowed only a handful of monopolies to dominate their respective sectors. The corporate sector wasn't allowed into many industry segments, which were dominated by the state controlled public sector resulting in stagnation of the economy right up to the early 1990s. Thereafter, when the Indian economy began liberalizing and the controls began to be dismantled or eased out, the securities markets witnessed a flurry of IPOs that were launched. This resulted in many new companies across different industry segments to come up with newer products and services.

A remarkable feature of the growth of the Indian economy in recent years has been the role played by its securities markets in assisting and fuelling that growth with money rose within the economy. This was in marked contrast to the initial phase of growth in many of the fast growing economies of East Asia that witnessed huge doses of FDI (Foreign Direct Investment) spurring growth in their initial days of market decontrol. During this phase in India much of the organized sector has been affected by high growth as the financial markets played an all-inclusive role in sustaining financial resource mobilization. Many PSUs (Public Sector Undertakings) that decided to offload part of their equity were also helped by the well-organized securities market in India.

The launch of the NSE (National Stock Exchange) and the OTCEI (Over the Counter Exchange of India) during the mid-1990s, by the government of India were meant to usher in an easier and more transparent form of trading in securities. The NSE was conceived as the market for trading in the securities of companies from the large-scale sector and the OTCEI for those from the small-scale sector. While the NSE has not just done well to grow and evolve into the virtual backbone of capital markets in India, the OTCEI struggled and is yet to show any sign of growth and development. The integration of IT into the capital market infrastructure has been particularly smooth in India due to the country's world class IT industry. This has pushed up the operational efficiency of the Indian stock market to global standards and as a result the country has been able to capitalize on its high growth and attract foreign capital like never before.

The regulating authority for capital markets in India is the SEBI (Securities and Exchange Board of India). SEBI came into prominence in the 1990s, after the capital markets experienced some turbulence. It had to take drastic measures to plug many loopholes that were exploited by certain market forces to advance their vested interests. After this initial phase of struggle SEBI has grown in strength as the regulator of India's capital markets and as one of the country's most important institutions.

Classification of Financial Markets

Financial markets in India are classified into two kinds. (A) Organized market (B) Unorganized market. Unorganized market has no proper regulations relating to financial affairs. The financial instruments are not standardized and unscientific in character limited in supply. The settlements of transactions are also not effective. The organized financial market, has a set of rules and regulations, monitoring system, governing the financial affairs of the economy. These markets are fully controlled and monitored by the government. The day to day operations are carried out by regulatory bodies and a regular transmission of information to the government organs for taking a decision. The organized market consists of "CAPITAL MARKET, MONEY MARKET". The unorganized market is dominated by money lenders, indigenous bankers etc.

PRIMARY MARKET

Capital market is one of the most important segments of the Indian financial system. It is the market available to the companies for meeting their requirements of the long-term funds. It refers to all the facilities and the institutional arrangements for borrowing and lending funds. In other words, it is concerned with the raising of money capital for purposes of making long-term investments. The market consists of a number of individuals and institutions (including the government) that canalize the supply and demand for long-term capital and claims on it. The demand for long term capital comes predominantly from private sector manufacturing industries, agriculture sector, trade and the government agencies. While, the supply of funds for the capital market comes largely from individual and corporate savings, banks, insurance companies, specialized financing agencies and the surplus of governments.

Primary market is known as new issue market. The new issue market is also known as public issue. In the primary market, new securities are sold or exchanged for cash or credit or other sources. The new securities can be issued by either existing companies or newly established companies. It can be described as a market where new securities are bought and sold for the first time. The development of primary market depends upon the movement of secondary market. If the secondary market activities increase, then there will be demand for primary market issues. If there is no demand in secondary market, the primary market may be in a dull position. Hence, the activity in the primary market depends upon the secondary market. In the primary market, the funds are raised through the sale of new securities flow from the buyers of securities to the issuer of securities. The financial institutions occupy a dominant role in moving funds from the savings to investment. They act as a coordinator between savers and borrowers. They convert the entire savings into investment process. The investment process materializes the industrialization. The process of industrialization is only possible with sufficient financial resources. The securities are sold by the large industrial units to the public under supervision of government authorities. The financial activities and primary market activities are monitored by the regulatory authorized by the union government. The required funds can also be raised privately to a limited number of investors. This process is known as private placement. The primary market creates financial claims. In this market the public can only buy the shares. Two parties are involved in this market; they are lenders and the borrowers. The funds flow from the lenders to the borrowers.

Objectives of Capital Issues

Generally the companies require two kinds of capital. They are (a) Fixed capital (b) Working capital. Fixed capital is needed for financing the capital assets. It is raised for buying of fixed assets like machinery, plant, equipment, land, and building at the initial stage of a project. Sometimes existing companies can also raise funds from the primary market. The issue of capital can be raised for any of the following purposes.

(a) Promotion of new project.

(b) Expansion of the existing capacity.

(c) Diversification.

(d) Capitalization of reserves.

(e) Regular working capital requirement.

The primary market is where securities are created. It's in this market that firms sell (float) new stocks and bonds to the public for the first time. It is also known as initial public offering (IPO). IPO occurs when a private company sells stocks to the public for the first time. They can be very complicated because many different rules and regulations dictate the processes of institutions, but they all follow a general pattern:

1. A company contacts an underwriting firm to determine the legal and financial details of the public offering.
2. A preliminary registration statement, detailing the company's interests and prospects and the specifics of the issue, is filed with the appropriate authorities. Known as a preliminary prospectus, or red herring, this document is neither finalized nor is it a solicitation by the company issuing the new shares. It is simply an information pamphlet and a letter describing the company's intent.
3. The appropriate governing bodies must approve the finalized statement as well as a final prospectus, which details the issue's price, restrictions and benefits and is issued to those who purchase the securities. This final prospectus is legally binding for the company.

SEBI Guidelines

Any company or a listed company making a public issue or a rights issue of value of more than ₹ 50 lakhs is required to file a draft offer document with SEBI for its observations. The company can proceed further only after getting observations from SEBI. The company has to open its issue within three months from the date of SEBI's observation letter.

Through public issues, SEBI has laid down eligibility norms for entities accessing the primary market. The entry norms are only for companies making a public issue and not for listed company making a rights issue.

The entry norms are as follows:

Entry Norm I (EN I): The company shall meet the following requirements

- Net Tangible Assets of at least ₹ 3 crores for 3 full years.
- Distributable profits in at least three years.
- Net worth of at least ₹ 1 crore in three years.
- If change in name, at least 50% revenue for preceding 1 year should be from the new activity.
- The issue size does not exceed 5 times the pre-issue net worth.

SEBI has provided two other alternative routes to company not satisfying any of the above conditions to provide sufficient flexibility and also to ensure that genuine companies do not suffer on account of rigidity of the parameters, for accessing the primary market. They are as under

Entry Norm II (EN II)

- Issue shall be through book building route, with at least 50% to be mandatorily allotted to the Qualified Institutional Buyers (QIBs).
- The minimum post-issue face value capital shall be ₹ 10 crore or there shall be a compulsory market-making for at least 2 years.

OR

Entry Norm III (EN III):

- The "project" is appraised and participated to the extent of 15% by FIs/Scheduled Commercial Banks of which at least 10% comes from the appraiser(s).
- The minimum post-issue face value capital shall be ₹ 10 crore or there shall be a compulsory market-making for at least 2 years.

  Note: The Company should also satisfy the criteria of having at least 1000 prospective allotters.

The following are exempted from the ENs

- Private Sector Banks
- Public sector banks
- An infrastructure company whose project has been appraised by a PFI or IDFC or IL&FS or a bank which was earlier a PFI and not less than 5% of the project cost is financed by any of these institutions.
- Rights issue by listed companies.

The Indian capital market is broadly divided into the gilt-edged market and the industrial securities market.

- The gilt-edged market refers to the market for government and semi-government securities, backed by the Reserve Bank of India (RBI). Government securities are traceable debt instruments issued by the government for meeting its financial requirements. The term gilt-edged means 'of the best quality'. This is because the government securities do not suffer from risk of default and are highly liquid (as they can be easily sold in the market at their current price). The open market operations of the RBI are also conducted in such securities.
- The industrial securities market refers to the market which deals in equities and debentures of the corporate. It is further divided into primary market and secondary market.
- **Primary market (new issue market)** deals with 'new securities', that is, securities which were not previously available and are offered to the investing public for the first time. It is the market for raising fresh capital in the form of shares and debentures. It provides the issuing company with additional funds for starting a new enterprise or for either expansion or diversification of an existing one, and thus, its contribution to company financing is direct. The new offerings by the companies are made either as an initial public offering (IPO) or rights issue.
- **Secondary market/stock market (old issues market or stock exchange)** is the market for buying and selling securities of the existing companies. Under this, securities are traded after being initially offered to the public in the primary market and/or listed on the stock exchange. The stock exchanges are the exclusive centers for trading of securities. It is a sensitive barometer and reflects the trends in the economy through fluctuations in the prices of various securities. It is defined as, "a body of individuals, whether incorporated or not, constituted for the purpose of assisting, regulating and controlling the business of buying, selling and dealing in securities". Listing on stock exchanges enables the shareholders to monitor the movement of the share prices in an effective manner. This assists those to take prudent decisions on

whether to retain their holdings or sell off or even accumulate further. However, to list the securities on a stock exchange, the issuing company has to go through set norms and procedures.

Regulatory Framework

In India, the capital market is regulated by the Capital Markets Division of the Department of Economic Affairs, Ministry of Finance. The division is responsible for formulating the policies related to the orderly growth and development of the securities markets (i.e., shares, debt and derivatives) as well as protecting the interest of the investors. In particular, it is responsible for (i) institutional reforms in the securities markets, (ii) building regulatory and market institutions, (iii) strengthening investor protection mechanism, and (iv) providing efficient legislative framework for securities markets, such as Securities and Exchange Board of India Act, 1992 (SEBI Act 1992); Securities Contracts (Regulation) Act, 1956; and the Depositories Act, 1996. The division administers these legislations and the rules framed thereunder.

The Securities and Exchange Board of India (SEBI) is the regulatory authority established under the SEBI Act 1992, in order to protect the interests of the investors in securities as well as promote the development of the capital market. It involves regulating the business in stock exchanges; supervising the working of stock brokers, share transfer agents, merchant bankers, underwriters, etc., as well as prohibiting unfair trade practices in the securities market. The following departments of SEBI take care of the activities in the secondary market:

- **Market Intermediaries Registration and Supervision Department (MIRSD)** – Concerned with the registration, supervision, compliance monitoring and inspections of all market intermediaries in respect of all segments of the markets, such as equity, equity derivatives, debt and debt related derivatives.
- **Market Regulation Department (MRD)** – Concerned with formulation of new policies as well as supervising the functioning and operations (except relating to derivatives) of securities exchanges, their subsidiaries, and market institutions such as clearing and settlement organizations and depositories.
- **Derivatives and New Products Departments (DNPD)** – Concerned with supervising trading at derivatives segments of stock exchanges, introducing new products to be traded and consequent policy changes.

Policy Measures and Initiatives

A number of initiatives have been undertaken by the government, from time to time, so as to provide financial and regulatory reforms in the primary and secondary market segments of the capital market. These measures broadly aim to sustain the confidence of investors (both domestic and foreign) in the country's capital market.

The policy initiatives that have been undertaken in the primary market during 2006-07 include:

- SEBI has notified the disclosures and other related requirements for companies desirous of issuing Indian depository receipts in India. It has been mandated that: (i) the issuer must be listed in its home country; (ii) it must not have been barred by any regulatory body; and (iii) it should have a good track record of compliance of securities market regulations.

- As a condition of continuous listing, listed companies have to maintain a minimum level of public shareholding at 25 per cent of the total shares issued. The exemptions include: (i) companies which are required to maintain more than 10 per cent, but less than 25 per cent in accordance with the Securities Contracts (Regulation) Rules, 1957; and (ii) companies that have two crore or more of listed shares and ₹ 1,000 crore or more of market capitalization.
- SEBI has specified that shareholding pattern will be indicated by listed companies under three categories, namely, 'shares held by promoter and promoter group'; 'shares held by public' and 'shares held by custodians and against which depository receipts have been issued'.
- In accordance with the guidelines issued by SEBI, the issuers are required to state on the cover page of the offer document whether they have opted for an IPO (Initial Public Offering) grading from the rating agencies. In case the issuers opt for a grading, they are required to disclose the grades including the unaccepted grades in the prospectus.
- SEBI has facilitated a quick and cost effective method of raising funds termed as 'Qualified Institutional Placement (QIP)' from the Indian securities market by way of private placement of securities or convertible bonds with the Qualified Institutional Buyers.
- SEBI has stipulated that the benefit of 'no lock-in' on the pre-issue shares of an unlisted company making an IPO, currently available to the shares held by Venture Capital Funds (VCFs)/Foreign Venture Capital Investors (FVCIs), shall be limited to: (i) the shares held by VCFs or FVCIs registered with SEBI for a period of at least one year as on the date of filing draft prospectus with SEBI; and (ii) the shares issued to SEBI registered VCFs/FVCIs upon conversion of convertible instruments during the period of one year prior to the date of filing draft prospectus with SEBI.
- In order to regulate pre-issue publicity by companies which are planning to make an issue of securities, SEBI has amended the 'Disclosure and Investor Protection Guidelines' to introduce 'Restrictions on Pre-issue Publicity'. The restrictions, *inter alia,* require an issuer company to ensure that its publicity is consistent with its past practices, does not contain projections/ estimates/any information extraneous to the offer document filed with SEBI.

Similarly, the policy initiatives that have been undertaken in the secondary market during 2006-07 include:

- In continuation of the comprehensive risk management system put in place since May 2005 in T+2 rolling settlement scenario for the cash market, the stock exchanges have been advised to update the applicable Value at Risk (VaR) margin at least 5 times in a day by taking the closing price of the previous day at the start of trading and the prices at 11:00 a.m., 12:30 p.m., 2:00 p.m. and at the end of the trading session. This has been done to align the risk management framework across the cash and derivative markets.
- In order to strengthen the 'Know Your Client' norms and to have sound audit trail of the transactions in the securities market, 'Permanent Account Number (PAN)' has been made mandatory with effect from January 1, 2007, for operating a beneficiary owner account and for trading in the cash segment.
- In order to implement the proposal on creation of a unified platform for trading of corporate bonds, SEBI has stipulated that the BSE Limited would set up and maintain the corporate bond reporting platform. The reporting shall be made for all trades in listed debt securities

issued by all institutions such as banks, public sector undertakings, municipal corporations, corporate bodies and companies.

- In line with the Government of India's policy on foreign investments in infrastructure companies in the Indian securities market, the limits for foreign investment in stock exchanges, depositories and clearing corporations, have been specified as follows:- (i) foreign investment up to 49 per cent will be allowed in these companies with a separate Foreign Direct Investment (FDI) cap of 26 per cent and cap of 23 per cent on Foreign institutional investment (FII); (ii) FDI will be allowed with specific prior approval of Foreign Investment Promotion Board (FIPB); (iii) FII will be allowed only through purchases in the secondary market; and (iv) FII shall not seek and will not get representation on the board of directors.
- The application process of FII investment has been simplified and new categories of investment (insurance and reinsurance companies, foreign central banks, investment managers, international organizations) have been included under FII.
- Initial issue expenses and dividend distribution procedure for mutual funds have been rationalized.
- Mutual funds have been permitted to introduce Gold Exchange Traded Funds.
- In the Government securities market, the RBI has ceased to participate in primary issues of Central Government securities, in line with the provisions of Fiscal Responsibility and Budget Management Act (FRBM Act).
- Foreign institutional investors have been allowed to invest in security receipts.

Thus, the capital market plays a vital role in fostering economic growth of the country, as it augments the quantities of real savings; increases the net capital inflow from abroad; raises the productivity of investments by improving allocation of investible funds; and reduces the cost of capital in the economy.

Rationalization of Guidelines for Public Issues

Keeping in view the changes in the capital market emanating from free pricing of shares and free access to market for funds by the issuers, the SEBI with the objective of broadening the investors' base, dispensed with the requirement of standard denomination of ₹ 10 and ₹ 100 (in terms of government circulars) and gave freedom to companies with dematerialized shares, to issue shares at any denomination but not below ₹ 1/- or decimal of a Rupee to be determined by them. This decision is also in conformity with the recommendation made by the Informal Group on Primary Market. The existing companies, which have issued shares at ₹ 10 and ₹ 100, also can avail of this facility by consolidating/splitting their existing shares.

In order to enable the investors to take informed investment decisions, the stock exchanges were directed to indicate the denomination value of shares as fixed by the company along with the market quotation. However, the companies availing of this facility are required to strictly adhere to disclosures and accounting norms.

As a further measure towards rationalization of existing guidelines, the SEBI decided that there would be only one set of disclosures and entry norms for all the issues irrespective of the issue price. Thus, the different requirements for making issues at par and premium were merged to create a common set of requirements.

Marketing Initial Public Offers through the Secondary Market

To facilitate the process of public offerings, the SEBI introduced the new system, *viz.,* 'Online Securities Offer System' which seeks to extend the benefits of online trading in the secondary market to the primary market. The system not only uses the existing infrastructure of the exchanges (*viz.,* terminals, brokers and systems) besides making necessary improvisations in software packages and improved means of connectivity.

- The present primary issue process involves printing of a large number of application forms and dispatching of refund orders and, therefore, leads to increase in cost and time required for the public issues. The new system would reduce the cost and time involved in a public issue process and does away with the blocking of funds of the investors.
- Compulsory linking of issuer companies with a depository and compulsory trading by new IPOs
- All new IPOs will be compulsorily traded in dematerialized form and guidelines of public issues were modified to make admission to a depository for dematerialization of securities, a pre-requisite for making a public or rights issue or an offer for sale. But the investors have been allowed to exercise option of either subscribing to securities in physical form or dematerialized form.

Disclosure of Credit Rating

On the basis of recommendations of the Committee set up to frame regulations for Credit Rating Agencies, the following additional requirements for companies issuing debt securities to public/on rights basis have been prescribed:

- All companies making public or rights issue of debt instrument (including convertible instrument) irrespective of their maturity/conversion period, shall obtain credit rating by at least one approved credit rating agency and disclose it in the offer document.
- Where credit rating is obtained from more than one approved credit rating agency, all the credit ratings, including the unaccepted ratings, shall be disclosed.
- The issuer shall give an undertaking in the offer document stating that they would give necessary cooperation to the credit rating agency in providing true and adequate information till the debt obligations in respect of the securities are outstanding
- Association of stock exchange personnel in allotment
- In order to improve the sanctity of the allotment procedure for public issues it was decided that Executive Director/Managing Director of the regional stock exchange along with the post-issue lead merchant banker and the registrar to the issue, shall be responsible to ensure that the basis of allotment is finalized in a fair and proper manner.

Lock in of Pre-issue Capital

- The practice of issuing shares at a price below the public issue price prior to the public issue, *prima facie,* gives a price advantage to such allottees. In order to discourage such practice, especially in view of high premiums to the issue price at which information technology stocks were being listed, it was decided to lock the entire pre-issue capital in case an allotment was made in above manner.

Disclosure and Investor Protection Guidelines

The Disclosure and Investor Protection Guidelines of SEBI were amended to provide for enhanced investor protection.

- The appraising agency would bring in the required contribution at least one day before the opening of the issue.
- The promoter's contribution has been made uniform at 20 per cent irrespective of the issue size.
- Only such securities have to be offered for promoter's contribution for which a specific written consent has been obtained from the shareholders for lock-in.
- Mandatory provision made for appointment of registrar for rights issues.

Malegam Committee for Disclosures in Offer Documents

- A Committee was set up under the Chairmanship of Shri. Y.H. Malegam to review the prevailing disclosure requirements in offer documents for public and rights issues and to recommend additions/modifications thereof in pursuance of SEBI's objectives for investor protection, promotion and development of transparent securities market.

Modifications in Eligibility Requirements for Information Technology Companies

- Companies in the information technology sectors submitted that in view of the factors like high valuation enjoyed by these companies coupled with low capital requirements, importance of employee stock options (as employees are the main asset for these companies) and attractiveness of ADR route for listing on overseas stock exchange with capital dilution as low as 10 per cent , they may be granted relaxation from requirement to offer to the public at least 25 per cent of the securities issued for the purpose of listing.
- In view of the fact that accumulation of excess capital by these companies would result in unproductive utilization and crowd out the other industries in need of capital, it was decided to allow these companies to list their shares by making a public offer of 10 per cent of the post issue capital instead of 25 per cent, subject to requirements of issue of minimum number of securities and a specified minimum issue size.
- A concern had arisen about the misuse of high valuation of IT industry by some unscrupulous promoters who may charge unreasonably high premiums from the investors. It was, therefore, thought necessary to stop the access to public funds by such promoters so that the interest of genuine promoters is protected.
- Thus, in continuation of efforts to ensure that the offer document contains adequate disclosures to enable the investors to make an informed investment decision, additional disclosure requirements were stipulated for companies which changed their names in the recent past to give an impression of being into information technology.
- To encourage only genuine information technology companies to be eligible to make initial public offer and to raise capital from public and to protect the interest of investors, it was stipulated that unlisted companies in the information technology industry should have a track record of distributable profits in three out of five years from the information technology activities. If a company fails to fulfill this criterion, it can access the market through the

alternative route of appraisal and financing by a bank or financial institution. The same conditions would apply to a listed company also which has changed its name to reflect the activities in information technology.

Amendments of Book Building Guidelines

- Book building is a price discovery mechanism used by the corporate issuing securities to discover the price of their securities. The mechanism also helps the small investors to subscribe to securities at a price, which is arrived at by a transparent process. The importance of this mechanism was recognized by the SEBI and book building guidelines were introduced in 1995. However, while book building became an accepted practice in the market for private placement of debt securities, it remained absent in the public issue market despite the regulatory framework being in place.
- This year saw the book building exercise being conducted for the first time for initial public offering as during the year, five initial public offers were made using the book building route. The practice of book building is comparatively new to the Indian capital market and the procedure is still evolving. On the basis of feedback from the market intermediaries, some areas of existing framework were identified for modification in order to improve the existing mechanism. The SEBI Board approved these modifications in October 1999. Under the modified guidelines an issuer has been given the option to book build either 90 per cent of the net offer to the public or 75 per cent of the net offer to the public. The balance issue is offered to the public at the fixed price determined through book building exercise. The book building mechanism is designed keeping in view the international practices and procedures for book building.

Modified Features of the Book Building Framework

- Additional disclosures with respect to the scheme to make up the deficit through book building in financing and the pattern of deployment of excess funds, shall be made in the offer document.
- Allotment in the book built portion may take place before that in the fixed price portion
- Excess subscription in fixed price portion can be spilt to book built portion reserved for allocation to individual investors bidding for up to 10 tradable lots, to the extent of shortfall in the latter
- In the 75 per cent book building scheme the allotment in the book built portion should be in dematerialized mode only.

Accounting Standards Committee

The Accounting Standards Committee, was set up by the SEBI as Standing Committee under the Chairmanship of Shri Y.H. Malegam, *inter alia* to review the continuous disclosures requirements under the listing agreement for the listed companies and provide inputs to Institute of Chartered Accountant of India (ICAI) for evolving new accounting standards and review the existing ones, wherever required in order to make disclosure standards and accounting practices at par with the international practices.

Major recommendations of the Committee that have been implemented by the SEBI are given below:

- With a view to make the unaudited financial quarterly results of the companies more transparent and meaningful, certain additional disclosure norms have been prescribed and also half yearly results have been subjected to a 'Limited Review' by the Auditors with effect from half year ending March 31, 2000.
- In order to harmonize the disclosure requirements under the Listing Agreement and the Accounting Standards issued by Institute of Chartered Accountants of India (ICAI), it has been prescribed that the Cash Flow Statement being disclosed by the companies in terms of Listing Agreement be prepared in accordance with the relevant Accounting Standard.
- In order to avoid excessive volatility in stock prices due to announcements of dividends, rights, bonus, etc., during the market hour, it has been prescribed that such announcements be made outside the market hours.
- The Committee has emphasized the need for formulation of accounting standards on Consolidation of Accounts, Segmental Reporting, Deferred Taxation and Related Party Disclosures and has urged the ICAI to expedite the issue of Accounting Standards on the above.

Employee Stock Options Scheme

The SEBI had issued guidelines on employee stock options in 1992 and modified them further in 1995. In view of the phenomenal growth in the knowledge-based industries, it was felt that there is a need to review the guidelines to suit the changed environment. As such a Committee was set up under the chairmanship of J.R. Verma to make recommendations and to frame the guidelines for Employee Stock Options and Stock Purchase Scheme. The guidelines were framed on the basic principles of complete disclosure and shareholder approval. The framework for employees stock option has been designed to give maximum flexibility to the corporate to formulate schemes keeping in mind the objectives of such a scheme subject to their following these basic tenets.

Guidelines on Employee Stock Options Scheme

- The ESOS/ESPS would mean the scheme under which a company grants option to employees and offers shares to its employees as part of public issue or otherwise.
- The employees have been given flexibility of exercising their option during the exercise period and to exercise option in accordance with the ESOS. The companies can offer equity shares and securities convertible into equity shares. The scheme includes American Depository Receipts (ADRs) and Global Depository Receipts (GDRs) or other Depository Receipts representing underlying equity shares or securities convertible into equity shares.
- The company has the freedom to determine the exercise price or pricing formula.

The employees have been given option to avail of such right but not an obligation to apply for shares of the company at a predetermined price.

- The employees can exercise the time period granted to them as a matter of their right to apply for shares against the option vested with them in accordance with the guidelines under ESOS.
- The right of option vested with the employees can lapse in case of termination of employment for misconduct.

- The ESOS can be offered to employees of the company provided the shareholders of the company approve the proposal by passing a special resolution in general meeting.
- There shall be a minimum period of one year between the grant of option and vesting of options. The company shall have the freedom to specify the lock-in period for the shares issued in accordance with the provisions of ESOS.
- The employee shall not have the right to receive any dividend or to vote or in any manner enjoy the benefits of a shareholder in respect of option granted to him till shares are issued on exercise of option.
- Option granted to an employee shall not be transferable to any person. The option granted to the employee shall not be pledged, hypothecated or mortgaged.
- In respect of options granted under ESOS during any accounting period, the accounting value of the option shall be treated as another form of employee compensation in the financial statement of the company.
- The accounting value of options shall be equal to the aggregate, over all employee stock options granted during the accounting period, of the fair value of the option.

India's top 10 IPOs

1. **Reliance Power: 11,700 crores in 2008**: This could easily be India's disastrous IPO. Anil Ambani has granted bonus shares to repair the damage done to the investors. That did not help as the stock never recovered. It is languishing at 170 rupees which is much below the IPO price including the bonus shares. There was no successful IPO after Reliance Power and markets are looking for Adani Power for a revival. Issue price of this IPO – 405-450 per share. Current Market Price: ₹ 172
2. **ONGC: 9,500 crores in March 2004:** It was the biggest IPO until Reliance Power came along. Issue price 680-750. Current Market Price: ₹ 1,125
3. **DLF: 9,188 crores in 2007:** It was one of the successful IPO's during the boom period. Though it did not give the listing gains as promised the stock has seen a dream run and went till the 1000 rupee level when Sensex was at 21000. The price band was 500-550. Current market price is: ₹ 393
4. **Cairn India: 5,788 crores in 2006:** Yet another oil and exploration company after ONGC. The price band was ₹ 160-190. Current market price is: ₹ 246
5. **Tata Consultancy Services: 5,420 crores in 2004:** One of the successful IPO's which has seen interest from around India. Current Market Price is, 482.
6. **NTPC: 5,368 crores in 2004:** Government has diluted 10.5% stake in this PSU to gather ₹ 5,368 crores. Current Market Price is ₹ 210
7. **Reliance Petroleum: 2,700 crores in 2006:** This debuted in the golden period or the boom period. This was the last successful IPO from Reliance stable. The initial price band was ₹ 57-62.
8. **Idea Cellular: 2,443 crores in 2007**: Price band is ₹ 65-75 per share. Current market price is ₹ 81. Only telecom IPO in the list. Airtel had a modest IPO of less than 1000 crores in 2002.

9. **Reliance Petroleum: 2,172 crores in 1993:** This is not a mistake. This was the initial IPO of Reliance Petroleum which was later merged with Reliance Industries which again came up with another IPO in 2006 (listed at #7). And now Reliance Petroleum is merged with Reliance Industries again. Something very common for Reliance.
10. **Jet Airways: 1,899 crores in 2005:** The biggest airline IPO until Air India IPO comes along. It was introduced in the price band of ₹ 950-1125. The current market price is – ₹ 247.

SECONDARY MARKET

Capital market is an inner element for the development of economy. The economic development of a country depends upon the maturity of its capital market. It is the nervous system of the economy. A strong economic situation creates wealth to the nation. The wealth creation is only possible with best asset formation. The asset formation is possible with capital formation. The capital formation depends upon the investment habits of the community. The economy may be either savings economy or spending economy. But the art of mixture of the economy is how much extent of saving should be done by the community and what level of spending may be done by the government. Capital market is the game of saving and spending. The saving and spending is based on risk and return. Risk and return is the game of financial markets.

The stock exchanges are known as the secondary markets. They play an important role in the securities market. The stock exchange is a place, where all kinds of financial products are available for buying and selling. In stock exchange, the government securities, municipal bonds, investment trust debentures and other financial instruments are traded. Secondary market means, the market for already issued shares. It is a medium of transfer of resources for the circulated securities. The development of primary market depends upon the activities of secondary market. If the secondary market is more active, the impact will be shown on primary markets. If the secondary market is inactive, there is no scope for primary market. The secondary market is run by speculation and gambling. The speculation is more important for the active trading. The speculation is oxygen to the stock market. It is desirable to some extent in the stock market. There is no secondary market without speculation. The activities in secondary market enhances the wealth of the corporate sector without any financial claims. The primary and secondary markets cannot be demarcated as two separate markets. Secondary market is resale market for shares and debentures. It represents an organized market in the trading of securities. The stock exchange activities are carried on by the members of the exchange. The securities are traded under certain set of rules and regulations. The stock exchange is an association or organization of members. Stock exchange was defined as follows:

"Stock exchange means an association, organization or body of individuals, whether incorporated or not, established for the purpose of assisting, regulating, and controlling the business in buying, selling and dealing in the securities."

— Securities Contract Regulation Act, 1956

"Security exchanges are market places where securities that have been listed thereon may be bought and sold for either investment or speculation" ***— J.F. Pyle***

Origin and Growth

The stock exchange is a systematic organized place where the securities are bought and sold. The organized stock exchanges in India are of recent origin. They are highly specialized and technically advanced organisations. They are competing with world stock exchanges. India is a SLEEPING LION AND ASIA'S TIGER in the global financial markets. The economy is in transformation stage. It is going to be called as digital economy. It has an excellent manpower with high information technology capability and emerging as a strong competitor to China. India is able to provide technical expertise to the American multinational firms. Strong and good policies may enhance the productivity and profitability levels of the corporate sector. The economic development is possible with a good chemistry of policies and extraction of information technology. India has excellent potential and talented skilled manpower to construct world class technology bourses. In India, the first stock exchange was set up in Bombay under the name of "native share and stockbrokers association of Bombay" in 1875. At present, there are 23 recognized stock exchanges under the SCRA, 1956. All the stock exchanges operate under the rules, by laws, and regulations, duly approved by the government. The objectives of the Securities Contract Act, 1956, are as follows:

A. To control the malpractices in the stock exchanges

B. To regulate the stock markets

C. To protect the investor's interests.

D. To improve the working conditions of the stock exchanges.

E. To create an efficient securities market.

The stock exchanges in India should work within the framework of the Acts. They are involved in accordance with the following laws.

1. Securities Contract Regulation Act, 1956
2. Companies Act, 1956
3. The Income Tax Act, 1961
4. Foreign Exchange Regulations Act.

1. Securities (Contract Regulation) Act, 1956

It was enacted to prevent undesirable transactions in securities by regulating the business of dealing therein and by providing for certain other matters connected therewith. The Securities Contracts (Regulation) Act, 1956 (hereinafter referred to as the Act), containing a mere 31 sections, keeps a tight vigil over all the Stock Exchanges of India since 20th, February, 1957. The provisions of the Act were formerly administered by the Central Government. However, since the enactment of The Securities and Exchange Board of India Act, 1992, the Board established under it (SEBI) concurrently has powers to administer almost all the provisions of the Act.

By virtue of the provisions of the Act, the business of dealing in securities cannot be carried out without a license from SEBI. Any Stock Exchange which is desirous of being recognized has to make an application under Section 3 of the Act to SEBI, who is empowered to grant recognition and prescribe conditions including that of having SEBI's representation (maximum three persons) on the Stock Exchange and prohibiting the Stock Exchange from amending its rules without SEBI's prior approval. This recognition can be withdrawn in the interest of the trade or public. SEBI is authorized to call for periodical returns from the recognized Stock Exchanges and make enquiries in relation to their affairs. Every Stock Exchange is obliged to furnish annual reports to SEBI. Stock Exchanges are allowed to make rules only with the prior approval of SEBI. The Central Government and SEBI can direct Stock Exchanges to frame rules. Recognized Stock Exchanges are allowed to make by-laws for the regulation and control of contracts but subject to the previous approval of SEBI and SEBI has the power to amend the said by-laws. The Central Government and SEBI have the power to supersede the governing body of any recognized stock exchange and to suspend its business.

A public limited company has no obligation to have its shares listed on a recognized Stock Exchange. But if a company intends to offer its shares or debentures to the public for subscription by issue of a prospectus, it must, before issuing such prospectus apply to one or more recognized stock exchanges for permission to have the shares or debentures intended to be so offered to the public to be dealt with in each of such stock exchange in terms of Section 73 of the Companies Act, 1956. SEBI can, however, under the provisions of Section 21 of the Securities Contracts (Regulation) Act, 1956 compel the listing of securities by public Companies if it is of the opinion that it is necessary or expedient in the interest of the trade or public. In the event of the Stock Exchange refusing to list the securities of any public company, an appeal to SEBI is provided under the Act. A Company as per the present provisions of law is obliged to get listed on the regional exchange, in addition to other exchanges. (There has been a recommendation that this restriction be removed).

A company on the grounds specified in Section 22A of the Act is entitled to refuse to register transfer of any of its securities, notwithstanding anything contained in its articles or Section 82 or Section 111 of the Companies Act, 1956 (See Table A).

2. Companies Act, 1956

The Companies Act, 1956 lays down rules and regulations to the stock exchanges with reference to allotment of shares. Sec. 73 of the Companies Act, 1956, deals with the issue and allotment of shares by the stock exchanges. Allotment of shares and debentures to be dealt in on stock exchange in the following way.

(1) Every company intending to offer shares or debentures to the public for subscription by the issue of a prospectus shall, before such issue, make an application to one or more recognized stock exchanges for permission for the shares or debentures intending to be so offered to be dealt with in the stock exchange or each such stock exchange.

(1A) Where a prospectus, whether issued generally or not, state that [an application under sub-section (1)] has been made for permission for the shares or debentures offered thereby to be dealt in one or more recognized stock exchanges, such prospectus, shall state the name of the stock exchange or, as the case may be, each such stock exchange, and any allotment made on an application in pursuance of such prospectus shall, whenever made, be void.

1. Ins. by Act 31 of 1988, s. 10 (*w.e.f.* 15-6-1988).
2. Subs. by Act 41 of 1974, s. 8 sub-section (1) (*w.e.f.* 1-2-1975) and renumbered as sub-section (1A) by Act 31 of 1988, s. 10 (*w.e.f.* 15-6-1988).
3. Subs. by Act 31 of 1988, s. 10 (*w.e.f.* 15-6-1988).
4. Omitted by s. 10, *Ibid.* (*w.e.f.* 15-6-1988).

If the permission has not been granted by the stock exchange or each such stock exchange, as the case may be, before the expiry of ten weeks from the date of the closing of the subscription lists: Provided that where an appeal against the decision of any recognized stock exchange refusing permission for the shares or debentures to be dealt in on that stock exchange has been preferred under section 22 of the Securities Contracts (Regulation) Act, 1956 (42 of 1956), such allotment shall not be void until the dismissal of the appeal.

(2) Where the permission has not been 1[applied under sub-section (1)] 2 [or, such permission, having been applied for, has not been granted as aforesaid], the company shall forthwith repay without interest all moneys received from applicants in pursuance of the prospectus, and, if any such money is not repaid within eight days after the company becomes liable to repay it 1[the company and every director of the company who is an officer in default shall, on and from the expiry of the eighth day, be jointly and severally liable to repay that money with interest at such rate, not less than four per cent. and not more than fifteen per cent, as may be prescribed, having regard to the length of the period of delay in making the repayment of such money.]

(2A) 4[Where permission has been granted by the recognized stock exchange or stock exchanges for dealing in any shares or debentures in such stock exchange or each such stock exchange and the moneys received from applicants for shares or debentures are in excess of the aggregate of the application moneys relating to the shares or debentures in respect of which allotments have been made, the company shall repay the moneys to the extent of such excess forthwith without interest, and if such money is not repaid within eight days, from the day the company becomes liable to pay it, 1[the company and every director of the company who is an officer in default shall, on and from the expiry of the eighth day, be jointly and severally liable to repay that money with interest at such rate, not less than four per cent. and not more than fifteen per cent., as may be prescribed, having regard to the length of the period of delay in making the repayment of such money.] 3

1. Subs. by Act 31 of 1988, s. 10 (*w.e.f.* 15-6-1988).
2. Subs. by Act 41 of 1974, s. 8, for certain words (*w.e.f.* 1-2-1975).
3. Omitted by Act 31 of 1988, s. 10 (*w.e.f.* 15-6-1988).
4. Ins. by Act 41 of 1974, s. 8 (*w.e.f.* 1-2-1975).

(2B) If default is made in complying with the provisions of sub-section (2A), the company and every officer of the company who is in default shall be punishable with fine which may extend to five thousand rupees, and where repayment is not made within six months from the expiry of the eighth day, also with imprisonment for a term which may extend to one year.]

(3) All moneys received as aforesaid shall be kept in a separate bank account maintained with a Scheduled Bank 1[until the permission has been granted, or where an appeal has been preferred against the refusal to grant such permission, until the disposal of the appeal, and the money standing in such separate account shall, where the permission has not been applied for as aforesaid or has not been granted, be repaid within the time and in the manner specified in sub-section (2)]; and if default is made in complying with this sub-section, the company, and every officer of the company who is in default, shall be punishable with fine which may extend to five thousand rupees.

(3A) 2[Moneys standing to the credit of the separate bank account referred to in sub-section (3) shall not be utilized for any purpose other than the following purposes, namely:

(a) Adjustment against allotment of shares, where the shares have been permitted to be dealt in on the stock exchange or each stock exchange specified in the prospectus; or

(b) Repayment of moneys received from applicants in pursuance of the prospectus, where shares have not been permitted to be dealt in on the stock exchange or each stock exchange specified in the prospectus, as the case may be, or, where the company is for any other reason unable to make the allotment of share.]

(4) Any condition purporting to require or bind any applicant for shares or debentures to waive compliance with any of the requirements of this section shall be void.

1. Subs. by Act 41 of 1974, s. 8, for certain words (*w.e.f.* 1-2-1975).
2. Ins. by s. 8, ibid. (*w.e.f.* 1-2-1975).

(5) 1[For the purposes of this section, it shall be deemed that permission has not been granted if the application for permission, where made, has not been disposed of within the time specified in sub-section (1).]

(6) This section shall have effect —

(a) In relation to any shares or debentures agreed to be taken by a person underwriting an offer thereof by a prospectus, as if he had applied there for in pursuance of the prospectus; and

(b) In relation to a prospectus offering shares for sale, with the following modifications, namely:

(i) References to sale shall be substituted for references to allotment;

1. Subs. by Act 41 of 1974, s. 8, for sub-section (5) (*w.e.f.* 1-2-1975).

(ii) The persons by whom the offer is made, and not the Company, shall be liable under sub- section (2) to' repay money received from applicants, and references to the company's liability under that sub-section shall be construed accordingly; and

(iii) For the reference in sub-section (3) to the company and every officer of the company who is in default, there shall be substituted a reference to any person by or through whom the offer is made and who is knowingly guilty of, or willfully authorizes or permits, the default.

(7) No prospectus shall state that application has been made for permission for the shares or debentures offered thereby to be dealt in on any stock exchange, unless it is a recognized stock exchange.

3. The Income Tax Act, 1961

The Income Tax Act, 1961, lay down rules and regulations for stock exchanges with reference to capital gains tax. Capital gains can be classified into two kinds, (a) short-term capital gains (b) long-term capital gains. The Income Tax Act, every year, the taxation procedure will be indicated in the budget of the central government.

4. Foreign Exchange Regulation

The stock exchange is required to act as per rules laid down by the Regulation Act.

The brokers, the investors, mutual funds and the financial institutions are the important constituents of the secondary market. The secondary market consists of the operations associated with the primary market. The secondary markets consist of regional stock exchanges, BSE, NSE, OTC etc.

Definitions

According to the Securities Contract (Regulation) Act of 1956, the stock exchange can be defined as "An association, organization, or body of individuals, whether incorporated or not, established for the purpose of assisting, regulating and controlling business in buying, selling and dealing securities.

According to Husband and Dockery "Securities or stock exchanges are privately organized markets, which are used to facilitate trading securities".

Functions of Stock Exchange

1. The stock exchange is established with the purpose of providing a market place for the members to deal with securities under well-laid down regulations and to protect interests of these: It extends liquidity to securities
2. It acts as a clearinghouse of business information.
3. It brings companies and investors together
4. It ensures wider ownership of securities
5. It provides capital to profitable sectors.
6. It ensures safety and fair dealings to all.
7. It facilitates market ability and transparency of securities.
8. It motivates managers of well-reputed companies to dominate the market.
9. It provides an orderly-regulated market for securities.
10. It facilitates continuous, ready and open market for selling and buying of securities.
11. It promotes savings and capital in the economy by attracting funds from the investors.
12. It facilitates the takeover by means of acquiring majority of share traded on the market.
13. It allows companies to float their shares on the market.
14. It induces managers to improve performance for converting the non-specified shares into specified group of shares in the exchange.

Classification of Securities Listed in Stock Exchange

The securities listed for trading in Bombay stock exchange are grouped into the following categories:

1. Group-A shares (specified securities)
2. Group-B shares
3. Permitted securities
4. Cleared securities
5. Non-cleared securities

1. Group A Securities

Listed securities are classified as cleared or specified or Group-A securities and non-cleared or unspecified or Group-B or cash securities. The security in which forward trading is allowed are called as Group-A shares. Group-A shares are included in the cleared list of exchange after the shares have satisfied the following conditions:

1. The shares should be fully paid up equity shares.
2. The companies paid up capital should be at least ₹ 5 crores.
3. The company should have a growth potential.
4. The company should be a dividend paying one.
5. The company's shares should have market capital,
6. The shares should have been actively traded on the floor.

2. Group-B Shares

The shares, which are traded on cash basis, are called Group-B shares. They are also called as cash scrips. The carry forward facility is not available to group B shares.

3. Permitted Shares

The securities, which are listed with some of the recognized stock exchanges, when permitted to be traded by those stock exchanges where they are not listed, are called as permitted securities. The permission is granted as per the rules and regulations of the stock exchange.

4. Cleared Securities

The securities, which are traded for fortnightly settlement is known as cleared securities. The payment and delivery will be completed in the third week following fortnightly clearing. The cleared securities are also called as specified securities. Speculation activity is permitted only for specified shares, which are included in the cleared securities list. The governing board of the concerned stock exchange has the power to pass special resolutions specifying the securities, which may from time to time be included in the specified securities list.

5. Non-cleared Securities

The securities which are traded between the brokers are called as non-cleared securities. These securities are not cleared through the stock exchange clearing house. Therefore, securities are not permitted carry-over facilities.

THE BOMBAY STOCK EXCHANGE

Bombay stock exchange is the oldest stock exchange in Asia and has the third largest number of listed companies in the world with 4,900 listed as on Feb. 2010. It is located at Dalal Street, Mumbai. On Feb., 2010, the equity market capitalization of the companies listed on the BSE was us $1.28 trillion, making it the largest stock exchange in south Asia and the 12th largest in the world. With over 4,900 Indian companies listed and over 7,700 scrips on the stock exchange, it has a significant trading volume. The BSE sensex (sensitive index), also called the BSE 30, is widely used as market index in

India and Asia. Though many other exchanges exist, BSE and NSE of India account for most of the trading shares in India.

BSE is the first exchange in India and the second in the world to obtain an ISO 9001:2000 certifications. It is also the first exchange in the country and second in the world to receive information security management system standard BS 7799-2-2002 certification for its BOLT (BSE ONLINE TRADING SYSTEM). Presently, it got an ISO 27001:2005 certificate; it is a version of BS 7799 for information security. The BSE index, SENSEX, is India's first and most popular stock market benchmark index. Exchange traded fund on SENSEX are listed on BSE and in HONG KONG. Futures and options on the index are also traded in BSE. Its achievements are presented below:

1. It became the first national stock exchange to launch its website in Gujarati, Hindi, and Marathi.
2. It purchased market place technologies in 2009, to enhance the in-house technology development capabilities and allow faster time to market new products.
3. It launched a reporting platform for corporate bonds christened the ICDM or India corporate debt market.
4. It acquired a 15% stake in United Stock Exchange to drive the development and growth of the currency and interest rate derivatives markets.
5. It launched BSE STAR MF mutual fund trading platform, which enables exchange members to use its existing infrastructure for transaction in mutual fund schemes.
6. It now offers AMFI certification for mutual fund advisors through BSE training institute.
7. It provides co-location facilities for algorithmic trading.
8. It successfully launched the BSE IPO INDEX and PSU website.
9. It revamped its website with wide range of new features like live streaming quotes for sensex companies, advanced stock reach, sensex view, market galaxy and members launched BSE SENSESX MOBILE STREAMER.
10. It has been undertaking corporate social responsibility initiatives with a focus on education, health and environment.
11. It has been awarded by world council of corporate governance, the golden peacock, global CSR award for its initiatives in corporate social responsibility.
12. It also received awards from ICAI for excellence in financial reporting in 2006-07.
13. The human resource department has received award from ASIA PACIFIC HRM awards for its efforts in employer branding through talent management at work, and excellence in HR through technology.

The Growth of Bombay Stock Exchange

1. 9-7-1875, the native share and stockbroker's association was formed.
2. 2-2-1921, clearing house started by bank of India.
3. 31-8-1957, BSE granted permanent recognition under SCRA.
4. 2-1-1986, SENSEX India's first equity index launched.
5. 10-7-1987, introduced investor's protection fund.

6. 3-1-1989, commenced BSE training institute.
7. 25-7-1990, SENSEX closes above 1000
8. 15-1-1992, sensex closes above 2000
9. 30-3-1992, closes above 4000.
10. 1-5-1992, SEBI Act established.
11. 29-5-1992, Capital issues control Act repealed.
12. 1992, Securities appellate tribunal established.
13. 14-3-1995, BOLT system introduced.
14. 19-8-1996, first time revamped sensex.
15. 12-5-1997, introduced trade guarantee fund.
16. 21-7-1997, broker's contingency fund introduced.
17. 1997, BOLT SYSTEM expanded nationwide.
18. 1-6-1999, interest rate swaps/forward rate agreement allowed.
19. 22-3-1999, central depository services ltd., established with other financial institutions.
20. 15-7-1999, CDSL commenced work.
21. 11-10-1999, sensex closed above 5000.
22. 11-2-2000, sensex crosses 6000 intra-day.
23. 9-6-2000, equity derivatives introduced.
24. 1-3-2001, corporatization of exchanges proposed by the union government.
24. 1-2-2001, BSE web launched.
25. 4-6-2001, BSE push index introduced.
26. 15-6-2001, wholesale debt market segment operations commenced.
27. 1-6-2001, index options launched.
28. 2-7-2001, VAR model introduced for margin requirement calculation.
29. 9-7-2001, stock options launched.
30. 11-7-2001, BSE tech launched, India's first free floated index.
31. 25-7-2001, dollex 30 launched.
32. 1-11-2001, stock futures launched.
33. 29-11-2001, 100% book building allowed.
34. 31-12-2001, all securities turn to T+5.
35. 1-4-2002, T+3 settlements introduced.
36. 15-2-2002, negotiated dealing system established.
37. 1-2-2002, two way fungibility for ADR/GDR.
38. 1-9-2003, SENSEX shifted to free-float methodology.
39. 1-1-2003, India's first etf (exchange traded fund) on sensex-spice introduced.
40. 16-1-2003, retail trading in G sec.

41. 1-4-2003, T+2 settlement introduction.
42. 1-6-2003, bankex launched.
43. 1-12-2003, T group launched.
44. 17-5-2004, second biggest fall of all time, circuit filters used twice in a day (564.71 points, 11.14%)
45. 2-6-2004, SENSEX closes over 6000 for the first time.
46. 20-5-2005, the BSE (corporatization and demutualization) schemes, 2005, (the scheme) announced by SEBI.
47. 8-8-2005, incorporation of Bombay stock exchange limited.
48. 12-8-2005, certificate of commencement of business.
49. 19-8-2005, BSE becomes a corporate entity.
50. 7-2-2006, BSE Gujarat website launched.
51. 21-10-2006, BSE Hindi website launched.
52. 2-11-2006, shares BSE SENSEX India trackers listed at Hong Kong stock exchange.
53. 7-3-2007, Singapore exchange limited entered into an agreement to invest in a 5% stakes in BSE.
54. 16-5-2007, appointed date" under this scheme, i.e., date on which corporatization and demutualization was achieved. Notified by SEBI in the official gazette on 29.06.2007.
55. 10-1-2008, SENSEX all-time high 21206.77.
56. 1-10-2008, currency derivatives introduced.
57. 18-5-2009, the SENSEX raised 2110.70 points (17.34%) and index-wide upper circuit breaker applied.
58. 7-8-2009, BSE-USE form alliance to develop currency and interest rate derivative markets.
59. 24-8-2009, BSE IPO index launched.
60. 1-10-2009, Bombay stock exchange introduced trade details facility for the investors.
61. 5-10-2009, BSE introduction new transaction fee structure for cash equity segment.
62. 25-11-2009, BSE launches FASTRADE- a new market access platform.
63. 4-12-2009, BSE launches BSE STAR MF- mutual fund trading platform.
64. 14-12-2009, Marathi website launched.
65. 18-12-2009, BSE's new derivative rates to lower transaction costs for all.
66. 4-1-2010, market time changed to 9.0 a.m.-3.30 p.m.
67. 20-1-2010, BSE PSU website launched.

The Bombay stock exchange is using the latest information technology for greater transparency, accurate, faster trading and easy settlements. It places a great deal of emphasis on information technology for its day to day operations and performance. The operations and trading department at the stock exchange continuously upgrades the hardware, software and networking systems. It enables the exchange to enhance the quality and standards of service provided to its members, investors, and other market intermediaries. It strictly adheres to IS policies and IS security policies and procedures for its day to day operation on 24 × 7 basis which has enabled it to achieve the BS7799 certification and the subsequent ISO 27001 certification. In addition, it has also been successful in maintaining systems and processes uptime of 99.99%.

BOLT

The BSE online trading facility was started in 1995. The stock exchange had replaced the system to facilitate smooth transactions. It is totally automated, screen-based trading in securities was put into practice nation-wide within a record time of just 50 days. It has been certified by DNV for conforming to ISO 27001:2005 security standards. The capacity of the BOLT platform stands presently enhanced to 80 lakhs orders per day. It has also introduced the world's first centralized exchange based internet trading system. The initiative enables investors anywhere in the world to trade on the BSE platform. It provides comprehensive information on the stock market. It is one of the most popular financial website in India and is regularly visited by financial organizations and other shareholders for updates. The stock exchange along with its strategic partners, have put into place several critical processes/systems such as:

- Derivates trading and settlement system (DTSS)
- Electronic contract notes (ECN)
- Unique client code registration (UCC).
- Real-time data dissemination system.
- Integrated back-office system-CDB/IDB.
- Book building system (BBS).
- Reserve book building system (RBBS).
- Debt market.
- Director's database.

Listing

Listing means admission of securities to deal on a recognized stock exchange. The securities may be of any public limited company, central or state government, quasi-governmental and other financial institutions/corporations, municipalities, etc., the objectives of the listing are mainly to:

1. Provide liquidity to securities.
2. Mobilize savings for economic development.
3. Protect interest of the investors by ensuring full disclosures.

The Bombay stock exchange has a dedicated listing department to grant approval from the listing of securities of companies in accordance with the provisions of the Securities Contract (Regulation) Act, 1956, Securities Contracts (Regulation) Rules, 1957, Companies Act, 1956 guidelines issued by SEBI and rules bye-laws and regulations of the bse. BSE has set various guidelines and forms that need to be adhered to and submitted by the companies. These guidelines will help the companies to expedite the fulfillment of the various formalities and disclosure requirement that are required at various stages of:

1. Public issues.
2. Initial public offering.

3. Further public offering.
4. Preferential issues.
5. Indian depository receipts.
6. Amalgamation.
7. Qualified institutions placements.

A company intending to have its securities listed on BSE has to comply with the listing requirements prescribed by it. Some of the requirements are as under:

1. Minimum listing requirements for new companies.
2. Minimum listing requirement for companies already listed on other stock exchanges.
3. Minimum requirement for companies de-listed by BSE seeking re-listing on BSE.
4. Permission to use the name of the BSE in an issuer company's prospectus.
5. Submission of letter of application.
6. Allotment of securities.
7. Trading permission.
8. Requirement of 1% security.
9. Payment of listing fees.
10. Compliance with the listing agreement.
11. Cash management services (CMS)-collection of listing fees.

1. Minimum Listing Requirements for New Companies

The following eligibility criteria have been prescribed effective August 1, 2006, for listing of companies on BSE, through initial public offerings (IPOs) and follow on public operations (FPOs):

1. Companies have been classified as large capital companies and small capital companies. A large capital company is a company with a minimum issue size of ₹ 10 crores and market capitalization of not less than ₹ 25 crores. A small capital company is a company other than a large capital company.

A. in respect of large capital companies

(i) The minimum post issue paid up capital of the applicant company shall be ₹ 3 crores

(ii) The minimum issue size shall be ₹ 10 crores; and

(iii) The minimum market capitalization of the company shall be ₹ 25 crores.

B. in respect of small capital companies

(i) The minimum post issue paid up capital of the company shall be ₹ 3 crores;

(ii) The minimum issue size shall be ₹ 3 crores and

(iii) The minimum market capitalization of the company shall be ₹ 5 crores and

(iv) The minimum income/turnover of the company shall be ₹ 3 crores in each of the preceding three 12 –months period; and

(v) The minimum number of public shareholders after the issue shall be 1,000.

(vi) A due diligence study may be conducted by an independent team of chartered accountants or merchant bankers appointed by BSE, the cost of which will be borne by the company.

The requirement of a due diligence study may be waived if a financial institution or a scheduled commercial bank has appraised the project in the preceding 12 months.

2. For All Companies:

(a) In respect of the requirement of paid-up capital and market capitalization, the issuers shall be required to include in the disclaimer clause forming a part of the offer document that in the event of the market capitalization (product of issue price and the post-issue number of shares) requirement of BSE not being met, the securities of the issuer would not be listed on BSE.

(b) The applicant, promoters and/or group companies, shall not be in default in compliance of the listing agreement.

(c) The above eligibility criteria would be in addition to the conditions prescribed under SEBI (disclosure and investor protection) guidelines, 2000.

2. Minimum Listing Requirements for Companies Already Listed on Other Stock Exchanges

The listing norms for companies already listed on other stock exchanges and seeking listing at BSE, made effective from August 6, 2002 are as under:

1. The company shall have a minimum issued and paid up equity capital of ₹ 3 crores.
2. The company shall have a profit making track record for the preceding three years. The revenues/profits arising out of extra ordinary items or income recurring nature shall be excluded while calculating the profit making track record.
3. Minimum net worth shall be ₹ 20 crores (net worth includes equity capital and free reserves excluding revaluation reserves).
4. Minimum market capitalization of the listed capital shall be at least two times of the paid-up capital.
5. The company shall have a dividend paying track record for at least the last 3 consecutive years and the dividend should be at least 10% in each year.
6. Minimum 25% of the company's issued capital shall be with non-promoter shareholders as per clause 35 of the listing agreement. Out of the above non-promoter holding, no single shareholder shall hold more than 0.5% of the paid-up capital of the company individually or jointly with others except in case of banks/financial institutions/foreign institutional investors/overseas corporate bodies and non-resident Indians.
7. The company shall have at least two years listing record with any of the regional stock exchanges.
8. The company shall sign an agreement with CDSL and NSDL for Demat trading.

3. Minimum Requirements for Companies Delisted by BSE Seeking Relisting on BSE

Companies delisted by BSE and seeking relisting at BSE are required to make a fresh public offer and comply with the extent guidelines of SEBI and BSE regarding initial public offerings.

4. Permission to use the Name of BSE in an Issuer Company's Prospectus

Companies desiring to list their securities offered through a public issue are required to obtain prior permission of BSE to use the name of BSE in their prospectus or offer for sale documents before filing the same with the concerned office of the Registrar of companies. BSE has a listing committee comprising of market experts, which decides upon the matter of granting permission to companies, use the name of BSE in their prospectus/offer documents. This committee evaluates the promoters, company, project, financials, risk factors and several other aspects before taking a decision in this regard.

Decision with regard to some types/sizes of companies has been delegated to the internal committee of BSE.

5. Submission of Letter of Application

As per section 73 of the Companies Act, 1956, a company seeking listing of its securities on BSE is required to submit a letter of application to all the stock exchanges where it proposes to have its securities listed before filing of the prospectus with the registrar of companies.

6. Allotment of Securities

As per the listing agreement, a company is required to complete the allotment of securities offered to the public within 30 days of the date of closure of the subscription list and approach the designated stock exchange for approval of the basis of allotment. In case of book building issues, allotment shall be made not later than 15 days from the closure of the issue, failing which interest @15% shall be paid to the investors.

7. Trading Permission

As per SEBI guidelines an Issuer Company should complete the formalities for trading at the stock exchanges where the securities are to be listed within 7 working days of finalization of the basis of allotment.

A company should scrupulously adhere to the time limit specified in the SEBI guidelines 2000, for allotment of all securities and dispatch of allotment letters/share certificates/credit in depository accounts and refund orders and for obtaining the listing permissions of all the exchanges whose names are stated in its prospectus or offer document. In the event of listing permission to a company being denied by any stock exchange where it had applied for listing of its securities, the company cannot proceed with the allotment of shares. However, the company may file an appeal before SEBI under section 22 of the Securities Contract Act, 1956.

8. Requirement of 1% Security

Companies making public/rights issues are required to deposit 1% of the issue amount with the designated stock exchange before the issue opens. This amount is liable to be forfeited in the event of the company not resolving the complaint of the investors regarding delay in sending refund orders/share certificates, non-payment of commission to underwriters, brokers etc.

9. Payment of Listing Fee

All companies listed on BSE are required to pay the BSE the annual listing fees by 30th April of every financial year as per the schedule of listing fees prescribed from time to time. The schedule of listing fees for the year 2010-11, is given hereunder.

Schedule of listing fees for the year 2010-11:

Securities *other than privately placed debt securities

- Initial listing fee ₹ 20,000
- Annual listing fee
- Companies with listed capital * up to ₹ 5 crores
- Above ₹ 5 crores and up to ₹ 10 crores
- Above ₹ 10 crores and up to ₹ 20 crore

Companies which have a listed capital * of more than ₹ 20 crores are required to pay an additional fee @ of ₹ 750/- for every additional ₹ 1 crore or part thereof.

₹ 10,000

₹ 15,000

₹ 30,000

* in case of debenture capital (not convertible into equity shares), the fees will be 25% of the above fees.

Includes equity shares, preference shares, fully convertible debentures, partly convertible debentures and any other security convertible into equity shares.

Privately placed debt:

1. Initial listing fees: Nil
2. Annual listing fees:

(a) Issue size

Upto ₹ 5 crores: 2,500

5 crores-10 crores: 3,750

Additional fee of ₹ 200 for every additional 1 crore or part thereof subject to a maximum of ₹ 30,000 per instrument. The capital on the annual listing fee of debt instruments per issue is ₹ 5 lakhs per annum.

10. Compliance with the Listing Agreement

If a company wants to get listing with BSE, it is required to enter into an agreement. It is known as listing agreement. According to the agreement, the company should follow disclosure norms as per Act. If any company fails to comply with existing rules, the company should face some disciplinary action, such as suspension/delisting of securities. As such, the listing agreement is of great importance and is executed under the common seal of a company. As per the listing agreement, a company undertakes, amongst other things, to provide facilities for prompt transfer, registration, sub-division and consolidation of securities; to give proper notice of closure of transfer books and record dates, to forward 6 copies of unabridged annual reports, balance sheets and profit and loss accounts to BSE, to file shareholding patterns and financial results on a quarterly basis; to intimate promptly to the exchange happenings which are likely to materially affect financial performance of the company and its stock prices, to comply with the conditions of corporate governance. The listing department of Bombay stock exchange monitors the compliance by the companies with the provisions of the listing agreement especially with regard to timely payment of annual listing fees, submission of results, shareholding patterns and corporate governance reports on a quarterly basis. Penal action is taken against the defaulting companies.

11. Cash Management Services (CMS)

The Bombay stock exchange introduced a simplified system for the payment of listing fee. It has entered into an arrangement with HDFC bank for collection of listing fees from 141 locations all over the country. The designated branches are available to the companies for payment of listing fee through HDFC. The interested companies to avail this opportunity should furnish the information to the cash management department.

Trading Timing

Trading on the BOLT system is conducted from Monday to Friday between 9:00 a.m. and 3:30 p.m. normally.

Groups

The scrips traded on BSE have been classified into various groups. BSE has, for the investors, classified the scripts in the equity segment into 'A', 'B', 'T', 'S', 'TS' and 'Z' groups on certain qualitative and quantitative parameters. The "F" group represents the fixed income securities. The "T" group represents scrips which are settled on a trade-to-trade basis as a surveillance measure.

The "S" group represents scrips forming part of the "BSE-indonex" segment.

The "TS" group represents scrips forming part of the "BSE-indonex" segment, which are settled on a trade-to-trade basis as a surveillance measure.

Trading in government securities by the retail investors is done under the "G" group.

The "Z" group was introduced by BSE in July, 1999 and includes companies which have failed to comply with its listing requirements and/or have not made the required arrangements with both the depositories, *viz.,* Çentral Depository Services (I) Ltd.(CDSL) and National Securities Depository Ltd. (NSDL) for dematerialization of their securities. BSE also provides a facility to the market participants for online trading of odd-lot securities in physical form in 'A', 'B', 'T', 'S', 'TS', and 'Z' groups and in rights renunciations in all groups of scrips in the equity segment. With effect from December 31, 2001, trading in all securities listed in the equity segment takes place in one market segment, *viz.,* compulsory rolling settlement segment (CRS).

The scrips of companies which are in dematting can be traded in market lot of 1. However, the securities of companies which are still in the physical form are traded in the market lot of generally either 50 or 100. Investors having quantities of securities less than the market lot are required to sell them as "ODD Lots". This facility offers an exit route to investors to dispose of their odd lots of securities, and also provides them an opportunity to consolidate their securities into market lots.

This facility of selling physical shares in compulsory Demat scrips is called an exit route scheme. This facility can also be used by small investors for selling up to 500 shares in physical form in respect of scrips of companies where trades are required to be compulsorily settled by all investors in Demat mode.

Listed Securities

The securities of companies, which have signed the listing agreement with BSE, are traded as "Listed securities". Almost all scrips traded in the equity segment fall in this category.

Permitted Securities

To facilitate the market participants to trade in securities of such companies, which are actively traded at other stock exchanges but are not listed on BSE, trading in such securities is facilitated as "Permitted Securities" provided they meet the relevant norms specified by BSE.

Tick Size

Tick size is the minimum differences in rates between two orders on the same side, i.e., buy or sell, entered in the system for particular scrip. Trading in scrips listed on BSE is done with the tick size of 5 paisa. However, in order to increase the liquidity and enable the market participants to put orders at finer rates, BSE has reduced the tick size from 5 paisa to 1 paisa in case of units of mutual funds, securities traded in "F" group and equity shares having closing price up to ₹ 15 on the last trading day of the calendar month. Accordingly, the tick size in various scrips quoting up to ₹ 15 is revised to 1 paisa on the first trading day of month. The tick size so revised on the first trading day of month remains unchanged during the month even if the price of scrips undergoes a change.

Computation of Closing Price of Scrips

The closing price of scrips is computed by BSE on the basis of weighted average price of all trades executed during the last 30 minutes of a continuous trading session. However, if there is no trade recorded during the last 30 minutes, then the last traded price of scrip in the continuous trading session is taken as the official closing price.

Basket Trading System

BSE has commenced trading in the derivative segment with effect from June 9, 2000, to enable investors to hedge their risks. Initially, the facility of trading in the derivatives segment was confined to index futures. Subsequently, BSE has introduced the index options and options and futures in select individual stocks. Investor in the cash market had felt a need to limit their risk exposure in the market to the movement in Sensex. With a view to provide investors the facility of creating sensex-linked portfolio and also to create a linkage of market prices of the underlying securities of sensex in the cash segment and futures on sensex, BSE has provided to the investors as well to its member a facility of basket trading system on BOLT with effect from August 14, 2000. In the basket trading system, the investors through the members are able to buy/sell all 30 scrips of sensex in one go in the proportion of their respective weight in the sensex. The investors need not calculate the quantity of sensex scrips to be bought or sold for creating sensex-linked portfolio and this function is performed by the system. The investor can also create their own baskets by deleting certain scrips from 30 scrips in the sensex. Further, the investors can alter the weight of securities in such profiled baskets and enter their own weights. The investors can also select less than 100% weightage to reduce the value of the basket as per their own requirements.

To participate in this system, the members need to indicate the number of Sensex basket(s) to be bought or sold, where the value of one sensex basket is arrived at the system by multiplying ₹ 50 to the prevailing sensex. For example, if the sensex is 15,000, the value of one basket of sensex would be 15,000 × 50 = i.e., ₹ 7,50,000.

The investors can also place orders by entering value of sensex portfolio to be bought or sold with a minimum value of ₹ 50,000 for each order.

The basket trading system provides the arbitrageurs an opportunity to take advantage of price differences in the underlying sensex and futures on the sensex by simultaneous buying and selling of baskets comprising the sensex scrips in the cash segment and sensex futures. This would provide a balancing impact on the prices in both cash and futures markets.

The basket trading system thus meets the need of investors and also improves the depth in cash and futures markets. The trades executed under the basket trading system are subject to intra-day trading and gross exposure limits available to the members. The VAR, MTM margins, etc., as are applicable to normal trades in the cash segment, are also recovered from the members.

The list of scrips in sensex as on 13-8-2010.

Market Capitalisation

Sensex	Market Capitalisation (₹ in Crores)	Days Weight 100	PE Ratio
SENSEX	13,12,712	100	21.55
1. RIL	1,43,795	10.95	18.3
2. INFOSYS	1,33,150	10.14	25.6
3. L&T	1,08,857	8.29	31.6
4. ICICI BANK	1,07,543	8.19	25.8
5. ITC	79,623	6.07	27.5
6. HDFC	76,893	5.86	29.5
7. HDFC BANK	76,972	5.86	30.3
8. SBI	71,743	5.47	15.1
9. ONGC	42,731	3.26	17.4
10. TCS	39,815	3.03	22.7
11. AIRTEL	39,614	3.02	13.2
12. BHEL	39,440	3.00	27.1
13. TATA MOTORS	30,729	2.34	22.7

14. TATA STEEL	30,467	2.32	-
15. HUL	28,207	2.15	26.8
16. M&M	25,909	1.97	16.3
17. ZINDAL STEEL	25,269	1.92	17.0
18. STERILITE	22,268	1.70	13.8
19. TATA POWER	21,051	1.60	16.0
20. WIPRO	20,922	1.59	20.6
21. HINDALCO	20,418	1.56	16.2
22. RELIANCE INFRA	16,742	1.28	24.8
23. NTPC	16,844	1.28	19.1
24. HERO HONDA	16,795	1.28	16.8
25. MARUTI SUZUKI	16,223	1.24	14.9
26. CIPLA	15,271	1.16	23.3
27. JAIPRAKASH	13,845	1.05	14.6
28. REL COMMN	11,675	0.89	7.7
29. DLF	11,443	0.87	30.7
30. ACC	8,461	0.64	11

Source: The Economic Times, dated 13-8-2010 page no: 14.

The method of compilation of the BSE sensitive index of equity prices is the same as used by the S & P; U.S.A. in construction of share price indices. The index for a day is calculated as per the percentage of the aggregate market value of the equity shares of all the companies in the sample on that day to the average market value of the equity shares of the same companies during the period for calculation of the Sensex as follows:

$$\text{S and P£} = \frac{£P_j£Q_{jt}}{£P_{jo}£Q_{jo}}$$

Where,

P_{it} = Price of the stock in period £

Q_{it} = Number of shares outstanding for stock I in period £

P_{io} = Price stock in the base period o

$£_{Io}$ = Number of shares outstanding for stock in base period and the base period is 1941-43.

Statement showing information related to BSE

Capital market	**End of fiscal year**				
	2005-06	**2006-07**	**2007-08**	**2008-09**	**2009-10**
BSE Sensitive index (1978 –79 = 100)	11280(73.7)	13072(15.9)	15644(19.7)	9707(-37.9)	175258(80.5)

BSE-100 (1983 – 84 = 100)	5904(69.6)	6587(11.6)	8233(25.0)	49439(-40)	9300(88.2)
BSE-200 (1989 – 90 = 1000)	1413(62.8)	1557((10.2)	1932(24.1)	1140(-41.0)	2200(92.9)
S&P CNX NIFTY (3 Nov 1995 = 1000)	3403(67.1)	3822(12.3)	4735(23.8)	3021(-36.2)	5249(73.8)
Skindia GDR index (2 Jan 1995 = 1000)	1749(49.4)	2230(27.5)	2633(18.1)	1153(-56.2)	2883(134.2)
Net FII investment in equities (US $ Mn) period end	45260(26.0)	50736(12.1)	63496(25.1)	51669(-18.6)	77159(43.1)

Source: www.bse.com

Statement showing the market capitalisation as on 29-7-10.

Company	Market Capitalization as on 29-7-10 (₹ in Crore)	P E
1. Reliance industries	1,49,444	19.0
2. Infosys tech	1,35,812	26.1
3. L&T	1,09,740	31.9
4. ICICI bank	1,03,359	25.7
5. ITC	80,590	27.9
6. HDFC bank	77,971	30.7
7. HDFC	76,320	29.2
8. SBI	63,734	13.4
9. ONGC	41,910	15.9
10. Bharathi Airtel	39,539	13.1
11. TATA consult	39,573	22.6
12. BHEL	38,891	26.7
13. TATA steel	31,270	
14. HIND. Unilever	27,199	25.9
15. M&M	26,378	17.8
16. TATA Motors	25,978	19.2
17. Jindal steel P	23,971	16.0
18. Sterlite Inds	23,727	14.8
19. Wipro	21,089	20.8
20. TATA Power	21,038	16.0
21. Hindal Co	19,678	16.1

22. Reliance infra	17,294	24.0
23. NTPC	17,268	19.6
24. Hero Honda	16,824	16.7
25. Cipla	15,942	24.3
26. Maruthi Suzuki	15,843	14.5
27. Jaiprakash	13,810	14.5
28. Reliance Comm.	12,245	8.1
29. DLF	11,209	30.4
30. ACC	8,498	11.0

Source: The Economic Times, 29-7-2010.

SETTLEMENTS

Compulsory Rolling Settlement

All transactions in all groups of securities in the equity segment and fixed income securities listed on BSE are required to be settled on T+2 basis. The settlement calendar, which indicates the dates of the various settlement related activities, is drawn by BSE in advance and is circulated among the market participants. Under rolling settlements, the trades done on a particular day are settled after a given number of business days. A T+2 settlement cycle means that the final settlement of transactions done on T, i.e., trade day by exchange of monies and securities between the buyers and sellers respectively takes place on second business day after the trade day.

The transactions in securities of companies which have made arrangements for dematerializations of their securities are settled only in Demat mode T+2 on net basis, i.e., buy and sell positions of a member-broker in the same scrip are netted and the net quantity and value is required to be settled. However, transactions in securities of companies, which are in "Z" group or have been placed under "trade-to-trade" by BSE as a surveillance measure ("T" and "TS" group) are settled only on a gross basis and the facility of netting of buy and sell facility on netting of buy and sell transactions in such scrips is not available.

BSE has introduced a new segment name "BSE indonex" *w.e.f.* January 7, 2005. The "S" group consists of scrips from B group on BSE and companies exclusively listed on regional stock exchange having a paid up capital of ₹ 3 crores to ₹ 30 crores. All trades in this segment are done through BOLT system.

The transactions in "F" group securities representing "Fixed income securities" and "G" group representing government securities for retail investors are also settled at BSE on T+2 basis.

In case of rolling settlements, pay-in and pay-out of both funds and securities is completed on the same day. Members are required to make payment for securities sold and/or deliver securities purchased to their clients within one working day after the pay-out of the funds and securities for the concerned settlement is completed by BSE. This is the timeframe permitted to the members to settle their funds/securities obligations with their clients as per the Bye-law of BSE.

The following table summarizes the steps in the trading and settlement cycles for scrips under CRS:

Day Activity

Trading on BOLT and daily downloading of statements showing details of transactions and margins at the end of each trading day. Downloading of provisional securities and fund obligation statement by member-brokers.

6A/7A*entry by the member-brokers/confirmation by the custodians.

Confirmation of 6A/7A data by the custodian's up to 1 p.m. downloading of final securities and fund obligation statement by the members.

T + 2

Pay-in of funds and securities by ll.00 a.m. and pay out of funds and securities by 1.30 p.m. The member-brokers are required to submit the pay-in instructions for fund and securities to bank and depositories respectively by 10.30 a.m.

T + 3

Auction on Bolt at 11.00 a.m.

T + 4

Auction pay-in and pay-out of funds and securities by 12.00 noon and 1.30 pm respectively.

The pay-in and pay-out of funds and securities takes place on the second business day, of the day of the execution of the trade.

The settlement of the trades done by a member on his own account on behalf of his individual, corporate or institutional clients may be either through the member himself or through a SEBI registered custodian, appointed by him/client. In case of the delivery/payment in respect of a transaction executed by a member is to be given or taken by registered custodian, the latter has to confirm the trade done by a member on the bolt system through 6 A-7A entries. For this purpose, the custodians have been given connectivity to the bolt system and have also been admitted as clearing member of the clearing house. In case a registered custodian does not confirm a transaction, a transaction done by a member within the time permitted, the liability for pay-in of funds or securities in respect of the same devolves on the concerned member.

The necessary documents and following statements can be downloaded by the members in their back offices on a daily basis.

(a) Statements giving details of the daily transactions entered into by the member.

(b) Statements giving details of margins payable by the member in respect of the trades executed by him.

(c) Statements of securities and fund obligation.

(d) Delivery/Receive orders for delivery/receipt of securities.

BSE generates delivery and receive orders for transactions done by the members A, B, S, F and G group scrips after netting purchase and sale transactions in each scrip whereas delivery and receive orders for "T", "TS", "C" & "Z" group scrips and scrips which are traded on Bombay stock exchange on "trade-to-trade" basis of generated on a gross basis, i.e., without netting of purchase and sell transactions in a scrip. However, the funds obligations, for the members or netted for transactions across all groups of securities. The deliveries order/receive orders provide information like scrips and quantity of securities to be delivered/received by the members through clearing house. The money statement provides scrip wise/item wise details of payments/receipts of monies by the members in the settlement. The delivery/receive orders and money statements can be downloaded by the members in their back office.

"PAY IN AND PAY OUT FOR A, B, T, S, TS, C, F, G & Z GROUP OF SECURITIES." The trades done on BOLT by the members in all securities in CRS are now settled on BSE by payment of monies and delivery of securities on T+2 bases. All deliveries of securities are required to be routed through the clearing house, the pay in pay out of funds based on the money statement and that of securities based on delivery order/receive order issued by BSE are settled on T+2 day.

Demat Pay In

The members can affect pay in of Demat securities to the clearing house through depositories. The members are required to give instructions to their respective depository participants specifying details such as settlement no., effective pay in date, quantity. Members may also effect pay in directly from the client's are required to mention the settlement details and clearing member id through whom they have sold the securities. Thus, in such cases the clearing members are not required to give any delivery instructions from their accounts. In case a member fails to deliver the securities, the value of shares delivered short is recovered from him at the standard/closing rate of the scrips on the trading day.

Auto Delivery Facility

Instead of issuing delivery instructions, for their securities delivery obligations in Demat mode in various scrips in a settlement/auction, a facility has been made available to the members for automatically generating delivery instructions on their behalf from their clearing members pool accounts maintained with NSDL and clearing member principal accounts, maintained with CSDL. This auto delivery facility is available for CRS (normal & auction) and for trade- to trade settlements, This facility is, however not available for delivery of non *pari passu* shares and shares having multiple ISINs, and members wishing to avail of this facility have to submit an authority letter to the clearing house. This auto delivery facility is currently available for clearing member pool accounts and principal accounts maintained by the members with the respective depositories.

Pay In of Securities in Physical Form

In case of delivery of securities in physical form, the Members are required to deliver the securities to the Clearing House in special closed pouches along with the relevant details like distinctive numbers, scrip code, quantity, etc., on a floppy. The data submitted by the Members on floppies is matched against the master file data on the Clearing House. If there is no discrepancy, the securities are accepted.

Funds Pay In

The bank accounts of Members maintained with the clearing banks, *viz.,* Bank of India, HDFC Bank Ltd., Oriental Bank of Commerce, Standard Chartered Bank, Centurion Bank Ltd., Axis Bank Ltd., ICICI Bank Ltd, Indusind Bank Ltd., Union Bank of India and Hong Kong & Shanghai Banking Corporation Ltd. are directly debited through computerized posting for their funds settlement obligations.

In case of Members whose funds pay in obligations are not cleared at the scheduled time, action such as levy of penalty and/or deactivation of BOLT TWSs, is initiated as per the prescribed penalty norms.

Securities Pay Out

Demat securities are credited by the Clearing House in the Pool/Principal Accounts of the Members. BSE has also provided a facility to the Members for transfer of pay out securities directly to the clients' beneficiary owner accounts without routing the same through their Pool/Principal accounts in NSDL/CDSL. For this, the concerned Members are required to give a client wise break up file which is uploaded by the Members from their offices to the Clearing House. Based on the break up given by the Members, the Clearing House instructs the depositories, *viz.,* CDSL & NSDL to credit the securities to the Beneficiary Owners (BO) Accounts of the clients. In case delivery of securities received from one depository is to be credited to an account in the other depository, the Clearing House does an inter-depository transfer to give effect to such transfers. In case of physical securities, the Receiving Members are required to collect the same from the Clearing House on the pay-out day.

Funds Pay Out

The bank accounts of the Members having pay out of funds are credited by the Clearing House with the Clearing Banks on the pay in day itself.

In case a member fails to deliver the securities, the value of shares delivered short is recovered from him at the standard/closing rate of the scrips on the trading day.

Penalty Norms

For Settlement (Pay-in) Defaults Revised norms as per Exchange Notice No. 20091211-20 for imposing late fees/fines/penalties on member brokers in case of delay/non-clearance of settlement obligations in the Cash Segment *w.e.f.* Monday, December 14, 2009.

Violation/s	Shortage amount	Late fees/fines/penalty
Non-fulfillment of funds obligation (*viz.*, Normal pay-in, securities shortage pay in and auction pay in) and failure to deposit additional capital towards capital cushion requirement as per SEBI norms within stipulated time.	(a) If the shortage amount is more than the Base Minimum Capital (at present ₹10 lakhs):	(a) - 1% of such shortage amount, and - additional 0.07% per day of the shortage amount. - Also, the trading facility of such member shall be withdrawn and the securities pay out shall be withheld.
	(b) If the funds shortage is less than the Base	(b) - 1% of such shortage amount, and - additional 0.07% per day of the shortage amount.

	Minimum Capital (at present ₹10 lakhs):	- In cases where the shortage amount exceeds 20% of the BMC but less than the BMC on 6 occasions within a period of three months, then also the trading facility of the member shall be withdrawn and the securities pay-out due to the member shall be withheld. (*In case the member's trading facility has been withdrawn on account of (b) above, then upon recovery of the complete shortages, the member shall be permitted to trade, subject to such members providing a deposit equivalent to his cumulative funds shortage amount as the 'funds shortage collateral'. Such deposit shall be kept with the Exchange for a period of ten rolling settlements and shall be released thereafter. Such deposit shall not be available against margin liabilities and also such deposit will not earn any interest. Such deposit may be by way of cash, fixed deposit receipts of banks and/or bank guarantee.)

Source: www.bse.com

Besides the aforesaid, all other norms as prescribed *vide* the aforesaid notice no. 20050520-20 dated May 20, 2005 and other notices issued from time to time in respect of the same will remain unchanged.

Further, if a member fails to meet his pay in obligations of a normal settlement, auction settlement and that of securities delivered short in the pay in for the same settlement, then such instances of default would be considered as a single instance for the purpose of counting violations and levying penalties as above.

Non deposit of additional capital under capital cushion requirement would be considered as a separate instance for the purpose of counting instances of violation and levying fines/penalties as above.

Shortages: The Clearing House arrives at the shortages in delivery of various scrips by the Members on the basis of their delivery obligations and actual delivery.

The Members can download the statement of shortages in delivery of scrips in A, B, T, S, TS, Z, F, Odd-lot & G group scrips on T+2 day, i.e., Pay in day. After downloading the shortage details, the Members are expected to verify the same and report discrepancy, if any, to the Clearing House immediately. If no discrepancy is reported within the stipulated time, the Clearing House assumes that the shortage of a Member is in order and proceeds to auction/close-out the same. Moreover, the value of shares delivered short is recovered from the Member at the standard/closing rate of the scrips on the trading day.

Auctions

An Auction Tender Notice is issued by BSE to the Members informing them about the names of the scrips short or not delivered, quantity slated for auction and the date and time of the auction session on the BOLT. The auction for the undelivered quantities is conducted on T+3 day between 11:00 a.m. and 12 noon for all the scrips under Compulsory Rolling Settlements except those in "Z" group and scrips on "trade to trade" basis which are directly closed-out. A Member who has failed to deliver the securities of a particular company on the pay-in day is not allowed to offer the same in auction. The Members, who participate in the auction session, can download the Delivery Orders in respect of the auction obligations on the same day, if their offers are accepted. The Members are required to deliver the shares in the Clearing House on the auction Pay in day, i.e., T+4. Pay-out of auction shares and funds is also done on the same day, i.e., T+4.

Self-auction

The Delivery and Receive Orders are issued by BSE to the Members after netting off their purchase and sell transactions in scrips where netting of purchase and sell positions is permitted. It is likely in some cases, a selling client has failed to deliver the shares sold in a settlement to a Member. However, this may not result in failure of the Member to deliver the shares to the Clearing House as there was a purchase transaction of his some other buying client in the same scrip and the same was netted off for the purpose of settlement. In such a case, the Member would require shares so that he can deliver the same to his buying client, which otherwise would have taken place from the delivery of shares by his selling client. To provide shares to the Members in such cases, they have been given an option to submit the details of such internal shortages on floppies on pay-in day for conducting self-auction (i.e., as if they have defaulted in delivery of shares to the Clearing House). These shortages are clubbed with the normal shortages in a settlement arrived at by the Clearing House and the auction is conducted by the Clearing House for the combined shortages.

Close-out

Close-out is affected for cases when no offer for particular scrip is received in an auction or when Members who offer the scrips in auction, fail to deliver the same or shortages pertaining to those groups of securities for which auctions are not conducted. The close-out rates for different segments are as under

'A', 'B', 'S' and 'F' group

The close-out rate is higher of the following rates:

(a) The highest rate of the scrip from the trading day to the day prior to the day on which the auction is conducted for the respective settlement.

(b) 20% above the closing rate as on the day prior to the day of auction/close out of the respective settlement.

"Odd Lot", "T", "TS" and "Z" group and Patawat objections

The closeout rate is higher of the following rates:

(a) The highest rate of the scrip from the day of trading to the day prior to the day of auction of the respective settlements;

(b) 10% above the closing rate as on the day prior to the day of auction/ close out of the respective settlement.

– "G" group In case of shortages in "G" group, the shortages are closed out at Zero Coupon Yield Curve (ZCYC) plus a 5% penalty. The closeout amounts are debited to the bank accounts of those Members who have failed to deliver the securities against their sale obligations and credited to the bank accounts of those Members who had bought the securities but did not receive the same.

Rectification of Bad Deliveries

One of the biggest problems faced by the investors in the secondary market while dealing in physical securities is that of bad delivery arising out of various reasons. Based on the reasons, these bad deliveries are classified into two categories, namely:

- Patawat (Settlement) Objections
- Company Objections

Patawat (Settlement) Objections

The physical securities received in payout are required to be checked by the Members for good delivery as per the norms of good and bad delivery of documents prescribed by the SEBI. If the securities are not considered good delivery, the receiving Member has to participate in "Patawat Objection Cycle" given below:

DAY	ACTIVITY	TIME
T + 3	Patawat Arbitration session : Arbitration awards to be obtained from officials of the Bad Delivery Cell	10:30 a.m. to 11:30 a.m.
	Securities under objection to be submitted in the Clearing House.	11:00 a.m. to 12:00 noon
	The delivering members to collect such securities under objection from the clearing house	2:00 p.m. to 3:00 p.m.
	Arbitration awards for invalid objection to be obtained from members of the Arbitration Review Committee/Officials of the Bad Delivery Cell.	5:00 p.m. to 5:30 p.m.
T + 4	Members and institution to submit rectified securities, confirmation forms and invalid objections in the clearing house.	1:00 p.m. to 2:00 p.m.
	Rectified securities/invalid objections will be delivered to the receiving members	3:00 p.m. to 4:00 p.m.
T + 5	Arbitration Awards for invalid rectification to be obtained from officials of the Bad Delivery Cell	11:30 a.m. to 12:30 p.m.
	Securities to be lodged with the clearing house unto	1:00 p.m

Source: www.bse.com

The transactions pertaining to un-rectified and invalid rectification of securities are directly closed-out by BSE as per the formula.

The shares in physical form returned under objection to the Clearing House as explained earlier are required to be accompanied by an arbitration award (Chukada) except in certain cases where the receiving Members are permitted to submit securities to the Clearing House without "Chukada" or arbitration award in the following cases:

(a) Transfer Deed is out of date.

(b) Cheques for the dividend adjustment for new shares where distinctive numbers are given in the BSE Notice are not enclosed.

(c) Stamp of the Registrar of Companies on the Transfer Deed is missing.

(d) Details like distinctive numbers, transferor's names, etc. are not filled in the Transfer Deeds.

(e) Delivering Member's stamp on the reverse of the Transfer Deed is missing.

(f) Witness stamp or signature on Transfer Deed is missing.

(g) Signature of the transferor is missing.

(h) Death Certificate (in cases where one or more of the transferors is/are deceased) is missing.

A penalty at the rate of ₹ 100 per Delivery Order is recovered by BSE on the delivering Members for delivering shares, which are not in order.

Company Objections

Bad deliveries arising out of rejection of physical shares sent to the companies by the buyers for getting them transferred in their names are termed as Company Objections. In order to help the buyers, BSE has set up a Bad Delivery Cell (BDC), which conducts its operations based on the Uniform Norms for Good/Bad Deliveries formulated by SEBI.

BDC follows a weekly cycle for acceptance of Objections and Rectifications. The cycle commences every Tuesday, when the Objections are accepted in the Clearinghouse. The Members have a facility of directly uploading the bad delivery claims in the BDC system, and download the various reports through the same. The physical/objection documents are accepted in the Clearing House only if the data has been successfully uploaded in the BDC system. The Objections, which have been forwarded to the Clearing House by the Buying Clearing Members on the first day of the cycle, need to be rectified by the Seller Clearing Members and submitted to Clearinghouse on the 21st day of that particular cycle.

BDC issues notices every Monday, Tuesday and Thursday informing the market about various activities to be carried out by them. The notice issued on Monday contains the details of the Clearing Members against whom the Buyer Member has lodged an Objection. The notice issued on Tuesday is information to the Market about the Bad Delivery Schedule for the next week's cycle. And the Thursday's notice contains the details about the shares going in Auction for the un-rectified securities, if any.

After receipt of the Objections, the Seller Member can approach the verification officers of the BDC for obtaining the Award for Invalid Objections, if any. The BDC officers, on the basis of the guidelines issued by SEBI for Good and Bad Deliveries of Documents and on the basis of provisions of other relevant Acts, give an Award stating "Not in Order/In Order". If the Award is given as "In Order", the Seller Member is required to accept the objections and to rectify the same within 21 days. If the objections are not rectified within the prescribed period of 21 days, the relevant transactions are auctioned or closed out as per the procedure laid down in this regard. If the Objection is "Not In Order", the Seller Members are required to deliver back the shares to the Clearing House, who in turn returns the same to the Buyer Members. After the award session for invalid objections, the deletion/modification entries are made and a statement titled Permanent Claim Status is generated. The same is available to the Seller Members and the Buyer Members in order to enable the Seller Members to submit rectifications on a floppy. To minimize the interfaces, the Members can also upload rectification directly through BDC system and can download the error report. The rectification will be accepted only if the data is properly uploaded in the BDC system.

Along with the award for invalid objections, the award for the invalid rectifications, if any, is also given. If the Seller Member has not properly submitted the rectifications, an award is given as "Not In Order". In that case the Buyer Members are required to deliver back the shares to the Clearing House who, in turn, returns the same to the Seller Member. Thus, all Invalid Rectifications go for auction/close-out along with all Uncertified Objections.

The auction is conducted on 30th day and the Buyer Member receives the shares in auction pay-in after 3 days. The Buyer Member also receives the close out amount, for the shares not received in auction offer, and for the un-rectified objections in Group Z, T and TS on the same day.

The disputed matters are referred to arbitration. The BDC accepts the objections only if the Company Objection Memo is forwarded or the Patawat Objection Memo duly signed by the Arbitrator is forwarded The share documents which have been returned under objection by a company for the second time, can be reported in the BDC system, as Second Time Objection. The seller in this case is not given a chance to rectify the objections and the claim is closed out on the 10th day after the commencement of the particular cycle.

In case of objection reported with the BDC as Fake/Forged and Missing/Lost/Stolen shares, the rectification is allowed only in Demat mode.

After every BDC auction, a report is generated for bad deliveries submitted under the reason 'fake/forged shares'. Members are cautioned against introducing fake/forged shares. They have to follow the policy of 'Know your client', and be careful while choosing their clients.

In case the amount of fake/forged shares introduced by a Member exceeds ₹ 10 lakhs in a year, he has to submit an explanation for the same to BDC In case where the value of fake/forged shares introduced by a Member exceeds a certain level, stringent action is taken against him. The list of members who have introduced fake/forged shares exceeding ₹ 5 lakhs in one quarter is also circulated to all the stock exchanges.

BDC also maintains the data of lost/stolen/fake/duplicate shares of all listed companies. BDC has informed all listed companies to forward updated database of such shares in soft copy or through E-mail, so that the Members and the Clearing House can download the same. This enables the Members to check the bad shares at the entry point, i.e., at the time when shares are delivered. This procedure prevents circulation of bad shares in the market, so that the same cannot be lodged with the company for transfer.

Bulk Deals Disclosures in the Cash Segment

Members are required to make a disclosure on a daily basis up to 5.00 p.m. through DUS (Data Upload software), with respect to all transaction in a scrip for a client where the total quantity bought/sold is more than 0.5% of the number of equity shares of the company listed at BSE.

All transactions' stated above are classified as under:

(a) **Single Trade:** Immediately upon the execution of the order where the traded quantity, either buy or sell, on account of any trade is more than 0.5% of the number of equity shares of the company listed on BSE.

(b) **Cumulative Trades for the Day:** Within one hour from the closure of the trading hours, where the cumulative quantity traded under any single client code on that day either purchase or sale is more than 0.5% of the number of equity shares of the company listed at BSE.

Block Deals Disclosures in the Cash Segment

Members are required to make a disclosure on a daily basis through DUS (Data Upload Software), with respect to all deals that have been executed by them on behalf of their 'client; or 'own' account in the Block Deal window. A trade, with a minimum quantity of 5,00,000 shares or minimum value of ₹ 5 crores executed through a single transaction on this window, qualifies as Block Deal.

- Risk Management
- Cash Market

The expansion of BOLT across the country has led to a significant increase in volumes and liquidity. This has also consequently increased the risk of default by the Members in meeting their settlement obligations. BSE has initiated several risk management measures in order to maintain the safety of the market and to avert defaults by the BSE Members in meeting their payment and delivery obligations.

Total Liquid Assets

The core of the risk management system is the liquid assets deposited by the Members with BSE. These liquid assets cover the following five requirements:

(a) *MTM (Mark-To-Market) Losses:* Mark-to-market losses on outstanding settlement obligations of the Member.

(b) *VaR Margins:* Value at risk margins to cover potential losses for 99% of the days.

(c) *Extreme Loss Margins:* Margins to cover the expected loss in situations that lie outside the coverage of the VaR margins.

(d) *Base Minimum Capital:* Capital required for all risks other than the market risk (for example, operational risk and client claims).

(e) *Special Margin:* Special margin collected as a surveillance measure.

Members are required to maintain the liquid assets (collateral) to cover all the above five requirements. There are no other margins in the risk management system.

Base Minimum Capital (BMC)

All Members are required to maintain a BMC of ₹ 10 lakhs with BSE in the prescribed manner at all times. The composite corporate Members are required to maintain BMC in multiple of the membership rights held by them. The BMC, as prescribed by SEBI, is required to be kept in the form of cash (minimum 12.5%), Fixed Deposit Receipt(s) or Bank Guarantee(s) issued by bank(s) (minimum 37.5%) and balance in the form of eligible shares. The eligible shares for the purpose of the securities portion of the BMC are A and B group securities forming part of Group I classified as per the parameters of volatility and liquidity as stipulated in SEBI circular No. MRD/DoP/SE/Cir-07/2005 dated February 23, 2005. BMC is not available for adjustment towards margins.

Additional Capital

(a) Members are also allowed to deposit Additional Capital (AC) over and above the BMC with BSE as follows:

(Liquid Assets):

Cash Equivalent.

Particulars	Haircut	Limit on Capital Deposit
(i) Cash	Nil	No Limit
(ii) Bank Fixed Deposit Receipts (FDRs).	Nil	No Limit
(iii) Bank Guarantee	Nil	Limit on BSE's exposure to a single bank exposure as stipulated in the SEBI circular No. MRD/DoP/SE/Cir-07/2005 dated February 23, 2005.
(iv) Securities of the Central Government *.	10%	No limit
(v) Units of liquid Mutual Fund (or) Govt. Sec. Mutual Fund (by whatever name called which invests in government securities) *.	10%	No limit.

Source: www.bse.com

Other Liquid Assets — Non-cash Component (Total of Other Liquid Assets should not exceed total of Cash Equivalent):

Particulars	Haircut	Limit on Capital Deposit
Non-cash equivalent :		
(i) Liquid (Group-I) Equity Shares (as per the criteria for classification of scrips on the basis of liquidity). (Only A and B group securities forming part of such Group I)	Same as the Value at Risk (VaR) margin for the respective shares.	Limit on BSE's exposure to a single issuer as stipulated in the SEBI circular No. MRD/DoP/SE/Cir-07/2005 dated February 23, 2005.

(ii)Mutual Fund units (other than those listed under cash equivalent).*	Same as the VaR margins for the units computed using the traded price on BSE, if available, or else, using the NAV of the unit treating it as a liquid security.	

Source: www.bse.com

* BSE, at present, does not accept such liquid assets towards collateral.

Cash equivalents should be at least 50% of the liquid assets. This implies that Other Liquid Assets in excess of the total Cash Equivalents is not regarded as part of the Total Liquid Assets.

The valuation of shares deposited by the Members with BSE is done on a daily basis, and a haircut equivalent to the respective VaR of individual scrip is applied, i.e., only the residual value of eligible shares deposited is considered for the purpose of evaluation of capital (collateral) deposited by the Members with BSE. The eligible shares deposited by the Members towards BMC are accepted by BSE in Demat form only.

The cash can be deposited by the Members towards capital by submitting instructions to their clearing banks to debit their bank accounts and credit the amount to BSE's account.

As regards the Fixed Deposit Receipts (FDRs) of banks, the duly discharged FDRs are required to be submitted by the Members to BSE in the name of "Bombay Stock Exchange Ltd. A/c - trade name of the Member" issued by any Mumbai-based branch or payable at any Mumbai-based branch of any scheduled commercial or cooperative bank.

The bank guarantees submitted by the Member towards the capital have to be in the approved format in favor of BSE either issued or payable by any Mumbai-based branch of a scheduled commercial bank only. However, in case FDRs/ bank guarantees are issued by the outstation branches of scheduled commercial banks (i.e., branches outside Mumbai), the payment of the proceeds on encashment of FDRs and invocation of bank guarantees by BSE has to be assured by a Mumbai-based branch of the concerned issuing bank.

(b) For every instance of deactivation of BOLT TWSs due to non-availability of total liquid assets, fines/penalties are levied as per the structure given below:

Description	No. of instances in a financial year	Fines/penalties (₹)
Fines/penalties for de-activation of BOLT TWSs due to non-availability of Total Liquid Assets (collateral) during the trading session and in case of de-activation of BOLT TWSs due to non-availability of total liquid asset at the end of day because of shortfall of Total Liquid Assets due to expiry of Bank Guarantees/Fixed Deposit	1st to 5th instance.	₹ 5,000/- per instance.
	6th to 15th instance.	₹ 10,000/- per instance or 0.25% of the amount of shortfall of total liquid assets on account of violation of trading limits, whichever is higher.
	16th to 30th instance	₹ 15,000/- per instance or 0.25% of the amount of shortfall of total liquid assets on account of violation of trading limits, whichever is higher.

Receipts, evaluation of securities, etc.	31st instance onwards.	₹ 20,000/- per instance or 0.25% of the amount of shortfall of total liquid assets on account of violation of trading limits, whichever is higher.

Source: www.bse.com

BSE, as a precautionary measure, provides online warnings to its Members on the BOLT TWSs when they reach 70%, 80% and 90% of the utilization of Total Liquid Assets (TLA). When a Member crosses 100% of the utilization of TLA, a message is flashed on his BOLT TWSs which says "Capital Violated: Member Trading Suspend" and immediately thereafter, all his BOLT TWSs get deactivated. The BOLT TWSs of the Members in such cases are reactivated only after they deposit the required additional liquid assets. To avoid deactivation of BOLT TWSs and levy of fines/penalties, the additional liquid assets should be deposited with BSE sufficiently in advance.

Liquidity Categorization of Securities

The securities are classified into three groups based on their liquidity:

Group	Trading Frequency (over the previous six months – see Note A)	Impact Cost (over the previous six months – see Note A
Liquid Securities (Group I)	At least 80% of the days	Less than or equal to 1%
Less Liquid Securities (Group II)	At least 80% of the days	More than 1%
Illiquid Securities (Group III)	Less than 80% of the days	N/A

Source: www.bse.com

Note: For securities that have been listed for less than six months, the trading frequency and the impact cost is computed using the entire trading history of the scrip.

Monthly Review

The trading frequency and impact cost is calculated on the 15th of each month on a rolling basis considering the previous six months for impact cost and previous six months for trading frequency. On the basis of the trading frequency and impact cost so calculated, the securities move from one group to another group from the 1st of the next month.

Categorization of Newly Listed Securities

For the first month and till the time of monthly review as mentioned above, a newly listed stock is categorized in that group where the market capitalization of the newly listed stock exceeds or equals the market capitalization of 80% of the stocks in that particular group. Subsequently, after one month, whenever the next monthly review is carried out, the actual trading frequency and impact cost of the security is computed, to determine the liquidity categorization of the security.

In case any corporate action results in a change in ISIN, the securities bearing the new ISIN is treated as newly listed scrip for group categorization.

Calculation of Mean Impact Cost

The mean impact cost is calculated in the following manner:

(a) Impact cost is calculated by taking four snapshots in a day from the order book in the past six months. These four snapshots are randomly chosen from within four fixed ten-minutes windows spread through the day.

(b) The impact cost is the percentage price movement caused by an order size of ₹ 1 Lakh from the average of the best bid and offer price in the order book snapshot. The impact cost is calculated for both, the buy and the sell side in each order book snapshot.

Dissemination of Information

The lists of securities forming part of groups I, II and III are disseminated on the BSE website on a monthly basis.

Margins

In order to contain the risk arising out of transactions entered into by the members in various scrips either on their own account or on behalf of their clients, BSE has a well designed risk-management system which *inter alia* includes collection of margins from the Members. BSE accordingly, imposes various kinds of margins on the Members based on their outstanding positions in the market. The margining system followed by BSE is described below:

- Computation of Margins
- VaR Margin

As mandated by SEBI, the Value at Risk (VaR) margining system, which is internationally accepted as the best margining system, is applicable on the outstanding positions of the Members in all scrips.

(a) The VaR Margin is a margin intended to cover the largest loss that can be encountered on 99% of the days (99% Value at Risk). For liquid stocks, the margin covers one-day losses while for illiquid stocks; it covers three-day losses so as to allow the Exchange to liquidate the position over three days. This leads to a scaling factor of square root of three for illiquid stocks. For liquid stocks, the VaR margins are based only on the volatility of the stock while for other stocks, the volatility of the market index is also used in the computation. Computation of the VaR margin requires the following definitions:

Scrip sigma means the volatility of the security computed as at the end of the previous trading day. The computation uses the exponentially weighted moving average method applied to daily returns in the same manner as in the derivatives market.

Scrip VaR means the highest of 7.5% or 3.5 scrip sigma.

Index sigma means the daily volatility of the market index (S&P CNX Nifty or BSE Sensex) computed as at the end of the previous trading day. The computation uses the exponentially weighted moving average method applied to daily returns in the same manner as in the derivatives market.

Index VaR means the highest of 5% or 3 index sigma. The higher of the Sensex VaR or Nifty VaR would be used for this purpose.

The VaR Margins are specified as follows for different groups of stocks:

Liquidity Categorization	One-Day VaR	Scaling factor for illiquidity	VaR Margin
Liquid Securities (Group I)	Scrip VaR	1.00	Scrip VaR
Less Liquid Securities (Group II)	Higher of Scrip VaR and three times Index VaR	1.73 (square root of 3.00)	Higher of 1.73 times Scrip VaR and 5.20 times Index VaR
Illiquid Securities (Group III)	Five times Index VaR	1.73 (square root of 3.00)	8.66 times Index VaR

Source: www.bse.com

Collection of VaR Margin

(a) The VaR margin is collected on an upfront basis by adjusting against the total liquid assets of the Member at the time of trade.

(b) The VaR margin is collected on the gross open position of the Member. The gross open position for this purpose is the gross of all net positions across all the clients of a Member including his proprietary position.

(c) For this purpose, there would be no netting of positions across different settlements.

(d) Dissemination of Information:

The VaR amount applicable in respect of the scrips is disseminated on the BSE website on a daily basis.

Extreme Loss Margin: The term Extreme Loss Margin replaces the terms “exposure limits” and “second line of defense” that have been used hitherto. It covers the expected loss in situations that go beyond those envisaged in the 99% value at risk estimates used in the VaR margin.

(a) The Extreme Loss Margin for any stock is higher of:

- 5%, and
- 1.5 times the standard deviation of daily logarithmic returns of the stock price in the last six months. This computation is done at the end of each month by taking the price data on a rolling basis for the past six months and the resulting value is applicable for the next month.

(b) The Extreme Loss Margin is collected/adjusted against the total liquid assets of the member on a real time basis.

(c) The Extreme Loss Margin is collected on the gross open position of the Member. The gross open position for this purpose means the gross of all net positions across all the clients of a member including his proprietary position.

(d) For this purpose, there is no netting of positions across different settlements.

(e) The Extreme Loss margin so collected is released along with the pay-in.

(f) *Dissemination of Information:* The ELM amount applicable in respect of the scrips is also disseminated on the BSE website.

Special Margin

Special margin may be imposed by BSE from time to time on certain scrips as a surveillance measure and informed to the Members through notices.

Mark-to-Market Margin (MTM):

(a) The MTM margin is collected on the gross open position of the Member. The gross open position for this purpose would mean the gross of all net positions across all the clients of a member including his proprietary position. For this purpose, the position of a client is netted across his various securities and the position of all the clients of a Member is grossed. Further, there is no netting across two different settlements.

(b) There is no netting off the positions and set off against MTM profits across 2 rolling settlements, i.e., T day and T-1 day. However, for computation of MTM profits/losses for the day, netting or set-off against MTM profits is permitted.

Collection and Release of Margins

All statements pertaining to daily margins, *viz.,* VaR, MTM, ELM and Special Margin computed by BSE on the outstanding positions of the Members are available for downloading by them in their back offices at the end of the day.

VaR Margin

The VaR margin is collected on an upfront basis by adjusting against the total liquid assets of the Member at the time of trade.

Extreme Loss Margin (ELM)

The ELM is collected/adjusted from the total liquid assets of the Member on a real time basis.

Mark-to-Market Margin (MTM)

The MTM is computed after trading hours on T day on the basis of closing price, of that day. In case the security has not been traded on a particular day, the latest available closing price is considered as the closing price. MTM margins is also recomputed in respect of all the pending settlements on the basis of closing prices of T day and the difference due to increase/decrease in MTM margins on account of such re-computation is adjusted in the MTM obligation of the Member for the day. Such MTM is collected from the Members in the evening on the T day itself, first by adjusting the same from the available cash and cash equivalent component of the liquid assets and the balance MTM in form of cash from the Members through their clearing banks on the same day.

Special Margins

The Special Margin as applicable is collected along with MTM from the Members, first, by adjusting the same from the available liquid assets and the balance Special Margin in form of cash from the Members through their clearing banks on the same day.

Release of Margins

The above-referred margins are released on completion of pay-in of the settlement Fines/Penalty for Margin Default cases where there are insufficient balances in bank accounts of the Members at the time of debit of margin amounts payable in cash on the relevant day, are treated as margin defaults. Revised norms as per Exchange Notice No. 20091211-20 for imposing late fees/fines/penalties on member brokers in case of delay/non-clearance of margin obligations in the Cash Segment w.e.f. Monday, December 14, 2009.

Violation/s	Revised norms (Instances of violations in a F.Y.)
Non-fulfillment of margin obligations to the Exchange.	In case of non-fulfillment of margin obligation, the trading facility of such members shall be withdrawn immediately and fine/penalty of 1% of the unpaid margin amount will be levied. The trading facility shall be restored after fulfillment of the margin obligation by the member.

Source: www.bse.com

Besides the aforesaid, all other norms as prescribed *vide* the aforesaid notice no. 20050520-20 dated May 20, 2005 and other notices issued from time to time in respect of the same will remain unchanged.

Exemption from Payment of Margins

Kindly refer Notice No. 20080416-15 for revised margin norms.

The following trades executed on the BOLT are exempted from payment of margins:

(a) Institutional business. For this purpose, institutional investors include :

1. Foreign Institutional Investors registered with SEBI.
2. Mutual Funds registered with SEBI.
3. Public Financial Institutions as defined under Section 4A of the Companies Act, 1956.
4. Banks, i.e., a banking company as defined under Section 5(1)(c) of the Banking Regulations Act, 1949.
5. Insurance companies registered with IRDA.

(b) In cases where early pay-in of securities is made, the outstanding position of the client to the extent of early pay-in.

Early Pay-in Facility:

- The early pay-in of securities done up to 3.00 p.m. on a day are considered for on-line release of blocked liquid assets on account of margins on that day. The benefits of early pay-in done after 3.00 p.m. on a day are available on the next trading day.
- Members are also able to do early pay-in of securities before execution of the trade on T day to avail benefit of margin exemption.

For availing the benefits of margin exemptions through early pay-in of securities, the members are required to upload a file containing details in respect of the early pay-in at client level to the Clearing House (BOISL). The detail in the file is matched against the transaction files received from CDSL and NSDL. Only the matched records are uploaded for Early Pay-In.

Capital Cushion Requirements

SEBI has advised BSE to build an administrative mechanism to encourage members to hold capital cushions while operating in the Cash and Derivatives Segments. Accordingly, the following methodology, as advised by SEBI, is being followed by BSE:

- At the end of each calendar month, Members who have exceeded 90% of utilization of capital during the day for more than 7 days in the current month are identified.
- In the derivatives segment, the utilization is monitored after considering initial margins, exposure margins and premium.
- The capital requirement to bring the utilization to a level of 85% at the time of violating the trigger point of 90% on each of those occasions is noted for the Members. The highest of such amounts for the identified members during the month is called for as additional capital.
- The requirement is communicated to the members on the first day of the subsequent month.
- The Members are provided a time limit of three working days to provide the amount of additional capital in the form of Cash, FDRs and Bank Guarantees only.
- The additional capital so collected is retained with the Clearing House for a period of one calendar month.
- No benefit including exposure, margin etc is available to the Member on the amount of additional capital so collected.
- In case of non-payment of additional capital within the stipulated time limit a penalty as applicable for funds shortage is levied on the Member for the period of default.
- In case a Member is liable to provide additional capital in the subsequent month, the amount of additional capital shall be recomputed and the excess/deficit is refunded/called for.

Monitoring Business of Brokers

BSE closely monitors the outstanding positions of the main Members on a daily basis. For this purpose, it has developed various market monitoring reports based on certain pre-set parameters. These reports are scrutinized by officials of the Surveillance Department to ascertain whether a Member has built up excessive purchase or sale position compared to his normal level of business. Further, it is examined whether purchases or sales are concentrated in one or more scrips, whether the margin cover is adequate and whether transactions have been entered into on behalf of institutional clients. Even the quality of scrips, i.e., liquid or illiquid, is looked into in order to assess the quality of exposure. Based on an analysis of these factors, the margins already paid and the total capital deposited by the Member with BSE, an advance pay-in is called from the concerned Member.

BSE also scrutinizes the pay in position of the Members and such Members who have larger funds pay-in positions are , at the discretion of BSE, asked to make advance pay-in on the T+1 day instead of on the T + 2 day.

BOLT Deactivation

The BOLT TWSs of a Member are deactivated for non-payment/late payment of margins or settlement dues or on apprehension of financial difficulties or on detection of serious irregularities or for frequent violations of trading restrictions. Such decisions are taken on a case-to-case basis. The overall objective in resorting to this ultimate step is to ensure that questionable trading behavior of a Member does not compromise the safety of the market or jeopardize the integrity of the market.

Arbitrage

In economics and finance, arbitrage is the practice of taking advantage of a price differential between two or more markets: a combination of matching deals are struck that capitalize upon the imbalance, the profit being the difference between the market prices. When used by academics, an arbitrage is a transaction that involves no negative cash flow at any probabilistic or temporal state and a positive cash flow in at least one state; in simple terms, a risk-free profit. A person who engages in arbitrage is called an arbitrageur. The term is mainly applied to trading in financial instruments, such as bonds, stocks, derivatives, commodities and currencies.

If the market prices do not allow for profitable arbitrage, the prices are said to constitute an arbitrage equilibrium or arbitrage-free market. Arbitrage equilibrium is a precondition for a general economic equilibrium. The assumption that there is no arbitrage is used in quantitative finance to calculate a unique risk neutral price for derivatives.

Conditions for Arbitrage

Arbitrage is possible when one of three conditions is met:

1. The same asset does not trade at the same price on all markets ("the law of one price").
2. Two assets with identical cash flows do not trade at the same price.
3. An asset with a known price in the future does not today trade at its future price discounted at the risk-free interest rate (or, the asset does not have negligible costs of storage; as such, for example, this condition holds for grain but not for securities).

Arbitrage is not simply the act of buying a product in one market and selling it in another for a higher price at some later time. The transactions must occur simultaneously to avoid exposure to market risk, or the risk that prices may change on one market before both transactions are complete. In practical terms, this is generally only possible with securities and financial products which can be traded electronically.

In the simplest example, any good sold in one market should sell for the same price in another. Traders may, for example, find that the price of wheat is lower in agricultural regions than in cities, purchase the goods, and transport it to another region to sell at a higher price. This type of price arbitrage is the most common, but this simple example ignores the cost of transport, storage, risk, and other factors. "True" arbitrage requires that there be no market risk involved. Where securities are traded on more than one exchange, arbitrage occurs by simultaneously buying in one and selling on the other.

Mathematically it is defined as follows:

$$P(V_T \geq 0) = 1 \text{ and } P(V_T \neq 0) > 0$$

Where V_T means a portfolio at time t.

Examples:

- Suppose that the exchange rates (after taking out the fees for making the exchange) in London are £5 = \$10 = ¥1000 and the exchange rates in Tokyo are ¥1000 = £6 = \$12. Converting ¥1000 to \$12 in Tokyo and converting that \$12 into ¥1200 in London, for a profit of ¥200, would be arbitrage. In reality, this "triangle arbitrage" is so simple that it almost never occurs. But more complicated foreign exchange arbitrages, such as the spot-forward arbitrage (see interest rate parity) are much more common.
- A common arbitrage involves borrowing at lower short-term rates and investing at higher long-term interest rates while pocketing the spread. The risk is that short-term loan rates rise higher.
- One example of arbitrage involves the New York Stock Exchange and the Chicago Mercantile Exchange. When the price of a stock on the NYSE and its corresponding futures contract on the CME are out of sync, one can buy the less expensive one and sell it to the more expensive market. Because the differences between the prices are likely to be small (and not to last very long), this can only be done profitably with computers examining a large number of prices and automatically exercising a trade when the prices are far enough out of balance. The activity of other arbitrageurs can make this risky. Those with the fastest computers and the smartest mathematicians take advantage of series of small differentials that would not be profitable if taken individually.
- Economists use the term "global labor arbitrage" to refer to the tendency of manufacturing jobs to flow towards whichever country has the lowest wages per unit output at present and has reached the minimum requisite level of political and economic development to support industrialization. At present, many such jobs appear to be flowing towards China, though some which require command of English are going to India and the Philippines. In popular terms, this is referred to as offshoring. (Note that "off shoring" is not synonymous with "outsourcing", which means "to subcontract from an outside supplier or source", such as when a business outsources it's bookkeeping to an accounting firm. Unlike off shoring, outsourcing always involves subcontracting jobs to a different company, and that company can be in the same country as the outsourcing company.)
- Sports arbitrage – Numerous internet bookmakers offer odds on the outcome of the same event. Any given bookmaker will weight their odds so that no one customer can cover all outcomes at a profit against their books. However, in order to remain competitive their margins are usually quite low. Different bookmakers may offer different odds on the same outcome of a given event; by taking the best odds offered by each bookmaker, a customer can

under some circumstances cover all possible outcomes of the event and lock a small risk-free profit, known as a Dutch book. This profit would typically be between 1% and 5% but can be much higher. One problem with sports arbitrage is that bookmakers sometimes make mistakes and this can lead to an invocation of the 'palpable error' rule, which most bookmakers invoke when they have made a mistake by offering or posting incorrect odds. As bookmakers become more proficient, the odds of making an 'arb' usually last for less than an hour and typically only a few minutes. Furthermore, huge bets on one side of the market also alert the bookies to correct the market.

- Exchange traded fund arbitrage – Exchange traded funds allow authorized participants to exchange back and forth between shares in underlying securities held by the fund and shares in the fund itself, rather than allowing the buying and selling of shares in the ETF directly with the fund sponsor. ETFs trade in the open market, with prices set by market demand. An ETF may trade at a premium or discount to the value of the underlying assets. When a significant enough premium appears, an arbitrageur will buy the underlying securities, convert them to shares in the ETF, and sell them in the open market. When a discount appears, an arbitrageur will do the reverse. In this way, the arbitrageur makes a low-risk profit, while fulfilling a useful function in the ETF marketplace by keeping ETF prices in line with their underlying value.
- Some types of hedge funds make use of a modified form of arbitrage to profit. Rather than exploiting price differences between identical assets, they will purchase and sell securities, assets and derivatives with similar characteristics, and hedge any significant differences between the two assets. Any difference between the hedged positions represents any remaining risk (such as basis risk) plus profit; the belief is that there remains some difference which, even after hedging most risk, represents pure profit. For example, a fund may see that there is a substantial difference between U.S. dollar debt and local currency debt of a foreign country, and enter into a series of matching trades (including currency swaps) to arbitrage the difference, while simultaneously entering into credit default swaps to protect against country risk and other types of specific risk.

Price Convergence

Arbitrage has the effect of causing prices in different markets to converge. As a result of arbitrage, the currency exchange rates, the price of commodities, and the price of securities in different markets tend to converge to the same prices, in all markets, in each category. The speed at which prices converge is a measure of market efficiency. Arbitrage tends to reduce price discrimination by encouraging people to buy an item where the price is low and resell it where the price is high, as long as the buyers are not prohibited from reselling and the transaction costs of buying, holding and reselling are small relative to the difference in prices in the different markets.

Arbitrage moves different currencies toward purchasing power parity. As an example, assume that a car purchased in the United States is cheaper than the same car in Canada. Canadians would buy their cars across the border to exploit the arbitrage condition. At the same time, Americans would buy US cars, transport them across the border, and sell them in Canada. Canadians would have to buy American Dollars to buy the cars and Americans would have to sell the Canadian dollars they received in exchange for the exported cars. Both actions would increase demand for US Dollars, and supply of

Canadian Dollars, and as a result, there would be an appreciation of the US Dollar. Eventually, if unchecked, this would make US cars more expensive for all buyers, and Canadian cars cheaper, until there is no longer an incentive to buy cars in the US and sell them in Canada. More generally, international arbitrage opportunities in commodities, goods, securities and currencies, on a grand scale, tend to change exchange rates until the purchasing power is equal.

In reality, of course, one must consider taxes and the costs of travelling back and forth between the US and Canada. Also, the features built into the cars sold in the US are not exactly the same as the features built into the cars for sale in Canada, due, among other things, to the different emissions and other auto regulations in the two countries. In addition, our example assumes that no duties have to be paid on importing or exporting cars from the USA to Canada. Similarly, most assets exhibit (small) differences between countries, transaction costs, taxes, and other costs provide an impediment to this kind of arbitrage.

Similarly, arbitrage affects the difference in interest rates paid on government bonds, issued by the various countries, given the expected depreciations in the currencies, relative to each other (see interest rate parity).

Risks

Arbitrage transactions in modern securities markets involve fairly low risks. Generally it is impossible to close two or three transactions at the same instant; therefore, there is the possibility that when one part of the deal is closed, a quick shift in prices makes it impossible to close the other at a profitable price. There is also counter-party risk that the other party to one of the deals fails to deliver as agreed; though unlikely, this hazard is serious because of the large quantities one must trade in order to make a profit on small price differences. These risks become magnified when leverage or borrowed money is used.

Another risk occurs if the items being bought and sold are not identical and the arbitrage is conducted under the assumption that the prices of the items are correlated or predictable. In the extreme case this is risk arbitrage, described below. In comparison to the classical quick arbitrage transaction, such an operation can produce disastrous losses.

Competition in the marketplace can also create risks during arbitrage transactions. As an example, if one was trying to profit from a price discrepancy between IBM on the NYSE and IBM on the London Stock Exchange, they may purchase a large number of shares on the NYSE and find that they cannot simultaneously sell on the LSE. This leaves the arbitrageur in an unheeded risk position.

In the 1980s, risk arbitrage was common. In this form of speculation, one trades a security that is clearly undervalued or overvalued, when it is seen that the wrong valuation is about to be corrected by events. The standard example is the stock of a company, undervalued in the stock market, which is about to be the object of a takeover bid; the price of the takeover will more truly reflect the value of the company, giving a large profit to those who bought at the current price — if the merger goes through as predicted. Traditionally, arbitrage transactions in the securities markets involve high speed and low risk. At some moment a price difference exists, and the problem is to execute two or three balancing transactions while the difference persists (that is, before the other arbitrageurs act). When the transaction involves a delay of weeks or months, as above, it may entail considerable risk if borrowed money is used to magnify the reward through leverage. One way of reducing the risk is through the illegal use of inside information, and in fact risk arbitrage with regard to leveraged buyouts was associated with some of the famous financial scandals of the 1980s, such as those involving Michael Milken and Ivan Boesky.

Types of Arbitrage

Merger arbitrage also called risk arbitrage; merger arbitrage generally consists of buying the stock of a company that is the target of a takeover while shorting the stock of the acquiring company.

Usually the market price of the target company is less than the price offered by the acquiring company. The spread between these two prices depends mainly on the probability and the timing of the takeover being completed as well as the prevailing level of interest rates.

The bet in a merger arbitrage is that such a spread will eventually be zero, if and when the takeover is completed. The risk is that the deal "breaks" and the spread massively widens.

Municipal bond arbitrage also called municipal bond relative value arbitrage, municipal arbitrage, or just municipal, this hedge fund strategy involves one of two approaches.

Generally, managers seek relative value opportunities by being both long and short municipal bonds with a duration-neutral book. The relative value trades may be between different issuers, different bonds issued by the same entity or capital structure trades referencing the same asset (in the case of revenue bonds). Managers aim to capture the inefficiencies arising from the heavy participation of non-economic investors (i.e., high income "buy and hold" investors seeking tax-exempt income) as well as the "crossover buying" arising from corporations' or individuals' changing income tax situations (i.e., insurers switching their munis for corporate after a large loss as they can capture a higher after-tax yield by offsetting the taxable corporate income with underwriting losses). There are additional inefficiencies arising from the highly fragmented nature of the municipal bond market which has two million outstanding issues and 50,000 issuers in contrast to the Treasury market which has 400 issues and a single issuer.

Second, managers construct leveraged portfolios of AAA or AA-rated tax-exempt municipal bonds with the duration risk hedged by shorting the appropriate ratio of taxable corporate bonds. These corporate equivalents are typically interest rate swaps referencing Libor [1] or SIFMA(Security Industry and Financial Markets Association) [2] (merged with and preceded by BMA [short for Bond Market Association] [3]). The arbitrage manifests itself in the form of a relatively cheap longer maturity municipal bond, which is a municipal bond that yields significantly more than 65% of a corresponding taxable corporate bond. The steeper slope of the municipal yield curve allows participants to collect more after-tax income from the municipal bond portfolio than is spent on the interest rate swap; the carry is greater than the hedge expense. Positive, tax-free carry from muni arb can reach into the double digits. The bet in this municipal bond arbitrage is that, over a longer period of time, two similar instruments — municipal bonds and interest rate swaps — will correlate with each other; they are both very high quality credits, have the same maturity and are denominated in U.S. dollars. Credit risk and duration risk are largely eliminated in this strategy. However, basis risk arises from use of an imperfect hedge, which results in significant, but range-bound principal volatility. The end goal is to limit this principal volatility, eliminating its relevance over time as the high, consistent, tax-free cash flow accumulates. Since the inefficiency is related to government tax policy, and hence is structural in nature, it has not been arbitraged away.

Convertible Bond Arbitrage

A convertible bond is a bond that an investor can return to the issuing company in exchange for a predetermined number of shares in the company.

A convertible bond can be thought of as a corporate bond with a stock call option attached to it.

The price of a convertible bond is sensitive to three major factors:

- *Interest rate.* When rates move higher, the bond part of a convertible bond tends to move lower, but the call option part of a convertible bond moves higher (and the aggregate tends to move lower).
- *Stock price.* When the price of the stock bond is convertible into moves higher, the price of the bond tends to rise.
- *Credit spread.* If the creditworthiness of the issuer deteriorates (e.g. rating downgrade) and its credit spread widens, the bond price tends to move lower, but, in many cases, the call option part of the convertible bond moves higher (since credit spread correlates with volatility).

Given the complexity of the calculations involved and the convoluted structure that a convertible bond can have, an arbitrageur often relies on sophisticated quantitative models in order to identify bonds that are trading cheap versus their theoretical value.

Convertible arbitrage consists of buying a convertible bond and hedging two of the three factors in order to gain exposure to the third factor at a very attractive price.

For instance an arbitrageur would first buy a convertible bond, then sell fixed income securities or interest rate futures (to hedge the interest rate exposure) and buy some credit protection (to hedge the risk of credit deterioration). Eventually what he'd be left with is something similar to a call option on the underlying stock, acquired at a very low price. He could then make money either selling some of the more expensive options that are openly traded in the market or delta hedging his exposure to the underlying shares.

Depository Receipts

A depository receipt is a security that is offered as a "tracking stock" on another foreign market. For instance a Chinese company wishing to raise more money may issue a depository receipt on the New York Stock Exchange, as the amount of capital on the local exchanges is limited. These securities, known as ADRs (American Depositary Receipt) or GDRs (Global Depositary Receipt) depending on where they are issued are typically considered "foreign" and therefore, trade at a lower value when first released. However, they are exchangeable into the original security (known as fungibility) and actually have the same value. In this case, there is a spread between the perceived value and real value, which can be extracted. Since the ADR is trading at a value lower than what it is worth, one can purchase the ADR and expect to make money as its value converges on the original. However there is a chance that the original stock will fall in value too, so by shorting it you can hedge that risk.

Regulatory Arbitrage

Regulatory arbitrage is where a regulated institution takes advantage of the difference between its real (or economic) risk and the regulatory position. For example, if a bank, operating under the Basel I accord, has to hold 8% capital against default risk, but the real risk of default is lower, it is profitable to securitise the loan, removing the low risk loan from its portfolio. On the other hand, if the real risk is higher than the regulatory risk then it is profitable to make that loan and hold on to it, provided it is priced appropriately.

This process can increase the overall riskiness of institutions under a risk insensitive regulatory regime, as described by Alan Greenspan in his October 1998 speech on The Role of Capital in Optimal Banking Supervision and Regulation.

In economics, regulatory arbitrage (sometimes, tax arbitrage) may be used to refer to situations when a company can choose a nominal place of business with a regulatory, legal or tax regime with lower costs. For example, an insurance company may choose to locate in Bermuda due to preferential tax rates and policies for insurance companies. This can occur particularly where the business transaction has no obvious physical location, in the case of many financial products, it may be unclear "where" the transaction occurs.

Telecom Arbitrage

Telecom arbitrage companies allow mobile phone users to make international calls for free through certain access numbers. The telecommunication arbitrage companies get paid an interconnect charge by the UK mobile networks and then buy international routes at a lower cost. The calls are seen as free by the UK contract mobile phone customers since they are using up their allocated monthly minutes rather than paying for additional calls. The end effect is telecom arbitrage. This is usually marketed as "free international calls". The profit margins are usually very small. However, with enough volume, enough money is made from the cost difference to turn a profit.

The Debacle of Long-term Capital Management

Long-term Capital Management (LTCM) lost 4.6 billion U.S. dollars in fixed income arbitrage in September 1998. LTCM had attempted to make money on the price difference between different bonds. For example, it would sell U.S. Treasury securities and buy Italian bond futures. The concept was that because Italian bond futures had a less liquid market, in the short-term Italian bond futures would have a higher return than U.S. bonds, but in the long-term, the prices would converge. Because the difference was small, a large amount of money had to be borrowed to make the buying and selling profitable.

The downfall in this system began on August 17, 1998, when Russia defaulted on its Ruble debt and domestic Dollar debt. Because the markets were already nervous due to the Asian financial crisis, investors began selling non-U.S. treasury debt and buying U.S. treasuries, which were considered a safe investment. As a Result, the return on U.S. treasuries began decreasing because there were many buyers, and the return on other bonds began to increase because there were many sellers. This caused the difference between the returns of U.S. treasuries and other bonds to increase, rather than to decrease as LTCM was expecting. Eventually this caused LTCM to fold, and their creditors had to arrange a bail-out. More controversially, officials of the Federal Reserve assisted in the negotiations that led to this bail-out, on the grounds that so many companies and deals were intertwined with LTCM that if LTCM actually failed, they would as well, causing a collapse in confidence in the economic system. Thus LTCM failed as a fixed income arbitrage fund, although it is unclear what sort of profit was realized by the banks that bailed LTCM out.

Etymology

"Arbitrage" is a French word and denotes a decision by an arbitrator or arbitration tribunal. (In modern French, *"arbiter"* usually means referee or umpire). In the sense used here it is first defined in 1704 by Mathieu de la Porte in his treatise "La science des magicians et teneurs de livres" as a consideration of different exchange rates to recognize the most profitable places of issuance and settlement for a bill of exchange ("L'arbitrage est. une combination que l'on fait de plusieurs changes, pour connote [connate, in modern spelling] quelled place est. plus advantageous pour tirer et remitter").

NATIONAL STOCK EXCHANGE

The national stock exchange of India limited has genesis in the report of the high powered study group on establishment of new stock exchanges. It recommended promotion of a national stock exchange by financial institutions (FIs) to provide access to investors from all across the country on an equal footing. It was incorporated in November, 1992.

On its recognition as a stock exchange under the Securities Contract (Regulation) Act, 1956, in April 1993, NSE commenced operations in the wholesale June 1994. The capital market (equities) segment commenced operations in November 1994 and operations in derivatives segment commenced in June 2000.

The following years witnessed rapid development of Indian capital market with introduction of internet trading, exchange traded funds (ETF), stock derivatives and the first volatility index – India VIX in April 2008, by NSE.

August 2008, saw introduction of currency derivatives in India with the launch of currency futures in USD INR by NSE. Interest rate futures were introduced for the first time in India by NSE on 31st August 2009, exactly after one year of the launch of currency futures. With this, now both the retail and institutional investors can participate in equities, equity derivatives, currency and interest rate derivatives, giving them wide range of products to take care of their evolving needs.

Mission

NSE's mission is setting the agenda for change in securities markets in India. The NSE was setup with the main objectives of:

- Establishing a nation-wide trading facility for equities, debt instruments and hybrids,
- Ensuring equal access to investors all over the country through an appropriate communication network,
- Providing a fair, efficient and transparent securities market to investors using electronic trading systems,
- Enabling shorter settlement cycles and book entry settlement systems, and
- Meeting the current international standards of security markets.

The standards set by NSE in terms of market practices and technology has become industry benchmarks and is being emulated by other market participants. NSE is more than a mere market facilitator. It's that force which is guiding the industry towards new horizon and greater opportunities.

Promoters

The NSE has been promoted by leading financial institutions, banks, insurance companies and other financial intermediaries:

- IDBI
- IFCI
- SBI
- ICICI BANK
- IL&FS TRUST COMPANY LTD
- STOCK HOLDING CORPORATION OF INDIA LTD
- SBI CAPITAL MARKETS LTD
- BANK OF BARODA
- CANARA BANK
- GENERAL INSURANCE CORPORATION OF INDIA
- NATIONAL INSURANCE
- THE NEW INDIA ASSURANCE COMPANY LTD
- THE ORIENTAL INSURANCE LTD
- UNITED INSURANCE LTD
- PNB LTD
- OBC
- INDIAN BANK
- UBI
- INFRASTRUCTURE DEVELOPMENT FINANCE COMPANY LTD.

Structure

NSE is one of the first de-mutualised stock exchanges in the country, where the ownership and management of the exchange is completely divorced from the right to trade on it. It has been set up as a public limited company owned by the leading institutional investors in the country. It is owned by a set of leading financial institutions, banks, insurance companies and other financial intermediaries. It is managed by professionals. They do not directly or indirectly trade on exchange. It is aggressively pursuing policies and practices within a public interest framework. The trading members don't involve in any involvement of activities in any different ways. The board of directors comprises with senior executives from promoters' institutions. They are eminent professionals in the fields of law, economics, accountancy, finance and taxation. The board includes public representatives, nominees of the SEBI and one full time executive of the exchange. The board deals with broad policy issues, decisions relating to market operations, are delegated by the board to various committees constituted by it. The committees include trading members, professionals, the public and the management. The managing director is supported by a team of highly experienced professional staff. The day to day affairs of the exchange is looked after by the managing director.

The chronological developments of NSE:

❍ Incorporation	: Novervmber 1992
❍ Recognition as a stock exchange	: April 1993
❍ Formulation of business plan	: May 1993
❍ Wholesale debt market segment	: June 1994
❍ Capital market segment	: Nov. 1994
❍ Establishment of investors grievance cell	: March 1995
❍ Establishment of NSE clearence corporation	: April 1995
❍ Introduction of centralised insurance cover for all trading	: June 1995
❍ Establishment of investor protection fund	: July 1995
❍ Became largest stock exchange in the country	: Oct. 1995
❍ Commencement of clearing and settlement by NSCCL	: April 1996
❍ Launch of S&P CNX nifty	: April 1996
❍ Establishment of settlement guarentee fund	: June 1996
❍ Setting up of national securities depository 1st depository in India	: November 1996
❍ Best IT usage award by computer society of India	: November 1996
❍ Commencement of trading/settlement in dematerialized securities	: December 1996
❍ Dataquest award for top IT's user	: December 1996
❍ Launch of CNX Nifty junior	: Decemer 1996
❍ Regional clearing facility goes live	: Feb. 1997
❍ Best IT usage award computer society of India	: November 1997
❍ Promotion of join venture, India index services & products Limited (IISL)	: May 1998
❍ Launch of NSE's certification programme in financial market	: July 1998
❍ Cyber corporate of the year	: August 1998
❍ Launch of automated lending and borrowing mechanism	: Febraury 1999
❍ Chip web award by Chip magazine	: April 1999
❍ Setting up of NSE.it	: October 1999
❍ Launch of NSE research initiative	: January 2000
❍ Commencement of internet trading	: Feb. 2000
❍ Commencement of derivative trading	: June 2000
❍ Launch of zero coupon yield curve	: Sept. 2000
❍ Launch of broker plaza by Dotex international.	: November 2000
❍ Commencement of swap trading	: December 2000
❍ Commencement of trading in index options	: June 2001

- Commencement of trading in options on individual securities : July 2001
- Commencement of trading in future on individual securities: November 2001
- Launch of NSE VaR for government securities : Dec. 2001
- Launch of exchange traded funds : Jan. 2002
- NSE wins Infosys award : May 2002
- Launch of NSE government securities index. : Oct.2002
- Commencement of trading in retail debt market : Jan. 2003
- Launch of interest rate futures : June 2003
- Launch of F&O in cnx IT Index : August 2003
- Launch of STP interoperablity : June 2004
- Launch of NSE electronic interface for listed companies : August 2004
- India innovation award : March 2005
- Launch of F&O bank Nifty index : June 2005
- Derivate exchange of year : December 2006
- Launch of NSE CNBC media centre : Jan. 2007
- NSE Crisil announce launch of India bond watch.com : March 2007
- NSE launches derivatives on Nifty junior and CNX 100 : June 2007
- NSE launches derivatives on Nifty midcap 50 : Oct. 2007
- Introduction of mini Nifty derivative contracts : January 2008
- Introduction of long term options contracts on S&P CNX nifty: April 2008
- Launch of India VIX : April 2008
- Launch of securities lending and borrowings scheme : April 2008
- Launch of currency derivatives : August 2008
- Launch of interest rate futures : Aug. 2008
- Launch of mutual fund service system : Nov. 2009
- Commencement of settlement of corporate bonds : Dec. 2009
- Launch of currency futures on additional currency pairs : Feb. 2010
- NSE-CME group & NSE-SGX product cross listing agreement : March 2010
- Financial derivative exchange of the year award by Asian Bank. : April 2010

Nifty (national index for fifty shares) market capitalisation as on 12.8.2010

Nifty	5416.45 Market Capitalisation ₹ in crores 15,60,703	100. Days in Weight (%)	PE Ratio
1. RIL	1,43,846	9.22	18.3
2. INFOSYS	1,32,867	8.51	25.6
3. L&T	1,08,724	6.97	31.6
4. ICICI BANK	1,07,471	6.89	25.8
5. ITC	79,596	5.10	27.5
6. HDFC BANK	76,907	4.93	30.2
7. HDFC	76,761	4.92	29.4
8. SBI	71,753	4.60	15.1
9. ONGC	42,718	2.74	17.4
10. TCS	39,738	2.55	22.7
11. BHARATI AIRTEL	39,533	2.53	13.1
12. BHEL	39,393	2.52	27.1
13. AXIS BANK	33,955	2.18	19.8
14. TATA MOTORS	30,750	1.97	22.8
15. TATA STEEL	30,476	1.95	
16. HUL	28,207	1.81	26.8
17. IDFC	25,948	1.66	23.1
18. M & M	25,926	1.66	16.3
19. ZINDAL STEEL	25,200	1.61	17
20. STERILITE	22,221	1.42	13.8
21. TATA POWER	21,065	1.35	16
22. WIPRO	20,846	1.34	20.6
23. HINDALCO	20,424	1.31	16.2
24. GAIL	20,171	1.29	16.9
25. NTPC	16,805	1.08	19.2
26. HERO HONDA	16,782	1.08	16.8
27. RELIANCE INFRA	16,734	1.07	24.8
28. MARUTI SUZUKI	16,220	1.04	14.9
29. CIPLA	15,251	0.98	23.3
30. PNB	15,084	0.97	8.6
31. CAIRN	14,663	0.94	50.3
32. KOTAK MAHINDRA	13,982	0.90	21.3

33. JAIPRAKSH ASSOCIATE	13,816	0.89	14.6
34. SUN PHARMA	13,065	0.84	20.6
35. UNITECH	12,647	0.81	31.9
36. IDEA CELLULAR	12,163	0.78	27.9
37. RELIANCE COMM.	11,675	0.75	7.7
38. DLF	11,435	0.73	30.7
39. SAIL	11,263	0.72	12
40. SIEMENS	10,455	0.67	32.1
41 AMBUJA CEMENTS	9,584	0.61	12.7
42. REL. CAPITAL	8,720	0.56	43.2
43. BPCL	8,719	0.56	
44. HCL TECHNO	8,671	0.56	25.8
45. ACC	8,490	0.54	11
46. ABB	7,944	0.51	69.8
47. RANBAXY	6,757	0.43	8.4
48. POWER GRID	5,727	0.37	19.1
49. RELIANCE POWER	5,685	0.36	60.6
50. SUZULON ENERGY	3,877	0.25	-

Source: The Economic Times, Dt. 14/8/2010.

The business of the national stock exchange was as follows:

1. Capital market segment:
2. Clearing and settlement
3. Derivatives (F&O) segment
4. Currency derivative segment

The financial information of capital market segment is presented below with the latest information available.

Settlement guarantee fund: ₹ 4,843.50 crores
As on 31st March 2009
Investor protection fund : ₹ 307.02 crores
As on 30- April- 2010
Numbers of securities available for trading : 1926
As on 30-June-2010
Record number of trades : 11260392
As on 19-May-2009
Record daily turnover (quantity): ₹ 19225 lakhs

As on 19-May-2009
Record daily turnover (value) : ₹ 40151.91 crores
As on 19-May-2009
Record market capitalization : ₹ 67,45,724 crores
As on 7-January-2008
Record value of S&P CNX nifty index : 6357.1
As on 8-January-2008
Record value of CNX nifty junior index : 13209.34
As on 4-January-2008

Clearing and Settlement

The financial information related to clearing and settlement segment of the available information is presented below:

1. Funds pay-in/pay-out (N2007200): ₹ 4,567.70 crores
   As on 23-October-2007*
2. Securities pay in/pay-out (value) (N2009088): ₹ 9,523.33 crores as on 21-May-2009*
3. Securities pay-in/pay-out (quantity) (M2009088): ₹ 4,385.75 lakhs as on 21-May-2009* * = settlement later

Derivatives (F&O) Segment

The derivatives futures and options segment is presented for the better understanding with the latest available information.

1. Settlement guarantee fund: ₹ 23,655.86 crores
As on 31-March-2008
2. Investor protection fund: ₹ 54.53 crores
As on 30-April-2010
3. Record daily turnover (value): ₹ 166,193.03 crores
As on 28-January-2010
4. Record number of trades: 1874697
As on 7-January-2009

Currency Derivatives Segment

The financial information of the currency derivative segment is presented with the latest available information for better understanding of the aspects.

1. Record daily turnover (value): ₹ 21,903.34 crores
As on 20-April-2010
2. Record number of trades: 78935

As on 11-January-2010
3. Record number of contracts: 4884935
As on 20-April-2010
4. Investor protection fund: ₹ 0.01 crores
As on 30-April-2010

Wholesale Debt Segment

The financial information related to wholesale debt segment is presented below with the latest available information.

1. Number of securities available for trading: 4,263
   As on 30-June-2010

National Stock Exchange of India Limited Rules

Arrangement of Chapters

Chapter

Description

I. Board
II. Executive Committee
III. Trading Membership
IV. Disciplinary Proceeding, Penalties
V. Suspension and Expulsion

I. Board

(1) The Board of Directors (herein referred to as Board) of National Stock Exchange of India Limited, constituted in accordance with the provisions of the Articles of Association of the Company, may organize, maintain, control, manage, regulate and facilitate the operations of the Exchange and of securities transactions by trading members of the Exchange, subject to the provisions of the Securities Contracts (Regulation) Act, 1956 and Rules thereunder, Securities and Exchange Board of India Act, 1992 and any directives there under and the trading regulations which RBI may prescribe from time to time for money market instruments.

(2) Directors of the National Stock Exchange of India Limited shall be appointed in accordance with the provisions of the Articles of Association of the Company as amended from time to time and in particular, provisions of Articles 108, 109, 110, 111, 112, 113, 114, 115 and 116 thereof. Any such appointment of Directors shall be considered as one being made under the provisions of these rules.

(3) Subject to the provisions of the Securities Contracts (Regulation) Act, 1956 and Rules there under, the Securities and Exchange Board of India Act, 1992 and any directives there under and the trading regulations which RBI may prescribe from time to time for money market instruments, the Board is empowered to make Bye-laws, Rules and Regulations from time to

time, for all or any matters relating to the conduct of business of the Exchange, the business and transactions of trading members between trading members inter-se as well as the business and transactions between trading members and persons who are not trading members, and to control, define and regulate all such transactions and dealings and to do such acts and things which are necessary for the purposes of the Exchange.

(4) Without prejudice to the generality of the foregoing, the Board is empowered to make Regulations, subject to the provisions of the Securities Contracts (Regulation) Act, 1956 and Rules thereunder, the Securities and Exchange Board of India Act, 1992 and any directives thereunder and the trading regulations which RBI may prescribe from time to time for money market instruments, for all or any of the following matters:

(a) Conditions for admission to membership of the Exchange;

(b) Conditions for any arrangement with another stock exchange pursuant to the *proviso* to Section 13 of the Securities Contracts (Regulation) Act, 1956 and all matters relating thereto

(c) Conduct of business of the Exchange;

(d) Conduct of trading members with regard to the business of the Exchange;

(e) Penalties for disobedience or contravention of the Rules, Bye-laws and Regulations of the Exchange or of general discipline of the Exchange, including expulsion or suspension of the trading members;

(f) Declaration of any trading member as a defaulter or suspension or resignation or expulsion from trading membership of the Exchange and consequences thereof;

(g) Conditions, levy for admission or subscription for admission or continuance of trading membership of the Exchange;

(h) Charges payable by trading members for transactions in such securities as may be laid down from time to time;

(i) Investigation of the financial condition, business conduct and dealings of the trading members;

(j) Appointment of Committee or Committees for any purpose of the exchange;

(k) Such other matters in relation to the Exchange as may be prescribed under the provisions of the Articles of Association, Bye-laws or these Rules or as may be necessary or expedient for the organization, maintenance, control, management, regulation and facilitation of the operations of the Exchange.

(5) The Board is empowered to delegate, from time to time, to the Executive Committee(s) or to the Managing Director or to any person, such of the powers vested in it and upon such terms as they may think fit, to manage all or any of the affairs of the Exchange and from time to time, to revoke, withdraw, alter or vary all or any of such powers.

(6) The Board may, from time to time, constitute one or more committees comprising of members of the Board or such others as the Board may in its discretion deem fit or necessary and delegate to such committees such powers as the Board may deem fit and the Board may from time to time revoke such delegation. The Committees constituted by the Board may inter alia include:

(a) Admissions Committee for admission of trading members of the exchange;

(b) Infrastructure Committee to recommend appropriate infrastructure and implement the same;

(c) Systems Committee to recommend setting up of systems for carrying on the functioning of the Exchange and to implement and monitor the same;

(d) Any other matter which the Board may think fit.

(7) The Board shall have the authority to issue directives from time to time to the Executive Committee or any other Committees or any other person or persons to whom any powers have been delegated by the Board. Such directives issued in exercise of this power, which may be of policy nature or may include directives to dispose off a particular matter or issue, shall be binding on the concerned Committee(s) or person(s).

(8) Subject to the provisions of the Securities Contracts (Regulation) Act, 1956 and Rules thereunder, the Securities and Exchange Board of India Act, 1992 and any directives thereunder and the trading regulations which RBI may prescribe from time to time for money market instruments, the Board is empowered to vary, amend, repeal or add to Bye-laws, Rules and Regulations framed by it.

(9) The Members of the Board and of such committees as may be identified by the Ethics Committee shall adhere to the Code of Conduct as may be prescribed by the Board or Ethics Committee from time to time. Guidelines for Fair Practices/ Code of Conduct for Public Representative and SEBI

Nominee Directors

(10) **(A) Meetings & Minutes**

Public Representative/SEBI Nominee Directors shall

(a) Endeavour to attend all the board meetings and shall be liable to vacate his office if he remains absent for three consecutive meetings of the Board of Directors or does not attend 75% of the total meetings of the Board in a calendar year;

(b) Not participate in the discussion of any subject matter in which any conflict of interest exists or arises, whether pecuniary or otherwise, and in such cases the same shall be disclosed and recorded in the minutes of the meeting;

(c) Not encourage the circulation of agenda papers during the meeting, unless circumstances require;

(d) Meet themselves at least once in 6 months separately, if necessary, to exchange views on critical issues;

(e) Offer their comments on the draft minutes and ensure that the same are incorporated in the final minutes;

(f) Insist on the minutes of the previous meeting being placed for approval in subsequent meeting;

(g) Endeavour to have the date of next meeting fixed at each Board Meeting in consultation with other members of the Board;

(h) Endeavour that in case where all the items of the agenda of a meeting were not covered for want of time, the next meeting is held within 15 days for considering the remaining items.

(B) Strategic Planning

Public Representative/SEBI Nominee Directors shall

(a) participate in the formulation and execution of strategies in the best interest of the exchange and contribute towards pro-active decision making at the Board level;

(b) give benefit of his experience and expertise to the Exchange and provide assistance in strategic planning and execution of decisions when the Board is in the throes of a raging controversy.

(C) Regulatory Compliances

Public Representative/SEBI Nominee Directors shall

(a) endeavour to ensure that the Exchange abides by all the provisions of the SEBI Act, Securities Contracts (Regulation) Act, Rules, Regulations framed thereunder and the circulars, directions issued by the Government/SEBI from time to time;

(b) endeavour compliance at all levels so that the regulatory system does not suffer any breaches;

(c) endeavour to ensure that the Exchange takes commensurate steps to honor the time limit prescribed(d) Not support any decision in the meeting of the Board which may adversely affect the interest of investors and shall report forthwith any such decision to SEBI;

(e) endeavour that the arbitral award is given within the period stipulated in the Bye-laws, Rules or Regulations of the Exchange and in any case, the award is delivered within 15 days after the final meeting.

II. Executive Committee

(1) Executive Committee(s) shall be appointed by the Board for the purposes of managing the day to day affairs of the different trading segment(s) in such manner as laid down in the Rules.

(2) The Executive Committee of each trading segment shall have such responsibilities and powers as may be delegated to it by the Board as provided for in the Rules.

Indices

An index is used to give information about the price movements of products in the financial, commodities or any other markets. Financial indexes are constructed to measure price movements of stocks, bonds, treasury bills and other forms of investment. Stock market indexes are meant to capture the overall behavior of equity markets. A stock market index is created by selecting a group of stocks that are representative of the whole market or a specified sector or segment of the market. It is calculated with reference to a base period and a base index value. Stock market indexes are very useful to all categories of people.

- They provide a historical comparison of returns on money invested in the stock market against other forms of investments such as gold or debt.
- They can be used as a standard against which to compare the performance of an equity fund
- It is a lead indicator of the performance of the overall economy or a sector of the economy.

- Stock indexes reflect highly up to date information.

Index is a tool to know about the market movement and it plays an important role in financial investments and risk management. The modern financial applications can be classified as:

(a) Index Funds
(b) Index Futures
(c) Index Options

(a) Index Funds

Index funds are a source of investment for long-term and less risky form of investment. The success of index funds depends on their low volatility of the price movement. The national stock exchange had an arrangement with India index services and products limited. It is a joint venture between NSE, CRISIL and IISL. The IISL has been formed with the objective of providing a variety of indices and index-related services and products for the capital market. IISL has a licensing and marketing agreement with Standard and Poor's (S&P), the world's leading provider of investible equity indices, for co-branding IISL's equity indices. The objectives of India index services and products limited are presented below. It is India's first specialized company focused upon the index as a core product.

- To develop, construct and maintain indices on Indian equities and commodities that serve as useful market performance benchmarks and are the underlying indices for derivatives trading.
- To develop related products and services this can be used by investors for managing their exposures in the equity and commodity markets.
- To provide data and information on the trading activity in the Indian stock markets.
- To provide market participants with value added research on the Indian equity and commodity market

The indices of NSE such as nifty, nifty junior, defty, crisil 500, crisil midcap 200 indexes have been transferred to IISL. Now the indices are maintained, developed and compiled by IISL. The index funds in India (IISL) are used by a number of WELL KNOWN MUTUAL FUNDS IN INDIA. The details of some of these funds are as follows:

1. Index Funds
2. Exchange Traded Funds

1. Index Funds

1. Principal index fund launched by principal PNB, AMC Private Limited in July 1999.
2. UTI nifty index fund launched by UTI, AMC Private Limited in March 2000.
3. Franklin India index fund launched by Franklin Templeton AMC India Pvt.Ltd in June 2000.
4. Franklin India tax fund launched by Franklin Templeton AMC India Pvt. Ltd in Feb. 2001.
5. SBI magnum index fund launched by SBI funds management Ltd in December 2001.
6. ICICI prudential index fund launched by ICICI prudential AMC ltd in Feb. 2002.
7. HDFC index fund nifty plan launched by HDFC AMC Ltd in July 2002.
8. BIRLA index fund launched by BIRLA Sun Life AMC Ltd in Sep. 2002.
9. LIC mutual index fund nifty plan launched by LIC MF AMC Ltd in Nov. 2002.

10. TATA index fund nifty plan launched by TATA AMC Pvt. Ltd in Feb. 2003.
11. ING vysya nifty plus fund launched by ING investment management India Ltd in January 2004
12. Canara robeco nifty index fund by Canara robeco AMC limited in September 2004
13. Benchmark S&P CNX 500 fund launched by benchmark AMC private limited in November 2008
14. JM nifty plus fund launched by JM financial AMC private limited in June 2009
15. IDFC nifty fund launched by IDFC AMC limited in May 2010.

2. Exchange Traded Fund

1. NIFTY BeES an exchange traded fund launched by benchmark AMC private limited in January 2002
2. Junior BeES and exchange traded fund on CNX nifty junior launched by benchmark AMC private limited in February 2003
3. SUNDER an exchange traded fund launched by UTI in July 2003
4. Bank BeES an exchange traded by benchmark AMC private limited in May 2004
5. Lyxor etf India launched by lyxor international asset management in September 2007
6. DB-X-Trackers S&P CNX nifty ETF launched by Deutsche bank AG in July 2007
7. PSU bank ETF launched by benchmark amc private limited in October 2007
8. Kotak PSU bank ETF launched by Kotak Mahindra AMC limited in October 2007
9. Reliance banking ETF launched by reliance Capital AMC limited in August 2008
10. Quantum index fund-ETF launched by Quantum AMC private limited in May 2008
11. Shariah benchmark ETF launched by benchmark AMC private limited in January 2009
12. Kotak Nifty ETF launched by Kotak Mahindra AMC limited in January 2010

(b) Index Futures

A futures contract is a forward contract, which is traded on an exchange. NSE commenced trading in index futures on June 12, 2000. The index futures contracts are based on the popular market benchmark S&P CNX Nifty index.

NSE defines the characteristics of the futures contract such as the underlying index, markets lot, and the maturity date of the contract. The futures contracts are available for trading from introduction to the expiry date.

- Contract specifications
- Trading parameters

Contract specifications

Security descriptor

The security descriptor for the S&P CNX Nifty futures contracts is:

Market type: N

Instrument type: FUTIDX

Underlying: NIFTY

Expiry date: date of contract expiry

Instrument type represents the instruments, i.e., futures on index.

Underlying symbol denotes the underlying index which is S&P CNX Nifty

Expiry date identifies the date of expiry of the contract

Underlying Instruments

The underlying index is S&P CNX NIFTY.

Trading Cycle

S&P CNX Nifty futures contracts have a maximum of 3-month trading cycle – the near month (one), the next month (two) and the far month (three). A new contract is introduced on the trading day following the expiry of the near month contract. The new contract will be introduced for three month duration. This way, at any point in time, there will be 3 contracts available for trading in the market i.e., one near month, one mid month and one far month respectively.

Expiry Day

S&P CNX Nifty futures contracts expire on the last Thursday of the expiry month, if the last Thursday is a trading holiday, the contract expires on the previous trading day.

Trading Parameters

Contract Size

The value of the futures contract on Nifty may not be less than ₹ 2 lakhs at the time of introduction. The permitted lot size for futures contracts and options contracts shall be the same for a given underlying or such lot size as may be stipulated by the exchange from time to time.

Price Steps

The price step in respect of S&P CNX Nifty futures contracts is ₹ 0.05.

Base Prices

Base price of S&P CNX Nifty futures contracts on the first day of trading would be theoretical futures price... the base price of the contracts on subsequently trading days would be the daily settlement price of the futures contracts.

Price Bands

There are no day minimum/maximum price ranges applicable for S&P CNX Nifty futures contracts. However, in order to prevent erroneous order entry by trading members, operating ranges are kept at +/- 10%. In respect of order which have come under price freeze, members would be required to confirm to the exchange that there is no inadvertent error in the order entry and that the order is genuine. On such confirmation the exchange may approve such order.

Quantity Freeze

Orders which may come to the exchange as quantity freeze shall be more than 15,000. In respect of orders which have come under quantity freeze, member would be required to confirm to the exchange that there is no inadvertent error in the order entry and that the order is genuine. On such confirmation, the exchange may approve such order. However, in exception may, at its discretion, not allow the orders that have come under quantity freeze for execution for any reason whatsoever including non-availability of turnover/exposures limit. In all other cases, quantity freeze orders shall be cancelled by the exchange.

Order Type/Order Book/Order Attribute

- Regular lot order
- Stop loss order
- Immediate or cancel
- Spread order

(c) Index Options

CNX Nifty options:

S&P CNX Nifty options: An option gives a person the right but not the obligation to buy or sell something. An option is a contract between two parties wherein the buyer receives a privilege for which he pays a fee (premium) and the seller accepts an obligation for which he receives a fee. The premium is the price negotiated and set when the option is bought or sold. A person who sells (or writes) an option is said to be short in the options. NSE introduced trading in index options on June 4, 2001. The options contracts are European style and cash settled and are based on the popular market benchmark S&P CNX Nifty index. (Selection criteria for indices)

- Contract specifications
- Trading parameters

Contract Specifications

Security descriptor: The security descriptor for the S&P CNX Nifty options contracts is:

Market type: N

Instrument type: OPTIDX

Underlying: Nifty

Expiry date: Date of contract expiry

Option type: CE/PE

Strike price: Strike price for the contract

Instruments type represents the instruments, i.e., options on index.

Underlying index, which is S&P CNX Nifty.

Expiry date identifies the date of expiry of the contract options type identifies whether it is a call or a put option. CE- call European, PE-put European.

Underlying instrument:

The underlying index is S&P CNX NIFTY.

Trading Cycle

S&P CNX Nifty options contracts have 3 consecutive monthly contracts, additionally 3 quarterly months of the cycle March/June/September/December and 5 following semi-annual months of the cycle June/December would be available, so that at any point in time there would be options contracts with at least 3 year tenure available. On expiry of the near month contract, new contracts (monthly/quarterly/half yearly contracts as applicable) are introduced at new strike prices for both call and put options, on the trading day following the expiry of the near month contract.

Expiry Day

S&P CNX Nifty options contracts expire on the last Thursday of the expiry month. If the last Thursday is a trading holiday, the contract expires on the previous trading day.

Strike Price Interval

The number of contracts provided in options on index is based on the range in previous day's closing value of the underlying index and applicable as per the following table:

Index level strike interval scheme of strike to be introduced	
Up to 2000	50 4-1-4
>2001 up to 4000	100 6-1-6
>4001 up to 6000	100 6-1-6
>6000	100 7-1-7

The above strike parameters scheme shall be applicable for all long-term contracts also.

Trading Parameters

Contract Size

The value of the option contract on Nifty may not be less than ₹ 2 lakhs at the time of introduction. The permitted lot size for futures contract and options contracts shall be the same for a given underlying or such lot size as may be stipulated by the exchange from time to time.

Price Steps

Base price of the options contracts, on introduction of new contracts, would be the theoretical value of the options contract arrived at based on black-scholes model of calculation of options premium.

The options price for a call, computed as per the following black-scholes formula:

$C = S * N(d_1) - X * e^{-rt} * N(d_2)$ and the price for a put is:

$p = X * e^{-rt} * N(-d_2) - S * N(-d_1)$

Where:

d_1= [In (S/X) + (r+ [] ^{2}/2) *t]/[] * sqrt (t)

d_2 = [In (S/X) + (r-[] ^{2}/2 * t]/ [] * sqrt (t) = d_1 – [] * sqrt (t)

c = price of a call option

p = price of a put option

s = price of the underlying asset

x = strike price of the option

r = rate of interest

t = time to expiration

[] = volatility of the underlying

N represents a standard normal distribution with mean = 0 and standard deviation = 1

'In' represents the natural logarithm of a number. Natural logarithms are based on the constant e (2.71828182845904). Rate of interest may be such relevant MBOR rate or such other rate as may be specified. The base price of the contracts on subsequent trading days will be the daily close price of the options contracts. The closing price shall be calculated as follows:

- If the contracts is traded in the last half an hour, the closing price shall be the last half an hour weighted average price.
- If the contracts is not traded in the last half an hour, but traded during any time of the day, then the closing price will be the last traded price (LTP) of the contract.

If the contract is not traded for the day, the base price of the contract for the next trading day shall be the theoretical price of the options contract arrived at based on black-scholes model of calculation of options premium.

Price Bands:

Quantity Freeze

Orders which may come to the exchange as quantity freeze shall be such that have quantity of more than 15,000. In respect of under quantity freeze, members would be required to confirm to the exchange that there is no inadvertent error in the order entry and that the order is genuine. On such confirmation, the exchange may approve such order. However, in exceptional cases, the exchange may, at its discretion, not allow the orders that have come under quantity freeze for execution for any reason whatsoever of turnover/exposures limit. In all other cases, quantity freeze orders shall be cancelled by the exchange.

Order type/order book/order attributes:

- Regular lot order
- Stop loss order
- Immediate or cancel
- Spread order.

Mutual Fund

Now the buying and selling of mutual fund have become easier for investors.

As investors who wishes to subscribe or redeem unit of a mutual fund scheme can now use mutual fund service system (MFSS) provided by NSE.

This service has been launched on November 30, 2009, at the hands of Mr. C.B. Behave, Chairman Securities exchange board of India (SEBI).

Mutual Fund Services Systems

Mutual fund services system (MFSS) is an online order collection system provided by NSE to its eligible member for placing subscription or redemption orders received from the investors.

Ordered Placing

The MFSS will be available for participants between 9 a.m. and 3 p.m.

The NSE MFSS shall facilitate entry of both buy and sell orders. In order to subscribe units, member will be required to place buy orders. A member who wishes to redeem units of mutual fund scheme will be required to place sell orders in the system. Participants can choose between physical mode and depository mode while putting their subscription/redemption requests on the MFSS. All orders shall be settled on order to order basis, on T+1 (working days).

Individual, HUF and body corporate can participate in MFSS subject to completing the KYC procedure. In case of a minor the guardian would have to be KYC compliant.

Confirmation of Order

The system will generate an order confirmation slip for each order which includes time stamp of the order being put on the system, on behalf of the investor. The order confirmation slip which is generated by the investor by the member and is the conclusive evidence of the transaction.

Eligibility Criteria for Members

Trading members of NSE who have obtained AMFI registration number (ARN) from association of mutual fund of India (AMFI) are eligible to participate in MFSS. Further, eligible members would be able to place orders only in respect of mutual fund companies where they have registered as distributor.

New Membership

NSE offers multi asset class products and services and operates trading platforms and the clearing and settlement platform is operated by NSCCL, a wholly owned subsidiary of NSE. Participation on the exchanges in each of the products is through the member of the exchange who is registered for the product. Membership of the exchange/NSCCL is opened to corporate entities, individuals and partnership firms who fulfill the eligibility criteria laid down by SEBI and NSE.

Categories of Membership

Members are admitted in the following categories:

- Only capital market – This category of membership entitles a member to execute trades and to clear and settle the trades executed on his own account as well as on account of his clients in the capital market segment.
- Capital markets and futures and options trading – A membership in this category entitles a member to execute trades and settle the trades executed on his own account as well as on account of his clients in the capital market segments and
  - (a) Execute trades on his own accounts as well as on account of his clients in the futures and the options segment, but clearing and the settlement of trades executed through the trading member would have to be done through trading-cum clearing member or professional clearing member of the exchange.
- Capital markets and futures and options trading and self clearing – A membership in this category entitles a member to
  - (a) Execute trades and to clear and settle the trades executed on his own account as well as on account of his clients in the capital market segment and
  - (b) Execute trades on his own account as well as on account of his clients and to clear and settle trades executed only on his own account as well as an accounts of his clients in futures and options segment
- Capital markets and futures and options trading and clearing- a membership in this category entities a member to
  - (a) Execute trades and to clear and settle the trades executed on his own account as well as on account of his clients in the capital market segment
  - (b) Executes trades on his own account as well as on account of his clients and to clear and settle trades executed by themselves as well as by other trading members who choose to use clearing services of the member in futures and options segments.
- Only WDM – a membership in this category acquires a right to execute trades and to clear and settle the trades executed by the members in the WDM segment. This membership can be also taken in combination with any of the four categories as stated above.
- Professional clearing members – a membership in this category entitles a member to clear and settle trades of such member of the exchange who choose to clear and settle their trades through this member. Further, to circular no: 648 with download no: NSE/MEMB/11148 dated August 19, 2008, the different categories of membership in the currency derivatives segment as follows:
  - (a) Only trading membership in currency derivatives – A membership in this category entitles a member to execute trades on his own account as well as on accounts of his clients in the currency derivative segment, but clearing and settlement of trades executed through the trading member would have to be done through trading-cum clearing member or professional clearing member of the exchange.
  - (b) Trading and clearing membership in currency derivatives – A membership in this category entitles a member to execute trades on his own account as well as on account of his clients

and to clear and settle trades executed by themselves as well as by other trading members who choose to use clearing services of the member in currency derivatives segments.

(c) Professional clearing members – A membership in this category entitles a member to clear and settle trades of such members of the exchange who chooses to clear and settle their trades through this member.

Eligibity Criteria

The following are eligible to apply for membership subject to the regulatory norms and provisions of SEBI and as provided in the rules, regulations, bye-laws and circulars of the exchange–

1. Individuals
2. Partnership firms registered under the Indian Partnership Act, 1932
3. Corporations, companies or institutions or subsidiaries of such corporations, companies or institutions setup for providing financial services
4. Banks for currency derivatives segments
5. Such other persons as may be permitted under the Securities Contracts Rules, 1957
   - Other eligibility criteria
   - Who cannot become a member

1. Individuals (Sole Proprietor)

Criteria

Age minimum	21 years
Status	Indian citizen
Education	at least HSC or equivalent qualification
Experience: Applicant should have an experience of not less than two years as A partner, with or an authorized assistant or authorized assistant clerk or remisier or apprentice to, a member.	

2. Partnership Firms

Where the applicant is a partnership firm, the applicant shall identify a dominant promoter group as per the norms of the exchange at the time of making the application. Any change in the shareholding of the partnership firms including that of the said dominant promoter group or their sharing interest shall be effected only with the prior permission of NSEIL/SEBI.

Criteria

Age: Minimum age of partner(s): 21 years

Status: Registered partnership firms under Indian Partnership Act, 1932

Education: Partner should be at least HSC or equivalent qualification.

Designated partners

Identify at least two partners are designated partners who would be taking care of the day to day management of the partnership firm.

Designated partners experience should have a minimum of two years experience in an activity related to dealing in securities or as portfolio manager or as investment consultant or as a merchant banker or in financial services or treasury, broker, sub broker, authorized agency or authorized clerk or authorized representatives or remisier, or apprentice to a member of recognized stock exchange, dealer, jobber, market maker, or in any other manner dealing in securities or clearing and settlement thereof.

Dominant promoter norms

Identify partners sharing interest as per exchange DPG norms

3. Corporations, Companies or Institutions

A company as defined in the Companies Act, 1956 (1 of 1956), shall be eligible to be admitted as a member of stock exchange provided:

I. Such company is formed in compliance with the provisions of sec. 12 of the said act;

II. It undertakes to comply with such other financial requirements and norms as may be specified by the securities and exchange board of India for the registration of such company under sub-section (1) of sec.12 of the securities and exchange board of India act, 1992 (15 of 1992);

III. The directors of such company are not disqualified for being member of a stock exchange under clause (1) of rule 8 [except sub-clause (b) and (f) thereof] or clause (3) of (8) [except sub-clause (a) and (f) thereof] of the securities contracts (regulations) rules, 1957 and the directors of the company had held the offices of the directors in any company which had been a member of the stock exchange had been declared defaulter or expelled by the stock exchange.

Criteria

Age

Minimum age of director (s) : 21 years

Status

Corporate registered under the companies act, 1956 (Indian)

Minimum paid up equity capital ₹ 30 lakhs

Designated directors

Identification of at least two directors or designated directors who would be managing the day to day trading operations

Education

Each of the designated directors should be at least HSC or equivalent qualification

Designated directors experience should have a minimum of two years experience in an activity related to and dealing in securities or as portfolio manager or as investment consultant or as merchant banker or in financial services or treasury, broker, sub broker, authorized agent, or authorized clerk, or authorized representative, or remisier or apprentice to a member of a recognized stock exchange, dealer, jobber, market maker, or in any other manner in dealing in securities or clearing and settlement thereof

Dominant promoter norms identify dominant group as per exchange DPG norms

4. Professional Clearing

The following persons are eligible to become PCMs of NSCCL for futures and options and/or capital market segment provided they fulfill the prescribed criteria:

1. SEBI registered custodians; or
2. Banks recognized by NSEIL/NSCCL for issuance of bank guarantees

5. Banks

Further to circular No: 648 with download no: NSE/MEMB/11148 dated August 19, 2008, the eligibility membership criteria banks in the currency derivatives segment as follows:

Banks authorized by the reserve bank of India under sec.10 of the Foreign Exchange Management Act, 1999, as 'AD category-I bank' are permitted to become trading and clearing members of the futures market and recognized stock exchange, on their own account and on behalf of their clients, subject to fulfilling the following minimum prudential requirements:

Minimum net worth of ₹ 500 crores

Minimum CRAR of 10%. Net NPA should not exceed 3%

Made net profit for last three years.

The AD category-I banks which fulfill the prudential requirements are required to lay down detailed guidelines with the approval of their boards for trading and clearance of currency futures contracts and management of risks.

The AD category-I bank which do not meet the above minimum prudential requirements and AD category I banks which are urban cooperative banks are state cooperative banks can participate in the currency futures market only as clients, subject to approval therefor from the respective regulatory departments of the reserve bank.

The requirement of approved users of being certified as per the certification as applicable in the F&O segment is waived off for banks for a period of 1 year from the date of issuance of SEBI circular SEBI/DNPD/Cir-38-2008 dated August 6, 2008.

6. Other Applicable Eligibility Criteria

1. At any point of time the applicant has to ensure that the proprietor/one designated director/ partner or the compliance officer of the applicant entity should be successfully certified either in securities market (basic) module or compliance officers (brokers) module or the relevant module pertaining to the segments wherein membership of the exchange has been sought, i.e.

(i) Capital market (dealers) module

(ii) Derivatives market (dealers) module

(iii) National institute of securities markets (NISM) series I-

- Currency
- Derivatives
- Certification
- Examination

The above norm would be a continued admittance norm for membership of the exchange.

2. An applicant must be in a position to pay the membership and other fees, deposits etc, as applicable at the time of admission within 3 months of intimation to him of admission as a trading member or as per the time schedule specified by the exchange.

3. The exchange may specify such standards for investor service and the infrastructure with regard to any category of applicants as it may deem necessary, from time to time.

7. Who Cannot Become a Member?

Further to the capital and network requirements, no entity shall be admitted as a member/partner or director of the member if

(a) It has been adjudged bankrupt or a receiver order in bankruptcy has been made against him or he has been proved to be insolvent even though he has obtained his final discharge;

(b) It has compounded with his creditors for less than full discharge of debts;

(c) It has been convicted of an offence involving a fraud or dishonesty;

(d) It is engaged as a principal or employee in any business other than that of securities, except as a broker or agent not involving any personal financial liability or for providing merchant banking, underwriting or corporate or investment advisory services, unless he undertakes to severe its connections with such business on admission, if admitted;

(e) It has been at any time expelled or declared a defaulted by any other stock exchange or he has been debarred from trading in securities by regulatory authorities like SEBI, RBI etc;

(f) It incurs such disqualification under the provisions of the securities contract (regulation) act, 1956 or rules made there-under so as to disentitle such persons from seeking membership of a stock exchange;

(g) It incurs such disqualification consequent to which NSE determines it to be not in public interest to admit him as a member on the exchange, provided that in case of registered firms, body corporate and companies the condition from will apply to, all partners in case of partnership firms, all directors in case of companies; NSE may from time to time modify/ expand the scope of activities that could be considered as relevant experience for the above purposes.

Disclaimer – the exchange reserves the right to accept or reject any application or amend the terms and conditions without assigning any reasons whatsoever. No members to be admitted shall be at sole discretion of the exchange.

Admission of a New Member in NSE

The admission of a new member in stock exchange depends upon several legal formalities and the aspirant needs to go through rigorous conditions to satisfy the authorities. At first step the aspirant should submit an application for a new membership to the office. The office will forward his application to MEMBERSHIP RECOMMENDATON COMMITTEE. The committee will scrutinize and if found genuine it approves and submits to the office. Again the office will send an offer letter of provisional admission for intended aspirant. The membership department of the national stock exchange will forward the documents for SEBI registration. After checking of all the documents if SEBI is satisfied, a certificate will be issued and sent to membership department of the national stock exchange. After receipt of the registration certificate from the SEBI, the office of NSE will forward the same to the concerned member. At the same time the office of the NSE transmits the information regarding an admission of a new member to the trading department. Then the newly accepted member will be allowed to participate in the trading system.

Recent Developments

The NSE is India's premier exchange which is quite giving a competition to the BSE. It announces launch of Real Time dissemination of India VIX.

- The first real time Volatility Index in India
- Goes live from 9 am today, July 19, 2010

It announces that for the first time in India, a volatility index is being disseminated, on a real time basis on an Indian exchange, from the 19th of July, 2010. The volatility index called the India VIX, indicates the investor's perception of the market's volatility in the near term. The index depicts the expected market volatility over the next 30 calendar days, i.e., higher the India VIX values, higher the expected volatility and *vice versa*. So far, the volatility index, which is expressed in a percentage figure, was shown at the end of the day. But now it will be displayed on a real time basis. NSE will be applying to SEBI for permission to start derivatives on the index, after it has been tracked for a suitable period. Once the futures and options start on the index, investors whose portfolios are affected by volatility in the market can use the product to hedge their risks. Once India VIX is available for trading after regulatory approvals, it will give a lot of security to investors and traders, who face uncertainty, because the new product will empower them with better information and foresight.

More importantly, it will give them the ability, to use the product to hedge their portfolios against the risk arising out of volatility. India VIX is a volatility index based on the index option prices of NSE's benchmark index NIFTY. India VIX is computed using the best bid and ask quotes of the out-of-the-money near and mid-month NIFTY option contracts, which are traded on the F&O segment of NSE. The factors which will be taken into account to calculate the index include the following

(1) Time to expiry of the options contracts of Nifty that are selected to calculate the index

(2) Interest rate: The NSE Mibor rate is being considered as risk-free interest rate for the respective expiry months of the NIFTY option contracts.

(3) A methodology called the forward index level is being used to select the contracts which will be used to calculate the index.

(4) From these selected contracts, the best bid and ask spreads will be chosen.

(5) Weightage is given to each of the options contracts that are chosen. As per the method adopted by the Chicago Board of Options Exchange (CBOE), The weightage of a single options contract is directly proportional to the average of best bid — ask spread of that option contract and inversely proportional to the option contract's strike price.

India VIX indicates the market's perception of the expected near term volatility. Portfolios are subjected to volatility. Before starting derivatives on the volatility index, the index will be disseminated on a real time basis, so that market participants can understand the behavior of the index, before trading on it. VIX is a trademark of CBOE Incorporated and Standard and Poor's has given a license to NSE, with permission from CBOE, to use this trademark in the name of India VIX and for purposes relating to India VIX.

Volatility refers to the amount of uncertainty or risk about the size of changes in a security or index value. A higher volatility means that a security's value can potentially vary over a larger range of values. This means that the price of the security can change dramatically. A lower volatility means that a security's value does not fluctuate dramatically, but changes in value at a steady pace over a period of time.

S&P CNX Nifty futures to be traded on CME from July 19, 2010, National Stock Exchange of India Limited is pleased to inform about the commencement of trading of S&P CNX Nifty Futures on Chicago Mercantile Exchange (CME) from July 19, 2010.

In March 2010, NSE and CME had announced cross listing arrangements including license agreements covering benchmark indexes for U.S. and Indian equities. Under the cross listing arrangements, the S&P CNX Nifty Index (Nifty 50), the leading Indian benchmark index accounting for 22 sectors of the Indian economy, has been made available to CME for the creation and listing of U.S. dollar denominated futures contracts for trading on CME. The license to the Nifty 50 from NSE's affiliate India Index Services & Products Ltd. (IISL) which is exclusive to CME group within the Americas and Europe is in addition to the existing licensing arrangement between Singapore Exchange Limited (SGX) and IISL.

From July 19, 2010, CME is introducing two new contracts designed to access India's market opportunities, *viz.,* E-mini and E-micro S&P CNX Nifty (Nifty 50) futures. The contract size of E-mini contracts will be $10 into the value of the Nifty index on that day and the E-micro contracts will be $2 into the value of the Nifty index on NSE on that day. These contracts will be traded on the CME Globex platform, providing access to participants around the world. Investors can trade for nearly 23 hours on CME Globex. These hours include the market hours in India (except the last one hour before the Indian market opens). These two new contracts are intended to give investors a more efficient means to gain exposure to India-related asset classes. They can also trade the contracts to hedge their risks from existing exposure to the Indian stock market Further, CME and SGX are extending their existing mutual offset arrangement to include the S&P CNX Nifty futures contract whereby investors can initiate a position at CME or SGX and offset it at the other exchange.

NATIONAL STOCK EXCHANGE AND LONDON STOCK EXCHANGE GROUP SIGN LETTER OF INTENT

Agreement to explore feasibility of mutual licensing of indices, enabling access to each other's markets, training and education on SME markets London Stock Exchange Group (LSEG) and India's National Stock Exchange (NSE) today signed a Letter of Intent to evaluate joint strategic business opportunities, and to cooperate together more closely in the future. As part of the Letter, both exchanges declared their intent to explore the feasibility of an agreement whereby FTSE Group may license the FTSE 100 Index to the NSE, and whereby the NSE may license the S&P CNX Nifty (Nifty 50) to LSEG for the purpose of issuing and trading options and other index contracts. It also conveys the intention of both parties to evaluate other joint strategic opportunities, such as allowing access to each other's market as and when regulatory framework permits.

Additionally, the two signatories will explore the possibility of holding joint training and education courses and seminars with a particular focus on Small and Medium sized Enterprises (SMEs). The Letter of Intent was signed in Mumbai by Xavier Rolet, Chief Executive of LSEG and Chitra Ramakrishna, Joint Managing Director of the NSE.

National Securities Clearing Corporation Ltd.

The national securities clearing corporation ltd. (NSCCL), a wholly owned subsidiary of NSE, was incorporated in August, 1995. It was the first clearing corporation to be established in the country and also the first clearing corporation in the country to introduce settlement guarantee. It was set up with the following objectives:

(1) To bring and sustain confidence in clearing and settlement of securities;

(2) To promote and maintain, short and consistent settlement cycles;

(3) To provide counter-party risk guarantee, and

(4) To operate a tight risk containment system.

NSCCL commenced clearing operations in April, 1996. It has since completed more than 2400 settlement (equities segment) without delays or disruptions.

National securities clearing corporation limited first Indian clearing corporation to get rated:

CRISIL has assigned its highest corporate credit rating of 'AAA' indicates highest degree of strength with regard to honoring debt obligations. NSCCL is the first Indian clearing corporation to get this rating. The rating reflects NSCCL's status as clearing corporation for NSE, India's largest stock exchange. The rating also factor in NSCCL's rigorous risk management controls and adequate settlement guarantee cover.

NSCCL carriers out the clearing and settlements of the trades executed in the equities and derivatives segments of the NSE. It operates a well-defined settlement cycle and there are no deviations or deferments from this cycle. It aggregates trades over a trading period, nets the positions to determine the liabilities of members and securities to meet respective liabilities.

NSCCL has empanelled 13 clearing banks to provide banking services to trading member and has established connectivity with both the depositories for electronic settlement of securities.

It also undertakes settlements of transactions on other stock exchanges like, the over the counter exchange of India.

Partners

(1) Clearing members

(2) Clearing banks

(3) Depositories

(4) Custodians

(5) Professional clearing members

(1) Clearing Members: Clearing members means a member of the clearing corporations who clears and settles deals for a segment in a manner and mode and subject to such terms and conditions and procedures prescribed for them. Further, a clearing member may clear and settle deals either on their own account or on behalf of their clients subject to the terms and conditions prescribed by the clearing corporation.

In the capital market segment, all trading member of the exchange are required to become the clearing member of the clearing corporation.

In F&O segment, trading members need not necessarily clear their own deals but can select another clearing member to clear and settle their dues. Trading members, who are also clearing members, can clear and settle their deals and also deals of other trading members who opt to settle their deals through the said clearing members. Self clearing members may clear and settle only their own proprietary trades and their clients' trades but cannot clear and settle trades of other trading members.

(2) Clearing banks: NSCCL offers settlement of funds through 13 clearing banks namely Axis Bank Ltd., Bank of India, Canara Bank, Citibank N.A, HDFC Bank, IDBI Bank, Indusind Bank, Kotak Mahindra Bank, Standard Chartered Bank, State Bank of India and Union Bank of India.

Members may open their clearing accounts with any of the empanelled clearing banks for the purpose of settlement of exchange transactions.

The clearing banks are required to provide the following minimum services as a single window to all clearing members of national securities clearing corporation ltd., as also to the clearing corporation:

(1) Branch network in cities that cover bulk of trading cum clearing members

(2) High level automation including electronic funds transfer (ETF) facilities

(3) Facilities like (a) dedicated branch facilities (b) software to interface with the clearing corporation (c) access to accounts information on a real time basis (d) backup procedures and fall back mechanism in case of failure of the bank system

(4) Value-added services to member such as free-of-cost funds transfer across centers etc.

(5) Providing working capital funds

(6) Stock lending facilities

(7) Services as professional clearing members

(8) Services as depository participants other capital market-related facilities

(9) All other banking facilities like issuing bank guarantees/credit facilities etc.

Multiple clearing bank provide advantages of competitive forces, facilitates introduction of new products, *viz.,* working capital funding, anywhere banking facilities, the options to member to settle funds through bank services suitable to the member.

(3) Depositories: In order to promote dematerialization of securities, NSE joined hands with leading financial institutions to establish the national securities depository ltd. (NSDL), the first depository in the country with the objective of enhansing the efficiency in settlement systems as also to reduce the menace of fake/forged and stolen securities. The second depository in the country, CDSL, promoted by the BSE and a few commercial banks, was granted certificate of commencement of business in February, 1999.

This has ushered in an era of dematerialized trading and settlement. SEBI has made dematerialized settlement mandatory in an ever-increasing number of securities in a phased manner, thus bringing about an increase in the proportion of shares delivered in dematerialized form. Today, more than 99% of settlement of securities takes place in dematerialized form NSCCL has established connectivity with both the depositories for electronic settlement of securities.

(4) Custodian: Custodians are clearing members but not trading members. They settle trades on behalf of their clients that are executed through other trading members. A trading member may assign a particular trade to a custodian for settlement. The custodian is required to confirm whether he is going to settle that trade or not. If the custodian confirms the trade, NSCCL assign the obligation to the custodian. If the custodian rejects the trade, the obligation is assigned back to the trading member.

Custodians clearing members are required to request allotment of custodian participant (CP) code for the clients for which they wish to clear and settle. The request has to be made along with documentation for the said purpose like SEBI registration number, PAN number, etc., depending on the category of the client.

- Axis Bank Ltd.
- Citibank N.A.
- DBS Bank Ltd.
- Deutsche Bank A.G.
- HDFC Bank Ltd.
- Honking Shanghai Banking Corporation Ltd.
- ICICI Bank Ltd.
- Infrastructure Leasing and Financial Services Ltd.
- JP Morgan Chase Bank N.A.
- Kotak Mahindra Bank Ltd.
- Orbis Financial Corporation Ltd.
- SBI Custodian Services Pvt. Ltd.
- Standard Chartered Bank Ltd.
- State Bank of India.
- Stock Holding Corporation of India Ltd.

(5) Professional clearing members: Clearing corporations admit a special category of member's namely professional clearing members. Professional clearing members (PCM) are clearing members who are not trading members. They are typically banks, custodians, etc., who clear and settle trades executed for their clients. In such an event the functions and responsibilities of the PCM would be similar to custodians. PCMs may also undertake clearing and settlement responsibilities for trading members. In such case, the PCM would settle the trading members connected to them. The onus for settling the trade would be thus on the PCM and not the trading member.

Securities and Exchange Board of India

The policies are enzymes and reforms are antibiotics. A strong policy with good reforms may yield better results. The implementation of policy with no deviations can show good impact to reach the destination. In financial aspect, a strict discipline is necessary to reach the objectives. Financial discipline is a key factor in getting success of the desired goals. The financial discipline will depend upon the best regulatory body functioning system. All countries in the world have established their financial regulatory authorities. In USA, the regulatory authority for stock markets are SECURITIES EXCHANGE COMMISSION (SEC), similarly in India, SECURITIES EXCHANGE BOARD OF INDIA was established. It was established in April, 1988. It has been functioning under the overall administrative control of the central government. It works under the guidance of ministry of finance. It is the formal authority of capital market. It was established for the regulation of capital market and stock exchanges. It also works for protecting the investor's rights, prevents malpractices in security trading and promote healthy growth of the capital markets. It has full authority to control, regulate, monitor and direct the capital markets. It is most powerful organ of the central government in the capital market. The SEBI has empowered full authority to regulate primary market in India. It has issued several guidelines to regulate financial intermediaries in the capital market. The guidelines were related to free pricing, disclosure of true and accurate information in prospectus. It has been established for the healthy development and regulation of the capital market.

Objectives of the SEBI

The main objectives of the SEBI are to protect the interest of the investors. It has three objectives by its act:

(a) To protect the interest of the investors in the market

(b) To promote the development of securities market.

(c) To regulate the securities market.

Powers of the SEBI

The following power had been given to the SEBI with their enactment of SEBI Act, 1992.

1. Regulating the business activities in the capital market.
2. Power to grant registration to financial intermediaries.
3. Registering and regulating the working of the depositories and custodians and FIIS, credit rating agencies.
4. Registering and regulating the working of venture capital funds and mutual funds.
5. Power to grant approval to bye-laws of the recognized exchanges.

6. Power to prohibit insider trading.
7. Power to compliance listing of the securities by the public companies.
8. Power to control and regulate stock exchange.
9. Power to call for any information or explanation from recognized stock exchanges or its members.
10. Power to levy fee
11. Power to regulate substantial acquisition of shares and takeover of companies.
12. Power to promote and regulate self-regulatory bodies
13. Prohibiting fraudulent and unfair trade practices relating to the securities' market.
14. Promoting investor's education and training of intermediaries of the securities markets.
15. Performing any other functions as may be assigned by the government from time to time.

Delegation of Powers

The Securities Contract Act Regulation 28 – indicate that SEBI has to exercise the following powers with a direction from union government.

1. It has the Power

(a) to call periodical returns from the stock exchanges.
(b) to regulate and control activities in spot delivery contracts.
(c) to grant of recognition to the stock exchanges.
(d) to withdraw the recognition of stock exchanges.
(e) to suspend the business of a recognized stock exchange.
(f) to give directions to the recognized stock exchanges.
(g) to grant licenses to the dealers in securities market.
(h) to hear appeal made by the companies.
(i) to exercise legal provisions of Securities Contract Regulation Act.
(j) to make or amend rules of Articles of Association of a stock exchange regarding the voting rights of members of stock exchange.

Powers to Make Rules

SEBI is the powerful organ of the central government regarding capital market affairs. The union government delegated authorities in 1995. It has the authority to make rules and regulations relating to the following INTERMEDIARIES:

(1) BROKERS AND SUB BROKERS.
(2) MERCHANT BANKERS.
(3) PORTFOLIO MANAGERS.
(4) REGISTRARS TO AN ISSUE.
(5) SHARE TRANSFER AGENTS.

(6) UNDERWRITERS.

(7) DEBENTURE TRUSTEES.

(8) BANKERS TO AN ISSUE.

Powers of Making Regulations

SEBI is regulatory authority of capital market. It has powers of making regulations with the approval of union government. All regulations will be published in official gazette. It is empowered to make regulations for the following aspects of the capital market.

(a) The registration process of financial intermediaries.

(b) The cancellation of registration of financial intermediaries.

(c) The suspension of licence of financial intermediaries.

(d) The powers for the regulation in respect of the registration process of the following financial intermediaries.

(1) MERCHANT BANKERS.

(2) LEAD MANAGERS.

(3) BROKERS AND SUB BROKERS.

(4) PORTFOLIO MANAGERS

(5) REGISTRARS TO AN ISSUE.

(6) SHARE TRANSFER AGENTS.

(7) BANKERS TO AN ISSUE.

(8) UNDERWRITERS.

(9) DEBENTURE TRUSTEES.

Organisation of the SEBI

SEBI is a powerful organ of the central government. It functions according to the guidance and approval of the government. The government will give all directions to regulate the capital market affairs. Capital market occupies an important role and dominant role in the economy. The development of a nation depends upon the peace of government policies. The government can implement its policies through various organs. All regulatory authorities will act as per the government orders. It is the representative of the union government in capital markets. It is a statutory body. It leads, monitors, and regulates the activities of the capital market. It has been divided into five departments. Each department will be headed by an executive director. The following are the main departments.

(1) PRIMARY MARKET DEPARTMENT.

(2) ISSUES MANAGEMENT AND INTERMEDIARIES DEPARTMENT.

(3) SECONDARY MARKET DEPARTMENT.

(4) INSTITUTIONAL DEPARTMENT.

(5) LEGAL DEPARTMENT.

(1) Primary Market Department

Primary market affairs of the capital market are looked after by the primary market department. It deals with the new issues market. It is headed by a division chief. It is the most important division in the SEBI organization. The development of industries in India depends upon the efficiency of this wing. It relates to the policy matters of the public issues. It will look after all regulatory issues of public issues in India. It also focuses on investor's grievances. It deals with the investor complaints for all aspects of the primary issues of the corporate sector. Therefore, it has full authority with reference to public issues.

(2) Issues Management and Intermediaries Department

This department will take care about the scrutiny of offer document. The offer document is the most important paper in public issue. It is the tool for attracting the investors. It is the basic document which is promised by the company to the newly becoming shareholders. The offer documents should contain only fact and a right projection about the future. Some companies can misguide the investors by creating a gloomy picture about their product and company. Therefore this department shall closely monitor the contents of the offer documents. This department is also involved in the registration of the financial intermediary. It also monitors the activities of various financial intermediaries.

(3) Secondary Market Department

The secondary market department occupies an important role in the regulation of the capital market operations. It involves in framing the policy matters regarding stock exchange activities. It regulates the secondary market activities. It guides, monitors the stock exchange administration. It continuously monitors the price movement in the stock market. It involves in the development of new investment products. It closely observes the market movements and gathers information through market surveillance. It also looks about the insider trading practices. It frames the policy and regulatory matters for the secondary market in India. It also looks into the affairs of stock exchanges administration inspection by making inquiry towards financial intermediaries. It also regulates the subbrokers activities.

(4) The Institutional Investment Department

This department frames the policy matters regarding the institutional investors. The institutions investors are more important in the capital market. They will put the higher amount of investment in the stock markets. They involve in buying and selling of shares on daily basis with crores of rupees investment. The following members will be treated as institutional investors

1. MUTUAL FUNDS
2. FIIS
3. CORPORATE INVESTORS
4. INSTITUTIONAL INVESTORS

It looks after mergers and acquisitions of the corporate sector. It also concentrates on research and publications. It maintains international relations in the process of globalization. It frames the policy matters for institutional investors. The legal department will take care of all the legal matters under the supervision of General Counsel. The investigation wing is also the part of institutional investment department. It carries out inspection and investigation under the supervision of the chief.

(5) Legal Department

The legal department will look after the framework and operational of the following financial intermediaries.

1. MERCHANT BANKERS.
2. LEAD MANAGERS.
3. UNDERWITERS.
4. BANKERS TO AN ISSUE.
5. BROKERS TO AN ISSUE.
6. REGISTRARS TO AN ISSUE.
7. DEBENTURE TRUSTEES.
8. PORTFOLIO MANAGERS.

In additional to the above departments the SEBI have two advisory committees. Each committee works for primary and secondary markets. These committees' inputs are useful in framing policies and regulations. These committees are constituted with market players, recognized investors associations and experts in the capital market. But these committees will have no statutory power and the SEBI may or may not abide by suggestions made by them. Further the SEBI has also expanded its activities by opening their regional offices at New Delhi, Chennai, Kolkata and Mumbai. The regional offices shall cover all operations in northern, southern, eastern and western effectively.

Compositions of the SEBI: The government proposes to make strengthening the SEBI. It granted additional powers for the smooth functioning of the capital market operations. The SEBI act provides for the establishment of a statutory board constituted by 6 members. The board will constitute with a chairman and two members who are appointed by the central government. The other member is to be appointed by the RBI, the remaining two members will be drawn from securities market with those persons having rich experience in that field. Therefore, the board will maintain the best talented expertise for the better functioning of the operations of the capital market. The central government has sanctioned the SEBI as an autonomous body status with perpetual succession and common seal. The Preamble of the Act states that it has been established to protect the interest of the investors in securities and to promote the development and regulate the securities market. The Sec.11 of the act deals with the power of the board. It clearly states that the board has to work to protect the interest of the investors. The statutory board was established on 21.2.92. The act further lays down that the various rules and regulations will be issued to enable the SEBI to register, regulate and monitor various financial intermediaries in the capital market.

Licencing Authority

The SEBI is the most powerful organization in the capital market. It has the right to grant the licences to the financial intermediaries. All financial intermediaries dealing in securities markets must compulsorily registered with the SEBI in accordance with the regulations made under the SEBI Act. The financial intermediaries, without licence do not have opportunity to take up the business activities in the capital market. Therefore, every financial intermediary shall get licence from the SEBI. The following intermediaries are required to get licence from the SEBI for commencing business activities in the capital market.

1. Stock brokers.
2. Share transfer agent.
3. Bankers to an issue.
4. Registrars to an issue.
5. Underwriter.
6. Merchant bankers.
7. Trustees.
8. Portfolio managers.
9. Investment advisers.
10. Custodians.
11. FIIS.
12. Credit rating agencies.
13. Depositories.
14. Venture capital fund.
15. Mutual funds.
16. Other intermediaries.

On application made by the above Intermediaries in a prescribed form to the SEBI, then SEBI will scrutinise the application form and if found satisfactory, then it will grant the certificate of registration. The certificate of registration contains the rules and regulations for the conduct of business by the intermediaries. Every financial intermediary shall apply in a prescribed form with a fee to the SEBI. The SEBI has the right to cancel/suspend a certificate of registration issued to the financial intermediaries in accordance with rules and regulations. If an intermediary is dissatisfied with the behavior of the SEBI, he may appeal to the central government. The central government issues various orders from time to time to implement the rules strictly in accordance with the provisions of the Act. The central government may also issue various directions to the SEBI matters relating to the policies in writing from time to time. The SEBI has to implement the orders, which are received from the central government for the smooth functioning of the capital market. The central government has authority to review the policy matters relating to the capital market.

Primary Markets

1. Introduced an innovative product "STOCK INVEST".
2. Flexibility in issue pricing.
3. Vetting of prospectus and letter of offer by SEBI.
4. Abridged prospectus.
5. Fixation of promoter's contribution.
6. All financial intermediaries brought under the purview of SEBI.
7. Public sector bonds brought under the purview of SEBI.
8. Deployment of Issue proceeds.
9. Guidelines for preferential allotment of shares.

10. Risk factors shall be disclosed prominently in prospectus.
11. Companies permitted to open private collection prospectus.
12. Guidelines to develop financial institution for disclosure and investor protection.
13. Obligation on merchant bankers and underwriters.
14. Fixation of lock in period for promoter's quota shares.
15. The allotment process must be finalized in the presence of the SEBI representative.
16. Registration of FIIs for the development and growth of the market.
17. In public issue, the number of minimum shares increased to 500 shares.
18. Codes of conduct to advertisers are announced.
19. Proportional allotment permitted in case of oversubscription.
20. Substantial firm allotment permitted in case of oversubscription.
21. Shareholders to decide price and time of conversion.
22. Underwriting for issue is made mandatory.
23. Credit rating is made compulsory.
24. Reduced the validity period of stock invest.

Secondary Market

1. Registration of share shops for spot shares.
2. Insider trading is declared as illegal.
3. Forward and carryover system banned.
4. Odd lot trading facilities provided at stock exchanges.
5. Financial requirements and norms for corporate members.
6. Uniform settlement system.
7. Introduction of jumbo transfer deeds.
8. Regulations and transactions between brokers and clients.
9. Introduction of circuit filters system at stock exchange to check wide fluctuations.
10. Private mutual funds have been permitted for the welfare of the small investors.
11. Private placement of shares banned.
12. Capital adequacy norms are prescribed for stockbrokers and other intermediaries.
13. NSE was introduced in July 1994.
14. Steps to ensure transparency in secondary market operations.
15. Brokers shall keep client's money in separate account.
16. Constitution of governing council of stock exchange.
17. Appointment of an executive director.
18. Audit inspection for members of the stock exchange.
19. Precautions in transactions between clients and brokers.
20. Norms for multiple membership of stock exchange.
21. Issue of contract notes is made compulsory.

Factors to be Considered for Investment in Primary Market

At present, the investors must be aware that free pricing environment makes the issuers free to fix the issue price subject to some conditions. These conditions are levied by the SEBI to regulate the primary market activities. The set of guidelines issued to educate the investors to be cautious while investing in the primary market. They are advised to check the contents of the prospectus before making any investment in any issue. For every detail relating to the issue, they should study the detailed prospectus which is available with the company or merchant banker. They have to make more efforts about the public issue. Public involves so many organizations and activities. The merchant bankers are responsible for drafting a prospectus. Therefore, they must take care about the disclosure of all the relevant information in the prospectus. The following factors are to be examined by the investor before making investment in any public issue.

(a) Promoter's record.

(b) Professional management of all company,

(c) Object of the present issue.

(d) Analysis of project details.

(e) Product analysis.

(f) Government stability.

Therefore, the investors are advised to go through the contents of the prospectus and avail the advices of the expert from media in this regard.

SEBI Guidelines

SEBI is the powerful organ of the central government. It receives directions from the ministry of finance and regulates the capital market from time to time as per the policy matters of the government. It reflects the policies of the government for the development of capital market. It will issue guidelines from time to time to control the affairs of the capital market. These guidelines are related to new issue market, secondary market, mutual funds, merchant banks, registrars, transfer agents, underwriters, brokers, subbrokers, and portfolio managers. The guidelines include for all financial intermediaries in the capital market. The code of conduct is also laid down for each category separately. All the financial intermediaries in the capital market should follow the guidelines and code of conduct and finding any violation, the SEBI has the authority to levy penalty. All the financial intermediaries have to seek first time licence and registration for operating in the capital market. The terms of condition for registration process will depend upon the type of financial intermediary. The SEBI has the authority to grant licences to foreign financial institutions, foreign institutional investors, NRIs, OCBs

Reforms in the Primary Market

The capital market consists of primary and secondary market. The primary market is related to issue of capital to the public. It consists of large volume of financial resources for the right companies at right time. The savers of money will be converted into investors. The retaining of investor is more important for the capital market, because additional funds will be poured by the existing investors. Hence the government will protect investors, through SEBI. The major reforms are carried out by SEBI in the following situations.

(1) Reforms in Primary Market
(2) Reforms in Secondary Market
(3) SEBI guidelines to Capital Markets.

(1) Reforms in Primary Market

SEBI is charged with the responsibility of protecting the integrity of the market and safeguarding the interest of the investors.

- Free entry into primary market with some limitations.
- Free pricing of new issues.
- Minimum public offer reduced to 20% of paid-up capital.
- Minimum subscription by promoters and directors at 25% for issues less than ₹ 100 crores and 20% for paid up capital of more than ₹ 100 crores.
- Preferential allotment to FFIs and OCBs are reduced to 20% and lock-in period of 5 years was removed in 1996.
- Foreign security firms and FFIs are allowed to operate through Indian brokers.
- Stock invest was introduced as a mode of making payments.
- The concept of anchor investor has been introduced very recently.
- Simplified procedure to rights issue in terms of disclosure requirements.
- SEBI has prohibited the issue of shares with superior voting rights by listed companies.
- An unlisted company should list on at least one stock exchange providing nation-wide trading terminals in order to provide a liquid trading platform to investors.
- The holding period of one year for an offer for sale of shares will include the period when fully paid convertible instruments have been held prior to conversion into equity shares.
- No entry load for mutual fund schemes.
- Private placement of non transferable shares of promoters and directors was prohibited.
- Minimum number of shares to be applied for, was raised from 100 shares to 500.
- Allotment on a proportional basis was introduced in the event of oversubscription.
- Recently, it has been decided to complete the public issue process within 12 days.

(2) Reforms in Secondary Markets

Stock markets are helpful for the development of a nation's economy. The markets should be guided in a right way as a part of financial discipline. Financial discipline is the important factor for the development of a nation or to an individual or to any commercial enterprise. The SEBI regulations of stock exchanges and their members had started in February 1992. The reforms later introduced have been on a continuous growth. It started with the licensing and registration of brokers and sub brokers in the recognized stock exchanges. The regulations were extended to underwriters, portfolio managers, and other categories of players in the market including foreign players. The guidelines are fluctuating from time to time. It is better to refer the media for updates of SEBI regulations and directions. However, the following reforms are presented for better understanding of the basic factors.

1. Automatic lending borrowing mechanism was introduced by national stock exchange.
2. Disclosure norms for listed companies tightened.
3. NIDHIS were brought under the control of SEBI.
4. Dematerialization of scrip's made mandatory.
5. New guidelines were introduced for corporate members of limited liability of directors.
6. Mutual funds and financial institutions were allowed trading in derivatives for hedging purposes.
7. Rolling settlement was made compulsory in some scrip on T+ basis.
8. Transparency in brokerage and share prices.
9. Continuous net settlement was permitted.
10. Trading in derivatives were allowed as per Securities Amendment Act, 1999.
11. Badla and carry forward was reintroduced in October 1996.
12. Broker account and client account should be maintained and the same to be reported to the stock exchange.
13. The stock exchange board should consist of brokers, public representatives and government representatives of 50% extent.
14. Capital adequacy norms laid down for stock exchange members according to their turnover and other factors.

(3) SEBI Guidelines to Capital Markets

In keeping with the broad thrust of the ongoing programs of economic reform, the mechanism of administrative controls over capital issues has been dismantled and pricing of capital issues is now essentially market determined. Regulation of the capital market and protection of investor's interest is now primarily the responsibility of the SEBI. Keeping in view of its functions, it issued a new set of comprehensive guidelines governing issue of shares, and other financial instruments, and has laid down detailed norms for stockbrokers and sub brokers, merchant bankers, portfolio managers, and mutual funds. On the recommendations of the Patel committee report, it permitted on 27th July, 1995, for carry forward system in the stock exchanges. On 26 January, 1995, the government promulgated an ordinance amending the SEBI Act and the Securities Contracts Act, 1956. SEBI is vested with power to take action against fraudulent and unfair trade practices in the capital market. It has the powers of a civil court in respect of discovery and production of books, documents and records, accounts, summoning and enforcing attendance of company/person and examining them under oath. It has the full authority in maintenance of discipline in the capital market. Recent reforms made by the SEBI:

1. On March 6th, 2010, it has announced the decision of the board meeting. The following is analysis of the decision.

"Margin requirements for qualified institutional buyers(QIB) bidding in a book built public issue revised so as to ensure level playing field among all categories of investors". It has decided that all types of investors should bring 100% of the application money as margin along with the application for securities in public issues.

"Reservation for employees in public/rights issues" it has decided that the reservation for employees in public/rights issues associates of the issuer whose financial statements are consolidated with the issuer's financial statements.

"Reforms in derivatives market", "Equity derivatives contracts with tenures up to 5 years have been allowed in the stock exchanges". "Derivative contracts on volatility indexes which have suitable track record". "Physical settlement of equity derivatives is allowed". The various recent bills regarding various aspects of the capital market is presented below.

"The Securities and Insurance Laws (amendment and validation) Bill, 2010. It is related to ULIP issue. SEBI vs IRDA".

"Report of takeover regulations, advisory committee."

"Pre-open session to be introduced by NSE and BSE."

"Stock exchanges to introduce physical settlement in F&O."

SECURITIES AND EXCHANGE BOARD OF INDIA NOTIFICATION

Securities and Exchange Board of India (Issue of Capital and Disclosure Requirements) (Amendment) Regulations, 2009 No. LAD-NRO/GN/2009-10/23/186926. In exercise of the powers conferred by Section 30 of the Securities and Exchange Board of India Act, 1992 (15 of 1992), the Board hereby makes the following regulations to amend the Securities and Exchange Board of India (Issue of Capital and Disclosure Requirements) Regulations, 2009, namely:

1. (i) these regulations may be called the Securities and Exchange Board of India (Issue of Capital and Disclosure Requirements) (Amendment) Regulations, 2009.

   (ii) These regulations except clauses (a) and (b) of sub-regulation (ix) of regulation 2 shall come into force on the date of their publication in the Official Gazette.

   (iii) Clause (a) of sub-regulation (ix) of regulation 2 of these regulations shall come into force on 1st April, 2010.

   (iv) Clause (b) of sub-regulation (ix) of regulation 2 of these regulations shall come into force on 1st January, 2010.

2. In the Securities and Exchange Board of India (Issue of Capital and Disclosure Requirements) Regulations, 2009 –(i) in regulation 2, in sub-regulation (1), — (a) for clause (k), the following clause shall be substituted, namely:- '(k) "convertible security" means a security which is convertible into or exchangeable with equity shares of the issuer at a later date, with or without the option of the holder of the security and includes convertible debt instrument and convertible preference shares;' (b) in clause (zd), after sub-clause (x), the following sub-clause shall be inserted, namely:- "(xi) insurance funds set up and managed by army, navy or air force of the Union of India;"

   (ii) In regulation 10, in sub-regulation (1), (a) in clause (b), for the words "ten thousand crore rupees" occurring towards the end, the words "five thousand crore rupees" shall be substituted;

   (b) After clause (c), the following proviso shall be inserted, namely: "Provided that for issuers, whose public shareholding is less than fifteen per cent. Of its issued equity capital, the annualized trading turnover of its equity shares has been at least two per cent. Of the weighted average number of equity shares available as free float during such six months' period."

(c) In clause (e), the following proviso shall be inserted, namely:

"Provided that if the issuer has not complied with the provision of the equity listing agreement relating to composition of board of directors, for any quarter during the last three years immediately preceding the reference date, but is compliant with such provisions at the time of filing of offer document with the Registrar of Companies or designated stock exchange, as the case may be, and adequate disclosures are made in the offer document about such non-compliances during the three years immediately preceding the reference date, it shall be deemed as compliance with the condition;"

(iii) In regulation 29, in clause (a), after the words "retail individual shareholders" and before the words "may be offered", the words "or employees of the issuer entitled for reservation made under regulation 42 making an application for specified securities of value not more than one lakh rupees," shall be inserted;

(iv) In regulation 42,- (a) in sub-regulation (4), in clause (a), for the words "ten per cent of the issue size" occurring at the end, the words "five per cent of the post-issue capital of the issuer", shall be substituted; (b) after clause (f), the following clause shall be inserted, namely:- "(g) value of allotment to any employee in pursuance of reservation made under sub-regulations (1) or (2), as the case may be, shall not exceed one lakh rupees."

(v) In regulation 50, in sub-regulation (1), the following proviso shall be inserted, namely: - "Provided that value of specified securities allotted to any person in pursuance of reservation made under clause (a) of sub-regulation (1) or clause (a) of sub-regulation (2) of regulation 42, shall not exceed one lakh rupees."

(vi) After regulation 55, the following regulation shall be inserted, namely: - "Reservation for employees along with rights issue. 55A.

Subject to other applicable provision of these regulations, the issuer may make reservation for its employee's along with rights issue subject to the condition that value of allotment to any employee shall not exceed one lakh rupees."

(vii) In regulation 96, in sub-regulation (2),- (a) in clause (e), figure and mark "43," shall be omitted; (b) after clause (I), the following clause shall be inserted, namely:- "(a) regulation 43, except sub-regulation (3) there

(viii) In regulation 98, in clause (e), the following proviso shall be inserted, namely: - "Provided that at least thirty per cent of the said fifty per cent, IDR issued shall be allocated to retail individual investors and in case of undersubscription in retail individual investor category, spill over to the extent of undersubscription shall be permitted to other categories."

(ix) in schedule VIII, in Part A, in Para (2), in item (IX),- (a) after the title "Financial Statements", the following notes shall be inserted, namely:- "[Notes: 1. The financial informations specified in this item shall be certified by only those auditors who have subjected themselves to the peer review process of the Institute of Chartered Accountants of India (ICAI) and hold a valid certificate issued by the 'Peer Review Board' of the ICAI. (2) All financial information's specified in this item must be reaudited for one full financial year and the stub period, by the auditor certifying them in case where the financial statements were audited by an auditor who had not been subjected to peer review process of ICAI.]"

(b) in sub-item (B), after clause (21), the following clause shall be inserted, namely:-"(22) If the issuer has entered into any scheme of arrangement during the period for which the financials are disclosed in the offer document, lead merchant banker to the issue shall ensure that the following disclosure requirements as specified in Accounting Standard 14 has been complied with:-

(i) A description of the accounting treatment followed in respect of financials contained in the schemes of arrangement and the reasons for following the treatment if it is different from those, which has been prescribed in applicable Accounting Standards.

(ii) In case of deviations, disclosure of the accounting treatment had the applicable standard been followed.

(iii) Impact on the financials, if any, arising due to such deviation."

(c) After sub-item (B), the following sub-item shall be inserted, namely: - "(BA) Alternate Financial Information of the issuer in further public offers:

(1) An issuer making further public offer may disclose the financial information specified in clause (2) of this sub-item, in lieu of information specified under sub-item (B) if:

(i) the issuer is making further public offer in accordance with provisions of regulation 10;

(ii) The specified securities offered in further public offer are of the same class of those already listed on a recognized stock exchange;

(iii) Financial reports of the issuer are available on the website of any recognized stock exchange having nationwide trading terminals or on a common e-filing platform specified by the Board;

(iv) There has not been any change in management of the issuer;

(v) Specified securities of issuer have not been listed pursuant to relaxation granted from clause (b) of sub-rule (2) of rule 19 of Securities Contracts (Regulation) Rules, 1957. (2) The issuer satisfying the conditions specified in clause (1) may disclose its financial statements as under:

(i) Stand-alone and consolidated financial statements of the issuer:

(1) A report by the auditors of the issuer with respect to profit or loss and assets and liabilities (indicating changes in accounting policies, if any) in respect of the last completed accounting year for which audit has been completed.

(2) A report by the auditors of the issuer on a limited review of the profit or loss and assets and liabilities (indicating changes in accounting policies, if any), as at a date not earlier than six months prior to the date of the opening of the issue, where audited accounts as at such date are not available.

(3) For the purpose of sub-clauses (1) and (2) above, it shall be sufficient if:

(a) In the statement of the assets and liabilities, the main heads of assets and liabilities as provided in Part I of Schedule VI of the Companies Act, 1956 have been provided. If an issuer is governed by a statute other than the Companies Act, 1956, the main heads of assets and liabilities as specified in such statute shall be provided in the statement of assets and liabilities.

(b) In the statement of profit or loss, the information required to be disclosed under the heads of income and expenditure as per clause 41 of the equity listing agreement in respect of quarterly financial information to be filed with the recognized stock exchanges, has been provided.

(ii) In addition, the following information for the period between the last date of the balance sheet and profit and loss account sent to the shareholders and up to the end of the last but one month preceding the date of the offer document shall be furnished.

(1) Working results of the issuer under following heads:

(a) (i) Sales/turnover (ii) Other income

(b) Estimated gross profit/loss (excluding depreciation and taxes)

(c) (i) Provision for depreciation (ii) Provision for taxes

(d) Estimated net profit/loss (2) Material changes and commitments, if any affecting financial position of the issuer.

(3) Weekend prices for the last four weeks; Current market price; and highest and lowest prices of equity shares during the period with the relative dates.

(iii) Stock market quotation of shares/convertible instruments of the company (high/low price in each of the last three years and monthly high/low price during the last six months).

(iv) Accounting and other ratios: The following accounting ratios shall be given for each of the accounting periods for which financial information is given:

(1) Earnings per share: This ratio shall be calculated after excluding extraordinary items.

(2) Return on Net Worth: This ratio shall be calculated excluding revaluation reserves.

(3) Net Asset Value per share: This ratio shall be calculated excluding revaluation reserves.

(4) Accounting and other ratios shall be based on the financial statements prepared on the basis of Indian Accounting Standards.

(v) Capitalization Statement:

(1) A Capitalization Statement showing total debt, net worth, and the debt/ equity ratios before and after the issue is made shall be incorporated.

(2) In case of any change in the share capital since the date as of which the financial information has been disclosed in the prospectus, a note explaining the nature of the change shall be given.

SUMMARY

Financial markets are a particular geographical area of location where the fund savers and borrowers meet at a particular place in a particular time for settlement of their transaction. Financial transactions are under which financial assets are created and or transferred. Financial markets exist whereever financial transactions occur, creation and transfer of financial assets or claims occur. A financial market may or may not have a particular physical existence. It facilitates buying and selling of financial claims, assets, services and securities. In financial markets, funds are flown from abundant supply of sources to needy, dearth place of requirement. Fund is a scarce commodity; it is available for a price for a particular period of time. Fund suppliers in the market exist from individual savers, corporate entities, banking institutions, finance institutions and fund borrowers arise from firms, individuals, banks, commercial enterprises, government organizations, etc.

Capital market is one of the most important segments of the Indian financial system. It is the market available to the companies for meeting their requirements of the long-term funds. It refers to all the facilities and the institutional arrangements for borrowing and lending funds. In other words, it is concerned with the raising of money capital for purposes of making long-term investments. The market consists of a number of individuals and institutions (including the government) that canalize the supply and demand for long-term capital and claims on it. The demand for long-term capital comes predominantly from private sector manufacturing industries, agriculture sector, trade and the government agencies. While, the supply of funds for the capital market comes largely from individual and corporate savings, banks, insurance companies, specialized financing agencies and the surplus of governments.

Capital market is an inner element for the development of economy. The economic development of a country depends upon the maturity of its capital market. It is the nervous system of the economy. A strong economic situation creates wealth to the nation. The wealth creation is only possible with best asset formation. The capital formation depends upon the investment habits of the community. The economy may be either savings economy or spending economy. But the art of mixture of the economy is how much extent of saving should be done by the community and what level of spending may be done by the government. Capital market is the game of saving and spending. The saving and spending is based on risk and return. Risk and return is the game of financial markets.

The stock exchanges are known as the secondary markets. They play an important role in the securities market. The stock exchange is a place, where all kinds of financial products are available for buying and selling. In stock exchanges, the government securities, municipal bonds, investment trust debentures and other financial instruments are traded. Secondary market means, the market for already issued shares. It is a medium of transfer of resources for the circulated securities. The development of primary market depends upon the activities of secondary market. If the secondary market is more active, the impact will be shown on primary markets. If the secondary market is inactive, there is no scope for primary market. The secondary market is run by speculation and gambling. The speculation is more important for the active trading. The speculation is oxygen to the stock market. It is desirable to some extent in the stock market. There is no secondary market without speculation. The activities in secondary market enhance the wealth of the corporate sector without any financial claims. The primary and secondary markets cannot be demarcated as two separate markets. Secondary market is resale market for shares and debentures. It represents an organized market in the trading of securities. The stock exchange activities are carried on by the members of the exchange. The securities are traded under certain set of rules and regulations. The stock exchange is an association or organization of members.

Key Terms

1. **Floating Debt:** A debt consisting of short-term obligation. The term is used in contradiction to long-term or funded debts.
2. **Funded Debt:** That part of the national debt which the government is not obliged to repay at any particular time, e.g., console. A debt that does not have to be repaid should especially be one represented by an irredeemable security.
3. **Household Sector:** It is a sector which sells or gives on hire the various factor services like land, labour, etc., to the production sector. The household sector receives income in the form of wages, rent, interest etc and with the money thus earned the household sector purchases the goods produced by the production sector.
4. **Infrastructure:** It refers to such basic requirements like the railways, roads, ships, internal waterways, telecommunication, power, and such other public utility concerns without which the functioning and growth of an economy, especially at fast pace, is not possible.
5. **Primary Market:** It is a market for new issues or new financial claims. It is also known as new issue market. It deals with those securities which are issued to the public for the first time.
6. **Merchant bankers:** They are issue managers, lead managers, co-managers, who are responsible to the company and SEBI. They offer a number of services like portfolio management, credit syndication, acceptance credit, counseling insurance.
7. **Registrars:** They are appointed by the company in consultation with the merchant bankers to the issue. Registrars have a major role next to the merchant bankers in respect of servicing of investors.
8. **Brokers:** Brokers along with the network of sub brokers market the new issues. They send their own circulars and applications to clients and do follow-up work to market the securities.
9. **Security:** A document given by a person or corporation or government called the "issuer" and acknowledging that the issuer has received money, or some other valuable consideration, for issuing the security and that some specified persons is, in return, entitled to certain rights against the issuer.
10. **Companies Act, 1956:** The Companies Act, 1956, came into force with effect from 1-4-1956. It is both a consolidating and amending Act. This Act presents the whole body of the company law in complete form and repeals earlier Companies Act and their amendments. It contains 651 sections and 13 schedules and numerous forms. This Act is based largely on the report of the company law committee 1952. With the growing complexities of modern business and the increasing role of joint stock enterprise in the economic development of the country, the company law is fast developing in order to protect the joint stock companies from the inroads of undesirable persons, and to ensure that the activities of the companies are carried on in furtherance of our economic goal establishing a socialistic pattern of society. The companies Act, 1956 has been amended for about dozen times with the last being in the series, the Companies Act, 1977.
11. **Stock Market:** It is an organized market for securities.
12. **Share:** A unit for reckoning investor's interest in the contributed capital of a company. Each share is assigned a nominal value, which is the minimum value of capital that must be

contributed for the share. A share is said to be par when it is sold at the nominal value or face value. When the share is sold at the price above the face value, it is said to be at a premium and it is said to be at discount when it is sold at a value less than the face value. Normally the face value of the share of the company is ₹ 10.

Questions

1. What is primary market? Explain its importance in industrialisation of the country.
2. Explain the relation between primary market and secondary market.
3. Who is merchant banker? Explain his relevance in issue of new securities.
4. Explain the role of broker in the capital market.
5. Secondary markets are the barometer for the economic development of a nation. Do you agree?
6. What is reforms? Explain the capital market reforms in India.
7. What is secondary market? Explain its objectives.
8. Explain the provisions of Securities Contract Regulation Act, 1956 with reference to stock markets.
9. Explain the provisions of Companies Act, 1956 with reference to stock exchanges.
10. What are the provisions of Income Tax Act, 1961 which deals with stock exchanges?
11. What are the functions of stock exchanges?
12. Explain different kinds of securities listed in stock exchanges.
13. Write an essay on Bombay Stock Exchange.
14. What is BOLT?
15. What is listing?
16. What is sensex? Explain its importance.
17. What is value at risk margin?
18. Explain the importance of national stock exchange.
19. What is nifty? Explain its components.
20. What is indices? Explain diferent kinds of indices.
21. Write an essay on SEBI by SEBI for corrective

4 Security Analysis

INTRODUCTION

All investments are risky. The return is always chased by risk. The difference between return and risk is the gain or loss to the investors. Millions of the investors are entering the stock market for this risk and return relationship. An intelligent investor must escape the risk and capture the return by entering in stock market at right time, at right prices and at right shares. Entering and exit of the stock market are the most important factor in determining the earnings of the investors. It is a simple principle, buy at low prices and sell at higher prices. The difference between two prices is the return to the investors. Buying at low price of scrip requires knowing the actual worth of scrip. This method is known as "security analysis". Security analysis refers to find out intrinsic value of a security. The intrinsic value represents the true economic worth of a financial asset. Generally every asset has its own value. The financial asset is called as "security analysis". If you are able to find out the actual value of the asset, we can say whether it is overpriced or underpriced. The common investor does not know these intricacies, and involves in either in profit or loss. Buying scrip at over priced leads to incurring losses and buying at under priced provides a hefty margin to the investors. The investor always invites return and avoids risk. The behavior of stock in the market depends upon latest information. Information in the stock market can discount or stimulate the share prices. The intrinsic value of a share depends upon earning potential of the company at present and also in future. Hence the information about performance of a company leads to know the intrinsic value of the share.

The intrinsic value is basically determined by the expected net earnings flow over a number of years. A strong financially sound company will have a potential growth in future. Large resources of reserves, surplus and undistributed profit may strengthen the company activities and leads to get better returns on their investments. Market is an inflow of new and existing scrips. It emerges always flooded with large number of securities. The securities are issued by companies, government, local bodies and public sector undertakings. Securities of more than one year came into the categories of capital and stock. A buyer who visits the shops, is always interested to purchase goods at low price and higher quality. In the same way the investor will think about the financial asset, which is available at lower prices and high quality. The selecting process of best scrip is known as "security analysis". Security analysis refers to analysis of trading securities from the point of view of their prices return and risks. It will help in understanding the behavior of security prices. If it is an analysis of particular scrip, it is called as micro analysis. If it is an analysis of market of securities, it is known as macro analysis. The analysis of trading securities reveals various facts about the market behavior. The following factor will influence security market analysis:

(a) Information
(b) Level of saving
(c) Trading methods
(d) Financial instruments
(e) Valuation of financial assets
(f) Market players
(g) Intermediaries.

(a) Information

Information is the powerful tool in the hands of intelligent investors. It provides a good data and an insight analysis for making investment decisions. A vast resource of information provides a good environment for making right investment decisions. Accumulation of knowledge leads to better investment making decisions. Knowledge-based decisions never fails in the prediction. In India, investment means simply handing over a cheque to the broker. The investors making their decisions based on market tips, rumors and hunches. Stock markets are highly influenced by information and money flow. The flow of information must be perfect and free, the market will adjust to the situation. Wrong information leads to imperfect market and the price formation will be unpredictable and volatile. The published source of information is available to all the investors. But the investors, who respond immediately, may gain advantage from the market. The market is based on demand and supply forces. The information acquired by the investors needs analytical capabilities and future projection. If the information is free and unbiased, the markets behave rationally and nobody can gain additional profits. Hence, the investors should be more cautions in the stock market while making investment decisions. The consequences are different when the information is perfect or imperfect or biased or unbiased. Profit booking in the stock market requires a lot of skills such as market behaviors, security behaviors, fundamental analysis, technical analysis and market valuation.

(b) Levels of Savings

Savings are the most important factor in the capital market. Capital markets will be active, when the levels of savings are very high. Market is based on supply and demand forces of money. The flow of money into the stock market may stimulate the growth of its securities. The micro analysis of saving flow would depend on the objectives such as return, capital appreciation, hedge against inflation liquidity and safety to the investors. The level of savings in the country depends upon many factors. The interest level of savings may lead to the growth of capital markets. The interest rates on savings may also influence the markets. A low rate of interest rates on bank deposits, bonds and debentures leads to increase the secondary market operations because the money will be diverted to the secondary market operations. If the rate of interest on savings is very high, the secondary market activities will decline significantly. Hence, the markets are influenced by the interest rates. The macro analysis of savings reveals that, the higher level of savings in the community may lead to the capital formation in the country. Capital formation can boost the growth of the corporate sector. The asset creation in the country is only possible with the primary market or initial public offering. The higher level of asset creation enhances the purchasing capacity of the community. A high rate of savings in the economy curtails the present consumption. A reduction in present consumption leads to fall of an industrial production. A fall of industrial production leads to closure of many units. The economy will be disturbed.

(c) Trading Methods

Trading is known as buying and selling of a financial product in the market. Market is a place, where buyers and sellers meet at a fixed place in a fixed time. Market is a coordinator between seller and buyer. It is influenced by the forces of supply and demand factors. These factors, the volume of trading turnover and also the prices. The trading turnover is one of the macro indicators for studying the market behavior. Market behavior reveals about the movement of the share such as buying pressure and selling pressure. The buying pressure in the stock market rises in the bear phase. The bear phase requires more supply of scrips. If the prices are falling, the bear will enter into the market and makes purchases. Hence, the market will stabilize and protection will be made from the falling of prices. If the prices are increasing, there will be more demand for scrips. The bulls enters into the market is known as bullish phase. The trading in scrips will be analyzed in the form of deals per day, or deals per hour. The scrips which are regularly traded in the stock exchange with high volume are known as "active scrips". The active scrips will command goodwill and enjoy reputation in the markets among the millions of investors. These scrips are being sold in the market as hot cakes. These scrips will be available for sale or purchase at any time in the market. These scrips are treated on par with the cash. They are treated as current assets in the market by the corporate sector. These scrips provide liquidity to the investors and market. It is related to the intrinsic value of the company and other internal factors of the company.

(d) Financial Instruments

The mobilization of resources from the market to the corporate sector can be done through issue of various financial instruments. The issuing company has to select best financial instrument among the various alternatives. The selection of financial instruments depends upon many factors. The capital structure of the company plays an important role in selection of financial instruments. DEBIT-EQUITY ratio occupies a dominant role in selection of financial instrument. It is a statutory ratio, which determines the companies either go for equity or debt. A number of different instruments which are available in the market are presented in the following:

1. Equity share.
2. Preference shares.
3. Debentures.
4. Bonds.
5. Convertible preference shares.
6. Fully convertible debentures.
7. Partly convertible debentures.
8. Non-convertible debentures.

9. Zero coupon bonds.
10. Warrants.
11. Deep discount bonds.
12. Option bonds.
13. Secured premium notes.
14. Non-voting equity shares.

(e) Valuation of Equity Shares

The aim of security analysis is to find out the worth of financial assets which is available at a market price. The market price can be either excess price or a lower price is known by the investors for making their investments decisions. Sometimes, the shares are available in the market at lower prices. The market consists of thousands of securities whose prices change from day to day and time to time. The detailed information about the share prices makes the investors to take a decision regarding buying and selling of securities. Hence it is necessary to make security valuation as important part of market analysis. The trend of price and volume of trading are interrelated. The investors should know full information about the market indicators such as PRICE, VOLUME OF TRADING VELOCITY, OF PRICE CHANGES AND INTENSITY OF TRADING, etc., all the information enables investor to take right instrument decisions. The valuation of financial assets can be categorized into two kinds.

(a) Market valuation

(b) Scrip valuation

Market valuation is associated with macro level of analysis. The macro level of analysis is done with the help of suitable price indices of the reputed scrips in the market and their PE ratio. The details of various indices for different scrips are prepared by the BSE national index. The investor can use all those information for making his investment in the market. The information is powerful tool in the hands of an intelligent investor. Published information is a public property to all the investors particularly in stock market is an adventure activity which shall be carried out by a skillful person. Nowadays the investors simply ignore the analytical tools and make investment decision, based on market tips and rumors. It is highly impossible to be a success in the stock market without a basic knowledge and proper skills. Ability to provide the money is not the critical in the stock market, but identification of best scrip is the most important factor to that success. The best scrips which are exposed to the market is mixed with thousands of secrets. The intelligent investor has to pick up best scrip from the market himself.

Scrip valuation is another important factor in the security valuation. It refers to the study about the behavior of a particular scrip. It is associated with the micro level of analysis. Micro level of analysis deals with the intrinsic value of a security. The intrinsic value of a security reveals that the market price of a security is either overpriced or undervalued. This determination enables the investor to take a decision regarding his investment. The intrinsic value of a share can be determined by the expected net earnings flow over a number of years discounted to the present time by a suitable discount rate. But it is difficult to project future earning of a company. Hence, the analysts will take PE ratio for future earnings of a company. Traditionally there are three approaches to market valuation. They are presented below:

(1) Efficient Market Hypothesis

(2) Fundamental Analysis

(3) Technical Analysis

The above valuation models are dealt with in detail in subsequent chapters. Further the valuation models in shares have three approaches. These are presented below:

(1) Discount of further inflows

(2) Payback period (PE ratio)

(3) Conceptual framework.

Discount of future inflows is the most important factor in valuation approach. The earning capability in future of a scrip, command a good reputation and it is a hidden talent. We may assess best scrip based on not only on present capabilities but also in future course of time. Talented people who are not exposed and the society will not recognize them. Like in the same way some scrips which are having good potential growth in future is ignored by the normal investors. An intelligent investor must find out such scrips from the market. The value of future income streams can be assessed as follows:

1. Compound method,
2. Discounting method.

In valuation of compound method takes 6 per cent interest rate and capital of ₹ 1.

In one year, it becomes ₹ (1 + 0.06) = 1.06

In two years, it becomes ₹ (1 + 0.06)2 = 1.1236

In three years, it becomes ₹ (1 + 0.06)3 = 1.2624.

in discounting method for example:

(a) The present value of ₹ 100, 10 years will be ₹ 39 at a discount rate of 10 per cent.

(b) The present value of the principal of ₹ 100 after 5 years at 8 per cent will be ₹ 68.

The process will apply to valuation of debt instruments. It will be discussed in latter chapters.

Payback period is associated with one of the valuation approaches. It is also known as multiplier approach. It is useful for valuation of equity shares. It is used in the form of PE ratio, for example, a company's earning is ₹ 20 and the scrip price is ₹ 100.

Therefore, PE ratio = 100/20 = 5

Hence, the payback period is 5 years.

Conceptual framework is related to study about investment decision activities influencing the productive process of the economy. Investment enhanced the output level of a nation and strongly influences the income component in the economy. According to Keynes, investment is an income multiplier in the economy. An additional investment may lead to an additional output and income. The following factors reveal the theoretical framework regarding investment decisions:

(a) Savings investment theory.

(b) Participants in trading.

(c) Fundamental in trading.

(d) Technical analysis.

(e) Risk and return relation.

Savings investment theory is the most theoretical tool study about the flow of investment. The savings flow into investments enhances the output and income levels. It is called as the capital output ratio or investment multiplier. Hence, the savings promote capital formation and economic growth. Economic growth stimulates the GDP level and influence per capita income of the public. A growth in purchasing power stimulates the demand for more additional quality goods. The standard of living of a common man increases and his lifestyle will also change significantly. For Ex., at present a common man, who is in below poverty line uses cellular services. He wants more comforts for his life. The savings will be attracted towards productivity by way of capital market. The capital market is a vehicle, to provide sufficient resources for the corporate sector by issuing a number of financial assets. The CAPITAL MARKET comprises new issues and secondary market. The new issues capital provides OXYGEN to newly established concerns. The primary market should be strengthened and it must be flexible to the market. The primary market in India has vast potential capabilities to meet the requirements of the corporate sector. The public issue should be made as "ONLINE" issues, the investor's allotment of shares should be finalized within 48 hours of the closing of issue. There is a strong need to make structural changes in the public issue. Investors should also be open "Demat" accounts for participation in the primary market. The SEBI should take steps to reduce the time in the public issues. The primary market can create wonders in the world of finance. It must be technologically updated purchasing shares at primary market should be done on par with secondary market operations. The IPOs should be available in "INTERNET". The procedure for applying and allotment of shares should be completed within 48 hours after the closure of issue. These transactions must be carried through the application of information technology. The primary market can be utilised for the commencement of mega project "interlinking of rivers". The mega project of the decade required an amount of ₹ 6,00,000 crores. It can be raised through public issue very easily and the unaccounted money diverted towards this mega project. This project will change the lives of 100 crores people of India.

Participation in trading is another important factor in making investment decisions by investors. The market behavior depends upon the market players and their role in trading. The trading in stock exchange is publicly available information to each and every interested investor. The volume of trading in particular scrip, the value of trading in a counter, the trading per hour, intraday trading information, and all other information is available to the public. The free flow of correct and unbiased information is always available in the market. The market absorbs all the information available in the market. Hence, the investor will know about the market behavior immediately. THE CAPITAL MARKET EFFECIENCY THEORY, RANDOM WALK THEORY and many other theories will clearly explain about price behavior in the market. Sometimes the share price movements may be erratic and biased. They may be overvalued and undervalued at any point of the time. The market consists of various factors such as "rumours, insider information, cornering, price rigging and other malpractices", which are unrelated to the prevailing fundamentals of a company. The theoretical analysis of the market should enable the investors to understand the movement. Hence, the investor can take a decision regarding his investment commitments towards the future by entering the stock market.

Fundamental analysis is one of the most important tools in investment analysis. It deals with the factors affecting the market in the macro and micro senses. In macro analysis, a close observation will be made about economic, industry and company aspects for the regular activities. The micro analysis reveals the intrinsic value of a share through security valuation models. It indicates whether a share is overvalued or undervalued. It will examine the balance sheet and profit and loss account of a company, whose share is being examined. RATIO ANALYSIS is the powerful tool to analyze the company performance. However, the fundamental analysis will enable us to decide what shares to buy and what shares to sell. The conceptual framework reveals about the factors influencing the market behavior.

(a) External factors (environmental, economic and political development)

(b) Internal factors (financial performance of the company)

(c) Capital structure

(d) Investment habits of the public

The market price depends upon the supply and demand factors of the share. The security is valued in terms of the returns or earning capacity of the company. The following factors are influencing the share price in the market:

1. Market efficiency theory (fundamental analysis)
2. Random walk theory (fundamental analysis)
3. Capital asset pricing method (fundamental analysis)
4. Trend walk theory (fundamental analysis)
5. Dow theory (technical analysis)
6. Elliot's theory (technical analysis)

In addition to the above factors, a lot of other factors such as psychological and emotional elements, will influence the share prices in the stock market.

Technical analysis is another important factor in conceptual framework. It reveals about the price behavior of the aggregate market and of individual share. It is a knowledge-based activity. It requires a lot of skills to understand the situations. It indicates the information with the help of the charts about share prices, trading volume, and moving averages. It will help us to know about trends in price changes and suggest buy and sell points in the charts. It informs us the past price of the individual scrip to take a good investment decision. The Dow Theory and Elliot wave theory are the part of technical analysis. These two theories will explain the price behavior in the past and help us in the future.

Yet another kind of analysis is the observation of RISK AND RETURN. The risk and return is the most important factor in determining the amount of investment. RETURN is always chased by the RISK. RISK is an estimated future loss of the business activity. Risk cannot be avoided. It is an escapable element. But in some situations, it cannot be escaped. It is an accepted level of loss by the investor. The return always depends upon the level of accepted risk. If the investor is always depending upon the level of accepted risk then the investor is willing to take more risk, the higher return is waiting for the investor. The risk and return analysis is to be achieved by the use of portfolio theory and portfolio management. The degree of risk depends upon the financial asset preferences, income requirements and other investment characteristics. The portfolio theory always thinks about the minimization of risk and maximization of return. All the theories are integrated to help the decision making by investors. The valuation is an important aspect of security analysis. Security valuation is an important part of market analysis.

(a) The capital market provides long-term funds to corporate sector, it coordinates the suppliers and borrowers at fixed place and time. The fund suppliers generally consist of individual investors, companies, firms, finance companies and non-banking finance companies, government and other organisations. Recently, a number of mutual funds, public financial institutions, non-resident Indians have also started as players in the market.

(b) Intermediates are coordinates between the fund suppliers and borrowers. They act as mediators for both the parties, in the financial markets, brokers, merchant bankers, financial institutions and investment consolidation firms. They activate the primary and secondary market. The number of players is more in primary market. The success of public issue mainly depends upon the assistance of intermediates. Brokers will play an important role in new issue market. Investors are regular clients of the brokers. The brokers will guide, motivate and inspire millions of investors through their wide network. Hence, the brokers are powerful financial intermediates in mobilization of resources in primary market. Secondary market operations are also handled by the brokers. Basically the secondary market operates through brokers only. They work for clients on communication basic. They render the services to the clients in buying and selling shares in market. The brokers occupy dominant role in secondary market. The primary market was involved with many intermediates such as merchant bankers, registrars, underwriters, share transfer agents and collecting bankers. The success of public issue depends upon their financial intermediates services. Hence all the above aspects are integrated to help in decision making by investors scientifically. SCIENTIFIC ANALYSIS is the important factor before making investments. PROFIT BOOKING in stock market is possible only with proper careful analysis. But in practice, an investment in stock market is made by the investors by handing over a cheque to the broker. They simply do not know about the company reputation, brand image financial performance of the company, EPS, PE ratio, past price, relation to government policy, etc., Therefore, the SAVINGS INVESTMENT THEORY explained the flow of the savings into investment which helps the growth process in the economy

Security analysis reveals about the behaviour of the market, if it finds out the true value of the security. The INTRINSIC VALUE is also known as real value of security. The following topics:

1. Fundamental analysis
2. Technical analysis
3. Dow theory
4. Elliot wave theory
5. Efficient market theory

1. Fundamental Analysis

It is one of the tools of scientific analysis in stock market operations. Any investor or analyst cannot ignore the importance of fundamental analysis. It relates its examination of the intrinsic value of the share. It is powerful tool to measure the efficiency of company. If the state of economy can show an impact on profitability of the company then fundamental analysis allows for selection of securities of different sectors of economy. The Indian economy mainly depends upon agriculture. Agriculture is based on monsoons. The following factors are considered to be essential for better performance of corporate sector:

(a) Good monsoon
(b) Performance of agriculture sector
(c) Monetary policy
(d) Economic system
(e) Political stability
(f) Economic policy
(g) Business cycles
(h) Labor legislations

The security analysis will be made by the investors before making investment decisions. It will be useful for understanding business and market environment in the country. It enables the investors to assess the potentiality of the particular company's earning capacity. The total analysis of the investment environment can be categorized into the following three types:

(a) Economic analysis
(b) Industry analysis
(c) Company analysis

(a) Economic Analysis

The state of economy is the most important factor in fundamental analysis. Indian economy is basically agricultural dominated market. Mixed economy is a participation of public and private sector. The government shall have to coordinate the intricacies of both the sectors. The government should encourage the private sector and also protect the public sector. The encouragement of private sector depends upon the government's industrial policy. The industrial policy is greatly helpful in the formation of capital in the country. The formation is the MOST IMPORTANT factor in the development of a nation and the capital formation asset creation in the economy. Asset creation is the indicator for measuring the PROSPERITY OF A NATION. The PROSPERITY depends upon the level of economic activity played by different forces. If the economy grows rapidly, industry can also be expected to show rapid growth. Growth is a strong and powerful element in the development of the nation. GROWTH is an element for assessing the capabilities of a nation. It depends upon the efforts made by the economy. If the level of economic activity is HIGH, the stock prices are HIGH and if level of economic is low, stock prices are also low. Hence, the stock price in stock market is a reflection of PROSPEROUS outlook for sales and profits of the corporate sector. The analysis of MACROECONOMIC environment enables to understand the behaviour of the stock prices. MACRO ANALYSIS deals with the following factor:

1. Gross domestic product
2. Savings potential
3. Monsoon

4. Taxation
5. Foreign exchange
6. Inflation
7. Budget
8. Infrastructure
9. Prediction
10. Interest rates
11. Economic assessment
12. Economic indicators.

1. Gross Domestic Product

Gross domestic product is a tool for analysis of the level of economic activities in the country. It represents the aggregate value of the goods and services produced by a country. It indicates all efforts made by a nation of people. It is the society contribution. It takes all factors into consideration for arriving the value of amount of goods and services produced by a whole nation. It is the most important factor in the macro analysis. It consists of personal consumption, expenditure, gross private domestic investment and government expenditure and net exports of goods and services. The estimates are available on annual basis. It is a combination of all sectors of the economy.

2. Savings Potential

Savings are the most important element in the economy. The influence the present level of investment. Though savings curb the present consumption but in long-term they help in growth of the economy. The saving will be directed towards various financial assets such as EQUITY SHARES, DEPOSITS, MUTUAL FUND UNITS, REAL ESTATE AND BULLIONS. India has a strong savings potential and the middle class families commands the higher level of saving. Saving towards new issue market leads to capital formation. Capital formation stimulates the value of assets. Asset creation is the most important factor in the PROSPERITY of the nation. Prosperity is the barometer of development. It is the indicator of the efforts made by human resources of a nation. CHINA And JAPAN are the best examples for the development of their economy. The patterns of savings in the society will be highly influenced by various factors such as interest rates, taxation, purchasing power, disposable income, etc., if the interest rates are at lower levels in the economy, the investors are not interested saving. The low rate of interest may curtail the savings habits in the economy. The debt market will be inactive but equity market can grow to higher level due to funds available at cheaper rate of interest. Hence, the level of rate of interest will influence the level of savings. TAX SYSTEM in the economy is one of the factors to increase the level of savings. Taxpayers in India are encouraged to save up to ₹ 1.00 lakh for reducing their tax burden. Hence, the direct tax can also influence the level of savings. Purchasing power in the community is another important factor in influencing the investment levels. Higher income with low spending habits may cause an increase in the level of savings. Disposable income at higher level with the community helps to mobilize the savings. The savings mobilized through various factors may be useful to produce more goods for the economy. Higher level of production is a value addition to the worth of assets. Higher level of asset creation in the economy might lead to better living standards and can reduce the citizen's problems. We can construct the modern India and can afford better quality of living standards on par with AMERICAN

CITIZENS. For achieving this purpose India should concentrate on political reforms rather than economic reforms. India can create miracles in the economy. Politicians in India should change their mindset. They should be trained in economic aspects. They should be in a position to run the government with corruption free environment. The economy should be "FREE ECONOMY" to achieve the goal like in China. We can do lot of things by observing the developed economy. But we should not copy them or indulge in theft. Development enhances the capabilities and efficiency. The restricted economy will halt the development and progress. Hence, the power of savings will be useful to construct modern India. The digital economy can enhance the living standards of the poor citizens. The below poverty line people are facing many problems. Their problems will be solved with proper financial planning of the economy. The poverty can be attacked with the change in mindset of the society. Development is not involved with monetary help. It is achieved with proper utilization of available financial resources. The proper utilization of funds can definitely achieve growth.

3. Monsoon

Agriculture is occupying a dominant role in the economy. It is based on rainfall in India. The rainfall depends upon good climate and pollution free environment, i.e., non-pollution environment. It is directly and indirectly linked with the industries such as sugar, cotton, textiles, food processing, etc. These industries depend upon agriculture for raw material. Fertilizers and chemical industries are supplying inputs to the agriculture. A good monsoon leads to higher demand for inputs and results in good crops. This situation enables stock index performance a good, leading to a good healthy environment in the country and it may attract more foreign direct investments. If the monsoon is very bad, agriculture and hydel power production would suffer a lot and lead to industrial unrest in the economy. A disturbance in the industrial process lead to a fall in the level of GDP. A negative growth in GDP is a dangerous situation. Hence, the monsoon is the most important factor in the Indian economy. Good rainfall depends upon the environment. The encouragement of eco-friendly industries leads to non-pollution environment. The government has also taken steps to create pollution free environment through various legislation and statutory clearances.

4. Taxation

In India, every year in the month February, the government presents its budget in the Parliament by the financial minister. The business community and the whole of India eagerly await the government's announcement regarding the tax policy. Tax policy is the part of the finance act. Finance act is the part of the union government's budget. Budget is the most important tool to the central government to change the lives of crores of people. Budget is a document consisting of income and expenditure of the government. The government collects its revenues through direct and indirect taxes. Direct taxes are regulated in India by the central board of direct taxes. The indirect taxes are controlled by central board of excise and customs duties. Both these wings are working under the control of finance ministry. They make arrangements to give tax relief to various industries in the form of concessions and incentives. Direct taxes are levied and collected by the central government. Income tax, gift tax and wealth tax are the best examples of direct taxes. Central excise, customs and central sales tax are examples of indirect taxes. Tax reliefs are given to savings for encouragement.

5. Foreign Exchange

Foreign exchange is the most important element in the economy. A favorable balance in foreign exchange reserves will stimulate the growth of the Indian economy. The foreign exchange relates to the country's receipts earned through export by the corporate sector. The country also requires the payments to other nations for import of goods for the domestic consumption. The difference between receipts and payments may be surplus or deficit. Balance of payment is a measure of the strength of rupee on external account. If the deficit increases, the rupee may depreciate against other currencies. The depreciation in rupee value leads to the weakening of the economy. The import may become more costly. The companies which are involved in export and import business will be affected by the changes in foreign exchange rate. The volatility of the foreign exchange rate severely affects the flow of foreign currency into the stock market through foreign institutional investors. The stock markets will be activated by the entry of FIIs. FIIs will occupy a dominant role in the stock market. Enter and exit of the FIIs from the stock markets will greatly influence the prices of Indian stock market. A favorable balance of payments in foreign exchange balances can create a positive effect on the Indian stock market.

6. Inflation

Inflation is another important factor in the economy. It refers to increase in the prices of different commodities and services available in the market. It increases along with the growth of GDP. Hence, the real rate of growth would be less. The demand in the consumer product industry is significantly affected. The growth in demand for more products will stimulate the production levels of the industry. Hence, the industries will come under the price control of the government. They may lose the market, for example, sugar. The profitability of the industry depends upon the government price control. Inflation is useful to the economy up to some extent but higher rate is harmful to the stock market.

7. Budget

Budget is an important tool to the government. It can influence the lives of crores of people. It contains the receipts and payments of the central government for a specific period. It is a guiding force of the government machinery. The budget may show either deficit or surplus balance. Deficit budget may lead to high rate of inflation which adversely affects the cost of production. Surplus budget leads to deflation. Deflation results in a lower level of prices for all commodities. Profits will be low and production levels decline. Therefore, balanced budget is more useful to the stock market.

8. Infrastructure

The development of the economy depends upon the good infrastructure facilities. Infrastructure is an essential for the growth of industrial and agriculture sector. It is useful for overall development of the nation. The governments need not develop every sector, but creation of better infrastructure automatically facilitates and stimulates the growth of every sector. Providing good transport mode, quality supply of power, provision for better natural resources, good communication facilities, better legislation, and good labor relations will enhance the industrial productivity.

9. Prediction

Prediction is one of the important factors in assessing market situation. Assessment of future in the right way enables the investors to book profits in the stock market. The assessing capabilities depend upon many factors such as foresight, good understanding of the economic environment, rapid changes in the technological aspects etc. A change in customers' attitudes, a change in government policy, etc., must be known by the predictor. The success of the prediction basically depends upon the abilities of the predictor.

10. Interest Rates

Interest is the reward to the fund owner. It is treated as an expense in cost of production of a commodity. The rate of interest can show impact on cost of production of a commodity. Interest rates are fluctuating in the market, which is determined by the RBI. Reserve bank is the full authority in determining the interest rates in the country. If the interest rates decrease, the profitability of the firms will be increased. A lower rate of interest will stimulate the earning capacity of the commercial enterprises. A flow of higher amount of money available at lower interest rate for the brokers may stimulate the speculative activities in the secondary market. A rise in share prices encourages more investors towards stock markets. The availability of resources at lower rate of interest will definitely stimulate the growth of the stock markets. A rise in secondary markets leads to more demand for the new issues. The demand for new issues creates capital formation. Capital formation is the indicator of the development of economic progress. Economic progress creates more employment opportunities to the 100 crores people of India. A good government can provide job opportunities in the corporate sector by providing funds at lower rate of interest. A rise in interest rates leads to higher cost of production. The goods sold in the market at higher prices reduce the demand. A fall in demand for goods will decline the sales of the corporate sector and profitability will decline. Hence, the interest rates are influencing factor in determining the growth of the corporate sector. The government will take a decision regarding the rate of interest in the market according to its monetary policy. The decisions of the government will be implemented by the Reserve Bank of India. Reserve bank is the supreme authority in determination of supply of money in the market.

11. Economic Assessment

A study of economic environment is necessary for the success in the stock market. The macro-economic analysis is more useful to book the profits in the stock market. The economic activities of the country affect the corporate profits and show an impact on the economy. Gross Domestic Product is the most important influencing factor in determining security prices. A fall in GDP may lead to a fall in corporate profit and consequently in the security prices. The success in stock market depends upon the correct forecasting techniques. The investor or analyst should know advantages and disadvantages of various techniques. The general techniques used by the analyst are presented below:

(a) Economic Barometer

(b) Statistical Techniques.

Acquiring various techniques by the investor for investment purpose will definitely be a success. The techniques will help him to decide the right time to invest and the type of security to be purchased. Stock market is not an ordinarily involved business. It requires intelligent analytical skills, talent, expertise, scientific analysis and good understanding about various economic aspects and its intricacies arising in the economy. Statistical techniques will be useful for analyzing the situation to take a good investment decision in the stock market

12. Economic Indicators

Economic development is the most important factor to a nation. The development of a nation can be measured through powerful economic indicators. The economic indicators indicate the present status of the economy. It reveals about the progress or slows down the economy. The indicators are the barometers of the economy. They reveal the actual situation which involved many factors such as capital investment, business profits, money supply, gross national product, interest rate and unemployment rate, etc. All these indicators inform about what is going to happen in the economy. The indicators show a signal to predict the way of the economy. The popular indicators in our economy are fiscal policy, monetary policy, rainfall index, productivity, capital formation, foreign direct investment and the stock indices. The fiscal policy is related to the central government. The aim of the policy is to reduce the fiscal deficit or increase the surplus balance in the economy. The Indian economy has always a deficit balance in its balance sheet. The central government will take measures to reduce the deficit in the economy. In order to increase the revenue of the government, a levy of direct and indirect taxes are necessary. Hence, the tax policy of the government may enhance the revenue levels of the economy. The reduction in expenditure levels of the government is not possible in the democratic country. Hence, the government is always trying to boost its revenue and reduce deficit in the economy. The tax policy of the central government will be reflected in the finance bill. Finance bill is the part of the union budget. The budget also contains about the incentives provided to the export-oriented units in order to encourage the exports contribution in the global economy. After globalization process, every nation is trying to capture the global market. The global markets provide excellent opportunities to the competitive nations. The global market requires a high quality of goods with lower prices. Hence, those countries which are able to meet these standard parameters can export their goods and earn foreign exchange. The commendable and favorable balance of the foreign reserves will make the "rupee" stronger in the global market. Generally, the global market is dominated by the dollar. The dollar is powerful weapon in the global market. The global market is an indicator to the efficiency of a nation. The major contribution of the global business is influenced by efficient utilization of resources by a nation. Competition in the global market is very high and the efficient countries only can capture the business. The efficiency is the barometer in the global market. The monetary policy is also related to the central government aspect. The RBI is the official agency to prepare the monetary policy on behalf of the union government. Monetary policy is associated with the money supply in the economy. The cheap money or the tight money policy adopted by the authorities will show impact on the industry. The stock market will discount all the affairs of the policy matters of the central government. The aspect in any government's policies will be observed by the stock market participants. The rise of BSE sensex and NSE NIFTY are the delicate tools and they will react to every small incident occurred in the economy of the country. A significant rise in the two index numbers will reflect the economic strength of India. India will definitely become a strong nation if it utilizes the available manpower in the right way. It should encourage research activities and a sophisticated legislation toward corporate sector to reach the goal. The development of India is not based on finance, but depends upon the attitude of the 100 crores public. The government is only a weapon to counter the poverty. Development activity should be taken as patriotism. Every citizens' attitude should be changed to work hard for the building of modern India. China is the guiding force for development of our nation, the awareness in the population. The other indicators are identified in our economy such as unemployment rate, consumer price index and flow of foreign funds. The predictions are known as econometrics.

b. Industry Analysis

Industry is a group of firms producing similar characteristic goods. The firms are producing goods to meet the requirements of their customers. The commercial firms will survive in the market due to patronage of the customers. The customers' tastes are changing, their needs are fluctuating, their buying habits are highly volatile, and all these factors will show a strong impact on the growth of an industry. Industry is consisting of a number of companies. Companies are classified as per their activities of manufacturing goods. The reserve bank of India has classified the following industry groups:

(a) Food products
(b) Textiles
(c) Beverages, tobacco
(d) Wood and wood products
(e) Rubber and plastic products
(f) Transport equipment and parts
(g) Basic metals, alloys and metal products
(h) Machinery and machinery tools.
(i) Non-metallic mineral products.
(j) Other manufacturing industries.
(k) Chemicals and chemical products.

The industries are different from one another. They are classified on the basis of the business cycles. The business cycle is a combination of different phases:

1. Growth industry.
2. Cyclical industry.
3. Industry life cycle.

Growth industry is a combination of different companies producing similar characteristic of goods. The growth industries have some special features in the business cycle. They have a high rate of earnings, high brand loyalty growth in expansion. They are independent of the business cycle. They are well established and stabilized in the market. They are ready to face any situations that exist in the market. The industry will go for expansion with the help of latest technology. Technology is the most important and influencing factor in the business sector. The latest technology reduces cost of manufacturing expenses very significantly. Nowadays all industries are taking cost reduction measures in order to get substantial savings of expenses. But the technology involves higher amount of capital expenditure. The information technology created a new wave in the corporate sector. The IT provides solutions to many business enterprises to attract the customers. For example, the commercial banks attracting the customers by providing ATM services throughout the nation. ATM facility provides flexibility to the customers for their withdrawal of cash. At the same time the banks also get substantial savings in the form of salaries to their limited workforce. E-Commerce is a sophisticated technology which saves time and money of the customer. It is also a cost effective tool to counter the cost of finished products. Business cycles continued to grow in the economy such as color television, telecommunications, drugs and pharmaceuticals. These industries have shown remarkable growth recently. The liberalization policy created a best environment to grow in the economy for the corporate sector. Some industries move along with business cycles such as boom and depression. While goods command a good market in the boom period and demand declines during depression period. Hence, the refrigerators, washing machines and home appliances enjoy a higher growth in the boom time. Some industries differ from the movement of business cycles. They are known as defensive industry. The basic need of the human being is associated with this industry. Generally, food and housing sectors will come under this classification. The food industry commands a good demand during recession and depression. The defensive industry scrips may be purchased by the investors for income earning purpose. Sometimes the government protection is available for this sector. Some industries are based on cyclical growth industry. They are technology-based performance sectors. They will face stagnation period and experience decline in sales. But they grow immediately with the changes occuring in the technological aspects. For example, automobile sector introduces new models to help the industry for the growth of its firms. Hence, the investor should always think about the latest changes occurring in the market. Industry life cycle is the most important theory in the fundamental analysis. This theory is contributed by Julis Gordensky. They study of different stages over a firm's life period. Generally all companies are entering in every stage of the industry life cycle. The life cycle of the industry can be classified as follows:

1. Preliminary stage
2. Growth stage
3. Stability
4. Declining stage

1. Preliminary Stage

Preliminary stage is an initial period for the newly established companies. Manufacturers try to develop brand name. In this stage, prospective demand for the product is promising and the technology of the finished product is low. There are many producers in the market producing the same quality of goods and creates a tough competition. The demand for that product attracts many entrepreneurs to survive with the market. The market creates a severe competition and only fittest companies survive in the market. Every company in the market wants to capture the market share. The major portion occupied by a company is known as market leader. In this stage, survival is the most critical and influencing factor in life of a business concern. The producers will provide heavy amount of budget for advertising to push the product at the disposal of the customers. Hence, in this stage it is difficult to recommend the companies for investment purpose. Hence, the survival is not known and the investor is unable to select the companies. Competition in the market will change the position of firms. The business in this stage is involved with high risk. Risk is always haunting the business men. Risk is in-escapable. Risk can be countered by the skills and intelligence of business concern.

2. Growth Stage

Growth stage is another important position in the industry life cycle. The preliminary stage eliminates some inefficient companies which are unable to better their performance. The survived companies can only enter in this stage. In this stage the companies must face any competition for capturing the market share of the product. Technology occupies an important position to get higher margins from the market. The latest technology will provide the substantial savings of expenses and generates more quality products. Quality and price dictates the market. Every company should provide goods with high quality of goods and lower prices. The companies have stable growth rate in this stage and they show the best financial performance to the shareholders in the form of declaration of higher rate of dividend. Dividend is the reward to the shareholders. It is advisable to invest in this company's shares. The example for this stage is that the growth rate is generally higher than the industry's average growth rate. It is the dynamic stage. The future will be decided and determined in this stage.

3. Stability

Maturity position will reveal all the consequences to the industry. It is the perfection stage and the growth rate tends to moderate. The growth rate would be more or less equal to the gross domestic product growth rate. The technology adopted by the industry may become obsolete. Technology must be upgraded and the new products should be introduced in this stage. It is also a cautious position of the industry. The investors have to closely observe the series of events that occur in the stage. Hence, the investors should take an investment decision after a careful study of events occuring in the industry.

4. Declining Stage

Declining stage is the end of the industry life cycle. In this stage demand for the specified product in the industry will decline. The sales of firms will fall. The earnings of the companies reduce drastically. Margins are under pressure. The product will become outdated. New products replace the old brands. Innovative products will appear in the market. For example, at present there is no demand for black and white TVs. There is no demand for VCRs, VCPs and are replaced by CD players and DVD players. There is no demand at present for mopeds. After the liberalization, automobile industries produce and provide a number of models in the motorcycle industry. The rural market of the mopeds is replaced by the motorcycle vehicles. There is less demand for ambassador product of four wheelers as new brand of cars enter the market. All these changes occurred due to changes in consumer's preference. Hence, the consumer behaviour is the most important factor in determination of the future. Even in the boom period, the growth of industry is negligible and leads to declining position. Any product, any company will survive in the market due to the patronage of consumers. Hence, the investors should be cautious and investment in this kind of company shares leads to erosion of capital. The investment decision in this kind of shares is involved in high risk.

Industry analysis is a reflection of all aspects regarding different stages in the economy. All industries are that part of gross domestic product. GDP is the most important factor in our mixed economy. GDP occupies a dominant role in economic development of our country. An increase in GDP stimulates the value of prosperity and leads to asset creation. Asset creation in the country enhances the richness of a nation. GDP is an indicator of the efficiency of a nation and it reveals the historical cost of different models manufactured by various kinds of industries. In addition to the above factors, the investors in India have to analyze the other influencing elements. They are presented below for acquiring more knowledge about the Indian industry. These factors are only helpful in prediction of the different alternatives available in the market at the disposal of investors:

- Growth of the industry
- Earning capabilities
- Product
- Competition

- Research
- Industrial peace
- Government policies

Growth of industry: Industry is a combination of different firms producing similar characteristic of products. GDP is a combination of various industries' efforts. Economy constitutes various factors. The performance of various industries is monitored by different agencies. The research agencies are regulatory organs of the various industries closely observing the situation that arises in the economy and publishes different reports. The reports are more useful in analyzing and assessment of stock markets for the investors. The common investor in India should make careful analysis about the market analysis before making his investment decisions. For this purpose he has to search for valuable information. The industry-wise information is published periodically by different agencies such as the "center for monitoring the Indian economy". "National council of applied economic research", "Indian bulletins", "and National institute of financial management", "Society for capital market research", etc., in the marketing aspects of the corporate world, various research organizations conduct surveys and makes periodical reports about the sales of different companies. Indian market research bureau, operations and research group, marketing and research group, publishes various periodical reports. Information provides knowledge. Knowledge about the economic environment creates an in-depth analysis about the functioning of the corporate world. The past earnings and present growth stimulates the economic value of the corporate sector. The macro-economics factors provide an insight into the future. The past performance is not repeated in the business but it can show a direction to predict the future. The information technology created a wave in the Indian economy. A tremendous growth in IT scrips occurred and created history in the stock markets. The IT sector dominates the other industries and plays a vital role in all sectors. The computerization process is introduced by almost all industries including government departments. Hence the future of GDP is based on utilization of IT sector. India is becoming a knowledge-based economy. The digital economy will completely change the corporate sector. Therefore, the investors should observe all these changes occurring in the economy and they should make investment decisions according to the latest situation in the market.

Earning capabilities: Profit is a glamour of the corporate sector. The efficiency of a business council can be measured through the quantum of money earned as profit. The sale price of a commodity by the manufacturer includes fixed and variable cost. The ratio of fixed and variable cost affect the cost of production, which ultimately tell on the profitability of a company. The fixed cost is different from one industry to another. For example: the fixed cost is very high in case of oil and natural gas industry and iron steel, etc., high fixed cost requires a great sales volume to meet the firms break-even point (BEP). The BEP is the most influential factor in determining the volume of profit available to the company. If the company crosses BEP and the production is going on, the margins can be increased naturally. Hence, the plant capacity utilization indicates the actual earnings made by the company. The full utilization of installed capacity needs additional capital to be invested for fixed equipment. Therefore, lower the fixed cost will definitely show impact on the corporate earnings. The variable expenses will be fluctuated according to the production schedule of the company. The latest situation in the market, reveal that the quality of goods must be high and price should be low. Hence, in order to meet such situation, every company is trying to cut the cost substantially by adopting innovative techniques. For this purpose the companies are introducing the cost reduction programs in order to reduce the pressure on the earnings of the company. Hence, the investors must observe all these factors while taking investment decisions.

Product: The goods which are in demand by the consumers in the market are manufactured and delivered by the corporate sector. Nowadays the goods should be manufactured according to the needs and convenience of the customers. The customer is king in the market. He dictates the terms of the corporate sector. The products maybe classified as industrial and consumer goods. For example, cement, steel and iron goods are produced. The demand for them depends upon the construction industry. The automobile component sector depends upon the growth of the automobile sector. Hence, there will be a relation between two factors. The investors have to make careful observation, analyze the conditions for related goods producing industry and the ultimate end uses of the product. The nature of the product is also occupying an important role in investment decisions of the investors.

Competition: Competition in the market is a common phenomenon in the business. The demand and supply of the goods are based on several factors. High competition in the market reduces margins to the company. Competition enhances the skills and abilities of the corporate sector. There will be competition between domestic and multinational companies. The competition maybe organized and unorganized. The competition would lead to a decline in the price of the product. The investors should be careful before investing in this type of scrips.

Research: Technology occupies a vital role in the manufacturing of goods. Traditional methods of production of goods require a higher amount of expenditure and time consuming process. The manufacturing of goods at factory levels are changing very fast by adopting latest technological methods. Latest technology saves time and money. The technology will be available only on a continuous effort made towards research and development. The R&D facilitates to acquire new method of manufacturing process in order to reduce the expenses. The economies of scale and new markets can be obtained through R&D. The higher percentage of allocation of budget for R&D leads to the emerging new methods of process.

Industrial peace: The labor relations in the industrial sector are also occupying a vital role in the performance of corporate world. Good labor relations and labor legislation may be helpful for the smooth functioning of the production of goods. The trade unions activities and attitudes will have impact on the labor productivity. Any disturbance in industrial peace leads to the interruption of the production of goods. The product targets of the industry will be fulfilled with the support of labor trade unions. The availability of adequate skilled persons may stimulate the productivity of the industry. An increase in productivity reduces the cost of production substantially. Therefore, the investor must observe these things before making his investment decisions.

Government policy: Policy is a long-term strategy. The government policies affect the profitability of the various industrial sectors. Government will give protection to some kind of units such as tax holidays and subsidies are provided for export-oriented units. Every government policy will affect any industrial sector either positively or negatively. For example, control and de-control of sugar prices affect the profitability of the sugar industry. Fertilizers are subsidized by the government, pharmaceutical prices are also under the control of government. The government provides tax incentives for companies which are established in backward areas. The tourism department will provide tax incentives for five star hotels. The domestic industries are protected by the government by way of giving incentives and subsidies. Hence, the investors are required to analyze themselves by observing all these factors. The government policy regarding aviation sector is quite encouraging and more aviation companies are entering into this segment. At present, new companies are entering this sector such as Sahara airlines, jet airways, Deccan aviations, etc., with the intensified competition, the private airlines offering a lower price of tickets to their passengers. It is surprising that ₹ 500 can afford air travel to the common man in India by the Deccan aviations. Hence, the aviation sector gets full support from the government.

Company Analysis

Knowledge about company's performance and their working environment is helpful to the investors in evaluating the performance of different companies. Stock market activities involve knowledge-based skills and persons who are fully equipped with a lot of information may become the stars of the stock market. Hence, acquiring information about corporate sector is necessary. From the available information, the investor assimilates the related company's data and evaluates the present and future value of a stock. The risk and return is associated with the purchase of financial asset from the stock market. Risk is always chased by the return. Return is always haunted by risk. The investor must get better returns by avoiding risk. The valuation of financial asset process depends upon the investor's skills, abilities, knowledge foresight, and analytical process to elicit information from various related variables. Any decision in company's boardroom will definitely show an impact on the company's earning capabilities. There are so many factors which influence the corporate profits. The evaluation of share prices can be classified as follows:

1. Future price
2. Present price

Any major decision of the company management can influence the share price either in present or in future. The selected company is a good company now but it will turn into an obsolete one tomorrow.

1. Future Price

The investors in the stock market are searching for a good company. They collect the information about the various companies which show better performance and achieving their targets and goals. But they are not in focus but tomorrow they will become a blue-chip company. The companies which are working silently and without much publicity can explore the hidden talents. They provide many returns to their shareholders. The companies which perform very well and maintain good labor relations with their workforce can turn tomorrow as blue-chip organization. Hence, the investor must assess the capabilities of different companies by keeping not only present situation but also future aspects. The following factors will affect share prices in future:

(a) Capabilities
(b) Profits
(c) Capital structure
(d) Board skills
(e) Operating efficiency
(f) Financial analysis

Capabilities: Economy is consisting of a number of industries. Industry is consisting of a number of individual firms producing similar characteristic of goods. Hence, the market contains thousands of individual organizations. Even through a large number of organizations exists in the market, but a few companies will become more popular and enjoys a lot of goodwill. The popular and reputed companies control the major market share. In all industries some companies rise to the position of excellence and dominance. Heavy companies are successful in facing the severe competition. Once the companies occupy the market leadership position, they will have to return and keep their position in the market. Companies working in the market will have to prove their efficiency with the existing competition and capture a sizable share in the market. The ability and skills, competitiveness of the company can be increased with the help of the following factors:

1. Market position
2. Sales performance
3. Stability

Market position: Market position or market share is an important factor in evaluation of a company's performance. All companies are working for the desired targets of the sales. They work for becoming a market leader in the market. The market share occupied by the company helps to determine the company's abilities and competitive edge. If a company captures higher rank in market share, the organization would be able to meet the severe competition successfully. For example, Hero Honda topped the list in term of sales in 2004 automobile sector for two wheelers. In evaluation of the market share, the size of the company should be considered. The smaller companies in the market have less scope for survival in the future. The large companies have higher potential to face any situation in the market, even for a long period of time. The star companies of today's market will continue to retain the position in the future. The investor should make a comparison before taking investment decision between companies in the market. For example, an automobile company should be compared with other automobile companies to choose the best company in that industry. A comparison between two companies in the same industry would draw better conclusions in the analysis. The skills, efficiency and capabilities of an organization will be exposed in comparison of the company's performance. A well reputed company always occupies the market share and stands at number one position. A leading company will always have competitive edge over other companies. The reputation and brand image will be achieved by the companies by putting many efforts in reaching its destination.

Sales performance is one of the important factors in capturing market share. A sale is the oxygen to any commercial enterprise. The basic activities of the commercial enterprise involves buying and selling of goods. All leading companies may not be showing higher sales. The growth in sales is different from one company to another. Market is just like a game of musical chair. All participants in the game require more attention and be cautious towards reaching their destination. Any negligence in the market leads to decline in sales and losing its market share and giving a chance to grow in the market for competitor. Hence, the companies are required to move in the *market with more attention*. The remarkable growth in sales is happy moment for company shareholders. The shareholders will become prosperous due to a growth in sales, because the value of scrip in the stock market increases tremendously. The scrip will be sold in the market with higher prices and its market capitalization will be stimulated. Generally, the large companies with inadequate growth in sales will not be preferred by the investors. The sales in the market are highly influenced by the brand loyalty. Brand name is the most important factor in the world of marketing. Brand loyalty creates guaranteed sales to the company. Brand image is the basis for establishing the brand loyalty relation. The satisfaction of the customer for a brand is reflected in the form of brand loyalty. Hence, if any company wants to become market leader, it should be remember about the brand positioning. Once the customer is satisfied with the particular company he may not change his attitude.

The evaluation of brand image is based on the following characters:

(a) Quality
(b) Perceived popularity
(c) Value for money
(d) Feeling of friendliness
(e) Repurchase intention

The final brand rating is arrived at in four steps. (Brand attributes):

(a) Always maintains a high level quality
(b) It is worth the price it commands
(c) It is going to be a popular brand for many years
(d) It evokes a feeling of confidence and pride among users

Stability is most important for survival in the market. If a firm has stable sales, the earning of that firm also will have stable profits. Continuous and constant profits are more useful for company which enjoys brand reputation and the market leader position. A wide variation in sales leads to fluctuation in capacity utilization, financial planning and dividend. An indication of hundred per cent capacity utilization leads to better sales performance. The investor can assume that the 100% capacity utilization is an indication of growth in sales regularly. Generally, all the financial newspapers, journals and magazines add information about the market share of different organization in an industry. A decline in the market share shows the declining trend of the company. If a company shows stability in sales, it should be compared with the market share and the competitor's market share. A right direction to the marketing department stimulates the sales volume of a company. The sales performance of a company mainly depends upon accurate "sales forecast". The sales forecast is a prediction about the process of market capturing by the concerned organization. A good reputed company enjoys a superior position capturing more sales but the investors in the stock market should have an idea whether the sales will continue in future or not. Hence, the study about future sales can be made in different methods. The investor can apply the trend line method either linear or non-linear which is found more suitable for his sales forecasting. Another method can be used for finding sales forecast by the investors known as "least square" technique. A comparison will be made about historical sales of the company and industry sales. This method of comparison easily reveals about the company's position in the market according to the microeconomic analysis technique. The sales volume of the company can be compared with GDP, per capita income and population growth. According to the demand analysis technique, a product is demanded by many different sources such as from customers and direct from industries. Hence, the total demand for a product should be taken into consideration. For example, steel and petroleum products are demanded by consumers and industries.

Profits: Increasing sales may not reflect an increase of profits levels. The cost and expenses of the company influence the levels of earnings. Sometimes sales, will decline, but profits will be at stimulating levels. In some situations, the sales performance of the company is very good but level of profit declines. Hence, the expenses occupy a dominant role in earnings part of the company's profit. A rise in costs and expenses shows an impact on earnings of the company. Hence, the investor needs a careful analysis regarding sales volume, because the earnings are most important factor than sales. The earnings of the company are a combination of operating and non-operating sources. Operating income is the basic earning of the company. Operating income is involved with sales activities of the produced goods and commodities by the company. The sources of income vary from industry to industry. For example, the cement industry generates operating income from sales of manufactured cement. For example, the income of a commercial bank arises from lending the loans on interest basis. Basically, every company gets operating income through the business activities, i.e., buying and selling or purchasing raw material and selling finished products. The operating income is also known as "revenue income". Usually, companies get revenue either from sales or from other sources. The revenue from other sources is known as "non-operating income". The corporate sector generally acquires non-operating income from various sources. There are many sources for getting non-operating income which are presented below:

1. Interest from debentures and bonds.
2. Rents from own buildings etc.
3. Sale of assets.
4. Dividends from securities.

The investor should be more cautious while analyzing the data for his reference. He should know particularly about the operating and non-operating incomes of a company. Sometimes the earning of a company appear more, due to dominance factors of non-operating income. But earnings must be more generated through the business activities of the company. The investor should know that the earnings of the company may have highly influenced by such factors as "change in sales, cost reduction programme, the method of depreciation adopted, change in direct and indirect taxes".

Capital Structure: Capital structure is another important and influential factor in determining the earnings of the company. At present, earning of profit by increasing selling price is not possible due to severe competition in the market. Hence, the companies are forced to reduce their revenue expenses substantially. The reduction in expenses may stimulate the earnings level of the company. Capital is necessary for every business enterprise. Capital is available at specified cost. The cost of capital is a financial expense, which is chargeable to the profit and loss account. A higher amount of financial expense, leads to show impact on earnings of the company. At present environment, only share capital is not sufficient to run the companies smoothly. In addition to equity, debt is necessary for smooth functioning of the company. Debt is compulsory like death is natural to human being. All companies exist in the market, may not be in a position to avoid the debt content in their capital structure. The combination of debt and equity is known as capital structure. The debt equity mix ratio is necessary for all legal formalities as per the provisions of the Companies Act. A high debt composition in the capital structure may show pressure on earnings of the company.

Boardroom Skills: The companies are managed by the board of directors. The board of directors is the legal organs to run the business enterprise. The board is a combination of different persons with a lot of skills in their respective fields. Hence, the efficiency of the top level management may influence the earning capacity of a company. A strong top level management can easily generate more revenue with their experience, talent and skills. At present all companies are giving priority to appoint professional managers. Professionalism in corporate sector will definitely stimulate the levels of earnings. The basic objective of financial management is to maximize return and minimize risk. The business is a game between risk and return; the efficient management escapes the risk and captures return. The good management has some essential characteristics which are presented below:

1. Getting things done by people
2. Leadership qualities
3. Analytical skills
4. Influencing behavior

In professional management environment, every level of managerial performance is evaluated against their targets and objectives. The investor further analyzes the capabilities and abilities of managerial personnel are presented below:

(a) Background, educational qualifications and experience of the managers
(b) The review of top level management record over the past years.
(c) The managerial skill can be found by observing the market share of the business.
(d) The investor should verify about the company's future plan of expansion. He must observe the strength of the company either in expansion or diversification. The horizontal or vertical expansion is a good sign of an efficient management.
(e) The investor should further analyze about the managements' capability in carrying out proper production schedules and maintaining good level of inventory stocks.
(f) The financial strength of the company should also be analyzed.
(g) The relationship between employees and management of the company must be taken into consideration. A good relation between workforce, employees and management enhances the productivity levels of the company.
(h) The adoption of scientific management technique influences the profitability of the company. Therefore, the investor should analyze all the influencing factors to boost the company's earnings.

Operating Skills: The earnings of a company depends upon operating skills of a business concern. The growing company must work for utmost satisfaction of the consumers. A high operating efficiency company produces goods at lower cost. A stable form creates stable profit. The operating efficiency can be measured through operating leverage. Operating leverage means, involving fixed cost component in the company's total cost. If the fixed cost is high in the total cost of a production it is said to be high degree of operating leverage. Therefore, the operating efficiency of a firm determines the earning capabilities of the company.

Financial Performance: Financial performance occupies a dominant role in making investment decisions by the investors. It can be observed with the help of the financial analysis. An analysis of a business concern will be with reference to the financial analysis. Analysis means methodical classification of the given data. The data is more useful in analysis of a business concern. Financial statement is an organized collection of data according to logical and accounting procedures. The aim of financial analysis is to know whether the firm is working efficiently or not? Financial statements provide historical and present information about the company's operations. Historical data helps to predict the future. Financial statements can be classified into the following aspects:

1. Income statement
2. Balance sheet
3. Statement of retained earnings
4. Statement of changes in financial position

1. Income Statement

Income statement is also known as profit and loss a/c. it is associated with the financial data. It reveals the result of operations between two balance sheet dates. It consists of revenue expenditure and revenue receipts. It shows the net profit earned or net loss by a firm during a particular period. The excess of revenue expenditure is known as net profit. Net profit earned by the company during a financial year is the barometer for study of analysis.

2. Balance Sheet

Balance sheet is a document which contains liabilities and assets of a business organization. It reflects the financial position of a company at a specified moment of time. Every commercial enterprise should prepare balance sheet to fulfill the legal provisions of the various acts. It represents all assets owned by the business at a particular moment of time and claims of the owners. It shows all the financial information related to the company during a particular period of time. Financial strength of a business concern can be observed from balance sheet. Balance sheet is an accumulation of fact data. It consists of historical data. Historical data is useful for prediction.

3. Statement of Retained Earnings

The accumulation of excess earnings over expenses is known as "retained earnings". The available net profit is transferred from income statement to balance sheet is called as "retained earnings". It is relational factor between income statement and balance sheet. The large amount of retained earnings shows the financial muscle of the company. A vast amount of reserve, retained earnings makes a company to grow substantially for expansion and diversification. Every year the available surplus amount of profits will be transferred to balance sheet. The pool of funds can be utilised by the company for business purpose. A higher amount of surplus funds will halt the borrowings of the company. The reduction of borrowing saves substantial amount of revenue expenditure.

4. Statement of Changes in Financial Position (SCFP)

The income statement exposes the net profit earned by a company. The balance sheet reveals the financial status of a commercial enterprise at a specified moment of time. But these two statements never show about the movement of circulating capital. Hence, the SCFP reveals about the movement of working capital. It also reveals about the flow of cash from the business. The changes in working capital position reflect in the SCFP. The SCFP is popularly known as "funds flow statement". The funds flow statement reveals the movement of funds. A change in cash position reveals the cash flow statement. A change in overall financial position will be reflected in "SCFP".

Financial statements are indicators of the two significant factors such as profitability and financial soundness. Profitability can be obtained from the income statement. The balance sheet exposes the financial soundness of a commercial enterprise.

Types of Financial Analysis

Financial analysis can be made through the study of various financial statements. Financial analysis can be done by various persons for various purposes. It can be classified into different categories depending upon the following sources:

1. Information
2. *Modus operandi*

On the basis of data, the financial analysis can be categorized as external analysis and internal analysis. External analysis will be carried out by outsiders of the company. They include investors, credit agencies, government agencies, other creditors. These people will depend on the published financial statements. This kind of analysis serves only a limited purpose. Internal analyses are carried out by company executives and employees. Sometimes the officers will also carry out this analysis and instruction received from court or from a government. This analysis will be done with specific objectives.

On the basis of *modus operandi*, financial analysis can be of two types. A. horizontal analysis, B. vertical analysis.

A. **Horizontal analysis:** In case of this type of analysis, financial statement for a number of years are reviewed and analyzed. The current year's figures are compared with the standard or base year. The analysis statement usually contains figures for two or more years and the changes are shown regarding each item from the base year usually in the form of percentage. Such an analysis gives the management considerable insight into levels and areas of strength and weakness. Since this type of analysis is based on the data from year to year rather than on one data, it is also termed as 'dynamic analyses'.

B. **Vertical analysis:** In case of this type of analysis a study is made of the quantitative relationship of the various items in the financial statements on a particular date. For example, the ratios of different items of cost for a particular period may be calculated with the sales per that period. Such an analysis is useful in comparing the performance of several companies in the same group or divisions or departments in the same company. Since this analysis depends on the data for one period, this is not very conducive to a proper analysis of the company's financial position. It is also called 'static analyses' as it is frequently used for referring to ratios developed on one date or for one accounting period.

Analysis of Financial Statement

Financial statement contains available information regarding the worth of a company. A statement can be analyzed in different ways as per the intention of the analyst. Hence, the financial statements expose a number of hidden facts about the organization. The statements deal with the financial aspects of a company during a particular period of time. The following steps are involved in financial statement analysis:

(a) Methodical classification

(b) Financial tools

(a) Methodical classification: Analysis requires a careful study of data in a chronological order. In order to have a meaningful analysis, it is necessary that the data should be arranged in a systematic manner. The statements are prepared in a manner to suit the needs and convenience of the analyst. The data will be arranged in two kinds of statement which are presented below:

1. Income statement/Operating statement
2. Balance sheet

(b) Financial tools: The analyst can make analysis with help of the company data. There are many techniques available to make a more meaningful comparison:

1. Comparative financial statements
2. Common size financial statements
3. Trend percentage
4. Fund flow analysis
5. Cash flow analysis
6. Cost volume profit analysis
7. Ratio analysis

Comparative financial statement reveals about the financial position of the company. In this statement data for two or more periods are placed side by side to facilitate comparison more meaningful. The statements consist of comparative income statement and comparative balance sheet. The income statement reveals the net profit or net loss from business activities of the company. The statement indicates the absolute data for two or more periods. The analyst can make a comparison between two periods about the profitability of company. The analyst can understand the performance of the company by seeing the statement which is arranged in a meaningful way. Hence, it will be more useful to the reader. Comparative balance sheet is useful to study about the trends in a business enterprise. The statement indicates about changes in increase or decrease in assets and liabilities of the company. A single balance sheet is enough for study about the financial performance of the company during a particular period of time.

Common size financial statement is another kind of financial technique. In this statement, figures are converted into percentages to some common base. The base is assumed to be 100 and all figures are expressed as a percentage of the total. These statements are useful for studying the comparative financial position of two or more businesses.

Trend percentages are useful in making a comparative study of financial statements for several years. Any year will be taken as base for company. An adjustment should be made in the light of price level changes rising during a specified period of time.

Funds flow analysis is one of the important tools to the financial analyst. Funds flow statement reveals the changes in working capital position. It reveals about the utilization and procurement of funds. The analysis will be useful in estimating about the company's financial position and policies.

Cost volume profit analysis is another important tool of profit planning. It is realized that, this technique is not used for analysis of financial statement. But it is an important tool for the management for decision making. It indicates about the relationship cost, volume of production, sales and profit. It further indicates about the break-even point, cost of production, volume of sales, selling price and cost. It also reveals about the quantity to be produced and sold in order to get the desired profit levels of the company.

Ratio analysis is the most important tool available to the analysts. Ratios are the powerful tools in analyzing the two figures. Ratios are calculated for different purposes. Ratios indicate a mathematical relationship between two figures. Gross profit ratio, current asset ratio, etc., are used as a yardstick for evaluating the financial status and performance of a business concern. There are many ratios which express information about the financial performance of a commercial enterprise. They are expressed in two ways: (a) times, (b) percentage. They can be classified into different categories. Basically they are classified into two kinds:

(a) Traditional

(b) Functional

(a) Traditional: Ratios are the tools for financial analysis. The traditional ratios are further classified as follows:

1. Profit and Loss a/c ratios
2. Balance sheet ratios
3. Composite ratios:

Profit and Loss a/c ratios will be calculated from the items of income statement. Income statement is also called as profit and loss a/c., these items are drawn from the P&L a/c only. For example, gross profit ratio, stock turnover ratio, net profit ratio.

Balance sheet ratios are related with balance sheet items. The components of balance sheet items will be taken for calculation purpose. For example, current ratio, debt equity ratio etc.

Composite ratios are also called as inter statement ratios. Ratios are related to profit and loss a/c and balance sheet. For example, fixed assets turnover ratio, overall profitability ratios.

(b) Functional: Functional classification of ratios is the other kind of tool for financial analysis. They have to be studied together in order to determine the profitability and solvency of the business. Functional classification of ratios, presented below:

1. Profitability ratios
2. Coverage ratios
3. Turnover ratios
4. Financial ratios

Profitability ratios are useful to bankers, financial institutions and creditors. It shows the efficiency of a company regarding its performance. The operational performance can be measured through this kind of ratios. Poor operational performance reveals poor sales and lower profits. A lower profit is an indication of the lack of control over expenses. The top level management and owners of the firms are interested to know the profitability regarding deployment of their funds and efforts. They are further classified as follows:

(a) Overall profitability ratio
(b) Earnings per share
(c) Price earnings ratio
(d) Gross profit ratio
(e) Net profit ratio
(f) Operating ratio
(g) Payout ratio
(h) Dividend yield ratio

Overall profitability ratios are also called as return on investment. The return on investment is also known as return on capital employed. It reveals the efficient utilization of funds by the company during a particular period of time.

Earnings per share are the most important ratio in the stock market. It is more useful to the investors in the stock market for taking a decision regarding his investment. It is the part of the overall profitability ratio. The EPS helps in assessment of a market share price of the equity share of the company. It measures the capacity of the earning power of a company. A high EPS is the measurement of better utilization of resources of the company.

Price earnings ratio is another important ratio in the stock market. The ratio indicates the number of times the earning per share is covered by its market price. It helps the investors in making investment decisions in the stock market. It indicates about a particular share, whether the share price is overvalued or underpriced.

Gross profit ratio is another important ratio to measure the operating efficiency of the company. It reveals relationship between gross profit and net sales of the company.

Net profit ratio indicates about the capability of the earning power by commercial enterprises. The ratio is more useful to the investors in the stock market for taking investment decisions. An increase in the net profit over the previous year indicates the efficiency of the company. An investor can take a decision whether to buy scrip or not.

Operating ratio deals with the operating expenses of a company. It is also known as expenses ratio. It indicates the expenses incurred by a company with high or low leverage. The operating costs include the cost of material, direct labor and factory or office or selling overheads. Financial expenses such as taxation and interest elements will be excluded. It gives caution to the top level management regarding control of expenses.

Payout ratio is associated with the payment of dividend to shareholders. The dividend will be paid by the company as per the profits earned by it. If the retention ratio is low, naturally the payout ratio will be more and shareholders enjoy the dividend amount. The payout ratio is also called as retained earnings ratio.

Dividend yield ratio is associated with investor's interest. A high rate of dividend may please the investors to patronage the company in future.

Coverage Ratio

Coverage ratios are associated with either shareholders or debentureholders of the company. It indicates about the repayment of agreed interest amount or dividend. The interest or dividend may be paid as per the agreement made by both parties. It can be further classified into three types, such as:

(a) Fixed interest cover ratio

(b) Fixed dividend cover ratio

(c) Debt service coverage ratio

Fixed interest cover ratio is related to the payment of interest to lenders of the company. It reveals that if the business earns sufficient profits, the lenders will be happy, otherwise they are involved in risk.

Turnover Ratios

Turnover ratios are related to the efficient utilization of funds by the company. It reveals about the efficiency regarding the capital employed/deployed in the business. It indicates about the overall profitability of the business enterprise. The turnover ratios can be classified into two methods:

(a) Net profit ratio

(b) Turnover ratio

The turnover ratios further can be divided into two kinds. They are:

1. Fixed assets turnover ratio
2. Working capital turnover ratio

Financial Ratios

Financial ratios are the most important tools in financial analysis. They indicate about the financial status of the company. They are classified into two kinds:

(a) Liquidity ratio

(b) Stability ratio

Liquidity ratio is related to the solvency of a business concern. Liquidity ratio is also called as short-term solvency ratio. They are classified into the following kinds:

1. Current ratio
2. Quick ratio
3. Super quick ratio
4. Defensive interval ratio

Stability ratios are related to long-term solvency of the company can be classified as follows:

(a) Fixed assets ratio

(b) Capital structure ratio

The ratios are power tools in the hands of financial analysts or researchers. Purpose wise classifications of ratios are presented below for ready reference:

1. Liquidity ratios

2. Assets utilization ratios
3. Profitability ratios
4. Appropriation ratios
5. Capitalization ratios
6. Coverage ratios
7. Coverage of senior charges
8. Financial stability ratios

Hence, the ratios have some advantages and disadvantages. But simply the ratios are conveying more messages to the analyst and the future of a particular company. However, it is more useful for prediction.

Present Price

The share prices in the stock market are highly influenced by a number of factors. The share value of a particular company depends upon the following factors:

(i) Past price
(ii) Price earnings ratio
(iii) Economic environment
(iv) Stock market situation

Past price of stock is the most important factor before going to buy particular scrip. Though past performance is not a guarantee for the future price of the stock, but it reveals about the attitude of the stock market. The historical price of stock reveals about the 52 weeks with high and low price ranges of the scrip. It enables the investor whether to buy or not to buy a scrip.

Price earnings ratio is the most common financial parameters used in the stock market. It associates the share price with earnings per share. The media will provide the PE ratios for all traded shares in the stock market. A high PE ratio reveals high expectation of the market regarding the growth of future earnings of the company. The PE ratio is influenced by other factors such as dividend growth rates and low cost of funds. It helps investor to make a comparison about the PE ratio with the company and industry. It is better to purchase the scrip when it is available underpriced. A PE ratio is lower than industry ratio is known as under expected PE ratio, the stock is overpriced. Therefore, it is better to sell when the share commands overprice. However, the investor should know about the intrinsic value of the share. The true economic worth of the share is called as intrinsic value of share.

Economic environment is another important factor in determination of present price levels of a share in the stock market. The monetary policy, the fiscal policy, finance bill, industrial policy and legislation of various acts can influence the stock market prices immediately. The routine activities of the RBI, SEBI, Department of company affairs, company law board, ministry of finance also influences the present prices of shares in the stock market.

Stock market environment is one of the influential factors of the share price. Stock market is a highly volatile market. The share prices are fluctuated for a small incidence in the economy. For example, a change in interest rates, a change in gold prices, a change in foreign exchange prices, hence, the investor should be more cautious in the stock market.

Shareholder Value Creation

The concept of finance has been changed due to liberalization, globalization and privatization. All these policies have been putting pressure on money. These policies encourage the industrialists to deploy their financial resources in the business environment. Hence, a lot of pressure arises on the supply of money. Hence, the importance of finance has been noticed and recognized by the business sector on global basis. The globalization policy has changed the situation in reduction of distance between two nations by providing international communication, global transport and foreign technological collaboration etc. The aviation policy of the central government has shown a great impact on business environment. The flights of international carriers became just like city bus service. Therefore, availability of transportation made the foreigners to think about investments in India. The central government is also proactive to attract the FDI. The globe is rotating on the supply of money. The digital economy requires higher skills, talent, and experts in all aspects of the business. Privatization policy aims to encourage the private persons in the business aspects to meet the growing needs of the global citizens. In the same situation the government reduces its role from the business environment due to its inefficient management of business enterprises under their control. A loss making public sector enterprise forced the government to disappear from the market and pushing the private parties before the customers. Privatization will make some benefits to the customers due to heavy competition in the market. Therefore, the government occupied a place only as an industry regulator. It is the better situation to the customers to enjoy the benefits from the market due to competitive environment. The government need not do business, but must only encourage more players in the market. Competition is the most important factor in the business aspects. The government should create a good healthy competitive environment in the market. In the competitive world, only efficiency will get success. Liberalization policy provides a good environment for establishing the industries. It encourages entrepreneurs by removing unnecessary clearances from the government. The time clearance of the licences and all legal formalities had been reduced drastically. Now the central government and all state governments are approaching the big industrial houses for setting up of units in their respective states. Therefore, all state governments are maintaining good relations with prospective entrepreneurs. After implementation of these policies, a lot of demand for finance has increased. India has a strong potential investor's base to develop the industrial sector. The power of middle class family savings cannot be ignored. They contribute higher amount of financial resources in the form of shares and debentures. All initial public offerings are being over-subscribed in the primary market. All companies are raising financial resources from the market for their expansion or diversification process. A lot of competition emerged among the companies to attract the public money. Hence, the companies are giving assurance to their shareholders for stimulating the value for their money. All financial and corporate policies have been framed according to the needs and convenience of the shareholders. The financial policies and strategy are directed towards the shareholders value creation. The traditional method of management techniques have been replaced by the modern and innovative technology. The latest technology and trends have changed the way of corporate sector. The corporate finance policy should be developed in the context of the strategic decision making power. Strategy is a plan for achieving a major goal. The corporate sector at present is always thinking about the shareholder value creation. The shareholder value can be created by the following factors:

(a) Strategic decision making framework

(b) Financial goals of the firms

(a) Strategic decision making framework: Strategy consists of multiple goals and objectives pursued by the corporate sector to satisfy its desires. The success of the corporate sector depends upon competitive edge and resources deployment of the firms. The shareholder should examine the competitiveness, capabilities and managerial skills of the company before purchasing the scrip. The firm's effectiveness is determined by the efficiency. Financial policies can influence the efficiency of a business enterprise. The primary focus on strategy is efficiency and it depends upon the following factors:

1. Strategic choice
2. Strategic financial management
3. Strategic investment policy
4. Strategic financing policy

1. Strategic choice: Strategic choice is one of the important factors in strategic decision making framework. It consists of various portfolio models. The business portfolio models are more popular to understand market situation. The investor should observe about the understanding capabilities of the market situation by the company. The existence of the firm is based on market growth, market share, cost and cash flow patterns, capital intensity and product maturity. The assessment of market growth is an important factor which influences the market capture. The market growth, market share model is the simple model of business portfolios. It is popularized by the Boston Consulting Group. The business enterprises are grouped in specified categories. They are presented below:

(a) Stars
(b) Cows
(c) Wild cats
(d) Dogs

Star category companies are well known companies. They are well reputed and regulated brands in the market. They are best performers and shows higher capabilities, efficiency in capturing market. Their brands are well established and well recognized in the market. They acquired customer satisfaction by providing higher quality goods, lower price, after sales service, etc., they are generally financial muscled companies. They acquire large amount of profits and having large amount of reserves and accumulated surplus.

Cows are another category companies which are declining stars. They provide cash to be utilised in the firm.

Dogs are one of the grouped companies and financially a weak competitive position held in the market. There is as little chance to grow in the market. They are facing many problems to generate little amount of profit. Existence and survival in the market is not a simple task for these companies. They will attempt to liquidate or selling their assets to survive in the market.

Wild cats category companies are attempting to become as star companies. They are trying to capture the market in a rapidly growing market. They are waiting for bigger opportunities. They are interested to enhance the firm's abilities, skills, efficiency and talents. They require higher amount of funds to achieve desired goals. These firms are mostly concentrated on reducing inefficiency and enhancing the efficiency.

The Boston Consulting Group developed a model to achieve the desired goals by the companies. The model implies that cash surplus from cash cows should be transferred to wild cats, for achieving their financial goals. The BCG indicates that dogs have no chance of improvement. The group reveals that experience in business stimulates the market share. The market leaders usually have a competitive dominance. They enjoy the lower cost due to mass production undertaking. It is not a simple task to get dominant role in the market share from competitors. Every company shall deploy its abilities and resources to capture the market from its competitors. The high competitive environment in the market forces the firms to reduce the prices substantially. A pressure on profits is necessary in the competitive environment. The success of a business firm needs a balanced portfolio of products or business. The strategic position of a firm is determined by market share and profitability.

2. Strategic financial management: The basic task of a finance manager involves in acquisition of funds and allocation of resources. The main aim of the business is to maximize the wealth of shareholders. The finance manager shall make decisions that will increase the shareholders stake in the firm. The efficient capital markets enable investors to lend or borrow funds. The capital markets are always discounted by the information.

Strategic management considers all markets, including product, labor and capitals as imperfect and changing. Strategies are made to manage the firm in uncertain situation. Therefore, the management has to analyze changing market conditions and environment to make predictions and allocation of resources. The shareholders are not only interested in the firm's activities but also other influentials constitutes such as lenders, employees, customers, suppliers, competitors, government and society. The strategic management focuses on growth, profitability and flow of funds rather than on the maximization of the market value of share.

3. Strategic investment policy: Investment decisions shows impact on the profitability of the firm. Strategic investments are generally involving large amount of expenditure. Strategic investment decisions are based on both quantitative and qualitative analysis. The business portfolio approaches can be very useful in identifying investment opportunities. A balanced portfolio of projects can create a lot of synergistic values. The financial theory reveals that the firm's diversification is not useful to shareholders. In undeveloped capital market diversification is an appropriate corporate strategy. It reduces corporate risk. Risk is an important aspect in the business. Its analysis is an important task of strategic management. Strategic management involved in managing total risk. At present, the survival in the business is a successful phenomenon in the corporate environment. A commercial enterprise is always threatened by many factors such as competition, technological obsolescence, labor relations, government policies, etc., hence, the invest policy may stimulate the shareholders value by making appropriate decisions in the business.

4. Strategic financing policy: Finance is the provision of money. Money is the essential element on the earth. Money is a facilitator for the smooth functioning of the firms. Money earns money and rotates with commercial motive. The procurement and allocation of financial resources depends upon the firm's policies. Generally all firms will depend upon the following financing aspects:

(a) External financing

(b) Internal financing

External financing means procuring financial resources from outside the firm. The procurement of funds depends upon the debt policy of the firm. Borrowing from the capital market or money market is known as external finance. Usually every company desires to keep high credit worthiness for their issuing financial assets. The firms will generally avoid debt component of their capital structure. But debt is necessary in changing business environment. At present debt component dominates the capital structure of the corporate sector. Debt threatens the profitability of the company.

Internal financing is the reflection of financial soundness of the firm. The reserves and surplus accumulated profit undistributed profits, depreciation funds are best examples of internal finance. A large amount of earnings may not be distributed by the company to its shareholders. A high retention policy of the company facilitate for provisions or internal finance. A low payout ratio dissatisfies the shareholders. But high retention policy may stimulate the shareholders values with a large amount of savings in the form of financial costs. Internal financing is the cheapest and best sources of the money supply.

(b) Financial goals of the firm: Goal is a long-term phenomenon. Financial goals are framed by the company itself. It is associated with the quantitative expressions of a company's mission. The empirical research in America reveals that profit is not always a priority element. Financial priorities are changed due to changes in economic and competitive environment. Financial goals are changeable and unstable. The finance managers find it difficult to understand and accept the goal. There are demand-related goals and supply-related goals. Demand-related goal is associated with sales growth of a company. Supply-related goals concentrates on earning of better returns. It also focuses on payment of dividend to shareholders and reduction of financial cost through internal financing. The Indian companies are rotating in the market for achieving the following financial goals:

(a) Maximizing the levels of network, profit and market value.

(b) Maximizing the ROI, net profit, market share

(c) Maximizing the growth in assets and sales

(d) Sufficient funds at disposal

However, the common investor should observe the following parameters before making his investment decisions in specified company scrip:

1. Cash flow per share
2. Price earnings ratio
3. Market value per share
4. Book value of net worth
5. Operating profit
6. Market rate of return
7. Net profit to net worth
8. Earnings per share
9. Market share
10. Return on investment

TECHNICAL ANALYSIS

Stock market is a highly volatile market. It requires higher talent, skills, imagination, foresight and risk bearing attitude by the investor. The share prices movement can be analyzed in two approaches. They are "fundamental and technical analysis". The fundamental analysis reveals about the intrinsic value of a share. It also analyses various factors such as economic environment of the nation, Industry position and company efficiency. Therefore, the intrinsic value of a share is influenced by these factors. The investor should buy shares when the share price is available at less than intrinsic value. The investor should sell the shares when the share price is higher than intrinsic value of the scrip. In stock market, knowing the intrinsic value of scrip is the most important factor. If any investor ignores this element, he will fall in risk. Technical analysis is associated with the study of price movement of the security. It deals with the trend position of the market. The investor can know the market trend whether the prices show uptrend or downtrend. The investor will make purchases, if the share prices reveal uptrend the investor may sell his shares in the downtrend for avoiding his risk position from the portfolio. It is helpful information of buying and selling strategy of the scrips in stock market. It analyses the relationship among price volume supply and demand factors. The market is based on supply and demand forces. The volume of share business in the market influences for further trading in the market. Hence, the technical analysis will help when to buy or sell the scrips. In stock market investment timing is the most important factor to get success. Enter and exit in the stock market involves either risk or return. It is based on the following assumptions:

(a) The share prices are determined by the interaction of supply and demand factors.

(b) The market knows everything.

(c) The market always reveals the trend position.

(d) The market is based on past prices to predict the future.

The above assumptions are considered while making technical analysis. The market discounts information about the business environment, and corporate financial performance. Technical analysis is based on Dow Theory. Charles H. Dow wrote a series of articles in the Wall Street Journal in 1984. Dow Theory was closely associated with the share price movement analysis. However, the technical analysis consist the following aspects:

1. Dow Theory
2. Technical indicators
3. Triangles

1. Dow Theory

Dow Theory was proposed by Charles H. Dow. He was the first editor of the Wall Street Journal. The theory reveals about the movement of prices of securities on the stock exchange. The stock prices can be studied in the following ways:

(a) Primary movements

(b) Secondary movements

(c) Daily movements

Primary movements are related to study the share price movements for a period of three years. It is associated with the study of share prices on long-term movements. The market is balanced by bulls and bears. If the market is dominated by bull operators, then it will be called a "bull phase". In bull phase the share prices increase and there is demand for more scrips. If the market is dominated by the bears, then it will be known as bear phase. The share prices are declining and more supply of shares exist in the market. The full supply of scrips reduces the market prices. If the share prices increase, it will be known as bullish market. If the share prices declines marginally, it will be known as bearish market. Hence, the primary movements may be upward or downward. The trend between upward and downward is called "intermediate trend" or corrective movements. This corrective movement is related to 3 weeks to 3 months.

Secondary movements are related to study the share price movements for short-term period. The share prices will be closely observed in stock exchanges from three weeks to three months. They are opposite in direction to the primary movements. In the bullish market the secondary trend would result in the fall of share prices. In the bearish market the secondary trend carries the price upward and corrects the main trends.

Daily movements are associated with the observation of share prices for each and every day. It represents irregular fluctuations in the stock exchange prices. They move without any definite trend. The fluctuations do not show any particular trend. These movements will arise due to speculative transactions. Speculation is oxygen to the stock market. The fluctuations will be rise due to participation of speculators in the stock exchange. Some investors will make gains out of these fluctuations only by a chance factor. Winning in the stock market is a chance factor for some situations. A finance manager should not depend upon these movements because he is basically an investor and not a speculator. Generally speculators will depend upon these movements for short-term gains. They are making buying and selling shares on daily basis for even a small amount of margins. In stock market, times are the most important element to enter and exit. An intelligent investor may purchase shares at lower and will sell as market prices rise. Hence, the investor should be termed as identification of the turn in the stock exchange prices. Identification of the "turn" is a difficult task. If you are able to identify the turn position, you may get success in the stock market. Primary, secondary and daily movements are part of the Dow Theory. In stock market, the investors can depend upon primary and secondary movements. Speculators can depend upon daily movements, because they accept the risk. Technical analysis is the important tool in analyzing the support and resistance level of the stock market. Support level is associated with individual stock prices. A considerable demand for a particular stock is expected to prevent further fall in the price level. Hence, the fall of a share price can be halted for time being. In this situation demand for the particular share is expected in the stock market.

Resistance level is associated with reduction of share price from further increase in share price. The share price halted for the time being is called as resistance. In this situation the supply of shares would be greater than demand. The increased supply of shares will halt the further increase in share price. These two levels occupy an important role and then automatically drops, this situation is called as resistance level. If a particular share price reaches down to a certain level and then its rises is called as support level. Hence, these two levels may switch over from one level to another level. They need not be formed only on tops or bottoms. They can be depicted on the graph. It is known as trend line or gaps of the chart. Gaps mean a difference in price level between two trading days. For example, if the high price of the ACC scrip on April 2nd is ₹ 350 and on April 3rd low is ₹ 375, a gap is said to have occurred on the chart. It indicates that the share is not traded between the level ₹ 375 and ₹ 350. This gap indicates further rise in price level. The same situation is applicable in falling price levels of the share prices. A gap is formed if the low price on May 2nd is ₹ 200 and the high price on May 3rd is ₹ 180. It indicates that there was no transaction between 200 and 180.

2. Technical Indicators

Technical indicators are one of the important aspects in the technical analysis. The indicators provide valuable information about the stock market. They will indicate about the direction of the overall market. It reflects the overall market situation. It indicates about macro aspects of the secondary market operations. The overall market movements will show greater impact on the individual share price. In stock market macro analysis is useful than micro analysis of the environment. Forecasting is an important factor in the stock market. Aggregate forecasting is considered to be more reliable than the individual forecasting. Technical indicators are price and volume of trade and short sales.

Volume of trade: Technical analysis is the study about the market data. It provides full information about the stock market operations. The investors will generally collect the data before making investment decisions. They collect the past share prices, past volume of business done in particulars scrip will make the investor take decisions. Investors will get confidence in a particular scrip trading volume. The trend is based on the volume of trade for particular scrip. In bullish market, large volume of trade will be occurring. Volume expands in bullish market and down in the bearish market. The volume of trade is influenced by the price behaviour of the stock. It is a matter of concern for the investor and the trend may not continue for a longer time.

The breadth of the market: Stock market is a highly volatile market. The prices are changing on daily basis, and sometimes even on hourly basis. Hence, the investors should be always cautious before making investment decisions. The breadth of the market is associated with the study of price changes in the stock exchange. The breadth of the market consists of advances, declines and net. Advances mean the number of shares whose prices have increased from the previous day's trading. Decline means the number of shares whose prices have fallen from the previous day's trading. All these information is available in all business dailies. The net difference between the number of stock advanced and declined during the same period is the breadth of the market.

Short selling: Short selling is one of the technical indicators. It is known as short interest. It refers to the selling of shares which are not owned. It is a speculation activity. The bears are the short sellers who sell now in the hope of purchasing at a lower price in the future to acquire profits. A demand for a particular share indicates future rise of prices. This position shows the general business situations. It requires higher talent and knowledge from the investors.

Oddlot trading: Shares are generally sold in a denomination of 100. The shares, which are sold below 100 is called as Oddlot. The buyers and sellers of small lots are known as Oddlot traders. The buying and selling Oddlot make Oddlot index. The Oddlot index will be constructed on the basis of volume of business. An increase in purchase of Oddlot increases the value of Oddlot index. Selling of Oddlot leads to fall in the index. All these information is known by the professional investors. Professional investors are stronger than the oddlotters. If professional investors dominate the market, it is called as strong market. If the oddlotters dominate the market, it is known as weak market. The big Oddlot purchases make a fall in the market price.

Moving average: Generally the share prices are moving towards either increasing or decreasing way. Market indices are constructed with selected share prices. Moving means a change in mobility of a particular thing. Moving average means that the body of data moves ahead by absorbing latest things. The trend can be studied by smoothing of the data. The moving average is useful to study movement of the stock market. It also reveals the individual scrip price movement. It indicates the underlying trend in the scrip price. Trend can be determined on the basis of the period. The short-term trend is associated with the study of moving averages for 10 days to 30 days. In case of medium-term trend 50 days to 125 days. The long-term is related to 200 days. Hence, the study can be made for the factors, i.e., index and individual stock prices. The professional investors will observe the individual stock prices before making investment decisions. They will compare the individual stock price with the indices to know the bullish or bearish trend. The technical analysis may plot the movements on graph paper. If NSE or BSE index is above stocks moving average line, it indicates bullish trend. If the BSE or NSE is below the stocks moving average, it indicates bearish market. If the moving average of the individual stock is above the index average, it indicates sell signal and the same situation in reverse indicates buy signal. The moving average is useful when to buy and sell shares in the stock market. A comparison should be made between stock price and stock prices moving average. A comparison can also be made between long-term and short-term moving averages. The comparison will reveal the buy or sell signal.

Oscillators: Oscillator means moving from one place to another place. The share prices are changing in the stock market on day to day basis. The investor should always be cautious in the stock market before making his investment decisions. Oscillators indicate the market momentum or scrip momentum. It refers to the velocity of price changes. It is measured by the rate of change of prices. It covers the short or a longer period. The short-term oscillators may reveal the price change for 5 or 10 days. The long-term period 3 to 6 months may also be covered by oscillators. The oscillators may move in the same direction, either positive or negative depending on the trends of the market.

Relative strength index: Relative strength index is one of the oscillators. It is used for identifying the inherent strength or weakness of a particular scrip. This theory was developed by Wells Wilder. It can be calculated for particular scrip by applying the following formula:

RSI = 100 – 100/1+RS

RS = average gain per day/average loss per day

It is calculated for 5, 7, 9 and 14 days.

A case study of Siemens India presented below:

Date	Price	Gain	Loss
8-4-11	1690.60	---	---
11-4-11	1701.35	10.75	---
12-4-11	1715.20	13.85	---
13-4-11	1742.20	27.00	---
15-4-11	1744.75	2.25	---
		53.85	---

53.85/4 = 13.46

RSI = 100 – 100/1 + 13.46 = 100 – 7.42 = 92.58

Charts: Charts are one of the tools in the technical analysis. They represent the information which is more easily understood by a layman. It is the easiest tool to analyze the data. It helps to know the trend of the share prices. It reveals the current situation of the stock market. It shows the past movements of particular scrip. The analysts can use these charts according to their needs and convenience. The charts require higher skills to handle the situation, otherwise they will become dangerous. The charts can be classified as follows:

(a) Figure charts

(b) Bar charts

3. Triangles

Figure charts help the investor to find out the trend of the price without any difficulty. They are useful for technical analysts. The share price movement of a particular stock or market indices can be found with the help of these charts. They are one dimensional presentation of data. They are unable to indicate about time or volume. A comparison of current price with previous prices can be made with the help of figure charts. They are drawn in the ruled paper. They are simple but have certain limitations such as non-indication of intraday price movement. Volume will not be taken into consideration in picturisation of charts. Volume and trend of direction is the most important for taking investment decisions by the investors. In bull market price rise is accompanied by high volume of trading. The bear market is related to low volume of trading due to decrease in share prices. Bar chart is another kind of charts. It is the simplest and most commonly used tool of a technical analysis.

Triangles are one of the tools in technical analysis. They are easily predictable and popular method. They can be classified into three kind's (a) symmetrical, (b) ascending, and (c) descending. Symmetrical triangle is built up with series of fluctuations. It does not have any bias towards the bull and bear operators. Ascending triangle reveals about the upward movement of the share price. Descending triangle indicates downward movement of share price. It is associated with the bear operator's movement.

Elliot Wave Theory

Stock market is highly volatile market. The investors should always be cautious in the stock market. The behavior of the stock market can be studied through various number of theories. Technical analysis is the study of data regarding stock market prices. It is fully involved in analysis of the stock market behavior. Ralph Elliot introduced a theory about the stock market behavior. He conducted various empirical studies and tested rules for his theory. According to this, the stock market is unfolded through the basic rhythm or pattern. The basic rhythm consist of five up waves and three down waves to form a complete cycle of 8 waves. The rhythm is reflected in various cycles and waves. One complete cycle consists of bullish and bearish phases. Hence, the waves are balancing each other and the stock market will be in stabilized manner. In a complete cycle there are 5 bullish and 3 bearish waves occuring. The cycle consist total number of 8 waves. The waves are based on the principle that action is followed by reaction. After the completion of 8 waves, there will be a fresh cycle starting with similar impulses arising out of market trading, change of sentiment in the market. The stock market is continuously rotating like these cycles consisting of 8 waves. This theory was empirically tested and found accurate and timeliness of rising waves. The waves and cycles are useful in identifying the buy and sell signal in the stock market. A lot of empirical study has been carried out by the researchers that the behavior of prices on the stock market confirms to the cycles and waves. It is proved that the theory is acceptable to predict the prices of shares. The wave is the most important element in this theory. The wave indicates the movement of the market price. The waves are emerging from the demand and supply pressures on the market. A demand exceeds supply; there will be a rise in share prices. A supply exceeds demand, there will be a chance leading to a down trend in the prices. Bullish phase rises when supply exceeds demand position of the market. Hence, the waves are generated depending upon the pressure of the situation. This theory had also explained that the stock market behavior was in a consistent manner. Therefore, wave theory is fully based on waves and cycles. The waves are an integral part of the reflection of mass psychology. In some situation, these waves' counts are not clear, the shape and length may vary depending on the buying and selling pressures. But an experienced analyst can discern the waves in both upward and downward directions. This theory offers the tools of identifying the market turns and their approach. It has some limitations that, the rhythms may not be consistent and the count number may not be possible.

Efficient Market Theory

Markets are generally dynamic. They are influenced by many factors. Stock markets are very delicate and they will react even to a small incident occurring in the economic, political, and business environment. They are influenced by money flows and information flows. Information is most powerful tool in the hands of experts. The market prices are determined by the supply and demand factors. Hence, demand and supply elements in business cannot be ignored. They are the foundation for growing dynamic market. The markets are becoming more competitive and they discount every information. The prices are the reflection of the present situation after absorbing the latest information. Hence, this situation is called as "efficient market". The free flow of information is discounted by the market and absorbed by it in the form of reflection of price changes. Efficiency means abilities and acquiring skills. The efficient market theory is based on free flow of information and malpractices. Malpractices in the market exist in many ways. There are no monopoly elements in the market. Information flow is free and costless. In the normal business environment, money flows towards profit. Profitability is the indication of efficiency and competitiveness. Money flows from less profitable to more profitable avenues. Hence, the profit element dictates the flow of money. The information is available to all the investors, which is immediately reflected in the stock prices and nobody can gain additional profit. All financial instruments will be correctly priced and all the information is absorbed by then and any investor entering the market at anytime will have the same advantage. There is no excess profit available to any investor. If the information is exposed to the public, there is no extra profit waiting for any investor. The profit is available to those who react immediately to the latest information available in the market. The risk or return depends upon the reaction of the exposed market information content and the investor's acceptance level of risk. If the demand and supply forces are playing their role freely, the prices are reflecting suitable to the situation. The prices are fair and move in a random manner. Prices are changing in the market on day to day forces and move in an independent and random manner. This situation has lead to concept of randomness. The randomness leads to random walk theory. Random walk theory is associated with market price behavior. It is better to understand the random walk theory before going to study about the efficient market theory.

Random Walk Theory

Random walk theory explains that changes in stock prices are independent and no factor can be influenced. The current prices are independent of the past trends. The information can influence the price levels. This theory was tested by researchers on the basis of empirical work on the market price behavior. The equilibrium price of a stock is determined by demand and supply forces. This theory is based on the following assumptions:

Assumptions

1. Market is dynamic and no one can influence it.
2. Market knows all current information and prices are reflected by absorbing latest development.
3. All investors have free access to the same information and no one can gain additional profits.
4. Market prices are changing due to changes in the fundamentals.
5. There is no scope for insider information.
6. Market cannot be influenced by institutional investors and bulk purchasers.
7. There is no scope for manipulations in the market.
8. Competition in the market exists at all times.

The prices are changing in the market due to change in the fundamental factors. Fundamental analysis is associated with the assessment of intrinsic value of a share. The fundamental factors influence the equilibrium prices. This theory is based on the capital market efficiency theorem. It is considered as restatement of efficient market theory by some analysis. According to this theory stock exchange prices can never be predicted since they are based on statistical ups and downs. Therefore, the behaviors of stock prices are absolutely unpredictable. Information is a powerful weapon in the hands of professional investors and fund managers. Usually there are three kinds of information and inside information. All these sources of information are same to all kinds of investors but all these types are not absorbed perfectly by the market. There is a possibility of some gaining return from the investment.

A lot of research has been carried out to test random walk theory. Empirical tests were conducted both in the past and present in India and abroad. These tests to some extent support the theory. The price changes of today are independent of the past price. The following tests have been carried out by researchers in connection with the validity of random walk theory:

(a) Filter test

(b) Run test

(c) Correlation test

(d) Other tests

Filter means fixing of a ceiling rate in price variation of scrip. The change in prices are permitted to a particular scrip must be in the horizon of 10 per cent. The scrips are not permitted to grow beyond the certain levels of prices. Filtering is the observation of important information affecting the prices from unimportant things. Filter tests were conducted by well known researchers Fama, Blume and Alexander. They found that filter tests did not give conclusive proofs.

Run test is associated with the study of price changes in same direction. This test is conducted by Fama. It is based on time series data and used to test the theory. Run tests are conducted by the following method.

For example: associated cement company share prices.

350, 352, 356, 362, 360, 365, 370, 360-10

An increase in price changes in the same direction shows + sign. The count number of signs with no change will be assigned 0. A change in price declines will be assigned – sign. The above data shows that there are no price dependencies. As per the test, yesterday's price neither indicates today's price nor tomorrow's price. Several research works have been conducted and found that security prices moved in a random manner.

Correlation Test

Correlation test is associated with the study of movement of stock prices. It is used to measure the extent of association of one series of security prices with a series in the past. Moore is associated to test this theory. He measured the correlation coefficient of price changes of particular scrip for one week. He also measured the changes for later week of same scrip. He found that a price rise did not show the tendency to the price fall in any predictable manner.

Other Tests

Several empirical studies have been conducted to test the hypothesis. Brownian is one of the persons to study motion of a share price. Several persons involved in research to study the price changes in the market. Levy, Jensen, Bennington and Osborne were associated with the tests. All these tests reveal that price changes in the present period are independent of the past trends. Similarly some of the authors conducted empirical tests in mutual fund performance. Sharpe, Jenson were associated with the study of mutual fund performance. They found that insider information is not found to earn any additional profits.

Efficient Market Theory

Efficient market theory is the study about price behaviour of the market. A market in which asset price will reflect all available information quickly and accurately. The market efficiency theory reveals that prices are the result of free flow of information which the market absorbs quickly and efficiently. It is based on correct information. In stock market, information plays a vital role in making investment decisions. Information provides a clear picture about future trend. Professional investors must acquire information to update their portfolio. Information enhances the skills and provide a confidence way. It is a value addition factor. There are three types of information which affect the market, i.e., past prices, public information and inside information. These three types of information may show impact on the stock prices. The analysts have placed the market absorption under the following heads:

(a) Weak form

(b) Semi-strong form

(c) Strong form

(a) Weak form of efficient market hypothesis: The weak form absorbs only market price information. A lot of research has been carried about the weak form. The research proves that the weak form holds good as it is not possible to gain more from the price information of the market. The weak form is closely related to the random walk hypothesis. The past prices are not necessarily representing the present prices. The present prices move independently and there is no relation to predict the future.

(b) Semi-strong form: Semi-strong form is the second component in the information content. It is associated with price information and also other public information. According to this formula, the market absorbs quickly and efficiently, not only the price information but also publicly available information. We have already discussed about the power of information. Information in India is easily available in the market. Public information is available to the investors in the form of financial reports balance sheet, P&L a/c, earnings, dividend reports, financial results, etc., a number of financial dailies, magazines, journals carry a wide variety of reports concerning financial aspects. A plenty of information is available at the disposal of investors. The success of stock market depends upon the utilization of available information. The extraction of information stimulates the level of knowledge of the investors. All information relating to corporate activity is published in the media and immediately reported in business channels. After the spread of satellite channels, communication flow is very easy to the investors. The mega business channel CNBC provides an excellent source of information. CNBC is providing reports with analytical content and interviews with experts, general managers, managing directors, board of directors, finance managers and professional, etc., the media also report such materials like financial structure, liquidity, solvency and absorbed by the market in the price information. In the flow of information, some wrong flow in as news affecting the market. Any revision of data or changes in functioning of the company affects the share prices. Some aspects like earnings reports, bonus issues, right issues affect the market even before official announcement. Empirical research has been conducted to test the effect of any public information released, on the share prices. The studies found absorption of the information on share price was inefficient and varied from scrip to scrip and the time period. Hence, the semi-strong form is empirically not well supported. But abroad, it is found to be applicable and markets quickly absorb all published information. The public information effect has been tested through capital asset pricing model or some economic models. However, the investor's behavior should be changed. All these theories, bars, charts are ignored by them and blindly they invest in the stock market. They simply handover the cheque to the broker and they do not know about the company activities, brand names, product line, EPS, dividend declaration, experience of the top level management, skills of employees, market share of the company, market potential, consumer behavior, government policies, etc., the revolution in information and communication technology has changed the common man's lifestyle significantly.

(c) Strong form: Strong form is one of the tools in flow of information. The hypothesis is the study about the private information of insider information and unpublished data. These sources of information are absorbed by the market and represents stock prices. If any unknown information is exposed to the public, the profits are waiting for all the investors equally. The reaction to the exposed information content is in fact getting the success of highly volatile market. Any investor can gain the average return from the market. Acquiring latest information and superior analysis by professional investors can make better returns. It is also possible to get good returns for inside traders, floor brokers and institutional investors. The price movements can be forecast which only results in superior return.

The efficient market theory in its strong form is not applicable in the market. In India, it is not useful to the investors for some factors. In the Indian capital market, prices are rigged up, manipulation of prices, lack of knowledge of the investors; unqualified empirical analysis had made the failure of this theory. Institutional investors, professional investors can make use of strong form of information by appointing qualified equity market analyst. Equity market research is one of the tools for forecasting prices and identification of undervalued scrips. Equity research analysts are the right persons to capture the strong form contents. In Indian market speculation carries 80 per cent of transactions and markets are not perfect and the absorption of all types of information is also not timely and efficient. The fundamental analysis is useful for the assessment of overvaluation and under-valuation of the scrip. Investment analysis contains market research, fundamental analysis and technical analysis. Fundamental analysis is useful to a large extent and technical analysis occupies a lesser role in the context of market situations however, the efficient market hypothesis is based on certain limitations. They are presented below for a wide discussion of this topic:

1. Random walk hypothesis holds good.
2. Semi-strong form is found less useful to the investors.
3. The perfect markets do not exist in India.
4. The stocks are not representing the intrinsic value of a share.
5. Speculation and sentiment occupies a dominant role in the stock prices.
6. Information does not spread evenly among all segments of the market.
7. Investor's knowledge is very low in the stock market aspects.

Suggestions

SEBI is the most powerful organization in the capital market. It is conducting investor's conference for primary market operations. But it should provide training facilities to the secondary market investors. Empirical studies have been encouraged by the foreign markets. In India, the focus on research studies should be made by the government. Research organizations should be established and R&D wing is necessary for enhancing the levels of knowledge of the investors.

SUMMARY

All investments are risky. The return is always chased by the risk. The difference between return and risk is the gain or loss to the investors. Millions of the investors are entering the stock market for this risk and return relationship. An intelligent investor must escape the risk and capture the return by entering in stock market at right time, at right prices and right shares. Entering and exit of the stock market are the most important factor in determining the earnings of the investors. It is a simple principle, buy at low prices and sell at higher prices. The difference between two prices is the return to the investors. Buying at low price of scrip requires knowing the actual worth of scrip. This method is known as "security analysis". Security analysis refers to find out intrinsic value of a security. The intrinsic value represents the true economic worth of a financial asset. Generally, every asset has its own value. The financial asset is called as "security analysis". If you are able to find out the actual value of the asset, we can say whether it is overpriced or underpriced. The common investor does not know these intricacies, and involves in either in profit or loss. Buying an overpriced scrip leads to incurring losses and buying underpriced provides a hefty margin to the investors. The investor always invites return and avoids risk. The behavior of stock in the market depends upon latest information. Information in the stock market can discount or stimulate the share prices. The intrinsic value of a share depends upon earning potential of the company at present and also in future. Hence the information about performance of a company leads to knowledge of the intrinsic value of the share.

Key Terms

1. **Risk:** The probability of failure or loss associated with a particular course of action. A hazard covered by a contract of insurance.
2. **Risk Management:** The process, activity or study of reducing the risk of loss to a firm, particularly loss caused by accidents. Risks, once they have been identified may be reduced by: taking preventive action; setting aside a fund to pay for losses; transferring the risk to someone else, e.g., by insurance.
3. **Rigging the Market:** Rigging the market is the financial technique designed to create an artificial market which benefits a businessman. Examples are found in bull and bear activities taking place in a free economy on a large-scale.
4. **Secondary Market:** That part of the money market which deals in the exchange of marketing of securities already in issue and where dealings can be arranged in such property as unquoted stocks and shares, second mortgages, etc., which are not generally handled by the primary market.

Questions

1. What is security?
2. What do you mean by security analysis?
3. Explain about fundamental analysis?
4. What is technical analysis?
5. How can we predict the stock markets?

5 Portfolio Theory and Asset Pricing

PRECAUTIONS FOR INVESTMENT

Investment is a curb in the present consumption. The curb in consumption leads to enhancing the investment levels. All investors should make proper planning of their investments first to provide for their requirements of comfortable life with a basic need of house, real estate, physical assets, etc. He should also take care about comforts and insurance for life and make a provision for a provident fund and pension fund for a future day. Before entering into stock market, the investor should think about his prior commitments by avoiding financial crisis in his life period. They make investments in the stock market on the advice of friends, relative, agents or brokers. Hence, they should take all precautions prior to entering the stock market. The risk and return are two important factors in the portfolio management. If we want more return, we must accept more risk and if no risk is taken, simply bank deposits are opted for investment. The return is a reward to the investor. Portfolio is a combination of different financial assets. The ratio of different combination of different kinds of ingredients stimulates the taste of the drink. The portfolio return is related to risk. In the market the risk free return assets are also available to the investors. Bank deposits, post office deposits or certificates are the best examples for risk free assets. Hence, the investors may also keep these assets in their portfolios to reduce the risk levels of the portfolio. There are also high return assets available in the market. The higher return depends upon many factors like accepted level of risk, expertise in selection of financial assets, return due to diversification, etc. The return in stock market depends upon many factors.

Portfolio is a combination of different financial assets such as shares, bonds and money market instruments. The aim of the portfolio management is to minimize the risk and maximize return. The mix of blending different broad assets will provide better return with minimum risk is known as "portfolio construction". The risk can be reduced through diversification. The return can be found by altering the original portfolio. Portfolio can be classified as family. The family's good will be enhanced by some members and at the same time, it will be damaged by the other members. Hence, the portfolio return can also be enhanced through some assets. The other assets will pull down the asset values of the portfolio. In portfolio, some securities may not show performance as expected by the portfolio managers. Some other securities may show excellent performance as expected by the portfolio manager. A single security may lead to a greater actual return.

APPROACHES IN PORTFOLIO CONSTRUCTION

Portfolio is a mix of different kinds of financial instruments. All of these asset combinations may generate return. That return is reward to the investor. The return earned through portfolio indicates the capabilities and skills of the portfolio manager. Hence, the construction of portfolio is the most important factor in portfolio management. A well structured portfolio may generate sufficient and expected return. Construction of portfolio can be done in two methods:

(a) Traditional method

(b) Modern approach

(a) Traditional Method

Portfolio theory is the basis of portfolio management. It relates to the construction of a good portfolio. It is associated with efficient portfolio management in financial and physical assets including shares, debentures and bonds of various companies. A portfolio mean holding of different kind of physical assets with a view to earn return from them. In this approach, the portfolio manager needs some information about the client. He considers the needs of the client in terms of income and capital appreciation. The collected information about the client's position enables the portfolio manager to frame a good portfolio to satisfy the needs of his client. In this traditional approach, the portfolio manager will evaluate the entire financial plan of the individual or client. The traditional approach is related to construction of a good portfolio by considering the following factors:

1. Objectives of the portfolio
2. Composition of securities

1. Objectives of the Portfolio:

Portfolio is a combination of different kinds of financial assets. Financial assets will generate some rate of return or some risk. Hence, the investor's intelligence is to avoid risk or escape risk and capture the return. The game of risk and return is the yield of portfolio. The return is the barometer of efficiency. The efficiency of portfolio manager is reflected in the returns of the portfolio. Minimize the risk and maximize the return is the main motive behind in construction of best portfolio. The construction of best portfolio is influenced by many factors. Before formulating the objective of the portfolio, the hurdles faced by the client should be analyzed. Hence, the portfolio manager should frame the investors to be compensated with efficient portfolio construction. The following are the important factors in traditional approach:

(a) Hurdles

(b) Time

(a) Hurdles

Generally, the investors will invest their amount of savings in the form of portfolio. Portfolio is a combination of financial instruments which generate appropriate returns. A common man should have to face many hurdles to pool his investment in the form of portfolio. The following hurdles are faced by the common investors:

1. Revenue
2. Safety
3. Liquidity
4. Time horizon

Revenue – it is very common to expect regular revenue from his investment by the investor. Every investor expects some return from his commitment. Every investor needs some income to meet all or part of the living expenses. The inflation also erodes the purchasing power. The investor need to offset the effect of the inflation and needs income in constant rupees. Generally, investor needs money in two situational factors:

(a) Desire for present revenue
(b) Regular flow of income.

Generally, common investors desire some amount of money for present consumption. He fulfills all his needs with the availability of present income levels. The current income level depends upon the current financial plan of the investors. He needs some money to cover his certain level of standard of living expenses. He needs some amount of money for his routine expenditure. Once the information is arrived at, it is very easy to assess the needs of money. It enables the portfolio manager to decide how much income must be provided for by the construction of the portfolio. The design of portfolio can be made very easily to achieve the client's financial goals.

Another important aspect is inflation. Inflation reduces the purchasing power of money. The rupee value is determined by the levels of inflation. A low level of inflation in the economy stimulates the value of rupee. A high level of inflation exists in the economy reduces the value of rupee. Therefore, the investor should take all considerations while designing the portfolio for his investment process. He must try to build a best portfolio which could offset the effect of inflation. The portfolio manager should take a decision and funds should be invested according to the impact of inflation. Hence, the inflation element cannot be ignored in portfolio management. In order to achieve the goals of the client, the portfolio manager should invest the funds in growth stocks. Identification of growth stock is the main important task in the portfolio management. The growth stock may also be known as sunrise industries' stocks. They are also known as blue chip shares. A strong earning potential, large amount of reserves, undistributed amount of profits, retained earnings are the main characteristics of the blue chip companies. Hence, the selection of growth stocks can show impact on the portfolio.

Safety – Investment means, just parking one's idle fund. The investors will invest the fund for the time being. After the completion of their time, they demand their amount of money from the parking place. Hence, the investor always thinks about the safety of his investment rather than return. Investment in debentures and bonds are safer than equity. Investing in regularly trading securities is not risky. Investing in unquoted, less traded, un-traded may not provide adequate safety to the investors. Investing in blue chip company shares will enhance the safety levels of investment.

Liquidity – Liquidity is the most important factor in the stock market operations. Some kind of financial assets provide high liquidity. High quality short-term debt instruments provide higher liquidity. Money market instruments, commercial papers and shares that are widely traded create high liquidity. Active trading, large volume of trading securities indicates the levels of liquidity in the market. Some sectors lack liquidity due to their nature of business. For example, we can take real estate. Some kind of shares are poorly traded in stock market creates no liquidity to that financial instruments. The portfolio manager should design the portfolio according to the needs of the levels of liquidity as desired by the investor or client.

Time horizon — Time is the essential factor in designing best portfolio in order to meet the financial goals of the client or investor. Generally investors are making their investment for a special purpose for their future. After a specific period of time, they pull their investment from the portfolio. Hence, the push and pull strategy will be applied by the common investor. He will push the funds when it is available freely at his disposal for a specific period of time. After the expiry of time he will pull his money from a basket of investment. Portfolio means a basket of different kinds of financial assets. The time horizon varies from individual to individual. Investment planning periods is also known as "time horizon". Gaining in the stock market is a game of risk and return elements. The mix of risk and return is the pleasure of the investor. The enjoyment of risk and return depends upon the life cycle of the common investor. The life cycle of the investor can be studied in the following ways:

(a) Career stage

(b) Mid-career level stage

(c) Retirement stage

(d) Tax considerations

Career stage is an early stage of life cycle of a common man. The stage of the life cycle determines the nature of investment. A student of higher education/lower education enters into life cycle of a common man. He will be placed in a suitable career according to his qualifications and capabilities. A bright future awaits him. His talent, skills, abilities may be exposed more if he settles early in a better career. At the early stage, the investor will have fewer assets than their liabilities. He wants to purchase more goods for his comfortable life. He needs more money for his consumption of goods. He will be thinking of construction of own house. In order to fulfill his dreams he may avail the housing loan scheme. The housing loan scheme deduction from the salary reduces the level of flow of money. The salary amount will be declined to the extent of level of finance taken by home. His next priority is towards savings for liquidity purpose. He provides a shelter for his family by way of taking insurance policies for protecting his life members from financial crisis on his expiry or death. In this stage, the time horizon has long life expectancy with a possibility of higher growth income. Hence, this stage is more important in designing the portfolio for his clients by the portfolio manager. It is more important that the average life expectancy of the common man has increased exponentially. The level of increase in life expectancy of the man stimulates the value of money due to longer period of holding time. The holding period of long-term nature of portfolio leads to the higher levels of income.

Mid-career stage is another important factor in time horizon factor. At this period the investor acquires more assets than his liabilities. The balance sheet of the individual reflects with surplus amount. He has limited time period to invest in this stage. He needs to think about potential pension benefits at this stage. At this stage he has limited period to invest in high risk and high return securities. Mid-career is a chance of opportunity to invest in the form of portfolio.

The third and final stage is retirement stage. In this period of time horizon investment is very much limited. At this final stage, he needs stable way of income because he loses his regular salary income. He thinks about the alternative regular flow of income. In this stage all this financial resources may be exhausted and all his loans must be cleared off by him. He will take utmost care about financial planning to end his life. He is in completion of all life insurance policies and shifts his investments to low return and low risk category of investments. At this stage he gives priority to the safety of the principal amount.

Tax is an element which changes from year to year. The direct taxes in India change in every budget period. The taxation system will be indicated through Finance Act. Finance Act deals with direct and indirect taxes in India. Income tax is one of the most influential factors in determining of the investment decisions. Investors in income tax horizon always consider reducing the tax liability. The Finance Act provides some savings for getting tax exemption under the law.

The Finance Act provides some tax concessions to the tax payers for investing in savings instruments. The investors always think about to reduce the tax liability by investing in provisions of the Act. Hence the investors should make their tax planning according to the latest provisions of the Act. The interest or dividend will be tax able under the head of income from other sources. The profit or loss will be shown as capital gains or capital loss. The capital gains will be taxable as per the existing income tax rates. The capital appreciation will be liable to taxable as per the Income Tax Act. The loss on capital may also be adjusted from capital gains. Hence any appreciation or depreciation in capital should be adjusted as per the provisions of the Income Tax Act. Investing in government bonds and national saving certificates can avoid taxation. If the investor wants to reduce tax burden, he can invest in these securities in addition to his portfolio.

Investment decisions are based some times on psychological factors. The temperament of the investor is one of the important factors in framing investment objectives. Investors are different kinds. Some of them risk takers. They would like to take up higher risk in order to earn more return from portfolio. Some of them are not interested towards risk. They would like to deploy the funds in risk free return instruments. Hence, the temperament of the investor occupies an important role in framing the portfolio for the clients.

2. Composition of Securities

Portfolio is a basket of different kinds of investments. It has the basic objective of financing current and future expenditures from a part of assets. The pool of assets are called portfolio. The investors return is based on acceptance level of risk by the client. The basic intention of construction of a portfolio is to get a regular revenue and capital appreciation. Generally, all the investors have the following objectives in construction of a portfolio:

1. Revenue income
2. Accumulated growth
3. Capital appreciation
4. Provision for future

Revenue income is a regular flow of income to the investors. Generally, the regular flow of income is an additional source of income to the client. He will depend upon the additional income to meet the livelihood expenses. This additional source of income stimulates the level of client's income. It is a value addition activity.

Accumulated growth of shares reflects the wealth of the investors. A long-term strategic investor can invest in growth oriented scrips. Risk will be balanced in long-term nature of investments. Identification of the growth scrip is the important task of the portfolio manager.

Capital appreciation means, an appreciation in the value of financial asset. Every asset has either appreciation or depreciation in its value. Investors will enter the stock market at lower prices and the securities will be sold in higher price market. The difference between purchase and sale price during the holding period is known as capital appreciation. The investor will gain in the stock market in the form of capital appreciation. The appreciation in value is based on market situations. Market is a combination of various factors. It will be fluctuated according to the situation. But in the stock market, there will be equal likelihood of losing the capital.

Provision for future is an essential element for every investor. Generally, investors will have some idle fund for saving purpose. They think that future will be not so bright and the stored money will help them in old age. Old age is the most important stage in the man's life for financial needs. He will be in a good position to store the money for his old age period. Hence, investment vehicle is a reservoir of finance.

As per the life cycle of an investor, objectives of investment, the portfolio manager should select the best portfolio in order to get the financial needs of the client. The selection of portfolio depends upon the following factors:

(a) Asset composition.

(b) Diversification.

Asset composition: The portfolio manager will make a good portfolio for his client. He selects the portfolio in accordance with the needs and convenience of the client. The skills and capabilities of the portfolio manager shall be reflected in the appreciation value of a selected portfolio. The asset composition will be based on client's preference. If the client requires in getting adequate amount of current income, 60 per cent of funds should be invested in debt instruments and 40 per cent on equities. The combination of debt and equity depends upon the individuals preferences. If the client's objective is stable income and safety of capital, the funds will be invested in short-term bonds. The bonds provide a stable return and safe custody of principal amount. The asset proportion in portfolio is based on the factor:

(i) Asset mix (Income based)

(ii) Asset mix (Capital appreciation)

(iii) Asset mix (Safety of principal)

(iv) Asset mix (Risk and return)

Asset mix (Income based): Already, we discussed that, the asset combination is prepared by the portfolio manager as per the desire of his client. If the investor requires a regular flow of income from his investment the portfolio may consist of 60 per cent to 100 per cent in equities and 0 to 40 per cent in debt instruments. The proportion of the asset mix is known as portfolio. The debt composition of the portfolio can attract income tax exemption. The equity component enhances the value of portfolio. For example, non-conventional energy companies, computer software and hardware company shares, etc.

Asset mix (Capital appreciation): The portfolio manager will keep the asset composition as per the intention of the client. Capital appreciation means the value of the original investment increases over the years. Some investments may provide a faster rate of capital appreciation. For example, real estate. Stock markets also provide much higher than their original issue price. The market capitalization has also increased exponentially. Nowadays stock market is becoming more popular formulating investments in the capital market. A careful analysis and observation of stock market movements can definitely achieve the desired goal of the client. The portfolio manager shall prepare the portfolio for capital appreciation motive and the funds must be invested in the equity from 90% to 100%. Equity consisted portfolio may generate sufficient and reasonable return through capital appreciation.

Asset mix (Safety of the principal): Risk is a future chance of loss. The return is based on level of accepted risk. Normally, all investors are very particular about safety of principal amount. No investor likes to lose his capital. In this kind of portfolio, debt instruments dominate the asset composition. The investment in short-term debt instruments will keep the principal amount more safely. Debt-based portfolios may generate a regular flow of income by way of interest but lack in capital appreciation.

Asset mix (risk and return): Risk and return are two important factors in stock market. Risk is always involved in the market. Return is chased by the risk. The yield earned by an investor is a game of risk and return. The traditional approach is based on some assumptions such as risk, return and non-risk factors. Generally the individual investors prefer more returns from the equity. Hence, the investors is involved in high risk in order to get more returns. The return is based on the accepted level of risk.

High risk ⇧	→	high return ⇧
No risk	→	no return
Low risk ⇩	→	low return ⇩

The risk factor in stock market cannot be ignored. The risk cannot be escaped. But it can be avoided in some situation. It depends upon the efficiency of risk management. The risk can be classified in many ways. They are interest rate risk, purchasing power risk, financial risk and market risk. The portfolio manager should also take into consideration of non-risk factors such as taxation, marketability, etc., the ability of the portfolio manager can be assessed through the earning capacity of asset composition.

Diversification: The portfolio will be designed as per the intention and wishes of the client. The portfolio manager will take all precautions before finalizing the construction of a portfolio. Once the asset mix and combination is determined and the risk return are analyzed, the final step is the diversification of portfolio. Risk is a future chance of loss. Return is always haunted by risk. The investor should escape the risk and capture the return. The yield or appreciation in portfolio value is the indication of efficiency of the portfolio manager. Risk can be minimized and return may be maximized. In the stock market, there will be a chance of financial risk. Financial risk can be reduced by introducing top quality bonds. Bonds will provide poor resistance for inflation. Inflation in the economy is a continuous phenomenon and it cannot be avoided. Shares will provide better protection from inflation effect. But they are more vulnerable to financial risk. There are many kinds of debentures available in the market. But good convertible debentures may balance the financial risk and purchasing power risk. The portfolio can be categorized as bond portfolio and stock portfolio. Bond portfolio may be constructed with long and short-term bonds. The investor should make a chance of balance between these two term bonds. Short-term bonds offer more risk to income. Long-term bonds involve more risk to principal. In the category of stock portfolio, the investor has to follow the steps.

I step → sectorial analysis → selection of industry

II step → selection of companies in the industry

III step → size of the portfolio

The portfolio should be constructed ultimately within the goals of the investor. The needs of the financial goals must be reached through better construction of good portfolio. Portfolio is a mix of different kinds of securities drawn from the capital market. Capital market provides a number of kinds different financial assets. The investor has to choose among them to his needs and convenient. The portfolio manager should take all precautions about the safety and liquidity of the different kinds of financial assets. The portfolio manager should tune the portfolio according to the dreams of investors. The investor has to analysis about the fundamental factors of the industry and company. There are so many industries the Indian economy. For example, manufacturing industries, coal steel, automobiles, consumer durable goods, heavy machinery engineering, cement, aluminum, banking, insurance, hotels, shipping, transport, health care, drugs and fast moving consumer goods. Each and every industry exists in the economy with the business cycle. All industries move cyclically. The investors should know about the intricacies of the economy principles such as business cycle, demand and supply factors and life cycle of the various industries. The investors should know about the industries advantages and disadvantages regarding the economy cycle. The investors have to select industries at first moment, company at second moment and the size of the portfolio at final stage. The investor has to select two scrips from each industry. The selection of company is the most important factor in the portfolio construction. The selection of scrips is in influenced by many factors such as growth, yield, expected earnings, past profits, reserves assets, price earnings ratio, earnings per share, dividend rate, retention ratio, expenditure on research and development etc., selection of best scrip is the ability and expertism of the investor. It reflects the investor's knowledge and perception regarding the corporate sector. Investor's knowledge about the various companies functioning, performance reports, studying and news gathering from the financial periodicals, observing experts interviews with business channels will make him more perfect about the stock market. The investor's knowledge and perception has no horizon in the stock market. After acquiring knowledge and other information about the corporate sector, the investor has to select the number of shares of each stock to be purchased. It involves the diversification process of the portfolio management. The portfolio manager has to build the portfolio as per the goals of the client. The investor's selection of different kind of financial assets enables the portfolio to balance the risk and return forces.

Markowitz Theory

Markowitz model is associated with the concept of risk measurement. It is based on study of risk and return relationship. Stock market is a game of risk and return. This theory is associated with his selection of portfolios. It is based on average investor's desire. Markowitz published an article, in the *Journal of Finance* in March 1952. After the publication of this article, numerous investment firms and portfolio managers developed "Markowitz algorithms". It is a theoretical framework for analysis of risk and return and their interrelationship. It fully utilised the statistical tools of measurement of risk. It is based on mathematical programming for selection of assets in a portfolio. It emphasized the quality of a portfolio.

Risk and return are two important aspects of the investments. They are expected by assumptions. Risk is measured by the variance and covariance. Markowitz model contributes about the qualification of risk and need for maximizing return. Portfolio is a combination of different financial assets. A portfolio is said to be efficient, if it is expected to yield the highest return possible for the lowest risk or a given level of risk. The theory of Markowitz is based on the following assumptions.

Assumptions

1. Investors desires is to minimize risk and maximize return
2. Investors have rational behaviour
3. There will be perfect markets in the economy
4. Investors have free access to fair and correct information on the returns and risk.

The theory indicated the importance of correlation among different kinds of stock's return in the construction of a portfolio. He proved that on security in the portfolio dominates the other at an expected level of return. He focused more on knowledge of the correlation between all securities in a portfolio.

Markowitz diversification: Portfolio means, a group of financial assets with different levels of returns. A group of securities combined for the purpose of desired return. Return is reward to the portfolio owner. The group of assets may vary different characteristics and returns at the accepted level of risk. The financial assets may be stocks, debentures, bonds and money market instruments. Sometimes a vast number of different kinds of industries and companies' scrips will be inserted in the portfolio. A large number of different kinds of industries' scrips are added to the portfolio, the total risk tends to decrease. The diversification can reduce the unsystematic risk in case of common stock portfolio. As per the experts and analyst guidelines, 15 stocks are ideal portfolio to reduce the unsystematic risk at zero level. If the portfolio exceeds 15 stocks, additional risk reduction cannot be gained. Diversification cannot reduce systematic risk. In case of simple diversification, securities are selected on random basis. There is no usage of statistical tools, mathematical and analytical tools in simple diversification. Hence, simple diversification reduces the total risk. The total risk of the portfolio consists of systematic and unsystematic risk. Total risk is measured by the various rates of returns over a time period. The research studies show that the systematic risk contains a quarter of total risk. The increase in portfolio size, the total risk will decline beyond that levels of limit, risk cannot be reduced. The vast diversification of portfolio is based on the following factors.

Vast diversification: Diversification means, expansion of the existing portfolio. Portfolio can be described as a joint family. For example, a family consists of wife, husband and three sons. One of the sons will add goodwill to his family by good behaviour, another son damages the reputation of the family through his nature. Hence, the goodwill of the family constructed by one member and dismantled by another. Suppose if the three sons show good behaviour, sincerity, honesty and maintain a good relation with society, the family will be high in reputation. If the three sons indulges in malpractices and shows worst performance, the family reputation will decline automatically.

Vast diversification means expansion of the existing portfolio with wide areas of different kinds of industries. Spreading the investment base towards a wide variety of different industries is known as vast diversification. By expanding the existing portfolio, there will be some problems which are presented for thorough understanding of the intricacies of the stock market operations. The following problems arise in vast diversification:

(a) Wrong selection of scrips
(b) Sources of information
(c) Transaction cost
(d) R&D

(a) Wrong selection of scrips: Portfolio means a set of different kinds of financial assets. An ideal portfolio is a combination of 15 different kinds of financial assets. Of these, some scrips may add returns to the portfolio and the remaining provides risk. Hence, the portfolio is a game of chance of risk and return elements. Sometimes the investors may buy scrips which will not yield adequate returns. Therefore, there will be a chance to increase the risk element in the portfolio. A wrong selection of scrip may disrupt the growth of the portfolio. The investor should always be cautious in selection of scrips.

(b) Information: The portfolio manager should observe the movements of the scrips which are in the portfolio combination. If the portfolio is very large and consisting of a number of different kinds of financial assets it is very problematic to collect all the information regarding all securities. The task of portfolio manager is not only constructing the portfolio but also to observe the information regarding the performance of companies and industries. He has to collect the financial information, marketing information, production schedules and other information regarding the company's performance. Financial information provides an excellent source of direction about the individual performance of the company. The portfolio manager should have to face many problems in collection of the information about the companies existing in the portfolio. Financial information like gross profit, net profit, profit before tax, profit after tax, provision of depreciation, provision of reserves, earning per share, pre-earnings ratio, dividend declarations, retention ratio, payout ratio, etc., will be useful for analyzing the company performance. Marketing information contains brand image, brand loyalty, product life cycle, market share, market leader, market penetration, consumers' preference, consumer behaviour, lifestyle of consumers, purchasing capacity, etc., factors indicate about the future of the company. Hence, the portfolio manager will face a lot of problems in acquiring all these information contents for all companies in the portfolio.

(c) Transaction cost: Buying and selling of financial assets attracts brokerage charges. A frequent purchase of small quantities of shares leads to higher transaction cost. A large amount of bulk shares attracts less transaction cost for less frequent intervals, i.e., mutual funds. Big financial institutions purchase different stocks at different levels of quantities. Hence, individual investor has to pay more transaction cost than large institutions.

(d) Research and development: Stock market is a game of risk and return. To play in stock market without knowledge is not safe. It is foolish, entering without sufficient knowledge, skills, talent and techniques of stock market. Research is the most important factor for acquiring knowledge. Knowledge is the powerful tool in the hands of individual investors. Knowledge about the company's performance, government policies, economic conditions current business affairs, consumers' attitude, demand and supply factors is necessary for making investment decisions especially in vast diversification. Knowledge is a store of valuable information. Information acquiring enhances the skills of the investors. Hence, investment in stock market is not only simply handing over a cheque to broker, but it also requires more knowledge about the stock markets. Observation, concentration regarding stock market movements makes the investors to move in the market more confidently. The individual investors will not take care about all these things. But the mutual funds, financial institutions, foreign institutional investors may appoint research staff and acquire knowledge and skills and they render scientific advices to buy, sell or hold the securities. Therefore, the establishment of research wing involves high cost. But all firms may not be in a position to incur the expenditure.

The Markowitz Model

It is a fundamental belief in the stock market that, holding two stocks is less risky than holding one. For instance holding stocks in information, communication and technology is better than investing all the money in a textile company's stock. Hence, the building of a good portfolio is a difficult task. But Markowitz provides a solution to it with the help of risk and returns. The risk and return occupies a dominant role in getting success in the stock market. Intelligent investors escape risk and capture the returns.

Assumptions

Markowitz model is based on the following assumptions:

(a) The investor estimates the risk on the basis of returns.

(b) Investors always prefer for higher returns at accepted level of risk.

(c) Investors would prefer to a given level of return, for lower risk than higher risk.

Theory

Markowitz theory is based on risk and return relationship in the market. He developed his theory and found that diversification can reduce the risk. A single stock portfolio will be good, if the investor expectation is perfect. But in the world of uncertainty it is not possible to say with a single portfolio. Hence investors prefer Markowitz model, because a provision is made in the portfolio to reduce the risk through diversification. The aim of the diversification is not only to reduce risk of a security, but also to reduce the covariance or interactive risk of two or more securities in a portfolio. It gives more importance to standard deviation. The portfolio risk is more important factor in determination of diversification.

CAPITAL ASSET PRICING METHOD (CAPM)

Risk is ginger and return is jam in the stock market. Stock market is a game of risk and return factors. Return is the outcome of dominating factor over risk. Escaping risk and capturing the return is the reflection of efficiency of the portfolio manager. Risk can be categorized as two components, i.e., diversifiable risk and undiversifiable risk. Diversifiable risk can be eliminated through diversification. Undiversifiable risk cannot be eliminated. Market risk is uncontrollable by anyone. Therefore the investors would like to have assets with systematic risk. They would like to prefer the financial assets with low beta coefficient and if they provide high rates of earnings. The behaviour of the investors depends upon the acceptance level of risk. The capital asset pricing theory deals with relationship between risk and return factor. It also reveals how the scrips are priced in the capital market. This theory was submitted by Markowitz, William Sharpe and John Linter. They provided the fundamental structure for the CAPM. It is based on a model of linear general equilibrium return. The rate of return of an asset is associated with assets beta value. The capital asset pricing model is focused on a more practical approach in stock valuation. It is based on the mean-variance approach to risk assessment. A risk assessment model was developed by Markowitz. The capital asset pricing model is based on the following assumptions.

Assumptions

1. There is no transaction cost.
2. There is no personal income tax.
3. The stock markets are perfect; no one can influence the price.
4. The investors can buy any quantity of shares.
5. All investors will have some expectations in the market.
6. Investment decision will depend upon the expected rate of returns.
7. There are no limit short sales in the market.
8. The investors have access to riskless rate of interest assets.

Concept of CAPM

Nowadays stock market has rapid changes in the assessment of future. The IT revolution has changed the affairs of the stock market operation. Technical sources have been established. Any small incident of corporate sector is known by stock market within the fraction of minutes. Now, buying shares means a click of mouse with computer. Online trading has changed the entire stock market operations drastically. Information is readily available to the markets. The following factors will clearly explain the concept of CAPM:

(A) Access to riskless rate of interest assets
(B) Composition of assets
(C) Security market line
(D) Capital market line

(A) Access to Riskless Rate of Interest Assets

Capital market is a combination of different sources of flow of funds. The funds are available in the form of different kinds of financial assets. Money market is a combination of different kinds of financial assets. Some kind of sources of financial is available for cheap rate of interest rates. At the same time financial money instruments are available for investment at the riskless rate of interest. Hence, the investors could borrow or lend any amount of funds at riskless rate of interest. They can mix the blend of risk free assets with risky assets in order to reduce the risk level of the portfolio. The portfolio can be altered according to the needs and convenience of the investors. Portfolio is a mix of different kinds of financial assets. The expected return on the combination of risky and risk free assets can be computed through the following formula:

$R_p = R_f X_f + R_m (1 - X_f)$

R_p = return on portfolio

X_f = ratio of funds invested in risky assets

R_f = risk free rate of return

R_m = return on risky assets

$1 - x_f$ = proportion of funds invested in risky assets.

(B) Composition of Assets

The combination of different kinds of financial assets is known as "portfolio". The ratio of mixing blend of various kinds of stocks generates portfolio return. The portfolio either generates returns or incurs losses. Facing of loss is known as "risk". An intelligent investor always wants to escape the risk and capture return. Hence, the stock market is a game of risk and returns. As per the CAPM approach all investors hold only the market portfolio and risk less securities. The market portfolio is a combination of all stocks existed in the stock market. The portfolio will be constructed with a different proportion of various financial assets in order to yield better returns to the investor. Each asset will occupy its proportion according to the market value of the scrip. The investors can combine riskless assets with risky assets in order to reduce the risk levels of the portfolio. The funds may be procured by him through cheaper sources of finance. The expected return can be computed through the following formula:

Expected return = price of time + (price of risk × amount of risk)

(C) Security Market Line

Stock market is a game of return and risk. The risk component has two factors, i.e., systematic and unsystematic risk. The risk and return relation can be studied through capital market line. The capital market line does not show the risk-return trade-off for other portfolios and individual securities. Efficient portfolio of the risk and return relationship can be observed through capital market line. Inefficient portfolios cannot be observed through capital market line. It lies below the capital market line. The systematic and unsystematic risk consists of standard deviation. The portfolio contains the total risk component. But unsystematic risk can be diversified and eliminated from the portfolio. Systematic risk exist alone in portfolio. The lone risk component of the portfolio can be measured through beta. The beta is a powerful tool for analysis of risk component in portfolio whether efficient or inefficient. Generally all portfolios will be altered according to the desire of investors. Sometimes additional security will be added to the existing market portfolio. The addition of security enhances the risk levels also. Then the variance of a portfolio is equal to the weighted sum of the covariances of the individual scrips in the portfolio. The addition of a security to the portfolio may also stimulate the returns levels of earnings. Its marginal contribution to the variance of the market is the covariance between the individual scrip return and market portfolios return.

(D) Capital Market Line

Capital market line is associated with combination of riskless assets with risky assets. It reveals the importance of riskless rate of return financial assets. The money market instruments provide riskless assets. The riskless assets are the oxygen to the risky portfolio. The proportion of the riskless assets increases in the portfolio, the level of portfolio risk can be reduced and even sometimes fully eliminated. The treasury bills, short-term government bonds are best sources of riskless assets. They are issued for very short-term nature and assured by the central government. Hence, investments in these securities are 100 per cent safe and provide reasonable rate of return. Therefore, the proportion of these instruments in the portfolio cannot be ignored and neglected. These assets are best weapons, when the risk levels reached beyond the level of expectation. The capital market line also deals with the combination of risky and riskless assets with a cheap source of finance availability to the investor. In this theory, the borrowing and lending rate of interest occupies a dominant role in analyzing the portfolio return.

Limitations

The CAPM is useful to provide insights for investors but it has some limitations. They are:

(a) it is unrealistic for any professional investor or a portfolio manager, who believes the fundamental factors strongly.

(b) the researchers conducted many empirical tests of the model have not proved very useful.

(c) it is built on all investors have the same expectations about future. But the expectations of the future vary from one person to another.

(d) it is a nice theoretical concept, but in real life it is not useful to the common investors. The empirical tests have not given support to this theory.

(e) the calculation of beta is not useful in prediction of future price of the scrip. The past betas may not reflect the future risk or return.

(f) the inputs cannot be estimated precisely, the expected return found is also subjected to criticism.

(g) investors are concerned with company-related risks. It focuses more attention about the market risk.

SUMMARY

Investment is a curb in the present consumption. The curb in consumption leads to enhancing the investment levels. All investors should make proper planning of their investments first to provide for their requirements of comfortable life with a basic need of house, real estate, physical assets, etc., he should also take care about comforts and insurance for life and make a provision for a provident fund and pension fund for a future day. Before entering into stock market, the investor should think about his prior commitments by avoiding financial crisis in his life period. They make investments in the stock market on the advice of friends, relative, agents or brokers. Hence they should take all precautions prior to enter into the stock market. The risk and return are two important factors in the portfolio management. If we want more return, we must accept for more risk and if no risk is taken, simply bank deposits are opted for investment. The return is a reward to the investor. Portfolio is a combination of different financial assets. The ratio of different combination of different kinds of ingredients stimulates the taste of the drink. The portfolio return is related to risk. In the market the risk free return assets are also available to the investors. Bank deposits, post office deposits or certificates are the best examples for risk free assets. Hence, the investors may also keep these assets in their portfolios to reduce the risk levels of portfolio. There are also high return assets available in the market. The higher return depends upon many factors like accepted level of risk, expertise in selection of financial assets, return due to diversification, etc., the return in stock market depends upon many factors.

Questions

1. What is portfolio? What are the basics of portfolio management?
2. Explain the recent trends in banking and capital marketing sector.
3. Explain about traditional approach of portfolio theory.
4. What is arbitrage theory?
5. Write about modern portfolio theory? Explain the importance of beta.
6. What is diversification of a portfolio? Explain the importance of Markowitz theory.
7. What is capital asset pricing theory? Explain its assumptions.
8. Distinguish between capm and arbitrage price theory.
9. Explain the Sharpe index model. How can one be arriving at the optimum portfolio?

6 Financial Services in India

Finance is the provision of money. The development of a nation's economy depends upon the efficiency of the financial system. A system is interrelated activity. It consists of a number of set of regulatory and implicative authorities. A speedy regulatory authority system may bring radical changes in the economy. The development of economy depends upon the velocity of money. The velocity of money is based on several factors. The Indian economy is transforming into digital economy. In earlier days, GDP was dominated by the contribution of agriculture sector. But at present, the GDP will be strongly dominated by services sector. The service sector has bright future in India, because of its excellent technical and non technical human resources availability. The development of economy depends upon the pace of services provided in its infrastructure. A strong financial infrastructure will change the economic environment. After the process of liberalization, privatization and globalization policy in our country, the opening of the economy to multinationals and free market concept have assumed much significance. After the information technology revolution, entire banking and financial sector scenario had changed. At present, the funds are transfered with a click of mouse. Now banking is becoming like shopping. The hassle free rules and regulations of the financial supermarkets will definitely change the Indian economy. As a result, phenomenal changes are being witnessed in the money market, securities market, capital market, debt market and foreign exchange market. The information technology revolution, regulatory reforms has transformed the financial services sector from being a conservative industry to a very dynamic one. The financial regulatory bodies include Reserve Bank of India, Securities and Exchange Board of India, Insurance Regulatory Development Authority, Board for Industrial and Financial Reconstruction, Department of Banking of the Union Government, etc.

The increasing role of private sector, market-oriented economy, liberalization, privatization, globalization policies made a high degree of competition and situation forced them to become highly efficient organisations. The market is a combination of different elements and every organization is forced to face it. The efficiency is the survival of the financial services industry. The main objective of management is to increase the efficiency, productivity and lowering cost and thus, enhancing profits. The quality of service depends upon the technology. The analysis of any firm involves the technological relationship between input and output.

Meaning of Financial Services

The services which are offered by the finance companies are known as "financial services". Financial companies are known as asset management compaies and liability management companies. The asset management company consists of leasing companies, mutual funds, merchant bankers, and portfolio managers. Liability management companies include bill discounting companies and acceptance house companies. The development of the economy depends upon the quality of services offered by the finance companies. The financial services may also be known as financial intermediation. Financial intermediation is a process where it coordinates savers and borrowers. They are financial mediators to materialize the transactions actively in the market. The process of materialization keeps the nation more active in financial sectors of the economy. Financial market is a combination of both savers and borrowers. The savers' amount of finance will be utilized efficiently and diverted towards productive way in the form of investment. The investment enhances the productivity levels of the industry which is more useful to the economy. A strong investment potential will definitely change the economy. The financial services mobilize the savings and enroute the resources towards required sector and serves as a key area for industrial development of the country. The financial services market comprises of four important constituents.

- Market players (Commercial banks, financing institutions, merchant bankers, consultants, stock brokers, etc.)
- Specialized institutions (Credit rating agencies, factoring, discount houses, acceptance house) and
- Regulatory bodies (SEBI, RBI, IRDA, Banking and insurance department of central government)
- Financial instruments (Equity instruments, debt instruments and zero coupon bonds).

Objectives of Financial Services

The financial intermediation process creates wealth of the nation. The wealth of a nation will be built up by a strong foundation of financial architecture. The good design of financial architecture will create asset formation. The growth of asset formation enhances the living standards of a layman. The following are the objectives of financial services which are offered by finance companies.

- Mobilization of resources.
- Parking of resources.
- Skillful services.
- Economic stability.
- Regulation.

Mobilisation of Resources

The market is a combination of savers and borrowers. The saver includes individual investors, institutional investors, corporate sector and financial institutions. The funds are required by the corporate sector, government sector, individuals, and institutions. The finance companies will channelize the savings amount into productive way.

Parking of Resources

The finance companies will show to the investors, to park their resources in a better and safety place of financial market. They assist in decision making regarding the services such as factoring, bill discounting, credit rating, money market instruments, e-commerce and securitization of debts. They provide best services in order to ensure efficient utilization of funds.

Skillful Services

The financial services require a specialized knowledge domain. This sector requires a greater efficiency. The efficiency is the barometer in the financial transaction. The efficiency will have to be procured from high knowledge. The knowledge is key factor and one will have to take decisions instantly. The speed of decision making and implementations will indicate the profitability of the firms. The productivity and profitability depends upon the level of skills deployed by the organisations. The skillful areas include, stock lending, credit rating, mutual funds, depository services, factoring, lease financing, banking and insurance. All of these areas require a greater knowledge.

Economic Stability

Stability is the most important factor in the economy. A strong policies and reforms will stabilize the economy. The stability of economy depends upon the infrastructure of the financial system. The financial services occupies a dominant role in the growth of economic development. The wealth creation is only possible with efficiency of financial services. Financial services will render a continuous effort for the rapid growth of development. It develops different places through the mobilization of savings from a cross section of society and diverts them to the corporate sector for productivity nature.

Regulation

The financial regulatory authority in India includes securities and exchange board of India, reserve bank of India, insurance regulatory development authority and banking department of the central government. The sebi is watchdog of the capital market. Reserve bank is big brother of the banking sector. The insurance sector is regulated by Insurance regulatory development authority (IRDA). All of these organisations are organs of the union government. A strong regulatory authority is necessary for the developing nations. Policies are enzymes and reforms are antibiotics. The financial sector reforms will occupy a dominant role in capital formation of the economy. A plethora of various legislations regulate the better functioning of the financial service institutions.

Classification of Financial Services

The financial services are nerves of the Indian financial system. The active participation of financial service institutions will make speedy development of economy. The financial services traditionally is classified into two categories

(a) Money market intermediaries.

(b) Capital market intermediaries.

The money market is a market for short term sources of finance. It consists of commercial banks, cooperative banks, and other agencies which supply only short-term funds. Capital market intermediaries consists of long-term lending institutions, and investing institutions which mainly provide long-term funds.

Scope of Financial Services

The financial service provides a wide range of activities. They can be categorized into two kinds:

(1) Traditional approach.

(2) Modern approach.

1. Traditional Approach

The traditional financial service industry provides a wide range of activities. The activities include both money and capital market aspects. They deeply involve in financial markets. According to the traditional approach, they are categorized into two methods.

(a) Fund-based Activities

(b) Fee-based Activites.

The fund-based activities require an investment by the financial services institutions. They involve in providing of finance to the corporate sector. The financial market is a combination of different kinds of investors, savers and borrowers. The following activities are treated as fund-based services.

- Underwriting of shares, debentures and bonds of new issues.
- Buying and selling of shares in secondary market.
- Participation in money market instruments.
- Financial involvement in leasing, hire purchase and venture capital.
- Participation in foreign exchange markets.

The following activities are classified as fee-based services:

- Pre-issue activities.
- Post issue activities.
- Placement of capital and debt instruments.
- Arrangement of funds from financial institutions to their clients.
- Advisory services to the corporate sector.

2. Modern Approach

Financial services are dynamic activities. The economic development will only be possible with the help of financial services. In order to achieve the goal of corporate sector, the need and help of the financial services sector is necessary. At present, it provides the following activities.

- Project advisory services.
- Clearance of government approval.
- Mergers and acquisitions.
- Capital structuring services to the corporate sector.

- Trustee to the debentureholders.
- Management advisory services.
- Portfolio management.
- Insurance services.
- Buy back options.
- Determining optimal debt mix.
- Safe custody of securities.
- Collection of income on securities.
- Share transfer and registration.

The financial services institution provides different kinds of activities and requires a greater knowledge to perform these activities. The fund based organisations will get income from interest spread. They get gains from lease rentals, income from real estate and capital markets. The fee-based organisations does not involve much risk. But they require a greater knowledge to perform these activities.

An entity whose income exceeds its expenditure can lend or invest the excess income. On the other hand, an entity whose income is less than its expenditure can raise capital by borrowing or selling equity claims, decreasing its expenses or increasing its income. The lender can find a borrower, a financial intermediary such as a bank or buy notes or bonds in the bond market. The lender receives interest, the borrower pays a higher interest than the lender receives and the financial intermediary earns the difference for arranging the loan.

A bank aggregates the activities of many borrowers and lenders. A bank accepts deposits from lenders on which it pays interest. The bank then lends these deposits to borrowers. Banks allow borrowers and lenders, of different sizes, to coordinate their activity.

Finance is used by individuals (personal finance), by governments (public finance), by businesses (corporate finance) and by a wide variety of other organizations, including schools and non-profit organizations. In general, the goals of each of the above activities are achieved through the use of appropriate financial instruments and methodologies, with consideration to their institutional setting.

Finance is one of the most important aspects of business management and includes decisions related to the use and acquisition of funds for the enterprise.

In corporate finance, a company's capital structure is the total mix of financing methods it uses to raise funds. One method is *debt financing*, which includes bank loans and bond sales. Another method is *equity financing* - the sale of stock by a company to investors. Possession of stock gives the investor ownership in the company in proportion to the number of shares the investor owns. In return for the stock, the company receives cash, which it may use to expand its business or to reduce its debt. Investors, in both bonds and stock, may be *institutional investors* - financial institutions such as investment banks and pension funds - or private individuals, called *private investors* or *retail investors*.

- Identify relevant objectives and constraints: institution or individual goals, time horizon, risk aversion and tax considerations;

- Identify the appropriate strategy: active v. passive – hedging strategy
- Measure the portfolio performance

Financial management is in duplicate with the financial function of the accounting profession. However, financial accounting is more concerned with the reporting of historical financial information, while the financial decision is directed toward the future of the firm.

MERCHANT BANKING

Introduction

Funds are tapped from the capital market to finance various mega industrial projects. In attracting public savings, merchant bankers play a vital role as specialized agencies. The resource raising function remains to be the primary business of a merchant banker. The primary market holds the key to rapid capital formation, growth in industrial production and exports. There has to be accountability for the end use of funds risen from the market. The trends in the primary market in India suggest that merchant bankers have been playing a very significant role in the corporate sector's drive for mobilizing funds from the public. The increase in the number of issues and amount raised by the number of merchant bankers. Therefore the field becomes a highly competitive market where it requires a specialized skill in handling the situation. The Financial assets sold to the public should represent the genuine claims on future cash flows and viable assets. The merchant bankers have a social responsibility in building an industrial structure in India.

Origin of Merchant Banking

In the 19th century, a British merchant used to send an agent out to little known parts of the world. The agent took with him or had shipped with him the manufactured goods produced in the home country which he would sell and at the same time he would buy the products of that country and ship them home. For this trade, money had to be remitted from one country to another and the bill of exchange, an instrument that was in usage throughout the Europe since a long time, came to be used more and more. The bill of exchange in London became the means of financing the trade practically in the whole world. The well established merchant argued to do for commission and gradually the practice of accepting bills to finance their own trade by degrees. The merchant became a banker for acceptance of credits or the accepting house. These firms in London are styled Merchant Banks. The oldest merchant bank in London was Barring brothers. It was very prominent in Europe in the 19th century. Industrial revolution made England into powerful trading nation. Rich merchant houses had made their fortunes in colonial trade diversified into banking. They involved in the acceptance of commercial bills pertaining to domestic as well as international trade. They became as "Acceptance house, discount houses and issue houses". A Merchant banker was primarily a merchant than a banker. The merchant banker was entrusted with funds by his customers. Merchant's banks in the Britain involved in

(a) Issue capital

(b) Foreign trade

(c) Manage individual funds an undertake

(d) Foreign security business foreign loan business

(e) Finance etc.

They also involved in financing savereign government in the form of long-term loans.

Several merchant banks were set up in the U.S.A to arrange capital and enterprise to promote railways, industrial projects and trade and commerce. The investment bankers had replaced brokers and promoters in issue of securities. They were actively involved in launching private companies into public owned companies. The growth of investment bankers were facilitated by the enactment of Federal Act of 1914, on the emergence of U.S.dollar as leading global currency and expansion of US banking system. The investment bankers involved in buying and selling of corporate bonds, securities, trading and investing in securities, originating and distributing new issues, etc. After the great crash of 1929 and depression, their business considerably contracted and faced heavy financial losses. Then the federal government enacted several laws to reform the wall street practices to protect the interests of investors. The increased regulation and control made the U.S. banks to undertake the merchant bank functions in global capital markets. They were responsible for the development of the global capital market. Investment bankers were fully involved in finding investors for "Initial Public Offering (IPO)" of securities sold in the New Issue Market. They brought the buyers and sellers together. They created market and made arrangements for the public issue. They also helped a finder for the private placement of securities.

Definition of Merchant Banking

Merchant banking services is mainly related to issue house activities. Webster dictionary defines the merchant banking as "a bank that specializes in bankers acceptances and underwriting or syndicating equity or bond issues."[1]

According to Rosenberg MJ[2], merchant banking means "an organization that underwrites securities for corporations, advises such clients on mergers and is involved in the ownership of commercial ventures." The meaning of the merchant bank refers those organizations that underwrites securities and advises such clients on issues like corporate managers in the ownership commercial ventures. The Securities and Exchange Board of India (Merchant Bankers) Rules of 1992, defined a merchant banker[3] "as any person who is engaged in the business of issue management either by making arrangement regarding selling, buying or subscribing to securities as manager, consultant, advisor, or rendering corporate advisory service in relation to such issue management."

According to Cox.D, merchant banking is defined as "merchant banks are the financial institutions providing specialist services which generally include the acceptance of bills of exchange, corporate finance, and portfolio management and banking services."[4]

1 Promod Kumar Agarwal, *Merchant Banking in India,* Financial Services Delta Publication, Delhi, 1997, p. 45.

2 *Ibid.*

3 A. Sudhakar, *Merchant Banking – Capital Markets,* Financial Services Delta Publishing House, Delhi, 1997, p. 65.

4 P.K. Agarwal, *Merchant Banking in India,* Financial Services Delta Publishing House, 1997, p. 46.

The notification of the ministry of finance defines a merchant banker as, "any person who is engaged in the business of issue management either by making arrangements regarding selling, buying or subscribing to securities as manager, consultant, adviser or rendering corporate advisory service in relation to such issue management."[5]

Merchant banks undertake the tasks of new issue management, project counseling, preparation of feasibility reports, selection of underwriters/brokers and bankers to issue. The merchant bankers are responsible for clearing off all legal formalities from the SEBI for making the public issue. Merchant bankers have been handling growing number of public and rights issues with elan. The profession of merchant banking is concerned with catering the needs of trade and industry by playing a role of intermediary, consultant, liaison officer and a banker. There is a strong need for the merchant banking agencies because of a major chunk of public savings lying untapped. However, they have been playing a useful role in procuring the support of capital market for the corporate sector for financing their operations. Merchant bankers are working for the long-term and of the markets that create a niche for specialized banks.

Main Objects of a Merchant Banking Company

Merchant bankers render their specialized assistance in achieving the main objectives, which are presented below:

1. To carry on the business of merchant banking, assist in the capital formation manage advice, under write, provide standby assistance, securities and all kinds of investments issued, to be issued or guaranteed by any company corporation, society, firm, trust, person, government, municipality, civic body, public authority established in India.
2. The main object of merchant banker is to create a secondary market for bills and discount or re-discount bills and acts as an acceptance house.
3. Merchant bankers involve in assistance and promotion of economic endeavor, identification of projects, promoters, and preparation of project reports, project feasibility studies, market research, pre investment studies and investigation of industries at micro and macro level.
4. Merchant bankers another objective is to set up and provide services for the venture capital technology funds.
5. They also provide services to the finance housing schemes for the construction of houses and buying of land.
6. They render the services like foreign exchange dealer, money exchange authorized dealer and to buy and sell foreign exchange in all lawful ways in compliance with the relevant laws of India.
7. They involve in acquiring and holding one or more membership in stock exchange/national stock exchange, trade associations, commodity exchanges clearing houses or associations or otherwise in India or any part of the world.
8. They help to promote or procure incorporation, formation or setting up of concerns and undertakings whether as a company, body corporate, partnership or any other association or

[5] H.R. Machragn, *Merchant Banking Rules and Regulations,* New Addition 1995, p. 12.

persons for engaging in any other association or persons in any industrial, commercial or business activities.

9. Their objective is to perform financial services including factoring and syndication of both the loans short and long-term with the financial institution banks and others to manage mutual funds and to provide financial software programs.
10. The objective of the merchant banking is to carry on the business of financing industrial enterprises.
11. They invest in buying and selling of transfers hypothecate and deal with disposal of shares, stocks, debentures, securities and properties of any other company.

Financial systems comprise of four major components.

These components are

1. Financial Institutions
2. Financial Markets
3. Financial Instruments
4. Financial Services

FINANCIAL INSTITUTIONS

Introduction

Beginning from 1891, India's financial system took a radically new turn towards the market model. This envisaged an increased role for the capital market, along with a fundamental restructuring of banks and financial institutions. Such restructuring has been rather slow. The bulk of the banking system and major financial institutions are still largely owned and controlled by the government.

The corporate sector desiring long-term funds can raise it by issuing shares and debentures to the members of the public. The corporate sector can also approach financial institutions for satisfying their long-term financial needs. The financial institutions are concerned with mobilizing resources from different sections of society for their channelization in productive way. The financial institutions provide a convenient and effective link between savings and investment. They pool the savings of the society and are used by them to cater to the needs of the corporate sector.

In India, we have a battery of financial institutions operating in capital market and rendering financial assistance to needy enterprises. These financial institutions can be categorized into three major groups:

1. Commercial Banks
2. Development Banks
3. Investing Institutions

1. Commercial Banks

Introduction

The Commercial Banks are the oldest institutions having wide network of branches commanding utmost public confidence and having the lion's share in the total banking operations. The Commercial Banks operating in India fall under a number of sub categories on the basis of ownership and control of management. They constitute a vital role in Indian financial system. These financial institutions have been major suppliers of working capital finance to the corporate sector.

The Commercial Banks assist enterprises by granting term loans and various kinds of financial modes. They render help to the corporate sector in raising long-term funds from capital market through merchant banking activity. Let us discuss the nature of long-term financing of business by the Commercial Banks:

(a) Term lending
(b) Underwriting
(c) Direct subscription
(d) Merchant banking activity

(a) Term Lending: Term Lending by Commercial Banks is a recent phenomenon. This facility is dispensed by Commercial Banks under refinancing schemes. The government of India had formulated a scheme in 1958.

A formal scheme under which the banks were to provide refinancing facilities through Refinance Corporation of India (RCI). The RCI was set up in June 1958, for the purpose. The RBI urged the Commercial Banks to set up their term lending divisions for providing finance to the following areas:

(a) Deferred export payments
(b) New potential for export business
(c) Agriculture sector
(d) Industries in backward areas
(e) Capital industries
(f) Deferred payment arrangements for purchase of capital goods in the domestic market

Under the refinance scheme a Commercial Bank can grant term loan to an enterprise. Under the refinance scheme gets priority to road transport organization, units in backward areas and specified categories. The refinance could be up to 90% of the loan to these categories. Banks are not expected to insist on security and personal guarantee particularly in the case of priority sector applicants. The role of the banks is very likely to assume significant proportion in view of the latest measure taken by the RBI.

(b) Underwriting: Commercial Banks in India were engaged in underwriting business since 1935. The corporate sector can raise funds through a Commercial Bank by getting its security issue under advantage of boom condition in the market the banks have been engaged in underwriting work on a continuous basis. The banks give an assurance depending upon the financial strength and reputation of the company. The banks are not interested in acquiring the securities underwritten by them.

(c) Direct Subscription: Commercial Banks render financial support to industrial undertakings by investing directly in their shares and debentures.

(d) Merchant Banking: Commercial Banks in India are now assisting the firms in raising desired funds from capital market by performing merchant banking functions. Commercial Banks in India sponsor the security issue as a merchant banker. They also undertake credit syndication activity. For sponsoring issues, the banks should obtain consent from the SEBI. They help in preparation of the prospectus, arrangements for underwriting appointment of brokers and bankers to the issue, press publicity, compliance with stock exchange listing requirements. They also render service in the preparation of project profits on loan application for assistance from various term financing institutions. A number of nationalized banks have launched subsidiaries to take up the merchant banking activities as full-scale. The following institutions are providing these services:

1. SBI Capital Market Ltd.
2. Can Bank Financial Services Ltd.
3. PNB Financial Services Ltd.

2. Development Banks

The Development banks are also known as Industrial banks. The development banks supply capital, knowledge and enterprise. They meet the requirements of industries. They provide long term investments. They are able to finance the long-term investments. They employ financial experts to render the services to the prospecting projects. These banks acquire funds by issuing their own shares and debentures and obtain loans from the Central government and international agencies. They are performing important functions for rapid industrialization of the country. They inquire and investigate the prospects of the industry feasibility and activities of the various schemes. They advise the industries in financial and non-financial matters of the corporate sector. They have been specialized in investment and financial aspects of the various sectors. These banks have assisted in the development of developed countries lie USA, Japan and Germany. These development banks have also contributed a lot to the economic development of India.

Functions: The functions of industrial banks can be categorized into three parts:

(a) Accepting of long-term deposits
(b) Permitting of long-term investments
(c) Consultancy services

The deposits are mobilized by these banks by giving higher rate of interest to the depositors. These banks grant direct financial aids to the industries. Long-term loans are sanctioned usually on the mortgagee of land, machine and other fixed assets. The companies require short-term funds for purchase raw materials and other payments. The short-term credit is provided by Commercial Banks. The important industrial banks in India are

1. IDBI
2. ICICI
3. IFCI

INDUSTRIAL DEVELOPMENT BANK OF INDIA (IDBI)

Introduction

The Industrial Development Bank of India was established in 1964. It has been empowered to finance all types of industrial concerns. It provides direct and indirect finance to the corporate sector. As direct financier it renders assistance to the corporate sector in the following ways:

(a) Sanctioning term loans and advances

(b) Underwriting the issue of shares or debentures of the companies

(c) Sanctioning third party loans to business community

The direct financial assistance is usually granted for purchase of fixed assets, for expansion and modernization of existing units. The direct financial assistance is the most useful to the large-scale manufacturing units. As an indirect financier, it assists in the following ways:

(a) Refinancing of industrial loans provided by Commercial Banks and SFCs

(b) Providing financial assistance to the financial institutions by subscribing the shares and debentures of them.

(c) Rediscounting of bills

(d) Refinancing of export credit sanctioned by Commercial Banks to exporters.

(e) Renders Consultancy services to the corporate sector.

The bank provides loans that are normally repayable over a period of 10 years. The authorized capital of the IDBI was ₹ 2,000 crore. It can be further increased to ₹ 5,000 crore. The main sources of the funds for the IDBI are:

1. Borrowing from Central Government & RBI
2. Issue of Shares and Banks
3. Grant and Loans from world bank

Management

The IDBI is managed by the board of directors. The Board of Directors consisting of 22 persons including Chairman and Managing Director.

The Chairman and Managing Director is appointed by the Central Government. The other members of the board comprise of a representative of the RBI, a representative each of the All India financial institutions two officials of the Central Government, 3 representatives from each public sector bank and SFCs, 5 members having special knowledge and experience of industry. The Board of directors has constituted an Executive Committee consisting of 10 members.

Role

IDBI was set up as the principal financial institution for industrial development in the country. Now it is playing an important role in the capital market. The role of IDBI for the purpose of exposure can be categorized into three phases:

I[st] Phase

IInd Phase

IIIrd Phase

First Phase (1964-75)

The IDBI was set up as a statutory corporation in July 1964. It is a wholly owned subsidiary of the RBI. The ownership of the IDBI was transferred to the government. In 1995, the IDBI act was amended to provide greater operational flexibility. The amendment of the act was made during the dynamic phase of the Bank. The life cycle of the IDBI starts from 1964 to 1975, as first phase. The transformation of the IDBI takes more than 35 years. The first phase was the most important stage in the life of the IDBI. The first phases have been concentrated towards industrialization of the nation. The bank had focused on establishing the core industries such as textiles, fertilizers, chemical products, basic metals and machinery. The industrialization strategy also required encouraging the small ancillary industries to create more employment opportunities in the country. At this point of time SFCs, SIDCs were already in place to promote and encourage these segments of the industry. The IDBI took over the activities of the Refinance Corporation in 1964. Therefore it started providing financial support to the SFCs and other primary lending institutions in the country by refinancing facility. The IDBI had introduced the rediscounting of machinery bills schemes to encourage the capital goods industry. Hence the IDBI is fully involved in direct project loans, Refinance and Bill rediscounting schemes to the industries.

The IDBI played an important role for the development of exports sector, balanced regional development and coordination between financial institutions. The IDBI started a scheme during this phase for financing projects export of capital goods on deferred payments basis. It actively participated in the formation of Export and Import Bank of India. The IDBI played an important role in achieving the balance regional development strategy. It initiated steps to conduct surveys for identify industrial potential in backward areas and other specific locations. It played an important role in setting up of technical consultancy organization in collaboration with other financial institutions. The Central government provided long term loans to IDBI at concessional rate of interest. The RBI created a separate national Industrial credit fund to meet the long-term received loans from this fund at concessional rate of interest. The government had exempted from income tax, which were issued by IDBI due to its recognition of developmental role. It also focused on developing linkages with other financial institutions.

Second Phase (1976-85)

The Second phase starts from 1976 to 1985. Because the IDBI was delinked from the RBI on 16-02-1976. It was accorded as principal financial institution, wholly owned by the Government of India. This period was the most important in the life of the IDBI. The RBI had transmitted all its responsibilities to the IDBI. It also transferred the initial capital of the IFCI and the UTI. The share capital of the SFCs was also transferred to the IDBI by the RBI. It became an autonomous institution. During this period, it actively involved in the process of industrialization of the country. It focused on widening of the entrepreneurial base of the country, modernization and upgrading of technology. It had achieved a certain degree of maturity during the second phase. The IDBI introduced a soft loan scheme involving loans at concessional rates of interest during this phase. The scheme was designed to meet the modernization program in industries such as Jute, Cotton, Textiles, Sugar, Cement and Engineering goods. Later, a revised modernization package was introduced for all industries. The Central Government created a special technical development fund for modernization of industries to boost the process of technology upgradation. According to this scheme, the IDBI provided concessional assistance for the import of balancing equipment acquiring technical know-how and consultancy services for upgrading existing technology of the approved units. It also actively participated to provide assistance to sick units. It had taken various measures during this period to meet the requirements of small, village and cottage industry. It initiated package of refinance to small and medium sectors towards meeting the modernization requirements. The technology upgradation required a higher amount of foreign currency. It diversified its resources base and borrowed the foreign currency from the global markets.

The term lending is an important aspect of industrial financing system. It is the oxygen for promotion of industrial growth. The term lending widens the entrepreneurial base and the related infrastructure, services, etc. The industrial activities will be increased only when the entrepreneurial base widens. Therefore the IDBI took initiative to educate the entrepreneurs by setting up a number of institutes for entrepreneurship development in association with other financial institutions. It encouraged the entrepreneurs by introducing scheme, which is known as seed capital scheme.

Third Phase (1986.....)

The Third phase was one of tremendous growth in activities of the IDBI. It provided several new challenges due to economic restructuring program initiated by the Government. During this period the IDBI introduced new products to meet the growing needs of entrepreneurs. It also focused on balanced regional development of the country, sectoral growth of the industries and capital market in India. The Central Government announced the technology upgradation scheme in 1987 to upgrade the technology of select capital goods industries. It was assigned to formulate the system for this scheme. It also established in 1986, a textile modernization fund to provide a point for modernization efforts in the industry. The World Bank helped the IDBI to modernization of cement industry.

The IDBI introduced an export incentive scheme in 1986. It encouraged the export units by providing incentives in the form of rebate of interest on rupee loans. The IDBI established a Venture Capital fund in 1986, to provide financial assistance for industrial concerns. It was also giving top priority to emerging conservation sector and environmental audit aspects. The World Bank provided assistance to pollution control projects.

The IDBI played a major role in the development of the capital market in India. It took initiative steps to set up several subsidiaries and associate concerns. These concerns offer a wide range of products and services. It set up the stockholding corporation of India in 1987. It provides depository services to financial institutions. The Central Government had also assigned the responsibility of setting up the SEBI. The NSE was also established by the IDBI with the instructions from the Central Government. The NSE provides nationwide screen based trading system. It became the India's premier stock exchange. It had thrown a challenge to the Bombay Stock Exchange. The IDBI promoted/established the following institutions with the directions from the government.

(a) National Securities Depository Ltd.

(b) Credit Analysis and Research Ltd.

(c) IDBI Capital Market Securities Ltd.
(d) IDBI Investment Management Company Ltd.
(e) IDBI Bank Ltd.
(f) Northeastern Development Finance Corporation Ltd.
(g) Infrastructure Development Finance Company Ltd.
(h) Over the Counter Exchange of India (with Others)
(i) Tourism Finance Corporation of India (with others)
(j) Shipping Credit and Investment Corporation of India
(k) Biotech Consortium of India Ltd.

The IDBI decentralized its offices and processing of projects to meet the competition of projects from the market. It devised a host of new products to meet the needs of modern corporate sector. It is also empowered to manage its own foreign currency.

INDUSTRIAL CREDIT AND INVESTMENT CORPORATION OF INDIA (ICICI)

Introduction

The Industrial Credit and Investment Corporation of India was incorporated on 5-1-1955. It was founded by the Government of India, World Bank and others. It was promoted as a public limited company. It has been established for the purpose of assisting industries in the private sector. The aim of setting up ICICI was to provide foreign currency finance to industrial projects and promote industries in private sector. It provides financial packages for R&D, commercialization of technology, Venture Capital, pollution control and environment protection. It had diversified into a number of other activities. It has also been managing United States Agency for international development and World Bank funds through its technological financing programs.

ICICI principal business was to provide medium and long-term project financing, underwriting to shares guarantees to suppliers of equipment and foreign lenders. It has entered into new areas of business like commercial banking, Investment banking, Non-banking finance, broking, investor servicing, Venture Capital financing and infrastructure financing. It operates in general in accordance with the guidelines of RBI/SEBI. It has the status as a public financial institution. This status is useful in getting the benefits of taxation. Its bonds are treated as public securities for investment by trusts.

Financial Resources

The resources of the ICICI comprise of two kinds:

1. Foreign Currency Resources
2. Rupee Resources

The resources of the ICICI consisted with interest free loan from the GoI and an advance in foreign currency from the World Bank.

The rupee resources of the ICICI comprise the following components:

(a) Share Capital
(b) Reserves
(c) Borrowings
(d) Public deposits

(a) Share Capital

It started with initial resources of about ₹ 17.5 Crore. At the end of the March, 96 paid up capital amounted to ₹ 376.3 Crore and reserves and surplus amounted to ₹ 2,059.4 Crore. A large part of the capital is held by public sector institutions such as banks, LIC, GIC and its subsidiaries, IDBI, UTI etc. It issued ADRs and GDRs and a significant change has resulte in its share ownership structure.

(b) Reserves

It has been consistently building up a large chunk of reserves. Reserves are the most important element for financial companies. The higher amount of reserves is the financial strength of the company. The reserves consist of capital reserve, capital redemption reserve, share premium account, general reserve and special reserve.

(c) Borrowings

It mobilizes the funds from domestic and foreign markets. The domestic borrowings by the ICICI are from:

(a) The Government of India
(b) Institutional Borrowings
(c) Government Backed Bonds
(d) Public issue of Bonds
(e) MIS

The foreign currency resources consists of the following borrowings:

(a) Multilateral Borrowings
(b) Commercial Borrowings

The Multilateral Borrowings have been from the multilateral institutions. The World Bank played an important role in setting up of the bank. It has been providing financial assistance at regular times on credit. It also received financial assistance from ADB, Commonwealth Development Corporation, UK. It has also getting assistance from the government export credit agencies. All of these lines of credit are guaranteed by the Government of India. It has received assistance from the overseas development administration of the UK through the Government of India. It has been receiving financial assistance from various foreign agencies.

Commercial borrowings played an important role of the financial architecture of the ICICI. It has diversified its resources base with a view to establish in the global market. It raised a public issue of SF 8 million bonds in the Swiss markets in 1973. It depends upon the commercial borrowings which has increased. The commercial borrowings from various countries made it a financial stability to survive in the global market stability. It borrowed the commercial borrowings in the following ways:

(a) Euro credits and other loans
(b) Bond issues in Switzerland
(c) Private placements in Japan
(d) Euro convertible debt market

It received strong support from the international banking and financial community. It also achieved its objectives of interest and currency diversification by borrowing in various markets in Dollar, Swiss, France, Yen, Pound, Sterling. It is constantly searching for financial assistance in the international markets. It launched a Global Medium Term Note program in 1996-97, to facilitate borrowing in small amounts at competitive rates.

(d) Public Deposits

It started accepting public deposit from 1979. It is only a marginal source of funds. It also invites public deposits from the public by offering competitive rates of interest.

Business Operations

The business operations of the ICICI can be categorized into 5 kinds:

(a) Lending Operations
(b) Capital Market Operations
(c) Advisory Services
(d) Sponsorship
(e) Subsidiaries

(a) Lending Operations

Lending is the basic operation of any financial institution. This activity refers to the provision of funds for asset creation to the business concerns. The lending operations generate income to the ICICI by charging different rates of interest from the corporate sector. The lending operations of the ICICI consists the following activities:

A. Project finance
B. Technology finance
C. Non-project finance

Project finance is the most important activity of the bank. It grants the loan to business concerns in the form of Rupee and foreign currency loans, underwriting and direct subscription to issue of shares and debentures. It also provides financial assistance for the modernization, expansion of manufacturing and processing units. The Rupee project loans are involved in financing the purchase of equipment and machinery. It also finances under this scheme towards cost of land, construction of factory and preliminary expenses etc. The rupee currency loans dominated the portfolio of loans disbursed by ICICI. The share of rupee loans in the total financial assistance provided by the bank increase substantially. Foreign currency project loans are provided to finance the purchase of imported capital goods. The World Bank channelizes foreign currency resources for the private industry through ICICI. It did not sanction any foreign loans during the commencement of its operations. It started financing the foreign currency loans from 1958, with the emergence of foreign exchange crisis. After

1971, the component of foreign currency loan declined substantially. This was due to the recessionary state of the economy. At present the Indian companies are directly accessing international capital markets through the issue of GDR.

It started guaranteeing loans from the private investment sources. It charges 1% P.A. on the outstanding balances of guarantee issued in rupees and 1.8% in case of foreign currencies. It also offers assistance to corporate sector by underwriting the issue of shares and debentures. Now it has been following a policy of direct subscription of shares to the extent of ₹ 1 crore.

Technology financing has emerged as one of the sources of finance. The ICICI is the largest financiers of technology in India. This source of finance is run with help of United State Agency of International Development and World Bank. They are providing funds for various schemes of financing. It offers a wide variety of financial packages for R&D commercialization of technology. It also offers package relating to pollution control and environmental protection. The following schemes are offered by the ICICI.

1. SPREAD
2. ACE
3. TEST
4. PACT
5. PACER

Sponsored Research and Development program (SPREAD) is one of the schemes, which are offered by ICICI. It encourages Indian corporate sector to set up their R&D activities. It links up the technology and industry. The package offers for the projects, which are involved in development of new product or process. The product modification will also be considered by this package. The package allows activities like preparation of feasibility studies, laboratory trials and pilot plant operations. The project under this scheme should have feasible and quantifiable objectives. The project should not take longer than two years to be completed. The company should bear 50% of the total cost of the project. The remaining amount will be granted as eligible project specific expenses which include equipment, facilities, materials, payment to consultant, fee payable to technology institutions, project related travel and overhead expenses. The financial assistance provided by the ICICI will be charged with an interest rate of 6% during the implementation period of the R&D project. The repayment period is up to 10 years. At the final stage of the project, the rate of interest will be increased to 15%.

The Agricultural Commercialization Enterprise (ACE) is the program which is funded by the ICICI. This scheme is formulated for the development of agricultural business in India. It provide financial assistance for setting up innovative projects in horticulture floriculture, mushrooms, fruits, essential oils, herbal products, enzymes, etc., these project activities involves loans to private sector, providing technical assistance and conducting travels. It conducts field trips to members of industry for observing and knowing of technical aspects.

The ICICI is conducting another research-based program, which is related to commercialization of energy. It provides funds for development of the technology in India towards energy sector. The financial assistance is provided for the technology development of energy such as renewable, sources of energy, energy conservation, fossils, etc.

The ICICI is also financing Indo-Us Joint ventures in R&D for the development of technology process in specified areas. The scheme is applicable to agriculture, health and other area. It aims at improving the availability of quality products and services in the segments of child health, AIDS and reproductive health. It also finances for the technology development of the environmental and pollution control.

The ICICI is also providing non-project finance to the industry with medium and long-term maturity period. It provides short-term loans to the corporate sector to meet working capital needs. It provides assistance to the corporate sector with a number of schemes.

(b) Capital Market Operations

The ICICI mobilizes funds through debt and equity. It is actively involved in capital market operations. It encourages entrepreneurs by making investments in their companies by direct subscription to public issues. It participates in capital market operations by taking up rights issues of the companies, conversion option of loan assisted companies, participating in private placement of the corporate sector and provide rehabilitation package for the sick industries. It does not acquire securities in the secondary market. The investment operations of the ICICI have been increasing at present. It also offers fee-based services to its clients. These activities are advisory in nature provide consultancy services. It has been offering project advisory services since 1991, to PSUs, and private sector companies. It acts as a trustee for the holders of convertible and non-convertible debenture issues. These financial instruments are issued by the companies to the public in the form of Rights issue, private placement, etc. it offers comprehensive custodial services since 1992. Its clients include FIIs, overseas depository banks.

The ICICI has been actively involving in promoting a number of institutions, which are strengthening the institution structure of the money and capital market. The Credit Rating information services of India Ltd. had been established in association with UTI in 1987. It provides a variety of consultancy services to the corporate sector. CRISIL is involved in rating various types of financial instruments offered to the investing public. It is also instrumental in promoting the following institutions.

(1) Technology Development and Information Company of India (TDCI)

(2) Over The Counter Exchange of India Ltd. (OTCEI)

(3) Stock Holding Corporation of India Ltd. (SHCI)

(4) Discount and Finance House of India (DFHI)

(5) Management Development Institutes (MDIs)

After the liberalization, privatization and globalization, the ICICI entered new areas of business like investment banking, asset management, commercial banking etc. it has set up specialized subsidiaries, which are presented below:

(1) ISEC Ltd.

(2) ICICI Brokerage

(3) ICICI Banking

(4) ICICI Info tech

(5) ICICI Personal Financial Services Ltd.

(6) ICICI Capital Services Ltd.

(7) ICICI Venture Ltd.

(8) ICICI International

(9) ICICI Properties

Merger of ICICI with ICICI Bank:

The ICICI have been merged with ICICI bank on 28-03-2002. The Universal Bank plans major thrusts on the retail and international fronts. The ICICI and ICICI bank have been moving towards a merger for over two years now. The formal announcement was made on 25-2-01. There has been frenetic activity in the ICICI group to conform to the statutory obligations on the way to the turning into a Universal bank. The merger process required the ICICI to show ₹ 23,000 crores by way of SLR for the combined entity. The ICICI bank already having ₹ 5,000 crores[6] in its SLR portfolio an additional ₹ 18,000 crores was required from ICICI. Then the ICICI mobilized the fund through a combination of retail deposits and asset swaps. The remaining ₹ 10, 000 Crore was brought in by way of retail deposits. The merger regulations did not allow merged entity to have any subsidiary that was involved in non-banking activities. The swap ratio has been fixed at one share of ICICI bank for every two shares of ICICI. Therefore, the final 2:1 ratio falls within the ambit of all the valuation norms. The aim of the post merger was: aggressive capital management, optimal size technology, intensive multi channel delivery architecture, world class skill bases and enduring customer relationship. The post merger will bring several advantages. The ICICI itself gets access to cheaper retail funds. The merged entity is focusing on the new avenues. They are fee income, trade finance, for ex., remittances, cash management services, dividend management, agri business, small and medium enterprises, consumer finance, auto loans, credit and debit cards, housing finance, personal loans, Internet banking, retail business, third party products, Mutual funds, insurance, pension products, smart cards and fund transfer.

Recently it introduced "e-cheque" system, in fund transfer process. According to the scheme, the customer can transfer money to any account in any bank in any of 14 cities is becoming pretty popular. Another service has been launched in Delhi; any cell phone owner can tap up with the ICICI ATM. It also focuses on cross selling instead of individual marketing. The major advantage of cross selling is that the customer acquisition cost comes down massively customer loyalty and satisfaction is reflected in cross selling. The major thrust areas are the international division. The international business is to provide 10-15% of ICICI bank's turnover and profits in the forthcoming 5 years but zero today. It identified four geographies setting up representative offices in the US, UK, Dubai, Singapore and London. The International division will be setting up a consultancy to provide services to banks and other financial sector players internationally.

The Indian economy requires large banks to cater to its requirements. The ICICI merger will be a significant player. The merger is clearly a reflection of the overdue consolidation the banking industry needs.

[6] The Big Picture, *Business India,* April 1-14-2002, p. 51.

A Merger Snapshot

		As on September, 2001 ICICI Bank Merged			March 31, 2001
	ASSETS				
1	Total Credits	61235	11660	72895	65000
2	SLR Investments	489	5400	5889	23500
3	Cash Reserves	-	1450	4500	4500
4	Other Assets	12650	2290	14940	15000
5	Total Assets	74374	20800	95174	108000
	LIABILITIES				
1	Equity Capital	786	220	613	600
2	Reserves	7996	124	9612	9600
3	Borrowings	59668	685	60353	60000
4	Deposits	-	17515	17515	32000
5	Other Liabilities	74374	20800	95174	108000

The expressions by the analysts and experts are that the new merged entity may be sitting on mountain of non-performing assets that may come home to roost. Their conclusion is that its loan portfolio cannot be too different from that of IDBI or IFCI. All of them were lending to the same sectors and companies with similar profiles. ICICI comes with net NPAs at around ₹ 3,000 crores or 5.3%. The ICICI bank has now NPAs at 1.36%.

Industrial Finance Corporation of India (IFCI)

Introduction

The industrial Finance Corporation of India was set up in July, 1948, by the government of India. It was established under the IFCI Act, 1948, with the basic objective of providing finance to the industries in private sector. At present it also provides financial assistance to cooperative, joint, public sector units. It provides loans for expansion, diversification and modernization of existing units. It also underwrites and directly subscribes to industrial securities, merchant banking services and lease finance. It renders financial assistance both in rupees and foreign currencies to the corporate sector.

The small-scale industries, proprietary and partnership concerns were not eligible for financial assistance from the IFCI. It did not grant assistance for the purpose of working capital. It did not provide assistance for the acquisition of capital goods for commercial or trading purposes. It did not grant loans in foreign currencies for purchasing of raw materials, imports or payments of royalties, interest and dividends. The IFCI Act was amended in 1986; the authorized business of the IFCI is as follows:

(a) It acts as agent to World Bank.

(b) It provides technical administrative assistance legal and marketing assistance to any industrial concern.

(c) It provides consultancy services in and outside India.

(d) Appointed as administrator.

Financial Resources

The sources of the funds are Share Capital, Retained earnings by the issue of bonds, borrowings from the Government, Repayment of past loans and sale of investments, borrowings from IDBI, borrowing from foreign lending institutions, foreign capital markets and public deposits.

The paid-up capital of the IFCI was held directly by the Central Government and the RBI. The holdings of the two concerns were transferred to the IDBI.

The balance of the paid-up capital contributed by the commercial banks, insurance organizations and cooperative banks. It made a first public issue of equity shares in December, 1993. The authorized capital has now been increased to ₹ 339.1 crores. It had consistently increased and built up sizeable reserves. The reserves of the IFCI consists the following elements:

(a) General Reserves

(b) Reserve fund

(c) Benevolent reserve

(d) Special Reserve

(e) Specific grant from the GoI

(f) Share Premium Account

It mobilizes funds for the sale of bonds. It grants Rupee currency and foreign currency loans, the Rupee currency loans are met from the domestic market and foreign market respectively. The IFCI policy is to reduce its dependence on government. It focused on market borrowing by issue of bonds. The bonds are guaranteed by the government and redeemable at par at coupon rates ranging from 8.75% and 13.5%. It depends on bonds which are privately placed and issued to public. The issued bonds to the public carry a maturity of 7 to 30 years. The privately placed bonds have a maturity of one to 27 years. It offered a variety of innovative bonds targeting different segments. It also issued deep discount bonds, education bonds, gift bonds, and retirement bonds, floating millionaire bonds.

It was authorized in 1952 to borrow in foreign currency. It has been borrowing from foreign agencies/financial institution and was allowed to borrow from the global market. It obtains financial assistance from USA, Germany, France and UK. The borrowings from international capital market are from:

(a) Euro Currency markets

(b) Germany markets

(c) Japanese capital market

It diversified its resources by raising short-term funds through certificate of deposits and commercial papers. It reduced its dependence on GoI and RBI. Its main funding source is market borrowings through a variety of innovative family bonds.

Business Activities

IFCI actively participated in industrialization of the country. It provides financial assistance to corporate sector through different schemes. The industrial financing activities consist of two segments. They are

(a) Project Finance

(b) Financial Services

Project Finance covers the entire funding new projects, expansion, diversification and modernization in the form of foreign currency and rupee term loans. The project finance is the main activity of the IFCI. The projects will be financed through term loans. The IDBI directly subscribes to equity shares of smaller new companies to encourage the new breed of entrepreneurs.

It is also involved in capital market operations. Its investment portfolio consists of acquisition of shares for underwriting obligations, direct subscription to shares, bonus issues subscription to shares, bonus issues subscription to right shares, conversion of convertible debentures proportion, conversion of dues into shares or debentures. It also guarantees to finance the amount to the industry. IFCI now also provides indirect finance for leasing companies. It has started providing short-term loans to corporate for meeting working capital financing.

Financial services is the secondary activity of IFCI in order to improve its profitability. The financial services include fund-based, fee-based, project counseling, issue management, loan syndication, financial restructuring, mergers and acquisitions, debentures, trusteeship, equipment leasing, etc. It provides financial assistance to enterprise in the private corporate sector, public sector and joint sector. It actively participated in sugar cooperative sector. The government directed the IFCI to continue the support to textile industry also. The assistance given to industrial cooperative has in all cases been in the form of loans only. The financial assistance to the cooperative sector has substantially declined over the years. The IFCI sanctioned loans to the private sector. Its assistance to the private sector projects has increased substantially over the years. It was providing financial assistance to PSUs, Government companies since 1969. This financial assistance was provided for expansion, diversification provided satisfying the following clauses:

(a) Public limited companies

(b) Had declared a maiden dividend

(c) Had built up sufficient internal resources

(d) Should not have approached for budgetary support

It provides financial assistance to a wide variety of industries. The sanctioning of loans depends upon changing conditions of national priorities. Initially, it was given preference to sugar and textile projects. It also diversified its investment strategy and concentrated in power generation, telecom services, textiles, electronics, synthetic resins, plastics, fertilizers, basic chemicals, petroleum refining and cement. It provides finance to industrial enterprises spread over AP, Gujarat, Maharashtra, Tamil Nadu, MP and WB. It also provides assistance to enterprise in the backward regions. It initiated measures to achieve the balanced regional development.

It actively involved in promotional activities like project identification, formulation implementation and operations. It provides consultancy fee subsidy scheme and interest scheme and assistance schemes.

The consultancy fee subsidy scheme is providing services to industrial units, which are identified as the small, tiny and ancillary units. The scheme is applicable to small entrepreneurs in rural, cottage, and tiny and small-scale sectors, to new entrepreneurs for meeting the cost of market survey. Interest subsidy scheme is to provide encouragement to the unemployed youth and women entrepreneurs. This scheme is implemented through SFCs. It also provides assistance schemes to the existing industrial projects in the medium and small-scale sector.

It encourages professionalism in management to improve the quality in day to day management. The IFCI sponsored in 1973, a management development institute to provide training and research in the field of banking. It established in 1977, a Development Banking Center as its autonomous wing. The MDI and DBC have been continuously working for the development of managerial manpower in public, private, joint and cooperative sectors in the industry. It diversified its business activities into the following areas:

(a) Merchant Banking

(b) Project Counseling

(c) Credit syndication

(d) Consultancy to sick industrialization

(e) Sponsoring of financial institutions

Importance of Financial Institutions

After the Second World War many countries felt that there was a strong need for establishment of financial institutions. In undeveloped countries, it is necessary to establish the financial institutions to boost the activities of industrialization like our nation. In 1918, the Industrial commission has recommended the establishment of financial institutions in India. After independence, a number of financial institutions have formed all India bases. These institutions are rendering specialized services not only in finance but also technical services and guidance. The following table may reveal the importance of All India Financial Institutions in our economy.

SECTOR	SANCTIONS					DISBURSEMENTS					UTILISATION (%)			
	94-95	95-96	96-97	97-98	98-99	94-95	95-96	96-97	97-98	98-99	94-95	95-96	96-97	97-98
1. Food Products	2151	2100	1091	1688	2027	1459	1500	1232	12302	1391	68	71	113	73
2. Textiles	7531	4624	3576	5206	5208	4385	4296	3286	3934	4723	58	93	92	76
3. Paper Products	676	1754	1052	909	1139	471	935	1058	942	916	70	53	101	104
4. Rubber	286	364	462	1067	694	162	293	346	278	427	57	81	75	26
5. Chemicals	6462	7548	6342	5631	5767	4588	4681	5149	4913	5297	71	62	81	87
6. Crude Oil	477	100	9	1	8	49	57	28	31	4	10	57	327	2354
7. Refineries	3522	2483	1348	4037	7792	1265	510	892	4391	4796	36	21	66	109
8. Fertilizers	983	2676	1824	1997	2753	663	907	1559	1740	2060	68	34	85	87
9. Cement	1986	2710	1710	1968	1754	1363	1256	2485	1857	1440	69	46	145	94
10. Basic metal														
Iron steel	4607	3868	3877	7343	4432	2748	2732	3103	5492	3563	60	71	80	75
(b) Non ferrous	358	267	960	571	1047	189	158	347	586	593	53	59	36	103
11. Metal Products	864	2239	2063	1422	1289	709	1527	1486	996	1049	84	68	72	70

12. Machinery	1464	1662	1904	1460	2004	907	1276	1958	1301	1398	62	77	103	89
13. Electrical equipment	713	972	1209	1467	1299	395	377	732	815	1102	55	39	61	55
14. Electronic equipment	1721	2686	1427	2616	2160	1090	1725	1295	1295	1899	63	64	91	73
15. Transport equipment	1304	1996	2696	2189	2669	755	1067	1797	1518	1947	58	53	67	69
16.Infrastructure														
(a)Power Generation	5517	5705	5024	12534	17768	1994	2600	3447	4465	4038	36	46	69	36
(b) Tele Communication	1021	1029	797	4752	4151	165	619	294	1170	1030	16	60	37	25
(c) Roads/Ports/ Bridges	354	162	490	2260	3186	9	45	39	1775	2276	3	28	8	79
17. Services	4865	5263	5150	9180	9788	3279	4675	4534	6540	7166	68	88	88	71
18. Other Industries	7183	4732	3021	4650	8054	4046	3584	3386	4461	6143	56	76	112	96
GRAND TOTAL	**54026**	**54942**	**46030**	**72849**	**88988**	**30691**	**34821**	**38454**	**50331**	**52992**	**57**	**64**	**84**	**69**

Source: The Economic Times, dt: 7-4-2000.

The All India Financial Institutions have been helping the corporate to mobilize the resources by sanctions, the take away of funds as represented by disbursement. As percentage of sanctions showed a downslide during the last years, i.e., 1997-98 & 98-99. The year 1998-99 saw a number of monetary measures to boost the investment, fuel growth promotes healthy atmosphere for the industrial recovery. The All India Financial Institutions have been playing a vital role; they provide a variety of customized financial products and services in tandem with the emerging needs of the industry by sanctioning the substantial financial assistance in the competitive and deregulated environment since the liberalization. The investment activity, which reflected in the disbursement of funds as a percentage of sanctions, had shown a downtrend since 1996-97. The latest annual report in the development banking published by the IDBI revealed this fact. The under utilization of funds was partially responsible for the sluggish market conditions and cost cutting exercise adopted by the corporate, whose profits have been dwindling.

The All India Financial Institutions constitutes the following institutions:

1. Industrial Development Bank of India (IDBI)
2. Industrial Finance Corporation of India (IFCI)
3. Industrial Credit and Investment Corporation of India (ICICI)
4. Small Industries Development Bank of India (SIDBI)
5. Industrial Investment Bank of India (IIBI)

Specialized Financial Institutions

(a) Risk Capital and Technology Finance Corporation (RCTFC)

(b) ICICI Venture

(c) Tourism Finance Corporation of India (TFCI)

Investment Institutions

1. Life Insurance Corporation (LIC)
2. Unit Trust of India (UTI)
3. General Insurance Corporation (GIC)

During 1998-99, the sanctions and disbursements of these institutions increased from 18.9% and 8.4% to ₹ 89,877 crores and ₹ 56,204 crores respectively. With the sanctions and disbursement of All India development banks they went up 20.5% and 7.7% respectively to ₹ 79,483 crores and ₹ 46,332 crores respectively institutions decreased to 32% and 28.4% respectively to ₹ 243 crores and ₹ 161 crores respectively during 1998-99.

The Investment institutions recorded an increase of 8.9% and 12.9% in sanctions and disbursements to ₹ 10,151 crores and ₹ 9,721 crores respectively during the year under review. However, there has been a decelerating trend in the effective utilization of funds as indicated in the disbursement: As percentage of sanctions by the All India Financial Institutions to industries to meet their varying needs during the last two years.

The disbursements as a percentage of sanctions by the All India Financial Institutions, which was at the peak of 82.21% in 96-97 plunged to 68.58% in 1997-98 and further to 62.63% in 1998-99. The fall in these ratios was mainly attributed to the slow pace of growth of funds disbursed as against sanctions by the leading Financial Institutions like IFCI, ICICI and specialized Financial Institutions like RCTFC.

In case of the IFCI, the proportion of disbursement to sanction was as high as 112.1% in 1996-97. It declined to 72.5% in 1997-98 and further to 54.7% in 1998-99.

Similarly in case of the ICICI the share of disbursement in the total sanction, which peaked at 79.4% in 1996-97, dropped to 63.9% in 1997-98 and further to 54.7% in 1998-99.

The disbursement as a proportion of sanctions had shown substantial improvement in the case of IDBI, IIBI and investment institutions like GIC during 1998-99. Such ratio works out as much higher at 134.5% in 1998-99 in the case of IDBI as against 63.3% in the previous year while for GIC the ratio ruled higher at 105.4% as compared to 97.5% in the previous year.

The Investment Institutions extends assistance to the industries through loans underwriting or through direct subscription to equities and debentures.

Industry wise trends in sanctions and disbursements shows that there has been perceptible shift in the utilization of funds during 1998-99, in favor of industries such as textiles, rubber and rubber products, chemical and chemical products. Electronic equipment, transports equipment, Tele communication and service industry.

Although food products, paper and paper boards, crude petroleum, refineries and oil exploration cement, basic metals, metal products, electricity generation and road, ports and bridges showed a significant growth in sanctions, there has been down trend in the ratio of disbursement to sanction in these cases during 1998-99.

Another dimension of analysis can also be found in the state wise of sanctions a disbursements shows that the ratio of disbursements to sanction of as worked out lower during 1998-99, when compared to previous year despite a surge in sanctions in the case of Nagaland, Arunachal Pradesh. Delhi, Jammu & Kashmir, Punjab, Maharashtra, Meghalaya and Tamil Nadu. Other states, which showed a lower utilization of fund, than sanctioned when compared to previous year, include AP, Assam, Bihar, Gujarat, Himachal Pradesh, Manipur, Meghalaya and West Bengal. On the other side Goa, Haryana, Kerala. Madhya Pradesh, Maharashtra, Mizoram, Orissa, Rajasthan, Sikkim, Tripura and Uttar Pradesh recorded substantial improvement in disbursement than sanctioned during 1998-99.

The further analysis of sector wise reveals that the public sector recorded the highest increase in sanctions at 86.3% followed by joint sector (8.6%) and private sector (6.5%) however, the ratio of disbursement to sanction showed a fall from 83.2% in 1997-98 to 61.5% in 1998-99 in the case of public sector, which claimed nearly 20% of the total sanction. The private sector, which accounts for the bulk of the sanctions when a fall in disbursement to sanction ratio from 66.4% to 61.7%.

With the increasing needs of the industry, the Financial Institutions had reoriented their policies and assistance structure with much sharper customer focus by developing and introducing variety of products and services in the post reform period. These Financial Institutions had set up several subsidiaries for offering a wide range of newly developed products and services as also for capital market infrastructure development, covering areas such as commercial banking, investment banking, Non-banking finance, investor servicing, broking, venture capital financing, infrastructure financing, custodial services, electronic trading in stock exchanges capital market regulation, registrar and transfer services and credit rating etc.

Obligations and Responsibilities

Merchant bankers have the following obligations and responsibilities:

(a) Merchant banker should maintain proper books of accounts, record, and submit half yearly/annual financial statements to the SEBI within stipulated period of time.

(b) No merchant banker should associate with another merchant banker who is not registered in the SEBI.

(c) Merchant bankers should not enter into any transactions on the basis of unpublished information available to them in the course of their professional assignment.

(d) Every merchant banker must submit himself to the inspection by the SEBI when required for and submit all the records.

(e) Every merchant banker must disclose information to the SEBI when it requires any information from him or her.

(f) All merchant bankers must abide by the code of conduct prescribed for them.

(g) Every merchant banker who acts as a lead manger must enter into an agreement with the issuer selling out mutual rights, liabilities obligations, relating to such issues with particular references to disclosures, allotment, refund, etc.

Code of Conduct

According to the regulation 13 of the SEBI of 1992 (Merchant Bankers), every merchant banker should comply with the following codes of conduct. They are:

(a) The merchant banker must observe high standards of integrity and fairness in all his dealings.

(b) He shall render at all times high standard of services, exercise due diligence exercise independent professional judgement.

(c) If necessary he must disclose to his clients the possible sources of conflict of duties and interest.

(d) The merchant banker should not indulge in unfair practice or unfair competition with other merchant bankers.

(e) He neither should nor make any exaggerated statement about his capacity or achievement.

(f) He should always endeavor to give the best possible advice and prompt, efficient and cost effective service.

(g) He should maintain secrecy of all the confidential information received during the course of service to his client.

(h) He should not engage in the creation of a false marker or price rigging or manipulations.

Merchant Banking in India

After the termination of the managing agency system in India, there was a strong need of legal and financial services to the corporate sector, which required an alternative agency. On such situation the emergence of merchant banking raised. The merchant banking system in India was introduced by Grindlays Bank in 1967. It was the first bank, which received license from the RBI. It started with the management of capital issues, rendering the services according to the needs of emerging new class entrepreneurs for diverse financial services ranging from production to marketing research. It also provided the services to large and medium range companies. The Citi bank established its merchant banking wing in 1970. Later on the Banking Commission which was established in 1972, felt the need for the establishment of the merchant institutions to offer services like syndication or financing, promotion of projects, investment management advisory services to the corporate sector. The SBI became the first commercial bank in India to launch its merchant banking division in 1972, consequent to the recommendations of the banking commission in 1972, that Indian banks were allowed to enter into this segment. Later other commercial banks and financial institutions like Indian Bank, Punjab National Bank, Indian overseas Bank, Bank of Baroda, Syndicate Bank, Chartered Bank, LIC, GIC, UTI, etc., also started merchant banking divisions. Some brokerage houses were diversified into this area like J.M.Financial and Investment Consultancy Services Pvt. Ltd. The DSP Financial Consultancy Ltd., Bajaj Capital Investment centers Pvt. Ltd., Tata Consultancy Service Ltd. etc., Among the development banks the ICICI started the merchant banking activities in 1973, followed by the IFCI in 1986 and the IDBI in 1991.

Activities/Services Rendered by Merchant Banks

Merchant banks are rendering diverse services and functions as organizing and extending of finance for the investment in projects acceptance house business, issue of foreign currency bonds, financing of loan authorities, financing export of capital goods, hydro power installations, financing of hire purchase transactions, raising of Euro dollar loans, equipment leasing, mergers and acquisition, valuation of assets, investment management and promotion of investments, all these securities are not offered by all the merchant bankers but different merchant bankers are specialized in different services. The merchant bank is a mute service oriented agency. Merchant banking is a creative activity .In India the merchant banks are engaged in the following activities:

(a) Corporate finance services (Management of public issues, credit syndication)
(b) Advisory services (Project counseling, financing, capital restructuring)
(c) Services NRIS (Evaluation of investment portfolio, promotion of industries)
(d) Leasing (Equipment, machinery e.g.).

Merchant banking activities are regulated in India by

1. Guidelines of the SEBI.
2. Guidelines of the Ministry of Finance.
3. Companies Act of 1956.
4. Securities Contracts (Regulation) Act of 1956.
5. Listing guidelines of the stock exchanges.

1. Guidelines of SEBI

After the abolition of the CCI, the place was occupied by a legal organ called as "Securities and Exchange Board of India". The issue of capital and pricing of issues by companies has become free prior approval. The SEBI has issued guidelines for the issue of capital by the companies. The guidelines broadly covers the requirement of the first issue by a new company or the first issue of a new company set up by the existing company, the first issue by the existing private companies and public issues by the existing listed companies. The SEBI is the most powerful organization to control and lead both the primary market and secondary market. According to SEBI guideline, if any company approaches the public, by issuing share capital through public issues must be kept open for three working days and it should be mentioned in the prospectus. In the case of rights issue, the subscription time should not be kept more than 60 days. The gap between rights and public issue should not exceed 30 days. The issued capital must be fully paid up within 12 months of the date of issue. The minimum amount of subscription by the investors in the public issue either at par or premium has been fixed at ₹ 5,000, the amount of issue should not exceed the amount specified in the prospectus. Oversubscription amount retention by the company is not permitted under any circumstances. The SEBI has announced the new guidelines for the disclosures by the companies leading to the investor protection. They are presented below:

(a) If any company's other income exceeds 10% of the total income, the details should be disclosed.
(b) The company should disclose any adverse situation, which affects the operations of the company and occurs within one year prior to the date of filing of the offer document with the registrar of companies or stock exchange.
(c) The company should also disclose the information regarding the capacity utilization of the plant for the last 3 years.
(d) The promoters of the company must maintain their holding at least at 20% of the expanded capital.
(e) The minimum application money payable should not be less than 25% of the issue price.
(f) The company should disclose the time normally taken for the disposal of various types of investor's grievances.

(g) The company can make firm allotments in public issues as follows:

1. India Mutual Funds (20%)
2. FIIs (24%)
3. Regular employees of the company (10%)
4. Financial Institutions (20%)

(h) The company should disclose the safety net scheme or buy back arrangements of the shares proposed in public issue. This scheme is applicable to a limited number of 500 shares per allotee and the offer should be valid for a period of at least 6 months from the date of dispatch of securities.

(i) According to guidelines, in case of the public issues at least 30 mandatory collection centers should be established.

(j) According to the SEBI guidelines regarding rights issue, the company should give advertisements in not less than two newspapers about the dispatch of letters of offer. No preferential allotment may be made along with any rights issue.

(k) The company should also disclose about the fee agreed between the Head Managers and the company in the memorandum of understanding

Registration of Merchant Bankers and Regulations

The Ministry of Finance the department of Economic Affairs has issued guidelines for the merchant bankers. According to the guidelines any person or body proposing to engage in the business of merchant banking would need the authorization from the SEBI. The authorized activities covers issue management, corporate advisory services relating to the issue, underwriting, portfolio management and managers, consultant or advisers to the issue. The SEBI categorized merchant bankers into 4 kinds.

They are:

1. *Category - I* to carry on any activity of the issue management and also act as adviser, consultant, co-manager, underwriter, portfolio manager.
2. *Category - II* to act as adviser, consultant, co-manager, underwriter, portfolio manager.
3. *Category – III* to act as underwriter, adviser, consultant to an issue.
4. *Category – IV* to act only as adviser, consultant to an issue.

The minimum net worth prescribed for the categories are ₹ 1 crore, ₹ 7.5 crores, ₹ 10,000 lakhs, ₹ 20,00,000 and nil for category I, II, III and IV respectively. The general obligations and responsibilities according to the regulations, related to their code of conduct, books of accounts, records, submission of the half yearly results, their appointment, restriction on appointment, responsibilities as the head managers submission of diligence certificate documents to be furnished to the board.

Authorized Activities

The merchant bankers will be permitted to involve in activities as per guidelines issued by the SEBI. Every activity performed by the merchant banker should be allowed by the SEBI. Without the SEBI's permission no merchant banker will act in public issues and other activities. The authorized activities of the merchant banker would include issue management and other authorized activities would be portfolio management services. The criteria for the authorization of different activities are based on several factors such as

(a) Professional qualification in Financial or Business Management.

(b) Infrastructure like adequate office space, manpower and equipment.

(c) Experienced members in merchant banking business as an employee status.

(d) Capital adequacy

(e) Post track record, experience, general reputation and fairness in all transactions. The merchant bankers should seek the permission from the SEBI within 3 months.

Terms of Authorization

The following are the terms of authorization issued by the SEBI:

(a) All the merchant bankers must have a minimum net worth as prescribed.

(b) The authorization will be for an initial period of 3 years.

(c) Every merchant banker should pay initial authorization fee, annual fee and a renewal fee.

(d) All issues should be managed by at least one authorized merchant banker in issues of over ₹ 100 crore, the number could go up to a maximum of four.

(e) The responsibilities of each Head Manager must be submitted to the SEBI before the public issue.

(f) Merchant bankers should verify the prospectus contents and they should submit a certificate to the SEBI

(g) Merchant bankers should have to submit all the information to the SEBI from time to time such as documents, returns and reports as prescribed and called for.

(h) The authorization of merchant banker can be suspended or cancelled in case of violation of the guidelines.

(i) The involvement of merchant bankers in an issue should continue at least and till the completion of the essential follow up steps, i.e., listing of the instrument and dispatch of certificates/refunds.

(j) Merchant bankers have to adhere to code of conduct prescribed by the SEBI.

(k) The guidelines should be followed by the company when its function arises. No exemption will be given to them if it fails in any responsibility.

Penalty System

The SEBI can inspect the books of accounts, records, the documents etc of the merchant bankers with the interest of the investors. If anything was found wrong the SEBI can give reasonable notice to the merchant banker. If the situation is severe the SEBI may appoint a qualified auditor to investigate the books of account, penalties will be imposed for the defaults made by the merchant bankers. The SEBI categorized the following defaults as penalty points.

(i) General defaults	Penalty Points	01
(ii) Minor defaults	Penalty Points	02
(iii) Major defaults	Penalty Points	03
(iv) Serious defaults	Penalty Points	04

(i) General Defaults

For the purpose of penalty point, the following activities are categorized as general defaults which attract *one* penalty point.

1. Non-receipts of draft prospectus from the lead manager by the SEBI before filing with ROC.
2. Non-receipts of interreallocation of responsibilities of Head Manager in an issue by the SEBI prior to the opening of issue.
3. Non-receipt of due diligence certificate in prescribed manner by the SEBI before opening of the issue.
4. Failure to ensure submission of certificate of minimum 90% subscription to the issue as required under the government of India, press note number F2/14/CCI/90, dated 6-4-1990.
5. Failure to ensure publishing the dispatch of refund orders, shares/debenture certificates, filing of listing application by the issuer as required under Government of India press notification No. 2/6/CCI/89, dated 10-1-1990.

(ii) Minor Defaults

The following activities are categorized under minor defaults and it attracts *two* penalty points.

1. Advertisement, circular, brochure, press release and other issue related materials not being in conformity with the contents of the prospectus.
2. Exaggerated information to the prospectus is given by issuer or merchant in any manner.
3. Delay in refund/allotment securities.
4. Non-handling of investor grievances promptly.
5. Failure to provide adequate and fair disclosure to the investors about the risk factors in the prospectus.
6. Failure to exercise due diligence in verifying contents of prospectus.
7. Violation of the government of India, lr.No.F1/23/SERVICES/86, dt: 24/3/86 and Government of India lr No.F/23/SERVICES/86, Dt 24-07-1987 regarding the advertisements on new capital issues.
8. Failure to substantiate matters containing highlights to the issue in the prospectus.

(iii) Major Defaults

The following activities are categorized under major defaults and it attracts *three* penalty points:

1. The Head Manager does not take up mandatory underwriting.
2. The association of unauthorized merchant banker in an issue.
3. If excess number of lead managers are involved than permitted under the SEBI guidelines. The SEBI released a press note on 28-2-91 on this regard.

(iv) Serious Defaults

The following activities are categorized under serious defaults and it attracts *four* penalty points:

1. Unethical practice followed by the merchant banker and/or in violation of code of conduct.
2. Non-cooperation with the SEBI in furnishing desired information, documents, and evidence as may be called for.

A merchant banker who reaches cumulative penalty points of 8 attracts the termination/suspension of authorization by the SEBI. The merchant banker takes the corrective action. The maximum penalty points awarded in a single issue managed by the merchant banker are restricted to four.

Defaults in Prospectus

If highlights are provided, the following deficiencies can be treated as negative points:

1. Absence of risk factors in highlights.
2. Absence of listing in highlights.
3. Extraneous contents to the prospectus.

The total points allotted to the prospectus are 10. A merchant banker who scored 8 or more than 8 points will be assigned A+ grade. The merchant banker who scored 6 or less than 8 points as an and with 4 or less than 6 points will be B. The banker with a score of less than 4 points will be assigned C category. A merchant banker on reaching the cumulative penalty points of 8 shall deserve the action from the SEBI. It may be added that the above list is not an exhaustive one and the action could be taken by the SEBI for other reasons like non-fulfillment of authorization criteria (Net worth), carrying out business detrimental to the interest of the public, conviction in any economic offence by the merchant banker or any of its directors or its principal officer, violation of any other guidelines /notification, which has a bearing on the functioning of merchant bankers.

In the wake of important developments in the recent times, merchant having financial services have become more sophisticated unlike before and therefore there is a great demand for highly specialized skill in planning, decision making and controlling in these areas. To cope with these challenges in the areas of merchant banking and financial services, the country now needs a large body of trained professionals. To provide, the necessary institutional infrastructure for imparting specialized training, the Institute of Chartered Financial Analyst of India (ICFAI) has launched an innovative programme, "Merchant banking and Financial Services (MBFS). This program need post graduation qualification. It is meant for those managers who are involved in finance area. The objective of the program is to improve the conceptual, managerial and operational skills of the managers engaged in merchant banking and financial services and to help them render the best services to their clients. The program seeks to impart the knowledge of basic concepts in Merchant Banking, and to improve the ability to rationally evaluate the alternatives in the decision making process. This program is divided into five groups. Foundation group, Group A, Group B, Group C and Group D. The subjects under the groups are divided as follows:

1. Foundation group (Financial & Cost Accounting, Financial Management Quantitative methods)
2. Group A (Financial Services, New Issue Management, Asset-based Financing)

3. Group B (Security evaluation and investment, Portfolio management and mutual funds, Venture Capital)
4. Group C (International Finance, Capital Markets, Corporate Finance Services)
5. Project work and viva.

SUMMARY

Funds are tapped from the capital market to finance various mega industrial projects. In attracting public savings, merchant bankers play a vital role as specialized agencies. The resource raising function remains to be the primary business of a merchant banker. The primary market holds the key to rapid capital formation, growth in industrial production and exports. There has to be accountability to the end use of funds risen from the market. The trends in the primary market in India suggest that merchant bankers have been playing a very significant role in the corporate sector's drive for mobilizing funds from the public. The increase in the number of issues and amount raised the number of merchant brokers. Therefore the field becomes a highly competitive market where it requires a specialized skill in handling the activities.

Key Terms

1. **Merchant Banks:** These, unlike the clearing or joint stock banks, evolved from the need to finance foreign trade. They tended, historically, to trade on their specialized knowledge of overseas financial organisations and institutions and their contacts with them. Their major concern has always been with the facilitation of international trade; also with the problems of exporters seeking assurance of payment for goods delivered abroad and importers looking for convenient methods of settling indebtedness to overseas suppliers. They are the principal brokers for international trade though much of their business in this sphere is connected with the acceptance or negotiation of bills of exchange.

   A merchant bank may be a firm whose main activity is the provision of finance for trade and industry. The older merchant banks originated as merchants who turned to financing other people trading activities. Merchant banks now provide a wide variety of financial services, including advice on public offers and mergers and acting as issuing houses and accepting houses.
2. **Term Loan:** A loan by a bank to a firm for a period of between 1 and 15 years which is to be repaid according to an agreed schedule of installments.
3. **Revolving Credit:** A facility granted to a specific person whereby he may borrow money, or buy goods on credit, upto a known initial limit; when money is borrowed or goods are bought, the credit limit is reduced by the value of the borrowing, etc. it can be increased again by the amount of any money paid to the granter of the facility, but never to more than the initial limit.
4. **Risk Management:** The process, activity or study of reducing the risk of loss to a firm, particularly loss caused by accidents. Risks, once they have been identified may be reduced by: taking preventive action; setting aside a fund to pay for losses; transferring the risk to someone else, e.g., by insurance.

Questions

1. What is merchant banking? Explain its origin.
2. Define merchant banking, explain its objectives.
3. What are the important components of Indian financial system?
4. Explain the traditional functions of commercial banks.
5. What is development bank? Explain its functions.
6. Explain the difference between commercial banks and development banks.
7. Explain the project financing process in industrial credit and investment corporation of India.
8. What are the obligations and responsibilities of a merchant banker in India?
9. Explain the code of conduct of a merchant banker.
10. What are the services rendered by merchant bankers in India?
11. Explain the penalty system imposed by the SEBI, for violation of rules and regulations made by merchant bankers in India.

7 Mutual Funds in India

Mutual funds are supposed to be the best mode of investment in the capital market since they are very cost beneficial and simple, and do not require an investor to figure out which securities to invest in. A mutual fund could simply be described as a financial medium used by a group of investors to increase their money with a predetermined investment.

The responsibility for investing the pooled money into specific investment channels lies with the fund manager of the mutual fund. Investment in a mutual fund means that the investor has bought the shares of the mutual fund and has become a shareholder of that fund. By diversification of investment investors are able to purchase securities with much lower trading costs by pooling money together in a mutual fund rather than try to do it on their own. However, the biggest advantage that mutual funds offer is diversification which allows the investor to spread out his money across a wide spectrum of investments. Therefore, when one investment is not doing well, another may be doing taking off, thereby, balancing the risk to profit ratio and considerably covering the overall investment. The best form of diversification is to invest in multiple securities rather than in just one security. Mutual funds are set up with the precise objective of investing in multiple securities that can run into hundreds. It could take weeks for an investor to investigate on this kind of scale, but with investment in mutual funds all this could be done in a matter of hours.

The investment preferences of households have changed dramatically. In India, the household sector accounts for over 80% of the GDP, this plays a significant change in their investment preferences. The investor's preference may show an impact on the economy. In the emerging economic environment of competitive markets, the investment pattern has seen changes all over the financial landscape as a result of financial liberalization. The household sector is the main provider of savings in the economy. Hence, the direction into which such savings are channeled determines the direction of growth of the financial sector. The financial development occurred because of the technical invention and through the mode of popular joint stock company. The joint stock form made the large-scale industry possible by collecting large amount of capital. Subsequent Financial innovations have carried the process further — the risk reduction and liquidity. The capital is generated out of savings leading to investment, which is a part of the financial system. The organized Finance comprises of money market, capital market, new issue market, stock market, etc., led by RBI, DFHI, banks, financial institutions, mutual funds, merchant banks and all other intermediaries regulated by the SEBI and the RBI. There are specialized investment institutions, which help those savers who do not understand the functioning of the capital market and remain away from the capital market because of the complicated procedure involved in analyzing and interpreting the investment opportunities. These institutions which act as investment conduits, pool the savings of many individual investors and combine them in to fairly large and well-diversified portfolio investments. All these features are available in mutual fund. Mutual funds are an investment vehicle for the investors to enjoy the expert management skills of professional and maximize the return with an accepted risk. These are the trusts for the public savers to pool their savings. In the entire globe, the trend has been for the individual investor shifting from the direct investment in equities to the mutual fund role routes.

Definition

Mutual fund can be defined as "a form of collective investment that is useful in spreading risks and optimizing returns". A Mutual fund offers safety; it provides the services to the investors and offers a wide variety of securities within the reach of the most modern investors. Mutual funds are fast developing in to magic wands for the retail investor. Mutual funds have been defined as "a non-depository, non-banking financial intermediary which acts as an important vehicle for bringing wealthholders and deficit units together indirectly".

— ***Pierce James***

According to Weston I Fred and Brigham, "Mutual fund is a corporation which accepts money from the investors and uses the same to buy stocks, long-term bonds, short-term debt instruments issued by the issuers"

The SEBI has defined Mutual funds in sec s (m) "Mutual funds mean a fund established in the form of a trust by a sponsor to raise money by the trustees through the sale of units to the public under one or more schemes for investing in securities in accordance with issue regulations" .

A Mutual fund is an investment company or a trust that pools the resources of thousands of unit holders and invests on behalf of them in security markets. The Mutual funds have been functioning as an agent to mobilize the resources from various investors, the Unit Trusts, Investment Trusts, Mutual funds, banks. Investment Companies, real estate, investment trusts, trust companies and personal trust funds, etc., all these names contain some common characteristics the investment trust is an investment holding company and very popular in U.K. This investment trust will be incorporated under the Companies' Act. It has the same type of capital structure like the Industrial Company. The Unit Trust is established and is obliged to buy back units whenever an investor wants to sell them. But investment trust cannot buy back its shares and the investor has to sell his shares on the Stock Market. Investment trusts can mobilize long-term and can retain a part of its income. The Unit Trust cannot do either of these things. The Unit Trust always maintains a direct relation between the value of the unit and the value of the fund. Mutual savings banks are popular in USA. They offer professional fund management entrusted to them by pension plans of business and institutions. Mutual funds are very popular in USA, Canada and India. Mutual fund is a trust at law. A Mutual fund performs the basic function of buying and selling securities on behalf of its unit holders. Mutual fund provides opportunity to the investors to secure a better rate of return on their savings by utilizing the benefit of professional management of portfolios. Mutual funds help the small investors to obtain high return low risk combinations from their scientifically managed portfolios. Mutual funds are convenient and efficient investment vehicles. They can take a portfolio of securities including the blue chip companies. The Mutual fund cult has spread much faster and over a wider area than the equity cult within a very short period.

The Society for Capital Market Research and Development conducted a study regarding the investor's preference towards the Mutual funds; the study finally concluded that there are 2/3rd of middle class households in India. The study further reveals that the shift towards Mutual funds has resulted in the declining popularity of certain other financial assets like LIC Policies, bank fixed deposits, National savings certificates and company deposits. The Unit Trust is basically a pure intermediary, which involves the capital appreciation. The small investors cannot directly invest in the instruments such as certificate of deposit, commercial paper and treasury bills because they require heavy amount of investment. Mutual funds provide continuous supervision, analysis, investment consultancy, judicious investment decision, experienced expert, professional management at low costs. The investors have to pay expenses like administrative fee, management and transaction costs for getting these services.

Advantages

The advantages of Mutual fund relative to the Stock Market are as follows.

- Low transaction costs
- Benefits of high talent and expertism
- Diversification
- Tax deductions
- Low risk and better return
- Investor's protection

1. Low transactions cost: The Mutual fund is a specialized institution, which acts as an investment intermediary and channelizes savings of a large number of people. The Mutual funds are able to get the economies of large-scale because pooling of the large amount at their disposal for investment in the market. This reduces the costs in the form of brokerage fee, commission, etc. Thus a small investor gets the benefits of economies.

2. Benefits of high talent expertism: The investors in India have no knowledge about the Stock Market operations. They are unable to know the position of market situation. They do not know about the economy, per capita income, demand, consumption, companies operations, efficiency, their earning capability, profit booking, etc. The Stock Market is a highly volatile and even sometimes the experts may feel confused. The entire Stock Market depends upon many factors. The common investor has no observation about all these movements the Stock Market is heaven for those with high expertism, in-depth knowledge, scientific analysis, through understanding about the industry, company and pulse of the customer, dynamism, courage, mental stability, financial muscle, etc. The Indian investors are highly influenced by the broker's decision. They do not take any investment decisions regarding a particular scrip. They simply hand over the cheque to the broker on their recommendations. They do not know when to buy when to sell, what price, at what price the scrip should be sold, etc. The buying price of particular scrip in the Stock Market is the most important factor in determining the profits. The sale price/disposal of a financial asset in the market is also a very important element in designing and constructing a portfolio. The portfolio management is a highly specialized skillful activity. It requires a continuous monitoring and evolution. A small investor cannot be an expert in the portfolio management. If the investor invests in Mutual funds he gets all the benefits of the above said factors. All these activities are performed by the Mutual funds. They will appoint highly talented, specially trained experts in the portfolio management, equity analysts, fund managers, etc. To achieve the targeted return assured by the fund to the investors. The funds can be professionally employed through the Mutual fund ensuring good returns. The fund managers have research facilities at their disposal. They are able to analyze the performance and prospectus of various companies and take good decisions in making the investments fruitful.

3. Diversification: In Mutual funds a large number of investor's small savings can be pooled. The investor can also buy shares of one or two companies. Therefore, the Mutual funds can be used to buy shares of many different companies. Diversification reduces the risk of a portfolio. Diversification requires an additional amount of investment. In diversification, sometimes more risk may be evolved. Thus, the portfolio's construction, expansion and diversification are very easy in the Mutual funds.

4. Tax deductions: The Income Tax Act of 1961, provides some tax deductions and exemptions to the Mutual funds which can be designed to suit the tax payers needs. A large number of Mutual funds have come up with the schemes ensuring tax benefits to the subscribers. Generally, the taxpayers contribute in these funds. According to these schemes the investors are required to keep the money in the funds for a certain period called "Lock Up" which at present is 3 years. These funds distribute the profits among the Unit holders. The units will be repurchased by the fund at current NAV. The pooled amount is used to acquire shares and debt instruments. The NAV of the Units varies with values of the financial assets held by the mutual fund.

5. Low risk and better returns: A Mutual fund will be operated by the efficient fund managers. The fund managers have basic and extraordinary skills in their areas. They are well versed with the market movement. They know how to move in a highly volatile market. They are able to reduce the risk factor and increase high return to his Unit fund. A small investor on the other hand, may not be in a position to minimize such risks. Therefore the Mutual funds can reduce risk and maximize return to the holders.

6. Investor's protection: Mutual funds in India are regulated by the SEBI. The SEBI regulations of 1996, provide better protection to the investors. The Mutual funds activities are also monitored by the SEBI (Mutual funds) regulations. The SEBI regulations impart a great degree of flexibility and facilitate competition.

7. Mutual funds in India: The first Mutual fund in India was started in 1964. The Unit Trust of India was set up under a special UTI act in 1963. All Mutual funds have to be registered with the SEBI. The UTI is involved in mobilizing small savings and canalizing them in to productive avenues. The Government of India permitted the commercial banks to launch Mutual funds in India by amending the banking regulation act in 1987. A number of commercial banks have started Mutual funds to mop up savings in the society. The SBI has launched a Mutual fund called the SBI Mutual fund in 1987. The first scheme launched was known as "Magnum Regular Income Scheme" and another scheme was "Magnum Monthly Income Scheme". It had also introduced "Magnum Tax savings Scheme" with a tax benefit U/S & 80C and "Magnum Regular Income" with 12% minimum assured rate of return per annum. The Canara Bank formed the Can bank Mutual fund with the objective of housing investment expertise for the benefit of investors. It had also started two schemes Can stock and Can share in 1987. The object of these schemes was long-term capital appreciation by adopting strategies. The objective was to secure a regular income and growth. The Indian Bank had also established a mutual fund called the Indian Bank Mutual Fund in 1990. It floated schemes such as "Saran Pushpa, 2nd Ratna, 2nd 88A,

2nd Jyothi, Saran Jyothi". 2nd 88A were a tax saving growth scheme. The Punjab National Bank set up a mutual fund called the PNB Mutual fund in 1990. It had floated a PNB Regular Income plus Scheme. It provides buy back facility after one year. The Bank of India introduced rising monthly income scheme schedule with an objective of doubling the amount after 5 years period. The LIC Mutual fund was set up in 1989 by the LIC. It had introduced open schemes such as "Dhamaraksh 1989, Dhanavirichi Dhana sahayog and Dhanavidya, Dharma Shree, Dhana 80CCB, Dhana Tax Saver, Dhanasamirdhi etc". The GIC Mutual fund was set up in 1990. It had launched schemes like GIC SAFE, GIC Rise, and the government of India allowed the private sector corporate to join the Mutual fund sector on 14-2-1992. Afterwards a number of private sector companies had approached the SEBI for permission to set up private Mutual fund. The alliance capital had set up the Alliance equity (D) (G). The Birla Mutual fund had introduced Birla advantage, Birla MNC (D) (G). The ING Mutual fund had set up IG portfolio (D) (G), ING Income portfolio. The Templeton Mutual fund had introduced Templet on India, Income, and Template on MIP. The Tata Mutual fund had set up Tata Income (D) (G). The sun mutual fund had set up sun F and C money value. Kotak Mahindra Mutual fund had set up K-30, K-Tech, Kgiit, K-Liand, Chola Mutual fund had introduced cholagit Saving, Cholgit investments. The Pioneer ITI prima plus (D), pioneer (IT Index). The DSP Mutual fund had set up DSPML balanced (D) (G). The JM Mutual fund had introduced JMI India Bond, (D) (G) JM Income bond (D) (G), Reliance Mutual fund introduced "Reliance Income (DH) (DX) Sundaram Mutual fund has set up Sundaram bond savers (D) (G) schemes, Zurich Mutual fund introduced Zurich India prudence D, Zurich India Prudence-G, Scheme Prudential ICICI Mutual fund has set up prudential ICICI MP prudential ICICI MP (G), prudential Liquid Plan. The IDBI Mutual fund introduced IDBI principal, IDBI Income scheme, Grind lays bank has set up Grind lays SSI, Grind lays SSIDQ, Schemes, HDFC introduced HDFC Income (D) (G) HDFC (Liquid) schemes etc. All of these Mutual funds have entered the market with the liberalization of rules and regulations by the government. In November 1995, the government has permitted private sector Mutual funds to set up Money Market Mutual fund. The SEBI Mutual fund regulation of 1996, provides registration constitution, management and schemes of Mutual funds in India. Money Market Mutual fund emerged in the US in 1972 and is now coming up in many countries. MMF is established for the purpose to purchase large pools of short-term financial instruments. Abroad the average maturity period of investments is about 40 days. The investors will use the MMMF with the prior approval of the RBI and SEBI. Since 1-4-96 the MMMF is available to only corporate and mutual funds. The maturity period of MMMF has also been reduced. Bank of Madurai, Amro Bank, UTI, IDBBIMF were given clearance to set up MMMFs. The first MMMF established by the Kothari Pioneer in 1997, did not succeed the UTI started its MMMF on 23-4-97 and collected about ₹ 30 crores. The scheme is offered to resident individuals, HUFs, trusts, societies and corporate. The MMMF is involved in buying and selling off with treasury bills, government securities call money commercial paper, and commercial bill certificates of deposits etc. The period 1996-99, was the worst in the history of the Mutual funds. But several AMCs used the opportunity to restructure their portfolios and were ready for the 1999, boom in equities. In the year 1999-2000, the value of assets under the management swelled to ₹ 1079.46 crores when the equity meltsdown happened. At present there are 34 Mutual fund houses managing 614 schemes and ₹ 90,577 crores in asset. All of them will not survive, but performance and transparency will prove in the long run.

Year	Corpus fund (AMC) (₹ in Crore)
1964-69	65
1969-74	172
1974-79	402
1979-84	1,261
1986-87	4,563
1987-88	6,739
1989-90	13,456
1990-91	19,111
1991-92	23,060
1992-93	37,480
1993-94	46,988
1994-95	61,301
1995-96	75,050
1996-97	80,539
1997-98	68,984
1998-99	68,472
1999-2000	1,07,946
2000-2001	90,587
2001-2002	94,571

Private sector funds recorded higher fresh sales as compared from May 2000-July 2001. Redemptions were also higher than in June. It resulted in a net inflow of ₹ 2,430 crores private sector funds utilized this period to increase their product offering. Taurus Mutual fund launched a debt and gilt fund. Bank sponsored funds net inflow of ₹ 61 crores. Institutions backed funds also saw a sharp fall in net inflows. Mutual funds can be classified as "by category" or based on functioning of schemes. The relevant data for the period May 2000 to July 2001 for Mutual funds (category) presented is below:

Mutual Funds by Category

- UTI Mutual fund
- Private sector Mutual funds (excluding UTI, Banks sponsored and Institutions backed.)
- Bank sponsored Mutual funds (BOB, BOI, Can Bank, PNB, and SBI)
- Institutions backed Mutual funds

(₹ in Crore)

1. UTIMF	Particulars	May 2000	June 2000	July 2000	May 2001	June 2001	July 2001
	Sales	1,224	1,410	774	376	1,858	237
	Redemption	1,100	557	1,134	2,302	2,265	87

	Net Sales	124	853	640	–1926	–407	–63
2. PSMF							
	Sales	5,015	3,931	4,208	6,815	986	112
	Redemption	4,034	3,529	3,580	4,030	6,787	88
	Net Sales	981	403	628	2,785	3,099	243
3. BSMF							
	Sales	95	101	373	389	835	330
	Redemption	161	92	90	136	187	27
	Net Sales	–66	9	283	253	648	6
4. IBMF							
	Sales	95	105	66	357	561	531
	Redemption	216	91	117	245	245	397
	Net Sales	–121	14	–51	112	112	134
5. AMF							
	Sales	6,429	5,547	5,421	7,937	13,140	1,235
	Redemption	5,511	4,268	3,921	6,713	6,713	1,037
	Net Sales	918	1,279	1,500	1,224	1,224	198

UTIMF: UTI Mutual Fund

PSMF: Private Sector Mutual Funds (Excluding UTI, banks sponsored, institutions backed)

BSMF: Banks Sponsered Mutual Funds

IBMF: Instituions Backed Mutual Funds

AMF: All Mutual Funds (Including UTI)

Mutual Funds by Schemes

The Mutual funds can also be classified according to the schemes:

- Growth Schemes
- Income Funds
- Balanced Funds
- Liquid and Money Market Fund
- Gilt Funds
- Equity Linked Savings Schemes

Particulars	May 2000	June 2000	July 2000	May 2001	June 2001	July 2001
A. Growth Schemes						
Sales	1,018	741	1,325	87	112	59
Redemption	482	481	960	190	80	135
Net Sales	536	260	365	–103	32	–76
B. Income Funds						
Sales	2,043	2,068	1,423	2,909	6,297	375
Redemption	1,963	1,400	1,003	1,074	496	368
Net Sales	80	688	420	1,835	4,801	78
C. Balanced Funds						
Sales		517	499	64	43	9
Redemption	285	290	98	1,725	2,105	115
Net Sales	413	227	401	–1,661	–2,062	–10
D. Liquid Money Market Fund						
Sales	2,147	1,847	1,850	4,348	5,991	8,074
Redemption	2,247	1,563	1,387	3,378	5,550	6,038
Net Sales	–100	274	463	970	491	2,036
E. Gilt Funds						
Sales	481	363	318	526	695	489
Redemption	522	513	466	152	258	390
Net Sales	–41	–150	–148	374	437	99
F. Equity Linked Savings Schemes						
Sales	42	11	6	3	2	3
Redemption	12	11	7	194	25	11
Net Sales	30	0	–1	–191	–23	–8

Funds Flow by Category

All Mutual funds taken together recorded a net inflow of ₹ 1,989 crores. While fresh sales fell to ₹ 12,359 crores redemption increased to ₹ 10,370 crores.

The Unit Trust of India saw another month of Net out Flow. The Redemptions also fell subsequently to ₹ 873 crores. There was a net out go of ₹ 636 crores. The private sector Mutual funds recorded higher fresh sales as compared to June. Redemptions were also higher than in June and this resulted in a net inflow of ₹ 2,430 crores. Private sector funds utilized this period to increase their product offerings. Taurus Mutual fund launched a debt and gilt fund. Banks sponsored funds saw a net inflow of ₹ 61 crores. Institution backed funds also saw a sharp fall in net inflows. The amount in this case was ₹ 134 crores.

Funds Flow by Type

The Mutual funds can be classified as growth schemes income funds, Balanced funds, Liquid Funds, Gilt Funds and Equity linked Savings funds. All of these schemes were discussed in preceding pages. Debt funds saw fresh sales fall by 40%. Redemptions on the other hand were higher by 46%. The net results were that net sales fell to double-digit levels. The fresh sales were dismally low, reaching single digit levels. In Us-64 had fully closed the exit route in July there were no Redemptions from this fund. Liquid and Money Market funds were the winners during the period May 2000-July 2001. The fresh sales increased by ₹ 5,000 crores over June. Redemptions increased by a little over ₹ 500 crores on the whole, this type of fund received a net inflow of ₹ 2,036 crores. This is a record for the analysis period. The strong inflows into liquid and Money Market funds could also be an indicator of investor's perception that the rally in bond markets is coming to an end. Gilt funds saw fresh sales of ₹ 1,489 crores. The Redemptions stood at ₹ 390 crores and the net result was an inflow of ₹ 99 crores. Most funds were moving into medium tenure paper and Gilt funds can also expect returns to slow down, tax saving funds continued to remain due. Inflows were minimal and there was a net flow of ₹ 8 crores.

Investment Trust

The Investment Trust is a financial institution. It collects a small amount of invisible funds from a large number of investors. The trust pools the amount of savings and invests them in Stock Market by constructing a suitable portfolio. A small investor may not have large funds to purchase the securities in many companies. It is fully authorized to deploy the funds, as it likes. It is very usual in the Stock Market. The prices are highly volatile, and then there is a danger of loss due to fluctuations. Diversification is the process of risk reduction. The portfolio risk can be reduced by diversification. The investment trust collects the funds from the public by selling the shares of trusts. The trust deploys the funds in the market, as it desires. The trustees decide the selections of securities. The trust distributes the income among its members in the form of dividend. The trust will make investments from the consolidated fund created from the subscriptions of various members of the trust. The first investment trust was established by the Royal family of Belgium Scottish America investment trust was established in 1873. In USA the investment trusts were established due to the substantial expansion of finance area and speculative spirit in that period.

Investment Trust in India

The first Industrial Investment Trust was established in 1933, by M/S Premchand Roy Chand in Mumbai. After the establishment of this fund the number of other trusts was formed such as Investment and Finance Company, Kolkata, General Investment and Trust Company, Kolkata, Tata Investment Trust Mumbai. Most of the investment trust is established by the industrial groups. These trusts try to make managerial control of the companies whose securities they are going to purchase the trusts are organized as private companies. The investment trusts are used as a tool to control more and more units by owning and controlling the shares. The investment trusts are categorized in to two types:

- Management Investment Trust
- Fixed Investment Trust

The Management Investment trusts have full freedom over the funds which they collect. The fixed investment trust is confined to a fixed fund, and is not empowered to change the portfolio except in unforeseen situation. The Fixed Investment trust is also known as "Unit Trust". The objective of the fund is to protect the investors from managerial manipulations. These trusts suffer from a number of drawbacks. There is no opportunity for diversification of investments. All of these funds are kept in few companies scrips only. The expenses for running the trust are very high. At present there is no existence of fixed investment trusts. These trusts are almost obsolete these days. The trusts in India can play an important role in the economy. The trusts should be regulated properly by better management.

Organization

The Mutual funds in India are regulated by SEBI. The SEBI has the authority to register both public and private sector's Mutual fund. The Mutual funds set up by LIC and GIC are regulated by the investment division, Ministry of Finance. All the intermediaries and players in the capital market are brought under the SEBI authorization and regulation. If the Mutual funds are started by the commercial banks, they should get the RBI permission also. The SEBI has taken over the responsibility of regulating; inspecting and controlling the activities of all the Mutual funds except MMF. The Mutual funds in India have five key parties involved:

- The Sponsors
- The Board of Trustees
- The Asset Management Company
- The Custodian
- The Unit Holders

The Sponsors are the important party in establishing a Mutual fund. Every Mutual fund is formed by a sponsor. According to the SEBI guidelines, Sponsors can be defined as "Sponsor means anybody corporate who, acting alone or in combination with another body corporate, establishes a Mutual fund after completing formalities thereof. "The Sponsors could be registered company or a scheduled bank or all India or state level financial institution. The sponsors must have a good track record, a positive net worth and consistent record of profitability and a good financial standing during the last 5 years. The board of Trustees is another party, which plays an important role in the formation and management of the Mutual fund. Acceding to the guidelines issued by SEBI, it has defined as "Trustee is a person who holds the property of Mutual fund in trust for the benefit of the Unit Holders". The trustee eligibility is determined on the basis of eligibility and suitability examined from the composition of the board of directors. The SEBI will examine and approve the "Memorandum of Association" of the trustee company. SEBI has the authority to examine and approve the draft of the trust deed. Asset Management company means a company formed and registered under the Companies, Act 1956 and was approved by the board under regulations 20. The approval of the AMC was based on good track record, Professional experience, net worth etc. Custodian means a person carrying on the activity of safe keeping of the securities or participating in any clearing system on behalf of the clients to effect deliveries of the securities. The custodian is an independent organization for setting up Mutual fund as a part of the composite authorization. The custodian is responsible for the coordination with the brokers, the actual transfer and storage of stocks and handling the property of the trust. The custodian is answerable to the AMC. The AMC conducts the research and based on it, manages the fund or portfolio. The AMC is responsible for floating, managing, redeeming the schemes etc. It receives the fee for the services rendered by it. The guidelines of SEBI should be implemented by the trust board. The AMC has to report on a Quarterly basis its activities, investments and operations through AMC. It should report to the trustees and to the SEBI separately in respect to their operations and results. The Mutual fund should prepare annual report and submit to the investors of the fund and to the SEBI. The Board of trustees is governed by the Deed and the policy in respect of each scheme should be laid down for getting the approval from SEBI. The management of Mutual fund is a top decision making function rests with the board of trustees as per the latest guidelines of the SEBI. The brain of the Mutual fund is the trustees and it is governed by a trust deed. The experts and specialists will be on the board of trustees. The AMC will look after the routine functions of fund. All MFs should be managed by the experts, high talented skill fund managers and professionals. The experts in this area are finance professionals. The AMC will manage the funds by making investment decisions. The funds to be invested in major categories are regular income investment, growth oriented and Money Market instruments. The Mutual fund should concentrate before taking decisions about fundamental analysis of the economy, industry and company. The fund can invest towards research and appoint experts, investment analysts, portfolio managers and a host of other specialists.

Organization Structure of Mutual Fund

The Mutual funds in India are regulated by SEBI. The SEBI has the authority to register both public and private sectors Mutual fund. The Mutual fund set up should be done according to the norms of the SEBI. The SEBI has provided "Four Tier" system for managing the affairs of the fund. The Mutual funds are designed to suit the needs and preferences of the investors. The choice of the fund will be determined by the investor himself. The investor should frame his investment objectives regarding whether he expects a regular income or capital appreciation or his earnings or low risk, etc. Then the objective will help to choose the best fund among different alternatives. The Mutual funds will adopt different strategies to meet the investor's objectives. In India, the Mutual funds can be classified into five categories. The classification of funds can be based on various factors.

- Based on Ownership Status
- Based on Schemes of Operation
- Based on Portfolio Objectives
- Based on Location
- Others

Ownership Status: The Mutual funds can be established by either public sector or private sector. The public sector Mutual funds have been functioning since 1963-64. The UTI has been functioning since 1964. In 1987, the second public sector Mutual fund was launched by SBI. SBI Mutual fund was the first among all the commercial banks. The government has given the permission to PSBs for entering the Mutual fund sector to curb the monopoly of the UTI, Can Bank, BOI, PNB, GIC; LIC Mutual funds have joined operations in the business at a short span of time. Private sector corporate has been permitted by the government on Feb. 14th, 1992. Since then a number of Private companies have approached SEBI for the approval of Mutual fund. The SEBI has provided the guidelines for registration, constitution and management of the funds.

Scheme of Operation: Mutual funds can be classified on the basis of their operations. The Mutual funds can be divided in to 3 categories, i.e., Open-ended, Close-ended and Open cum Close ended Schemes.

Open ended schemes: Mutual fund which offer units for sales without specifying any duration for redemption. An investor can subscribe it at any time. The scheme will be opened throughout the year and investor can redeem his holding at any time. Enter and exit of the scheme is very easy. The Mutual fund repurchases the units at periodically announced rates. The repurchase prices are based upon the Net Asset Value (NAV). The NAV of the scheme will depend upon the Stock Market prices. The Open-ended funds provide high liquidity of the investors. The sale prices of units are also announced by the fund from time to time for subscription. For Ex: U.S.E4, ULIP of UTI Dhanavirichi, Dhamaraksh; Magnum balance fund Magnum Insta Cash fund of the SBI.

Close ended Scheme: A Mutual fund which offers units for sale to the public only at the time of initial issue. The scheme is also offered to the investors at a specified period of time. After closing the time, the investor can not subscribe to the scheme. A close ended scheme of Mutual fund, the period of maturity will be announced in advance. The investor can buy or sell the units of the scheme in Secondary Market. The price in the Secondary Market is determined on the basis of demand and supply. The close-ended scheme can be easily managed by the fund managers. The fund manager can evolve long term investment strategies depending upon the life of the scheme. Master gain-92, Grand Master, of UTI, Dhana Samithis, Dhana Sere of LICMF can double, Can Star, Can growth of Canara Banks, 2nd Jyothi, Saran Jyothi of Indian bank are some of the examples of close ended schemes.

Open cum close-ended scheme: The scheme is offered by the Mutual fund is kept open for a specific interval and it runs the scheme as a close-ended funds. These kinds of schemes are permitted by SEBI in recent years only. In offer document the scheme rules and regulations will be announced. The units of the scheme may be listed in Stock exchange. These units may be traded in the Stock exchange regularly.

Portfolio Basis: Mutual funds can be classified on the basis of portfolio. The schemes are classified as follows:

- Balanced Funds
- Equity Funds
- Bond Funds
- Growth Funds
- Tax Benefit Funds
- Specialized Funds
- MMMF
- Leveraged Funds

Balanced Fund means the amount collected from this scheme is deployed in the market by purchasing equity and fixed income bearing securities. The combination of both the financial assets will be fixed Mutual fund. Some Mutual funds spent some amount on the equity preference and debentures. Therefore the situation may ensure certain amount of interest and dividend. Some Mutual funds maintain a ratio between equity and preference share in 50:50. The balanced fund ensures both capital appreciation and regular return in the form of dividend and interest. The investors have advantage both in return and capital appreciation. It is also known as Income and Growth funds. Examples for balanced fund schemes can triple of commercial bank – Canara Bank, Dhamaraksh 1989 of LIC. ULIP (Unit Linked Insurance Policy) 1971, Unit Scheme 95(D), HDFC balanced fund. Tata balanced fund, Prudential ICICI balanced Alliance 1995 etc.

Equity fund scheme units will be offered to the investors by the Mutual funds. This scheme proceeds will deploy for purchase of shares. According to these scheme objectives, the funds will be spent for the acquisition of the blue chip company shares. The fund undertakes risks associated with the investment in equity of the reputed companies. This scheme is also further classified as Income fund and growth funds. Examples for equity fund scheme: UGC 10000, UTI Pharma and Health Care, UTI Service Sector, UTI Software, K-Tech Alliance Millennium, Magnum IT, Prudential ICICIFMCH etc.

Bond funds proceeds will be spent for acquiring bonds. The bonds ensure fixed and regular income. It ensures regular income to the investors. The bonds are available in the market at lower prices in some situations. Therefore the net income on these bonds will go higher. Some companies offer non-convertible bonds including shares. Any investor who subscribes for the share will have to take up bonds also. EX: UTI Bond, UTI Mahila Unit Scheme, UTI NRI, Tata Income, Alliance Income fund 54EAD, IDBI Principal, K-bond deposit, K-bond wholesale Sundaram Bond saver, Templeton Income fund IDBI Principal Deposit, Chola triple funds, Alliance Income fund, Prudential ICICI, Pioneer ITI Income builder, LIC bond-G, Sun F &C Money Value bond, Zurich India high interest- D, IL & FS bond.

Growth funds objective is to provide capital appreciation for the value of investments. The scheme concentrates on value appreciation of securities. The risk involved in this scheme is very high. The scheme will not give preference for regularity of income. Growth fund is also called as long haul investments. The scheme is a long-term based fund.

Perhaps Tax schemes are designed to meet the tax payer's needs. The investor who contributes the scheme is entitled to get the tax concession in income tax. The lock in period is 3 years. The scheme distributes the profits among the unit holders. A large number of Mutual funds have come up with many schemes. These schemes provide benefits like Income, Capital appreciation and tax concessions. The proceeds of these shares would be deployed to acquire equity and debentures. Usually all the taxpayers will contribute for these funds. For Ex: Magnum tax gain, Pioneer ITI tax shield.

Specialized fund/sector fund invests in a particular type of securities. The scheme objective is to make investments in a particular area or industry. If any investor who wants to invest in a particular security he will prefer a fund, which deals in such securities. EX: Birla MNC, UTI, Pharma, K-Tech, Magnum IT, and UTI Software, Pioneer ITI.

Money Market Mutual funds (MMMF) is a scheme, which has been set up with the objective of investing in Money Market instruments. The fund involves in buying of instruments from the Money Market like treasury bills, call money, Commercial paper, Commercial bill, certificate of deposits, and Government securities. The maturity period will be less than 1 year for all these instruments. The MMMF constitutes the only portfolio of MMMF. EX: UTI MMMF, IDBI Principal, Money Market fund.

The aim of leveraged portfolio is to maximize the capital appreciation to the investors. In this type of scheme, the financial assets will be purchased by borrowing the fund at a cost. The cost of invests and the gain from holding shares is the profit of leveraged fund. Leverage funds involves in speculative activity to earn more and more profit.

Based On Location: Mutual funds can be categorized on the basis of location where they mobilize funds as Domestic savings from public within the country offshore Mutual funds are the mobilized funds from abroad for investment in India.

Other types of Mutual funds such as Loan funds and Non-Loan funds. These are not very popular in the country.

Objectives of a Mutual Fund

The objectives of the Mutual fund are presented below:

- To provide a better opportunity to low income group investors.
- To provide better expertise, talent, skillful, scientific approach towards Stock Market activities.
- To manage small investor's portfolios that provides regular income, growth, safety liquidity and diversification.

Importance of Mutual Fund

The Mutual funds mobilize a large amount of savings from the small investor's savings. The fund attracts resources mainly from middle class families. Their savings potential is very high in India. The pooling of the large amount of resources, operating economies and the ability to commit the large sums of money for long periods. The Mutual funds will enjoy ample resources at their disposal by mobilizing from various investors. The Mutual funds gain a lot of significance from the investors. It has been proved in the case of Master gain 92 scheme of the Unit Trust. The scheme has mobilized ₹ 4,500 crores from the market and created history in the market. But the Unit Trust failed to manage that scheme. In India then investors do not have any basic knowledge about the portfolio management. Therefore the investors are investing in Mutual funds. They are important due to the following reasons:

- The Mutual funds have been functioning like financial intermediaries in mobilizing the savings of the public.
- The Mutual fund invests in a variety of securities where there is a demand.
- Mutual funds appoint experts, to get the benefits of speculation activities.
- Mutual funds lead to a general prosperity to the investors.
- The Mutual funds will handle the investor's fund with utmost care and try to fulfill the needs of Unit holders.
- The fund managers will apply all the Stock Market techniques to enhance the NAV of the fund.
- The Mutual funds will attract foreign investments by offering offshore funds.

- The per capita income of rural and urban middle class people are increasing and their savings are canalized towards Mutual fund sector. The fund diverts the resources towards industrial undertaking units by acquiring the financial assets of various companies.
- The Mutual funds have tremendous scope for growth in the country,

The liberalization and industrial policies gave a scope for the growth of the country. The government should prepare an agenda about the utilizing of the vast resources available with the Mutual funds. There are certain areas to be developed such as water resources, roads, agriculture etc. The government of India can divert the resources towards construction of dams, water sheds and creation of irrigation facilities, development of agriculture sector, development of cooperative service sector, benefits will pass on to the farmers. The Mutual funds may also enter into power sector to improve the production of power by providing large amounts of savings. In future the Mutual funds may be like UTI (Agr), UTI (Power), UTI (Roads), UTI (Housing) etc.

Regulatory Framework

The Mutual funds in India are governed by the UTI act of 1963, Indian Trust act of 1882, company's act of 1956, securities act of 1956, and the other tax laws. The overall monitoring and supervising are done by the Ministry of Finance, the RBI and the SEBI. The RBI had issued guidelines for the bank sponsored Mutual funds in 1987. Afterwards it also received the guidelines from the Ministry of Finance in 1991. The SEBI also issued guidelines in 1991 and a comprehensive set of regulations in 1993. After the successful growth of the Mutual fund industry, it became necessary that all Mutual funds in India should follow uniform norms for the valuation of investments and accounting practices. This leads to better comparison for the evaluation of fund performance. The SEBI issued new Mutual fund regulation in December 1996, based on the recommendations of the Mutual fund 2000 report. All Mutual funds in India including the UTI is regulated by the SEBI. The off shore funds are governed by the Ministry of Finance, the Government of India, and the RBI. MMMFs are governed by the RBI. The SEBI regulations aim at facilitating competition, transparency, investors' protection etc.

Registration of Mutual Fund

According to the SEBI guidelines the following process is involved for the registration of a Mutual fund:

- Every Mutual fund should be registered with the SEBI under regulation.
- An application for registration should be made in Form A by the fund sponsor and shall be addressed to the SEBI.

Not with by a sponsor prior coming in sub regulation (1) any application made by a sponsor prior coming into force of these regulations containing such particulars are mentioned in the form shall be treated as an application made in pursuance of the sub regulation (1) and should be dealt with accordingly; provided that the fee payable in respect of the application made under sub regulation shall be the same as is referred to in the sub regulation of regulation (4) every application for registration under the regulation (3) shall be accompanied with an application fee as specified in schedule II by means of a cheque or bank draft in favor of the SEBI payable at Mumbai.

Regulation (5)

The SEBI regulation indicates that subject to the provisions that under sub-regulation (3) of regulation 3, any application which is not complete in all aspects and does not confirm to the particulars specified in the form, shall be rejected provided that before rejecting any such application, the applicant shall be given an opportunity to remove within the time specified, such objections as may be indicated by the board.

Regulation (6): (1):

The regulation 6 deals with the furnishing information clarification and personal representation. The SEBI may require the sponsor to furnish such further information or clarification as may be considered necessary for the grant of registration. The sponsor should appear before the SEBI for personal representation.

Regulation (7):

This regulation indicates the consideration of application. The board on the basis of information furnished in the application and after obtaining such further information as may be required should decide on the application for registration not more than 3 months from the date of receipt.

Regulation (8):

This regulation deals with the conditions for the registration of a Mutual fund. For the purpose of granting the registration the board should take into account all the matters which are relevant to efficient and orderly conduct of the affairs of a Mutual fund and in particular the following.

The sponsor must possess a sound track record and experience in the relevant field of financial services, for a minimum period of 5 years. He should possess professional competence, financial soundness and general reputation of fairness and integrity in his business transactions "Sound track record" means net worth, dividend paying capacity and the profitability of the sponsor.

Mutual fund is in the form of a trust and the trust deed has been approved by the board.

An asset management company who hold an approval of the board has been appointed to manage the affairs of the Mutual fund and operations the schemes of such funds.

The sponsors contributes at least 40% to the net worth of the AMC.

The sponsor or any of its director to the principal officer is to be employed by the fund. The management looks after the affairs of its business at any time when it is convicted for any offence involving moral turpitude or guilty of any economic offence.

Regulation (9):

It deals with the grant of registration. The board on being satisfied that the application is complete in all respects and all particulars sought has been furnished and that the Mutual fund is eligible for registration may register with fund subject to:

Receipt of registration fee indicated in schedule II of the act in a manner specified by the board.

The terms and conditions specified in regulation 12.

Where a Mutual fund is found to be eligible for grant of registration, the board shall grant a certificate in Form B.

Regulation (10):

According to the regulation every Mutual fund registered under these regulations should pay annual fee for every financial year, from the year following the year of registration as specified in schedules II.

The annual fee should be remitted to the board in the manner specified in such regulation (1) of regulation 4 before the beginning of each financial year.

Regulation (11):

The Regulation deals with the failure of the payment of fee by the Mutual fund. If any fund fails to remit the annual fee as provided in sub regulation (2) of regulation 10, the board may prohibit the Mutual fund from launching any new schemes till the fee has been remitted.

Without prejudice to these Regulations, the board may, on being satisfied with the reasons for the delay and subject to such conditions as it may deem fit, permit the sponsor to pay the annual fee at any time within 2 months from the commencement of the financial year to which such fee relates.

Regulation (12):

According to the Regulation every fund which is granted registration is subjected to fulfill the following terms and conditions.

Complying with the provisions of these regulations.

Informing forth with the board, as soon as it comes to the knowledge of the sponsor or the trustees that any information or particulars submitted to the board were either misleading or false in any material respect.

Information forth with the board of any material change in the information or particulars previously furnished, which have a bearing on the registration granted by it.

The sponsor, the AMC trustees and the custodian should comply with the provisions of the Regulations.

Allowing examination of the directors, officers and other employees in the course of inspection and extending full cooperation on unit's behalf.

Agreeing to produce books of accounts, documents and such other information as sought for by the board in the course of inspection.

Regulation (13):

It deals with the situation procedure where registration is not granted by the SEBI. The following process involved while denying registration.

Where an application does not satisfy the requirements mentioned in Regulation 8 the board shall reject the application.

The information about the rejection of application will be communicated to the applicant in writing, stating there in the grounds on which the application has been rejected.

The applicant who is aggrieved by the decision of the board under sub Regulation (2) may within a period of 30 days from the date of receipt of such intimation can apply to the board for reconsideration of its decision.

The board shall, as soon as possible, in the light of the submissions made in the application and whenever necessary, after giving an opportunity for personal hearing, convey its decision in writing to the applicant.

Regulation (14):

According to this Regulation, it deals with the constitution and management of the Mutual fund. The Mutual fund shall be constituted in the form of a trust in accordance with the provisions of the Indian Trust Act 1882, (of 1882).

Regulation (15):

The Regulation informs about the appointment procedure of the trust the process for the appointment of the trust is as follows.

A company shall be appointed as a trustee to manage the Mutual fund provided that, the board may regarding the special circumstances can permit the appointment of a board of trustees, as trustees of a Mutual fund.

The appointment of the trustees should be subjected *inter alia* to the following conditions namely:

The trustees are persons who have experience in financial services and are not found guilty of any economic offence.

The names of the trustees should be forwarded to the board.

Any change in the appointment of the trustees should be subjected to the approval of the board.

No trustee should retire unless another person is appointed in the place of retiring trustee.

No person should be a trustee or a director of a trustee company in more than one Mutual fund.

At least 50% of the trustees should be independent members and no such trustee should be an affiliate or subsidiary of the sponsor.

An AMC, any of its directors, officers or employees should not act as a trustee of any Mutual fund.

Regulation (16):

The Regulation deals with the process of registration of a deed under this registration act. The investment of the trust shall be in the form of a deed duly registered under the provisions of the Indian Registration Act of 1908, executed by the sponsor in favor of the trustees named in such instruments and shall contain such clauses as mentioned in schedule III and such clauses which are necessary for safeguarding the interest of the Unit Holder.

No trust deed shall contain a clause which has the effect of:

Limiting or extinguishing the obligations and liabilities of the trust in relation to any Mutual fund or the Unit holders; or

Indemnifying of the trustees or the Asset Management Company for the loss of damage caused to the Unit holders by their acts of negligence or acts of commissions or omissions.

The trust deed should be made available for the inspection by any member from the public at the registered office or the principal place of business of the Mutual fund and if so desired a copy of the same should be made available to any person on payment of a nominal fee as decided by the Mutual fund.

Regulation (17):

The section deals with the obligations of the trustees as per the law. The trustees' shall have a right to obtain from the AMC such information as relevant to the management of the affairs concerning the operations of the trust and may also call for periodical report from the AMC.

(2) Where the trustees have reason to believe that the conduct of the business of the Mutual fund is not in conformity with these Regulations, they should wish to take such remedial steps as necessary to rectify the situation and keep the board informed of the same with full particulars.

The trustees should take the steps to execute all the documents, which are necessary to secure the acquisitions disposals, it also assures the transactions that a Regulation entered in to by the AMC are properly made in accordance with these Regulations

The trustees should be responsible for ensuring that the AMC complies with these regulations.

The trustee should enter in to an agreement with the AMC which contains the clauses as specified in the schedule IV and such other clauses which are necessary for the purpose of investment if the funds of the Mutual fund then such agreement will be approved by the board.

The trustees should be accountable for and be the custodian of the property of the respective schemes and should hold the same in trust for the benefit and the interest of the trust.

The trustees should take stapes to ensure that the transactions concerning Mutual funds are in accordance with the provisions of the trust deed and schedule III of these regulations.

The trustees should be responsible for the calculation of any income due to be paid to the fund and also income received in the Mutual fund for the holders of the units of any scheme in accordance with to these regulation and the trust deed:

The trustees should receive a quarterly report from the AMC and submit a 6 monthly report to the board on the activities of the fund.

The trustees should call for the meeting of the unit holders:

Whenever required to do so by the board in the interest of on a requisition of ¾ Th of the unit holders of any scheme or all of the schemes together, or

When the majority of the trustees decides to wind up or prematurely redeem the units or modify any scheme.

Regulation (18):

The regulation deals with the process of setting up of the AMC. According to the rules and regulations the following steps required for the approval of the AMC.

The application for the approval of the AMC shall be made in form A.

The memorandum and articles of association of the AMC shall be submitted to the board along with the application for approval under the sub-regulation (I).

The provisions of regulations 5, 6 and 7 should apply to the applications made under sub-regulation (1) of this regulation as they apply to the application for registration of a mutual fund.

Regulation (19):

The regulation explains the process of getting of an appointment of the AMC. The act indicates that the sponsor. The trustee should appoint an AMC who is approved by the board to manage the affairs of the Mutual fund and operate the schemes of the fund.

The appointment of an AMC can be terminated by majority of the trustees or by 75% of the unit holders of the scheme.

Any change in the appointment of the AMC should be subject to prior approval of the board.

Regulation (20):

The regulation deals with the approval of the AMC. For the grant of approval from the AMC, the board may take into account all the matters, which are relevant to efficient and orderly conduct of the affairs of the AMC and in particular, the following namely.

The existing AMC has a sound track record, general reputation and fairness in transactions.

The directors of AMC are persons of high, fame and stand having at least 5 years of professional experience in the relevant fields, such as portfolio management, investment analysis, and financial administration.

The board of directors of the AMC has at least 50% directors, who are not affiliated. Or associated in any manner with the sponsor or any of its subsidiaries or the trustees.

The chairman of the AMC should not be the director of a Trustee Company or trustee of the board of trustees.

The AMC shall have a minimum networth of ₹ 5 crores.

Regulation (21):

The regulation explains about the terms and conditions of approval of the AMC. The grant of approval of the AMC under regulation 20 shall be subject to the following terms and conditions, namely.

The AMC has professional with adequate experience in the management of mutual funds.

Any directors of the AMC shall not hold the position of a director in another AMC or of a trustee in any Mutual fund.

The AMC shall forth with inform the board of any material change in the information or particulars previously furnished, which have a bearing on the approval granted by it.

No change in the management of the AMC shall be made without prior approval of the board.

The AMC undertakes to comply with these regulations.

Regulation (22):

This section deals about the situation, if the approval is not granted to an AMC.

Where an application made under regulation 18 for grant of approval does not satisfy the requirements laid down in regulation 21 the board may reject the application.

The decision to reject the application shall be communicated to the applicant in writing stating the grounds on which the application has been rejected.

The AMC which is aggrieved by the decision of the board under sub regulation (1) may within a period of 30 days from the date of receipt of such intimation, apply to the board for reconsideration of its decision.

The board shall as soon as possible in the light of the submission made in the application under sub regulation (3) and whenever necessary after giving an opportunity for personal hearing, communicate its decision in writing to the applicant.

Regulation (23):

The regulation informs about the restriction on business activities of the AMC. No asset management company shall

Act as trustee of any Mutual fund.

Undertake any other business activities except activities like financial services consultancy, exchange of research on commercial basis as long as any such activities of one not in conflict with the activities of the Mutual fund.

Act as an AMC for any other Mutual fund to hold the position of a trustee in a trust or act as a director in any other AMC.

Permit any director of the AMC.

Regulation (24):

The regulation defines the role and obligations of an AMC the following process tells us about the rule position regarding the obligations of the AMC.

The AMC shall take all reasonable steps and exercise all efforts and ensure that the investment of funds pertaining to any scheme is not contrary to the provisions of the regulation and the trust deed.

The AMC shall be responsible for the acts of commission and omission by its employees or the person whose services have been obtained by the company.

The AMC shall submit to the trustee, quarterly reports on March 31, June 30, September 30 and December 31 on its activities and the compliance with these regulations.

The AMC shall be expected to meet all its expenses and make provisions

For office space, personnel including security analysts and portfolio managers Regulatory compliance and reporting services

Preparation and distribution of the fund's prospectus, annual and periodic reports and other investor's communications.

Advertising and other sales material.

Accounting services and preparation of tax returns.

Insurance coverage and other services.

The trustees of the Mutual fund may terminate the assignment of the AMC at any time after receiving a reasonable notice in writing from the AMC.

Not with standing anything contained in any contract or agreement, the AMC or its directors or the officers shall not be absolved of any civil liability to the Mutual fund for their acts of commissions and omissions, while holding such position or office.

Regulation (25):

The Mutual fund shall have a custodian. He is not associated with AMC in any way.

Regulation (26):

The regulation explains about the process of approval of custodian.

The custodian shall make an application in form A for registration.

The provisions of 5, 6 and 7 shall so far as may be applying to the application make under sub-regulation (1) of this regulation.

For grant of approval of the custodian, the board may take into account all matters which are relevant to efficient and orderly conduct of the affairs of the custodian and in particular the following namely:

The existing custodian has a sound track record, general regulation and fairness in transactions.

The applicant himself or the employees or the persons who have experience in providing custodian services.

The applicant has the infrastructure, office space and personnel to provide custodian services.

The applicant or the director, or the partner are not found guilty of any economic offence

The applicant is not the sponsor or trustee, of any Mutual fund.

(d) The grant of approval to the custodian shall be subjected to the following terms and conditions, namely

The custodian or its directors, partners will not in any way be directly or indirectly affiliated or associated with any AMC.

The custodian will not act as sponsor or the trustee of any fund.

The custodian will not act as a custodian of more than one Mutual fund without the approval of the SEBI.

The rules and regulations framed by the SEBI: Every Mutual fund in India has to follow the rules and the regulation from 27 to 39 which indicate about the schemes of the Mutual funds.

Regulation (27):

It deals with the procedure for the announcement of schemes.

Regulation (28):

It reveals the contents of publicity material.

Regulation (29):

It contains the rules regarding misleading statement.

Regulation (30):

It indicates about the steps involved in listing of the schemes with the concerned Stock exchange.

Regulation (31):

This clause explains about the minimum amount to be raised from the market through various schemes. Close ended ₹ 20 crores. Open ended ₹ 50 crores.

Regulation (32):

This section tells us that the schemes should be kept open for the public subscription for a period of 45 days.

Regulation (33):

It indicates about the process of refund to an investor when the Mutual fund scheme fails.

Regulation (34):

It reveals that the allotted applicant should receive the unit certificates from the fund within 10 weeks in case of close ended schemes and 6 weeks in case of an open ended scheme.

Regulation (35):

This provision deals with the transfer process of unit certificates.

Regulation (36):

It indicates the winding up process of a Mutual fund.

Regulation (37):

It tells the effect of winding up of the schemes.

Regulation (38):

It explains the procedure and manner of winding up of schemes.

Regulation (39):

This provision deals with the declaration of winding up of scheme.

The regulations from 40 to 46 indicate about the investment objectives and valuation policies of the Mutual fund. The rules from 47 to 65 tell about the general obligations of the Mutual funds on various aspects. Regulations 65 to 75 inform about the procedure for an action in case of default regarding various conditions.

RBI Guidelines

The commercial banks are considered to follow the guidelines, which are issued by the RBI on certain aspects as indicated below.

Every Mutual fund should be constituted as a trust under the Indian Trust act and the sponsoring bank should appoint a board of the trustees to manage it. The board of trustees should have at least two outside trustees.

The trustees in addition to ability and integrity should have the proven capacity to deal the investment decisions and investors protection.

The overall direction, control, superintendence and management of the affairs and business should vest in the board of trustees.

The routine functions of the schemes should be looked after by a full fledged executive trustee.

The executive trustee should not discharge any other responsibility in the concerned bank.

A healthy relationship should be maintained between the sponsor and the board of trustees.

Care should be taken so that there will be no clash of interest between the trustee board and the concerned bank.

The sponsor bank should contribute the corpus fund as specified by the RBI. No additional contribution should be made by the sponsor bank to the corpus without the prior approval of the RBI.

The sponsor bank should contribute in addition to the corpus fund and maintain in each of the funds schemes by the way of its stake, an amount equivalent to 1 % of the amount outstanding.

The banks should obtain the RBI's prior approval before announcing any scheme of a Mutual fund.

The investment objectives and policies of the Mutual fund should be laid down in the trust deed and every scheme launched by the fund must be in accordance with such broad objectives and policies.

The Mutual fund should make a clear statement while inviting the public about the investment objectives of the fund and its policies.

The subscription amounts collected by the Mutual funds are primarily intended to be channelized in to the capital market instruments.

The Mutual funds should not undertake direct or indirect lending portfolio funds management, under writing, bill discounting, money operations etc, which are essentially banking/merchant banking functions etc.

There is no objection to the Mutual funds in investing the amounts initially collected for a scheme in the Money Market instruments, rediscounting of bills or bank deposits for a period of not exceeding 6 months.

The Mutual funds may also invest their temporary surplus fund in similar instruments up to not more than 25% of their total investible funds. Such short term/temporary investments can however be made only if they are permissible under the charter of the fund.

The Mutual funds should take delivery of scrips purchased and in the case of scripts sold, give delivery thereof to the purchases. The scrips purchased should be transferred in the fund's name.

A Mutual fund should not make short sale/purchase of securities or carry over the transactions from one settlement period to the next settlement period.

The Mutual funds should not make investment in any other Mutual funds of similar collective investment companies/corporations.

The Mutual funds should not hold under any one scheme, more than 5% of issued share capital or debenture stock of any company.

In case the Mutual fund operates more than one scheme, the holding in respect of all its schemes put together should not exceed 15% of the paid up capital or debenture stock of a company.

The total amount invested by a fund from any of its schemes in the shares, debentures, of any specific industry should not exceed 15% of a scheme fund. This provision wills not, however apply to a scheme which has been floated for investments in one or more specified industries and a declaration has been made to that effect.

The maximum spread between the purchase and selling prices of units/shares of any scheme should not be more than 5%.

The total cost of managing any scheme under a fund should be kept within 5% of the total income of the scheme.

Income distribution by the way of dividend or capitalization of gains should not be made on the basis of evolution of the stock holdings or unrealized capital appreciation.

The fund should create depreciation on investment to hold and provision for bad or doubtful debts the auditors should satisfy before declaring any dividend.

Further the fund should create a dividend equalization fund for each scheme by appropriating a part of its surplus income.

A mutual fund should maintain separate accounts of each scheme launched by it, aggregating the assets under each scheme. No switching of assets between the schemes should take place, except with the prior approval of the board of trustees and at the prevailing market rates.

The board of trustees of Mutual funds should prepare an annual statement of accounts in respect of each of the schemes which should contain, statements of assets and liabilities and income and expenditure accounts, duly audited by the qualified auditors. Further an abridged version of the annual account together with the reports of auditors and the board of trustees, should be published for the information of subscribers to the concerned scheme.

The board of trustees of Mutual funds should disclose the NAV of each of the schemes and the method of valuation for the benefit of the concerned subscribers.

The sponsor bank should furnish to the RBI in duplicate, the following reports on a regular basis:

A half yearly report indicating the performance of the Mutual fund as a whole as well as each scheme.

Audited annual statement of accounts, together with the reports of auditors and the report of the board of trustees.

Scheme wise details of investment portfolio of the funds, value of such investments, changes in the portfolio since the previous annual report and industry wise exposure.

Company Law Guidelines

Mutual funds generally invest in shares, debentures and other securities of the blue-chip companies and in the money market instruments. The guideline issued by the government indicates that a mutual fund in a private sector can be sponsored by one or more limited companies having a sound track record. The company or companies who want to establish a mutual fund should establish the fund as a trust under the Indian Trust Act of 1882. The sponsoring company should incorporate an AMC. The AMC should have a net worth prescribed by the government the sponsoring company should have at least a 40% stake in the paid up capital of the AMC. In order to meet this requirement of 40% stake, the sponsoring company or companies have to subscribe to the shares of the AMC by complying with the provisions of sec 372 of the Companies, Act (rule 11). According to the rule 11(c) the sponsoring company can invest only up to 25% of the subscribed equity capital. Since the sponsoring company has to invest to the extent of at least 40% in the paid up capital of the AMC less than the sponsoring company has to get the approval of its shareholders in a general meeting and the central government as required by the Sub section (4) of Section 372 of the Act for investing in the shares of the AMC. As stated above, the mutual fund is required to be established as a trust. Indian Trust Act Section (3) defines the term trust as "an obligation annexed to the ownership of property and arising out of a confidence reposed in and accepted by the owner or declared and accepted by him for the benefit of another, or of another and the owner". Section 41(2) of the act provides that person and the owner". Section 41(2) of the act provides that a person who has agreed in writing to become a member and whose names entered in the register of members shall be a member of the company. A person means a natural person or a corporation. A trust is not a legal entity. It is only a legal arrangement, it is not a person. According to Section 153 of the act, no notice of trust shall be entered on the register of members. To overcome, Section 153 of the act, in practice mutual funds get the shares registered with either in the name of the sponsoring company or in the name of the Asset Management Company or in the name of the Custodian Company. According to the Government rules and regulations, every mutual fund should avail the services of the custodian. According to the government regulations every mutual fund should get the shares purchased and transferred to the funds name and scheme also.

If the shares are not registered in the name of the mutual fund, the mutual fund should comply with section 187-C of the Act by giving the declaration in form II as prescribed by the companies rules of 1975, as contemplated in sub section (2) of Section 187-C of the Act, within 30 days from the date of registration of transfer of the shares should be done by concerned company. Consequently, the company in whose name the mutual funds shares are registered has to file form No.1 as prescribed by the Companies, Act rules 1975, with the company concerned, within 30 days from the date of registration of transfer of shares as required by the subsection (1) of section 187 C of the act. When firms is required to file form No. III prescribed under the companies rules, 1975, with the registrar of companies within 30 days from the date of receipt of forms I & II from the shareholding company and the mutual fund by paying the appropriate filing fees as prescribed in schedule X of the act. Section

187-C of the Act does not apply to the shares purchased or acquired by the mutual fund since the shares are registered in the company's name and to the account of mutual fund.

Sec 153-B of the Act provides that where any shares or debentures exceeding a certain value are held in trust by any person, such person has to make a declaration to the public trustee appointed by the Central Government under section 153-A of the Act, within 60 days in form No.1 annexed to trustees Rules, 1964 and send a copy of the declaration to the company concerned within 21 days after the declaration is sent to the public trustee. Or incase of stock Holding Corporation of India, such declaration in Form I shall be made in respect of the shares or debentures held by it as such on or before 31st March, company wise, by the 30th of May every year. If there is any change in the share holding or debenture time holding given in the declaration in Form I, the person who has given the declaration has to send a report in Form II appended to the trustee's rules 1964, to the public trustee notifying such change within 30 days from the date of such change.

According to companies act 187-B section indicates that the public trustee gets all the powers and rights exercisable by Mutual fund. The Mutual funds and the sponsoring companies are required to comply with some of the cumbersome provisions of the Companies Act, 1956.

Risk Factors of a Mutual Fund

Risk is the essence of the valuation of a financial instrument. The value of a financial asset depends upon many factors. Risk means a chance that expected gain; profit or return may not materialize. The actual outcome of the investment may be less than the expected out come. If the certainty of outcomes expected variance is zero it is called as risk free. Risk can be defined as "the variability of returns from those that are expected". The actual return on the investment may differ substantially from the expected return, the risk must be considered in determining the value and making the investment choices. Risks return can be defined as "Income received on an investment, plus any change in market price, usually expressed as a percentage of the beginning market price of the investment". The return comes from two sources income plus any price appreciation. For common stock the one-period return can be computed with the following formula.

$$R = Dt + (pt - pt - 1)$$

Where, Dt = Cash dividend at the end of the time period t

Pt = Stocks price at time period t

R = Actual return

T = A particular time period in the past/future

(Pt – 1) = stock Price at time period t –1

The return, which we expect, is different from the return, which we receive. For highly risky services, the actual rate of return can be viewed as a random variable subject to a "Probability distribution". It can be defined as "A set of possible values that a random variable can assume and their associated probabilities of occurrence". The probability distribution is based on two factors of the distribution.

- The expected return
- The standard deviation.

The Expected Return is a weighted average of the possible returns, with the weights being the probabilities of occurrence. The expected return can be defined as "the weighted average of possible returns, with the weights being the probabilities of occurrence". The expected return can be calculated by the following formula.

Ŕ= Σni=1(RI) (Pi)

Ŕ = Expected return

RI = Return for the ith possibility

Pi = the probability of a return occurring

N = the total number of possibilities

The other factor, which influences the probable distribution, is the standard deviation. The expected return is based around the dispersion or variability of a financial asset. The conventional measure of dispersion is the standard deviation. Standard deviation can be defined as "A Statistical measure of the variability of a distribution around its mean, it is the square root of the variance" . The Standard Deviation of returns depends upon the variability of returns. The Standard Deviation

σ = √ ∑in=1(RI – R –) 2 (Pi)

where, σ = Standard Deviation

RI = return investment

R- = the expected return on investment

Pi = Probability occurrence of the Financial asset

The Standard Deviation sometimes confines and some times make to fall in dilemma when compared with the risk of a financial asset. To overcome the limitations of the Standard Deviation it can be better to find out its coefficient of variation. The coefficient of variation can be defined as "the ratio of the deviation of a distribution to the mean of that distribution. It is a measure of relative risk" The coefficient of variation can be calculated by the following formula.

CV = σ / Ř

Where, Ř = Expected return

σ = Standard Deviation

Thus the coefficient of variation is a measure of the risk per unit of expected return. The larger the CV, the larger the relative risk of the Financial asset. The average investor is averse to risk. The risky investments should offer higher expected returns than less risky investments in order to make the people and hold it. Therefore the risk averse can defined "Term applied to an investor who demands a higher expected return the higher the risk". The low risk investment sometimes produces higher returns. Investors usually make their investments in a single Financial asset or they deploy their wealth in a combination of investments are called as "portfolio". Portfolio can be defined as "A combination of two or more securities or assets". Mutual funds performance depends upon the management of portfolio. The NAV is the barometer of performance of any type of Mutual fund. The reflection of better management of portfolio is an indication of the high NAV of the units. The expected return of a portfolio is a weighted average of the expected returns of the securities comprising the portfolio. The weights are equal to the proportion of total funds invested in each security. The formula for the expected return of a portfolio can be as follows:

Up = Σjm=1 Wj RJ

Up = The Expected return on portfolio

Wj = the Proportion of the investments in security j

RJ = the expected return for security j

m = the total number of different securities in the portfolio

The fund managers of the Mutual fund will have to concentrate on many factors like portfolio. Standard Deviation, Covariance, Correlation etc. The portfolio management also concentrates on the diversification. The concept of diversification is to spread the risk across a number of assets or investments. The meaningful diversification reduces risk. The portfolio risk comprises two components.

Total risks = Systematic risk + Unsystematic risk

The Systematic risk means the overall movements of the general market or economy. It is caused y number of factors. This type of risk is inescapable. The systematic risk is also called as market risk or non-diversification risk. The Systematic risk can be defined as "the variability of return on stocks or portfolios associated with changes in return on the market as a whole" the diversification cannot reduce this risk. The Unsystematic risk is also called as "non-market risk" or "diversifiable risk". The non-systematic risk can be reduced by the diversification. The security's total return is not related to the overall market variability. The Unsystematic risk can be defined as "The variability of return on stocks or portfolios not explained by general market movements. It is avoidable through diversification". The Unsystematic risk is related to a particular company or industry. Unsystematic risk is independent of economic, political and the factors that affect all the assets in a systematic manner. All the risk associated with the market portfolio is the systematic risk. In this context, the capital market and portfolio theories have developed a critical important concept "Beta". Beta is a measure of relative risk of a security. Beta is a coefficient measuring a security's relative volatility. It indicates the extent of the risk for a given financial asset, which is non-diversifiable. It is the covariance of a security return with that of the market for a security class. Beta can be defined as "An index of systematic risk. It measures the sensitivity of a stock's returns to changes in returns of the market portfolio. The beta of a portfolio is simply a weighted average of the individual stock betas in the portfolio". The security with a higher (than 1) beta is more volatile than the market, and the net asset with a lower (than 1) beta would rise or full slowly than the market. For ex: $\beta = 1$ is for every one percentage change in the market return, on an average, the security return also will change by one percent.

To understand the financial market in a better way it is necessary to know the value of a financial asset, the values of financial assets are highly influenced by the return and risk. The fund managers should keep in mind about these components in their portfolios. These two elements can not be ignored under any circumstances; the fund manager's skill reflects in the risk reduction of a portfolio and enhances the returns to one efficient portfolio. The risks may be classified in a number of ways.

The following are said to be the major types of risks which mutual funds, should not ignored while designing, the innovative schemes to meet the needs of the unit holders. They are default risk liquidity risk, financial risk, maturity risk, inflation risk, currency risk, country risk, business risk, interest rate risk. Default risk means the failure of repayment on the part of the debtor. The debtor fails to pay the capital and income risk. It has the capital risk and income risk. It affects the fund-based activities liquidity risk means a situation where the assets may not be disposed off or sell in the market. The assets will be sold in the market after a great inconvenience, which costs in terms of money and time. If an asset can be bought and sold quickly without any price concessions and transaction costs it is called as liquid. Financial risk is concerned with the use of debt financing by the companies. It is generally associated with debt equity ratio of the company. The higher the debt equity ratio of the company. The higher the financial risk. The more debt component of the capital structure leads to financial risk. The use of heavy debt by the firm causes variability of return for both the creditors and the shareholders. Maturity risk means the risk will arise when the financial assets maturity happens to be longer. The time factor leads the risk. The long-term debt involves greater risk. Inflation risk is closely associated with the fixed income securities. It is the risk that the real income on a financial asset is less than the nominal income. It is also known as purchasing power risk. Purchasing power risk is associated with a chance of the purchasing power of the invested money declines due to inflation. The inflation is actually the risk of uncertain inflation. Currency risk refers that the firms, which are, involved in the global transaction affects the variability in cash flow according to the fluctuations of Forex market. It arises mainly when the demand and supply for the foreign currency changes. It is also known as "exchange risk". Banks and FIs are also normally affected by these sources of risk. Country risk means the uncertainty in respect of an investment in a particular country. The country risk has many elements. The political risk and economic stability are the other important element. Business risk arises due to the nature of a firms business. The business risk has two elements i.e. controllable and un-controllable. The controllable risk means the firm can control that component by an efficient operating process. The uncontrollable business risk means, the operating conditions are beyond its control. Business risk can be measured by the analysis of the earning capability of a firm over a time. Interest rate risk refers that the variability in income of a financial asset due to changes in the level of market interest rates. It exists in all types of securities.

Unforeseen risk proves that every long-term stock investor will dump a fund at the worst time. A fund past performance tends to be an unreliable guide except for the worst funds. Volatility in the market is a routine. The fund managers have much more control over the risks than returns. The investor may expect ups and downs in the market and can use the risk indicators to choose a relatively well placed fund. Speculators can bear higher risks for higher returns. The technique reveals the risks that are likely to be most rewarding.

Risk indicators involve mathematics. Beta is the most common measure of the risk. A beta of 1, matches market risk, less than 1, a fund is calmer than the market Alpha is a performance measure adjusted for the risk. A fund that responds more to the markets advances then the declines has a positive alpha.

Growth funds concentrates on the companies which have rapidly increasing earnings and riskier than the value funds, which hunt for those stocks at low multiples of earnings or book value. To reduce the overall risk a balanced portfolio of funds should be placed across the spectrum with perhaps a slight tilt towards small stocks and value for the period.

Performance Valuation of Mutual Funds

The SEBI has come out with a standard format of the balance sheet for Mutual funds in India. The Mutual fund industry does not have a standard accounting policy and comparison may be done after the adjustments the Mutual fund performance is based on the Net Asset value. The NAV of the unit is an important concept and it is the basis for the unit pricing. In the case of open ended and closed end schemes. The NAV can be calculated as follows:

$$\text{NAV} = \frac{\text{Total market value of the assets in the portfolio of the fund} - \text{Liabilities}}{\text{Number of funds units outstanding}}$$

In the case of open-ended schemes the NAV is calculated on daily basis and the sale and purchases are to be made on each day. The following formula can be applied to calculate the sale and repurchase prices of units:

$$\text{Sale Price} = \frac{\begin{array}{c}(\text{MVA} - \text{Liabilities excluding CL, ISC, Reserve and unit capital})\\ + \text{Brokerage issue on tax and others}\end{array}}{\text{Number of units outstanding}}$$

$$\text{Repurchase price} = \frac{\begin{array}{c}(\text{MVA} - \text{Liabilities excluding CL, ISC, Reserve and unit capital})\\ - \text{Brokerage issue commercial}\end{array}}{\text{Number of units issued or outstanding}}$$

The expected rate of return on units can be calculated as

$$\text{ERR} = \frac{(\text{NAV}_t - \text{NAV}_{t-1}) + \text{dividends} - \text{capital gains}}{\text{NAV}_{t-1}}$$

ERR = Expected rate of return on units

MVA = Market value of assets

CL = current liabilities

ISC = Initial share capital

t = current year

t – 1 = previous year

The NAV is determined by the stock market prices. The stock market prices are influenced by the supply, the demand and the other factors the units are discounted to the extent value of the net asset value, and the average discount have been about 25% and in certain cases the discounts are as high as 30 to 50%. The following factors may give rise to discounts:

The close ended fund units are very limited trading in value and volume.

The close ended scheme unit floating is very small.

High administrative expenses and management fee causes low dividend which in turn lower the prices.

The unit's prices are very low because the brokers offer low prices which they have to hold them for more time.

Overall the market for these units is limited while comparing with the corporate shares.

The NAV includes dividends, interest accruals and reduction of liabilities, expenses besides market value of investments. The causes for the non-satisfactory performance of the mutual funds are as follows:

- Poor Investment planning.
- Too much diversification of portfolio.
- Blue-chip scrips do not yield more than average return.
- High turnover of portfolio leads to huge payment of brokerage
- Wrong prediction about income, profitability, interpretation of government policies etc.

Efficiency of Mutual Fund

A good Mutual fund always works for the satisfaction of the unit holders. The evaluation of a Mutual fund can be done by taking the following factors into consideration.

- *Liquidity:* A good Mutual fund should create liquidity to its unit holders in the form of listing on a Stock exchange.
- *Stability:* A Mutual fund should be stable and offer a wide range of schemes for a long term period.
- *Growth:* The fund must concentrate on increasing the NAV's consistent growth in dividend and capital appreciation.
- *Returns:* A fund should assure better returns to its unit holders and try to achieve the goal.
- *Credibility:* Previous track record of issuer. An investor before investing should decide and verify the track record.
- *Management approach:* The management of a fund depends upon many factors, i.e., diversification, and risk bearing, returns maximization.

Method of valuation of the investments:

- Every Mutual fund in India should have investments. According to the following valuation norms.
- Traded securities
- Non-traded securities
- Rights shares

While valuing the traded securities, the following factors should be taken into consideration:

- The securities should be valued at the last quoted closing price on the bourse.
- If the scrips are traded on more than one Stock exchange, generally the AMC is left to select the appropriate Stock exchange. The reasons for selection should be recorded in writing. Usually all the scrips can be valued at the prices quoted on the Stock exchange where a majority in value of the securities is principally traded.

- In a particular valuation day, if a security has not been traded on the selected Stock exchange, the value at which it is traded on another Stock exchange may be taken.
- In some situations, when a scrip is not traded on any Stock exchange on a specific valuation day, the earliest previous day quotation may be used for consideration. But such date should not be more than 60 days prior to the valuation date.
- The non-traded securities will be valued in the following manner.
- Scrip may be treated as non-traded scrip, if it is not traded on any Stock exchange for a period of 60 days prior to the valuation date.
- The Asset Management Company has the authority to value the non-traded securities in the following procedure.
- The board of directors of the AMC should prescribe the norms for valuation of non-traded securities.
- The decision of the board of directors of the AMC must be documented in the minutes and the supporting data in respect of each security so valued must be preserved.
- The methods used to find out the value of non-traded security should be periodically reviewed by the trustees of the Mutual fund.
- The auditors of the MFs should be report as "fair and reasonable" in their report on the annual accounts of the Mutual fund.
- The equity instrument should be valued on the basis of capitalization of earnings or NAV method.
- The debt instruments should be valued on a yield to maturity basis.
- The value of investments like call money, short-term deposits, and rediscounted bills should be valued at cost plus accrual.
- The value of other money market instruments should be valued at the yield for which they are currently traded.
- The government securities should be valued at yield to maturity based on the current market rate.
- For the valuation of the non-traded instruments follow:
- Cost of the non-traded instrument + interest accrued at the beginning of the day + (redemption value – the cost (spread over to the remaining maturity period of the instrument)
- For the valuation of non-convertible debenture, it will be treated as debt instrument and valued accordingly.
- In case of convertible debentures, the convertible component should be valued as an equity instrument.
- If the financial instruments have been bought on repo basis, the instrument must be valued as:
- The resale price – interest up to the date of resale.

  If the financial instrument has been sold on repo basis:
- Repurchase price- interest (up to the date of repurchase price) – the value of the instrument. If the repurchase price exceeds the investment value the depreciation should be provided. If the

repurchase price is lower than the value of the instrument, adjustment must be taken into consideration.

- In case of valuation of equity, the warrants to subscribe for shares attached to instruments can be valued at the value of the share minus the cost of warrant.

The value of rights shares should be calculated as:

The price of the rights share may either cum-right price or an "ex-right price". The cum right price gives the buyer, besides the ownership of shares already held, the right to apply for new shares offered by the company, while the ex-right price gives the buyer only the ownership of the existing shares held by the seller and not the right to apply for additional shares offered by the company. Ex-right price is quoted either after the rights shares have already been allotted by the company or the time to apply for right shares has already expired. The value of the right can be calculated by the following formula:

$$R = \frac{M - S}{N + 1}$$

R = Value of one right

M = Cum-right market price of a share

S = Subscription price for a new share

N = No. of shares (old) required to purchase one new share.

The valuation of a share ex-right can be obtained by the following formula:

$$P = \frac{MN + S}{N + 1}$$

P = Theoretical market value of a share ex-right

M = Cum-right market price

N = Number of old shares entitling to purchase one new share

S = Subscription price for a new share

Alternatively the value of a right can also be calculated by the following formula:

$$R = \frac{P - S}{N}$$

R = Value of one right

P = Ex-right market price of a share

N = Number of old shares entitling to new one share

S = Subscription price for one new share

Alternatively until they are traded, the value of the rights shares can also be calculated by applying the following formula.

$$V = N/M \times (P_{ex} - P_o)$$

V = Value of right share

N = No. of rights offered

M = No. of original shares held

Pex = Ex-rights price

Po = Rights offer price

While calculating the NAV of the MFs, all expenses and incomes accrued up to the valuation date should be taken into consideration. The management expenses, and other expenses accrued on daily basis shall be adjusted. Any changes in portfolio of the Mutual fund are to be recorded in the book up to a period of seven days following the date of the transaction. The NAV calculation should not be effected by more than two percent.

The price of the units must be determined with reference to the last determined NAV unless, the sale price is determined with or without a fixed premium added to the future NAV which is declared in advance.

While determining the prices of the units, it must be ensured that the repurchase price is not lower than 93% and the sale price is not higher than 107% of the NAV.

General Obligations

Every Mutual fund in India should work according to the general obligations, which were imposed by the act. Generally the Mutual funds should fulfill following obligations

- Maintenance of proper books of accounts.
- Accounting policies and standards
- Financial year
- Initial expenses treatment/Issue expenses
- Issue of warrants
- Annual report
- Auditor's report
- Disclosure norms
- Procedure for action in case of default.

The important obligation of a Mutual fund is to maintain the proper books of accounts. According to the sub-regulation (2) of the SEBI regulations 1993, the Mutual funds should keep the books of accounts to explain its transactions and to disclose it at any point of time the financial position of the fund in particular give a true and fair view of the state of the affairs of the fund. The Mutual fund shall inform the SEBI the place where the books, records and documents are maintained and available.

The Mutual fund shall follow the accounting policies and standards to provide appropriate details in the following manner.

The Mutual funds should present all investment in the balance sheet at market value.

The Mutual fund while determining the holding cost of investment and the gain or loss on sale of investments, the average cost procedure should be followed.

The income of a scheme generally earned by a Mutual fund is in the form of dividend. Dividend income should be recognized by the fund on the date the share is quoted on an ex-dividend basis.

If the shares are not quoted on the Stock exchange the dividend income should be recognized on the date of declaration by the concerned company.

In case of debt instruments income must be calculated on a daily basis for the concerned period of the time.

The financial statement of the Mutual fund should reflect the transactions for the purchase or sale of investments for a particular trade date but not as of the settlement date.

While evaluating the income of a scheme, bank shares are also to be taken into consideration. The original shares are valued on ex-banks basis.

In case of rights entitlements, it should be recognized only when the original shares on which the rights entitlement accrues are traded on Stock exchange on an ex-right basis.

If the accrued income has not been received beyond due date, the provision should be made in revenue account of the scheme.

In case of open ended scheme units are sold if any positive amount is arised it should be credited to reserves. And if negative amount found it should be debited to reserves, the face value will be credited to capital account.

If units are repurchased on open ended scheme, if any positive amount is arised should be debited to reserve and if negative should be credited to reserves, the face value being debited to the capital account.

Every Mutual fund should maintain an equalization account for open-ended scheme, on sale of the units an appropriate part of the proceeds should be credited to it. When the units are repurchased by the Mutual fund an appropriate amount should be debited to equalization account. The net balance of this account should be adjusted in revenue account.

Every Mutual fund should maintain capital account for each close-ended scheme. In this scheme, if the Mutual fund repurchases its units, the par value of the unit should be debited to capital account. If any positive amount is available it should be credited to reserves and if negative it should be debited to reserves.

A proportionate initial expense should also be transferred to the reserves.

The investment in different financial instruments should include stamp charges, brokerage charges etc.

In case of debt instruments, if any discount is found in purchasing moment, it should be reduced from the cost of the investment.

If any underwriting commission is received by the Mutual fund, it should be treated as revenue only when there is no devolvement on the scheme. If there is devolvement, the underwriting commission should be adjusted according to the proportion.

Financial Year

The accounting year for the entire scheme shall end on the same date which shall be March 31. In case of a new scheme, which is commenced in the accounting year. The disclosure and reporting requirement would apply for the period beginning from the date of its commencement and ending on the last date of the relevant accounting year of the Mutual fund.

Treatment of Issue Expenses

Every Mutual fund should identify all expenses clearly and must be appropriate for each scheme. The Asset Management Company (AMC) is important organ in Mutual fund; it will undertake the functions of buying and selling securities of each scheme. The AMC renders the investment and advisory services on turn over basis of the schemes. It will charge the fee to Mutual fund, which is fully disclosed in the offer document subject to the following:

If the net assets do not exceed ₹ 100 crores, the commission or fee is one and a quarter of one percent of the weekly average net assets in each accounting year for each scheme.

If the net assets exceed ₹ 100 crores, one percent of the excess amounts over ₹ 100 crores will be charged.

In addition to the above fee the AMC may charge the Mutual fund with the following expenses.

Initial issue cost of sponsoring the fund and its schemes.

Recurring expenses such as brokerage, marketing and selling expenses, registration's services for transfer of shares, agents commission all of these initial expenses in respect of any one scheme shall not exceed 6% of the fund raised under that scheme. In addition to the above expenses the following expenses may also be charged to the Mutual fund.

- Fee and expenses of trustees.
- Audit fees
- Custodian fee
- Cost of funds from location to location
- Winding up costs for terminating a Mutual fund /scheme
- Cost of statutory advertisements
- Cost regarding to investor communication
- Any such other costs approved by the SEBI.

The treatment of initial expenses:

The initial expenses must be accounted in the books of account of each scheme specified as below

The issue of scheme can be classified into two categories.

- Load or
- No load basis

(i) Sometimes it may issue as mixed basis. The type of issue should be clearly explained to the investors in the offer document. In the case of a close ended scheme floated on a load basis, the initial issue expenses should be amortized on a weekly basis over the period of the scheme.

(ii) In case of open ended schemes, floated on the load basis, the initial expenses may be amortized over a period not exceeding 5 years. The expenses incurred during the life of an open ended scheme cannot be amortized.

(iii) In case of load basis open end and close end schemes, the unamortized portions of the expenses are to be included in the calculation of Net Asset Value. But such portion should not be included for calculation of the advisory service to the AMC.

(iv) If the schemes floated on a no load basis, the AMC can levy an additional management fee not exceeding 1% of the NAV. The AMC is entitled to levy contingent charges as follow.

(v) It may be entitled to levy a contingent deferred sales charge for redemption during the first four years after purchase should not exceed 4% of the redemption proceeds in the first year.

- It is 3% in the second year
- It is 2% in the third year
- It is 1% in the fourth year

(vi) The distribution charges, in case of load schemes should be borne by the scheme of the Mutual fund.

(vii) The distribution charges, in case of no load schemes should be borne by the Asset Management Company.

All the initial expenses together should not exceed 6%. If any amount exceeds 6%, it should be borne by the AMC. The total expenses of the scheme excluding issue/redemption expenses, but including the investment management and advisory fee are subject to the following limits.

- On the first ₹ 100 crores of the average weekly net assets 2.5%
- On the next ₹ 300 crores of the average weekly net assets 2.25%
- On the next ₹ 300 crores of the average weekly net assets 2%
- On the balance of the assets 1.75%

Any expenditure exceeding limits should be borne by the AMC/Trustee/Sponsor. The SEBI cannot approve the expenses beyond the certain level of percentage.

Issue of Warrants

The issue of warrants or dividends to the unit holders must be within 42 days of the declaration of the dividend. Repurchase proceeds must be paid to unit holder within 10 days from the date of repurchase/redemption.

Annual Report

Every Mutual fund should prepare annual report scheme wise basis or an abridged summary. It shall be published through an advertisement within 6 months from the date of closure of the relevant financial year. The Annual report or abridged summary shall contain details as specified in schedules VII and VIII of the Act. The Annual report of every Mutual fund shall be made available for inspection at the head office of the Mutual fund. If any member so required, a copy there of shall be made available on payment of nominal fee as specified by the Mutual fund.

Auditor's Report

The books of accounts of every Mutual fund should be audited by an auditor. The auditor shall be different from the auditor of the AMC. According to the SEBI regulation 65, the auditor may be defined as "Auditor means a person who is qualified to audit the accounts of a company U/S 224 of the Companies' Act, 1956." An auditor of the Mutual fund should be appointed by the trustees. The auditor shall submit his report to the trustees. The audit report shall form part of the annual report of the Mutual fund. The auditor's report should comprise of a certificate to the effect that:

He has obtained all information and explanations, which to the best of his knowledge and belief were necessary for the purpose of his audit.

The statement of accounts has been prepared in accordance with accounting policies and standards as specified by the SEBI.

The balance sheet and the revenue account give a fair and true view of the scheme, state of affairs and surplus or deficit in the fund for the accounting period to which the balance sheet or as the case may be the Revenue Account relates.

Disclosure Norms

The scheme wise annual report of a Mutual fund or its abridged summary thereof should be published through an "advertisement". And an abridged scheme wise annual report shall be mailed to all unit holders within 6 months from the date of closure of the relevant accounting year. The report shall contain all the information as specified by the SEBI. The report should reflect a true and fair view of the operations of the Mutual fund. But the abridged information shall not contain full portfolio disclosure but must contain details regarding fund activities. According to the SEBI norms, if any Mutual fund publishes full accounts in news papers, the full portfolio disclosure is not required. Every Mutual fund should submit all the information to the SEBI within 6 months from the date of closure of each financial year. The Mutual fund, AMC, Trustees, Custodian, Sponsor of the Mutual fund should make such disclosure or submit such documents as they may be called upon to do so by SEBI. The Mutual fund should furnish the periodical reports to the SEBI as follows:

Copies of the duly audited annual statement of accounts including the balance sheet and P&L account for the Mutual fund and in respect of each scheme once a year.

- A copy of six monthly Un-audited accounts
- A quarterly statement of movements in net assets for each of the schemes of the fund.
- A quarterly portfolio statement including changes from the provision periods for each scheme.

The sale of units should be done by the trustees or the AMC after providing sufficient information made available for the investors to take an informed decision. The trustees of the Mutual fund are bound to make disclosures to the unit holders. It is the responsibility of the trustees to keep the investors informed about all the available information. SEBI is the most powerful organization in the financial sector of the nation. It has the full authority in the primary market, secondary market, money market and Mutual fund industry. All the Mutual funds in India shall act as per the guidelines/

norms issued by the SEBI from time to time. SEBI is the watchdog of the stock market and Mutual fund sector. The SEBI is empowered to suspend registration of a Mutual fund, if a it fails in the following situations.

- Fails to furnish any information.
- Furnish wrong information relating to its activities.
- Fails to submit periodical returns.
- Fails to comply with directions.
- Fails to resolve invest or complaint
- Guilty of misconduct/unprofessional ethics
- Fails to pay any fee
- Fails to maintain net worth of the Asset Management Company.

The SEBI has the authority to cancel the registration of a Mutual fund or impose a penalty on the following grounds.

If the Mutual fund, Asset Management Company, trustees of the Mutual fund involved in price rigging or manipulation or concurring activities affecting the securities market and the investor's interest.

The Mutual fund or AMC or trustees or custodian is guilty of fraud or is convicted of a criminal offence.

The Mutual fund has been guilty of repeated defaults which result in suspension of the registration.

The financial position of the Mutual fund deteriorates to such an extent that the board is of the opinion that its continuance is not in the interest of investors and other Mutual funds.

Therefore, the SEBI has the full authority in either cancellation of a registration of a Mutual fund or suspension of registration of the license of the fund/AMC/trustees. The suspension/cancellation of a certificate of the Mutual fund should be preceded by an Enquiry. The SEBI has the authority to appoint an inquiry officer under regulation 69 of the Act for holding an inquiry. The enquiry officer shall issue a notice of the Mutual fund/AMC/trustee/custodian as the case may be at the registered office or the principal place of business of the concerned. The Mutual fund/AMC/trustee/custodian may within 30 days from the date of receipt of such notice furnish to the enquiry officer a reply together with copies of documentary or other evidence relied on by him or sought by the board from him.

The enquiry officer shall give to the concerned person a reasonable opportunity of being heard to enable him to make submissions in support of his reply under the sub regulation (3). The alleged person or any other person on behalf of him should be present before the enquiry officer. But no advocate is permitted on behalf of the person. But some times, the SEBI will give permission to an advocate to attend on behalf of the Mutual fund/AMC/trustees. The enquiry officer shall after taking into account all relevant facts and submissions made by the party submit a report to the board and recommend the penalty to be awarded as also the grounds on the basis of the report the SEBI would issue a show cause notice which the Mutual fund must reply within 14 days. After hearing the reply it would approve the action for default. Every order passed under sub regulation (3) shall be self contained and give reasons for the conclusions stated there including justification of the penalty imposed by that order. The board shall send a copy of the order under sub regulation (3) to the Mutual fund and Central government. On and from the date of the suspension, the Mutual fund shall cease to carry on any activity related to Mutual fund during the period of suspension. On and from the date of cancellation the Mutual fund shall cease to carry on any activity related to that Mutual fund. The order of suspension or cancellation of registration passed under sub-regulation (3) of regulation 71 shall be published in at least two daily newspapers by the board. Any person aggrieved by an order of the board may prefer an appeal to the Central government.

Winding up of Scheme

In Mutual fund, there are basically two kinds of schemes available to the investors. They are categorized as

- Open ended scheme
- Close ended scheme.

An open ended scheme shall be wound up, if the total number of units outstanding after repurchases at any point of time falls below 50% of the originally issued number of units. A close ended scheme of a Mutual fund may be wound up.

On the expiry of the period of time if any, fixed for the duration of the scheme by that scheme or

On the happening of any event which in the opinion of the trustees, requires the scheme to be wound up; or

If 70% of the unit holders of a scheme pass a resolution that the scheme be wound up; or

If the board so directs in the interest of the unit holders.

If a scheme is to be wound up in pursuance to sub-regulation of the act, the trustees shall give notice of the circumstances leading to the winding up of the scheme. On and from the date of advertisement of the winding up the trustees or the AMC as the case may be, shall

- Cease to carry on any business activities
- Cease to create and cancel units in the scheme.
- Cease to issue and redeem units in the scheme.

Procedure and manner of winding up: The Mutual fund of the trustee shall call a meeting of the unit holders to consider and pass necessary resolutions by simple majority of the unit holders present and voting at the meeting for authorizing the trustees or any other person to take steps for winding up of the scheme.

The trustee or the person authorized under the act shall dispose of the assets of the scheme concerned in the best interest of the unit holders of that scheme.

The proceeds of sale made in pursuance of clause (a) above shall in the first instance be utilized towards discharge of such liabilities as are properly due under the scheme and after making appropriate provisions for meeting the expenses connected with such winding up the balance shall be paid to the unit holders in proportion to their respective interest in the assets of the scheme as on the date when the decision for winding up was taken.

On the completion of the winding up was taken shall forward to the SEBI and after the receipt of the report, if the board is satisfied that all measures for winding up of the scheme have been completed, the scheme shall cease to exist.

- Disclosing through the WEB Mutual funds style

Recent Developments

Over the course of the past year, the returns of much equity Mutual funds remained in negative territory. This has been largely due to the direction taken by the markets. The fund managers could not give returns due to market situation. The Mutual funds now viewed as investments, which empower investors to participate in the growth of financial market fund investments, are transparent as investors are regularly informed about their portfolio. The latest development in the market is mutual funds. Mutual funds are also providing information on websites. The websites of different funds focus on the information required by the investors. Daily disclosures of the NAV, regular monthly updates and information on dividends and changes in the load structure are the things, which all the investors should be aware of before investing.

Alliance capital, the site provides the first hand information about the Net Asset Value of the fund. The previous days NAV of all the schemes is provided in an easily accessible manner on the site and is updated regularly. The site contains the information such as news about dividend declaration, fund's holding in its different schemes, etc., the quarterly reports also contains the same information. The information about the portfolio usually contains only, the top ten holdings of the particular scheme. The website provides the financial data about the fund's returns over different time periods as well as the benchmark of the sector.

The site provides offer document for all funds' schemes. These can be downloaded in a format. These can also be requested through e-mail as well as post. A facility for receiving the NAV of the funds schemes as well as news updates through e-mail is also provided on the site.

The site also provides information about the funds as well as its key personnel along with the directors and the trustees. Details about the qualification and the experience of the key personnel are also provided. Telephone numbers and addresses of the funds offices in different cities as well as those of its transfer agents are provided. The fund's site has a learning centre, which has a section on Frequently Asked Questions and an archive of useful articles from the investment manager. Here also some of the information is out dated. A glossary and a simple savings calculator are also present on the site.

WWW.pioneeriti.com

The PIONEERITI can be reached through above address. The fund is up to the mark by presenting the latest information on NAVs of its different schemes. A facility for the daily receipt of NAV through e-mail is also provided.

The portfolio of the funds and different schemes are presented under the heading of the monthly performance reports. PIONEERITI is among the few funds, which provides full disclosure of their portfolios for each month of the year. The information about returns will be provided and is also to be updated on a weekly basis.

The funds site provides a number of tools for the financial planning. These include a savings, net worth and inflation calculator. The savings and net worth calculator require detailed inputs and ones financial position. These concerned parameters provide a realistic time frame for developing a saving plan. The inflation calculator is a simple tool to demonstrate the effect of inflation on the current prices.

Forms required for making the investments, redemption or switches are provided in a downloaded format. These also include the slips for the information about the change of address; change of account number and other routine communication between and investor and the fund.

The funds CEO communicates with the investors on a monthly basis through the site. This is usually same as the communication as that provided in the monthly fact sheet. This is based on the issues faced by the investor and provides inputs for targets oriented investing. As the proliferation of ranking surveys is being carried out the funds are eager to impress the investors about their performance. This information is also provided by the fund and usually shows the results of the latest ranking exercises. The fund also provided the data of different volatility measures of its different schemes. The significance of these are also communicated. The fund provides the detailed information about itself and its sponsors. Information about the funds key personnel and trustees is also now present. The sites section on the FAQ's provides a series of questions which take investors through the entire process of investing and the possible questions which arises in an investors mind. These also indicate general questions on Mutual funds and the concept of fund investing. Reports about the funds in different sections of the press are included in site. The site provides the addresses and telephone numbers of its offices in different cities.

1. Basics of fund management: The key objective behind every investment is to get better returns out of the same, with a moderate degree of risk associated with it. But, in order to reap the benefits from an investment, be it equity, bonds, MFs, FDs... the investor should be better informed and should be in a position to take a call based on certain analysis, and not just be a layman putting the hard earned money on rumors and information floating around in the market place.

In case of the assets of a Mutual fund, which is the pool of assets from the individual investors, the most significant risk is the poor fund performance. While analyzing the performance of a fund, crisil in its research 'tries to address only portfolio (market) risk and not the credit, counter party. In case of pension funds and insurance companies, sufficient research has taken place on asset liability management. In the banking sector, already there exists sophisticated operations. Fund advisors demands are increasing to understand how performance has been achieved for the risk assumed.

For a majority of funds, performance is assessed as against the prescribed benchmark for the same. A number of methods to assess portfolio risk do exist and many of the funds adopt Standard Deviations as a measure of risk, along with a few others for the simple fact that no single model can predict risk accurately. The basic idea of evaluation of a Mutual fund can be implemented more accurately by taking into account the whole organization. Also, once the management process is put in place in a fund house, it would prove better for key people: Chief Investment Officers (CIO), fund managers, research analysts, and dealers to take conscious decisions based on the set of defined parameters.

In the context of a fund's performance, diversification is in inverse proportion with the risk, within certain limits. The market linked risk from economy-related factors like fiscal policy, industrial policy, money supply; inflation etc… cannot be eliminated. Thus, the risk that can be explained by the market conditions is called: systematic risk and the unexplained residual risk (which could be company or industry or instrument specific) are called unsystematic risk.

2. Top of the pops: These are a few of the favorite sectors: The scores have changed, so has the popularity. The pharmaceutical sector-riding high on expanding global demand for generic drugs has emerged as the most popular sector among Mutual funds for the quarter ended September '01. However, even after having lost its sheen during their three months, Infosys Technologies still tops the funds' Popularity Index Chart.

In spite of the ET-CRISIL Fund Popularity Index Chart, for the September quarter, indicating a 44.8% fall in propensity to invest in Infosys Technologies by Mutual funds, it still ruled as the most popular stock held by funds.

The propensity to invest by funds in pharmaceutical stocks rose sharply by 37.76%. However the propensity to invest fell to 55.62% in case of information technology stocks, for the quarter ended September'01.

During the same period, most fund their holdings in Infosys Technology by 23%. The total percentage to net asset value (NAV) of the scrip fell 26% to 2.400.

For the same period, stock preferences of private sector Mutual funds (excluding UTI) indicator four of the top 20 stocks in their portfolio are pharmaceutical stocks. Two information technology stocks and not a single one from the media and telecom sector.

The value-weighted holdings

Scrips	Sept 29'01	June 30'01	Cbg (%)
Ranbaxy Labs	2.96	0.96	208.84
Acc	2.63	1.32	99.54
Dr. Reddy's Labs	4.93	2.84	73.68
Hero Honda Motors	3.61	2.13	69.55
CIPLA	5.79	4.23	36.76
HLL	3.57	2.64	34.97
Reliance Ind	4.74	3.85	23.12
ITC	3.6	3.01	19.74
Grasim Industries	3.19	2.82	13.02
Satyam Computers	2.65	2.47	7.41
MTNL	1.05	0.98	7.06
AVANTIS Pharma	2.07	2.03	1.86
VSNL	2.16	2.12	1.68
HPCL	1.81	1.82	–0.13
BHEL	2.57	2.66	–3.68
BPLL	2.57	2.66	–3.68
SBI	1.81	1.99	–5.23

Hindalco Industries	1.81	2.05	–11.88
L&T	3.66	4.22	–13.33
Infosys Technologies	4.92	8.49	–42.04

On the other hand, the remaining 14 of these tops 20 stocks belonged to core sector like capital goods, engineering, cement, steel, petroleum products and petro chemicals.

As is evident from the ET-Crisil analysis of the changing performances of fund managers, the study excludes all overseas registered foreign Institution (FII) without portfolio details as well as domestic Mutual fund monolith-Unit trust of India – due to non-availability of its portfolio for the period ended September 01.

Analysis of the top equity holding are based on 2 factors – the number of schemes comprising a particular stock and the simple average of the percentage holdings of each scheme in the particular stock (without considering the absolute value of the holdings). It is therefore, an amalgamation of how commonly owned, the scrip is and the extent to which the funds are willing to allocate their portfolios (irrespective of the size of that portfolio) to that scrip. We call this the popularity Index.

The sample size includes 98 equity and balanced schemes which account for over 70 per cent of the total assets of the private sector domestic Mutual funds in the two categories (please see accompanying tables).

The Value, Volume, Price

	Value (₹ M)			Volume (000's)			Price(R)		
Scrips	**Sep'01**	**June'01**	**Chgl (%)**	**Sep'01**	**June'01**	**Chgl (%)**	**Sep'01**	**June'01**	**Chgl(%)**
Infosys Tech	746.74	1543.46	–51.62	311.14	406.18	–23.40	2400.00	3799.95	– 36.8
Cipla	883.86	901.40	–1.95	792.70	789.32	0.43	1115.00	1142.00	–2.3
HLL	547.77	537.19	1.97	2646.23	2632.66	0.53	207.00	204.05	1.4
L&T	554.56	801.27	–30.79	3532.23	3647.11	–3.15	157.00	219.70	–28.5
Reliance Industry	719.45	921.36	–21.91	2705.72	2481.11	9.05	265.90	317.35	–28.0
ITC Ltd.,	550.59	558.94	–1.49	949.78	741.3	28.12	579.70	754.00	–23.1
ACC	398.98	308.37	29.38	3221.45	2259.95	42.55	123.85	136.45	–9.2
BHEL	474.10	685.84	–30.87	3984.03	3853.02	3.40	119.00	178.00	–33.1
HPCL	275.59	297.74	–7.44	2256.20	1878.48	20.11	122.15	158.50	–22.9
Satyam Computers	400.23	590.51	–32.22	3151.41	3485.91	–9.60	127.00	169.40	–25.0
VSNL	328.60	322.79	1.80	1557.73	1010.46	54.16	210.95	319.45	–33.4
SBI	277.38	399.34	–30.54	1681.10	1827.67	–8.02	165.00	218.50	–24.0
Hero Honda Motors	548.75	411.42	33.38	2935.30	2837.38	3.45	186.95	145.00	28.0
Hindalco Industries	276.15	406.65	–31.92	542.17	472.78	14.68	509.35	853.00	–40.1
MTNL	160.47	196.15	–18.19	1236.57	1556.16	–18.80	127.00	126.05	0.75

Source: The Economic Time, Dt: 9-11-2002.

So, which stocks are in and which ones are out of favor with fund managers? The popularity Index of September 2001, has as many as eight new entrants. These include three pharmaceuticals stocks, two Tele communications stocks and one each from automobiles, cement and steel industry. The eight new entrants comprise of Grasim Industries (in the 9th position), Dr.Reddy's (10th position). Aventis Pharma (11th position), VSNL (16th position). Hero Honda (18th position) and Hindalco industries and MTNL taking the last two positions respectively.

Information Technology stocks such as Digital global software, HCL technologies, WIPRO and Hughes software, all of which were among the most sought after stocks by funds for the quarter ended. June'01, have dropped out of the top 20. Stocks held by funds during the following quarter. Pharmaceuticals ranked 11th in June quarter moved out of the top 20 holdings of funds in the September.

Let us take a closer look at the most popular stocks. At the top, Infosys remains the most preferred stock yet, however, the extent of its popularity has been eroding since December '00. That is evident from the intensity of preference or propensity to invest which is measured by the percentage change in the combined score of how commonly owned, the stocks is and the simple average portfolio allocations to it between periods.

The propensity to invest in Infosys technologies dropped by nearly 44.87 per cent for the quarter ended sept'01. In fact the intensity of preference for just three stocks of the top ten in the popularity index, dipped dramatically for the September quarter. Satyam Computers slipped 60.18 per cent between June-September, while HCL Technologies fell 63.77 per cent.

Reliance Industries dipped 26.95 per cent and Bharat Heavy Electrical fell by 14.87 per cent. A look at the value-volume figures will corroborate this trend. In the case of Infosys, the private sectors Mutual funds shed as much as 23 per cent of their volume holding in the stock.

This, coupled with nearly 36 per cent erosion in the price of stock between June-September, 2001, has resulted in a 51.63 per cent decline in the actual value of the funds' Infosys holding, which came down to ₹ 746.74 m as of September 30.'01.

On the other hand, Cipla, the second most popular stock witnessed a 14.8 per cent increase in the property to invest by funds in September '01 over June '01.funds shed 0.43 per cent of the volume of their Cipla holdings even as price dipped 2 percent in the same period.

So the pure value of the funds' holdings in Cipla came down by nearly 1.9 per cent to ₹ 883.86m. other pharmaceutical stocks like Dr. Reddy's Laboratories and Ranbaxy Laboratories entered the popularity index chart in septembe'01. The sharpest jump in popularity is seen in new entrant Ranbaxy laboratory. It is the only stock in top 20 list, in which funds value holding jumped a whopping 22.9 percent to ₹ 453.4m. The same can be attributed to a 147 per cent increase in the volume holdings of the scrip in funds. The share price of the stock rose 33 per cent to ₹ 645 in September'01.

Revised Methodology

The redefined new methodology uses superior returns score criteria instead of the sharp ratio, which was used for previous five quarters. The new CPR methodology is based on the following criteria. Superior return score, concentration of the scheme portfolio, liquidity and asset size of the scheme.

Final performance score is computed over four half-year periods with time weighing of 20 per cent, 24 per cent, 26 per cent and 30 per cent. This is drawn so that the latest performance gets a higher weightage.

SUMMARY

Mutual funds are supposed to be the best mode of investment in the capital market since they are very cost beneficial and simple, and do not require an investor to figure out which securities to invest into. A mutual fund could simply be described as a financial medium used by a group of investors to increase their money with a predetermined investment. The responsibility for investing the pooled money into specific investment channels lies with the fund manager of said mutual fund. Therefore investment in a mutual fund means that the investor has bought the shares of the mutual fund and has become a shareholder of that fund. Diversification of investment Investors are able to purchase securities with much lower trading costs by pooling money together in a mutual fund rather than try to do it on their own.

Key Terms

1. **Fund Mutual:** A mutual fund can be defined as a financial institution which mobilizes the savings from the general public and invest the money so collected in different ways. The profits earned by the funds are distributed to the shareholders of the fund.
2. **Regulating System:** A control system the purpose of which is to hold constant the controlled conditions or to vary these under a pre-determined program.
3. **Remisiers:** Remisier is also known as sub-brokers. They are the agents of fullfledged members of a stock exchange. They cannot carry on business in their own name. They have to secure business for the members and are paid commission by the member.
4. **Return on Investment:** Ratio of net income after taxes have been paid of a firm or a division of a firm over a period to the average value during that period of the operating assets of the firm. Synonym for rate of return.

Questions

1. Define mutual fund, explain its objectives.
2. Explain the advantages and disadvantages of mutual funds.
3. Explain different kinds of mutual fund schemes.
4. Narrate the role of UTI in mutual fund industry.
5. What is asset management company? Explain its role in functioning of a mutual fund.
6. What are the differences between open ended scheme and close ended scheme?
7. Explain the regulatory framework of a mututal fund organisation.

8 Money Market Operations

MONEY MARKET

Money market is a market for raising of short-term sources of finance to the business enterprises, banking institutions and other financial institutions. It is an important source of finance for trade and industry. It is centre for dealings, in money assets related to short-term requirements of the borrowers. It provides liquidity to the lenders. It works as a coordinator between lender and borrower for short-term finance. It offers short-term sources of finance to the government. It works as non-inflationary avenue of raising short-term funds through bills which are subscribed by commercial banks and the public.

Definitions of Money Market

1. Money Market is "the centre for dealings, mainly short-term character, in money assets. It meets the short-term requirements of the borrowers and provides liquidity or cash to the lenders. It refers to the market for short-term assets that are close substitutes of money, usually with maturities of less than a year.
2. Money market means, market, where money or its equivalent can be traded.
3. "Money Market is a wholesale market of short-term debt instrument and is synonym of liquidity"
4. "A market for short-term financial assets that are close substitute for money, facilitates the exchange of money in primary and secondary market". RBI

The money market is defined by A. Crowther: The money market is the collective name given to the various firms and institutions that deal with the various grades of near money. Money market deals with trade bills, promissory notes and treasury bills for short period.

The central bank occupies an important role in the money market by providing funds either by lending or through purchasing securities. The central bank administers the money market through open market operations to regulate the flow of money to financial sector of the economy as a whole. The money market contributes to an effective implementation of monetary policy. The Indian money market is not developed on par with London and New York markets. Indian money market consists of the organized and unorganized sector. The organized sector comprises of reserve bank of India, state bank of India together with seven associated state banks, public sector commercial banks, private sector commercial banks including foreign banks, regional rural banks, non-scheduled commercial banks and other non bank financial intermediaries comprising of the LIC, GIC, UTI. The UNORGANISED SECTOR is basically comprised of indigenous bankers, money lenders, and chit funds.

Money market deals only with short-term funds which are available for a day, a week, a month, or for three months, for six months against different types of securities such as bill of exchange, bankers' acceptances, and bonds. It does not refer to a particular place where money is borrowed and lent by the parties concerned. In money market the personal presence of two parties is not essential for completing a financial transaction. The transactions may be carried out through a mail or on telephone. The borrowers in money market are generally:

- Merchants
- Traders
- Brokers
- Manufacturers
- Speculators
- Government institutions.

The lenders in money market are:

- Commercial banks
- Insurance companies
- Non-banking finance companies
- Central bank

Functions of the Money Market

The money market is the most important weapon for the Indian economy to stabilize the market through various alternatives. It performs a diversity of functions in the banking structure of the economy:

- It provides outlets to commercial banks, non-banking financial companies, business enterprises and investors.
- It provides short-term funds to business man, industrialists, and traders to meet their day to day requirement of working capital.
- It also provides short-term funds to government and its agencies.
- It serves as a medium through which the central bank exercises control on the creation of credit.

Importance of Money Market:

- Development of trade and industry.
- Development of capital market.
- Smooth functioning of commercial banks.
- Effective central bank control.

- Formulation of suitable monetary policy.
- Non-inflationary source of finance to government.

A developed money market facilitates the flow of funds to the most important uses of the economy. It serves to provide funds to finance production and distribution and contribute to the economic growth of the country. Money market helps the smooth functioning of the financial system in any economy in the following ways:

1. Money markets finance the short-term working capital requirements of trade and industry. It facilitates the development of industry and trade both national and international.
2. In money market, the commercial banks can temporarily employ their surplus funds in easily realizable assets. They can get back the funds quickly, in times of need by resorting to the money market. It is possible for the commercial banks to utilize their funds profitable and with liquidity.
3. The short-term rates of interest and the conditions that prevail in the money market influence the long-term as well as the resource mobilization in capital market.
4. Money market helps the effective functioning of the central bank in the implementation of the monetary policy. The central bank, through the money market, regulates the flow of money to promote the economic growth with stability.
5. Conditions prevailing in a money market serve as a true indicator of the monetary state of an economy. It serves as a guide to the government in formulating and revising the monetary policy based upon the existing conditions.
6. A developed money market also helps the government to raise short-term funds through the treasury bills floated in the market. Besides trade and industry, money market offers to the government avenues of rising short-term funds through bills that are subscribed by the commercial banks and the public.

Characteristics of Money Market

The following are the characteristics of Money Market.

(a) It involves in the arrangement of short-term funds.

(b) It is a tool for the preparation of monetary policy fiscal management.

(c) It deals with high liquid instruments.

(d) The players in this market are RBI and commercial banks and companies.

(e) It is subject to the RBI regulations.

(f) It tells about the trends in liquidity and interest rates.

(g) It provides funds at low transaction cost.

(h) It sets the requirements of borrow for the short-term funds.

(i) It encourages the open market operations.

Objective of Money Market

- To provide a parking place to employ short-term surplus funds.
- To provide room for overcoming short-term deficits.
- To enable the central bank to influence and regulate liquidity in the economy through its intervention in this market.
- To provide a reasonable access to users of short-term funds to meet their requirement quickly, adequately at reasonable cost.

Characteristics of Developed Money Market

1. **Well-organized banking system:** The money market exists under a highly organized banking system. The commercial banks serve as the nerve system of the whole money market to deal with short-term transactions. On the other side, the central bank occupies the highest place in the money market.
2. **Existence of central bank:** Money market should have a central bank, to act as the banker's bank. The central bank is the guide and controller of the money market. It enables the commercial banks and other institutions to convert their assets into cash in times of financial crisis and provide additional liquidity in the busy seasons.
3. **Adequate availability of credit instruments:** The existence of developed money market has a continuous and adequate availability of credit instruments like bills of exchange, treasury bills, short-term government bonds, etc., which are easily negotiable. Also the presence of dealers and brokers in large numbers to transact in these securities are needed.
4. **Large number of sub markets:** The existence of a large number of sub markets determines the structure of the money market. The several sub markets together make a coherent money market, besides being competitive to each other.
5. **Availability of sufficient funds:** There must be availability of sufficient funds and also perfect mobility of funds throughout the money market. The funds may come from within the country and also be able to attract funds from foreign countries.
6. **Other influencing factors:** A developed money market is also very sensitive to the impact of internal and international influences in trade. The other factors such as political stability, heavy foreign investments, rapid industrialization, price stabilization etc also contribute to the development of money market.

The need for a Money Market:

1. The Money Market is a coordinator between borrowers and lenders of the short-term funds.
2. It provides the transmission of funds from surplus concerns to shortage funds concerns.
3. Money market is a device to the Government to balance its cash inflows and outflows.
4. Money Market is a weapon to business firms to meet their short-term funds.
5. Money Market creates a minimum rate of return on idle fund lying at the disposal of corporate sector and banking sectors.
6. Money Market is a tool to the finance managers in order to more utilization of funds to enhance the shareholders wealth.

The Goals of Money Market Investor:

1. The main objective of the investors in Money Market is about the safety and liquidity of the principal amount. They also think of some gains along with their amounts.
2. Money Market is a parking place of idle fund.
3. The investors will escape wisely from long-term market rises.
4. Money Market instruments generally offer more protection against political risk and inflation risks.
5. In Money Market the investors never face default rises.

Statement showing money market information for the period 2007-10

(₹ in Crores)

Money and Banking (₹ Crore)	Full fiscal year		
	2007-08	2008-09	2009-10
Money supply (M3)	701790(21.2)	759187(18.9)	802498(16.8)
Currency with public	85504(17.7)	97866(17.2)	101772(15.3)
Deposits money with banks of which	614727(21.8)	664802(19.3)	702514(17.1)
• demand deposits	102685(21.6)	3143(0.5)	132642(22.8)
• time deposits	512041(21.8)	661659(23.1)	569872(16.2)
Net bank credit to government	61954(7.4)	378206(42.0)	390535(30.6)
Bank credit to commercial sector	4489112(21.1)	441527(17.1)	462737(15.3)
Net foreign exchange assets	381952(41.8)	57053(4.4)	–77145(–5.7)
Banking sector's net non-monetary liabilities of which	191992(33.5)	118429(15.5)	–25507(–2.9)
RBI	29874(16.6)	177706(84.5)	–77627(–20.0)
Reserve money(2nd July , 2010)	219312(30.9)	59695(6.4)	167689(17.0)
Net RBI credit to center	–116772	176397(–)	149820(–)
MSS, deposits with RBI	105418(167.4)	–80315(–47.7)	–85340(–96.9)

Source: EPW ON July 30, 2010, vole XVLV No 29.

Statement showing money circulation through scheduled comercial banks in India during the period (2007-10) (₹ in crores)

Schedule commercial banks	Full Fiscal year		
	2007-08	2008-09	2009-10
Aggregate deposits	585005(22.4)	637169(17.2)	658717(17.2)
Demand	94580(22.0)	–1224(-0.2)	122525(23.4)
Time	490428(22.5)	638395(23.9)	53192(16.2)
Investments	180199(22.8)	194694(20.0)	218342(18.7)

Bank credits	430724(22.3)	413636(17.5)	469239(16.9)
Non-bank credits	432847(23.0)	411824(17.8)	46696(17.1)
Commercial investments	11961(14.3)	9267(9.7)	13298(12.7)
Total bank assistance to comml sector	444808(22.6)	421091(17.5)	480259(16.9)

Source: EPW on July 30, 2010, vol. XVLV, No. 29.

Financial Institutions in the Money Market

Financial institutions occupy a vital role in Indian economy through money market. Money market is a place where the borrowers and lenders will meet to reach their fulfillments of financial affairs. However, financial institutions will dominate the affairs of the money market. The following financial institutions will participate in the money market for their routine business operations:

- Commercial banks
- Non-banking financial institutions
- Discount houses
- Central bank

Report of the Technical Group on Money Market

Introduction

1. Money market constitutes an important segment of the financial market by providing an avenue for equilibrating the surplus funds of lenders and the requirements of borrowers for short periods ranging from overnight up to a year. In this process, it also provides a focal point for central bank's intervention in influencing the liquidity in the financial system and thereby transmitting the monetary policy impulses.
2. The Indian money market till mid-1980s, was relatively underdeveloped with few instruments and strict regulations with regard to participants and interest rates. Another issue of concern was that the distribution of liquidity in the market was skewed with a few large lenders and some chronic borrowers. The basic pre-requisite of a deep and liquid market that participants should alternate between borrowing and lending activity (i.e., providing two-way quotes) was also absent.
3. In pursuance of the recommendations of the Committee to Review the Working of the Monetary System (Chairman: Professor Sukhamoy Chakravarty) [1985] and the Working Group on the Money Market (Chairman: Shri N. Vaghul) [1987], a number of measures were taken by RBI to widen and deepen the money market through institution building and instrument development. Measures were also initiated to increase the number of participants in the money market. The Discount and Finance House of India Ltd. (DFHI) was set up jointly by the Reserve Bank, public sector banks and financial institutions to deal in short-term money market instruments with the primary objective of imparting improved liquidity to such instruments.

4. Accordingly, while introduction of new instruments, broadening of participants' base and strengthening of institutional infrastructure have been pursued during the 1990s, based on the framework provided by the Vaghul Committee, the Narasimham Committee (1998), recommended rationalization, *inter alia,* of the participation of different classes of entities in various segments of money market as also underscored the importance of money market in the context of discretionary liquidity management of RBI. Pursuant to these recommendations, coupled with the need to keep the credit risk at a minimum in the financial market, encouraging inter-linkages across various segments of money market as also to foster a more balanced development of different markets, RBI has been initiating a number of structural and instrument-specific measures which have further contributed to the growth and sophistication of Indian money market, particularly since 2000-01.
5. There are three broad policy objectives that are being pursued now for the development of the Indian money market which include (a) ensuring stability in short-term interest rates, (b) minimizing default risk and (c) achieving a balanced development of various segments of money market.
6. With regard to the first objective, i.e., ensuring stability in short-term interest rates, it is stated that RBI has been reasonably successful in minimizing volatility as well as in aligning these rates through active operation of Liquidity Adjustment Facility (LAF) combined with outright transactions under Open Market Operations (OMO) and more recently, Market Stabilization Scheme (MSS). An important feature of these operations is that the present LAF framework, where the reverse repo rate attempts to provide the floor to the movement of call rates, has been in a position to hold all other short-term rates in reasonable alignment with the reverse repo rate. In other words, the RBI reverse repo rate has not only become the benchmark rate for call rates, it has also become the reference rate for market repo/Collateralized Borrowing and Lending Obligation (CBLO) rates with the spread between them declining over the years
8. Reflecting this, the relative turnover in various segments of money market has undergone significant changes over the years. This is partly policy driven and partly on account of the substantial improvement in underlying liquidity condition in the economy during this period. While the relative share of call/notice money market has declined from as high as 81 per cent during 2000-01, to only 29 per cent during 2004-05, that of market repo has increased from only 1 per cent to as much as 22 per cent over this period. CBLO, after a slow start, has been gathering significant momentum and now accounts for about 14 per cent during 2004-05. The situation, however, changes if the average volume accepted under RBI's reverse repo window is taken into account along with these instruments. It is evident that with substantial improvement in liquidity, the share of RBI's reverse repo rose from 8 per cent to 48 per cent over this period.
9. Further, it is heartening to note that the attempt to develop a deep collateralized market, *viz.,* market repo and CBLO *vis-à-vis* the uncollateralized call/notice market has already witnessed significant success. As regards other money market instruments, the outstanding amount under CP has been scaling new peaks with every passing month in the recent period. All these factors have brought about a relatively more balanced development of various segments of money market though the prospect for further development is immense.

10. In order to identify further expected changes in money market over a medium-term period based on cross-country practices and the changing dynamics of the Indian financial market, RBI constituted an Internal Technical Group on Money Market. (Annexure-1) The Report thus prepared was discussed with members of the Technical Advisory Committee (TAC) on Money, Foreign Exchange and Government Securities Markets on April 12, 2005. The Group places on record the valuable contributions made by the members during their deliberations on the Report.

11. The Report is organized into four Sections. Section I discusses the importance of money market and related issues in the conduct of monetary operations against the backdrop of sustained capital inflows. Against this macro scenario, Section II explores the expected future transformation in various segments of money market over a medium-term horizon. Section III captures the macro issues and their consequent implications for money market. A summary of recommendations of the Group is given in Section IV.

Section I

12. The money market, particularly the overnight market, is important from the point of view of any central bank. This is because a vibrant, deep and broad-based money market is the key for efficient distribution of liquidity among various economic agents in the economy. Therefore, it is through this segment, the central bank attempts to influence the systemic liquidity and stabilize short-term interest rates. In the process, it transmits the impulse of monetary policy. However, the pre-requisites for achieving a vibrant, deep and efficient money market are that there should be adequate number of liquid instruments, wider base of participants with diverse liquidity needs and sound institutional infrastructure including efficient payment and clearing mechanism. Further, the financial market in general, and money market in particular, perform best when the enabling environment is conducive in that the economy runs on a low fiscal deficit and the regulatory and prudential regime incentivizes the functioning of the market and makes the economic agents accountable for their actions. These issues have become particularly important as the Indian economy has become progressively more globalised.

13. Assessing the status of Indian money market against the above-mentioned perspective, one may maintain that the market has not only been transformed markedly, particularly during the last five years in terms of depth and more varied instruments, it has also brought in a wider level of participation in these markets. The institutional infrastructure, particularly with the up gradation of payment system infrastructure, *viz.,* operationalization of Clearing Corporation of India Ltd. (CCIL), Negotiated Dealing System (NDS), Real-Time Gross Settlement (RTGS) system and the Centralized Funds Management System (CFMS) has brought about immense benefit to the financial market at large. The substantial growth of collateralized market vis-à-vis uncollateralized market as mentioned earlier is reflective of the combined result of the developmental process set in motion by RBI and adapted by the market.

14. The above process would be further strengthened with the implementation of FRBM Act, 2003. Under this mandate, direct credit from RBI through its participation in primary auctions of central government securities would come to an end since April 1, 2006. This would functionally lead to separation of debt management operation from monetary operations. All these would give rise to an environment where RBI would have greater control over the

composition of its balance sheet and further flexibility in monetary operations. This, however, presupposes that there would be close co-ordination between the fiscal authority and the monetary authority for ensuring stability in the financial market as a whole.

15. With the ensuing enabling environment within the domestic economy expected to be more conducive, it is envisaged that the money market in India is poised for a big leap. However, the principal challenge that the economy may experience over the medium-term following its increasing openness could be the management of liquidity in the face of strong capital inflows. This is particularly important because if India could sustain the present high level of growth rate combined with a benign inflation environment, lower fiscal deficit and other strong macroeconomic fundamentals, the economy could be expected to receive more than its normal share of capital inflows, notwithstanding changes in policy stance in major advanced economies.
16. The challenges before RBI in managing capital flows had been dealt with extensively in the Report of the Internal Group on Liquidity Adjustment Facility (November 2003) and the RBI Working Group on Instruments of Stabilisation (December 2003). It was underscored therein that 'In order for the LAF to function as the principal monetary policy instrument for signaling the Reserve Bank's stance on interest rates, it is desirable that LAF operates to primarily manage liquidity at the margin on a day to day basis'. The dilemma before any central bank under that situation was put forth as 'while operationally it is difficult to distinguish between the stabilisation operations and liquidity management operations under LAF, conceptually there is a need to distinguish surplus liquidity of 'temporary' nature from surplus liquidity of a somewhat 'enduring' nature'. Considering these issues, the LAF Group recommended that in order to improve the effectiveness of LAF, introduction of additional instruments of stabilisation against the backdrop of declining stock of government securities with RBI should be explored. Accordingly, the RBI Working Group on Instruments of Stabilisation, after considering pros and cons of various instruments, recommended that 'Government may consider setting up of a Market Stabilisation Fund (MSF) .... For mopping up enduring surplus liquidity from the system'. Taking into account all these issues, the revised LAF scheme as well as the Market Stabilization Scheme were operationalized in April 2004.
17. The issue that needs to be appreciated here is that continued stabilisation has a financial cost in terms of the outgo of coupon on the stabilisation amount. The trade-off here is that in the absence of stabilisation, there could be excessive volatility in financial markets, interest rates and exchange rate leading to erosion of competitiveness of the economy; this would have adverse impact on the economy at large and on the non-government sector in particular. This brings forth the core issue of stabilization of short-term interest rates in money market consistent with expected growth of GDP and inflation in an environment of large capital inflows. The framework for achieving this objective in a corridor setting was given by the Report of the Internal Group on LAF. This framework, based on the experiences of select developed economies, has been modified to suit the needs of Indian situation. Accordingly, under surplus mode, while the fixed reverse repo rate at 5.00 per cent at which RBI absorbs liquidity from the market provides the floor to the movement of call money rates, the ceiling is provided by the fixed repo rate at 6.0 per cent at which RBI is prepared to lend to eligible market participants. In this context, the reverse repo rate acts as the policy rate reflecting the

stance of RBI besides being the rate for liquidity management. It is important to note here that outright purchase and sale of securities, often known as open market operations (OMOs), should be so conducted as to stabilize interest rates and minimize their volatility. The essential distinction between the reverse repo rate under LAF and the outright buy/sale of securities under OMO is that under the former, RBI determines the rate to provide clarity to the stance of RBI whereas under the latter, buy/sale of securities at a particular price is linked to the secondary market conditions. Therefore, while the reverse repo rate under LAF is a fixed one, the outright buy/sale of securities could be done at a variable price with reference to the corresponding secondary market price.

18. A related issue here is the width of the corridor. International experiences show that it varies between 50 basis points (bps) and 200 bps. In India, it stands at 100 bps now. Ideally, the spread should reflect the society's tolerance level of volatility in short-term interest rates. Even then, in the Indian context, RBI may find it difficult to tolerate daily fluctuations in call rates by 100 bps over a sustained period. Therefore, for all practical purpose, this spread of 100 bps should be interpreted as the maximum tolerance level under extreme one-off circumstance. This is also corroborated by the market practice as call rates generally fluctuate within 5/10 bps in the relation to the RBI's reverse repo rate. The success in keeping call rates in a narrower bound in relation to the RBI's reverse repo rate would, therefore, depend upon how successfully RBI would conduct LAF and OMO.

Section II

Call/Notice Money Market

19. RBI has implemented a series of prudential measures not only to minimize the default risk in call/notice market but also to achieve a balanced development of various segments of the financial market, particularly in favor of the collateralized segment. The major policy measures relevant for this purpose are enumerated below.

    - *Following the recommendations of the Narasimham Committee (1998), RBI is in an advanced stage of making call/notice market a pure inter-bank market.*
    - *Prudential limits have been placed on borrowings and lending of banks and PDs in call/notice market.*

Prudential Limits on Call/Notice Money Market Operations: Review of Benchmark

20. With a view to facilitating balanced development of various segments of money market, it was decided to stipulate prudential limits in a symmetric way on both borrowing and lending of banks and PDs in call/notice money market. The prudential limits as applicable to various classes of entities are indicated below:

    Scheduled Commercial Banks:

    - Lending of scheduled commercial banks, on a fortnightly average basis, should not exceed 25 per cent of their owned funds (OF) (i.e., sum of Schedules I and II); however, banks are allowed to lend a maximum of 50 per cent of their owned funds on any day during a fortnight.

- Borrowings by scheduled commercial banks, on a fortnightly average basis, should not exceed 100 per cent of their owned funds or 2 per cent of aggregate deposits, whichever is higher; however, banks are allowed to borrow a maximum of 125 per cent of their owned funds on any day during a fortnight.

Cooperative Banks:

- Borrowings by urban cooperative banks (UCBs)/State Cooperative Banks (SCBs) and District Central Cooperative Banks (DCCBs) in call/notice money market on a daily basis should not exceed 2.0 per cent of their aggregate deposits as at end March of the previous financial year.

Primary Dealers:

- *PDs are permitted to lend, on average in a reporting fortnight, up to 25 per cent of their net owned funds (NOF) as at end-March of the preceding financial year.*
- *PDs are allowed to borrow, on average in a reporting fortnight, up to 200 per cent of their NOF as at end-March of the preceding financial year.*

Non-Bank Entities:

- Non-bank participants are allowed to lend, effective January 8, 2005, on average in a reporting fortnight, up to 30 per cent of their average daily lending in call/notice money market during 2000-01.

21. It is; therefore, evident that at present, different classes of eligible participants have different benchmarking norms for their transactions in the call/notice money market. The limits are linked to owned funds, net owned funds (NOF) and aggregate deposits. However, keeping in view the risks, it may be desirable to have capital funds (sum of Tiers I & II) as the benchmark for fixing of call/notice money limits.

II. Feasibility of Migrating from Owned Funds (OF) to Capital Funds (Sum of Tiers I&II)

22. An exercise has been carried out here to examine the feasibility of migrating from owned funds to capital funds as the benchmark in an effort to standardize the benchmarking of norms. Accordingly, the limits with respect to the new benchmark of capital funds *vis-a-vis* those under Owned Fund (OF) for different classes of eligible participants in the call/notice money market are examined below.

Scheduled Commercial Banks

(a) Lending Limit:

23. It is evident that if the lending limit at 25 per cent is linked to the capital funds (sum of Tiers I & II), then the aggregate lending limit of scheduled commercial banks would increase by ₹ 2,440 crores (Table 1). Though there would be a decline in the lending limit of foreign banks by ₹ 95 crores, they would not be affected much since they are generally net borrowers.

Table 1: Lending Limit

(₹ in Crore)

Type of Bank	Current	Proposed	Difference between 2 & 1
	25% of	25% of Capital Funds	
	1	2	3
Public Sector	19,806	21,503	1,697
Foreign	3,594	3,499	–95
Private Sector	5,502	6,340	838
Total	28,902	31,342	2,440

(b) Borrowing Limit:

24. As with lending limit, if the norm of 100 per cent is changed to the alternate norm of 100 percent of capital funds, then apparently there would be a sharp jump in the aggregate borrowing limit of scheduled commercial banks by ₹ 10,031 crores (Table 2). While foreign banks would have marginally lower limits than their current limits, the entitlements of public sector banks and private sector banks would increase by ₹ 6,788 crores and ₹ 3,622 crores respectively in the process. However, since public sector banks are generally surplus, the effective increase in borrowing limit should be around the level of that of private sector banks, i.e., about ₹ 3,500 crores.

Table 2: Borrowing Limit

(₹ in Crore)

Type of Bank	Current	Proposed	Difference between 2 & 1
	100% of OF	100% of Capital Funds	
	1	2	3
Public Sector	79,224	86,012	6,788
Foreign	14,377	13,998	–379
Private Sector	22,008	25,630	3,622
Total	1,15,609	1,25,640	10,031

Co-operative Banks

25. At present, borrowings by Urban Cooperative Banks (UCBs)/State Cooperative Banks (SCBs) and District Central Cooperative Banks (DCCBs) in call/notice money market on a daily basis should not exceed 2.0 per cent of their aggregate deposits as at end-March of the previous financial year. To bring it in line with the norms applicable to scheduled commercial banks, their borrowing limit could be linked to their capital funds also. However, the capital adequacy norms as applicable for scheduled commercial banks have not been made

applicable for District Central Cooperative Banks and State Cooperative Banks though the same has been extended to UCBs. Hence, it may not be desirable to prescribe different benchmarking norms for different types of banks within the cooperative segment. Accordingly, the Group recommends for continuing with the current benchmark of 2 per cent of aggregate deposits for these banks in call/notice money market.

Primary Dealers

26. The Group examined the feasibility of adopting Capital Funds as the benchmark. However, it has been found that unlike the banking sector, since the difference between Capital Funds and NOF for PDs as at end March 2004 was only marginal, it may not matter much if Capital Funds is used as the benchmark instead of the present benchmark based on NOF (Table 3). Therefore, the Group proposes that the current norm of NOF for benchmarking limits for PDs may be continued.

Table 3: Norms for Primary Dealers

(₹ in Crore)

Category	Current	Proposed	Difference between 2 & 1
	As %age of NOF	As %age of Capital Funds (Tier I + II)	
	1	2	3
I. Lending	1,493	1,525	32
II. Borrowing	11,944	12,186	242

Non-bank Entities:

27. Currently, the non-bank participants are allowed to lend, on average in a reporting fortnight, up to 30 per cent of their average daily lending in call/notice money market during 2000-01. Since they are in an advanced stage of being phased out from call/notice money market, the Group suggests that the present norm may not be changed.

II.1.3 Dealings on an Electronic Negotiated Quote Driven System:

28. At present, call/notice money transactions are essentially voice based. In order to improve transparency and to facilitate real-time dissemination of information, the Group suggests that dealings in call/notice market transactions should be conducted on a screen-based negotiated quote driven platform.

II.1.4 Participation in Call/Notice Market:

29. The process is underway to make the call/notice market a pure inter-bank one by phasing out non-bank participants from this market following the recommendations of the Narasimham Committee (1998). Accordingly, the process commenced after due consultations with market participants in May 2001 as non-bank participants were allowed to lend, on average in a reporting fortnight, up to 85 per cent of their average lending in 2000-01. This limit was brought down in successive stages following full scale operationalization of CCIL and reasonable development in alternative markets such as repo and CBLO. In view of market

developments, the Group recommends that non-bank participants may be encouraged to move out of the call/notice market completely by the middle of 2005-06 and this market would then be purely an inter-bank one. In such a scenario, there could be a case for further review of prudential guidelines for banks and PDs for their transactions in call/notice money market.

II.1.5 Borrowing Limit:

30. The main reason for placing limit on the borrowing in call/notice market is that an entity should not borrow an unsustainable amount from this market relative to the size of its balance sheet. Ideally, the implementation of an efficient ALM framework should be the first best solution to manage exposure to such uncollateralized market. During the last four years, major changes have taken place in risk management guidelines being followed by banks and PDs. This is also reflected in the market behavior as cooperative banks intending to borrow have virtually moved out of the call market to the collateralized CBLO segment. Similarly, some banks, perceived to be weak by the market, have been apparently finding it difficult to borrow from call market. In such a scenario, the Group felt that, as underscored by RBI earlier, there could be a need to allow more flexibility to banks/PDs to borrow in call/notice market provided they have appropriate risk management systems in place and such need is warranted by their balance sheet structure.

II.1.6 Lending Limit:

31. On the lending side, though the fundamental objectives of placing restriction are to limit the exposure to this uncollateralized market as also to develop term money, repo and CBLO markets, these have not contributed to the growth of term money market at the desirable level, as banks/PDs, especially the former, have the softer option of placing funds in RBI's LAF window where return has been, on average, higher than those from repo and CBLO markets. The latter two markets have, however, developed largely because non-banks, particularly mutual funds and financial institutions, which, on being phased out from call/notice market, have become the largest supplier of funds in these two segments. Implementation of DVP III and roll over of repo has also contributed markedly to their growth. With call/notice money market being eventually an inter-bank one, the Group feels that with appropriate level of risk management capacity, participants could be afforded larger freedom to undertake their transactions.

II.2 Collateral for Repo and CBLO Markets:

32. Increasing use of collateral, both in India and the major economies in the world, has been becoming the most important tool for mitigation of risk in the wholesale financial market. The motivation for increasing use of collateral could come from three areas. First, it could be ‘security–driven’, e.g., for compliance with statutory liquidity ratio (SLR) norm or 'cash-driven' in order to reduce funding costs as borrowing under the collateralized repo/CBLO is cheaper than that under uncollateralized call/notice market. Second, increasing use of collateralization of positions in derivatives market has been coming in place to offset counterparty risk. Third, higher demand for collateral is expected to emanate from more sophistication in payment and settlement system, particularly in the wake of full-scale operationalization of RTGS system which is very liquidity intensive. Due to all these reasons, cross-country experiences show that the volume of repo transactions have been increasing markedly in major markets such as in the US, the UK, Euro area and Japan. A notable trend in

these economies is that with the reduction in fiscal deficit and consequent decline in stock of government bonds, high quality corporate papers such as mortgage–backed securities and Pf and brief (i.e., bonds issued by German mortgage banks and collateralized by either loans to the public sector or mortgages) are increasingly being used as the underlying assets in repo transactions. Further, equities belonging to major indices in stock markets are also being increasingly accepted for repos on account of their high quality.

33. Broadening the range of assets as collaterals for repo/CBLO also underscores the need for appropriate collateral management. This is particularly because managing of credit risk becomes important for private corporate papers compared to a situation when collaterals are essentially government papers, as the issue sizes of private papers tend to be smaller and more heterogeneous than those of government papers. Further, there could be virtually no liquid derivative market for private sector fixed income securities. In that case, it would be difficult to value and hedge these securities. Considering these issues, there could be a need to broad base the pool of securities beyond central government securities and treasury bills to act as collaterals for market repo and CBLO. While state government securities are eligible for repo, there have been very few repo transactions based on these securities largely on account of lack of liquidity in this segment. It is in this context, development of state government securities market assumes importance as these could also provide a pool of securities as collaterals for the use of market participants.

II.2.1 Dealings on an Electronic Anonymous Order Driven System:

34. In order to improve transparency and to facilitate real-time dissemination of information, the Group recommends that the possibility of conducting repo transactions on an electronic anonymous order driven trading system may be explored.

II.3 Term Money:

35. Term money market is where funds with maturity from 15 days to one year are borrowed and lent without collateral. Two distinct policy measures were taken to activate the term money market. First, term money of original maturity between 15 days and 1 year was exempted from CRR in August 2001. Second, no limits were stipulated for transactions in term money market unlike those under call/notice money market. Apparently, the growth of term money market, as reported on NDS, has been very sluggish as can be observed by the fact that the average daily term money transactions at ₹ 195 crores in 2001 increased to ₹ 519 crores in 2003 before declining to ₹ 477 crores in April 2005. However, an analysis of data as reported by banks under Section 42 (Annex A to Form A) to RBI reveals that the outstanding amounts were as high ₹ 15,000-20,000 crores. With regard to term money market, there seems to be some reporting issues.

36. In this connection, it may be noted that in order to improve transparency and strengthen efficiency in the money market, it is mandatory for all NDS members to report all their call/notice money market transactions through NDS within 15 minutes of concluding the transaction. Both RBI and the market participants have access to this information on a faster frequency and in a more classified manner, thereby improving transparency and price discovery.

37. It is widely accepted that the banking sector needs a deep and liquid term money market for managing its liquidity as also a smoother rupee yield curve. In order to improve transparency

and strengthen efficiency in the term money market, the Group recommends that the reporting of term money deals on NDS may be made mandatory. Further, in order to improve transparency and facilitate a better price discovery process, the Group recommends that dealings in term money transactions should be conducted on a screen based negotiated quote driven platform.

II.4 Certificates of Deposit

38. Certificates of Deposit (CDs) were introduced in India in 1989, as a short-term unsecured promissory note. It has a maturity period ranging from 15 days to 365 days for banks. In this context, it may be noted that in the mid-term review of annual policy statement for the year 2004-05, the minimum tenor of retail domestic term deposits (under ₹ 15 lakhs) was reduced from 15 days to 7 days. Apart from bulk deposits (₹ 15 lakhs and above), with effect from November 1, 2004, banks at their discretion can also reduce the minimum tenor of retail term deposits from 15 days to 7 days. Further, minimum maturity period of commercial paper (CP) was also reduced from 15 days to 7 days in the mid-term Review of annual policy Statement for the year 2004-05. In view of reduction of minimum maturity period for fixed deposits and CP, the Group recommends that the minimum tenure of CD for banks may be reduced from 15 days to 7 days.

II.5 Commercial Paper:

39. With a view to developing the commercial paper (CP) market further, a Status Paper was prepared by RBI and placed on its website in July 2003. After deliberating on the suggestions of the Status Paper with market participants and experts, three measures, *viz.,* (i) reduction of minimum maturity period from 15 days to 7 days, (ii) reporting of issuance of CP on the negotiated dealing system (NDS) platform by issuing and paying agents (IPAs) and (iii) constitution of a Group comprising market participants to rationalize and standardized, wherever possible, various aspects of processing, settlement and documentation of CP issuance with a view to achieving the settlement at least on T + 1 basis, were announced in the mid-term review of annual policy statement for the year 2004-05. The position in this regard is as follows:

- The minimum maturity period has already been reduced to 7 days.
- The reporting of CP issuance by IPAs on NDS platform has commenced since April 16, 2005 and would be made available on RBI website shortly.
- As regards standardization, while the documentations and other market practices were already standardized by FIMMDA, settlement of CP on T+1 basis could be achieved if funds settlement is ensured on T+0 basis. The Group recognized that this would be possible after full operationalization of RTGS system.

II.5.1 Asset-backed Commercial Paper:

40. Asset-backed commercial paper (ABCP) is reportedly the largest component of CP market in the US. It is issued by a company, which purchases receivables from one firm or a group of firms, and finances the purchase with funds raised in the commercial paper market. In other words, asset backed issuer's securities a portfolio of cash generating assets funded by liabilities including CP. The sole business activity of the special company is the purchase and finance of the receivables so that risk of the company and the CP it issues is isolated from the risk of the firm or firms, which originated the receivables. With asset-backed paper, the

paper's risk is instead tied directly to the creditworthiness of specific financial assets, usually some form of receivables. Asset-backed paper is one way whereby smaller, riskier firms can access the CP market. Traditionally, banks have used ABCP as a device to put their current asset off their balance sheets and yet provide liquidity support to their clients. The Group recommends that in India, ABCP may be introduced for further deepening the CP market. In this context, it may be noted that RBI issued the draft guidelines on securitization of standard assets on April 4, 2005.

II.6 Forward Rate Agreements (FRAs)/Interest Rate Swap (IRS):

41. In the 'Mid-term Review of Monetary and Credit Policy for 1998-99' announced on October 30, 1998, it was indicated that with a view to further deepening the money market as also to enable banks, primary dealers and all-India financial institutions to hedge interest rate risks, with effect from July 7, 1999, the Reserve Bank had allowed Scheduled Commercial Banks (SCBs) excluding Regional Rural Banks, primary dealers and all India financial institutions to undertake Forward Rate Agreements/Interest Rate Swaps (FRA/IRS) as a product for their own balance sheet management and for market making/trading purposes. Also, effective November 1, 1999, with a view to providing further flexibility in the use of FRA/IRS, mutual funds were allowed to participate in the market for the purpose of hedging their own balance sheet risks. Further, effective April 27, 2000, the use of 'interest rate implied in the foreign exchange forward market' as a benchmark had been permitted in addition to the domestic money and debt market rates.

42. Presently, banks/PDs/FIs can undertake different kinds of plain vanilla FRAs/IRS. Swaps having explicit/implicit option features such as caps/floors/collars are not permitted. The rupee derivative market has grown significantly since 1999. It has increased from 104 contracts for the notional principal amount of ₹ 2,065 crores as on January 14, 2000 to 35,634 contracts for ₹ 10,12,671 crores as on April 1, 2005. In this context, it is worthwhile to note that exchange-traded derivatives were introduced by way of futures in Stock Exchange, Mumbai (BSE) and National Stock Exchange (NSE) from June 2000. Further, with regard to OTC products, Foreign Exchange Management Act, 2000, permits banks to provide risk management tools like swaps, options, caps, collars and FRAs to clients to hedge interest rate risk arising out of foreign currency liabilities. Against this background, since considerable time has elapsed after the introduction of guidelines on FRAs/IRS in 1999, there is a need to consider more complex features of swaps and options.

43. In order to examine all these issues, following the announcement in the mid-term review for the year 2002-03 on October 29, 2002, the Reserve Bank had constituted a Working Group. The Group was required to suggest the modalities for introducing dealing in the derivatives having explicit option features such as caps/collars/floors in the rupee derivative segment and also the norms for capital adequacy, exposure limits, swap position, asset liability management, internal control and other risk management methods for these derivatives. Thereafter, due to various issues relating to OTC derivatives such as ambiguity over legality of OTC derivative contracts, absence of netting laws, etc., further relaxation could not be afforded so far.

44. In this regard, in the Union Budget 2005-06, the Honorable Finance Minister has stated ' Over the Counter (OTC) derivatives play a crucial role in mitigating the risks of corporate, banks

and other financial entities. There is however, some ambiguity regarding the legality of OTC derivative contracts, which has inhibited their growth. I, therefore, propose to take measures to provide clear legal validity of such contracts'. In view of the above, the Group proposes that the Government should amend appropriately the RBI Act, 1934, to provide legality to OTC derivatives. Further, it is felt that the recommendations given by the Jaspal Bindra Group can be implemented in a phased manner after putting in place the revised risk reporting system by market participants and the robust accounting standards, and legality of OTC derivatives is clarified.

II.7 MIBOR - Linked Short-term Papers:

45. The jurisdiction of RBI over various segments of financial market was clarified following the issuance of notification by the Government of India on March 1, 2000 under Section 16 of the Securities Contracts (Regulation) Act (SCRA), 1956, whereby, it was decided that 'in relation to any contracts in Government securities, money market securities, gold related securities and in securities derived from these securities and in relation to ready forward contracts in bonds, debentures, debenture stock, securitized debt and other debt securities shall also be exercisable by the Reserve Bank of India constituted under section 3 of the Reserve Bank of India Act, 1934 (2 of 1934)'.

46. There are some new instruments such as Mumbai Inter-bank Offered Rate (MIBOR) linked short-term papers up to 365 days with/without daily call/put options. In this market, top rated corporate generally raise funds from non-bank entities, particularly from mutual funds. There is a need to address regulatory issues pertaining to such papers for an orderly development of the market.

Section III

47. Though the money market has transformed markedly during the course of the last five years, it is expected to witness more remarkable changes in the coming years. The principal macro drivers of such changes could be the following:

- Sustained effort in deregulation and rationalization of economic policies and
- Continued technological progress, particularly in the context of up gradation of payment system infrastructure.

48. All these changes are expected to have profound implications for the Indian money market in future. The Report has attempted to capture the possible progression of some of these major changes and their consequent implications for Indian money market below.

III.1 Deregulation and Rationalization of Economic Policies:

49. Since money market is part of the overall financial market, any change in the broader macro scenario is expected to impact the money market also. Though it is difficult to gauge how the money market would evolve in future, it is likely that there could be two macro factors that might affect this market significantly in future, *viz.,* (i) increasing concentration of activities of market players arising out of mergers, acquisition and consolidation and (ii) increasing activity in fixed income market.

50. An analysis of transactions of top 10 participants in various segments of money market reveals that there already exists high level of concentration in all these markets except in

CBLO. For example, in call/notice money market, the shares of top 10 borrowers have increased substantially from 40 percent during 2000-01 to as much as 58 percent during 2004-05 (Annex II). This should, however, be seen against the background of contraction in the turnover of call/notice market from about ₹ 36,000 crores to about ₹ 16,000 crores over this period following substantial improvement in liquidity. Similarly, in market repo segment, while the shares of top 10 borrowers have increased from 62 per cent during August-December 2001 to 73 per cent during 2004-05, those in lending have also spurted from 66 per cent to 90 per cent over this period. In contrast, CBLO is the only segment among these three funding markets where the concentration has gone down markedly reflecting broader basing of its market structure over the period (Annex II). While consolidation per se may be a desirable process, particularly in the context of increasing internationalization of our economy, all these might also create an oligopolistic structure in the economy.

51. The fixed income market, particularly the corporate debt segment, is expected to witness greater activity in future. Additional demand is expected to emanate from deregulation in the pension and insurance sectors, financing demand arising on account of consolidation/merger/acquisition, foreign portfolio capital, phasing out of non-bank participants from call/notice money market as also from the payment system, in particular the RTGS system *vis-à-vis* expected shrinkage in supply of government papers following implementation of the FRBM Act, 2003. Further, there could be substantial demand for asset-backed securitized instruments due to increased awareness in credit risks, especially from the pension, insurance and mutual funds segments.

52. In the pension sector, it is likely that the pressure to migrate from defined benefit plan to defined contribution plan would increase in coming years. This coupled with the liberalization of investment norms for pension funds permitting them to invest a part of their corpus in equity and fixed income corporate papers facilitated recently, would create a large pool of savings which would demand both long and short-term assets for investment. Since a part of savings from insurance players might come through mutual funds, the demand for both capital market and money market instruments would most likely increase significantly.

53. The implications of all these expected developments would be that while investment interests in money market instruments are likely to go up substantially in future, the market could also be more volatile in future on account of rise in concentration. This implies that RBI would have to be more proactive with LAF and OMO in stabilizing short-term interest rates and preserving financial stability.

III.2 Technological Progress:

54. The Indian financial market has witnessed huge technological advancement in recent period. These include the operationalization of CCIL, NDS, RTGS system, centralized funds management system (CFMS) and electronic clearing system (ECS), and the expected completion in a short period of time of cheque truncation; national electronic funds transfer (NEFT), virtual PDO and virtual DAD. All these have been bringing about some fundamental changes in the financial market in the form of the ability to shift not only funds from one place to the other but also from one market to the other and take positions in various segments of financial market.

55. The implications are that market participants have been exploiting the arbitrage opportunities existing in different segments of money market and thereby, aiding the convergence of different money market rates subject to only the degree of credit risk prevalent in these instruments. This is clearly evident in recent period when not only a large part of call borrowing has migrated to repo and CBLO due to relatively cheaper funding costs in the latter two markets *vis-à-vis* call market but also select participants have been borrowing cheaper in call/repo/CBLO and placing them in RBI's reverse repo window so long as the latter rate is higher than the other rates. All these have led to marked reduction in the spread among call, repo and CBLO rates *vis-à-vis* RBI's reverse repo rate under LAF (Chart 1, p. 2).

56. The advantage of this convergence is that different segments are getting increasingly interlinked and hence, price discovery process is more efficient now. The ensuing environment while improving the overall transmission process of monetary policy would pose greater challenges to RBI in its conduct of monetary operations. This is because coupled with progressive scaling down of CRR to very low level, the upgradation of payment system infrastructure in the form of full-scale operationalization of RTGS system would result in faster and more efficient funds transfer. In the process, the likely volatility in the call money market may have to be carefully managed. In this situation, the need for both marginal liquidity and collateral (for securing both intra-day and inter-day liquidity) for the system as a whole may increase substantially. All these may call for conduct of multiple LAF on intra-day basis and active OMO by RBI to smoothen the behavior of short-term interest rates.

57. The Group noted that intra-day liquidity (IDL) would be available to eligible participants under RTGS system till 5.00 p.m. as of now. Since it has been mandated that IDL has to be extinguished by the end of the day, a dilemma arises with regard to holding of late hour repo auction. This is because conversion of IDL into overnight facility would have an unanticipated money supply impact. Further, IDL should be availed of by market participants against assured cash flows. Therefore, if IDL is allowed to be extinguished through borrowing from RBI's repo window, it would tantamount to shifting of cash management responsibilities of market participants on to RBI and unwarranted expansion of money supply in the economy. On balance, the Group felt that there is merit in exploring late hour intra-day LAF as and when warranted in future. Ideally, late hour intra-day LAF towards the closing hours of the market should aim at absorption of residual resources (i.e., reverse repo).

Section IV

Summary of Recommendations

58. The Group maintained that the policy thrust should be to encourage collateralized market, develop the rupee yield curve, ensure transparency and better price discovery, provide avenues for better risk management and strengthen monetary operations. Recommendations of the Group in this regard have been summarized below:

IV.1 Call/Notice Money Market:

- RBI may migrate from OF (Owned Fund) to capital funds (sum of Tier I and Tier II capital) as the benchmark for fixing prudential limits for call/notice money market for scheduled commercial banks. RBI may, however, continue with the present norm associated with cooperative banks (i.e., Aggregate Deposit), PDs (i.e., Net Owned Fund) and non-banks (i.e., 30 per cent of their average daily lending during 2000-01).

- Call/notice money market transactions should be conducted on an electronic negotiated quote driven platform.
- Banks and PDs with appropriate risk management systems in place and balance sheet structure may be allowed more flexibility to borrow in call/notice money market.
- Upon accomplishing the call/notice money market into a pure inter-bank one, larger freedom in lending in call/notice market should be afforded to banks and PDs.

IV.2 Repo/CBLO

- Consequent upon coming into effect of the FRBM Act 2003, there would be a need to broad-base the pool of securities to act as collateral for repo and CBLO markets.
- The possibility of conducting repo transactions on an electronic, anonymous order driven trading system may be explored.

IV.3 Term Money

- Reporting of term money transactions on NDS platform may be made compulsory to improve transparency.
- Term money market transactions on an electronic, negotiated quote driven platform should be introduced.

IV.4 CD

- Maturity period of CDs to be reduced to 7 days, in line with that under CP and fixed deposit.

IV.5 Commercial Paper

- Asset-backed CP should be introduced in the Indian market.

IV.6 FRAs/IRS

- Appropriate amendment to the RBI Act, 1934, may be done to provide legal clarity to OTC derivatives.
- Limited optionality should be permitted in rupee derivative segment in a phased manner after putting in place the revised risk reporting system by market participants and the robust accounting standard, and legality of OTC derivatives is clarified.

IV.7 MIBOR-Linked Short-term Papers

- There is a need to address regulatory issues pertaining to this type of new instruments for an orderly development of the market.

IV.8 Timing of LAF

- There is merit in exploring late hour intra-day LAF as and when warranted in future. Ideally, late hour intra-day LAF towards the closing hour of the market should aim at absorption of residual resources (i.e., reverse repo).

❍ Annex I: Constitution of Technical Group on Money Market

1. It is proposed to set up a Technical Group on Money Market with the following members:

   (i) Shri Deepak Mohanty, Adviser-in-Charge, MPD, Convenor

(ii) Shri Himadri Bhattacharya, CGM, DEIO, Member
(iii) Shri B. Mahapatra, CGM-in-C, IDMD, Member
(iv) Shri P.Vijaya Bhaskar, CGM, DBOD, Member
(v) Dr. Janak Raj, Director, DEAP, Member
(vi) Shri Amitava Sardar, Director, MPD, Member-Secretary

2. The terms of reference of the Technical Group are:
   (i) Review of developments and current status of Money Market in India
   (ii) Cross-country experience in money market
   (iii) Suggest measures for further development of the money market in India
3. The Group is expected to submit its report within a fortnight from its first meeting.

(ShymalGopinath)
Deputy Governor
February 23, 2005

- Annex II

II.1 Composition of Top Ten Players in Call/Notice Money Market

(In per cent)

Entity	Borrowing		Lending	
	2000-01	2004-05	2000-01	2004-05
I. Bank	40 (10)	49 (8)	24 (6)	44 (9)
II. Non-Bank	-	9 (2)	8 (4)	4(1)
Total (I + II)	40 (10)	58 (10)	32 (10)	48 (10)

Note: Parenthetic figures indicate number of entities.

II.2 Composition of Top Ten Players in Market Repo

(In per cent)

Category	Borrowing		Lending	
	Aug - Dec 2001	2004-05	Aug - Dec 2001	2004-05
I. Public Sector Bank	16 (1)	12 (2)	—	9 (1)
II. Foreign Bank	17 (3)	6 (1)	11 (2)	8 (1)
III. Private sector Bank	8 (3)	27 (3)	—	6 (1)
IV. Cooperative Bank	—	—	—	—
V. PD	21 (3)	28 (4)	—	—
VI. FI & MF	—		55 (8)	67 (7)
Total	62 (10)	73 (10)	66 (10)	90 (10)

Note: Parenthetic figures indicate number of entities.

II.3 Composition of Top Four/Five Players in CBLO

(In per cent)

Category	Borrowing		Lending	
	Jan - Mar 2003	May 04-Mar 2005	Jan - Mar 2003	May 04-Mar 2005
I. Coop. Bank	40 (2)	—	65 (3)	—
II. Public Sec. Bank	38 (1)	29 (2)	20 (1)	—
III. Pvt. Sec. Bank	—	12 (1)	—	—
IV. FIs & MF	—	—	—	58(5)
V. PDs	13 (1)	26 (2)	—	—
VI. Total	91 (4)	67 (5)	85 (4)	58 (5)

Note: Parenthetic figures indicate number of entities.

Source: www.rbi.org.in

Components of the Money Market

Money market is composed of several sub-markets, each one of which deals in different types of short-term credit. It has different types of sub-markets. In money market, several transactions will arise according to the needs and convenience of borrowers and lenders. For each of transactions, there is a different specialized sub-market in the economy. The various types of specialized sub-markets are presented below.

1. Call Money Market.
2. Commercial Bill Market.
3. Commercial Paper Market.
4. Certificate of Deposit.
5. Treasury Bill Market.

1. Call Money Market

The call money market is the market for extremely short period loans. It is the most active segment of the money market. The market is meant for the transfer of funds among the banks. It consists of an arrangement for making the surpluses of some banks available to the other banks in temporary deficit of cash. Hence, it is known as inter-bank call/notice money market. The call loan is one day or overnight loan and the short notice loan is for a short period of up to 14 days.

The Indian call money market remains largely confined to big industrial and commercial centers like Mumbai, Kolkata, Chennai, Ahmadabad, Delhi, and Bengaluru. Although both Mumbai and Kolkata, consume the two biggest centers in India both in terms of size and buoyancy of the market, Mumbai is in a predominant position because of its stature as the commercial capital of the country.

The participants in the call/notice money market are the schedule and non-schedule commercial banks, foreign banks, and co-operative banks. After the Vaghul Working Group Report in 1987, there has been enlargement in the number of participants by allowing the non-banking institutions to function as lenders. During October 1990, the list of participants as lenders increased to include all institutions participating in the commercial bills rediscounting market.

Advantages of Call Money Market

- **Liquidity:** The most important advantage in a call market is that, money lent can be called back at any time when needed. It is therefore, highly liquid. Call money market offers the advantages of easy and quick borrowing to meet the statutory liquidity requirement of banks.
- **Investment:** Call money market is cheap and safe in the sense that brokers have been prohibited from operating in the call market. It facilitates effective and profitable investment of temporary surplus funds. Further, the market provides the assurance of excellent liquidity of funds invested.
- **Profitability:** Banks invest their surplus funds in a period when call rates are high and volatile. It offers a parking place for employing the surplus funds of banks temporarily and makes their lending highly profitable.
- **Utilization:** Another advantage of call market is that it enables commercial banks to maintain their statutory reserve requirements. In the absence of call market, banks have to maintain idle cash to meet their reserve requirements.
- **Central Bank:** Call money market provides indication to the central bank in the changes in demand and supply of funds. In addition to this, the existence of an efficient call market helps the central bank to carry out its open market operations effectively and successfully.

Call Market Operations

In a call market the transactions are conducted over the telephone. Dealings are arrived at, after prolonged telephonic negotiations relating to the terms and conditions, between borrowers and lenders. Lender issues an RBI cheque in favor of the borrowing bank, which is acknowledged by the call money borrowing receipt. This will be commenced from 10.00 a.m. and closes by 2.30 p.m. on the next day, the borrowing bank repays the amount with interest by issuing RBI cheque and the lender returns the duly discharged receipt.

Where the transactions are to take place through the DFHI, the borrowers and lenders approach the DFHI by spelling out their terms as the quantum and availability of funds, interest rates, etc. the transaction when confirmed, results, in exchange of the Deal Settlement Advice (DSA). DFHI issues a call deposit receipt to the lender and in turn receives an RBI cheque for the amount lent in exchange for call deposit receipt. On the day of next, the lender surrenders the duly discharged call deposit receipt, and the borrower in turn issues an RBI cheque for the amount borrowed with interest.

Banks, non-scheduled banks, foreign banks, urban banks, cooperative banks, discount and finance house of India, and securities trading corporation of India. The DHFI and STC borrow as well as lend the money.

Call markets are located in commercial centers like Mumbai, Kolkata, Chennai, Delhi and Ahmedabad. The stock exchange is also located in these cities. Mumbai and Kolkata dominate call market in India. Mumbai is the financial capital of India and the head offices of RBI, LIC and UTI are located there. It also has the biggest stock exchange in Asia. The development of IT has facilitated for the flow of funds. The call rates are prevailing in different centers in different rates. There is a large number of local call markets developed and marketed by indigenous local bankers.

Turnover of the Call Market

The turnover of the call market in India has been smaller than that of the US and UK, because of the bill market in India being undeveloped. The call loans to the bill market cannot be available. The volume of call loans depends upon the extent of trading in bills of exchange, treasury bills etc. The banks in India are not willing to offer loans to brokers and dealers in bills and securities. Another important factor is that the commercial banks can rediscount their bills from the RBI as a result of which they have much less interest towards the loans from the money market. The commercial banks hold fairly large cash reserves. Therefore there is no need to get the funds from the call market. The other factor is that the government securities are directly sold by the RBI without much intervention by brokers and dealers. The turnover in securities traded on the stock exchanges is also relatively small. There is no scope in our financial system to extend support to the stock exchanges by banks. So many regulations have been imposed by the RBI on the banks in respect of loans against shares. Hence the trading activity in stock exchanges is carried out by the members using their own funds. Therefore the turnover in stock exchange has been derived by the members from private sources. There are fluctuations in the volume of demand and for supply of call loan due to various factors. The following are the causes for volatility of call market.

(1) The financial resources in the banking depends on the extent, of deposits accruals.

(2) Any increase in deposits with banks, needs to explore possibilities of investment overseas.

(3) The bank resources flow to call market which in some of overseas for investment would increase.

(4) All the banks accrue deposits, and then there will be an increase in volume of interbank call loan transactions.

(5) In a case such as the supply of funds to the outside of the banking system borrowers would increase.

(6) The differential growth in the deposits of different banks would lead to increase in volume of Interbank call loans market.

(7) The demand for call loans would depend upon the stock market situation, industrial sector needs and commercial requirements.

(8) The turnover of call market is determined by the possibility of quick investment or liquid assets.

(9) The opening of subscriptions to government loans would lead to increase for the demand to call loans.

(10) Usually the demand for call money tends to broaden in December, March, and June.

(11) The velocity of the remittance and clearance system in the country leads to show an impact on the day to day volume of call loans.

(12) The policies of the RBI leads to show an impact as the volume of call market.

(13) The pressure on call money market reaches a peak towards the end of banking week, i.e., Friday.

(14) The foreign exchange market activity becomes a significant factor in the turnover of call market.

- Call Money: Money lent for one day.
- Notice Money: Money lent for a period exceeding one day.
- Term Money: Money lend for 15 days or more in interbank market.
- Held till maturity: Securities which are not meant for sale and shall be kept till maturity.

Held for trading: Securities acquired by the banks with the intention to trade by taking advantage of the short-term price/interest rate movements will be classified under held for trading. Available for sale the securities which do not fall within the above two categories, i.e., HTM or HFT will be classified under available for sale. Yield to maturity Expected rate of return on an existing security purchased from the market

Coupon Rate Specified interest rate on a fixed maturity security fixed at the time of issue.

Treasury operations trading in government securities in the market. An investor Bank can purchase these securities in the primary market. Trading takes place in the secondary market.

Gilt-edged security Government security that is a claim on the government and is a secure financial instrument which guarantees certainty of both capital and interest. These securities are free of default risk or credit risk, which leads to low market risk and high liquid.

The money market is a market for short-term financial assets that are close substitutes of money. The most important feature of a money market instrument is that it is liquid and can be turned over quickly at low cost and provides an avenue for equilibrating the short-term surplus funds of lenders and the requirements of borrowers. The call/notice money market forms an important segment of the Indian money market. Under call money market, funds are transacted on overnight basis and under notice money market; funds are transacted for the period between 2 days and 14 days.

Banks borrow in this money market for the following purpose.

- To fill the gaps or temporary mismatches in funds
- To meet the CRR & SLR Mandatory requirements as stipulated by the Central bank
- To meet sudden demand for funds arising out of large outflows Thus call money usually serves the role of equilibrating the short-term liquidity position of banks.

Participants in the Money Market

Participants in call/notice money market currently include banks, Primary Dealers (PDs), development finance institutions, insurance companies and select mutual funds. Of these, banks and PDs can operate both as borrowers and lenders in the market. But non-bank institutions (such as all-India FIs, select Insurance Companies or Mutual Funds), which have been given specific permission to operate in call/notice money market can, however, operate as lenders only. No new non-bank institutions are permitted to operate (i.e., lend) in the call/notice money market with effect from May 5, 2001. In case any eligible institution has genuine difficulty in deploying its excess liquidity, RBI may consider providing temporary permission to lend a higher amount in call/notice money market for a specific period on a case-by-case basis.

Effective from Aug 06, 2005, non-bank participants except Primary Dealers are to discontinue to participate, to make the call money market pure inter-bank market.

Prudential Norms of RBI

Lending of scheduled commercial banks, on a fortnightly average basis, should not exceed 25 per cent of their capital fund. However, banks are allowed to lend a maximum of 50% on any day, during a fortnight.

Borrowings by scheduled commercial banks should not exceed 100 per cent of their capital fund or 2 per cent of aggregate deposits, whichever is higher. However, banks are allowed to borrow a maximum of 125 per cent of their capital fund on any day, during a fortnight.

Interest Rate

Eligible participants are free to decide on interest rates in call/notice.

Advantages of call money:

In India, commercial banks play a dominant role in the call loan market. They used to borrow and lend among themselves and such loans are called inter-bank loans. They are very popular in India. So many advantages are available to commercial banks. They are as follows:

- The surplus funds of banks temporarily lent.
- *Maintenance of SLR:* Call market enables commercial bank to minimise their statutory reserve requirements. Generally High Liquidity: Money lent in a call market can be called back at any time when needed. So, it is highly liquid. It enables commercial banks to meet large sudden payments and remittances by making a call on the market.
- *High Profitability:* Banks can earn high profits by lending their surplus funds to the call market when call rates are high by volatile. It offers a profitable parking place for employing banks borrow on a large-scale every reporting Friday to meet their SLR requirements. In absence of call market, banks have to maintain idle cash to meet their reserve requirements. It will tell upon their profitability.
- *Safe and Cheap:* Though call loans are not secured, they are safe since the participants have a strong financial standing. It is cheap in the sense brokers have been prohibited from operating in the call market. Hence, banks need not pay brokers on call money transitions.
- *Assistance to Central Bank Operations:* Call money market is the most sensitive part of any financial system. Changes in demand and supply of funds are quickly reflected in call money rates and give an indication to the central bank to adopt an appropriate monetary policy. Moreover, the existence of an efficient call market helps the central bank to carry out its open market operations effectively and successfully.

Drawbacks of Call Money

The call market in India suffers from the following drawbacks:

- *Uneven Development:* The call market in India is confined to only big industrial and commercial centers like Mumbai, Kolkata, Chennai, Delhi, Bengaluru and Ahmadabad.

Generally, call markets are associated with stock exchanges. Hence, the market is not evenly developed.

- *Lack of Integration:* The call markets in different centers are not fully integrated. Besides, a large number of local call markets exist without any integration.
- *Volatility in Call Money Rates:* Another drawback is the volatile nature of the call money rates. Call rates vary to greater extent in different centers in different seasons on different days within a fortnight. The rates vary between 12% and 85%, one cannot believe 85% being charged on call loans.

Recommendations of Three Committees

The issue of whether non-bank participants should constitute part of call/notice/term money market could be traced first in the Report of the Committee to Review the Working of the Monetary System (Chairman: S. Chakravarty) in 1985.

Since then, the Report of the Working Group on the Money Market (Chairman: N. Vaghul) in 1987 and the Report of the Committee on Banking Sector Reforms (Chairman: M. Narasimham) in 1998, had also deliberated on this issue.

It needs to be appreciated that the particular set of recommendations from these three Committees have to be assessed against the specific objectives for which these Committees had been constituted as well as the differing initial conditions reflecting the state of Indian financial market which were prevailing at that particular point of time.

The Chakravarty Committee (1985), viewed this issue essentially from the angle of efficacy of monetary regulation by the Central Bank. It felt that allowing additional non-bank participants into the call market would not dilute the strength of monetary regulation by the RBI as resources from non-bank participants do not represent any additional resource for the system as a whole and their participation in call money market would only imply a redistribution of existing resources from one participant to another.

Therefore, the monopoly power to affect the system's reserves continues to rest with the RBI. In view of this, the Chakravarty Committee recommended that additional non-bank participants may be allowed to participate in call money market. The Vaghul Committee (1987), on the other hand suggested that call money market should be purely an inter-bank market and therefore, the restrictions on entry into call market prevailing at that point of time should continue.

The essential rationale for such recommendation was that freeing of entry into the call market coupled with allowing call money rates to be determined entirely by market forces at a time when deposit rates of banks were administered would lead to, it was apprehended, substantial diversion of funds from the bank deposit segment to the call money market segment which would raise the cost of funds to banks markedly.

Therefore, while the Vaghul Committee decided in favor of making the call money market a pure inter-bank market, it felt that LIC and UTI which had been permitted in the market as lenders in 1971, would gradually come out of the market as other money market instruments develop with wider array of maturities.

The Narasimham Committee II (1998), concurred with the Vaghul Committee as it also observed that call/notice/term money market in India, like in most other developed markets, should be strictly restricted to banks.

It, however, felt that exception should be made for Primary Dealers (PDs) who have been acting as market makers in the call money market and are formally treated as banks for the purpose of their inter-bank transactions and, therefore, they should remain as part of call money market. With regard to non-banks, it expressed concern that these participants "are not subjected to reserve requirements and the market is characterized by chronic lenders and chronic borrowers and there are heavy gyrations in the market".

It felt that allowing non-bank participants in the call market "has not led to the development of a stable market with liquidity and depth .... and the time has come to undertake a basic restructuring of call money market". Like the Vaghul Committee, it had also suggested that the non-bank participants should be given full access to bill rediscounting, Commercial Paper (CP), Certificates of Deposit (CDs), Treasury Bills (TBs) and Money Market Mutual Funds (MMMFs) for deploying their short-term surpluses.

International Experiences

USA:

Federal funds market in USA is the counterpart of our call/notice money market in India. In this market, only those depository institutions that are required by the Monetary Control Act of 1980 to hold reserves with the Federal Reserve Banks are permitted to borrow include commercial banks, savings banks, savings and loan associations and credit unions. Non-bank participants such as corporate, state and local governments are prohibited from participating in the federal funds market directly. They supply funds to the overnight market through repurchase agreements (RPs) with their banks. Banks' borrowings from federal funds market as well as from RPs are free of reserve requirements. It is found that RP rates closely follow the federal funds rate with the former being lower than the latter as RP market is collateralized and, therefore, safer than the federal funds market and RP involves additional transaction costs in the form of documentation.

It was found that as resources raised under RPs were free of reserve requirements, banks attempted to minimize their burden of reserve requirements by raising more resources through the RP avenue *vis-a-vis* deposits thereby reducing the volume of required reserves banks had to hold with the Federal Reserve Banks. This in turn reduced the size of the Federal Reserve Banks' balance sheet and, therefore, reduced the interest payments that it could transfer to the US Government. In order to obviate this situation, the Federal Reserve Board passed a resolution in 1969, restricting the collateral to be used for RPs to only direct obligations of the US Government or its agencies. This somewhat offset the revenues that are likely to be lost due to reduced volume of reserves held by banks.

France:

Initially, some non-bank entities were allowed in the money market which was able to obtain a market rate of return on their investments. These non-bank entities included insurance companies, pension funds, stockbrokers' Boards, etc. In order to encourage the spread of negotiable securities among the public as well as to restrict the access to the market for "central bank money", the authorities favored the creation of a pure inter-bank money market accessible only to credit institutions. The non-bank entities that are no longer part of the inter-bank money market have moved to the repo market as well as sales of negotiable securities as part of their short-term liquidity management. The authorities felt that this sort of restructuring of the market should help in fostering development of short-term securities in the economy.

Among emerging economies also, overnight money markets in countries like Singapore, Malaysia and Thailand have only banks as participants.

Section II

Characteristics of the Indian Call Money Market

As indicated above, call money is the most important segment of the Indian financial system. It consists of overnight money and money at short notice for a period of up to 14 days. The call money market essentially serves the purpose of equilibrating the short-term liquidity position of banks and other participants. It is also the focal point through which the RBI attempts to influence the short-term interest rates. Its average daily turnover at more than ₹ 40,000 crores in recent periods is the highest among all money market instruments including Government securities market. In this market, while banks and primary dealers (PDs) are allowed to both borrow and lend non-bank participants such as financial institutions, mutual funds and select corporate are permitted to only lend. The demand for funds in this market is mainly governed by the banks' need for resources to meet their statutory reserve requirement; it also offers to some participants a regular funding source for building up short-term assets. It is however, felt that the demand for funds for reserve requirements dominates any other demand in the market. Viewed from this angle, it may be noted that total reserves transacted (i.e., aggregate borrowings) in the call money market as proportion of aggregate cash balances maintained by commercial banks with the RBI, on average, ruled around 32 per cent in recent period.

As regards the number of participants, apparently the market is very broad-based as on the borrowing side, there are as many as 169 participants (banks - 154 and PDs - 15) while on the lending side, apart from these 169 participants, there are additional 105 participants taking the total to 274 (Table 1).

Table 1: Number of Participants in Call/Notice Money Market

(as on March 12, 2001)

Category	Bank	PD	FI	MF	Corporate	Total
I. Borrower	154	15	—	—	—	169
II. Lender	154	15	20	35	50	274

A typical characteristic of this market is that except PDs who are participating in both sides of the market, there is hardly any bank that operates both as borrower and lender simultaneously on any given day. It is generally found that public sector banks with their vast branch network in the country are generally the supplier of funds in the market while foreign and private sector banks with their urban-centric structure coupled with their relatively advanced treasury operations are regular borrowers in the market. Keeping this as perspective, the overall shares of various constituents based on their daily transactions during the last two years are as follows:

Table 2: Market Shares of Constituents in Call/Notice Money Market

(In Per cent)

	Borrowings		Landings		
Year	**Banks**	**PDs**	**Banks**	**PDs**	**Others**
1999	68	32	52	11	37
2000	66	34	45	11	44

Note: (a) Figures do not include operations of co-operative banks.

(b) "Others" constitute financial institutions, mutual funds and select corporate.

An analysis of participant-wise shares in both borrowings and lending in call/notice money market reveals a highly skewed nature of the market. On the lending side, State Bank of India (SBI) is the largest participant accounting for as much as 15 per cent in 1999 which, however, declined to 13 per cent in the following year (Table 3). On the whole, four public sector banks and five financial institutions (FIs) supplied to the tune of 38 per cent of the aggregate supplies of funds in the market in 1999 which dropped to 31 per cent in 2000. What is important to note here is that though there are as many as 274 participants (Table 1) who are eligible to lend in the market, there are only 9 participants as indicated above who control about one-third of aggregate lending in the market.

Table 3: Shares of Select Participants in Call/Notice Money Market: Lending

(In Per cent)

Year	Banks	FIs	Total
1999	20 (15)	18	38
2000	17 (13)	14	31

Banks: Canara Bank, Central Bank, PNB and SBI

FIs: ICICI, IDBI, LIC, SIDBI and UTI

Parenthetic figures relate to those of the SBI.

Similarly, on the borrowing side, the shares of only ten foreign and private sector banks accounted for as much as 36 per cent of aggregate borrowings in 1999 which increased further to 39 per cent in the following year (Table 4).

Table 4: Shares of Select Banks in Call/Notice Money Market: Borrowings

(In Per cent)

Year	Banks
1999	36
2000	39

Select banks include ABN-AMRO Bank, Bank Nationale De Paris, Centurion Bank, CITI Bank, Deutsche Bank, Grindlays Bank, HDFC Bank, Hong Kong Bank, IDBI Bank and Standard Chartered Bank.

From this analysis, it needs to be noted that though apparently the market is quite broad based, in reality, the market is quite lopsided in both borrowing and lending segments. In other words, despite the market having the highest turnover in Indian money market, it lacks depth and liquidity as absence of one or two major participants in either of the segments may have the potential to cause sharp volatility in the market. This not only impairs efficient price discovery process in the market, but also necessitates more active liquidity management practices by the RBI in order to keep interest rates within a reasonable corridor.

Section III (Position Since 1990s)

Following the freeing of interest rates in call money market in June 1989, there had been bouts of extreme volatility in call rates on many occasions during 1989-90. Despite the Vaghul Committee recommendation that call money market should be made purely an inter-bank market, with a view to reducing volatility and widening the market, the policy relating to the entry into the call/notice money market was gradually liberalized since 1990. In May 1990, three more financial institutions (*viz.,* GIC, IDBI and NABARD) besides LIC and UTI were permitted to participate in the call/notice money market as lenders. In October 1990, with a view to further widening the call/notice money market and to bring about a greater integration in various segments of the money market, all the participants in the Bills Rediscounting Scheme who were not operating in the call/notice money market till then, were granted entry into the call/notice money market as lenders. Subsequently, eight mutual funds sponsored by public sector banks/financial institutions were also permitted to participate in the call/notice money market as lenders.

In April 1991, the policy relating to entry in the call/notice money market was further liberalized and it was decided to provide access as lenders to such entities as were able to provide evidence to RBI of bulk lendable resources. Such entities were required to observe a minimum size of operations of ₹ 20 crores per transaction and such transactions were to be routed through Discount and Finance House of India (DFHI) only. Furthermore, such entities were also required to give an undertaking that they had no outstanding borrowings from the banking system. In April 1997, the facility of routing of transactions by these entities was extended to all the PDs as against only DFHI earlier and the minimum size of operations was also reduced from ₹ 20 crores to ₹ 10 crores. The minimum size of operations was further reduced to ₹ 5 crores and finally to ₹ 3 crores in October 1997 and in May 1998 respectively. Consequent upon the relaxations granted to entities for routing of call transactions, the number of entities routing their call transactions through PDs rose sharply. At present, there are 50 such entities.

Earlier only the public sector mutual funds were allowed to operate as lenders in the call/notice money market but with a view to facilitating a level playing field, it was decided in April 1995 to provide access to mutual funds set up in the private sector and approved by the Securities and Exchange Board of India (SEBI) also as lenders in the call/notice money market after these entities obtained specific permission from the Reserve Bank. In 1996, 4 primary dealers, in addition to DFHI and STCI were permitted to operate both as lenders as well as borrowers in the call/notice money market. As of now, the number of PDs has increased to 15.

As on March 12, 2001, there are 55 financial institutions and mutual funds which are allowed to operate in the market as lenders, besides all scheduled commercial banks, co-operative banks and primary dealers which are operating as both lenders as well as borrowers. List of participants permitted to participate in the call money market.

Shift in Stance in RBI

There has been a change in policy stance regarding permission to non-bank participants to operate in the call/notice money market. This issue was also examined by the "Internal Group to Examine the Development of Call Money Market" in 1997, which had observed that the call money market was an inter-bank market the world over. Furthermore, when non-banks are allowed to participate in the call money market, it partly distorts the signals of liquidity conditions in the system. Analysis done by the Group revealed that intermediate lenders in call money were in a position to exploit the situation of tight money conditions and dictate terms to the banking system thereby causing undue volatility in the call/notice money market. The view was that non-bank institutions should instead be allowed to deploy their short-term funds in alternative money market instruments like Repos, Money Market Mutual Funds (MMMFs) and Certificates of Deposit (CDs), etc. and until these markets develop, the existing non-bank participants may be allowed to continue in the call money market.

Similarly, following the recommendations of the Narasimham Committee II (1998), the general consensus of members of the Standing Committee on Money Market (which was since reconstituted as Technical Advisory Committee on Money and Government Securities Markets) was that ultimately we should move towards a pure inter-bank market along with only primary dealers, and in the meantime steps should be taken to widen the repo market and increase non-bank participation in other money market instruments.

Accordingly, in the "Mid-term Review of Monetary and Credit Policy for 1998-99" announced in October 1998, the Reserve Bank indicated its intention to ultimately move towards a pure inter-bank call/notice/term money market including PDs. It was indicated that simultaneously measures would be taken to widen the repo market and improve non-bank participations in a variety of other instruments and this would be implemented in a manner that existing lenders in the market would have operational flexibility to adjust their asset-liability structures.

It was decided, as a first step, that permission only to non-bank participants for routing their call transactions through PDs be withdrawn and other non-bank institutions (financial institutions and mutual funds) be allowed to continue in the call/notice money market until such time the other avenues for short-term deployment of funds are available. Accordingly, in April 1999, it was indicated that permission given to non-bank entities to lend in the call/notice money market by routing their transactions through PDs would be available only up to end-December 1999. This permission was, however, extended in stages up to June 2001.

Simultaneously, Reserve Bank has taken several steps to widen the participation in repo market as indicated below:

(i) Following the amendment to the Securities Contract (Regulations) Act, 1956 (SCRA) in March, 2000, delegating regulatory powers to RBI to regulate, inter alia, dealings in Government securities and money market securities, all those non-bank entities maintaining current account and SGL account with RBI, Mumbai had been permitted to undertake both repo and reverse repo.

(ii) Minimum maturity for repo transactions was reduced to one day.

(iii) State Government securities have been made eligible for undertaking repos.

(iv) RBI also opens its purchase window to impart liquidity to Treasury Bills whenever situation warrants.

(v) Clearing Corporation is being set up for money and securities settlement.

In addition to the above, the minimum period for transferability in case of Certificates of Deposit has recently been abolished. This would provide an additional avenue to non-banks to lend short-term funds to the banking system.

Section IV

Policy Perspective and Recommendations

The Technical Group appreciated the need for non-banks to be phased out of the call/notice money market in the interest of development of a risk-free short-term yield curve in the economy. Towards this end, the Group concurred fully with the view expressed by Dr. Y.V. Reddy, Deputy Governor of the RBI that complete withdrawal of non-banks from call money market should be co-terminus with the full fledged operationalization of the Clearing Corporation. Keeping this in perspective, the Group deliberated on various suggestions in order to achieve a smooth transition to the repo/reverse repo market. These suggestions broadly relate to call money market and Government securities market including repo market.

Call Money Market

With regard to gradual phasing out of access to call money market by such non-bank participants as financial institutions and mutual funds, the Group recommends that such access may be reduced in three stages by placing cap in relation to their average daily lending during April 2000 - March 2001. In the first stage, each such non-bank participant should be allowed to lend only up to 70 per cent of their average daily lending in call money market during 2000-2001, for a period of three months which should come into effect at the earliest after March 31, 2001. In the second stage, access should be reduced further to 40 per cent of their average daily lending during 2000-01. The final stage should commence with the setting up of Clearing Corporation or after a period of three months from the conclusion of the second stage whichever is later. The final stage by which time the Clearing Corporation is expected to be established should last for a period of three months. During this phase, the Group feels that access to call money market should be permitted to these participants to the extent of 10 per cent of their average daily lending during 2000-01. This is considered necessary to enable these particular classes of non-bank participants to be familiar with the operations of the Clearing Corporations. After the end of this stage, these entities would not be permitted to lend in call money market at all.

While the Group appreciates that there is a strong need to gradualise the process of phasing out non-banks from the call money market for ensuring their smooth transition to the repo market as has been indicated above, there is a consensus that among the non-bank participants, select corporate who route their funds through PDs may be withdrawn immediately as these entities could always place their funds with PDs through the inter-corporate deposits (ICDs) route. Accordingly, the Group recommends that corporate permitted to lend in call money market should not be permitted to lend after end-June 2001.

Government Securities/Repo Market

With the phasing out of non-bank participants from call money market to repo/reverse repo market, it is expected that the latter would emerge as a vibrant short-term money market for both banks and non-banks. In fact, it is envisaged that in future, both call money market and repo/reverse repo market would constitute as a unified market for equilibrating short-term funds positions for both banks and non-bank participants because repo/reverse repo (henceforth, it is indicated as repo market for convenience unless otherwise stated) market would afford both borrowing and lending facility to non-bank participants. However, during the intermediate period, it is apprehended that funds flow between these two markets may not be as smooth as one expects it to be eventually. This is because distribution of surplus liquidity and that of surplus securities over statutory liquidity requirements (SLR) in the banking sector are such that those who are persistent borrowers in the market (i.e., foreign and private sector banks) do not maintain sufficiently large volume of surplus securities in their portfolio (Table 5) so as to enable them to borrow easily from the repo market.

Table 5: Distribution of Excess SLR Securities among Categories of Banks

(₹ in Crore)

Group of Bank		Average holding of Excess SLR Securities		Percentage share in total	
		1999	2000	1999	2000
1.	SBI Group	28,324	35,703	36.4	37.3
2.	Nationalized Banks other than SBI Group	39,355	46,455	50.6	48.5
3.	Private Sector Banks	6,054	8,749	7.8	9.1
4.	Foreign Banks	4,219	4,819	5.4	5.0
Total		77,952	95,726	100	100

Note: For this purpose, required SLR investments have been worked out as 25 per cent of "Liability to Others" for the category of banks concerned. Excess SLR securities have been defined as "Investments in Government and other Approved Securities" less required SLR investments.

It may be worthwhile to note that while the average daily aggregate lending in call money market by non-bank participants stood at ₹ 7,672 crores during the years 1999 and 2000, average net borrowings by banks and PDs were ₹ 3,488 crores and ₹ 4,184 crores, respectively, during the period. As against this, the average surplus securities available with the foreign and private sector banks were at ₹ 11,920 crores of which the average volume of surplus securities with foreign banks was at ₹ 4,519 crores during the period. Moreover, a part of securities held by PDs would also be available for undertaking repo transactions. Again, since these classes of entities are also more active in trading in Government securities market, the effective volume of surplus securities available for repo for borrowing of funds would be lower for them. While the Group is aware that chronic borrowers should need to reduce their call money borrowing keeping in view the asset-liability management (ALM) guidelines, it is generally perceived that these borrowers could face some transition problems. However, considering the fact that non-bank participants such as financial institutions and mutual funds would be permitted to lend up to 70 per cent of their average daily lending during 2000-2001 for three months in the first phase, it is expected that market participants on both lending and borrowing sides would have sufficient time to adjust their portfolios accordingly without any disruption in the market. Moreover, with the establishment of Clearing Corporation, repo operations would not only become more efficient and the need for securities would be relatively less, it would also be possible to undertake repo transactions in non-Government securities. Non-bank participants under the new set up may also like to build up a portfolio of repoable securities for meeting their occasional short-term borrowing needs over time. This may represent an additional demand in the debt market including Government securities. Eventually, it is envisaged that since call money rates would be higher than the repo rates, banks with surplus SLR securities may act as conduits for funds from repo market to call market.

Under the ambit of the Clearing Corporation, rollover of securities in repo transactions would also become possible (provided it is not considered a short sale). Similarly, the Group feels that securities obtained under reverse repo may be allowed to be used for undertaking repo. These apart, at present repo are permitted only at Mumbai. Such activities may be allowed in other centers as well. The Group feels that since repo market will attract larger volume of transactions in the wake of phasing out of non-bank participants from the call money market, there is a strong need for introduction of a master repo agreement with uniform documentation and accounting standards. The Group, however, appreciates that such an effort is underway under the aegis of the Fixed Income Money Market and Derivatives Association of India (FIMMDA). Though non-bank participants are allowed to invest in all other money market instruments with a much wider array of maturities, the Group has suggested that floating stock of Treasury Bills particularly at the shorter end may be increased for providing an additional avenue to non-bank participants for deploying their short-term surplus funds.

SUMMARY

Money market is a market for raising of short-term sources of finance to the business enterprises, banking institutions and other financial institutions. It is an important source of finance for trade and industry. It is centre for dealings, in money assets related to short-term requirements of the borrowers. It provides liquidity to the lenders. It works as a coordinator between lender and borrower for short-term finance. It offers short-term sources of finance to the government. It works as non-inflationary avenue of raising short-term funds through bills which are subscribed by commercial banks and the public.

Key Terms

1. **Call Money Market:** Market in which brokers and dealers borrow money to satisfy their credit needs, either to finance their own inventory of securities or to cover their customer's margin accounts.
2. **Certificate of Deposits:** It is a time deposit, a financial product, commonly offered to the consumers by banks, thrift institutions and credit unions.

3. **Treasury Bill Market:** It is a market where treasury bills are bought and sold. It is nothing like a promissory note issued by the government under discount for a specified period stated therein.
4. **Commercial Bill Market:** It is also known as discount market. It is the market where banker's acceptances are discounted is known as discount market.
5. **Acceptance Market:** THE market that deals with banker's acceptance market is known as acceptance market. It is related to short-term source of finance.

Questions

1. Define money market, explain its functioning system.
2. Explain the functions of money market.
3. Narrate the characteristics of money market.
4. What are the characteristics of the developed money market?
5. Explore the facts about money market in India.
6. What is call money?
7. Explain the concept of certificate of deposit.
8. What is commercial paper?
9. Write about commercial bill market in India.
10. Explain the functioning of Treasury bill market in India.

ANNEXURE I

Memorandum

Reserve Bank of India

Technical Group on Phasing out of Non-banks from Call/Notice Money Market

1. In the mid-term Review of Monetary and Credit Policy in October 2000, it was announced that a Group would be constituted to suggest a smooth phasing out of non-bank participants by a planned reduction in their access to call/notice money market and that the Group would also include representatives of non-bank institutions. Accordingly, it has been decided to constitute a Technical Group comprising the following members:
2. The Group would prepare a Technical Paper backed up by significant technical work analyzing, *inter alia,* (i) the international experiences on the functioning of inter-bank market, (ii) the background in which non-bank entities were permitted in call/notice money market and the trends in volume and extent of their participation, and (iii) the pre-conditions for phasing out of non-bank entities. Based on the analysis, the Group would suggest an approach to phasing out of non-bank entities from the call/notice money market in a non-disruptive manner to the functioning of money and securities markets in general and the participation of non-bank entities in particular.
3. The Technical Group would be free to associate as special invitee's representatives of other departments of RBI and banks/FIs, etc., as it deems fit.
4. The Technical Group will submit its Report within two months from the date of its first meeting.

ANNEXURE II

List of Institutions Permitted to Participate in Call/Notice Money Market only as Lenders - As on March 12, 2001

A. Financial Institutions

- Export Credit Guarantee Corporation of India Ltd.
- Export Import Bank of India
- General Insurance Corporation of India
- HDFC Standard Life Insurance Co. Ltd.
- ICICI Ltd.
- ICICI Prudential Life Insurance Co.
- Industrial Development Bank of India
- Industrial Finance Corporation of India Ltd.
- Industrial Investment Bank of India
- Life Insurance Corporation of India
- National Bank for Agriculture and Rural Development
- National Housing Bank
- National Insurance Co.
- New India Assurance Co.
- Oriental Insurance Co.
- Royal Sundaram Alliance Insurance Co. Ltd.
- Small Industries Development Bank of India
- Tourism Finance Corporation of India
- Unit Trust of India
- United India Insurance Co.

B. Mutual Funds

- Alliance Capital M. Fund
- ANZ Grind lays M. Fund
- B.O.B. Mutual Fund
- B.O.I. Mutual Fund
- Birla Mutual Fund
- CANBANK Mutual Fund
- Cholamandalam Cazenove Mutual Fund
- DSP Merril Lynch Mutual Fund
- Dundee Mutual Fund
- Escort Mutual Fund

- G.I.C. Mutual Fund
- HDFC Asset Management Co. Ltd.
- I.D.B.I. Mutual Fund
- IL and FS AMC Mutual Fund
- Indbank offshore Mutual Fund
- Indian Bank Mutual Fund
- ING Assets Management
- J.M. Capital Management
- Jardine Fleming Mutual Fund
- Kotak Mahindra
- Kothari Pioneer Mutual Fund
- L.I.C. Mutual Fund
- Morgan Stanley Mutual Fund
- P.N.B. Mutual Fund
- Prudential I.C.I.C.I. Mutual Fund
- Reliance Capital Mutual Fund
- S.B.I. Mutual Fund
- SBI Offshore Mutual Fund
- Sriram Mutual Fund
- Sun F and C Mutual Fund
- Sundaram Newton Mutual Fund
- Tata Mutual Fund
- Taurus Mutual Fund
- Templeton Mutual Fund
- Zurich India Mutual Fund

C. Select Corporates

- Bajaj Auto Ltd.
- Berger Paints India Ltd.
- BSES Ltd. (Bombay Suburban Electric Supply Co.)
- Citicorp Finance Ltd.
- Citicorp Maruthi Finance Ltd.
- Dabhol Power Co.
- DSP Merrill Lynch Ltd.
- Grasim Industries Ltd.
- Gujarat Industrial Investment Corp.
- Gujarat Mineral Development Corporation Ltd.

- Gujarat State Financial Services Ltd.
- Haldia Petrochemicals Ltd.
- HDFC Ltd.
- Hindustan Organic Chemicals Ltd.
- Hindustan Zinc Ltd.
- HLL (Hindustan Lever Ltd.)
- Housing and Urban Development Corporation Ltd.
- Indian Tobacco Co.
- Indoburma Petroleum Co. Ltd.
- Infrastructure Development Finance Co.Ltd.
- LIC Housing Finance Ltd.
- Lubrizol India Ltd.
- Madras Refineries Ltd.
- Mahindra & Mahindra Ltd.
- Max Telecom Venture Ltd.
- Minerals and Mining Trading Corporation
- Mishra Dhatu Nigam Ltd
- National Thermal Power Corporation Ltd. (NTPC)
- Peerless General Finance & Investment Co. Ltd.
- Power Finance Corporation
- Power Trading Corporation of India Ltd.
- Project Equipment Corporation Ltd.
- Rabo India Finance Pvt. Ltd.
- Reliance Industries Ltd.
- Reliance Telecom Ltd.
- Rural Electrification Corporation
- Sage Investments Ltd.
- Saiinfo Services Ltd.
- SBI Capital Markets Ltd.
- Southern Petrochemical Industries
- State Industrial and Investment Corporation of Maharashtra
- Stock Holding Corporation of India Ltd.
- Summit Investments Ltd.
- Tata Electric Companies
- Tata Iron & Steel Co. Ltd.
- The Great Eastern Shipping Co. Ltd.

- TVS Suzuki Ltd.
- Videsh Sanchar Nigam
- Vindhya Telelinks Ltd.
- Voltas Ltd.

Source: www.rbi.org.com

2. Commercial Bill Market

Commercial bill is one which arises out of a genuine trade transaction, i.e. credit transaction. As soon as goods are sold on credit, the seller draws a bill on the buyer for the amount due. The buyer accepts it immediately agreeing to pay amount mentioned therein after a certain specified date. Thus, a bill of exchange contains a written order from the creditor to the debtor, to pay a certain sum, to a certain person, after a creation period. A bill of exchange is a 'self-liquidating' paper and negotiable/; it is drawn always for a short period ranging between 3 months and 6 months.

Definition of a Bill

Section 5 of the negotiable Instruments Act defines a bill exchange as follows:

- "an instrument in writing containing an unconditional order, signed by the maker, directing a certain person to pay a certain sum of money only to, or to the order of a certain person or to the bearer of the instrument".

Types of Bills

Many types of bills are in circulation in a bill market. They can be broadly classified as follows:

1. Demand and usance bills.
2. Clean bills and documentary bills.
3. Inland and foreign bills.
4. Export bills and import bills.
5. Indigenous bills.
6. Accommodation bills and supply bills.

Demand and Usance Bills

Demand bills are otherwise called sight bills. These bills are payable immediately as soon as they are presented to the drawer. No time of payment is specified and hence they are payable at sight. Usance bills are called time bills. These bills are payable immediately after the expiry of time period mentioned in the bills. The period varies according to the established trade custom or usage prevailing in the country.

Clean Bills and Documentary Bills

When bills have to be accompanied by documents of title to goods like Railway receipt, Lorry receipt, Bill of Lading, etc., the bills are called documentary bills. These bills can be further classified into D/A bills and D/P bills. In the case of D/A bills, the documents accompanying bills have to be delivered to the drawer immediately after acceptance. Generally, D/A bills are drawn on parties who have a good financial standing. On the order hand, the documents have to be handed over to the drawer only against payment in the case of D/P bills. The documents will be retained by the banker. Till the payment of such bills. When bills are drawn without accompanying any documents they are called clean bills. In such a case, documents will be directly sent to the drawer.

Inland and Foreign Bills

Inland bills are those drawn upon a person resident in India and are payable in India. Foreign bills are drawn outside India and they may be payable either in India or outside India. They may be drawn upon a person resident in India also. Foreign bills have their origin outside India. They also include bills drawn on India made payable outside India.

Export and Foreign Bills

Export bills are those drawn by Indian exports on importers outside India and import bills are drawn on Indian importers in India by exports outside India.

Indigenous Bills

Indigenous bills are those drawn and accepted according to native custom or usage of trade. These bills are popular among indigenous bankers only. In India, they called 'Hundis' the Hundis are known by various names such as 'Shah Jog', 'Nam Jog', Jokhani', Termainjog'. 'Darshani', 'Dhanijog', and so on.

Accommodation Bills and Supply Bills

If bills do not arise out of genuine trade transactions, they are called accommodation bills. They are known as 'kite bills' or 'wind bills'. Two parties draw bills on each other purely for the purpose of mutual financial accommodation. These bills are discounted with bankers and the proceeds are shared among themselves. On the due dates, they are paid. Supply bills are those neither drawn by suppliers nor contractors on the government departments for the goods nor accompanied by documents of title to goods. So, they are not considered as negotiable instruments. These bills are useful only for the purpose of getting advances from commercial banks by creating a charge on these bills.

Operations in Bill Market: From the operations point of view, the bill market can be classified into two, *viz.,*

- Discount Market
- Acceptance Market

Discount Market

Discount market refers to the market where short-term genuine trade bills are discounted by financial intermediaries like commercial banks. When credit sales are affected, the seller draws a bill on the buyer who accepts it promising to pay the specified sum at the specified period. The seller has to wait until the maturity of the bill for getting payment. But, the presence of a bill market enables him to get payment immediately. The seller can ensure payment immediately by discounting the bill with some financial intermediary by paying a small amount of money called 'Discount rate' on the date of maturity; the intermediary claims the amount of the bill from the person who has accepted the bill.

In some countries, there are some financial intermediaries who specialize in the field of discounting. For instance, in London Money Market there are specialists in the field discounting bills. Such institutions are conspicuously absent in India. Hence, commercial banks in India have to undertake the work of discounting. However, the DFHI has been established to activate this market.

Acceptance Market

The acceptance market refers to the market where short-term genuine trade bills are accepted by financial intermediaries. All trade bills cannot be discounted easily because the parties to the bills may not be financially sound. In case such bills are accepted by financial intermediaries like banks, the bills earn a good name and reputation and such bills can readily be discounted anywhere. In London, there are specialist firms called acceptance house which accept bills drawn by trades and import greater marketability to such bills. However, their importance has declined in recent times. In India, there are no acceptance houses. The commercial banks undertake the acceptance business to some extent.

Advantages of Commercial Bills

Commercial bill market is an important source of short-term funds for trade and industry. It provides liquidity and activates the money market. In India, commercial banks play a significant role in this market due to the following advantages:

- **Liquidity:** Bills are highly liquid assets. In times of necessity, bills can be converted into cash readily by means of rediscounting them with the central bank. Bills are self-liquidating in character since they have fixed tenure. Moreover, they are negotiable instruments and hence they can be transferred freely by a mere delivery or by endorsement and delivery.
- **Certainty of Payment:** Bills are drawn and accepted by business people. Generally, business people are used to keeping their words and the use of the bills imposes a strict financial discipline on them. Hence, bills would be honored on the due date.
- **Ideal Investment:** Bills are for periods not exceeding 6 months. They represent advances for a definite period. This enables financial institutions to invest their surplus funds profitably by selecting bills of different maturities. For instance, commercial banks can invest their funds on bills in such a way that the maturity of these bills may coincide with the maturity of their fixed deposits.
- **Simple Legal Remedy:** In case the bills are dishonored\, the legal remedy is simple. Such dishonored bills have to be simply noted and protested and the whole amount should be debited to the customer's accounts.
- **High and Quick Yield:** The financial institutions earn a high quick yield. The discount is dedicated at the time of discounting itself whereas in the case of other loans and advances, interest is payable only when it is due. The discounts rate is also comparatively high.
- **Easy Central Bank Control:** The central bank can easily influence the money market by manipulating the bank rate or the rediscounting rate. Suitable monetary policy can be taken by adjusting the bank rate depending upon the monetary conditions prevailing in the market.

Drawbacks of Commercial Bills

In spite of these merits, the bill market has not been well developed in India. The reasons for the slow growth are the following:

- **Absence of Bill Culture:** Business people in India prefer O.D and cash credit to bill financing therefore, banks usually accept bills for the conversion of cash credits and overdrafts of their customers. Hence bills are not popular.
- **Absence of Rediscounting among Banks:** There is no practice of re-discounting of bills between banks who need funds and those who have surplus funds. In order to enlarge the rediscounting facility, the RBI has permitted financial institutions like LIC, UTI, GIC and ICICI to rediscount genuine eligible trade bills of commercial banks. Even then, bill financial is not popular.
- **Stamp Duty:** Stamp duty discourages the use of bills. Moreover, stamp papers of required denomination are not available.
- **Absence of Secondary Market:** There is no active secondary market for bills. Rediscounting facility is available in important centers and that too is restricted to the apex level financial institutions. Hence, the size of the bill market has been curtailed to a large extent.
- **Difficulty in Ascertaining Genuine Trade Bills:** The financial institutions have to verify the bills so as to ascertain whether they are genuine trade bills and not accommodation bills. For this purpose, invoices have to be scrutinized carefully. It involves additional work.
- **Limited Foreign Trade:** In many developed countries, bill markets have been established mainly for financing foreign trade. Unfortunately, in India, foreign trade as a percentage to national income remains small and it is reflected in the bill market also.
- **Absence of Acceptance Services:** There is no discount house or acceptance house in India. Hence specialized services are not available in the field of discounting or acceptance.
- **Attitude of Banks:** Banks are shy rediscounting bills even the central bank. They have a tendency to hold the bills till maturity and hence it affects the velocity of circulation of bills. Again, banks prefer to purchase bills instead of discounting them.

3. Commercial Paper in India

A commercial paper is an unsecured promissory note issued with a fixed maturity by a company approved by RBI, negotiable by endorsement and delivery, issued in bearer form and issued at such discount on the face value as may be determined by the issuing company.

In India, the commercial paper is a new instrument. It has been launched in 1989-90. They are both totally new on the Indian market scenario. It was very popular in abroad, in UK they were introduced in 1986, in France 1985, Japan 1987, Canada 1950, Sweden 1980, Spain, 1982, Norway 1984, Netherlands, 1986, Hongkong 1982 and Singapore 1984. It is a short-term usance promissory notes with fixed maturity issued mostly by the lending corporations. It is also known as industrial paper, finance paper, and corporate paper. It is issued by highly nationwide reputed, creditworthy and highly rated large organisations. It is unsecured instrument. It is backed by the general creditworthiness of the issuing company. It is negotiable by endorsement and delivery. It is regarded as highly safe and liquid instrument. It is believed to be one of the highest quality instruments available from the private sector. It is a simple and flexible instrument. It is normally a buy back instrument issued by the organisations. It is issued in a bearer form on discount to face value basis. It carries a fixed rate of interest. They are issued on large denominations. They will be issued through a bank or merchant banks or dealers or brokers in the open market.

Features of Commercial Paper

1. Commercial paper is a short-term money market instrument comprising usance promissory note with a fixed maturity.
2. It is a certificate evidencing an unsecured corporate debt of short-term maturity.
3. Commercial paper is issued at a discount to face value basis but it can be issued in interest bearing form.
4. The issuer promises to pay the buyer some fixed amount on some future period but pledges no assets, only his liquidity and established earning power, to guarantee that promise.
5. Commercial paper can be issued directly by a company to investors or through banks/ merchant banks.

Advantages of Commercial Paper

- **Simplicity:** The advantage of commercial paper lies in its simplicity. It involves hardly any documentation between the issuer and investor.
- **Flexibility:** The issuer can issue commercial paper with the maturities tailored to match the cash flow of the company.
- **Easy To Raise Long-term Capital:** The companies which are able to raise funds through commercial paper become better known in the financial world and are thereby, placed in a more favorable position for rising such long-term capital as they may, from time to time, as required. Thus, there is an inbuilt incentive for companies to remain financially strong.
- **High Returns:** The commercial paper provides investors with higher returns than they could get from the banking system.
- **Movement of Funds:** Commercial paper facilitates securitization of loans resulting in creation of a secondary market for the paper and efficient movement of funds providing cash surplus to cash deficit entities.

Commercial Paper Market in Other Countries

The roots of commercial paper can be traced way back to the early nineteenth century when the firms in the USA began selling open market paper as a substitute for bank loan needed for short-term requirements but it developed only in 1920s. The development of consumer finance companies in the 1920s and the high cost of bank credit resulting from the incidence of compulsory reserve requirements in the 1960s, contributed to the popularity of commercial paper in the USA. Today, the US commercial paper market is the largest in the world. The outstanding amount at the end of 1990, in the US commercial paper market stood at $557.8 billion. The commercial paper issues in the US are exempted from requirement of issue of prospectus so long as proceeds are used to finance current transitions and the paper's mortuary is less than 270 days.

Most of the commercial paper market in Europe is modeled on the lines of the US market. In the UK the Sterling Commercial Paper Market was launched in May 1986. In the UK, the borrower must be listed in the stock exchange and he must have assets of at least $50 million. However, rating by credit agencies is not required. The maturities of commercial paper must be between 7 and 364 days. The commercial paper is exempted from stamp duty.

In France, commercial papers were thought of as a fixable alternative to bank loans. The commercial paper was introduced in December 1985. Commercial paper can be issued only by non-bank France companies and subsidiaries of foreign companies. The papers are in bearer form. It can be either issued by dealers or placed directly. The maturity ranges from ten days to seven years. Rating by credit agencies is essential. To protect investors, law contains fairly extensive disclosure requirements and requires publication of regular finance statements of issue. The outstanding amount at the end of 1990, in France Commercial paper market was $31 billion.

The Canadian commercial paper market was launched in 1950s. The commercial paper is generally used for terms of 30 days to 365 days although terms such as overnight are available. The commercial paper issued by Canadian companies is normally secured by pledge of assets. The outstanding amount at the end of 1990, in the commercial market was $26.8 billion.

In Japan, the yen commercial paper market was opened in November 1987. The commercial paper issues carry maturities from two weeks to nine months. Japan stands second in the commercial paper market in the world and outstanding amount of $117.3 billion in 1990.

In 1980s, many other countries launched commercial paper market, notably Sweden (early 1980s), Spain (1982s), Hong Kong (1982), and Singapore (1984), Norway (1984).

Commercial Paper in India

In India, on the recommendations of the Vaghul working Group, the RBI announced on 27th March 1989, that commercial paper will be introduced soon in Indian money market. The recommendations of the Vaghul Working Group on introduction of commercial paper in Indian money market are:

1. There is a need to have limited introduction of commercial paper. It should be carefully planned and the eligibility criteria for the issuer should be sufficiently rigorous to ensure that the commercial paper market develops on healthy lines.
2. Initially, access to the commercial paper market should be registered to rated companies having a net worth of ₹ 5 crores and above with good dividend payment record.
3. The commercial paper market should function within the overall discipline of CAS. The RBI would have to administer the entry on the market, the amount of each issues the total quantum that can be raised in a year.
4. New issue restriction is placed on the commercial paper market except by way of minimum size of note. The size of single issue should not be less than ₹ 1 crore and the size of each lot should not be less than ₹ 5 lakhs.
5. Commercial paper should be excluded from the stipulations on insecure advances in the case of banks.
6. Commercial paper would not be tied to any transaction and the maturity period may be 7 days and above but not exceeding six months, backed up if necessary by a revolving underwriting facility of less than three years .
7. The using company should have a net worth of net less than ₹ 5 crores, a debt equity ratio of not more than 1:5, current ratio of more than 1:3, a debt servicing ratio closer to 2, and be listed on the stock exchange.

8. The interest rate on commercial paper would be market dominated and the paper could be issued at a discount to face value or could be interest bearing.
9. Commercial paper should not be subject to stamp duty at the time of issue as well as at the time transfer by endorsement and delivery.

On the recommendations of the Vaghul Working Group, the RBI announced on 27th March, 1989, that commercial paper will be introduced soon in Indian money market. Detailed guidelines were issued in December 1989, through non-Banking companies (acceptance of Deposits through commercial paper) Direction, 1989 and finally the commercial papers were introduced in India from 1st January, 1990.

RBI Guidelines on Commercial Paper Issue

The important guidelines are:

1. A company can issue commercial paper only if it has:
   (a) A tangible net worth of not less than ₹ 10 crores as per the latest balance sheet;
   (b) Minimum current ratio of 1.33:1,
   (c) A fund based working capital limit of ₹ 25 crores or more.
   (d) A debt servicing ratio closer to 2;
   (e) The company is listed on a stock exchange;
   (f) Subject to CAS discipline;
   (g) It is classified under Health Code no. 1 by the financing banks;
   (h) The issuing company would need to obtain p1 from CRISIL;
2. Commercial paper shall be issued in multiples of ₹ 25 lakhs but the minimum amount to be invested by a single investor shall be ₹ 1 crore.
3. The commercial paper shall be issued for minimum maturity period of 7 days and the maximum period of 6 months from the date of issue. There will be no grace period on maturity.
4. The aggregate amount shall not exceed 20% of the issuer's fund-based working capital.
5. The commercial paper is issued in the form of usance promissory notes, negotiable by endorsement and delivery. The rate of discount could be freely determined by the issuing company. The issuing company has to bear all flotation cost, including stamp duty, dealers, fee and credit rating agency fee.
6. The issue of commercial paper cannot be underwritten or co-opted in any manner. However, commercial banks can provide standby facility for redemption of the paper on the maturity date.
7. Investment in commercial paper can be made by any person or banks or corporate bodies registered or incorporated in India and un-incorporated bodies too. Non-resident Indians can invest in commercial paper on non-repatriation basis.
8. The companies issuing commercial paper would be required to ensure that the relevant provisions of the various statutes such as Companies' Act, 1956, the IT Act, 1961 and the Negotiable Instruments Act, 1981, are complied with.

Procedure and Time frame for Issue of Commercial Paper

1. Application to RBI through financing bank or leader of consortium bank for working capital facilities together with a certificate from credit rating agency.
2. RBI to communicate in writing their decision on the amount of commercial paper to be issued to the leader bank.
3. Issue of commercial paper to be completed within 2 weeks from the date of approval of RBI through private placement.
4. The issue may be spread but shall bear the same maturity date.
5. Issuing company to advise RBI through the bank/leader of the bank, the amount of actual issue of commercial paper within 3 days of completion of the issue.

Implications of Commercial Paper

The issue of commercial paper is an important step in disintermediation bringing a large number of borrowers as well as investors in touch with each other, without the intervention of the banking system as financial intermediary. Directly from borrowers can get at least 20% of their working capital requirements at market rates, which can be more advantageous than borrowing through a bank. The first class borrowers have the prestige of joining the elitist commercial paper club with the approval of CRISIL, the banking system and the RBI, however RBI has presently stipulated that the working capital limits of the banks will be reduced to the extent of issue of commercial paper, industrialists have already made a plea that the issue of commercial paper should be outside the scheme of bank finance and other guidelines such as recommendation of banks and approval of RBI has not accepted the plea at present as commercial paper is an unsecured borrowing and not related to a trade transaction. The main aim of the RBI is to ensure that commercial paper develops a sound money market instrument. In the initial stages emphasis should be on the quality rather than quantity.

Impact on Commercial Banks

The impact of issue of commercial paper on commercial banks would be of two dimensions. One is that banks themselves can invest in commercial paper and show this as short-term investment. The second aspect is that the banks are likely to lose interest on working capital loan which has been hitherto lent to the companies, which have, now started borrowing through commercial paper.

Further, the larger companies might avail of the cheap funds available in the market during the slack season worsening the bank's surplus fund position\, but come to the banking system for borrowing during the busy season when funds are costly. This would mean the banks are the losers with a clear impact on profitability.

However, the banks stand to gain by charging higher interest rate on reinstated portion especially it is done during busy season and by way of service charge for providing standby facilities and issuing and paying commission. Further when large borrowers are able to borrow directly from the market, banks will correspondingly be freed from the pressure on resources.

Impact on the Economy

The process of disintermediation is taking place in the free economies all over the world. With the introduction of CP financial disintermediation has been gaining momentum in the Indian economy.

If CP is allowed free play, large companies as well as banks would learn to operate in a competitive atmosphere more efficiently. This results in greater excellence in the service of banks as well as management of finance by companies.

Recent trends

- RBI has liberalized the terms of issues of CP from May 30, 1991. According to the liberalized terms, proposal by eligible companies for the issues of CP would not require the approval of RBI. Such companies would have to submit the proposal to the financing bank which provided working capital facility either as a sole bank or as a leader of the consortium. The bank, on being satisfied of the compliance of the norms would take the proposal on record before the issue of commercial paper.
- RBI has further relaxed the rules in June 1992, the minimum working capital limit required by a company to issue CP has been reduced to ₹ 5 crores. The ceiling on amount of which can be raised through CP has been raised to 75% of working capital. A closely held company has also been permitted to borrow through CPs provided all the criteria are met. The minimum rating required from CRISIL has been lowered to P2 from 1994-95, the standby facility by banks for CP has been abolished. When CPs are issued, banks will have to effect a pro-rata reduction in the criteria. While the minimum rating needed from ICRA is A2 instead of A1.
- According to the RBI monetary policy for the second half of 1994-95, the standby facility by banks for CP has been abolished. When CPs are issued, banks will have to effect a *pro rata* reduction in the cash credit limit and it will be no longer necessary for banks to restore the cash credit limit to meet the liability on maturity of CPs. This will import a measure of independence to CP as a money market instrument.

Future of Commercial Paper in India

Corporate enterprises requiring burgeoning funds to meet their expanding needs find it easier and cheaper to raise funds from market by issuing commercial paper. Further, it provides greater degree of flexibility in business finance to the issuing company in as much it can decide the quantum of CP and its maturity on the basis of its future cash flows. CPs have made a good start. Since the inception of CPs in India in January 1990, 23 companies have issued CPs worth ₹ 419.4 crores till June 1991. The total issues amounted to ₹ 9,000 crores in June 1994. The outstanding amount of CPs stood at ₹ 4,770 crores on March 31, 1999 and increased to ₹ 7,814 crores on March 31. 2000.

The issues of CPs declined to ₹ 5,663 crores on March 31, 2000. It shows that the CP market is moribund. There is no increase in issuer base. I.e. the same companies are tapping this market for funds. The secondary market is virtually non-existent. Only commercial banks pick these papers and hold till mortuary. No secondary market is allowed to develop on any significant scale. Further, trading is cumbersome as procedural requirements are onerous. The stamp duty payable by banks subscribing charged to non-banking entities like, primary dealer, corporate and non-banks instead of directly subscribing to them. The structural rigidities such as rating requirements, timing of issue, terms of issue, maturity ranges denominational range and interest rate stand in the way of developing commercial paper market. The removal of stringent conditions and imposing of such regulatory measures justifiable to issues, investors and dealers will improve the potentiality of CP as a source of corporate financing.

4. Certificate of Deposit

Introduction

CDs are negotiable money market instruments and are issued in dematerialized form or a usance promissory note, for funds deposited at a bank or other eligible financial institution for a specified time period. They are like bank term deposits accounts. Unlike traditional time deposits these are freely negotiable instruments and are often referred to as Negotiable Certificate while certificates of deposits, otherwise known as CDs or time certificates, have been around since the early periods of banking, as legislation was passed to create a national system of financial reserves, the CD became more popular among those seeking long-term earnings on their money. Banks can only loan money that they have under assets. In order to keep assets under management to loan out for a higher rate of return, banks began to use certificates of deposits to entice customers to leave their money in the bank for long duration of time. The interest paid is the cost of being able to loan the money out. It wasn't until 1961 that a fixed rate time certificate was established.

A Certificate of Deposit, or CD, is a relatively low-risk debt instrument purchased directly through a commercial bank or savings and loan institution. The certificate indicates that the investor has deposited a sum of money for specified period of time and at a specified rate of interest. CD rates, terms and dollar amounts will vary from institution to institution. CDs are not publicly traded securities. As such, you will not find them traded on any exchange. The certificates of deposit are basically time deposits that are issued by the commercial banks with maturity periods ranging from 3 months to five years. The return on the certificate of deposit is higher than the Treasury Bills because it assumes a higher level of risk.

Definition

"Receipt from a bank acknowledging the deposit of a sum of money. The most common type, the time certificate of deposit, is for a fixed-term interest-bearing deposit in a large denomination. It consequently pays higher interest than a savings account, though the investor who withdraws money before its maturity date is subject to a penalty. Introduced in the early 1960s, CDs have become a popular method of saving."

"A certificate of deposit is a promissory note issued by a bank. It is a time deposit that restricts holders from withdrawing funds on demand. Although it is still possible to withdraw the money, this action will often incur a penalty."

The characteristics of CD

- CDs can be issued by all scheduled commercial banks except RRBs (ii) selected all India financial institutions, permitted by RBI
- Minimum period 15 days
- Maximum period 1 year
- Minimum Amount ₹ 1 lack and in multiples of ₹ 1 lakh
- CDs are transferable by endorsement
- CRR and SLR are to be maintained
- CDs are to be stamped

- CDs may be issued at discount on face value
- Interest calculations are mostly based upon a standard 360 days in a year called actual/360 but some are actual/365
- Investment is dependent solely upon the credit worthiness of the bank deposits
  - **Credit Risk:** High. The investor should monitor the financial condition of the bank.
  - **Liquidity Risk:** High. CDs cannot be liquidated without paying penalty.
  - **Market Risk:** Moderate. Monitor collateral value and require adequate margins.

Advantages of Certificate of Deposit as a money market instrument

1. Since one can know the returns from before, the certificates of deposits are considered much safe.
2. One can earn more as compared to depositing money in savings account.
3. The Federal Insurance Corporation guarantees the investments in the certificate of deposit.

Disadvantages of Certificate of deposit as a money market instrument:

1. As compared to other investments the returns is less.
2. The money is tied along with the long maturity period of the Certificate of Deposit. Huge penalties are paid if one gets out of it before maturity.
3. Investors can redeem bank-issued CDs prior to maturity. However, you will typically be charged an early withdrawal penalty. These penalties are set by each bank and differ nationwide.
4. Unlike Treasury notes, the interest on CDs is not exempt from state and local taxes. CDs are fully taxable at the state, local and federal levels.
5. The investment is locked in at a specific rate, even if interest rates increase.

RBI Guidelines Issued on Certificate of Deposit

Certificate of Deposit (CD) is a negotiable money market instrument and issued in dematerialized form or as a Usance Promissory Note against funds deposited at a bank or other eligible financial institution for a specified time period. Guidelines for issue of CDs are presently governed by various directives issued by the Reserve Bank of India, as amended from time to time. The guidelines for issue of CDs incorporating all the amendments issued till date are given below for ready reference.

1. Eligibility

CDs can be issued by (i) scheduled commercial banks excluding Regional Rural Banks (RRBs) and Local Area Banks (LABs); and (ii) select all-India Financial Institutions that have been permitted by RBI to raise short-term resources within the umbrella limit fixed by RBI.

2. Aggregate Amount

2.1 Banks have the freedom to issue CDs depending on their requirements.

2.2 An FI may issue CDs within the overall umbrella limit fixed by RBI, i.e., issue of CD together with other instruments, *viz.*, term money, term deposits, commercial papers and inter-corporate deposits should not exceed 100 per cent of its net owned funds, as per the latest audited balance sheet.

3. Minimum Size of Issue and Denominations

Minimum amount of a CD should be ₹ 1 lakh, i.e., the minimum deposit that could be accepted from a single subscriber should not be less than ₹ 1 lakh and in the multiples of ₹ 1 lakh thereafter.

4. Investors

CDs can be issued to individuals, corporations, companies, trusts, funds, associations, etc. Non-Resident Indians (NRIs) may also subscribe to CDs, but only on non-repatriable basis, which should be clearly stated on the Certificate. Such CDs cannot be endorsed to another NRI in the secondary market.

5. Maturity

5.1 The maturity period of CDs issued by banks should be not less than 7 days and not more than one year.

5.2 The FIs can issue CDs for a period not less than 1 year and not exceeding 3 years from the date of issue.

6. Discount/Coupon Rate

CDs may be issued at a discount on face value. Banks/FIs are also allowed to issue CDs on floating rate basis provided the methodology of compiling the floating rate is objective, transparent and market-based. The issuing bank/FI are free to determine the discount/coupon rate. The interest rate on floating rate CDs would have to be reset periodically in accordance with a pre-determined formula that indicates the spread over a transparent benchmark.

7. Reserve Requirements

Banks have to maintain appropriate reserve requirements, i.e., cash reserve ratio (CRR) and statutory liquidity ratio (SLR), on the issue price of the CDs.

8. Transferability

CDs in physical form are freely transferable by endorsement and delivery. CDs in demat form can be transferred as per the procedure applicable to other demat securities. There is no lock-in period for the CDs.

9. Trades in CDs

All OTC trades in CDs shall be reported within 15 minutes of the trade on the FIMMDA reporting platform.

10. Loans/Buy-backs

Banks/FIs cannot grant loans against CDs. Furthermore, they cannot buy-back their own CDs before maturity. However, the Reserve Bank may relax these restrictions for temporary periods through a separate notification.

11. Format of CDs

Banks/FIs should issue CDs only in dematerialized form. However, according to the Depositories Act, 1996, investors have the option to seek certificate in physical form. Accordingly, if investor insists on physical certificate, the bank / FI may inform the Chief General Manager, Financial Markets

Department, Reserve Bank of India, Central Office, Fort, Mumbai - 400 001 about such instances separately. Further, issuance of CDs will attract stamp duty. A format (Annex I) is enclosed for adoption by banks/FIs. There will be no grace period for repayment of CDs. If the maturity date happens to be holiday, the issuing bank should make payment on the immediate preceding working day. Banks/FIs may, therefore, so fix the period of deposit that the maturity date does not coincide with a holiday to avoid loss of discount/interest rate.

12. Security Aspect

Since CDs in physical form are freely transferable by endorsement and delivery, it will be necessary for banks to see that the certificates are printed on good quality security paper and necessary precautions are taken to guard against tampering with the document. They should be signed by two or more authorized signatories.

13. Payment of Certificate

13.1 Since CDs are transferable, the physical certificates may be presented for payment by the last holder. The question of liability on account of any defect in the chain of endorsements may arise. It is, therefore, desirable that banks take necessary precautions and make payment only by a crossed cheque. Those who deal in these CDs may also be suitably cautioned.

13.2 The holders of dematted CDs will approach their respective depository participants (DPs) and give transfer/delivery instructions to transfer the demat security represented by the specific ISIN to the 'CD Redemption Account' maintained by the issuer. The holders should also communicate to the issuer by a letter/fax enclosing the copy of the delivery instruction they had given to their respective DP and intimate the place at which the payment is requested to facilitate prompt payment. Upon receipt of the Demat credit of CDs in the "CD Redemption Account", the issuer, on maturity date, would arrange to repay to holders/transferors by way of Banker's cheque/high value cheque, etc.

14. Issue of Duplicate Certificates

14.1 In case of the loss of physical certificates, duplicate certificates can be issued after compliance with the following:

a. A notice is required to be given in at least one local newspaper;

b. Lapse of a reasonable period (say 15 days) from the date of the notice in the newspaper; and

c. Execution of an indemnity bond by the investor to the satisfaction of the issuer of CDs

14.2 The duplicate certificate should be issued only in physical form. No fresh stamping is required as a duplicate certificate is issued against the original lost CD. The duplicate CD should clearly state that the CD is a Duplicate one stating the original value date, due date, and the date of issue (as "Duplicate issued on ________").

15. Accounting

Banks/FIs may account the issue price under the Head "CDs issued" and show it under deposits. Accounting entries towards discount will be made as in the case of "cash certificates". Banks/FIs should maintain a register of CDs issued with complete particulars.

16. Standardized Market Practices and Documentation

Fixed Income Money Market and Derivatives Association of India (FIMMDA) may prescribe, in consultation with the RBI, for operational flexibility and smooth functioning of the CD market, any standardized procedure and documentation that are to be followed by the participants, in consonance with the international best practices. Banks/FIs may refer to the detailed guidelines issued by FIMMDA in this regard on June 20, 2002.

17. Reporting

17.1 Banks should include the amount of CDs in the fortnightly return under Section 42 of the Reserve Bank of India Act, 1934 and also separately indicate the amount so included by way of a footnote in the return.

17.2 Further, banks/FIs should submit a fortnightly return, as per the format given in Annex II, to the Chief General Manager, Financial Markets Department, Reserve Bank of India, Central Office Building, Fort, Mumbai - 400 001, Fax: 91-22-22630981/22634824 within 10 days from the end of the fortnight date. Additionally banks are also required to send the requisite information in the format as per Annex II of this Master Circular in an MS Excel/ CSV file via e-mail to cgmfmd@rbi.org.in within 10 days from the end of the fortnight. With effect from the fortnight ending July 2, 2010, data on issuance of Certificates of Deposits (CD), which are being reported in physical form/through e-mail shall also be concurrently reported on the web-based module under the Online Returns Filing System (ORFS).

Source: www.rbi.org.in

5. Treasury Bills Market

Treasury bills are the main financial instruments of money market. These bills are issued by the government. The borrowings of the government are monitored and controlled by the central bank. On behalf of the central government the bills are issued by the RBI. The RBI is the agent of union government. They are issued by tender or tap. The bills were sold to the public by tender method up to 1965. These bills were put at weekly auctions. Treasury bills are also issued by the state government.

History of Treasury Bills

In the United States, the history of the Treasury bill dates back to December 1929. To tackle the unforeseen financial demands that occurred during, and after, World War I, the US Treasury issued bills, notes, and bonds. After World War II, along with their popularity over other short-term government securities, and there has been a gradual rise of acceptance of treasury bills as marketable treasury securities. This is because they:

- Have a very short maturity period
- Are easier to issue and hence less expensive for the Treasury
- There is no pre-determined interest rate

Definitions

"A short-term debt obligation issued by the government to finance government activities. These are commonly referred to as T-Bills. They are usually issued in maturities of one, three, or six months."

"T-bills are zero-coupon bonds, which mean that they don't pay out interest. Instead, an investor buys them at a discount to their par value and earns the difference"

"Treasury bills are a short-term marketable securities issued on discount basis rather than at par, the price of which is determined by competitive bidding. Purchase can be done primarily through these auctions, however, at the secondary level; the bills can be bought and sold from traders."

Treasury bills, commonly referred to as T-Bills are issued by Government of India against their short-term borrowing requirements with maturities ranging between 14 to 364 days.

All these are issued at a discount-to-face value. For example a Treasury bill of ₹ 100.00 face value issued for ₹ 91.50 gets redeemed at the end of its tenure at ₹ 100.00.

Banks, Primary Dealers, State Governments, Provident Funds, Financial Institutions, Insurance Companies, NBFCs, FIIs (as per prescribed norms), NRIs & OCBs can invest in T-Bills.

The Characteristics of Treasury Bills

- No coupon and trade at a discount, meaning that the investor is not paid interest in increments over the life of the investment, but instead the security is sold for an amount less than the face or par value of the security. When the security reaches maturity, the investor is paid face value.
  - Interest = par value minus cost
  - 3- and 6-month treasury bills are auctioned every Monday
  - One year treasury bills are auctioned every four weeks
- Treasury Bills mature on Thursdays unless it's a holiday, then they mature on the next business day
- Treasury Bills are quoted and traded on a discount yield that is converted to a bond equivalent yield.

At present, the Government of India issues three types of treasury bills through auctions, namely,

- 91-day,
- 182-day and
- 364-day.

There are no treasury bills issued by State Governments.

Amount

- Treasury bills are available for a minimum amount of ₹ 25, 000 and in multiples of ₹ 25,000. Treasury bills are issued at a discount and are redeemed at par.
- Types of Bills: on tap bills, ad hoc bills, auctioned T-bills. The Treasury bills are short-term money market instrument that mature in a year or less than that. The purchase price is less

than the face value. At maturity the government pays the Treasury bill holder the full face value. The Treasury Bills are marketable, affordable and risk free. The security attached to the treasury bills comes at the cost of very low returns.

- **Credit Risk:** Low. Treasury bills are backed by the full faith and credit of the US Treasury.
- **Liquidity Risk:** Low. Treasury bills are one of the most liquid securities in the market.
- **Market Risk:** Low. The short duration allows for less price volatility.

Merits of treasury bills:

- T-bills remain one of the safest investments for liquid position.
- The advantage of purchasing these short-terms, liquid instruments, is access to your funds at any time, with the peace of mind knowing that your funds will not be tied up in long-term investments, should an emergency arise.
- T-bills can be held to maturity, with constant roll over into other T-bill purchases, or can be sold at any time an investor chooses.
- Compared with commercial banks and other financial institutions rates, the Treasury Bills sometimes offer the highest interest rate available.
- Treasury Bills provide a regular income or cash flow which can be used to supplement your existing income or provide an income if you are retired.
- Treasury Bills can easily be converted to cash on maturity, or they may be sold if you need the money before the maturity dates.
- As Treasury Bills are an income generating asset, they can be used as collateral for loans from banks and other financial institutions.
- Treasury Bills offer a simple mode of preserving and protecting your investment.

Demerits of Treasury Bills

The main disadvantage of Treasury Bills is that income from Treasury Bills is fixed for the term of the investment. In times of high inflation, the purchasing power of your money will be reduced.

9 Foreign Direct Investment in India

After the introduction of liberalization, privatization and globalization policies, the entire Indian economy has changed drastically. The economy has changed from traditional to digital economy or wired economy. There has exponential growth in gross domestic product. The GDP is strongly built up by manufacturing sector, agriculture sector and service sector. In traditional economy, the GDP was dominated by agriculture sector. After 1991, the entire situation had changed in the components of GDP. In the digital economy, services sector dominate the components of GDP. Service sector is a highly intellectual component in human resource management. India has a vast pool of highly educated, talented and skilled resources. The increase in education levels of the community, a strong commitment made by the government towards education sector and an attitude towards a better education by the society enhanced the literacy levels. India is a reservoir of best talented human resource but lack of technical competency. The technical competency can be enhanced by giving proper training activities to the human resources. A strong and skilled manpower can build the technical modern India. The GDP is a combination of "agriculture, manufacturing, service sectors". The agriculture sector can be re-built with the adaption of interlinking of rivers in India. It is a cost of estimated worth of more than ₹ 15 lakh crores. This project will give an intellectual process for the development of entire Indian economy within a period of 10 years. The mega project can be built with the help of financial markets and services. In the financial markets abundant supply of financial resources will be available, to convert them into the productive way of interlinking of rivers for modern India. The abundant supply of financial resources can be tapped by proper efficient financial resources. Financial services are a highly intellectual and innovative activity. It is not a just routine activity. It requires a proper and better understanding of investor's psychology and market trends. Investor psychology was dealt by behavioral finance. It is an innovative and undeveloped subject in India. This subject should be introduced as a curriculum at the stages of schooling and collegiate education. The importance of money and its proper utilization should be taught to the responsible up-coming citizens. Hence, a proper financial discipline can be maintained in the society with the help of various powerful weapons such as schools, colleges, universities, educational institutions, commercial banks, financial institutions, reserve bank and ministry of finance.

GDP = Manufacturing Sector + Agriculture Sector + Services Sector.

SERVICE SECTOR IN INDIA

Services account for more than 60 per cent of world GDP and trade in services has grown. As an economy grows, the proportion of income spent on services increase more than proportionately when compared to income spent on manufactured items, which, in turn, accounts for a higher proportion of income spent on them as compared to agricultural items. The demand for services increase as income increases. On the supply side, the share of services in output also goes up. As the economy grows, firms restructure to use a supply intensive mode of production. This "splintering" refers to the activity where firms start focusing on core functions and sub-contract non-core functions to the services sector.

Services are categorized into four different modes. Mode 1, refers to services supplied from one country to another, such as international telephone calls and business process outsourcing. Mode 2, relates to consumption abroad where consumers or firms of one country make use of services in another country. Examples in this category include medical care, education, and tourism. Mode 3, refers to commercial presence, where foreign companies set up subsidiaries or branches to provide services in another country. Examples include banking, financial and telecommunication services. Lastly, Mode 4, refers to movement of neutral persons. Examples include IT professionals, scientists and other professionals, traveling from their own country to provide services in another country.

The modes of service delivery and respective share in world trade in services

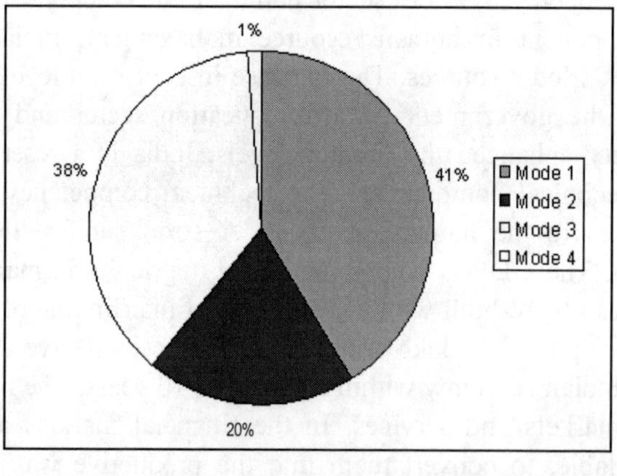

Source: www. thomex.com.

International trade in services has recorded rapid growth in the recent past. Global exports in commercial services grew by 10 % and amounted to USD 2,145 billion in 2005. It is expected that by 2050, world trade in services will exceed world trade in manufactured items. Trade in services within Asia went up 14% for the same year. Technological developments, demographics, growing globalization of production processes, and economic liberalization are the driving forces behind the increasing trade in services. While developed countries still dominate trade in services, developing countries are catching up fast. Among the top twenty exporters of commercial services in 2005, five are developing countries with India in the 11th position. In addition, in terms of the share of services export in total exports, India ranks 1st for the year 2005. India's share in world exports of services has grown from 0.6 % in 1995 to 2.3 % in 2005.

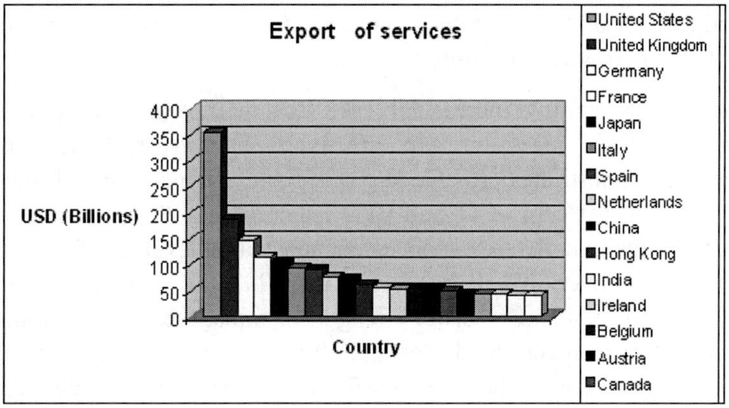

Source: www.thomex.com.

India's negotiating position on services has changed since the Uruguay Round (UR). During the UR, India had defensive stance on services. The country was one of the prime opponents of the inclusion of services in the ambit of the multilateral trade negotiations. It was apprehended that any concessions gained in traditional sectors like agriculture or textiles would be offset by the opening up of the government dominated services such as, banking, insurance and telecommunications. However, since the beginning of the GATS 2000 Negotiations and particularly after the Doha Ministerial in 2001, India has emerged as a leading proponent of the services trade liberalizations at the multilateral arena.

The change in India's approach towards trade and investment liberalization in services is clearly due to the growing importance of the services sector in India's economy and its trade and investment flows in the recent years. India's services sector recorded an average annual growth rate of 9 per cent in the 1990s, while India's GDP grew at an average annual rate of 7.5 per cent during the same period. According to the latest RBI Annual Report, in 2005-06, the services sector has recorded a growth rate of 10.3 per cent, contributing almost three-fourths of the overall real GDP growth of India. From a mere 28 per cent in 1950-51, the share of services (excluding construction) in the overall GDP of the economy went up to 53 per cent in 2004-05.

The impressive growth in the Information technology sector has been feasible because of low cost of operations, high quality of product and services and readily available skilled manpower. The ITES-BPO industry has witnessed significant growth in 2005-06, driven by increased offshoring by firms in America and Europe. Within ITES service lines, customer care and finance have been the two fastest growing segments. Apart from these two, some other important segments in the outsourcing industry include human resources, payment services administration and content development. While presently customer care remains the largest service line, finance and administration services are expected to grow significantly over the next few years.

The global ITES and BPO market is growing at around 9 per cent. With the industry structure undergoing change, established software service companies have entered into ITES-BPO arena driven by factors such as cross selling opportunities, critical mass and strong balance sheets, end-to-end service offerings. Even as Indian service providers continue to strengthen their position as providers of Information Technology Outsourcing (ITO) and Business Process Outsourcing (BPO) services to companies around the world, the possibility now exists for India to add new stream of services export growth, i.e., Engineering Services Outsourcing (ESO).

Most economies are getting increasingly skill-scarce in a relative cost-effective sense, and professionals in India could meet this gap effectively. Each year, India's universities, technical colleges and other tertiary institutes produce nearly 100,000 engineering and science graduates. India presently accounts for 28 per cent of IT and BPO talent among 28 low-cost countries in the world. India has emerged as a major software exporting country with a level of US $ 23.6 billion in 2005-06, growing at a steady rate of over 30% in the recent past. While this cost advantage due to cheap skilled labour and the fluency in English is a major strength for India, the pool is not big enough. Currently only about 25 per cent of technical graduates and 10 to 15 per cent of general college graduates are suitable for employment in the offshore IT and BPO industries, respectively. There is a shortfall of nearly 0.5 million qualified employees in the IT and BPO sector. The potential shortage of skilled labor has already led to an increase in wage. Wage costs are rising by around 17-20 per cent per year. India will need a 2.3 million IT and BPO workforce by 2010, to maintain its current market share.

Service Sector in India today accounts for more than half of India's GDP. According to data for the financial year 2006-2007, the share of services, industry, and agriculture in India's GDP is 55.1 per cent, 26.4 per cent, and 18.5 per cent respectively. The fact that the services sector now accounts for more than half the GDP marks a watershed in the evolution of the Indian economy and takes it closer to the fundamentals of a developed economy. Services or the "tertiary sector" of the economy covers a wide gamut of activities like trading, banking and finance, infotainment, real estate, transportation, security, management and technical consultancy among several others. The various sectors that combine together to constitute service industry in India are:

- Trade
- Hotels and Restaurants
- Railways
- Other Transport and Storage
- Communication (Post, Telecom)
- Banking
- Insurance
- Dwellings, Real Estate
- Business Services
- Public Administration, Defense
- Personal Services
- Community Services
- Other Services

There was marked acceleration in services sector growth in the eighties and nineties, especially in the nineties. While the share of services in India's GDP increased by 21 per cent points in the 50 years between 1950 and 2000, nearly 40 per cent of that increase was concentrated in the nineties. While almost all service sectors participated in this boom, growth was fastest in communications, banking, hotels and restaurants, community services, trade and business services. One of the reasons for the sudden growth in the services sector in India in the nineties was the liberalization in the regulatory framework that gave rise to innovation and higher exports from the services sector. The boom in the services sector has been relatively "jobless". The rise in services share in GDP has not been accompanied by proportionate increase in the sector's share of national employment. Some economists have also cautioned that service sector growth must be supported by proportionate growth of the industrial sector; otherwise the service sector growth will not be sustainable. In the current economic scenario it looks that the boom in the services sector is here to stay, as India is fast emerging as global services hub.

Telecom Industry in India

The telecom industry is one of the fastest growing industries in India. India has nearly 200 million telephone lines making it the third largest network in the world after China and USA. With a growth rate of 45%, Indian telecom industry has the highest growth rate in the world. History of Indian Telecommunications started in 1851 when the first operational land lines were laid by the government near Calcutta (seat of British power). Telephone services were introduced in India in 1881. In 1883, telephone services were merged with the postal system. Indian Radio Telegraph Company (IRT) was formed in 1923. After independence in 1947, all the foreign telecommunication companies were nationalized to form the Posts, Telephone and Telegraph (PTT), a monopoly run by the government's Ministry of Communications. Telecom sector was considered as a strategic service and the government considered it best to bring under state's control. The first wind of reforms in telecommunications sector began to flow in 1980s when the private sector was allowed in telecommunications equipment manufacturing. In 1985, Department of Telecommunications (DOT) was established. It was an exclusive provider of domestic and long-distance service that would be its own regulator (separate from the postal system). In 1986, two wholly government-owned companies were created; the Videsh Sanchar Nigam Limited (VSNL) for international telecommunications and Mahanagar Telephone Nigam Limited (MTNL) for service in metropolitan areas. In 1990s, telecommunications sector benefited from the general opening up of the economy. Also, examples of telecom revolution in many other countries, which resulted in better quality of service and lower tariffs, led Indian policymakers to initiate a change process finally resulting in opening up of telecom services sector for the private sector. National Telecom Policy (NTP) 1994, was the first attempt to give a comprehensive roadmap for the Indian telecommunications sector. In 1997, Telecom Regulatory Authority of India (TRAI) was created. TRAI was formed to act as a regulator to facilitate the growth of the telecom sector. New National Telecom Policy was adopted in 1999 and cellular services were also launched in the same year. Telecommunication sector in India can be divided into two segments: Fixed Service Provider (FSPs), and Cellular Services. Fixed line services consist of basic services, national or domestic long distance and international long distance services. The state operators (BSNL and MTNL), account for almost 90 per cent of revenues from basic services. Private sector services are presently available in selective urban areas, and collectively account for less than 5 per cent of subscriptions. However, private services focus on the business/corporate sector, and offer reliable, high-end services, such as leased lines, ISDN, closed user group and videoconferencing. Cellular services can be further divided into two categories: Global System for Mobile Communications (GSM) and Code Division Multiple Access (CDMA). The GSM sector is dominated by Airtel, Vodafone-Hutch, and Idea Cellular, while the CDMA sector is dominated by Reliance and Tata Indicom. Opening up of international and domestic long distance telephony services are the major growth drivers for cellular industry. Cellular operators get substantial revenue from these services, and compensate them for reduction in tariffs on airtime, which along with rental was the main source of revenue. The reduction in tariffs for airtime, national long distance, international long distance, and handset prices has driven demand. The telecom sector is also afflicted by a number of restraints. These include:

- Sluggish pace of reform process.
- Lack of infrastructure in semi-rural and rural areas, which makes it difficult to make inroads into this market segment as service providers have to incur a huge initial fixed cost.
- Limited spectrum availability. But notwithstanding these constraints, telecom sector has undergone a revolution in the past decade and has played a major part in bridging the rural-urban divide.

BPO Industry in India

Business Process Outsourcing (BPO) is one of the fastest growing segments of the Information Technology Enabled Services (ITES) industry in India. Business Process Outsourcing refers to the delegation of one or more IT-intensive business processes to an external provider that in turn owns administers and manages the selected process based on defined and measurable performance criteria. The trend to outsource work is on rise in today's competitive environment. There are number of reasons behind the increasing trend of outsourcing. Firstly, companies want to focus on mission-critical issues and are not interested in frittering away time and energy on non-core functions. Secondly, as businesses grow exponentially, the companies do not have resources to cope with the growth and as a result they outsource part of their business processes. Thirdly, companies may not have the best talent and skills to do the job themselves. Lastly, converging technologies of telecommunication, information technology and media have redefined the way we do business and have made outsourcing possible. There are a number of advantages of outsourcing. Major among them are: (1) Reduce overheads and free up resources, (2) Improves efficiency, (3) Offloads non-core functions, (4) Gives access to specialized skills, (5) Saves on manpower and training costs, (6) Reduces operating costs, (7) Enhances tactical and strategic advantages, (8) Spreads risks, (9) Provides the best quality services, products and people, and (10) Helps to focus scarce resources on time-critical projects. Some of typical services and processes that are outsourced include: Technical Support Services, Telemarketing Services, Insurance Processing, Data Entry Services/Data Processing Services, Data Conversion Services, Bookkeeping and Accounting Services, etc. The Indian BPO industry is constantly growing and a lot of Fortune 500 companies are outsourcing services to India. There are several reasons for India's emergence as one of leading outsourcing destinations. India is very rich in educated and talented human resource. India is one of the pioneers in software development. India has a mature industrial set up with world class systems. India has excellent technical facilities and infrastructure for setting up call centers. Time zone difference between India and America has also worked to the advantage of Indian BPO industry. India has an 8-12 hour time zone difference with respect to the US and other developed markets. Most of the Indian call centers servicing American customers have timings between 5:30 p.m. to 9:30 a.m. This time zone difference allows Indian companies BPOs to service American clients by working in the nights. Last, but not the least, India has a huge pool of English speaking workforce that provides excellent voice-based services at extremely competitive costs resulting in huge savings for companies. Some of the leading BPO companies in India are: GE Capital, Convergys, Wipro Spectra mind, WNS, Dell, Daksh e-

Services, ICICI OneSource, and Mphasis. Some of the problems afflicting Indian BPO industry are high attrition rate, and backlash in developed countries against perceived job losses due to outsourcing to India. To tackle the problem of attrition companies are adopting measures such as good rewards, bonding program, flexible working hours and stronger career path. As regards backlash against outsourcing, the backlash is mainly political. There is compelling economic logic for companies to outsource to India and also Indian BPO companies have taken initiatives to allay fears of job loss.

Hotel Industry in India

Hotel Industry in India has witnessed tremendous boom in recent years. Hotel Industry is inextricably linked to the tourism industry and the growth in the Indian tourism industry has fuelled the growth of Indian hotel industry. The thriving economy and increased business opportunities in India have acted as a boon for Indian hotel industry. The arrival of low cost airlines and the associated price wars have given domestic tourists a host of options. The 'Incredible India' destination campaign and the recently launched 'Atithi Devo Bhavah' (ADB) campaign have also helped in the growth of domestic and international tourism and consequently the hotel industry. In recent years government has taken several steps to boost travel and tourism which have benefited hotel industry in India. These include the abolishment of the inland air travel tax of 15%; reduction in excise duty on aviation turbine fuel to 8%; and removal of a number of restrictions on outbound chartered flights, including those relating to frequency and size of aircraft. The government's recent decision to treat convention centers as part of core infrastructure, allowing the government to provide critical funding for the large capital investment that may be required has also fuelled the demand for hotel rooms. The opening up of the aviation industry in India has exciting opportunities for hotel industry as it relies on airlines to transport 80% of international arrivals. The government's decision to substantially upgrade 28 regional airports in smaller towns and privatization and expansion of Delhi and Mumbai airport will improve the business prospects of hotel industry in India. Substantial investments in tourism infrastructure are essential for Indian hotel industry to achieve its potential. The upgrading of national highways connecting various parts of India has opened new avenues for the development of budget hotels in India. Taking advantage of this opportunity Tata group and another hotel chain called 'Homotel' have entered this business segment. According to a report, Hotel Industry in India currently has supply of 1,10,000 rooms and there is a shortage of 1,50,000 rooms, fueling hotel room rates across India. According to estimates demand is going to exceed supply by at least 100% over the next 2 years. Five-star hotels in metro cities allot same room, more than once a day to different guests, receiving almost 24-hour rates from both guests against 6-8 hours usage. With demand-supply disparity, hotel rates in India are likely to rise by 25% annually and occupancy by 80%, over the next two years. This will affect the competitiveness of India as a cost-effective tourist destination. To overcome, this shortage Indian hotel industry is adding about 60,000 quality rooms, currently in different stages of planning and development, which should be ready by 2012. Hotel Industry in India is also set to get a fillip with Delhi hosting 2010 Commonwealth Games. Government has approved 300 hotel projects, nearly half of which are in the luxury range. The future scenario of Indian hotel industry looks extremely rosy. It is expected that the budget and mid-market hotel segment will witness huge growth and expansion while the luxury segment will continue to perform extremely well over the next few years.

Entertainment Industry in India

Entertainment Industry in India comprises of Film Industry and Television Industry. The Indian entertainment industry is among the fastest growing sectors in the country. In the past two decades entertainment industry in India has witnessed explosive growth. In television alone, from a single state owned television network, Doordarshan in 1991, today there are over 300 national, regional and local channels being beamed across the country. Indian film industry is the largest film industry in the world, producing on an average, close to a thousand films a year in all languages. In terms of film production India exceeds Hollywood's production volume by over three times. Some of the fastest growing segments in the Indian entertainment industry include music, cable and satellite television, animation and FM. According to an estimate by FICCI and Ernst and Young, Indian entertainment industry would be worth more than ₹ 400,000 million in 2008. Several positive developments like the accordance of the 'industry' status to the film industry, satellite channel penetration, the retail boom in the channels for music sales (Music World & Planet M), the use of digital technology in all spheres of entertainment and the growth of multiplexes have contributed to the growth of this sector. Entertainment industry in India is presently in a consolidation phase as boundary lines between films, music and television are fast disappearing. Skills and resources are being pooled extensively. Besides adaptation to high-end digital technology, the entertainment industry is also witnessing rapid development of state-of-the-art studios and post production facilities. In terms of employment, an estimated 6 million people earn their livelihood from the entertainment industry and this number is all set to grow. Entertainment industry in India is projected to be one of the major economic driving forces of the country. In India, television is the major segment of entertainment industry. Presently, India has the third largest television market in the world behind only china and the USA. Today, television reaches about hundred million Indian households. India has the world's biggest movie industry in terms of the number of movies produced. Presently, the technology of film-making in India is perhaps the best among all developing countries. Indian film industry is now increasingly getting professional and a lot of production houses such as Yash Raj Productions, Dharma Productions, Mukta Arts, etc., are now working on corporate lines. The popularity of Indian entertainment industry goes well beyond the geographical frontiers of the country. Indian television channels and films are viewed and enjoyed across the entire South Asia. Across the Middle East, parts of South East Asia and Africa, large expatriate populations ensure that Indian TV channels and films are a regular part of their entertainment bouquet. In UK and North America (USA and Canada), Indian TV channels and films are increasingly finding a foothold beyond the expatriate pockets as the audience there has started to enjoy and identify with the contemporary Indian culture. Quite a few of Indian film stars are also getting good offers from Hollywood. The future prospects of Indian entertainment industry look to be extremely good. As India's profile rises on the global stage outside interest in India's culture and entertainment industry is also bound to grow.

Statement showing the gross domestic product of India (2006-10)

Gross Domestic Product at Factor Cost - Annual

All Institutions ₹ in Crore

Data Series : NAS-2004-05									
		2009-10		2008-09		2007-08		2006-07	
		Constant Prices	Current Prices	Constant Prices	Current Prices	Constant Prices	Current Prices	Constant Prices	Current Prices
(A)	Total Domestic Product	44,64,081	58,68,331	41,54,973	52,28,650	38,93,457	45,40,987	35,64,627	39,41,865
(A.1)	Agriculture, Forestry & Fishing	6,51,901	10,04,594	6,50,461	8,98,378	6,40,315	8,15,399	6,11,409	7,14,254
(A.10)	Net Indirect Taxes	3,14,078	3,72,910	3,10,387	3,45,799			3,10,005	3,42,114
(A.10.1)	Indirect taxes	5,42,469	6,67,899	5,36,926	6,30,788			4,60,404	5,08,090
(A.10.2)	Less subsidies	2,28,391	2,94,989	2,26,539	2,84,989			1,50,399	1,65,976
(A.1.1)	Agriculture			5,47,980	7,67,119			5,16,094	5,96,765
(A.1.2)	Forestry & Logging			68,826	88,823			65,447	82,124
(A.1.3)	Fishing			33,655	42,436			29,868	35,365
(A.2)	Mining & Quarrying	1,09,182	1,45,532	98,745	1,34,398	97,201	1,25,730	93,587	1,08,166
(A.3)	Manufacturing Total	7,19,975	9,31,101	6,49,635	8,14,025	6,29,446	7,31,078	5,70,765	6,34,304
(A.3.1)	Manufacturing – Registered			4,33,394	5,53,677			3,79,702	4,27,075
(A.3.2)	Manufacturing – Unregistered			2,16,241	2,60,348			1,91,063	2,07,229
(A.4)	Electricity, Gas & Water Supply	87,199	92,743	81,866	86,512	78,776	83,060	72,579	76,472
(A.5)	Construction	3,54,541	4,88,345	3,32,782	4,50,021	3,14,298	3,81,521	2,85,722	3,22,265
(A.6)	Trade, Hotels & Restaurant	11,85,190	14,36,650	10,84,764	12,86,380	10,08,603	11,29,387	5,96,174	6,69,282
(A.6.1)	Trade			6,24,193	7,91,470			5,37,690	6,04,006
(A.6.2)	Hotels & Restaurants			63,687	80,352			58,484	65,276
(A.7)	Transport, Storage & Communication							3,14,648	3,20,905
(A.7.1)	Transport by Railways			41,444	48,117			34,779	37,429
(A.7.2)	Transport by other means			2,30,936	2,86,462			2,02,104	2,22,435
(A.7.3)	Storage			2,632	3,300			2,256	2,511
(A.7.4)	Communication			1,21,872	76,679			75,509	58,530
(A.8)	Finance, Insurance, Real	7,69,390	9,52,309	7,01,338	8,39,232	6,37,223	6,95,861	5,62,878	5,86,159

	Estate &Business Services								
(A.8.1)	Banking & Insurance			3,19,395	2,99,562			2,40,105	2,17,196
(A.8.2)	Real Estate, Ownership of Dwellings & Business Services			3,81,943	5,39,670			3,22,773	3,68,963
(A.9)	Community, Social & Personal Services	5,86,703	8,17,058	5,55,382	7,19,704	4,87,595	5,78,951	4,56,865	5,10,058
(A.9.1)	Public Admn., Defense & Quasi-Govt. Bodies			2,42,640	3,11,637			1,84,975	2,05,683
(A.9.2)	Other Services			3,12,742	4,08,067			2,71,890	3,04,375
(B.1)	Total final consumption expenditure	33,35,629	43,39,408	31,67,659	38,71,330	29,24,530	33,31,021	26,63,127	29,10,387
(B.1.1)	Private final consumption expenditure	27,69,769	35,71,999	26,55,533	32,18,198	24,85,554	28,15,675	22,62,812	24,65,205
(B.1.2)	Government final consumption expenditure	5,65,860	7,67,409	5,12,126	6,53,132	4,38,976	5,15,346	4,00,315	4,45,182
(B.2)	Gross capital formation			15,57,757	19,44,328	16,22,226	18,65,899	13,88,239	15,20,312
(B.2.1)	Gross fixed capital formation	15,76,445	20,18,916	14,71,161	18,38,499	14,14,975	16,30,513	12,28,060	13,47,057
(B.2.2)	Changes in stocks	63,327	83,419	59,812	74,023	1,54,033	1,75,154	1,33,825	1,45,295
(B.2.3)	Valuables	63,503	81,017	58,673	71,656	47,456	53,591	46,182	49,709
(B.2.4)	Errors and omissions			–31,888	–39,850	5,762	6,640	–19,828	–21,749
(B.3)	Exports	10,22,029	12,82,846	10,94,929	13,10,849	9,17,455	10,18,931	8,72,357	9,13,408
(B.4)	Less Imports	12,69,570	15,73,518	13,69,202	16,14,048	11,13,113	12,19,752	10,12,045	10,44,007
(B.5)	Discrepancies	15,860	–916	–17,672	22,139	–97,417	–41,602	–37,046	–16,122
(C)	GDP at market prices	48,07,222	62,31,171	44,65,360	55,74,449	42,47,918	49,47,857	38,74,632	42,83,979
	(A.15)Population	1,170	1,170	1,154	1,154			1,122	1,122

Source: www.rbi.org.in

Statement showing gross domestic product at price level of 1999-2000 For 2006-09

Data Series: NAS-1999-2000					
		2008-09		2006-07	
		Constant Prices	Current Prices	Constant Prices	Current Prices
(A)	Total Domestic Product	33,39,375	49,33,183	28,71,120	37,79,384
(A.1)	Agriculture, Forestry & Fishing	5,66,045	8,61,753	5,31,315	6,86,044
(A.10)	Net Indirect Taxes	2,70,050	3,88,570	2,48,911	3,49,789
(A.10.1)	Indirect taxes	4,18,005	6,21,990	3,61,558	5,08,090
(A.10.2)	Less subsidies	1,47,955	2,33,420	1,12,647	1,58,301
(A.1.1)	Agriculture			4,87,010	6,25,161
(A.1.2)	Forestry & Logging			19,991	26,855
(A.1.3)	Fishing			24,308	34,050
(A.2)	Mining & Quarrying	64,244	1,25,414	60,038	1,06,024
(A.25)	Services (Including Construction)	21,55,448	30,86,132	17,79,029	22,99,212
(A.26)	Trade, Hotel, Transport and Communications	9,54,589	12,46,718	7,78,896	9,47,096
(A.3)	Manufacturing Total	4,87,739	7,80,405	4,40,193	6,17,648
(A.3.1)	Manufacturing - Registered			2,99,931	4,28,909
(A.3.2)	Manufacturing - Unregistered			1,40,839	1,89,045
(A.4)	Electricity, Gas & Water Supply	65,899	79,478	60,544	70,455
(A.5)	Construction	2,42,577	4,37,017	2,05,543	3,19,180
(A.6)	Trade, Hotels & Restaurant	9,54,589	12,46,718	7,78,896	9,47,096
(A.6.1)	Trade			3,98,367	5,70,888
(A.6.2)	Hotels & Restaurants			42,310	59,476
(A.7)	Transport, Storage & Communication			3,27,207	3,19,104
(A.7.1)	Transport by Railways			33,668	39,308
(A.7.2)	Transport by other means			1,51,042	2,00,722
(A.7.3)	Storage			1,768	2,535
(A.7.4)	Communication			1,40,729	76,539
(A.8)	Finance, Insurance, Real Estate & Business Services	4,93,356	6,91,221	4,09,472	5,24,019
(A.8.1)	Banking & Insurance			1,91,387	2,13,381
(A.8.2)	Real Estate, Ownership of			2,18,643	3,13,374

(A.9)	Dwellings & Business Services Community, Social & Personal Services	4,64,926	7,11,176	3,85,118	5,08,917
(A.9.1)	Public Admn., Defense & Quasi-Govt. Bodies			1,61,547	2,18,883
(A.9.2)	Other Services			2,28,473	2,89,703
(B.1)	Total final consumption expenditure	24,00,750	35,29,833	21,02,984	27,29,368
(B.1.1)	Private final consumption expenditure	20,01,488	29,13,386	17,93,691	23,07,822
(B.1.2)	Government final consumption expenditure	3,99,262	6,16,447	3,09,293	4,21,546
(B.2)	Gross capital formation			10,73,783	15,21,805
(B.2.1)	Gross fixed capital formation	11,63,503	18,52,354	9,52,344	13,43,843
(B.2.2)	Changes in stocks	1,08,739	1,87,548	69,673	1,08,956
(B.2.3)	Valuables	49,859	71,656	38,091	49,709
(B.2.4)	Errors and omissions			13,675	19,297
(B.3)	Exports	7,77,380	12,06,600	6,74,670	9,16,804
(B.4)	Less Imports	9,86,440	14,91,375	7,82,976	10,42,263
(B.5)	Discrepancies	95,634	-34,864	51,570	3,459
(C)	GDP at market prices	36,09,425	53,21,753	31,20,031	41,29,173
	(A.13) Industry	6,17,882	9,85,297	5,60,775	7,94,127
	(A.15) Population	1,154	1,154	1,122	1,122

Source: www.rbi.org.in

Meaning of Financial Services

Service offered by financial companies are known as financial services. Financial services require highly skilled talented and innovative capabilities. They are not offering routine and unskilled services. They provide innovative and highly skillful and time bound assignment. It requires higher efficiency. The efficiency depends upon the knowledge acquired by a person with the high intention of work culture ethics. The financial services require high degree of integration and a concentrated effort. The financial service can also be called as financial intermediation. It is a process which works as a coordinator between borrowers and lenders. Its dynamic activity helps to grow economy in a fast way. It mobilizes idle fund and diverts it towards a productive way. The diverting of funds into a productive way is known as creativity. The creativity or innovation depends upon the qualities of a person or intellectual who deploys his thoughts in the profession. The professional skill is important for this sector. The professionalism will provide expertism. The expertism will make a person more perfect in performing his concentrated activities. With the entrance of information technology, the entire financial sector scenario has changed drastically. The information technology created new waves in the banking sector in the form of ATMs. The ATMs are the brainchild of revolution of information technology. With the introduction of ATMs, the banks operational expenses had been reduced drastically. According to the financial expenses scenario, if a customer approached an ATM, it costs the bank ₹ 1.50 per his transaction. If the same customer visits the branch, the transaction cost for the bank is ₹ 25 for his visit. Therefore, we can understand the cost reduction to the banking sector. The future of the banking sector depends upon the extraction of the information technology capabilities. In India, five star treatment to bank customers are available at State Bank of India in Hyderabad Kohinoor Banzara Premium Branch; it is the first of its kind in India with the following facilities.

- 7 days and 24 hrs branch
- Bank lockers
- No holidays
- Five star facilities
- Nilam lounge
- Pearl coffee bar
- Ruby emerald business centre
- Video conference
- Dressing room
- Financial services
- Forex services
- NRI services
- Upto 8 p.m.
- SBI tax online payment
- E-investment
- Demat
- Online trading centre
- Minimum deposit balance must be ₹ one crore
- 50 accounts opened as on 4/9/2010
- 150 accounts in process as on 4/9/2010.

Financial Companies

Financial companies include both Asset Management Companies and Liability Management Companies. The asset management companies include "Leasing Companies, Mutual Funds, Merchant Bankers, Issue Managers and Portfolio Managers. Liability management companies consist of bill discounting and acceptance houses. The financial services are offered by a host of institutions and agencies that understand and meet the requirement of a wide spectrum of customers. It comprises of four major constituents. They are:

1. Market Players
2. Financial Instruments
3. Specialised Institutions
4. Regulatory Bodies.

In financial services market, the market players occupy a dominant role in attracting the investor's attention. The market players consist of banks, financial institutions, merchant bankers, stock brokers, and consultants. The success of the financial service market depends upon the dynamism of these market players.

The financial instruments or financial assets are the next important constituent in the financial markets. They are equity instruments, debt instruments and zero-coupon bond. The inflation levels in the economy and interest rates at different period of time will make demand for different kind of financial instruments.

The specialized institutions in the financial services market found acceptance house, discount house, factoring, credit rating agencies, etc. They render a highly specialized service to its customers. In India, these services are not yet popularized.

The regulatory bodies will monitor the activities of the financial services market components. The regulations are more important for dynamic growth of a nation. The expectation of development in the economy depends upon the strict regulations with a strong commitment towards achieving the growth. The financial services market regulator in India is SEBI, RBI, and Deparment of Banking and Insurance of the union government. The regulations depend upon the policies and reforms adopted by the government. Policies are enzymes and reforms are antibiotics.

The financial services market will make ease of speedy industrialization of the country, which depend upon the investment policies of the government and the level of degree of competition existing in the market. Therefore, the following regulatory policies will occupy a dominant role in financial services market.

1. Competition act.
2. Foreign direct investment.

1. Competition Act

The market is a battlefield for the corporate sector. Every business enterprise wants to capture the market and they dream for No.1 position in their field. The competition is the best element for the consumer. The intensified competition may bring the lower level prices to consumer with high quality of products. The government role is to create a high level of competition between market players and its duty is to wait and watch the situation. The monitoring activities will be looked after by the government. The economies are becoming market-oriented and in the competition, only real organisations with high potential will survive. The competition enhances the efficiency levels of the industrial units. The inefficient enterprises will lose their grip on the market and they will disappear from the business.

1. Short title, extent and commencement.

(1) This Act may be called the Competition Act, 2002.

(2) It extends to the whole of India except the State of Jammu and Kashmir.

(3) It shall come into force on such date as the Central Government may, by notification in the Official Gazette, appoint: Provided that different dates may be appointed for different provisions of this Act and any reference in any such provision to the commencement of this Act shall be construed as a reference to the coming into force of that provision.

2. Definitions.

In this Act, unless the context otherwise requires, —

(a) "Acquisition" means, directly or indirectly, acquiring or agreeing to acquire —

(i) shares, voting rights or assets of any enterprise; or

(ii) control over management or control over assets of any enterprise;

(b) "Agreement" includes any arrangement or understanding or action in concert, —

(i) whether or not, such arrangement, understanding or action is formal or in writing; or

(ii) whether or not such arrangement, understanding or action is intended to be enforceable by legal proceedings;

(c) "Cartel" includes an association of producers, sellers, distributors, traders or service providers who, by agreement amongst themselves, limit, control or attempt to control the production, distribution, sale or price of, or, trade in goods or provision of services;

(d) "Chairperson" means the Chairperson of the Commission appointed under sub-section (1) of section 8;

(e) "Commission" means the Competition Commission of India established under sub-section (1) of section 7;

(f) "Consumer" means any person who —

(i) buys any goods for a consideration which has been paid or promised or partly paid and partly promised, or under any system of deferred payment and includes any user of such goods other than the person who buys such goods for consideration paid or promised or partly paid or partly promised, or under any system of deferred payment when such use is made with the approval of such person, whether such purchase of goods is for resale or for any commercial purpose or for personal use;

(ii) hires or avails of any services for a consideration which has been paid or promised or partly paid and partly promised, or under any system of deferred payment and includes any beneficiary of such services other than the person who hires or avails of the services for consideration paid or promised, or partly paid and partly promised, or under any system of deferred payment, when such services are availed of with the approval of the first-mentioned person whether such hiring or availing of services is for any commercial purpose or for personal use;

(g) "Director General" means the Director General appointed under sub-section (1) of Section 16 and includes any Additional, Joint, Deputy or Assistant Directors General appointed under that section;

(h) "Enterprise" means a person or a department of the Government, who or which is, or has been, engaged in any activity, relating to the production, storage, supply, distribution, acquisition or control of articles or goods, or the provision of services of any kind, or in investment, or in the business of acquiring, holding, underwriting or dealing with shares, debentures or other securities of any other body corporate, either directly or through one or more of its units or is located at the same place where the enterprise is located or at a different place or at different places, but does not include any activity of the Government relatable to the sovereign functions of the Government divisions or subsidiaries, whether such unit or division or subsidiary including all activities carried on by the departments of the Central Government dealing with atomic energy, currency, defense and space.

Explanation

For the purposes of this clause,

(a) "activity" includes profession or occupation;

(b) "article" includes a new article and "service" includes a new service;

(c) "unit" or "division", in relation to an enterprise, includes —

(i) a plant or factory established for the production, storage, supply, distribution, acquisition or control of any article or goods;

(ii) any branch or office established for the provision of any service;

(i) "goods" means goods as defined in the Sale of Goods Act, 1930 (8.of 1930) and includes-

(A) products manufactured, processed or mined;

(B) debentures, stocks and shares after allotment;

(C) in relation to goods supplied, distributed or controlled in India, goods imported into India;

(j) "Member" means a Member of the Commission appointed under sub-section (1) of Section 8 and includes the Chairperson;

(k) "Notification" means a notification published in the Official Gazette

(l) "person" includes —

(i) an individual;

(ii) a Hindu undivided family;

(iii) a company;

(iv) a firm;

(v) an association of persons or a body of individuals, whether incorporated or not, in India or outside India;

(vi) any corporation established by or under any Central, State or Provincial Act or a Government company as defined in section 617 of the Companies Act, 1956 (1 of 1956)

(vii) any body corporate incorporated by or under the laws of a country outside India;

(viii) a co-operative society registered under any law relating to cooperative societies;

(ix) a local authority;

(x) every official jurisdical person, not falling within any of the preceding sub-clauses;

(m) "Practice" includes any practice relating to the carrying on of any trade by a person or an enterprise;

(n) "Prescribed" means prescribed by rules made under this Act;

(o) "Price", in relation to the sale of any goods or to the performance of any services, includes every valuable consideration, whether direct or indirect, or deferred, and includes any consideration which in effect relates to the sale of any goods or to the performance of any services although ostensibly relating to any other matter or thing;

(p) "Public financial institution" means a public financial institution specified under section 4A of the Companies Act, 1956 (1 of 1956) and includes a State Financial, Industrial or Investment

Corporation;

(q) "Regulations" means the regulations made by the Commission under section 64;

(r) "Relevant market" means the market which may be determined by the Commission with reference to the relevant product market or the relevant geographic market or with reference to both the markets;

(s) "Relevant geographic market" means a market comprising the area in which the conditions of competition for supply of goods or provision of services or demand of goods or services are distinctly homogenous and can be distinguished from the conditions prevailing in the neighboring areas;

(t) "Relevant product market" means a market comprising all those products or services which are regarded as interchangeable or substitutable by the consumer, by reason of characteristics of the products or services, their prices and intended use;

(u) "Service" means service of any description which is made available to potential users and includes the provision of services in connection with business of any industrial or commercial matters such as banking, communication, education, financing, insurance, chit funds, real estate, transport, storage, material treatment, processing, supply of electrical or other energy, boarding, lodging, entertainment, amusement, construction, repair, conveying of news or information and advertising;

(v) "Shares" means shares in the share capital of a company carrying voting rights and includes —

(i) any security which entitles the holder to receive shares with voting rights;

(ii) stock except where a distinction between stock and share is expressed or implied;

(w) "Statutory authority" means any authority, board, corporation, council, institute, university or any other body corporate, established by or under any Central, State or Provincial Act for the purposes of regulating production or supply of goods or provision of any services or markets therefor or any matter connected therewith or incidental thereto;

(x) "Trade" means any trade, business, industry, profession or occupation relating to the production, supply, distribution, storage or control of goods and includes the provision of any services;

(y) "Turnover" includes value of sale of goods or services;

(z) Words and expressions used but not defined in this Act and defined in the Companies Act, 1956 (1 of 1956) shall have the same meanings respectively assigned to them in that Act.

Prohibition of Agreements

Anti-competitive Agreements

(1) No enterprise or association of enterprises or person or association of persons shall enter into any agreement in respect of production, supply, distribution, storage, acquisition or control of goods or provision of services, which causes or is likely to cause an appreciable adverse effect on competition within India.

(2) Any agreement entered into in contravention of the provisions contained in sub-section (1) shall be void.

(3) Any agreement entered into between enterprises or associations of enterprises or persons or associations of persons or between any person and enterprise or practice carried on, or decision taken by, any association of enterprises or association of per sons, including cartels, engaged in identical or similar trade of goods or provision of services, which —

(a) directly or indirectly determines purchase or sale prices;

(b) limits or controls production, supply, markets, technical development, investment or provision of services;

(c) shares the market or source of production or provision of services by way of allocation of geographical area of market, or type of goods or services, or number of customers in the market or any other similar way;

(d) directly or indirectly results in bid rigging or collusive bidding, shall be presumed to have an appreciable adverse effect on competition:

Provided that nothing contained in this sub-section shall apply to any agreement entered into by way of joint ventures if such agreement increases efficiency in production, supply, distribution, storage, acquisition or control of goods or provision of services.

Explanation. For the purposes of this sub-section, "bid rigging" means any agreement, between enterprises or persons referred to in sub-section (3) engaged in identical or similar production or trading of goods or provision of services, which has the effect of eliminating or reducing competition for bids or adversely affecting or manipulating the process for bidding.

(4) Any agreement amongst enterprises or persons at different stages or levels of the production chain in different markets, in respect of production, supply, distribution, storage, sale or price of, or trade in goods or provision of services, including —

(a) tie-in arrangement;

(b) exclusive supply agreement;

(c) exclusive distribution agreement;

(d) refusal to deal;

(e) resale price maintenance, shall be an agreement in contravention of sub-section (1) if such agreement causes or is likely to cause an appreciable adverse effect on competition in India.

Explanation. For the purposes of this sub-section, —

(a) "tie-in arrangement" includes any agreement requiring a purchaser of goods, as a condition of such purchase, to purchase some other goods;

(b) "exclusive supply agreement" includes any agreement restricting in any manner the purchaser in the course of his trade from acquiring or otherwise dealing in any goods other than those of the seller or any other person;

(c) "exclusive distribution agreement" includes any agreement to limit, restrict or withhold the output or supply of any goods or allocate any area or market for the disposal or sale of the goods;

(d) "refusal to deal" includes any agreement which restricts, or is likely to restrict, by any method the persons or classes of persons to whom goods are sold or from whom goods are bought;

(e) "resale price maintenance" includes any agreement to sell goods on condition that the prices to be charged on the resale by the purchaser shall be the prices stipulated by the seller unless it is clearly stated that prices lower than those prices may be charged.

(5) Nothing contained in this section shall restrict —

(i) the right of any person to restrain any infringement of, or to impose reasonable conditions, as may be necessary for protecting any of his rights which have been or may be conferred upon him under —

(a) the Copyright Act, 1957 (14 of 1957)

(b) the Patents Act, 1970 (39 of 1970)

(c) the Trade and Merchandise Marks Act, 1958 (43 of 1958) or the Trademarks Act, 1999 (47 of 1999)

(d) the Geographical Indications of Goods (Registration and Protection) Act, 1999 (48 of 1999)

(e) the Designs Act, 2000 (16 of 2000)

(f) the Semi-conductor Integrated Circuits Layout Design Act, 2000 (37.of 2000)

(ii) the right of any person to export goods from India to the extent to which the agreement relates exclusively to the production, supply, distribution or control of goods or provision of services for such export. **Prohibition of abuse of dominant position.**

4. Abuse of dominant position.

(1) No enterprise shall abuse its dominant position.

(2) There shall be an abuse of dominant position under sub-section

(1), if an enterprise —

(a) directly or indirectly, imposes unfair or discriminatory —

(i) condition in purchase or sale of goods or service; or

(ii) price in purchase or sale (including predatory price) of goods or service.

Explanation. For the purposes of this clause, the unfair or discriminatory condition in purchase or sale of goods or service referred to in sub-clause (i) and unfair or discriminatory price in purchase or sale of goods (including predatory price) or service referred to in sub-clause (ii) shall not include such discriminatory condition or price which may be adopted to meet the competition; or

(b) limits or restricts —

(i) production of goods or provision of services or market therefor; or

(ii) technical or scientific development relating to goods or services to the prejudice of consumers; or

(c) indulges in practice or practices resulting in denial of market access; or

(d) makes conclusion of contracts subject to acceptance by other parties of supplementary obligations which, by their nature or according to commercial usage, have no connection with the subject of such contracts; or

(e) uses its dominant position in one relevant market to enter into, or protect, other relevant market.

Explanation. For the purposes of this section, the expression —

(a) "dominant position" means a position of strength, enjoyed by an enterprise, in the relevant market, in India, which enables it to —

(i) operate independently of competitive forces prevailing in the relevant market; or

(ii) affect its competitors or consumers or the relevant market in its favor;

(b) "predatory price" means the sale of goods or provision of services, at a price which is below the cost, as may be determined by regulations, of production of the goods or provision of services, with a view to reduce competition or eliminate the competitors.

5. Regulation of Combinations

Combination —

The acquisition of one or more enterprises by one or more persons or merger or amalgamation of enterprises shall be a combination of such enterprises and persons or enterprises, if —

(a) any acquisition where —

(i) the parties to the acquisition, being the acquirer and the enterprise, whose control, shares, voting rights or assets have been acquired or are being acquired jointly have —

(A) either, in India, the assets of the value of more than rupees one thousand crores or turnover more than rupees three thousand crores; or

(B) in India or outside India, in aggregate, the assets of the value of more than five hundred million US dollars or turnover more than fifteen hundred million US dollars; or

(ii) the group, to which the enterprise whose control, shares, assets or voting rights have been acquired or are being acquired, would belong after the acquisition, jointly have or would jointly have —

(A) either in India, the assets of the value of more than rupees four thousand crores or turnover more than rupees twelve thousand crores; or

(B) in India or outside India, in aggregate, the assets of the value of more than two billion US dollars or turnover more than six billion US dollars; or

(b) acquiring of control by a person over an enterprise when such person has already directly or indirectly control over another enterprise engaged in production, distribution or trading of a similar or identical or substitutable goods or provision of a similar or identical or substitutable service, if —

(i) the enterprise over which control has been acquired along with the enterprise over which the acquirer already has direct or indirect control jointly have —

(A) either in India, the assets of the value of more than rupees one thousand crores or turnover more than rupees three thousand crores; or

(B) in India or outside India, in aggregate, the assets of the value of more than five hundred million US dollars or turnover more than fifteen hundred million US dollars; or

(ii) the group, to which enterprise whose control has been acquired, or is being acquired, would belong after the acquisition, jointly have or would jointly have —

(A) either in India, the assets of the value of more than rupees four thousand crores or turnover more than rupees twelve thousand crores; or

(B) in India or outside India, in aggregate, the assets of the value of more than two billion US dollars or turnover more than six billion

US dollars; or (c) any merger or amalgamation in which —

(i) the enterprise remaining after merger or the enterprise created as a result of the amalgamation, as the case may be, have —

(A) either in India, the assets of the value of more than rupees one thousand crores or turnover more than rupees three thousand crores; or

(B) in India or outside India, in aggregate, the assets of the value of more than five hundred million US dollars or turnover more than fifteen hundred million US dollars; or

(ii) the group, to which the enterprise remaining after the merger or the enterprise created as a result of the amalgamation, would belong after the merger or the amalgamation, as the case may be, have or would have —

(A) either in India, the assets of the value of more than rupees four thousand crores or turnover more than rupees twelve thousand crores; or

(B) in India or outside India, the assets of the value of more than two billion US dollars or turnover more than six billion US dollars.

Explanation. For the purposes of this section —

(a) "control" includes controlling the affairs or management by —

(i) one or more enterprises, either jointly or singly, over another enterprise or group;

(ii) one or more groups, either jointly or singly, over another group or enterprise;

(b) "group" means two or more enterprises which, directly or indirectly, are in a position to —

(i) exercise twenty-six per cent. Or more of the voting rights in the other enterprise; or

(ii) appoint more than fifty per cent. of the members of the board of directors in the other enterprise; or

(iii) control the management or affairs of the other enterprise;

(c) the value of assets shall be determined by taking the book value of the assets as shown, in the audited books of account of the enterprise, in the financial year immediately preceding the financial year in which the date of proposed merger falls, as reduced by any depreciation, and the value of assets shall include the brand value, value of goodwill, or value of copyright, patent, permitted use, collective mark, registered proprietor, registered trade mark, registered user, homogenous geographical in location, geographical indications, design or layout-design or similar other commercial rights, if any, referred to in sub-section (5) of section 3.6. Regulation of combinations.

6. Regulation of combinations —

(1) No person or enterprise shall enter into a combination which causes or is likely to cause an appreciable adverse effect on competition within the relevant market in India and such a combination shall be void.

(2) Subject to the provisions contained in sub-section (1), any person or enterprise, who or which proposes to enter into a combination, may, at his or its option, give notice to the Commission, in the form as may be specified, and the fee which may be determined, by regulations, disclosing the details of the proposed combination, within seven days of —

(a) approval of the proposal relating to merger or amalgamation, referred to in clause (c) of section 5, by the board of directors of the enterprises concerned with such merger or amalgamation, as the case may be;

(b) execution of any agreement or other document for acquisition referred to in clause (a) of section 5 or acquiring of control referred to in clause (b) of that section.

(3) The Commission shall, after receipt of notice under sub-section

(4) Deal with such notice in accordance with the provisions contained in sections 29, 30 and 31. (4) The provisions of this section shall not apply to share subscription or financing facility or any acquisition, by a public financial institution, foreign institutional investor, bank or venture capital fund, pursuant to any covenant of a loan agreement or investment agreement.

(5) The public financial institution, foreign institutional investor, bank or venture capital fund, referred to in sub-section (4), shall, within seven days from the date of the acquisition, file, in the form as may be specified by regulations, with the commission the details of the acquisition including the details of control, the circumstances for exercise of such control and the consequences of default arising out of such loan agreement or investment agreement, as the case may be.

Explanation. For the purposes of this section, the expression —

(a) "foreign institutional investor" has the same meaning as assigned to it in clause (a) of the Explanation to section 115AD of the

Income-tax Act, 1961 (43 of 1961)

(b) "venture capital fund" has the same meaning as assigned to it in clause (b) of the Explanation to clause (23FB) of section 10 of the

Income-tax Act, 1961 (43 of 1961).

7. Establishment of Commission —

(1) With effect from such date as the Central Government may, by notification, appoint, there shall be established, for the purposes of this Act, a Commission to be called the "Competition Commission of India".

(2) The Commission shall be a body corporate by the name aforesaid having perpetual succession and a common seal with power, subject to the provisions of this Act, to acquire, hold and dispose of property, both movable and immovable, and to contract and hall, by the said name, sue or be sued.

(3) The head office of the Commission shall be at such place as the

Central Government may decide from time to time.

(4) The Commission may establish offices at other places in India.

8. Composition of Commission —

(1) The Commission shall consist of a Chairperson and not less than two and not more than ten other Members to be appointed by the Central Government : Provided that the Central Government shall appoint the Chairperson and a Member during the first year of the establishment of the Commission.

(2) The Chairperson and every other Member shall be a person of ability, integrity and standing and who, has been, or is qualified to be, a judge of a High Court, or, has special knowledge of, and professional experience of not less than fifteen years in international trade, economics, business, commerce, law, finance, accountancy, management, industry, public affairs, administration or in any other matter which, in the opinion of the Central Government, may be useful to the Commission.

(3) The Chairperson and other Members shall be whole-time Members.

9. Selection of Chairperson and other Members. The Chairperson and other Members shall be selected in the manner as may be prescribed.

10. Term of office of Chairperson and other Members.

(1) The Chairperson and every other Member shall hold office as such for a term of five years from the date on which he enters upon his office and shall be eligible for re-appointment: Provided that no Chairperson or other Member shall hold office as such after he has attained —

(a) in the case of the Chairperson, the age of sixty-seven years;

(b) in the case of any other Member, the age of sixty-five years.

(2) A vacancy caused by the resignation or removal of the Chairperson or any other Member under section 11 or by death or otherwise shall be filled by fresh appointment in accordance with the provisions of sections 8 and 9. (3) The Chairperson and every other Member shall, before entering upon his office, make and subscribe to an oath of office and of secrecy in such form, manner and before such authority, as may be prescribed.

(3) In the event of the occurrence of a vacancy in the office of the Chairperson by reason of his death, resignation or otherwise, the senior-most Member shall act as the Chairperson, until the

date on which a new Chairperson, appointed in accordance with the provisions of this Act to fill such vacancy, enters upon his office.

(4) When the Chairperson is unable to discharge his functions owing to absence, illness or any other cause, the senior-most Member shall discharge the functions of the Chairperson until the date on which the Chairperson resumes the charge of his function.

11. Resignation, removal and suspension of Chairperson and other Members —

(1) The Chairperson or any other Member may, by notice in writing under his hand addressed to the Central Government, resign his office: Provided that the Chairperson or a Member shall, unless he is permitted by the Central Government to relinquish his office sooner, continue to hold office until the expiry of three months from the date of receipt of such notice or until a person duly appointend as his successor enters upon his office or until the expiry of his term of office, whichever is the earliest.

(2) Notwithstanding anything contained in sub-section (1), the Central Government may, by order, remove the Chairperson or any other Member from his office if such Chairperson or Member, as the case may be —

(a) is, or at any time has been, adjudged as an insolvent; or

(b) has engaged at any time, during his term of office, in any paid employment; or

(c) has been convicted of an offence which, in the opinion of the Central Government, involves moral turpitude; or

(d) has acquired such financial or other interest as is likely to affect prejudicially his functions as a Member; or

(e) has so abused his position as to render his continuance in office prejudicial to the public interest; or

(f) has become physically or mentally incapable of acting as a Member.

(3) Notwithstanding anything contained in sub-section (2), no Member shall be removed from his office on the ground specified in clause (d) or clause (e) of that sub-section unless the Supreme Court, on a reference being made to it in this behalf by the central Government, has, on an inquiry, held by it in accordance with such procedure as may be prescribed in this behalf by the Supreme Court, reported that the Member, ought on such ground or grounds to be removed.

12. Restriction on employment of Chairperson and other Members in certain cases —

The Chairperson and other Members shall not, for a period of one year from the date on which they cease to hold office, accept any employment in, or connected with the management or administration of, any enterprise which has been a party to a proceeding before the Commission under this Act: Provided that nothing contained in this section shall apply to any employment under the Central Government or a State Government or local authority or in any statutory authority or any corporation established by or under any Central, State or Provincial act or a Government company as defined in section 617 of the Companies Act, 1956 (1 of 1956).

13. Financial and administrative powers of Member Administration —

The Central Government shall designate any Member as Member Administration who shall exercise such financial and administrative powers as may be vested in him under the rules made by the

Central Government: Provided that the Member Administration shall have authority to delegate such of his financial and administrative powers as he may think fit to any other officer of the Commission subject to the condition that such officer shall, while exercising such delegated powers continue to act under the direction, superintendence and control of the Member Administration.

14. Salary and allowances and other terms and conditions of service of Chairperson and other Members —

(1) The salary, and the other terms and conditions of service, of the Chairperson and other Members, including travelling expenses, house rent allowance and conveyance facilities, sumptuary allowance and medical facilities shall be such as may be prescribed.

(2) The salary, allowances and other terms and conditions of service of the Chairperson or a Member shall not be varied to his disadvantage after appointment.

15. Vacancy, etc., not to invalidate proceedings of Commission —

No act or proceeding of the Commission shall be invalid merely by reason of—

(a) any vacancy in, or any defect in the constitution of, the Commission; or

(b) any defect in the appointment of a person acting as a Chairperson or as a Member; or

(c) any irregularity in the procedure of the Commission not affecting the merits of the case.

16. Appointment of Director-General, etc. —

(1) The Central Government may, by notification, appoint a Director General and as many Additional, Joint, Deputy or Assistant Directors General or such other advisers, consultants or officers, as it may think fit, for the purposes of assisting the Commission in conducting inquiry into contravention of any of the provisions of this Act and for the conduct of cases before the Commission and for performing such other functions as are, or may be, provided by or under this Act.

(2) Every Additional, Joint, Deputy and Assistant Directors General or such other advisers, consultants and officers, shall exercise his powers, and discharge his functions, subject to the general control, supervision and direction of the Director General.

(3) The salary, allowances and other terms and conditions of service of the Director General and Additional, Joint, Deputy and Assistant Directors General or such other advisers, consultants or officers, shall be such as may be prescribed.

(4) The Director General and Additional, Joint, Deputy and Assistant Directors General or such other advisers, consultants or officers shall be appointed from amongst persons of integrity and outstanding ability and who have experience in investigation, and knowledge of accountancy, management, business, public administration, international trade, law or economics and such other qualifications as may be prescribed.

17. Registrar and officers and other employees of Commission —

(1) The Commission may appoint a Registrar and such officers and other employees as it considers necessary for the efficient performance of its functions under this Act.

(2) The salaries and allowances payable to and other terms and conditions of service of the Registrar and officers and other employees of the Commission and the number of such officers and other employees shall be such as may be prescribed.

18. Duties of Commission —

Subject to the provisions of this Act, it shall be the duty of the Commission to eliminate practices having adverse effect on competition, promote and sustain competition, protect the interests of consumers and ensure freedom of trade carried on by other participants, in markets in India: Provided that the Commission may, for the purpose of discharging its duties or performing its functions under this Act, enter into any memorandum or arrangement with the prior approval of the Central Government, with any agency of any foreign country.

19. Inquiry into certain agreements and dominant position of enterprise —

(1) The Commission may inquire into any alleged contravention of the provisions contained in sub-section (1) of section 3 or sub-section (1) of section 4 either on its own motion or on —

(a) receipt of a complaint, accompanied by such fee as may be determined by regulations, from any person, consumer or their association or trade association; or

(b) a reference made to it by the Central Government or a State Government or a statutory authority.

(2) Without prejudice to the provisions contained in sub-section (1), the powers and functions of the Commission shall include the powers and functions specified in sub-sections (3) to (7).

(3) The Commission shall, while determining whether an agreement has an appreciable adverse effect on competition under section 3, have due regard to all or any of the following factors, namely:

(a) creation of barriers to new entrants in the market;

(b) driving existing competitors out of the market;

(c) foreclosure of competition by hindering entry into the market;

(d) accrual of benefits to consumers;

(e) improvements in production or distribution of goods or provision of services;

(f) promotion of technical, scientific and economic development by means of production or distribution of goods or provision of services.

(4) The Commission shall, while inquiring whether an enterprise enjoys a dominant position or not under section 4, have due regard to all or any of the following factors, namely:-

(a) market share of the enterprise;

(b) size and resources of the enterprise;

(c) size and importance of the competitors;

(d) economic power of the enterprise including commercial advantages over competitors;

(e) vertical integration of the enterprises or sale or service network of such enterprises;

(f) dependence of consumers on the enterprise;

(g) monopoly or dominant position whether acquired as a result of any statute or by virtue of being a Government company or a public sector undertaking or otherwise;

(h) entry barriers including barriers such as regulatory barriers, financial risk, high capital cost of entry, marketing entry barriers, technical entry barriers, economies of scale, high cost of substitutable goods or service for consumers;

(i) countervailing buying power;

(j) market structure and size of market;

(k) social obligations and social costs;

(l) relative advantage, by way of the contribution to the economic development, by the enterprise enjoying a dominant position having or likely to have an appreciable adverse effect on competition;

(m) any other factor which the Commission may consider relevant for the inquiry.

(5) For determining whether a market constitutes a "relevant market" for the purposes of this Act, the Commission shall have due regard to the "relevant geographic market" and "relevant product market".

(6) The Commission shall, while determining the "relevant geographic market", have due regard to all or any of the following factors, namely –

(a) regulatory trade barriers;

(b) local specification requirements;

(c) national procurement policies;

(d) adequate distribution facilities;

(e) transport costs;

(f) language;

(g) consumer preferences;

(h) need for secure or regular supplies or rapid after-sales services.

(7) The Commission shall, while determining the "relevant product market", have due regard to all or any of the following factors, namely –

(a) physical characteristics or end-use of goods;

(b) price of goods or service;

(c) consumer preferences;

(d) exclusion of in-house production;

(e) existence of specialized producers;

(f) classification of industrial products.

20. Inquiry into combination by Commission —

(1) The Commission may, upon its own knowledge or information relating to acquisition referred to in clause (a) of section 5 or acquiring of control referred to in clause (b) of section 5 or merger or amalgamatei on referred to in clause (c) of that section, inquire into whether such a combination has caused or is likely to cause an appreciable adverse effect on competition in India: Provided that the Commission shall not initiate any inquiry under this sub-section after the expiry of one year from the date on which such combination has taken effect.

(2) The Commission shall, on receipt of a notice under sub-section (2) of section 6 or upon receipt of a reference under sub-section (1) of section 21, inquire whether a combination referred to in that notice or reference has caused or is likely to cause an appreciable adverse effect on competition in India.

(3) Notwithstanding anything contained in section 5, the Central Government shall, on the expiry of a period of two years from the date of commencement of this Act and thereafter every two years, in consultation with the Commission, by notification, enhance or reduce, on the basis of the wholesale price index or fluctuations in exchange rate of rupee or foreign currencies, the value of assets or the value of turnover, for the purposes of that section.

(4) For the purposes of determining whether a combination would have the effect of or is likely to have an appreciable adverse effect on competition in the relevant market, the Commission shall have due regard to all or any of the following factors, namely –

(a) actual and potential level of competition through imports in the market;

(b) extent of barriers to entry into the market;

(c) level of combination in the market;

(d) degree of countervailing power in the market;

(e) likelihood that the combination would result in the parties to the combination being able to significantly and sustainably increase prices or profit margins;

(f) extent of effective competition likely to sustain in a market;

(g) extent to which substitutes are available or are likely to be available in the market;

(h) market share, in the relevant market, of the persons or enterprise in a combination, individually and as a combination;

(i) likelihood that the combination would result in the removal of a vigorous and effective competitor or competitors in the market;

(j) nature and extent of vertical integration in the market;

(k) possibility of a failing business;

(l) nature and extent of innovation;

(m) relative advantage, by way of the contribution to the economic development, by any combination having or likely to have appreciable adverse effect on competition;

(n) whether the benefits of the combination outweigh the adverse impact of the combination, if any.

21. Reference by statutory authority —

(1) Where in the course of a proceeding before any statutory authority an issue is raised by any party that any decision which such statutory authority has taken or proposes to take, is or would be, contrary to any of the provisions of this Act, then such statutory authority may make a reference in respect of such issue to the Commission.

(2) On receipt of a reference under sub-section (1), the Commission shall, after hearing the parties to the proceedings, give its opinion to such statutory authority which shall thereafter pass such order on the issues referred to in that sub-section asit deems fit: Provided that the Commission shall give its opinion under this section within sixty days of receipt of such reference.

22. Benches of Commission —

(1) The jurisdiction, powers and authority of the Commission may be exercised by Benches thereof.

(2) The Benches shall be constituted by the Chairperson and each Bench shall consist of not less than two Members.

(3) Every Bench shall consist of at least one Judicial Member.

Explanation — For the purposes of this sub-section, "Judicial Member" means a Member who is, or has been, or is qualified to be, a Judge of a High Court.

(4) The Bench over which the Chairperson presides shall be the Principal Bench and the other Benches shall be known as the Additional Benches.

(5) There shall be constituted by the Chairperson one or more Benches to be called the Mergers Bench or Mergers Benches, as the case may be, exclusively to deal with matters referred to in sections 5 and 6.

(6) The places at which the Principal Bench, other Additional Bench or Mergers Bench shall ordinarily suit shall be such as the Central Government may, by notification, specify.

23. Distribution of business of Commission amongst Benches —

(1) Where any Benches are constituted, the Chairperson may, from time to time, by order, make provisions as to the distribution of the business of the Commission amongst the Benches and specify the matters, which may be dealt with by each Bench.

(2) If any question arises as to whether any matter falls within the purview of the business allocated to a Bench, the decision of the Chairperson thereon shall be final.

(3) The Chairperson may-

(i) transfer a Member from one Bench to another Bench; or

(ii) authorize the Members of one Bench to discharge also the functions of the Members of other Bench: Provided that the Chairperson shall transfer, with the prior approval of the Central Government, a Member from one Bench situated in one city to another Bench situated in another city.

(4) The Chairperson may, for the purpose of securing that any case or matter which, having regard to the nature of the questions involved, requires or is required in his opinion or under the rules made by the Central Government in this behalf, to be decided by a Bench composed of more than two Members, issue such general or special orders as he may deem fit.

24. Procedure for deciding a case where Members of a Bench differ in opinion.

If the Members of a Bench differ in opinion on any point, they shall state the point or points on which they differ, and make a reference to the Chairperson who shall either hear the point or points himself or refer the case for hearing on such point or points by one or more of the other Members and such point or points shall be decided according to the opinion of the majority of the Members who have heard the case, including those who first heard it.

25. Jurisdiction of Bench —

An inquiry shall be initiated or a complaint be instituted or a reference be made under this Act before a Bench within the local limits of whose jurisdiction —

(a) the respondent, or each of the respondents, where there are more than one, at the time of the initiation of inquiry or institution of the complaint or making of reference, as the case may be, actually and voluntarily resides, or carries on business, or personally works for gain; or

(b) any of the respondents, where there are more than one, at the time of the initiation of the inquiry or institution of complaint or making of reference, as the case may be, actually and voluntarily resides or carries on business or personally works for gain provided that in such case either the leave of the Bench is given, or the respondents who do not reside, or carry on business, or personally work for gain, as aforesaid, acquiesce in such institution; or

(c) the cause of action, wholly or in part, arises.

Explanation – A respondent, being a person referred to in sub-clause (iii) or sub-clause (vi) or sub-clause (vii) or sub-clause (viii) of clause (l) of section 2, shall be deemed to carry on business at its sole or principal place of business in India or at its registered office in India or where it has also a subordinate office at such place.

26. Procedure for inquiry on complaints under section 19.

(1) On receipt of a complaint or a reference from the Central Government or a State Government or a statutory authority or on its own knowledge or there exists a prima facie case, it shall direct the Director General to cause an investigation to be made into the matter. information, under section 19, if the Commissions of the opinion that

(2) The Director General shall, on receipt of direction under sub-section (1), submit a report on his findings within such period as may be specified by the Commission.

(3) Where on receipt of a complaint under clause (a) of sub-section (1) of section 19, the Commission is of the opinion that there exists no prima facie case, it shall dismiss the complaint and may pass such orders as it deems fit, including imposition of costs, if necessary.

(4) The Commission shall forward a copy of the report referred to in sub-section (2) to the parties concerned or to the Central Government or the State Government or the statutory authority, as the case may be.

(5) If the report of the Director General relates on a complaint and such report recommends that there is no contravention of any of the provisions of this Act, the complainant shall be given an opportunity to rebut the findings of the Director General.

(6) If, after hearing the complainant, the Commission agrees with the recommendation of the Director General, it shall dismiss the complaint.

(7) If, after hearing the complainant, the Commission is of the opinion that further inquiry is called for, it shall direct the complainant to proceed with the complaint.

(8) If the report of the Director General relates on a reference made under sub-section (1) and such report recommends that there is no contravention of the provisions of this Act, the Commission shall invite comments of the Central Government or the State Government or the statutory authority, as the case may be, on such report and on receipt of such comments, the Commission shall return the reference if there is no prima facie case or proceed with the reference as a complaint if there is a prima facie case.

(9) If the report of the Director General referred to in sub-section (2) recommends that there is contravention of any of the provisions of this Act, and the Commission is of the opinion that further inquiry is called for, it shall inquire into such contravention in accordance with the provisions of this Act.

27. Orders by Commission after inquiry into agreements or abuse of dominant position —

Where after inquiry the Commission finds that any agreement referred to in section 3 or action of an enterprise in a dominant position, is in contravention of section or section 4, as the case may be, it may pass all or any of the following orders, namely:

(a) direct any enterprise or association of enterprises or person or association of persons, as the case may be, involved in such agreement, or abuse of dominant position, to discontinue and not to re-enter such agreement or discontinue such abuse of determinant position, as the case may be;

(b) impose such penalty, as it may deem fit which shall be not more than ten per cent. of the average of the turnover for the last three preceding financial years, upon each of such person or enterprises which are parties to such agreements or abuse: Provided that in case any agreement referred to in section 3 has been entered into by any cartel, the Commission shall impose upon each producer, seller, distributor, trader or service provider included in that cartel, a penalty equivalent to three times of the amount of profits made out of such agreement by the cartel or ten per cent. of the average of the turnover of the cartel for the last preceding three financial years, whichever is higher;

(c) award compensation to parties in accordance with the provisions contained in section 34;

(d) direct that the agreements shall stand modified to the extent and in the manner as may be specified in the order by the Commission;

(e) direct the enterprises concerned to abide by such other orders as the Commission may pass and comply with the directions, including payment of costs, if any;

(f) recommend to the Central Government for the division of an enterprise enjoying dominant position;

(g) pass such other order as it may deem fit.

28. Division of enterprise enjoying dominant position —

(1) The Central Government, on recommendation under clause (f) of Section 27, may, notwithstanding anything contained in any other law for the time being in force, by order in writing, direct division of an enterprise enjoying dominant position to ensure that such enterprise does not abuse its dominant position.

(2) In particular, and without prejudice to the generality of the foregoing powers, the order referred to in sub-section (1) may provide for all or any of the following matters, namely:

  (a) the transfer or vesting of property, rights, liabilities or obligations;

  (b) the adjustment of contracts either by discharge or reduction of any liability or obligation or otherwise;

  (c) the creation, allotment, surrender or cancellation of any shares, stocks or securities;

  (d) the payment of compensation to any person who suffered any loss due to dominant position of such enterprise;

  (e) the formation or winding up of an enterprise or the amendment of the memorandum of association or articles of association or any other instruments regulating the business of any enterprise;

(f) the extent to which, and the circumstances in which, provisions of the order affecting an enterprise may be altered by the enterprise and the registration thereof;

(g) Any other matter which may be necessary to give effect to the division of the enterprise.

(3) Notwithstanding anything contained in any other law for the time being in force or in any contract or in any memorandum or articles of association, an officer of a company who ceases to hold office as such in consequence of the division of an enterprise shall not be entitled to claim any compensation for such cesser.

29. Procedure for investigation of combinations —

(1) Where the Commission is of the opinion that a combination is likely to cause, or has caused an appreciable adverse effect on competition within the relevant market in India, it shall issue a notice to show cause to the parties to combination calling upon them to respond within thirty days of the receipt of the notice, as to why investigation in respect of such combination should not be conducted.

(2) The Commission, if it is *prima facie* of the opinion that the combination has, or is likely to have, an appreciable adverse effect on competition, it shall, within seven working days from the date of receipt of the response of the parties to the combination, direct the parties to the said combination to publish details of the combination within ten working days of such direction, in such manner, as it thinks appropriate, for bringing the combination to the knowledge or information of the public and persons affected or likely to be affected by such combination.

(3) The Commission may invite any person or member of the public, affected or likely to be affected by the said combination, to file his written objections, if any, before the Commission within fifteen working days from the date on which the details of the combination were published under sub-section (2).

(4) The Commission may, within fifteen working days from the expiry of the period specified in sub-section (3), call for such additional or other information as it may deem fit from the parties to the said combination.

(5) The additional or other information called for by the Commission shall be furnished by the parties referred to in sub-section (4) within fifteen days from the expiry of the period specified in sub-section (4).

(6) After receipt of all information and within a period of forty-five working days from the expiry of the period specified in sub-section (5) the Commission shall proceed to deal with the case in accordance with the provisions contained in section 31.

30. Inquiry into disclosures under sub-section (2) of Section (6) —

(6) Where any person or enterprise has given a notice under sub-section (2) of section 6, the Commission shall inquire —

(a) whether the disclosure made in the notice is correct;

(b) whether the combination has, or is likely to have, an appreciable adverse effect on competition.

31. Orders of Commission on certain combinations —

(1) Where the Commission is of the opinion that any combination does not, or is not likely to, have an appreciable adverse effect on competition, it shall, by order, approve that combination including the combination in respect of which a notice has been given under sub-section (2) of Section 6.

(2) Where the Commission is of the opinion that the combination has, or is likely to have, an appreciable adverse effect on competition, it shall direct that the combination shall not take effect.

(3) Where the Commission is of the opinion that the combination has, or is likely to have, an appreciable adverse effect on competition but such adverse effect can be eliminated by suitable modification to such combination, it may propose appropriate modification to the combination, to the parties to such combination.

(4) The parties, who accept the modification proposed by the commission under sub-section (3), shall carry out such modification within the period specified by the Commission.

(5) If the parties to the combination, who have accepted the modification under sub-section (4), fail to carry out the modification within the period specified by the Commission, such combination shall be deemed to have an appreciable adverse effect on competition and the Commission shall deal with such combination in accordance with the provisions of this Act.

(6) If the parties to the combination do not accept the modification proposed by the Commission under sub-section (3), such parties may, within thirty working days of the modification proposed by the commission, submit amendment to the modification proposed by the Commission under that sub-section.

(7) If the Commission agrees with the amendment submitted by the parties under sub-section (6), it shall, by order, approve the combination.

(8) If the Commission does not accept the amendment submitted under sub-section (6), then, the parties shall be allowed a further period of thirty working days within which such parties shall accept the modification proposed by the Commission under sub-section (3).

(9) If the parties fail to accept the modification proposed by the commission within thirty working days referred to in sub-section (6) or within a further period of thirty working days referred to in sub-section (8), the combination shall be deemed to have an appreciable adverse effect on competition and be dealt with in accordance with the provisions of this Act.

(10) Where the Commission has directed under sub-section (2) that the combination shall not take effect or the combination is deemed to have an appreciable adverse effect on competition under sub-section (9), then, without prejudice to any penalty which may be imposed or any prosecution which may be initiated under this Act, the Commission may order that —

(a) the acquisition referred to in clause (a) of Section 5; or

(b) the acquiring of control referred to in clause (b) of Section 5;or

(c) the merger or amalgamation referred to in clause (c) of Section 5, shall not be given effect to: Provided that the Commission may, if it considers appropriate, frame a scheme to implement its order under this sub-section.

(11) If the Commission does not, on the expiry of a period of ninety working days from the date of publication referred to in sub-section (2) of section 29, pass an order or issue direction in accordance with the provisions of sub-section (1) or sub-sect on (2) or sub-section (7), the combination shall be deemed to have been approved by the Commission.

Explanation — For the purposes of determining the period of ninety working days specified in this sub-section, the period of thirty working days specified in sub-section (6) and a further period of thirty working days specified in sub-section (8) shall be excluded.

(12) Where any extension of time is sought by the parties to the combination, the period of ninety working days shall be reckoned after deducting the extended time granted at the request of the parties.

(13) Where the Commission has ordered a combination to be void, the acquisition or acquiring of control or merger or amalgamation referred to in Section 5, shall be dealt with by the authorities under any other law for the time being in force as if such acquisition or acquiring of control or merger or amalgamation had not taken place and the parties to the combination shall be dealt with accordingly.

(14) Nothing contained in this Chapter shall affect any proceeding initiated or which may be initiated under any other law for the time being in force.

32. Acts taking place outside India but having an effect on competition in India —

The Commission shall, notwithstanding that —

(a) an agreement referred to in section 3 has been entered into outside India; or

(b) any party to such agreement is outside India; or

(c) any enterprise abusing the dominant position is outside India; or

(d) a combination has taken place outside India; or

(e) any party to combination is outside India; or

(f) any other matter or practice or action arising out of such agreement or dominant position or combination is outside India, have power to inquire into such agreement or abuse of dominant position or combination if such agreement or dominant position or combination has, or is likely to have, an appreciable adverse effect on competition in the relevant market in India.

33. Power to grant interim relief —

(1) Where during an inquiry before the Commission, it is proved to the satisfaction of the Commission, by affidavit or otherwise, that an act in contravention of sub-section (1) of Section 3 or sub-section (1) of Section 4 or Section 6 has been committed and continues to be committed or that such act is about to be committed, the Commission may, by order, grant a temporary injunction restraining any party from carrying on such act until the conclusion of such inquiry or until further orders, without giving notice to the opposite party, where it deems it necessary.

(2) Where during the inquiry before the Commission it is proved to the satisfaction of the Commission by affidavit or otherwise that import of any goods is likely to contravene sub-section (1) of section 3 or sub-section (1) of Section 4 or Section 6, it may, by order, grant a temporary injunction restraining any party from importing such goods until the conclusion of

such inquiry or until further orders, without giving notice to the opposite party, where it deems it necessary and a copy of such order granting temporary injunction shall be sent to the concerned authorities.

(3) The provisions of rules 2A to 5 (both inclusive) of Order XXXIX of the First Schedule to the Code of Civil Procedure, 1908 (5 of 1908) shall, as far as may be, apply to a temporary injunction issued by the Commission under this Act, as they apply to temporary injunction issued by a civil court, and any reference in any such rule to a suit shall be construed as a reference to any inquiry before the Commission.

34. Power to award compensation —

(1) Without prejudice to any other provisions contained in this Act, any person may make an application to the Commission for an order for the recovery of compensation from any enterprise for any loss or damage shown to have been suffered, by such person as a result of any contravention of the provisions of Chapter II, having been committed by such enterprise.

(2) The Commission may, after an inquiry made into the allegations mentioned in the application made under sub-section (1), pass an order directing the enterprise to make payment to the applicant, of the amount determined by it as realizable from the enterprise as compensation for the loss or damage caused to the applicant as a result of any contravention of the provisions of Chapter II having been committed by such enterprise.

(3) Where any loss or damage referred to in sub-section (1) is caused to numerous persons having the same interest, one or more of such persons may, with the permission of the Commission, make an application under that sub-section for and on behalf of, or for the benefit of, the persons so interested, and thereupon, the provisions of rule 8 of Order 1 of the First Schedule to the Code of Civil Procedure, 1908 (5 of 1908), shall apply subject to the modification that every reference therein to a suit or excrete shall be construed as a reference to the application before the Commission and the order of the Commission thereon.

35. Appearance before Commission —

A complainant or defendant or the Director General may either appear in person or authorize one or more chartered accountants or company secretaries or cost accountants or legal practitioners or any of his or its officers to present his or its case before the Commission.

Explanation — For the purposes of this section —

(a) "chartered accountant" means a chartered accountant as defined in clause (b) of sub-section (1) of Section 2 of the Chartered Accountants Act, 1949 (38 of 1949) and who has obtained a certificate of practice under sub-section (1) of section 6 of that Act;

(b) "company secretary" means a company secretary as defined in clause of sub-section (1) of Section 2 of the Company Secretaries Act, 1980 (56 of 1980) and who has obtained a certificate of practice under sub-section (1) of Section 6 of that Act;

(c) "cost accountant" means a cost accountant as defined in clause (b) of sub-section (1) of Section 2 of the Cost and Works Accountants Act, 1959 (23 of 1959) and who has obtained a certificate of practice under sub-section (1) of Section 6 of that Act;

(d) "legal practitioner" means an advocate, vakil or an attorney of any High Court, and includes a leader in practice.

36. Power of Commission to regulate its own procedure —

(1) The Commission shall not be bound by the procedure laid down by the Code of Civil Procedure, 1908 (5 of 1908), but shall be guided by the principles of natural justice and, subject to the other provisions of this Act and of any rules made by the Central Government, the Commission shall have powers to regulate its own procedure including the places at which they shall have their sittings, duration of oral hearings when granted, and times of its inquiry.

(2) The Commission shall have, for the purposes of discharging its functions under this Act, the same powers as are vested in a civil court under the Code of Civil Procedure, 1908 (5 of 1908), while trying a suit, in respect of the following matters, namely:-

(a) summoning and enforcing the attendance of any person and examining him on oath;

(b) requiring the discovery and production of documents;

(c) receiving evidence on affidavits;

(d) issuing commissions for the examination of witnesses or documents;

(e) subject to the provisions of sections 123 and 124 of the Indian Evidence Act, 1872 (1 of 1872), requisitioning any public record or document or copy of such record or document from any office;

(f) dismissing an application in default or deciding it *ex parte;*

(g) any other matter which may be prescribed.

(3) Every proceeding before the Commission shall be deemed to be a judicial proceeding within the meaning of Sections 193 and 228 and for the purposes of Section 196 of the Indian Penal Code (45 of 1860) and the Commission shall be deemed to be a civil court for the purposes of Section 195 and Chapter XXVI of the Code of Criminal Procedure, 1973. (2 of 1974).

(4) The Commission may call upon such experts, from the fields of economics, commerce, accountancy, international trade or from any other discipline as it deems necessary, to assist the Commission in the conduct of any inquiry or proceeding before it.

(5) The Commission may direct any person —

(a) to produce before the Director General or the Registrar or an officer authorized by it, such books, accounts or other documents in the custody or under the control of such person so directed as may be specified or described in the direction, being documents relating to any trade, the examination of which may be required for the purposes of this Act;

(b) to furnish to the Director General or the Registrar or any officer authorized by it, as respects the trade or such other information as may be in his possession in relation to the trade carried on by such person, as may be required for the purposes of this Act.

(6) If the Commission is of the opinion that any agreement referred to in Section 3 or abuse of dominant position referred to in section 4 or the combination referred to in Section 5 has caused or is likely to cause an appreciable adverse effect on competition in the relevant market in India and it is necessary to protect, without further delay, the interests of consumers and other market participants in India, it may conduct an inquiry or adjudicate upon any matter under this Act after giving a reasonable oral hearing to the parties concerned.

37. Review of orders of Commission —

Any person aggrieved by an order of the Commission from which an appeal is allowed by this Act but no appeal has been preferred, may, within thirty days from the date of the order, apply to the Commission for review of its order and the Commission may make such order thereon as it thinks fit: Provided that the Commission may entertain a review application after the expiry of the staid period of thirty days, if it is satisfied that the applicant was prevented by sufficient cause from preferring the application in time: Provided further that no order shall be modified or set aside without giving an opportunity of being heard to the person in whose favour the order is given and the Director General where he was a party to the proceedings.

38. Rectification of orders —

(1) With a view to rectifying any mistake apparent from the record, the Commission may amend any order passed by it under the provisions of this Act.

(2) Subject to the other provisions of this Act, the Commission may make —

(a) an amendment under sub-section (1) of its own motion;

(b) an amendment for rectifying any such mistake which has been brought to its notice by any party to the order.

Explanation — For the removal of doubts, it is hereby declared that the Commission shall not, while rectifying any mistake apparent from record, amend substantive part of its order passed under the provisions of this Act.

39. Execution of orders of Commission —

Every order passed by the Commission under this Act shall be enforced by the Commission in the same manner as if it were a decree or order made by a High Court or the principal civil court in a suit pending therein and it shall be lawful for the Commission to send, in the event of its inability to execute it, such order to the High Court or the principal civil court, as the case may be, within the local limits of whose jurisdiction —

(a) in the case of an order against a person referred to in sub-clause (iii) or sub-clause (vi) or sub-clause (vii) of clause (l) of Section 2, the registered office or the sole or principal place of business of the person in India or where the person has also a subordinate office, that subordinate office, is situated;

(b) in the case of an order against any other person, the place, where the person concerned voluntarily resides or carries on business or personally works for gain, is situated, and thereupon the court to which the order is so sent shall execute the order as if it were a decree or order sent to it for execution.

40. Appeal —

Any person aggrieved by any decision or order of the Commission may file an appeal to the Supreme Court within sixty days from the date of communication of the decision or order of the Commission to him on one or more of the grounds specified in Section 100 of the Code of Civil Procedure, 1908 (5 of 1908): Provided that the Supreme Court may, if it is satisfied that the appellant was prevented by sufficient cause from filing the appeal within the said period, allow it to be filed within a further period not exceeding sixty days: Provided further that no appeal shall lie against any decision or order of the Commission made with the consent of the parties.

41. Director-General to investigate contraventions —

(1) The Director General shall, when so directed by the Commission, assist the Commission in investigating into any contravention of the provisions of this Act or any rules or regulations made there under.

(2) The Director General shall have all the powers as are conferred upon the Commission under sub-section (2) of Section 36.

(3) Without prejudice to the provisions of sub-section (2), Sections 240 and 240A of the Companies Act, 1956 (1 of 1956), so far as may be, shall apply to an investigation made by the Director General or any other person investigating under his authority as they apply to an inspector appointed under that Act.

42. Contravention of orders of Commission —

(1) Without prejudice to the provisions of this Act, if any person contravenes, without any reasonable ground, any order of the Commission, or any condition or restriction subject to which any approval, sanction direction or exemption in relation to any matter has been accorded, given, made or granted under this Act or fails to pay the penalty imposed under this Act, he shall be liable to be detained in civil prison for a term which may extend to one year, unless in the meantime the Commission directs his release and he shall also be liable to a penalty not exceeding rupees ten lakhs.

(2) The Commission may, while making an order under this Act, issue such directions to any person or authority, not inconsistent with this Act, as it thinks necessary or desirable, for the proper implementation or execution of the order, and any person who commits breach of, or fails to comply with, any obligation imposed on him under such direction, may be ordered by the Commission to be detained in civil prison for a term not exceeding one year unless in the to a penalty not exceeding rupees ten lakhs. Mean time the Commission directs his release and he shall also be liable

43. Penalty for failure to comply with directions of Commission and Director-General —

If any person fails to comply with a direction given by —

(a) the Commission under sub-section (5) of Section 36; or

(b) the Director General while exercising powers referred to in sub-section (2) of Section 41, the Commission shall impose on such person a penalty of rupees one lakh for each day during which such failure continues.

44. Penalty for making false statement or omission to furnish material information —

If any person, being a party to a combination —

(a) makes a statement which is false in any material particular, or knowing it to be false; or

(b) omits to state any material particular knowing it to be material, such person shall be liable to a penalty which shall not be less than rupees fifty lakhs but which may extend to rupees one crore, as may be determined by the Commission.

45. Penalty for offences in relation to furnishing of information —

(1) Without prejudice to the provisions of Section 44, if any person, who furnishes or is required to furnish under this Act any particulars, documents or any information —

(a) makes any statement or furnishes any document which he knows or has reason to believe to be false in any material particular; or

(b) omits to state any material fact knowing it to be material; or

(c) willfully alters, suppresses or destroys any document which is required to be furnished as aforesaid, the Commission shall impose on such person a penalty which may extend to rupees ten lakhs.

(2) Without prejudice to the provisions of sub-section (1), the Commission may also pass such other order as it deems fit.

46. Power to impose lesser penalty —

The Commission may, if it is satisfied that any producer, seller, distributor, trader or service provider included in any cartel, which is alleged to have violated Section 3, has made a full and true disclosure in respect of the alleged violations and such disclosure is vital, impose upon such producer, seller, distributor, trader or service provider a lesser penalty as it may deem fit, than leviable under this Act or the rules or the regulations: Provided that lesser penalty shall not be imposed by the Commission in cases where proceedings for the violation of any of the provisions of this Act or the rules or the regulations have been instituted or any investigation has been directed to be made under section 26 before making of such disclosure: Provided further that lesser penalty shall be imposed by the Commission only in respect of a producer, seller, distributor, trader or service provider included in the cartel, who first made the full, true and vital disclosures under this section: Provided also that the Commission may, if it is satisfied that such producer, seller, distributor, trader or service provider included in the cartel had in the course of proceedings —

(a) not complied with the condition on which the lesser penalty was imposed by the Commission; or

(b) had given false evidence; or

(c) the disclosure made is not vital, and thereupon such producer, seller, distributor, trader or service provider may be tried for the offence with respect to which the lesser penalty was imposed and shall also be liable to the imposition of penalty to which such person has been liable, had lesser penalty not been imposed.

47. Crediting sums realized by way of penalties to Consolidated Fund of India —

All sums realized by way of penalties under this Act shall be credited to the Consolidated Fund of India.

48. Contravention by companies —

(1) Where a person committing contravention of any of the provisions of this Act or of any rule, regulation, order made or direction issued there under is a company, every person who, at the time the contravention was committed, was in charge of, and was responsible to the company for the conduct of the business of the company, as well as the company, shall be deemed to be guilty of the contravention and shall be liable to be proceeded against and punished

accordingly: Provided that nothing contained in this sub-section shall render any such person liable to any punishment if he proves that the contravention was committed without his knowledge or that he had exercised all due diligence to prevent the commission of such contravention.

(2) Notwithstanding anything contained in sub-section (1), where a contravention of any of the provisions of this Act or of any rule, regulation, order made or direction issued there under has been committed by a company and it is proved that the contravention has taken place with the consent or connivance of, or is attributable to any neglect on the part of, any director, manager, secretary or other officer of the company, such director, manager, secretary or other officer shall also be deemed to be guilty of that contravention and shall be liable to be proceeded against and punished accordingly.

Explanation — For the purposes of this section —

(a) "company" means a body corporate and includes a firm or other association of individuals; and

(b) "director", in relation to a firm, means a partner in the firm.

49. Competition Advocacy —

(1) In formulating a policy on competition (including review of laws related to competition), the Central Government may make a reference to the Commission for its opinion on possible effect of such policy on competition and on receipt of such a reference, the Commission shall, within sixty days of making such reference, give its opinion to the Central Government, which may thereafter formulate the policy as it deems fit.

(2) The opinion given by the Commission under sub-section (1) shall not be binding upon the Central Government in formulating such policy.

(3) The Commission shall take suitable measures, as may be prescribed, for the promotion of competition advocacy, creating awareness and imparting training about competition issues.

50. Grants by Central Government —

The Central Government may, after due appropriation made by Parliament by law in this behalf, make to the Commission grants of such sums of money as the Government may think fit for being utilised for the purposes of this Act.

51. Constitution of Fund —

(1) There shall be constituted a fund to be called the "Competition Fund" and there shall be credited thereto —

(a) all Government grants received by the Commission;

(b) The monies received as costs from parties to proceedings before the Commission;

(c) the fees received under this Act;

(d) the interest accrued on the amounts referred to in clauses (a) to(c).

(2) The Fund shall be applied for meeting —

(a) the salaries and allowances payable to the Chairperson and other members and the administrative expenses including the salaries, allowances and pension payable to the

Director General, Additional, Joint, Deputy or Assistant Directors General, the Registrar and officers and other employees of the Commission;

(b) the other expenses of the Commission in connection with the discharge of its functions and for the purposes of this Act.

(3) The Fund shall be administered by a committee of such Members of the Commission as may be determined by the Chairperson.

(4) The committee appointed under sub-section (3) shall spend monies out of the Fund for carrying out the objects for which the Fund has been constituted.

52. Accounts and Audit —

(1) The Commission shall maintain proper accounts and other relevant records and prepare an annual statement of accounts in such form as may be prescribed by the Central Government in consultation with the Comptroller and Auditor- general of India.

(2) The accounts of the Commission shall be audited by the Comptroller and Auditor-General of India at such intervals as may be specified by him and any expenditure incurred in connection with such audit shall be payable by the Commission to the Comptroller and Auditor-General of India.

Explanation — For the removal of doubts, it is hereby declared that the orders of the Commission, being matters appealable to the Supreme Court, shall not be subject to audit under this section.

(3) The Comptroller and Auditor General of India and any other person appointed by him in connection with the audit of the accounts of the Commission shall have the same rights, privileges and authority in connection with such audit as the Comptroller and Auditor-General of India generally has, in connection with the audit of the Government accounts and, in particular, shall have the right to demand the production of books, accounts, connected vouchers and other documents and papers and to inspect any of the offices of the Commission.

(4) The accounts of the Commission as certified by the Comptroller and Auditor General of India or any other person appointed by him in this behalf together with the audit report thereon shall be forwarded annually to the Central Government and that Government shall cause the same to be laid before each House of Parliament.

53. Furnishing of returns, etc., to Central Government —

(1) The Commission shall furnish to the Central Government at such time and in such form and manner as may be prescribed or as the Central Government may direct, such returns and statements and such particulars in regard to any proposed or existing measures for the promotion of competition advocacy, creating awareness and imparting training about competition issues, as the Central Government may, from time to time, require.

(2) The Commission shall prepare once in every year, in such form and at such time as may be prescribed, an annual report giving a true and full account of its activities during the previous year and copies of the report shall be forwarded to the Central Government.

(3) A copy of the report received under sub-section (2) shall be laid, as soon as may be after it is received, before each House of Parliament.

54. Power to exempt —

The Central Government may, by notification, exempt from the application of this Act, or any provision thereof, and for such period as it may specify in such notification-

(a) any class of enterprises if such exemption is necessary in the interest of security of the State or public interest;

(b) any practice or agreement arising out of and in accordance with any obligation assumed by India under any treaty, agreement or convention with any other country or countries;

(c) any enterprise which performs a sovereign function on behalf of the Central Government or a State Government: Provided that in case an enterprise is engaged in any activity including the activity relatable to the sovereign functions of the Government, the Central Government may grant exemption only in respect of activity relatable to the sovereign functions.

55. Power of Central Government to issue directions —

(1) Without prejudice to the foregoing provisions of this Act, the Commission shall, in exercise of its powers or the performance of its functions under this Act, be bound by such directions on questions of policy, other than those relating to technical and administrative matters, as the Central Government may give in writing to it from time to time: Provided that the Commission shall, as far as practicable, be given an opportunity to express its views before any direction is given under this sub-section.

(2) The decision of the Central Government whether a question is one of policy or not shall be final.

56. Power of Central Government to supersede Commission —

(1) If at any time the Central Government is of the opinion —

(a) that on account of circumstances beyond the control of the Commission, it is unable to discharge the functions or perform the duties imposed on it by or under the provisions of this Act; or

(b) that the Commission has persistently made default in complying with any direction given by the Central Government under this Act or in the discharge of the functions or performance of the duties imposed on it by or under the provisions of this Act and as a result of such default the financial position of the Commission or the administration of the Commission has suffered; or

(c) that circumstances exist which render it necessary in the public interest so to do, the Central Government may, by notification and for reasons to be specified therein, supersede the Commission for such period, not exceeding six months, as may be specified in the notification: Provided that before issuing any such notification, the Central Government shall give a reasonable opportunity to the Commission to make representations against the proposed supersession and shall consider representations, if any, of the Commission.

(2) Upon the publication of a notification under sub-section (1) superseding the Commission —

(a) the Chairperson and other Members shall, as from the date of supersession, vacate their offices as such;

(b) all the powers, functions and duties which may, by or under the provisions of this Act, be exercised or discharged by or on behalf of the Commission shall, until the Commission is reconstituted under sub-section (3), be exercised and discharged by the Central Government or such authority as the Central Government may specify in this behalf;

(c) all properties owned or controlled by the Commission shall, until the Commission is reconstituted under sub-section (3), vest in the Central Government.

(3) On or before the expiration of the period of supersession specified in the notification issued under sub-section (1), the Central Government shall reconstitute the Commission by a fresh appointment of its Chairperson and other Members and in such as any person who had vacated his office under clause (a) of sub-section (2) shall not be deemed to be disqualified for re-appointment.

(4) The Central Government shall cause a notification issued under sub-section (1) and a full report of any action taken under this section and the circumstances leading to such action to be laid before each House of Parliament at the earliest.

57. Restriction on disclosure of information —

No information relating to any enterprise, being an information which has been obtained by or on behalf of the Commission for the purposes of this Act, shall, without the previous permission in writing of the enterprise, be disclosed otherwise than in compliance with or for the purposes of this Act or any other law for the time being in force

58. Members, Director General, Registrar, officers and other employees, etc., of Commission to be public servants —

The Chairperson and other Members and the Director General, Additional, Joint, Deputy or Assistant Directors General and Registrar and officers and other employees of the Commission shall be deemed, while acting or purporting to act in pursuance of any of the provisions of this Act, to be public servants within the meaning of Section 21 of the Indian Penal Code (45 of 1860).

59. Protection of action taken in good faith —

No suit, prosecution or other legal proceedings shall lie against the Central Government or Commission or any officer of the Central Government or the Chairperson or any Member or the Director-General, Additional, Joint, Deputy or Assistant Directors General or Registrar or officers or other employees of the Commission for anything which is in good faith done or intended to be done under this Act or the rules or regulations made there under.

60. Act to have overriding effect —

The provisions of this Act shall have effect notwithstanding anything inconsistent therewith contained in any other law for the time being in force.

61. Exclusion of jurisdiction of civil courts —

No civil court shall have jurisdiction to entertain any suit or proceeding in respect of any matter which the Commission is empowered by or under this Act to determine and no injunction shall be granted by any court or other authority in respect of any action taken or to be taken in pursuance of any power conferred by or under this Act.

62. Application of other laws not barred —

The provisions of this Act shall be in addition to, and not in derogation of, the provisions of any other law for the time being in force.

63. Power to make rules —

(1) The Central Government may, by notification, make rules to carry out the provisions of this Act.

(2) In particular, and without prejudice to the generality of the foregoing power, such rules may provide for all or any of the following matters, namely:-

(a) the manner in which the Chairperson and other Members shall be selected under section 9;

(b) the form and manner in which and the authority before whom the oath of office and of secrecy shall be made and subscribed to under sub-section (3) of Section 10;

(c) the financial and administrative powers which may be vested in the Member Administration under section 13;

(d) the salary and the other terms and conditions of service including travelling expenses, house rent allowance and conveyance facilities, sumptuary allowance and medical facilities to be provided to the Chairperson and other Members under sub-section ( ) of Section 14;

(e) the salary, allowances and other terms and conditions of service of the Director General, Additional, Joint, Deputy or Assistant Directors General or such other advisers, consultants or officers under sub-section (3) of section 16;

(f) the qualifications for appointment of the Director General, Additional, Joint, Deputy or Assistant Directors General or such other advisers, consultants or officers under sub-section (4) of Section 16;

(g) the salaries and allowances and other terms and conditions of service of the Registrar and officers and other employees payable, and the number of such officers and employees under sub-section (2) of Section 17;

(h) for securing any case or matter which requires to be decided by a Bench composed of more than two Members under sub-section (4) of Section 23;

(i) any other matter in respect of which the Commission shall have power under clause (g) of sub-section (2) of Section 36;

(j) the promotion of competition advocacy, creating awareness and imparting training about competition issues under sub-section (3) of section 49;

(k) the form in which the annual statement of accounts shall be prepared under sub-section (1) of Section 52;

(l) the time within which and the form and manner in which the Commission may furnish returns, statements and such particulars as the Central Government may require under sub-section (1) of Section 53;

(m) the form in which and the time within which the annual report shall be prepared under sub-section (2) of Section 53;

(n) the manner in which the monies transferred to the Central Government shall be dealt with by that Government under the fourth proviso to sub-section (2) of Section 66;

(o) any other matter which is to be, or may be, prescribed, or in respect of which provision is to be, or may be, made by rules.

(3) Every notification issued under sub-section (3) of Section 20 and Section 54 and every rule made under this Act by the Central Government shall be laid, as soon as may be after it is made, before each House of Parliament, while it is in session, for total period of thirty days which may be comprised in one session, or in two or more successive sessions, and if, before the expiry of the session immediately following the session or the successive sessions aforesaid, both Houses agree in making any modification in the notification or rule, or both Houses agree that the notification should not be issued or rule should not be made, the notification or rule shall thereafter have effect only in such modified form or be of no effect, as the case may be; so however, that any such modification or annulment shall be without prejudice to the validity of anything previously done under that notification or rule, as the case may be.

64. Power to make regulations —

(1) The Commission may, by notification, make regulations consistent with this Act and the rules made there under to carry out the purposes of this Act.

(2) In particular, and without prejudice to the generality of the foregoing provisions, such regulations may provide for all or any of the following matters, namely:

(a) the cost of production to be determined under clause (b) of the Explanation to section 4;

(b) the form of notice as may be specified and the fee which may be determined under sub-section (2) of Section 6;

(c) the form in which details of the acquisition shall be filed under sub-section (5) of Section 6;

(d) the fee which may be determined under clause (a) of sub-section (1) of Section 19;

(e) any other matter in respect of which provision is to be, or may be, made by regulations.

(3) Every regulation made under this Act shall be laid, as soon as may be after it is made, before each House of Parliament, while it is in session, for a total period of thirty days which may be comprised in one session or in two or more successive sessions, and if, before the expiry of the session immediately following the session or the successive sessions aforesaid, both Houses agree in making any modification in the regulation, or both Houses agree that the regulation should not be made, the regulation shall thereafter have effect only in such modified form or be of no effect, as the case may be; so, however, that any such modification or annulment shall be without prejudice to the validity of anything previously done under that regulation.

65. Power to remove difficulties —

(1) If any difficulty arises in giving effect to the provisions of this Act, the Central Government may, by order published in the Official Gazette, make such provisions, not inconsistent with the provisions of this Act as may appear to it to be necessary for removing the difficulty: Provided that no such order shall be made under this section after the expiry of a period of two years from the commencement of this Act.

(2) Every order made under this section shall be laid, as soon as may be after it is made, before each House of Parliament.

66. Repeal and saving —

(1) The Monopolies and Restrictive Trade Practices Act, 1969 (54 of 1969) is hereby repealed and the Monopolies and Restrictive Trade Practices Commission established under sub-section (1) of Section 5 of the said Act (hereinafter referred to as the repealed Act) shall stand dissolved.

(2) On the dissolution of the Monopolies and Restrictive Trade Practices Commission, the person appointed as the Chairman of the Monopolies and Restrictive Trade Practices Commission and every other person appointed as Member and Director General of Investigation and Registration, Additional, Joint, Deputy, or Assistant Directors General of Investigation and Registration and any officer and other employee of that Commission and holding office as such immediately before such dissolution shall vacate their respective offices and such Chairman and other Members shall be entitled to claim compensation not exceeding three months pay and allowances for the premature termination of term of their office or of any contract of service: Provided that the Director General of Investigation and Registration, Additional, Joint, Deputy or Assistant Directors General of Investigation and Registration or any officer or other employee who has been, immediately before the dissolution of the Monopolies and Restrictive Trade Practices Commission appointed on deputation basis to the Monopolies and Restrictive Trade Practices Commission, shall, on such dissolution, stand reverted to his parent cadre, Ministry or Department, as the case may be: Provided further that the Director General of Investigation and Registration, Additional, Joint, Deputy or Assistant Directors General of Investigation and Registration or any officer or other employee who has been, immediately before the dissolution of the Monopolies and Restrictive Trade Practices Commission, employed on regular basis by the Monopolies and Restrictive Trade Practices Commission, shall become, on and from such dissolution, the officer and employee, respectively, of the Central Government with the same rights and privileges as to pension, gratuity and other like matters as would have been admissible to him if the rights in relation to such Monopolies and Restrictive Trade Practices Commission had not been continued to do so unless and until his employment in the Central Government is duly terminated or until his remuneration, terms and conditions of employment are duly altered by that Government: Transferred to, and vested in, the Central Government and shall, provided also that notwithstanding anything contained in the Industrial Disputes Act, 1947 (14 of 1947), or in any other law for the time being in force, the transfer of the services of any Director General of Investigation and Registration, Additional, joint, Deputy or Assistant Directors General of Investigation and Registration or any officer or other employee, employed in the Monopolies and Restrictive Trade Practices Commission, to the Central Government shall not entitle such Director General of Investigation and Registration, Additional, Joint, Deputy or Assistant Directors General of Investigation and Registration or any officer or other employee any compensation under this Act or any other law for the time being in force and no such claim shall be entertained by any court, tribunal or other authority: Provided also that where the Monopolies and Restrictive Trade Practices Commission has established a provident fund, superannuation, welfare or other fund for the benefit of the Director General of Investigation and Registration, Additional, Joint, Deputy or Assistant Directors General of Investigation

and Registration or the officers and other employees employed in the Monopolies and Restrictive Trade Practices Commission, the monies relatable to the officers and other employees whose services have been transferred by or under this Act to the Central Government shall, out of the monies standing, on the dissolution of the Monopolies and Restrictive Trade Practices Commission to the credit of such provident fund, superannuation, welfare or other fund, stand transferred to, and vest in, the Central Government and such monies which stand so transferred shall be dealt with by the said Government in such manner as may be prescribed.

(3) All cases pertaining to monopolistic trade practices or restrictive trade practices pending before the Monopolies and Restrictive Trade Practices Commission on or before the commencement of this Act, including such cases, in which any unfair trade practice has also been alleged, shall, on such commencement, stand transferred to the Competition Commission of India and shall be adjudicated by that Commission in accordance with the provisions of the repealed Act as if that Act had not been repealed.

(4) Subject to the provisions of sub-section (3), all cases pertaining to unfair trade practices other than those referred to in clause (x) of sub-section (1) of section 36A of the Monopolies and Restrictive Trade Practices Act, 1969 (54 of 1969) and pending before the Monopolies and Restrictive Trade Practices Commission on or before the commencement of this Act shall, on such commencement, stand transferred to the National Commission constituted under the Consumer Protection Act, 1986 (68 of 1986) and the National Commission shall dispose of such cases as if they were cases filed under that Act: Provided that the National Commission may, if it considers appropriate, transfer any case transferred to it under this sub-section, to the concerned State Commission established under section 9 of the Consumer Protection Act, 1986 (68 of 1986) and that State Commission shall dispose of such case as if it was filed under that Act.

(5) All cases pertaining to unfair trade practices referred to in clause (x) of sub-section (1) of Section 36A of the Monopolies and Restrictive Trade Practices Act, 1969 (54 of 1969) and pending before the Monopolies and Restrictive Trade Practices Commission on or before the commencement of this Act shall, on such commencement, stand transferred to the Competition Commission of India, and the Competition Commission of India shall dispose of such cases as if they were cases filed under that Act.

(6) All investigations or proceedings, other than those relating to unfair trade practices, pending before the Director General of Investigation and Registration on or before the commencement of this Act shall, on such commencement, stand transferred to the Competition Commission of India, and the Competition Commission of India may conduct or order for conduct of such investigation or proceedings in the manner as it deems fit.

(7) All investigations or proceedings, relating to unfair trade practices, other than those referred to in clause (x) of sub-section (1) of Section 36A of the Monopolies and Restrictive Trade Practices Act, 1969 (54 of 1969) and pending before the Direct r General of Investigation and Registration on or before the commencement of this Act shall, on such commencement, stand transferred to the National Commission constituted under the Consumer Protection Act, 1986 (68 of 1986) and the National Commission m y conduct or order for conduct of such investigation or proceedings in the manner as it deems fit.

(8) All investigations or proceedings relating to unfair trade practices referred to in clause (x) of sub-section (1) of Section 36A of the Monopolies and Restrictive Trade Practices Act, 1969 (54 of 1969), and pending before the Director General of Investigation and Registration on or before the commencement of this Act shall, on such commencement, stand transferred to the Competition Commission of India and the Competition Commission of India may conduct or order for conduct of such investigation in th manner as it deems fit.

(9) Save as otherwise provided under sub-sections (3) to (8), all cases or proceedings pending before the Monopolies and Restrictive Trade Practices Commission shall abate.

(10) The mention of the particular matters referred to in sub-sections (3) to (8) shall not be held to prejudice or affect the general application of section 6 of the General Clauses Act, 1897 (10 of 1897) with regard to the effect of repeal.

FOREIGN DIRECT INVESTMENT POLICY

The new Economic Policy 1991, transformed successively towards a market-oriented economy. The entire globe is rotating on the flow of funds. After reforms, the financial sector has grown tremendously. The liberalization and deregulations have provided a new era for the capital market. India's liberalization policy has gained importance in the context of global business scenario. Modern economics is influenced by expansion and diversification.

The free market reforms have varied greatly among transition economies in initial conditions and political developments have constrained government's economic policies and influenced their reforms choice. Hungary and China began liberalizing gradually in the 1960s and the 1970s, respectively. Vietnam accelerated its liberalization in 1989, after partial reforms had failed to raise growth rates or to stabilize the economy sufficiently. Poland liberalize with one "big band", freeing 90 per cent of prices, eliminating most trade barriers, abolishing state trading monopolies, and making its currency convertible for current transactions all at once in January 1990. Albania, the Baltic countries, the former Czechoslovakia, and the Kyrgya republic followed this model of rapid and comprehensive liberalization. Bulgaria initially did the same, but strong interest group pressures for continued protection and state support to enterprises later brought something of a reversal. In Romania price reforms advanced fitfully for three years after half of all prices were freed in 1990, but liberalization has recently accelerated Russia substantially liberalized prices and imports in January 1992, but extensive export restrictions remained in place until 1995 (remaining export duties are set to be eliminated by mid 1996), and many consumer prices are still subject to local government intervention. Countries have usually been slower to adjust or liberalize housing rents and utility and public transport prices.

The world economy at the turn of the century has influenced the process of globalization, global partnership and capital flows as a portfolio of global socio-economic enrichment. The reallocation of goods and services without the movement of labour :emergence of developing countries like India and china as an exporter of goods and services and also as a provider of the largest consumer base for world trade, weakening of dollar and improvement of terms of trade have been some the remarkable trends in world investment.

Globalization has witnessed a tremendous flow of trade, capital and services as a resultant of the globalization and trade liberalization process of the 1990s. The reallocation of resources has been by far constructive towards building a more integrated socio-cost efficient economic system. Globalization and stable growth in qualitative capital flows in India has lead to faster growth in demand and productivity. The challenges of globalization today are: the resultant volatility in the international financial markets, emergence of e-finance and capital flows: the rise in productivity and the role of government and regulatory bodies cannot be adequately handled by a system that was largely designed for the world 50 years ago.

The global economy faces several destabilized factors such as volatility in the oil prices, global warming, disturbance in the world peace, exchange rate fluctuation on fore market, price fluctuation in gold and silver. Financial development contributes significantly to growth. Development is necessary for poverty reduction. Researchers have shown that the financial development directly benefits the poorer segments of society and income redistribution. Strong financial systems are the key factor for proper financial developments. For a strong financial system, one requires supporting financial institutions and well developed financial markets to reduce the information costs of borrowing and lending and making financial transactions. Financial institutions include institutions like banks, insurance companies, provident fund and pension funds, mutual funds, compulsory saving schemes, cooperative banks, credit unions. Informal financial intermediaries and securities markets. Generally, banks and financial institutions dominate most formal financial systems, but lately stock markets are gaining importance particularly with international capital flows. The entry of FIIs in the stock markets and relaxation of portfolio investments by the emerging markets is playing an important role in the growth and co-integration of financial markets globally.

In the 1990s, a major part of capital inflows to India was led by foreign investment, reflecting a shift from a prohibition of foreign investment in the pre-reform period to a liberal policy regime. Recognizing the macro economic implications of volatility associated with capital flows. India has adopted a policy of managing the capital account with a preference for non-debt flows. Consistent with the principle of hierarchy of capital flows, India has been making efforts towards encouraging inflows through FDI, and enhancing the quality of portfolio flows by a strict adherence to the know your investor principle. The foreign investment policy of India can be broadly classified into four phases;

(a) Cautious non-discrimination in controls during the period 1948 to the mid 1960s.

(b) selective restrictions and control from mid 1960s, to the end 1970s, with the promulgation of the Foreign Exchange Regulation Act, 1973 and the industrial licensing policy 1973 as the main instruments of control

(c) gradual and partial liberalization in the 1980s, with special incentives for investment in export oriented units and

(d) wide ranging liberalization since 1991, as per the existent policy FDI up to 100% is allowed under the automatic route in most activities with ceilings for some sectors crucial from the view point of strategic consideration or financial stability.

FDI inflows to India came from US, UK, GERMANY and MARITIUS. MARITIUS IS the second largest sources of FDI inflows to India in recent times, due to tax adjustment agreement. Indian policy makers responded positively to the role being played by overseas Indians. It can also be seen that the inflows from JAPAN, UK, NETHERLANDS AND GERMANY steadily increased during the later periods. The investment made by the NRIs was as much as US $ 2965 million. FDI approvals according to industrial sector in India during the period 1991-2000. It is interesting to note that unlike china, the fuel and power sector dominates in India. The telecommunications sector too contributes about 19% of the total investment during the period 1991-2000. FDIs India is concentrated in the services sector. Information technology has enabled a greater growth potential and tradability of a number of business and professional services. Within the services sector, financing, insurance, real estate, and business services has witnessed a large increase in their share in FDI inflows to India between 2002-03 and 2007-08. Computer sector have also remained a key sector for FDI as the captive business process outsourcing or subsidiaries have been the principal mode of offshore delivery.

Need and Importance of FDI

In view of the recent and ongoing economic reforms, India attracted capital inflows from various sources of different countries. The development of a nation depends upon two factors (a) DOMESTIC INVESTMENT (b) FOREIGN INVESTMENT. Domestic investment is unable to meet the present and future requirements of the country. In India, consumption is always an influencing factor for good investment. There is dearth of investment in all sectors of the economy. The increase in growth rate of GDP is gaining momentum even in universal recession situation. The world is moving towards an increased specialization wanting to gain from economies of scales, diffusion of information technology transfers and cross border movement of funds keeping risk diversification well in place. The effect of international trade on growth or critically dependent on the pattern of specialization and integration. The financial assistance from different nations should be utilized by the government towards agriculture sector, irrigation and water management, medical and health sectors, etc., there is a strong need to develop towards world standards.

With the advent of economic reforms and globalization, competition has become very severe and every nation is trying to attract foreign investment to develop their nations. In order to survive domestic as well as global competition more and more countries are recognizing the importance and necessity of the foreign investment. Foreign investment is necessary to survive in the global market. Global markets require higher quality of goods with world standards and specifications. In order to attract the foreign investment, bilateral agreements with other countries will occupy an influencing factor. FDI are generally expected, to originate from other countries with high levels of financial markets, infrastructure but low growth potential directed towards countries with a high growth potential relatively less developed financial markets.

Several researches had been conducted in the field of FDI area. Their findings and conclusions are presented below.

1. Davidson and Kogut: found that "foreign investments flow was influenced by product markets, human resources, production technology, consumer tastes and culture".

2. Teece: have identified that "satisfying strategies also played an important role in terms of FDI in the original neighborhood".

3. Twomey: found that, "US was the world's biggest borrower in 1913. It had begun investing abroad, predominantly in its local neighborhood – Canada, Mexico, and the Caribbean".

4. Dunning observed that, "US firms preferred to exploit markets with which the net start up costs were low as opposed to new markets with potential growth and the opportunity to maximize profit".

5. Hagedoorn and Neural explored that, "US companies started to diversify their production to exploit the advantage of the single market".

6. Pursell observed that, "borrowed on the basis of the general credit worthiness of the country, fungible between alternative investment projects and constitute part of the general fund of investible resources".

7. Leviathan and March have argued that, "the satisfying strategy of a firm should balance the exploitative and explorative since both are *"sine qua none"* for the present and future viability of firms".

8. Bacchetta and Win Coop have shown that, "the gradual nature of liberalization combined with costs of absorbing large inflows in emerging economies leads to rich dynamics of capital flows".

9. Marstar argued that, "deregulation and liberalization succeeded to an extent as interest rate in a single currency are nearly the same regardless of whether they are offered in national or euro-currency markets".

10. Beckaert studied, "the inter relationship between capital flows returns and dividend in 20 emerging markets and concluded that after liberalization, equity flows increase by 14% of the market capitalization".

11. Srivatsava observed that, "the FDI gap between China and India may not bear large as suggested by official's figures, it is recently that, the wrong signals conveyed to potential investors and the consequences, there of being appreciated".

12. Dunning and Neural hypothesis that, "firms make their international production decisions based on perceived ownership advantage, location advantage and internationalization advantage related factor".

13. Dunning argues that, "firms from developing countries are likely to perform activities in neighboring countries that are politically and economically stable".

14. Arndt finds that, "one of the innovative features of the current phase of globalization is the fragmentation of production into production networks based on component specialization and intra product trade, it offers groups of small countries the opportunities to make open regionalism work by enhancing their productivity and competitiveness as well as welfare of their nationals".

15. Kumar explored that, "many developing countries do not follow the international monetary fund guidelines completely while compiling and reporting their FDI data".

16. Reddy observed that, "India has been making efforts towards encouraging inflows through FDI and enhancing the quality of portfolio flows by a strict adherence to the "know your investor" principle".

17. Clavo found that, "the relative importance of domestic and external factors in determining portfolio investment flows towards a country, however remains in conclusive".

18. Bohn and Tesar revealed that, "the links between cross border portfolio flows and domestic stock returns, especially the direction of causality also continues to remain inconclusive".

19. Chakrabarthi explored that, "the determinants of portfolio flows to India find co-movement between FII flows and BSE sensex to be fairly high".

20. Gordan and Gupta stated that, "a combination of domestic, regional and global variables was found to be significant in determining equity flow to India".

21. Kim and Wei observed that, "a positive feedback of high stock prices on portfolio inflows in certain east Asian countries before the crisis, which did not hold true after the crisis".

22. Mohan found that, "large swings in capital flows over a very short period of time impose significant adjustment costs and large output and employment losses on the emerging market economies".

23. Mohan indicated that, "exchange rate volatility arising of volatile capital flows has significant adverse consequences, particularly for countries which specialize in labour intensive and low intermediate technology products in an intensely competitive global market".

24. Fernandez – Arias and P J Montiel explored that, "in the absence of central bank intervention, heavy inflows lead to an appreciation of the domestic currency, which eventually threaten competitiveness. Intervention leads to monetary expansion and inflation, unless sterilized".

25. Bhupal Singh found that, "a sudden shift in the risk perception to emerging markets emanating from the global financial crisis was evident that in the reversal of the capital flow cycle to India in 2008, with challenges of large inflows giving way to the concerns of sharp reversals and their implications for the domestic financial market stability and the real estate sector".

26. Bhupal Singh explored that, "the overseas commercial borrowings are significantly influenced by the peace of domestic activities, and interest rate arbitrage plays an important role".

27. Bhupal Singh stated that, "FDI inflows to India have been increasingly concentrated in the service sector. Such inflows have displayed stability even during the various episodes of major global financial shocks".

1. Industrial Policy

The Government's liberalization and economic reforms program aims at rapid and substantial economic growth, and integration with the global economy in a harmonized manner. The industrial policy reforms have reduced the industrial licensing requirements, removed restrictions on investment and expansion, and facilitated easy access to foreign technology and foreign direct investment.

Industrial Licensing

All industrial undertakings are exempt from obtaining an industrial license to manufacture, except for

(i) Industries reserved for the Public Sector (Annex I),

(ii) Industries retained under compulsory licensing (Annex II),

(iii) Items of manufacture reserved for the small-scale sector and

(iv) If the proposal attracts locational restriction.

Industrial Entrepreneurs Memorandum

Industrial undertakings exempt from obtaining an industrial license are required to file an Industrial Entrepreneurs Memorandum (IEM) in Part 'A' (as per prescribed format) with the Secretariat of Industrial Assistance (SIA), Department of Industrial Policy and Promotion, Government of India, and obtain an acknowledgement. No further approval is required. Immediately after commencement of commercial production, Part B of the IEM has to be filled in the prescribed format. The facility for amendment of existing IEMs has also been introduced.

Locational Policy

Industrial undertakings are free to select the location of a project. In the case of cities with population of more than a million (as per the 1991 census), however, the proposed location should be at least 25 km away from the Standard Urban Area limits of that city unless, it is to be located in an area designated as an ''industrial area'' before the 25th July, 1991. (List of cities with population of 1 million and above is given at Annexure-V). Electronics, Computer software and Printing (and any other industry which may be notified in future as "non polluting industry") are exempt from such locational restriction. Relaxation in the aforesaid locational restriction is possible if an industrial license is obtained as per the notified procedure.

The location of industrial units is further regulated by the local zoning and land use regulations as also the environmental regulations.

Policy Relating to Small-scale Undertakings

An industrial undertaking is defined as a small-scale unit if the investment in fixed assets in plant and machinery does not exceed ₹ 10 million. The small-scale units can get registered with the Directorate of Industries/District Industries Centre in the State Government concerned. Such units can manufacture any item including those notified as exclusively reserved for manufacture in the small-scale sector. Small-scale units are also free from locational restrictions cited. However, a small-scale unit is not permitted more than 24 per cent equity in its paid up capital from any industrial undertaking either foreign or domestic.

Manufacturing of items reserved for the small-scale sector can also be taken up by non small-scale units, if they obtain an industrial license. In such cases, it is mandatory for the non small-scale unit to undertake minimum export obligation of 50 per cent. This will not apply to non small-scale EOUs that are engaged in the manufacture of items reserved for the SSI sector, as they already have a minimum export obligation of 66 per cent of their production. In addition, if the equity holding from another company (including foreign equity) exceeds 24 per cent, even if the investment in plant and machinery in the unit does not exceed ₹ 10 million, the unit loses its small-scale status.

A small-scale unit manufacturing small-scale reserved item(s), on exceeding the small-scale investment ceiling in plant and machinery by virtue of natural growth, needs to apply for and obtain a Carry-on-Business (COB) Licence. No export obligation is fixed on the capacity for which the COB licence is granted. However, if the unit expands its capacity for the small-scale reserved item(s) further, it needs to apply for and obtain a separate industrial licence.

It is possible that a chemical or a by-product recoverable through pollution control measures is reserved for the small-scale sector. With a view to adopting pollution control measures, Government have decided that an application needs to be made for grant of an industrial license for such reserved items which would be considered for approval without necessarily imposing the mandatory export obligation.

Environmental Clearances

Entrepreneurs are required to obtain Statutory clearances relating to Pollution Control and Environment for setting up an industrial project. A Notification (SO 60(E) dated 27.1.94) issued under The Environment (Protection) Act, 1986 has listed 30 projects in respect of which environmental clearance needs to be obtained from the Ministry of Environment, Government of India. This list includes industries like petrochemical complexes, petroleum refineries, cement, thermal power plants, bulk drugs, fertilizers, dyes, paper, etc. However, if investment is less than ₹ 1,000 million, such clearance is not necessary, unless it is for pesticides, bulk drugs and pharmaceuticals, asbestos and asbestos products, integrated paint complexes, mining projects, tourism projects of certain parameters, tarred roads in Himalayan areas, distilleries, dyes, foundries and electroplating industries. Further, any item reserved for the small-scale sector with investment of less than ₹ 10 million is also exempt from obtaining environmental clearance from the Central Government under the Notification. Powers have been delegated to the State Governments for grant of environmental clearance for certain categories of thermal power plants. Setting up industries in certain locations considered ecologically fragile (e.g., Aravalli Range, coastal areas, Doon valley, Dahanu, etc.) are guided by separate guidelines issued by the Ministry of Environment of the Government of India.

Foreign Direct Investment

Foreign Direct Investment (FDI) is now recognized as an important driver of growth in the country. Government is, therefore, making all efforts to attract and facilitate FDI and investment from Non Resident (NRIs) including Overseas Corporate Bodies (OCBs) that are predominantly owned by them, to complement and supplement domestic investment. To make the investment in India attractive, investment and returns on them are freely repatriable, except where the approval is subject to specific conditions such as lock-in period on original investment, dividend cap, foreign exchange neutrality, etc. as per the notified sectoral policy. The condition of dividend balancing that was applicable to FDI in 22 specified consumer goods industries stands withdrawn for dividends declared after 14th July 2000, the date on which Press Note No. 7 of 2000 series was issued.

Foreign direct investment is freely allowed in all sectors including the services sector, except a few sectors where the existing and notified sectoral policy does not permit FDI beyond a ceiling. FDI for virtually all items/activities can be brought in through the Automatic Route under powers delegated to the Reserve Bank of India (RBI), and for the remaining items/activities through Government approval. Government approvals are accorded on the recommendation of the Foreign Investment Promotion Board (FIPB).

(a) Automatic Route

(b) New Ventures

All items/activities for FDI/NRI/OCB investment up to 100% fall under the Automatic Route except those covered under (i) to (iv) of Para 2.9. Whenever any investor chooses to make an application to the FIPB and not to avail of the automatic route, he or she may do so. Investment in public sector units as also for EOU/EPZ/EHTP/STP units would also qualify for the Automatic Route. Investment under the Automatic Route shall continue to be governed by the notified sectoral policy and equity caps and RBI will ensure compliance of the same. The National Industrial Classification (NIC) 1987 shall remain applicable for description of activities and classification for all matters relating to FDI/NRI/OCB investment: Areas/sectors/activities hitherto not open to FDI/NRI/OCB investment shall continue to be so unless otherwise decided and notified by Government. Any change in sectoral policy/sectoral equity cap shall be notified by the Secretariat for Industrial Assistance (SIA) in the Department of Industrial Policy and Promotion. (b) Existing Companies

Besides new companies, automatic route for FDI/NRI/OCB investment is also available to the existing companies proposing to induct foreign equity. For existing companies with an expansion program, the additional requirements are that — (i) the increase in equity level must result from the expansion of the equity base of the existing company without the acquisition of existing shares by NRI/OCB/foreign investors, (ii) the money to be remitted should be in foreign currency and (iii) proposed expansion program should be in the sector(s) under automatic route. Otherwise, the proposal would need Government approval through the FIPB. For this the proposal must be supported by a Board Resolution of the existing Indian company.

For existing companies without an expansion program, the additional requirements for eligibility for automatic approval are — (i) that they are engaged in the industries under automatic route, (ii) the increase in equity level must be from expansion of the equity base and (iii) the foreign equity must be in foreign currency.

The earlier SEBI requirement, applicable to public limited companies, that shares allotted on preferential basis shall not be transferable in any manner for a period of 5 years from the date of their allotment has now been modified to the extent that not more than 20 per cent of the entire contribution brought in by promoter cumulatively in public or preferential issue shall be locked-in.

The automatic route for FDI and/or technology collaboration would not be available to those who have or had any previous joint venture or technology transfer/trade mark agreement in the same or allied field in India.

Equity participation by international financial institutions such as ADB, IFC, CDC, DEG, etc. in domestic companies is permitted through automatic route subject to SEBI/RBI regulations and sector specific cap on FDI.

In a major drive to simplify procedures for foreign direct investment under the "automatic route", RBI has given permission to Indian Companies to accept investment under this route without obtaining prior approval from RBI. Investors are required to notify the Regional Office concerned of the RBI of receipt of inward remittances within 30 days of such receipt and file required documentation within 30 days of issue of shares to Foreign Investors. This facility is available to NRI/OCB investment also.

Government Approval for the following categories, Government approval for FDI/NRI/OCB through the FIPB shall be necessary:

(i) All proposals that require an Industrial License which includes — (1) the item requiring an Industrial License under the Industries (Development & Regulation) Act, 1951;

(2) foreign investment being more than 24 per cent in the equity capital of units manufacturing items reserved for small-scale industries; and

(3) All items which require an Industrial License in terms of the locational policy notified by Government under the New Industrial Policy of 1991.

(ii) All proposals in which the foreign collaborator has a previous venture/tie up in India. The modalities prescribed in Press Note No. 18 dated 14.12.1998 of 1998 Series, shall apply to such cases. However, this shall not apply to investment made by multilateral financial institutions such as ADB, IFC, CDC, DEG, etc. as also investment made in IT sector.

(iii) All proposals relating to acquisition of shares in an existing Indian company in favor of a foreign/NRI/OCB investor.

(iv) All proposals falling outside notified sectoral policy/caps or under sectors in which FDI is not permitted. Areas/sectors/activities hitherto not open to FDI/NRI/OCB investment shall continue to be so unless otherwise decided and notified by Government. Any change in sectoral policy/sectoral equity cap shall be notified by the Secretariat for Industrial Assistance (SIA) in the Department of Industrial Policy and Promotion.

RBI has granted general permission under Foreign Exchange Management Act (FEMA) in respect of proposals approved by the Government. Indian companies getting foreign investment approval through FIPB route do not require any further clearance from RBI for the purpose of receiving inward remittance and issue of shares to the foreign investors. Such companies are, however, required to notify the Regional Office concerned of the RBI of receipt of inward remittances within 30 days of such receipt and to file the required documents with the concerned Regional Offices of the RBI within 30 days after issue of shares to the foreign investors.

For greater transparency in the approval process, Government has announced guidelines for consideration of FDI proposals by the FIPB. The guidelines are stated in Annexure III. The sector specific guidelines for FDI and Foreign Technology Collaborations are stated in Annexure IV.

Issue and Valuation of Shares in case of existing companies:

Allotment of shares on preferential basis shall be as per the requirements of the Companies Act, 1956, which will require special resolution in case of a public limited company. In case of listed companies, valuation shall be as per the RBI/SEBI guidelines as follows: The issue price shall be either at:

(a) The average of the weekly high and low of the closing prices of the related shares quoted on the Stock Exchange during the six months preceding the relevant date or

(b) The average of the weekly high and low of the closing prices of the related shares quoted on the Stock Exchange during the two weeks preceding the relevant date.

The stock exchange referred to is the one at which the highest trading volume in respect of the share of the company has been recorded during the preceding six months prior to the relevant date.

The relevant date is the date thirty days prior to the date on which the meeting of the General Body of the shareholder is convened.

In all other cases a company may issue shares as per the RBI regulation in accordance with the guidelines issued by the erstwhile Controller of Capital Issues.

Other relevant guidelines of Securities and Exchange Board of India (SEBI)/(RBI) including the SAST (Substantial Acquisition of Shares and Takeover) Regulations, 1997, wherever applicable, would need to be followed.

Foreign Investment in the Small-scale Sector

Under the small-scale policy, equity holding by other units including foreign equity in a small-scale undertaking is permissible up to 24 per cent. However there is no bar on higher equity holding for foreign investment if the unit is willing to give up its small-scale status. In case of foreign investment beyond 24 per cent in a small-scale unit which manufactures small-scale reserved item(s), an industrial licence carrying a mandatory export obligation of 50 per cent would need to be obtained.

Foreign Investment Policy for Trading Activities

Foreign investment for trading can be approved through the automatic route up to 51% foreign equity, and beyond this by the Government through FIPB. For approval through the automatic route, the requirement would be that it is primarily export activities and the undertaking concerned is an export house/trading house/ super trading house/star trading house registered under the provisions of the Export and Import policy in force. The sectoral policy of trading activities is elaborated at S. No. 8, *viz.,* trading of Annexure IV (Sector Specific Guidelines for Foreign Direct Investment) of this Manual.

Other Modes of Foreign Direct Investments

Global Depository Receipts (GDR)/American Deposit Receipts (ADR)/Foreign Currency Convertible Bonds (FCCB): Foreign Investment through GDRs/ADRs, Foreign Currency Convertible Bonds (FCCBs) are treated as Foreign Direct Investment. Indian companies are allowed to raise equity capital in the international market through the issue of GDR/ADRs/FCCBs. These are not subject to any ceilings on investment. An applicant company seeking Government's approval in this regard should have a consistent track record for good performance (financial or otherwise) for a minimum period of 3 years. This condition can be relaxed for infrastructure projects such as power generation, telecommunication, petroleum exploration and refining, ports, airports and roads.

There is no restriction on the number of GDRs/ADRs/FCCBs to be floated by a company or a group of companies in a financial year. A company engaged in the manufacture of items covered under Automatic Route, whose direct foreign investment after a proposed GDR/ADR/FCCBs issue is likely to exceed the percentage limits under the automatic route, or which is implementing a project falling under Government approval route, would need to obtain prior Government clearance through FIPB before seeking final approval from the Ministry of Finance.

There are no end-use restrictions on GDR/ADR issue proceeds, except for an express ban on investment in real estate and stock markets. The FCCB issue proceeds need to conform to external commercial borrowing end user requirements; in addition, 25 per cent of the FCCB proceeds can be used for general corporate restructuring.

Preference Shares

Foreign investment through preference shares is treated as foreign direct investment. Proposals are processed either through the automatic route or FIPB as the case may be. The following guidelines apply to issue of such shares:

(i) Foreign investment in preference share is considered as part of share capital and fall outside the External Commercial Borrowing (ECB) guidelines/cap.

(ii) Preference shares to be treated as foreign direct equity for purpose of sectoral caps on foreign equity, where such caps are prescribed, provided they carry a conversion option. If the preference shares are structured without such conversion option, they would fall outside the foreign direct equity cap.

(iii) Duration for conversion shall be as per the maximum limit prescribed under the Companies Act or what has been agreed to in the shareholders agreement whichever is less.

(iv) The dividend rate would not exceed the limit prescribed by the Ministry of Finance.

(v) Issue of Preference Shares should conform to guidelines prescribed by the SEBI and RBI and other statutory requirements.

3. Investment by Non-resident Indians and Overseas Corporate Bodies

For all sectors, excluding those falling under Government approval, NRIs (which also includes PIOs) and OCBs (an overseas corporate body means a company or other entity owned directly or indirectly to the extent of at least 60% by NRIs) are eligible to bring investment through the automatic route of RBI. All other proposals, which do not fulfill any or, all of the criteria for automatic approval are considered by the Government through the FIPB.

The NRIs and OCBs are allowed to invest in housing and real estate development sector, in which foreign direct investment is not permitted. They are allowed to hold up to 100 per cent equity in civil aviation sector in which otherwise foreign equity only up to 40 per cent is permitted.

4. Foreign Technology Agreements

With a view to injecting the desired level of technological dynamism in Indian industry and for promoting an industrial environment where the acquisition of technological capability receives priority, foreign technology induction is encouraged both through FDI and through foreign technology collaboration agreements. Foreign technology collaborations are permitted either through the automatic route under delegated powers exercised by the RBI, or by the Government. However, cases involving industrial licenses/small-scale reserved items do not qualify for automatic approval and would require consideration and approval by the Government. Automatic route for technology collaboration would also not be available to those who have, or had any previous technology transfer/trade-mark agreement in the same or allied field in India. Further, automatic approval for EOU/EHTP/STP units is governed by provisions.

Automatic Approval

The Reserve Bank of India, through its regional offices, accords automatic approval to all industries for foreign technology collaboration agreements subject to

(i) The lump sum payments not exceeding US $ 2 Million;

(ii) royalty payable being limited to 5 per cent for domestic sales and 8 per cent for exports, subject to a total payment of 8 per cent on sales over a 10 year period; and

(iii) the period for payment of royalty not exceeding 7 years from the date of commencement of commercial production, or 10 years from the date of agreement, whichever is earlier (The aforesaid royalty limits are net of taxes and are calculated according to standard conditions). Payment of royalty up to 2% for exports and 1% for domestic sales is allowed under automatic route on use of trademarks and brand name of the foreign collaborator without technology transfer. In case of technology transfer, payment of royalty subsumes the payment of royalty for use of trademark and brand name of the foreign collaborator. Royalty on brand name/trade mark shall be paid as a percentage of net sales, *viz.,* gross sales less agents'/dealers' commission, transport cost, including ocean freight, insurance, duties, taxes and other charges, and cost of raw materials, parts, components imported from the foreign licensor or its subsidiary/affiliated company.

Payment of royalty up to 8% on exports and 5% on domestic sales by wholly owned subsidiaries (WOS) to offshore parent companies is allowed under the automatic route without any restriction on the duration of royalty payments.

Government Approval

For the following categories, Government approval would be necessary:

(a) Proposals attracting compulsory licensing

(b) Items of manufacture reserved for the small-scale sector

(c) Proposals involving any previous joint venture or technology transfer/trademark agreement in the same or allied field in India. The definition of ''same'' and ''allied'' field would be as per 4 digit NIC 1987 Code and 3 digit NIC 1987 Code.

(d) Extension of foreign technology collaboration agreements (including those cases, which may have received automatic approval in the first instance)

(e) Proposals not meeting any or all of the parameters for automatic approval as given.

The items of foreign technology collaboration, which are eligible for approval through the automatic route, and by the Government, are technical knowhow fees, payment for design and drawing, payment for engineering service and royalty.

Payments for hiring of foreign technicians, deputation of Indian technicians abroad, and testing of indigenous raw material, products, indigenously developed technology in foreign countries are governed by separate RBI procedures and rules and are not covered by the foreign technology collaboration approval. Similarly, payments for imports of plant and machinery and raw material are also not covered by the foreign technology collaboration approval. For any of these items, entrepreneurs may contact the RBI.

100% Export-oriented units/export processing zones/special economic zones:

A 100 per cent Export-oriented Units (EOUs) and units in the Export Processing Zones (EPZs)/Special Economic Zones (SEZs), enjoy a package of incentives and facilities, which include duty free imports of all types of capital goods, raw material, and consumables in addition to tax holidays against export.

100% FDI is permitted under automatic route for setting up of industrial park/industrial model town/special economic zone in the country. To encourage investment in this sector, 100% income tax exemption for 10 years within a block of 15 years is also granted for the industrial parks set up during the period 1.4.1977 to 31.3.2006".

Automatic Approval

The Development Commissioners (DCs) of Export Processing Zones (EPZs)/Free Trade Zones (FTZS))/Special Economic Zones (SEZs) accord automatic approval to projects where

(a) activity proposed does not attract compulsory licensing or falls in the services sector except IT enabled services;

(b) location is in conformity with the prescribed parameters;

(c) units undertake to achieve exports and value addition norms as prescribed in the Export and Import Policy in force;

(d) unit is amenable to bonding by customs authorities; and

(e) unit has projected the minimum export turnover, as specified in the Handbook of Procedures for Export and Import.

All proposals for FDI/NRI/OCB investments in EOU/EPZ units qualify for approval through automatic route subject to sectoral norms. Proposals not covered under the automatic route would be considered and approved by FIPB.

Conversion of existing Domestic Tariff Area (DTA) units into EOU is also permitted under automatic route, if the DTA unit satisfies the parameters mentioned above and there is no outstanding export obligation under any other Export Oriented scheme of the Government of India.

FDI upto100% is allowed through the automatic route for all manufacturing activities in Special Economic Zones (SEZs), except for the following activities:

(a) Arms and ammunition, explosives and allied items of defense equipments, defense aircraft and warships;

(b) Atomic substances;

(c) Narcotics and psychotropic substances and hazardous chemicals;

(d) Distillation and brewing of alcoholic drinks; and

(e) Cigarettes/cigars and manufactured tobacco substitutes.

For services, norms as notified would be applicable Government Approval:

All proposals which do not meet any or all of the parameters for automatic approval will be considered and approved by the Board of Approval of EOU/EPZ/SEZ set up in the Department of Commerce.

Electronic hardware technology park and software technology park schemes:

In order to provide impetus to the electronics industry, to enhance its export potential and to develop an efficient electronic component industry, Electronic Hardware Technology Park (EHTP) and Software Technology Park (STP) schemes offer a package of incentives and facilities like duty free imports on the lines of the EOU Scheme, deemed exports benefits and tax holidays.

Automatic Approval

The Directors of STPs in respect of STP proposals; and the Designated Officers in respect of EHTP proposals accord automatic approval if:

(a) Items do not attract compulsory licensing;

(b) Location is in conformity with the prescribed parameters;

(c) Export obligation laid down in the respective EHTP scheme or STP scheme is fulfilled;

(d) Unit is amenable to bonding by the Customs, and all the manufacturing operations are carried out in the same premises and the proposal does not envisage sending out of the bonded area any raw material or intermediate products for any other manufacturing or processing activity. All proposals for FDI/NRI/OCB investments in EHTP/STP units are eligible for approval through automatic route subject to parameters listed.

Government Approval

All proposals which do not meet any or all of the parameters for automatic approval need to be considered and approved by the Government. Government approval for FDI/NRI/OCB investment under EHTP/STP needs to be obtained through the FIPB in respect of proposals covered under paragraph.

Procedures

Approval Procedures

It has been the continuous effort of the Government to simplify the procedures for filing of the application for various approvals. Even the forms required for various purposes are also simplified and are available in downloadable format on the website of the Department. The following paragraphs give in brief the procedures involved in obtaining various approvals

General Procedures

Procedural Requirements for De-licensed Sector – Industrial Entrepreneurs Memorandum (IEM):

(a) All industrial undertakings exempt from the requirements of industrial licensing, including existing units undertaking substantial expansion, need to file information in the prescribed Industrial Entrepreneurs Memorandum, i.e., Form IEM. The form is available at all outlets dealing in Government Publications, Indian Embassies, the Entrepreneurial Assistance Unit (EAU) of the Secretariat for Industrial Assistance (SIA), Department of Industrial Policy and Promotion, Udyog Bhavan, New Delhi-110011, and can also be downloaded from the website of the DIPP. The Memorandum (IEM) after filling in can be submitted to the EAU of the SIA in person or by post. The IEM should be submitted along with a crossed demand draft of ₹ 1000 drawn in favor of "The Pay & Accounts Officer, Department of Industrial Development, Ministry of Industry", payable at the State Bank of India, Nirman Bhawan Branch, New Delhi up to 10 items proposed to be manufactured in the same unit. For more than 10 items, an additional fee of ₹ 250 up to 10 additional items needs to be paid through crossed demand draft.

(c) A computer acknowledgement containing the SIA Registration Number (for future reference) will be issued across the counter immediately if delivered in person or sent by post if received through post. No further approval from SIA is required.

(d) All Industrial undertakings also need to file information in Part 'B' of the Memorandum at the time of commencement of commercial production. The prescribed form is appended to Form IEM. Part - B of the Memorandum has to be filed with the EAU in SIA, but no fee is required.

(e) No amendment/modifications are made to any IEM filed before 30th June 1998 except for clerical errors. Where any amendment/modification is sought to be made in such IEMs, a fresh memorandum in Form IEM, along with the prescribed fee has to be filed for which a fresh acknowledgement will be issued. An IEM would be cancelled /deleted from the SIA records if, on scrutiny, it is found that the proposal contained in the IEM is licensable.

(f) In respect of IEMs filed in the new form made effective from 1st July 1998, amendments/ modifications will be made on the request of the entrepreneur, as per the notified procedure.

Procedural Requirements for Licensed Sectors

Industrial Licence

(a) All industrial undertakings subject to compulsory industrial licensing are required to submit an application in the prescribed format, i.e., Form FC-IL. Licences are granted under the provisions of the Industries (Development and Regulation) Act, 1951. The form is available in the EAU of the SIA, at all outlets dealing in Government Publications, Indian Embassies, and can also be downloaded from the website of the DIPP. Applications for the manufacture of chlorine and caustic soda, along with associated products should include information regarding the chlorine utilization program.

(b) Application in Form FC-IL should be submitted to the EAU of the SIA, Department of Industrial Policy and Promotion, Ministry of Commerce and Industry, Udyog Bhawan, New Delhi - 110011.

(c) The application, in Form FC-IL, should be submitted along with a crossed demand draft of ₹ 2500 drawn in favour of the Pay & Accounts Officer, Department of Industrial Development, and Ministry of Industry, payable at the State Bank of India, Nirman Bhawan, and New Delhi.

(d) Approvals will normally be available within 4-6 weeks of filling the application.
Carry on Business (COB) License:

(e) A COB license is required when a small-scale unit exceeds the prescribed small-scale limit of investment in plant and machinery by way of natural growth and continues to manufacture small-scale reserved item(s). Also, if exemption from Industrial licensing granted for any item is withdrawn, the industrial undertakings that are manufacturing such item(s) require COB license. Department of Industrial Policy and Promotion, along with a crossed demand draft of ₹ 2500 drawn in favor of the Pay & Accounts Officer, Department of Industrial Development, Ministry of Industry, payable at the State Bank of India, Nirman Bhawan, New Delhi.

Foreign Direct Investment

Procedure for Automatic Route

The proposals for approval under the automatic route are to be made to the Reserve Bank of India in the FC (RBI) form. In a major drive to simplify procedures for foreign direct investment under the "automatic route", RBI has given permission to Indian Companies to accept investment under this route without obtaining prior approval from Reserve Bank of India.

However, investors are required to notify the concerned Regional Offices of RBI of receipt of inward remittances within 30 days of such receipt and will have to file the required documents with the concerned Regional Office of the RBI within 30 days after issue of shares to foreign investors. This facility is available to NRI/OCB investment also.

Procedure for Government Approval:

Foreign Investment Promotion Board:

(a) All other proposals for foreign investment, including NRI/OCB investment and foreign investment in EOU/EPZ/STP/EHTP units, which do not fulfill any or all of the parameters prescribed for automatic approval, as given in paragraph 2.8, 3.1, and 3.2 are considered for approval by the Foreign Investment Promotion Board (FIPB). The FIPB also grants composite approvals involving foreign technical collaborations and setting up of Export Oriented Units involving foreign investment/foreign technical collaboration.

(b) Applications to FIPB for approval of foreign investment should be submitted in Form FC-IL. Plain paper applications carrying all relevant details are also accepted. No fee is payable.

The following information should form part of the proposals submitted to FIPB: -

(i) Whether the applicant has had or has any previous financial/technical collaboration or trade mark agreement in India in the same or allied field for which approval has been sought; and

(ii) If so, details thereof and the justification for proposing the new venture/technical collaboration (including trade marks).

(c) The application can be submitted with the FIPB Unit of the Department of Economic Affairs, Ministry of Finance, North Block, and New Delhi. Applications can also be submitted with Indian Missions abroad who will forward them to the Department of Economic Affairs for further processing.

(d) Foreign investment proposals received in the Department of Economic Affairs (DEA) are placed before the Foreign Investment Promotion Board (FIPB) within 15 days of its receipt.

The recommendations of FIPB in respect of project proposals involving a total investment of up to ₹ 6 billion are considered and approved by the Finance Minister. Projects with a total investment exceeding ₹ 6 billion are submitted to the Cabinet Committee on Economic Affairs (CCEA) for decision.

(e) The decision of the Government in all cases is conveyed by the DEA normally within 30 days.

(f) For inward remittance and issue of shares to NRI/OCB up to 100 per cent equity also, prior permission of RBI is not required. These companies have to file the required documents with the concerned Regional Offices of RBI within 30 days after the issue of shares to NRIs/OCBs.

Foreign Technology Collaboration

Procedure for Automatic Approval

Applications for automatic approval for such foreign technology agreements should be submitted in Form FT (RBI) with the concerned Regional Offices of Reserve Bank of India. No fee is payable. Approvals are available within 2 weeks.

Procedure for Government Approval

All other proposals for foreign technology agreement, not meeting any or all of the parameters for automatic approval, and all cases of extension of existing foreign technical collaboration agreement, are considered for approval, on merits, by the Government. Application in respect of such proposals should be submitted in Form FC-IL to the Secretariat for Industrial Assistance, Department of Industrial Policy & Promotion, Ministry of Commerce and Industry, Udyog Bhavan, New Delhi. No fee is payable. The following information should form part of the proposals submitted to SIA:

(i) Whether the applicant has had or has any previous financial/technical collaboration or trade mark agreement in India in the same or allied field for which approval has been sought; and

(ii) If so, details thereof and the justifications for proposing the new venture/technical collaboration (including trademarks).

On consideration of the proposal by the Project Approval Board/FIPB, decisions are normally conveyed within 4 to 6 weeks of filing the application.

100% export-oriented units and units set up in EPZ/FTZ

A. Procedure for Approval for EOUs

Applications in the prescribed form for 100 per cent EOUs should be submitted to the Development Commissioners (DCs) of the Export Processing Zones (EPZs) concerned for automatic approval and to the SIA for Government approval. The Form is printed in the Handbook of Procedures for Export and Import, 2002-2007 published by the Ministry of Commerce & Industry and is also available at all outlets dealing in Government Publications. The application should be submitted along with a crossed demand draft of ₹ 5000 drawn in favour of the "the Pay & Accounts Officer, Department of Industrial Development, Ministry of Commerce and Industry", payable at the State Bank of India, Nirman Bhavan Branch, New Delhi. Procedure for Automatic Approval for EOUs.

Applications in the prescribed form for 100 per cent EOUs should be submitted to the DCs of the EPZs. Wherever, the proposals meet the criteria for automatic approval, the DC of the EPZ would issue approval letters within 2 weeks.

Procedure for Government Approval for EOUs:

Proposals not covered by the automatic route shall be forwarded by the DC to the Board of Approval (BOA) for consideration. On consideration of the proposal by the board, the decision would normally be conveyed in six weeks.

Procedure for Foreign Direct Investment/NRI Investment

For proposals not covered under Automatic Route, the applicant should seek separate approval of the FIPB.

B. Procedure for Approval for units located In EPZ/FTZ/SEZ

Applications for setting up units in EPZs/SEZs are submitted to the concerned DC of the EPZ/SEZ. The Form is printed in the Handbook of Procedures for Export and Import, 2002-2007 published by the Ministry of Commerce and Industry and is also available at all outlets dealing in Government Publications. The application should be submitted along with a crossed demand draft of ₹ 5000/- drawn in favor of the "the Pay & Accounts Officer, Department of Industrial Development, Ministry of Industry", payable at the State Bank of India, Nirman Bhavan Branch, New Delhi.

Procedure for Automatic Approval for units located in EPZ/FTZ/SEZ:

Applications in the prescribed form for 100 per cent EOUs should be submitted to the DCs of the EPZs/SEZs. Wherever, the proposals meet the criteria for automatic approval, as given in paragraph 5.2, the DC of the EPZ/SEZ would issue approval letters within 2 weeks. Procedure for Government Approval for units located in EPZ/FTZ /SEZ.

Proposals not covered by the automatic route shall be forwarded by the DC to the Board of Approval (BOA) for consideration. On consideration of the proposal by the Board, the decision would normally be conveyed in six weeks.

Procedure for Foreign Direct Investment/NRI Investment

All proposals for FDI/NRI/OCB investment in EPZ/EOU/SEZ are eligible for approval under Automatic Route subject to parameters listed in Para 2.9. For proposals not covered under Automatic Route, the applicant should seek separate approval of the FIPB.

EHTP/STP Units

Procedure for Approval for EHTP/STP

Application, in the prescribed form, should be submitted to the concerned Directors of STPs or the Designated Officers of EHTPs for automatic approval, and to the SIA for Government approval. The application should be submitted along with a crossed demand draft for ₹ 5,000 drawn in favour of the "the Pay & Accounts Offer, Department of Industrial Development, Ministry of Industry", payable at State Bank of India, Nirman Bhawan, New Delhi. The form is available in any outlet dealing with Government Publications.

Procedure for Automatic Approval for EHTP/STP

Application, in the prescribed form, should be submitted to the concerned Directors of STPs or the Designated Officers of EHTPs for automatic approval. Wherever, the proposals meet the criteria for automatic approval, the approval letters are issued within 2 weeks. All other proposals shall be forwarded to the Inter Ministerial Standing Committee for consideration.

Procedure for Government Approval for EHTP/STP

Application, in the prescribed form, should be submitted to the Officer designated by the Ministry of Information Technology for the purpose. Such applications shall be forwarded by the Officer designated to the Inter Ministerial Standing Committee in the Ministry of Information Technology for consideration. On consideration by the Inter Ministerial Standing Committee, a decision would be normally conveyed within six weeks.

Procedure for Foreign Direct Investment /NRI Investment

All proposals for FDI/NRI/OCB investment in EHTP/STP Units are eligible for approval under Automatic Route subject to parameters. For proposals not covered under Automatic Route, the applicant should seek separate approval of the FIPB.

Procedure for Foreign Direct Investment in Industrial Park

As 100% FDI is permitted under automatic route for setting up of industrial park, the procedure will be applicable for seeking requisite approval.

Procedure for availing income tax benefit for the industrial park

For availing 100% tax exemption available under section 80 IA of the Income Tax Act, for setting up, operating, operating and maintenance of Industrial Park, proposal has to be submitted in IPS-I form, available on this departments, to the secretariat for Industrial Assistance. The proposals which meet the given criteria (please refer to Industrial Park Notification, 2002 available on the department's web site) are approved under automatic route.

Otherwise, they are considered under non-automatic route by an empowered committee. Application for automatic approval has to be submitted in duplicate and for non-automatic approval, in six sets. The approval in IPS-I form has to be accompanied with a demand draft of ₹ 6000 drawn in favour of "Pay & Accounts Officer, Department of Industrial Development" payable at State Bank of India, Nirman Bhavan branch, New Delhi.

NIC Codes

In all the forms required for various approvals National Industrial Classification (NIC) Codes for the activities to be undertaken have to be filled in. The description of activities seeking all industrial approvals including foreign direct investment are required to be given as per the National Industrial Classification of All Economic Activities (NIC), 1987, published by the Central Statistical Organization, Ministry of Statistics and Program Implementation, New Delhi. Copies of the publication can be obtained on payment from Controller of publications, 1, Civil Lines, Delhi-1 10054 or from any outlet dealing in Government Publications.

Investment Promotion and Facilitation

Secretariat for Industrial Assistance (SIA)

SIA has been set up by the Government of India in the Department of Industrial Policy and Promotion in the Ministry of Commerce and Industry to provide a single window for entrepreneurial assistance, investor facilitation, receiving and processing all applications which require Government approval, conveying Government decisions on applications filed, assisting entrepreneurs and investors in setting up projects, (including liaison with other organisations and State Governments) and in monitoring implementation of projects. It also notifies all Government Policy relating to investment and technology, and collects and publishes monthly production data for 209 select industry groups.

Foreign Investment Promotion Board (FIPB)

The FIPB is the competent body to consider and recommend Foreign Direct Investment (FDI) proposals, which do not come under the automatic route. The FIPB, till 18.2.2003, had the following composition:

(i) Secretary, - Department of Industrial Policy & Promotion, - Chairman

(ii) Finance Secretary – Member

(iii) Commerce Secretary – Member

(iv) Secretary (Economic Relations), Ministry of External Affairs – Member

The Board also had the Revenue Secretary, Secretary (SSI and ARI) and Chairman CBEC as co-opted members. The FIPB meets every week and applications made to it are, by and large decided within a time frame of 6-8 weeks. With the shifting of the FIPB to the Department of Economic Affairs, the FIPB has been re-constituted as under:

(i) Secretary, Department of Economic Affairs - Chairman

(ii) Secretary, Department of Industrial Policy & Promotion - Member

(iii) Commerce Secretary – Member

(iv) Secretary (Economic Relations), Ministry of External Affairs - Member

The Board would be able to co-opt Secretaries and other top officials of financial institutions, banks and professional experts of industry and commerce, as and when necessary.

Foreign Investment Implementation Authority (FIIA)

Foreign Investment Implementation Authority (FIIA) was established on 9.8.1999 to assist the foreign investors in getting necessary approvals and thereby facilitating quick translation of Foreign Direct Investment (FDI) approvals into implementation. Fast Track Committees have been set up in 30 Ministries/Departments for regular review of FDI mega projects (with proposed investment of ₹ 1 billion and above), and resolution of any difficulties in consultation with the concerned Ministries/State Governments. Unresolved issues are brought before FIIA. Details of the Fast Track Committees set up in various Ministries/Departments are available at the website www.dipp.nic.in.

Meetings of FIIA

FIIA's meetings are held on regional basis as also with investors from specific countries. In the meetings of FIIA, apart from GOI Ministries, senior officials from State Governments also participate. Besides approval holders of unimplemented FDI projects with proposed investment of ₹ 100 crores and above, representatives from apex industrial associations are also invited.

Regional Meetings of FIIA

For conducting meeting of FIIA, the Country is divided into 4th region as under:

Region States Covered

Northern: Delhi, Chandigarh, Haryana, Himachal Pradesh, J&K, Madhya Pradesh, Chhattisgarh, Punjab, Rajasthan and Uttar Pradesh, Uttaranchal

Southern: Andhra Pradesh, Karnataka, Kerala, Pondicherry and Tamil Nadu, Western Gujarat, Maharashtra, Dadra & Nagar Haveli, Daman & Diu, Goa and Lakshadweep

Eastern: Bihar, Jharkhand, Orissa, Sikkim, West Bengal, Assam, Arunachal Pradesh, Manipur, Meghalaya, Mizoram, Nagaland and Tripura, and Andaman & Nicobar Islands

Meetings with Investors from Specific Countries:

In addition to the regional meetings, separate meeting with Investors from major investing countries in India are also held. In the recent past following meetings with investors from specific investing countries have been held for special focus on their problems.

- Meetings with investors from Netherlands and Italy in January 2002.
- Meeting with investors from Switzerland in May 2002.
- Meeting with investors from European Union countries in December 2002.
- Meeting with investors from Republic of Korea in May 2003.

Issues Resolved by FIIA

Foreign Investment Implementation Authority has emerged as an effective problem-solving platform for the foreign investors. Nearly 70% of the issues received from investors in FIIA have been resolved /decided.

Association of Industrial Organizations

FIIA has been seeking co-operation of apex industrial organizations viz., CII, ASSOCHAM, and FICCI, JAPAN Chamber of Commerce in India and American Chamber of Commerce (AMCHAM), etc. Information about meetings of FIIA is sent to such organizations to advise their members to participate in the meeting, in case they are experiencing difficulties in implementation of their projects. Representatives of these organisations are also invited to these meetings. CII, FICCI and ASSOCHAM have also been requested to follow up with approval holders of mega projects to whom letters have been written by FIIA.

Direct Contact with Investors

Besides the meetings with the investors, FIIA has also taken the following initiatives to establish a direct contact with foreign investors for resolution of their difficulties:

(a) FIIA periodically writes to the approval holders of FDI mega projects, which are under implementation or about which no information is available, to get a direct feedback on any difficulties being faced by them in the implementation of their projects, which can be followed by FIIA with respective Ministries/State Governments.

(b) All fresh FIPB approvals issued since September 2001 contain information on FIIA and its e-mail address for investors to approach FIIA in case of any difficulties.

(c) Directors/Deputy Secretaries of DIPP have been designated as Nodal Officers to monitor FDI Mega projects with concerned State Governments. Names and e-mail addresses of nodal officers are available on DIPP's website (www.dipp.nic.in).

(d) Indian Missions abroad, who already receive FDI applications on behalf of FIPB, have been advised to monitor implementation of FDI approvals emanating from their regions.

(e) Embassies of top 10 investing Countries in India and Indian Embassies in these Countries have been informed about FIIA and requested to bring to its notice any issue hampering implementation.

(f) Investors experiencing difficulties in the implementation of their projects can also approach FIIA through the website (www.dipp.nic.in)

Nodal Officers

The Department of Industrial Policy and Promotion has nominated officers at the Deputy Secretary/Director level as Nodal officers for facilitation of the FDI. Details of the nodal officers are also available at the web site (www.dipp.nic.in) of the Department.

Focus Windows

The Department of Industrial Policy and Promotion also has opened Country Focus Windows for countries with sizeable investment interest in India. At present, the Focus Window covers countries such as USA, Germany, France, Switzerland, Australia, Japan and Korea. For each focus window a senior officer in the Department provides facilitation and assistance.

Foreign Investment Promotion Council (FIPC)

Apart from making the policy framework investor-friendly and transparent, promotional measures are also taken to attract Foreign Direct Investment into the country. The Government has constituted a Foreign Investment Promotion Council (FIPC) in the Ministry of Commerce and Industry. This comprises professionals from Industry and Commerce. It has been set up to have a more target oriented approach toward Foreign Direct Investment promotion. The basic function of the Council is to identify specific sectors/projects within the country that require Foreign Direct Investment and target specific regions/countries of the world for its mobilization.

SIA's Promotional Activities

As an investor friendly agency, it provides information and assistance to Indian and foreign companies in setting up industry and making investments. It guides prospective entrepreneurs and disseminates information and data on a regular basis through its two monthly newsletters the "SIA Newsletter" and the "SIA Statistics" as also through its Website address, i.e. http://dipp.nic.in. It also assists potential investors in finding joint venture partners and provides complete information on relevant policies and procedures, including those, which are specific to sectors and the State Governments.

Investment Promotion and Infrastructure Development (IP & ID) Cell:

In order to give further impetus to facilitation and monitoring of investment, as well as for better coordination of infrastructural requirements for industry, a new cell called the "Investment Promotion and Infrastructure Development Cell" has been created. The functions of the Cell include: -

[a] Dissemination of information about investment climate in India;

[b] Investment facilitation;

[c] Developing and distributing multimedia presentation material and other publications;

[d] Organizing Symposiums, Seminars, etc. on investment promotion;

[e] Liaison with State Governments regarding investment promotion;

[f] Documentation of single window systems followed by various States;

[g] Match-making service for investment promotion;

[h] Coordination of progress of infrastructure sectors approved for investment/technology transfer, power, telecom, ports, roads, etc.

[i] Facilitating Industrial Model Town Projects, and Industrial Parks, etc.

[j] Promotion of Private Investment including Foreign Investment in the infrastructure sector;

[k] Compilation of sectoral policies, strategies and guidelines of infrastructure sectors, both in India and abroad; and

[l] Facilitating preparation of a perspective plan on infrastructure requirements for industry.

20 Entrepreneurial Assistance Units (EAU) of the SIA

20.1 The Entrepreneurial Assistance Unit functioning under the Secretariat for Industrial Assistance, Department of Industrial Policy and Promotion provides assistance to entrepreneurs on various subjects concerning investment decisions. The unit receives all papers/applications related to industrial approvals and immediately issues a computerized acknowledgement, which also has an identity/reference number. All correspondence with the SIA should quote this number. In case of papers filed by post, the acknowledgement will be sent by post. The Unit extends this facility to all papers/applications relating to IEMs, Industrial Licences, Foreign Investment, Foreign Technology Agreements, 100 per cent EOUs, EHTP, STP Schemes, etc.

The Unit also attends to enquiries from entrepreneurs relating to a wide range of subjects concerning investment decisions. It furnishes clarifications and arranges meetings with nodal officers in concerned Ministries/Organisations. The Unit also provides information regarding the current status of applications filed for various industrial approvals.

Website, Online Chat and Bulletin Board Facilities

To facilitate the easy availability of information to the investors and provide information about the investment climate in the country, state industrial policies, projects on offer, different publications, notifications and press releases, Department is hosting a web site www.dipp.nic.in.

The web site contains the following

- Ready Reckoner for Investing in India
- Manual on Industrial Policy and Procedures
- Press Notes, Notifications and Press Releases

- Industrial Policy Statements
- Latest Annual Report
- Information about Intellectual Property Rights
- Status of PAB/IEM and LOI
- Profile of Selected Industrial Sectors
- Important Legislations
- Information about Attached and Subordinate Offices

The website has the facility of online chat between 4.00 p.m. to 5.00 p.m. (Indian Standard Time, GMT+5 ½) on all working days. Investors can ask any question relating to FDI Policies and related issues which is replied immediately. The online chat facility is being utilized by the investors. Nearly 2000 queries were responded during chat session in 2002.

The website also has a provision of a bulletin board. If the investor cannot avail the online chat facility, he/she can post the question on the bulletin board at any time of the day. All efforts are made to send a reply within 24 hours. On an average about 3 to 4 questions are received everyday on the bulletin board.

International Centre for Alternative Dispute Resolution

International Centre for Alternative Dispute Resolution (ICADR) has been established as an autonomous organization under the aegis of Ministry of Law, Justice and Company Affairs to promote settlement of domestic and international disputes by different modes of alternate dispute resolution. ICADR has its headquarters in New Delhi and has regional office in Lucknow and Hyderabad. More information on ICADR can be obtained from the website: http://www.icadr.org

Publications

SIA Newsletter

This is a monthly publication and covers information on data relating to Foreign Direct Investment, NRI investment, sectoral break-ups, country wise break-up, all approvals accorded for Foreign Direct Investment, and NRI investment during the month, FDI inflows, and policy notifications issued during the month. Annual issues of SIA Newsletter for 1999 and 2000, have been officially released and is now available and can be obtained on payment from Controller of Publications, 1 Civil Lines, Delhi - 110 054 or from any outlet dealing in Government publications.

SIA Statistics

This is also a monthly publication which contains data relating to Industrial Licences, approvals granted for setting up 100 per cent Export-oriented Units, details of approvals for Industrial Licences, EOUs, Foreign Technical Collaboration, etc., monthly data on industrial production of 209 select industry groups, as well as policy announcements by Government during the month. Annual issues of SIA Statistics have been officially released and is now available and can be obtained on payment from Controller of Publications, 1 Civil Lines, Delhi-110 054 or from any outlet dealing in Government publications.

Other Publications

These publications include this manual as well as sector specific publications, such as on the Indian Automobile industry, Cement industry, Engineering industries, Leather industries, etc. A set of publications relating to the Infrastructure sector with specific volumes on Ports, Roads, Power, Telecom and Railways is also published. Other publications include information on current taxation and duty structure, Entry options for business in India, and the like. All or any of these publications are available through the EAU of the SIA, the Investment Promotion and Infrastructure Development Cell, as also Indian Missions abroad. These can also be down loaded from the SIA website.

Submission of Monthly Production Returns

All industrial undertakings, whether exempt or not from compulsory industrial licensing, are statutorily required to submit a monthly production return in the proforma to the Deputy Director (Statistics), Industrial Statistics Unit, Department of Industrial Policy & Promotion, Room No. 326, Udyog Bhawan, New Delhi – 110 011 Fax: 011-301 4564/301 2626

Email: ipp_ddstat@ub.nic.in every month, so as to reach him by the 7th of the following month positively. This information is used to compile various industrial growths which is time bound monthly exercise. A copy of the monthly production returns should also be submitted to the Concerned Administrative ministry/Department and to the concerned technical authorities, *viz.,* Iron and Steel Controller; Coal Controller, Directorate of Sugar; Directorate of Vanaspati, Vegetable Oils and Fats and Textile Commissioner, as the case may be.

In the case of small-scale industrial undertakings, the monthly production return should be submitted to the appropriate State Government or Commissioner of Industries and to the Department of Small-scale and Agro and Rural Industries, Government of India along with a copy to the Small Industries Service Institute.

Information about Various Other Clearances and Approvals

In addition to the approval for bringing FDI in India, many other clearances and approvals, such as registration of company, environment and forest clearance, permission for import of plants and machinery, land acquisition, power and water connection, etc., are required for starting a business in India. Brief details of Departments/Agencies along with their website addresses are given in Annex VI.

Grievances and Complaints

Business Ombudsperson

To facilitate expeditious redressal of grievances and attend to complaints relating to delays in grant and implementation of industrial approvals and facilitate their disposal, the Government has appointed a BUSINESS OMBUDSPERSON in the Ministry of Commerce and Industry. Additional Secretary and Financial Adviser, Ministry of Commerce and Industry, Udyog Bhavan, New Delhi-110011, has been nominated to act as Business Ombudsperson.

Grievances Officer and Joint Secretary

Grievances and complaints are also received by the Grievances Officer-cum-Joint Secretary, Department of Industrial Policy and Promotion, Ministry of Commerce and Industry, Udyog Bhavan, New Delhi-110011, either through post or through the mail box in the EAU of the SIA and at Reception of the Ministry of Commerce and Industry at Gate No.13 of Udyog Bhavan, New Delhi-110011. Any such communication is handled expeditiously and steps are taken to redress the grievance.

Citizens Charter

The Department of Industrial Policy and Promotion has also got its own Citizens Charter, which outlines general procedures and standards of performance expected from the Department.

Frequently Asked Questions

1. What are the forms in which business can be conducted by a foreign company in India?

Ans. Foreign companies can make investments or operate their business in a number of ways such as Liaison/representative office, . Project Office, . Branch Office, . 100% Wholly owned subsidiary and. Joint venture company. The requisite approval can be granted by Reserve Bank of India (RBI) or Foreign Investment Promotion Board (FIPB). Any company set up with FDI has to be incorporated under the Indian Companies Act with the Registrar of the company, Department of Company Affairs and all Indian operations would be conducted through this company.

2. What proposals require an Industrial Licence (IL) and how is it obtained?

Ans. In the New Industrial Policy, all industrial undertakings are exempt from licensing except for those products given in Annexure I and II of this manual and those reserved for the small-scale sector. The project should not be located within 25 kilometres of a city with a population of more than one million as per 1991 Population Census. The Government has substantially liberalized the procedures for obtaining an Industrial License. The application in form IL-FC should be filed with the SIA. Approvals are normally granted within 6-8 weeks.

3. What is the procedure for a delicensed sector?

Ans. An Industrial undertaking exempted from licensing needs only to file information in the Industrial Entrepreneurs Memorandum (IEM) with the SIA, which will issue an acknowledgement. No further approvals are required.

4. What is the Taxation Policy in India?

Ans. Since the onset of liberalization in the country, tax structure of the country is also being rationalized keeping in view the national priorities and practices followed in other countries. Foreign nationals working in India are generally taxed only on their Indian income. Income received from sources outside India is not taxable unless it is received in India. The Indian tax laws provide for exemption of tax on certain kinds of income earned for services rendered in India. Further, foreign nationals have the option of being taxed under the tax treaties that India may have signed with their country of residence. Remuneration for work done in India is taxable irrespective of the place of receipt. Remuneration includes salaries and wages, pensions, fees, commissions, profits in lieu of or in addition to salary, advance salary and perquisites. Taxable payments include all allowances and tax equalization payments unless specifically excluded. The stock options granted by the employer are taxable as capital gains at the time of sale of shares acquired due to exercise of options.

5. What are the important Labour Rules/ Regulations applicable in India?

Ans. Under the Constitution of India, Labour is a subject in the Concurrent List where both the Central & State Governments are competent to enact legislation subject to certain matters being reserved for the Centre. Some of the important Labour Acts, which are applicable for carrying out business in India, are:

Employees' Provident Fund and Miscellaneous Provisions Act, 1952

Employees' State Insurance Act, 1948

Workmen's Compensation Act, 1923

Maternity Benefit Act, 1961

Payment of Gratuity Act, 1972,

Factories Act, 1948

Dock Workers (Safety, Health & Welfare) Act, 1986

Mines Act, 1972 | Minimum Wages Act |

Payment of Bonus Act, 1965

Contract Labour [Regulation & Abolition] Act, 1970

Payment of Wages Act, 1936

6. What is the situation regarding Intellectual Property Rights protection in India?

Ans. India is a signatory to the agreement concluding the Uruguay Round of GATT negotiations and establishing the World Trade Organization (WTO). This Agreement, *inter alia,* contains an Agreement on Trade Related Aspects of Intellectual Property Rights (TRIPS), which came into force from 1st January 1995. It lays down minimum standards for protection and enforcement of Intellectual Property Rights in member countries, which are required to promote effective and adequate protection of Intellectual Property Rights with a view to reducing distortions and impediments to international trade. The obligations under the TRIPS Agreement relate to provision of minimum standards of protection within the member country's legal systems and practices.

As regards the status of various Intellectual Property laws in India and standards in respect of various areas of intellectual property, a law on Trademarks has been passed by Parliament and notified in the gazette on 30.12.1999. This law repeals and replaces the earlier Trade & Merchandise Act, 1958. A new law for the protection of Geographical Indications, *viz.,* the Geographical Indications of Goods (Registration and the Protection) Act, 1999, has also been passed by the Parliament and notified on 30.12.1999. A law called the Designs Act, 2000, relating to Industrial Designs which repeals and replaces the earlier Designs Act, 1911, has also been passed by Parliament in its Budget Session, 2000. The Act has been brought into force from 11.05.2001. A Bill on Patents to amend the Patents Act, 1970, was passed by Parliament on 14.05.2002.

7. What are the Incentives offered by States?

Ans. India is a federal country consisting of States and Union Territories. States are also partners in the economic reforms being undertaken in the country. Most of the States are making serious efforts for simplifying the rules and procedures for setting up and operating the industrial units. Single Window System is now in existence in most of the States for granting approval for setting up industrial units. Moreover, with a view to attract foreign investors in their states, many of them are offering incentive packages in the form of various tax concessions, capital and interest subsidies, reduced power tariff, etc.

8. Is investment by Non-Resident Indians (NRIs) permitted?

Ans. The Government attaches importance to investments by NRIs and Overseas Corporate Bodies (OCBs), i.e., corporate bodies in which NRIs hold at least 60% of equity. Government has provided a liberalized policy framework for approval of NRI investments through both the Automatic and the Government route. NRI/OCBs are permitted to invest upto 100% equity in the Real Estate and Civil Aviation Sectors. Automatic Approval is given by the RBI to all NRI/OCB proposals with their investment upto 100% for all items/activities except a few mentioned in Press Note 2 (2000 series) read with sector specific guidelines. Government approval is given for all proposals not qualifying for Automatic Approval.

9. Can profits, dividends, royalty, knowhow payments are repatriated from India?

Ans. All profits, dividends, royalty, knowhow payments that have been approved by the Government/RBI can be repatriated. Some sectors like investment in development of integrated township, NRI Investment in real estates, etc., may attract a lock-in period.

10. What are the formalities a joint venture company has to complete to increase the foreign equity holding?

Ans. The following formalities are required for the joint venture that wants to increase in their foreign equity holding by acquisition of shares or by any other means. (a) If only the quantum of foreign equity increased without change in percentage then Press Note no. 7 (1999 series) may be followed. (b) For increase in percentage of foreign equity by way of expansion of capital base, automatic route or FIPB/Government route would apply depending upon the nature of proposal in terms of Press Note No. 2 (2000 series). (c) Cases involving increase in percentage in foreign equity by way of acquiring existing shares in an Indian company would necessarily require prior approval of FIPB/Government. (d) In cases involving inclusion of an additional foreign collaborator, guidelines laid down in Press Note No. 18 (1998 series) would have to be satisfied.

11. What is the policy of conversion of non-repatriable shares into repatriable shares?

Ans. FIPB approval is required. Where original investment was made in foreign exchange, the change is allowed without any conditions; if not, the sale proceed will have to be repatriated to India by opening an NRO account.

12. What is the mechanism for publicizing the changes in the FDI Policies?

Ans. Changes in FDI policies are brought out in the form of Press Notes by Department of Industrial Policy & Promotion (DIPP). Soon after releasing the Press Notes to the media, it is also loaded on the Departmental website (http://dipp.nic.in/).

13. What are the policies and procedures governing Indian Investment abroad?

Ans. The Direct Investment by Indian parties in Joint Ventures (JVs) and Wholly Owned Subsidiaries (WOSs) abroad is encouraged. This Direct Investment by Indian parties can be in newly promoted foreign concerns, to make initial or additional Direct Investment in existing foreign concerns and for acquisition of overseas business. The foreign concern in which the direct investment is proposed to be made may be engaged in industrial, commercial, trading or service activities including hotel or tourism industries. These also include financial services such as insurance, mutual funds, etc. There are two categories of applications for setting up overseas JVs and WOSs, *viz.,* category (a): Fast Track and category (b): Normal Cases. All applications are to be made to and processed by the Reserve Bank of India(RBI), For Fast Track category, an application for Direct Investment in a JV/WOS abroad from a private/public limited company will be eligible for automatic approval for RBI, provided the total value of the investment by the Indian party does not exceed US $ 15 million and in respect of Indian Rupee investment in Nepal and Bhutan, it does not exceed ₹ 600 million and the amount of investment is up to 25% of annual average export/foreign exchange earning of the Indian party (other than equity exports to existing JVs/WOSs abroad) in the preceding three years, etc. for Indian software companies norms are different.

All applications involving investment beyond US $ 4 million but not exceeding US $ 15 million or those not qualifying for Fast Track clearance on the basis of applicable criteria will be processed in the RBI through a Special Committee appointed by RBI in consultation with Government and Chaired by the Commerce Secretary with the Deputy Governor, RBI, as the alternate Chairman. Investment proposals in excess of US $ 15 million will be considered if the required resources beyond US $ 15 million are raised through the GDR route. Up to 50% GDR resources raised may be invested as equity in overseas JVs subject to specific approvals of the Government. Indian parties seeking to acquire overseas ventures through time-bound bidding/tender procedures are sometimes required to obtain "in-principle" approvals on an urgent basis. In such special circumstances, RBI may grant such 'in principle' approval. RBI would formulate separate guidelines/conditions on applications and approvals for such cases. The detailed guidelines regarding the Indian investment abroad may be seen at the website: (www.iic.nic.in) of India Investment Centre, Department of Economic Affairs, Ministry of Finance.

List of Industries Reserved for the Public Sector

1. Atomic Energy
2. Railway transport.

ANNEXURE - II

LIST OF INDUSTRIES FOR WHICH INDUSTRIAL LICENSING IS COMPULSORY under Industries (Development & Regulation) Act, 1951

1. Distillation and brewing of alcoholic drinks.
2. Cigars and cigarettes of tobacco and manufactured tobacco substitutes.
3. Electronic Aerospace and defense equipment: All types.

4. Industrial explosives including detonating fuses, safety fuses, gun powder, nitrocellulose and matches.
5. Hazardous chemicals.
   (a) Hydrocyanic acid and its derivatives
   (b) Phosgene and its derivatives
   (c) Isocyanides and di-Isocyanates of hydrocarbon, not elsewhere specified (example: Methyl Isocyanides)
6. Drugs and Pharmaceuticals (according to modified Drug Policy issued in September, 1994 and subsequently amended in February, 1999)

Note: Manufacture of SSI reserved items by other industrial undertakings and location of industrial undertakings in relaxation of the notified locational policy will attract compulsory licensing.

ANNEXURE - III

Guidelines for the consideration of foreign direct investment (FDI) proposals by the foreign investment promotion board (FIPB)

(To be read with paragraph 2.11 of the Manual)

The following Guidelines are laid-down to enable the Foreign Investment Promotion Board (FIPB) to consider the proposals for Foreign Direct Investment (FDI) and formulate its recommendations.

1. All applications should be put up before the FIPB by the SIA (Secretariat of Industrial Assistance) within 15 days and it should be ensured that comments of the administrative ministries are placed before the Board either prior to/or in the meeting of the Board.
2. Proposals should be considered by the Board keeping in view the time frame of 30 days for communicating Government decision (i.e., approval of C&IM/CCEA or rejection as the case may be).
3. In cases in which either the proposal is not cleared or further information is required, in order to obviate delays presentation by applicant in the meeting of the FIPB should be resorted to.
4. While considering cases and making recommendations, FIPB should keep in mind the sectoral requirements and the sectoral policies *vis-a-vis* the proposal(s).
5. FIPB would consider each proposal in totality (i.e., if it includes apart from foreign investment, technical collaboration/industrial licence) for composite approval or otherwise. However, the FIPB's recommendation would relate only to the approval for foreign financial and technical collaboration and the foreign investor will need to take other prescribed clearances separately.
6. The Board should examine the following while considering proposals submitted to it for consideration:
   (i) Whether the items of activity involve industrial license or not and if so the considerations for grant of industrial licence must be gone into;
   (ii) Whether the proposal involves technical collaboration and if so: - (a) the source and nature of technology sought to be transferred.

(iii) Whether the proposal involves any mandatory requirement for exports and if so whether the applicant is prepared to undertake such obligation (this is for items reserved for small-scale sector as also for dividend balancing, and for 100% EOUs/EPZ units);

(iv) Whether the proposal involves any export projection and if so the items of export and the projected destinations;

(v) Whether the proposal has concurrent commitment under other schemes such as EPCG Scheme etc.

(vi) In the case of Export Oriented Units (EOUs) whether the prescribed minimum value addition norms and the minimum turnover of exports are met or not;

(vii) Whether the proposal involves relaxation of locational restrictions stipulated in the industrial licensing policy;

(viii) Whether the proposal has any strategic or defense-related considerations, and

(ix) Whether the proposal has any previous joint venture or technology transfer/trademark agreement in the same or allied field in India, the detailed circumstance in which it is considered necessary to set up a new joint venture/enter into new technology transfer (including trademark), and proof that the new proposal would not in any way jeopardize the interest of the existing joint venture or technology/trade mark partner or other stake holders.

7. While considering proposals the following may be prioritized.

(a) Items/activities covered under automotic route (i.e., those which do not qualify for automatic approval).

(b) Items falling in infrastructure sector.

(c) Items which have an export potential

(d) Items which have large scale employment potential and especially for rural people.

(e) Items, which have a direct or backward linkage with agro business/farm sector.

(f) Item which have greater social relevance such as hospitals, human resource development, life saving drugs and equipment.

(g) Proposals, which result in induction of technology or infusion of capital.

8. The following should be especially considered during the scrutiny and consideration of proposals:

(a) The extent of foreign equity proposed to be held (keeping in view sectoral caps if any - e.g., 24% for SSI units, 40% for air taxi/airlines operators, 49% in basic/cellular/paging, etc., in Telecom sector).

(b) Extent of equity with composition of foreign/NRI (which may include OCB)/resident Indians.

(c) Extent of equity from the point of view whether the proposed project would amount to a holding company/wholly owned subsidiary/a company with dominant foreign investment (i.e., 75% or more) joint venture.

(d) Whether the proposed foreign equity is for setting up a new project (joint venture or otherwise) or whether it is for enlargement of foreign/NRI equity or whether it is for fresh induction of foreign equity/NRI equity in an existing Indian company.

(e) In the case of fresh induction of foreign/NRI equity and/or cases of enlargement of foreign/ NRI equity in existing Indian companies whether there is a resolution of the Board of Directors supporting the said induction/enlargement of foreign/NRI equity and whether there is a shareholders agreement or not.

(f) In the case of induction of fresh equity in the existing Indian companies and/or enlargement of foreign equity in existing Indian companies, the reason why the proposal has been made and the modality for induction/enhancement [i.e., whether by increase of paid-up capital/authorized capital, transfer of shares (hostile or otherwise) whether by rights issue, or by what modality]. Cases pertaining to FIPB approvals, which involve increase in the non-resident equity within the approved percentage of non-resident equity in a joint venture company and enhancement of paid-up capital in a wholly owned subsidiary do not require FIPB approval provided the intent for increase in the amount of foreign equity is duly notified to SIA and formal documentation by way of intimation is made to SIA within 30 days of receipt of funds and allotment of shares (to non-resident shareholders).

(g) Issue/transfer/pricing of shares will be as per SEBI/RBI guidelines.

(h) Whether the activity is an industrial or a service activity or a combination of both.

(i) Whether the item of activity involves any restriction by way of reservation for the small-scale sector.

(j) Whether there are any sectoral restrictions on the activity (e.g., there is ban on foreign investment in real estate while it is not so for NRI/OCB investment).

(k) Whether the item involves only trading activity and if so whether it involves export or both export and import, or also includes domestic trading and if domestic trading whether it also includes retail trading.

(l) Whether the proposal involves import of items which are hazardous, banned or detrimental to environment (e.g., import of plastic scrap or recycled plastics).

9. In respect of activities to which equity caps apply, FIPB may consider recommending higher levels of foreign equity as compared to the prescribed caps, keeping in view the special requirements and merits of each case.

10. In respect of other industries/activities the Board may consider recommending 51 per cent foreign equity on examination of each individual proposal. For higher levels of equity up to 74 per cent the Board may consider such proposals keeping in view considerations such as the extent of capital needed for the project, the nature and quality of technology, the requirements of marketing and management skills and the commitment for exports.

11. FIPB may consider recommending proposals for 100 per cent foreign owned holding/ subsidiary companies based on the following criteria:

(a) Where only "holding" operation is involved all subsequent/downstream investments to be carried out would require prior approval of the Government;

(b) Where proprietary technology is sought to be protected or sophisticated technology is proposed to be brought in;

(c) Where at least 50% of production is to be exported;

(d) Proposals for consultancy; and

(e) Proposals for industrial model towns/industrial parks or estates.

12. In special cases, where the foreign investor is unable initially to identify an Indian joint venture partner, the Board may consider and recommend proposals permitting 100 per cent foreign equity on a temporary basis on the condition that the foreign investor would divest to the Indian parties (either individual, joint venture partners or general public or both) at least 26 per cent of its equity within a period of 3-5 years.

13. Similarly in the case of a joint venture, where the Indian partner is unable to raise resources for expansion/technological upgradation of the existing industrial activity the Board may consider and recommend increase in the proportion/percentage (up to 100 per cent) of the foreign equity in the enterprise.

14. In respect of trading companies, 100 per cent foreign equity may be permitted in the case of the activities involving the following:

(i) Exports;

(ii) Bulk imports with ex-port/ex-bonded warehouse sales;

(iii) Cash and carry wholesale trading;

(iv) Other import of goods or services provided at least 75% is for procurement and sale of goods and services among the companies of the same group.

15. In respect of the companies in the infrastructure/services sector where there is a prescribed cap for foreign investment, only the direct investment should be considered for the prescribed cap and foreign investment in an investing company should not be set off against this cap provided the foreign direct investment in such investing company does not exceed 49 per cent and the management of the investing company is with the Indian owners.

16. No condition specific to the letter of approval issued to a foreign investor would be changed or additional condition imposed subsequent to the issue of a letter of approval. This would not prohibit changes in general policies and regulations applicable to the industrial sector.

17. Where in case of a proposal (not being 100% subsidiary) foreign direct investment has been approved up to a designated percentage of foreign equity in the joint venture company the percentage would not be reduced while permitting induction of additional capital subsequently. Also in the case of approved activities, if the foreign investor(s) concerned wished to bring in additional capital on later dates keeping the investment to such approved activities, FIPB would recommend such cases for approval on an automatic basis.

18. As regards proposal for private sector banks, the application would be considered only after "in principle" permission is obtained from the Reserve Bank of India (RBI).

19. The restrictions prescribed for proposals in various sectors as obtained, at present, is given in the annexure - IV and these should be kept in view while considering the proposals. The Guidelines are meant to assist the FIPB to consider proposals in an objective and transparent manner. These would not in any way restrict the flexibility or bind the FIPB from considering

the proposals in their totality or making recommendation based on other criteria or special circumstances or features it considers relevant. Besides these are in the nature of administrative Guidelines and would not in any way be legally binding in respect of any recommendation to be made by the FIPB or decisions to be taken by the Government in cases involving Foreign Direct Investment (FDI). These guidelines are issued without prejudice to the Government's right to issue fresh guidelines or change the legal provisions and policies whenever considered necessary. The above mentioned guidelines stands modified to the extend changes have been notified by Secretariat for Industrial Assistance from time to time.

ANNEXURE - IV

Sector specific guidelines for foreign direct investment:

Sl. No. Sector Guidelines

1. Private Sector 49% from all sources on the automatic route subject to guidelines issued from RBI from time-to-time. Consolidated guidelines are given at Appendix-A Non Banking (a) FDI/NRI/OCB investments allowed in the following 19 NBFC activities shall be as per levels:

(a) Financial Companies indicated below: (NBFC)

- (i) Merchant banking
- (ii) Underwriting
- (iii) Portfolio Management Services
- (iv) Investment Advisory Services
- (v) Financial Consultancy
- (vi) Stock Broking
- (vii) Asset Management
- (viii) Venture Capital
- (ix) Custodial Services
- (x) Factoring
- (xi) Credit Reference Agencies
- (xii) Credit rating Agencies
- (xiii) Leasing & Finance
- (xiv) Housing Finance
- (xv) Forex Broking
- (xvi) Credit card business
- (xvii) Money changing Business
- (xviii) Micro Credit
- (xix) Rural Credit

(b) Minimum Capitalization Norms for fund-based NBFCs:

- (i) For FDI up to 51% - US$ 0.5 million to be brought upfront
- (ii) For FDI above 51% and up to 75% - US $ 5 million to be brought upfront

(iii) For FDI above 75% and up to 100% - US $ 50 million out of which US $ 7.5 million to be brought up front and the balance in 24 months

(c) Minimum capitalization norms for non-fund-based activities: Minimum capitalization norm of US $ 0.5 million is applicable in respect of all permitted non-fund-based NBFCs with foreign investment

(d) Foreign investors can set up 100% operating subsidiaries without the condition to disinvest a minimum of 25% of its equity to Indian entities, subject to bringing in US $ 50 million as at (b) (iii) above (without any restriction on number of operating subsidiaries without bringing in additional capital)

(e) Joint Venture operating NBFC's that have 75% or less than 75% foreign investment will also be allowed to set up subsidiaries for undertaking other NBFC activities, subject to the subsidiaries also complying with the applicable minimum capital inflow, i.e., (b) (i) and (b) (ii) above

(f) FDI in the NBFC sector is put on automatic route subject to compliance with guidelines of the Reserve Bank of India. RBI would issue appropriate guidelines in this regard Insurance FDI up to 26% in the Insurance sector is allowed on the automatic route subject to obtaining license from Insurance Regulatory & Development Authority (IRDA)

2. Domestic Airlines (Detailed guidelines have been issued by Ministry of Civil Aviation) In the domestic Airlines

(i) FDI up to 40% permitted subject to no direct or indirect equity participation by foreign airlines

(ii) 100% investment by NRIs/OCBs

(iii) The automatic route is not available

Airports up to 100% with FDI, beyond 74% requiring Government approval

3. Telecommunication (i) In basic, cellular, value-added services and global mobile personal communications by satellite, FDI is limited to 49% subject to licensing and security requirements and adherence by the companies (who are investing and the companies in which the investment is being made) to the license conditions for foreign equity cap and lock-in period for transfer and addition of equity and other licence provisions

(ii) In ISPs with gateways, radio-paging and end-to-end bandwidth,

FDI is permitted up to 74% with FDI, beyond 49% requiring Government approval. These services would be subject to licensing and security requirements

(iii) No equity cap is applicable to manufacturing activities

(iv) FDI upto 100% is allowed for the following activities in the telecom sector:

(a) ISPs not providing gateways (both for satellite and submarine cables)

(b) Infrastructure Providers providing dark fiber (IP Category 1)

(c) Electronic Mail; and

(d) Voice Mail

The above would be subject to the following conditions:

(a) FDI up to 100% is allowed subject to the condition that such companies would divest 26% of their equity in favour of Indian public in 5 years, if these companies are listed in other parts of the world

(b) The above services would be subject to licensing and security requirements, wherever required

(c) Proposals for FDI beyond 49% shall be considered by FIPB on case to case basis

4. Petroleum.

(a) Under the exploration policy, FDI up to 100% is allowed for small fields through competitive (other than Refining) bidding; upto 60% for unincorporated JV; and up to 51% for incorporated JV with a No Objection Certificate for medium size fields

(b) For petroleum products and pipeline sector, FDI is permitted up to 51%

(c) FDI is permitted up to 74% in infrastructure related to marketing and marketing of petroleum products

(d) 100% wholly owned subsidiary (WOS) is permitted for the purpose of market study and formulation

(e) 100% wholly owned subsidiary (WOS) is permitted for investment/Financing

(f) For actual trading and marketing, minimum 26% Indian equity is required over 5 years. The automatic route is not available Petroleum a. FDI is permitted up to 26% in case of public sector units (PSUs). PSUs will hold 26% and balance (Refining) 48% by public. Automatic route is not available

(g) In case of private Indian companies, FDI is permitted upto 100% under automatic route

5. Housing. No foreign investment is permitted in this sector except for development of integrated townships and Real Estate settlements where FDI upto 100% is permitted with prior Government approval. NRIs/OCBs are allowed to invest in the following activities

(a) Development of serviced plots and construction of built up residential premises

(b) Investment in real estate covering construction of residential and commercial premises including business centers and offices

(c) Development of townships

(d) City and regional level urban infrastructure facilities, including both roads and bridges

(e) Investment in manufacture of building materials, which is also open to FDI

(f) Investment in participatory ventures in (a) to (e) above

(g) Investment in housing finance institutions, which is also, open to FDI as an NBFC

6. Coal and Lignite

(i) Private Indian companies setting up or operating power projects as well as coal or lignite mines for captive consumption are allowed FDI up to 100%

(ii) 100% FDI is allowed for setting up coal processing plants subject to the condition that the company shall not do coal mining and shall not sell washed coal or sized coal from its coal processing plants in the open market and shall supply the washed or sized coal to those parties who are supplying raw coal to coal processing plants for washing or sizing

(iii) FDI up to 74% is allowed for exploration or mining of coal or lignite for captive consumption

(iv) In all the above cases, FDI is allowed up to 50% under the automatic route subject to the condition that such investment shall not exceed 49% of the equity of a PSU

7. Venture Capital Offshore. Venture Capital Funds/Companies are allowed to invest in domestic venture capital undertaking Fund (VCF) and as well as other companies through the automatic route, subject only to SEBI regulations and sector Venture Capital specific caps on FDI Company(VCC)

8. Trading. It is permitted under automatic route with FDI up to 51% provided it is primarily export activities and the undertaking is an export house/trading house/super trading house/star trading house.

However, under the FIPB route:

(i) 100% FDI is permitted in case of trading companies for the following activities:

- exports
- bulk imports with ex-port/ex-bonded warehouse sales
- cash and carry wholesale trading
- other import of goods or services provided at least 75% is for procurement and sale of goods and services among the companies of the same group and not for third party use or onward transfer/distribution/sales

(ii) The following kinds of trading are also permitted, subject to provisions of EXIM Policy:

(a) Companies for providing after sales services (that is not trading per se)

(b) Domestic trading of products of JVs is permitted at the wholesale level for such trading companies who wish to market manufactured products on behalf of their joint ventures in which they have equity participation in India

(c) Trading of hi-tech items/items requiring specialized after sales service

(d) Trading of items for social sector

(e) Trading of hi-tech, medical and diagnostic items

(f) Trading of items sourced from the small-scale sector under which, based on technology provided and laid down quality specifications, a company can market that item under its brand name

(g) Domestic sourcing of products for exports

(h) Test marketing of such items for which a company has approval for manufacture provided such test marketing facility will be for a period of two years, and investment in setting up manufacturing facilities commences simultaneously with test marketing

(i) FDI up to 100% permitted for e-commerce activities subject to the condition that such companies would divest 26% of their equity in favor of the Indian public in five years, if these companies are listed in other parts of the world. Such companies would engage only in business to business (B2B), e-commerce and not in retail trading.

9. Investing Companies. In respect of the companies in infrastructure/service sector, where there is a prescribed cap for foreign in infrastructure/ investment, only the direct investment will be considered for the prescribed cap and foreign investment in service sector an investing company will not be set off against this cap provided the foreign direct investment in such investing company does not exceed 49% and the management of the investing company is with the Indian owners. The automatic route is not available

10. Atomic minerals. The following three activities are permitted to receive FDI/NRI/OCB investments through FIPB (as per detailed guidelines issued by Department of Atomic Energy vide Resolution No.8/1(1)/97-PSU/1422 dated 6.10.98):

(a) Mining and mineral separation

(b) Value addition *per se* to the products of (a) above

(c) Integrated activities (comprising of both (a) and (b) above.)

The following FDI participation is permitted:

(i) Up to 74% in both pure value addition and integrated projects

(ii) For pure value addition projects as well as integrated projects with value addition upto any intermediate stage, FDI is permitted upto 74% through joint venture companies with Central/State PSUs in which equity holding of at least one PSU is not less than 26%

(iii) In exceptional cases, FDI beyond 74% will be permitted subject to clearance of the Atomic Energy Commission before FIPB approval

11. Defense and Foreign Direct Investment, including NRI/OCB investment, is permitted up to 26% with prior Government strategic industries approval subject to licensing and security requirements. Detailed guidelines for participation of private sector and foreign investors in this sector are given in Appendix-B

12. Agriculture. No FDI/NRI/OCB investment is permitted other than Tea sector, where (including plantation) FDI permitted up to 100% in Tea sector, including tea plantations, with prior Government approval and subject to following conditions:

- Compulsory divestment of 26% equity in favor of Indian partner/Indian public within a period of five years, and
- Prior State government approval required in case of any future land use change.

The above dispensation would be applicable to all fresh investments (FDI) made in this sector.

13. Print media. The following FDI participation in Indian entities publishing Newspapers and periodicals is permitted:

(a) FDI up to 74% in publishing scientific/technical and specialty magazines/periodicals/journals

(b) FDI up to 26% in publishing Newspapers and Periodicals dealing in News and Current Affairs subject to verification of antecedents of foreign investor, keeping editorial and management control in the hands of resident Indians and ensuring against dispersal of Indian equity. The detailed guidelines had been issued by Ministry of Information and Broadcasting.

14. Broadcasting.

(a) TV Software Production 100% foreign investment allowed subject to:

(i) all future laws on broadcasting and no claim of any privilege or protection by virtue of approval accorded, and

(ii) not undertaking any broadcasting from Indian soil without Government approval

(b) Setting up hardware facilities, such as uplinking, HUB, etc. Private companies incorporated in India with permissible FII/NRI/OCB/PIO equity within the limits (as in the case of telecom sector FDI limit up to 49% inclusive of both FDI and portfolio investment) to set up linking hub (teleports) for leasing or hiring out their facilities to broadcasters Foot note: As regards satellite broadcasting, all TV channels irrespective of management control to uplink from India provided they undertake to comply with the broadcast (program & advertising) code

(c) Cable Network: Foreign investment allowed up to 49% (inclusive of both FDI and portfolio investment) of paid up share capital. Companies with minimum 51% of paid up share capital held by Indian citizens are eligible under the Cable Television Network Rules (1994) to provide cable TV services

(d) Direct-to-Home: Company with a maximum of foreign equity including

FDI/NRI/OCB/FII of 49% would be eligible to obtain DTH License. Within the foreign equity, the FDI component not to exceed 20%

(e) Terrestrial Broadcasting FM: The licensee shall be a company registered in India under the Companies Act. All share holding should be held by Indians except for the limited portfolio investment by FII/NRI/PIO/OCB subject to such ceiling as may be decided from time to time. Company shall have no direct investment by foreign entities, NRIs and OCBs. As of now, the foreign investment is permissible to the extent of 20% portfolio investment

(f) Terrestrial TV: No private operator is allowed in terrestrial TV transmission

15. Power. Up to 100% FDI allowed in respect of projects relating to electricity generation, transmission and distribution, other than atomic reactor power plants. There is no limit on the project cost and quantum of foreign direct investment

16. Drugs & FDI. Up to 100% is permitted on the automatic route for manufacture of drugs and pharmaceutical. Pharmaceuticals provided the activity does not attract compulsory licensing or involve use of recombinant DNA technology, and specific cell/tissue targeted formulations FDI proposals for the manufacture of licensable drugs and pharmaceuticals and bulk drugs produced by recombinant DNA technology, and specific cell/tissue targeted formulations will require prior Government approval

17. Roads & Highways. FDI up to 100% under automatic route is permitted in projects for construction and maintenance of roads, highways, vehicular bridges, toll roads, vehicular tunnels, ports and harbors

18. Hotels & Tourism. 100% FDI is permissible in the sector on the automatic route. The term hotels include restaurants, beach resorts, and other tourist complexes providing accommodation and/or catering and food facilities to tourists. Tourism related industry include travel agencies, tour operating agencies and tourist transport operating agencies, units providing facilities for cultural, adventure and wild life experience to tourists, surface, air and water transport facilities to tourists, leisure,

entertainment, amusement, sports, and health units for tourists and Convention/Seminar units and organisations for foreign technology agreements, automatic approval is granted if—

(i) up to 3% of the capital cost of the project is proposed to be paid for technical and consultancy services including fees for architects, design, supervision, etc.

(ii) up to 3% of net turnover is payable for franchising and marketing/publicity support fee, and

(iii) up to 10% of gross operating profit is payable for management fee, including incentive fee

19. Mining.

(i) For exploration and mining of diamonds and precious stones FDI is allowed up to 74% under automatic route

(ii) For exploration and mining of gold and silver and minerals other than diamonds and precious stones, metallurgy and processing FDI is allowed up to 100% under automatic route

(iii) Press Note No. 18 (1998 series) dated 14.12.98 would not be applicable for setting up 100% owned subsidiaries in so far as the mining sector is concerned, subject to a declaration from the applicant that he has no existing joint venture for the same area and/or the particular mineral

20. Postal Services. FDI up to 100% is permitted in courier services with prior Government approval excluding distribution of letters, which is reserved exclusively for the state

21. Pollution Control. FDI up to 100% in both manufacture of pollution control equipment and consultancy for integration and management of pollution control systems is permitted on the automatic route

22. Advertising and Films.

(a) Advertising sector

FDI up to 100% allowed on the automatic route

(b) Film sector (film production, exhibition and distribution including related services/products)

FDI up to 100% allowed on the automatic route with no entry level condition

23. Mass Rapid Metro. FDI up to 100% is permitted on the automatic route in mass rapid transport system in all metros. Transit System including associated real estate development

24. Township. FDI up to 100% is permitted for development of integrated townships including houses, commercial development premises, hotels, resorts, city and regional level urban infrastructure facilities such as roads and bridges, mass rapid transit system; and manufacture of building materials. Development of land and providing allied infrastructure will form an integral part of township's development. FDI in this sector would be permissible with prior Government approval. Detailed guidelines regarding investment in this sector are given at Appendix-C

25. Establishment and FDI up to 74% is permitted with prior Government approval for Operation of satellite

26. Lottery business. Government has reiterated prohibition of foreign direct investment gambling & betting (FDI)/Foreign technical collaboration (FTC) in any form in lottery business, gambling and betting sector.

APPENDIX - A

Guidelines for foreign direct investment (FDI) in the banking sector

1. Limit for FDI under automatic route in private sector banks

   (a) In terms of the Press Note no. 4 (2001 series) dated May 21, 2001 issued by Ministry of Commerce & Industry, Government of India, FDI up to 49% from all sources will be permitted in private sector banks on the automatic route, subject to conformity with the guidelines issued by RBI from time to time.

   (b) For the purpose of determining the above-mentioned ceiling of 49% FDI under the "automatic route" in respect of private sector banks, following categories of shares will be included.

      (i) IPOs,

      (ii) Private placements,

      (iii) ADRs/GDRs, and

      (iv) Acquisition of shares from existing shareholders [subject to (d) below]

   (c) It may be clarified that as per Government of India guidelines, issue of fresh shares under automatic route is not available to those foreign investors who have a financial or technical collaboration in the same or allied field. This category of investors requires FIPB approval.

   (d) It may be further clarified that, as per Government of India guidelines, automatic route is not applicable to transfer of existing shares in a banking company from residents to non–residents. This category of investors require approval of FIPB followed by "in principle" approval by Exchange Control Department (ECD), RBI. The "fair price" for transfer of existing shares is determined by RBI broadly on the basis of SEBI guidelines for listed shares and erstwhile CCI guidelines for unlisted shares. After receipt of "in principle" approval, the resident seller can receive funds and apply to ECD, RBI for obtaining final permission for transfer of shares.

   (e) Under the Insurance Act, the maximum foreign investment in an insurance company has been fixed at 26%. Application for foreign investment in banks, which have joint venture /subsidiary in insurance sector, should be made to RBI. Such applications will be considered by RBI in consultation with Insurance Regulatory and Development Authority (IRDA).

   (f) Foreign banks having branch presence in India are eligible for FDI in the private sector banks subject to the overall cap of 49% mentioned above with the approval of RBI.

2. Limit for FDI in public sector banks FDI and portfolio investment in nationalized banks are subject to overall statutory limits of 20% as provided under Section 3 (2D) of the Banking Companies (Acquisition and Transfer of Undertakings) Acts, 1970/80. The same ceiling would also apply in respect of such investments in State Bank of India and its associate banks.

3. Voting rights of foreign investors In terms of the statutory provisions under the various banking Acts, the voting rights, when exercised, which are stipulated as under:

Private sector banks – [Section 12 (2) of Banking Regulation Act, 1949] No person holding shares, in respect of any share held by him, shall exercise voting rights on poll in excess of ten per cent of the total voting rights of all the share holders Nationalized Banks – [Section 3(2E) of Banking Companies (Acquisition and Transfer of Undertakings) Acts, 1970/80] No shareholder, other than the

Central Government, shall be entitled to exercise voting rights in respect of any shares held by him in excess of one per cent of the total voting rights of all the share holders of the nationalized banks

State Bank of India (SBI) – (Section 11 of State Bank of India Act, 1955) No shareholder, other than RBI, shall be entitled to exercise voting rights in excess of ten per cent of the issued capital (Government, in consultation with RBI can raise the above voting rate to more than ten per cent). SBI Associates – [Section 19(1) & (2) of SBI (Subsidiary Bank) Act, 1959] No person shall be registered as a shareholder in respect of any shares held by him in excess of two hundred shares. No shareholder, other than SBI, shall be entitled to exercise voting rights in excess of one per cent of the issued capital of the subsidiary bank concerned.

4. Approval of RBI and reporting requirements

(i) Under extant instructions, transfer of shares of 5 per cent and more of the paid-up capital of a private sector banking company, requires prior acknowledgments of RBI. For FDI of 5 per cent and more of the paid–up capital, the private sector banking company has to apply in the prescribed form to the Department of Banking Operations and Department in the Regional Office of RBI, where the bank's Head Office is located.

(ii) Under the provisions of FEMA 1999, any fresh issue of shares of a banking company, either through the automatic route or with the specific approval of FIPB does not require further approval of Exchange Control Department (ECD) of RBI from the exchange control angle. The Indian banking company is only required to undertake 2- stage reporting to the ECD as follows:

(a) In the first stage, the Indian company has to submit a report within 30 days of the date of receipt of amount of consideration indicating the name and address of foreign investors, date of receipt of funds and their rupee equivalent, name of bank through whom funds were received and details of Government approval, if any.

(b) In the second stage, the Indian banking company is required to file within 30 days from the date of issue of shares, a report in form FC-GPR together with a certificate from the Company Secretary of the concerned company certifying that various regulations have been complied with. The report will also be accompanied by a certificate from a Chartered Accountant indicating the manner of arriving at the price of the shares issued.

5. Conformity with SEBI Regulations and Companies Act provisions wherever applicable, FDI in banking companies should conform to the provisions regarding shareholding and share transfer, etc., as stipulated by SEBI, Companies Act, etc.

6. Disinvestments by Foreign Investors

In terms of regulation 10 and 11 of RBI Notification No. FEMA/20/2000-RB dated May 3, 2000 issued under FEMA 1999; disinvestments by foreign investors would be governed by the following:

(i) Sale of shares by non-residents on a stock exchange and remittance of the proceeds thereof through an authorized dealer does not require RBI approval.

(ii) Sale of shares by private arrangement requires RBIs prior approval. RBI grants permission for sale of shares at a price that is market related and is arrived at in terms of guidelines indicated in Regulation 10 above.

7. All commercial banks, which either have foreign investments or intending to have foreign investments, need to observe the above guidelines.

APPENDIX - B

Guidelines for licensing production of arms & ammunitions:

In pursuance of the Government decision to allow private sector participation up to 100% in the defense industry sector with foreign direct investment (FDI) permissible up to 26%, both subject to licensing as notified *vide* Press Note No. 4 (2001 series), the following guidelines for licensing production of arms and ammunitions are hereby notified:

1. Licence applications will be considered and licences given by the Department of Industrial Policy & Promotion, Ministry of Commerce & Industry, in consultation with Ministry of Defense.
2. Cases involving FDI will be considered by the FIPB and licences given by the Department of Industrial Policy & Promotion in consultation with Ministry of Defence.
3. The applicant should be an Indian company/partnership firm.
4. The management of the Applicant Company/partnership should be in Indian hands with majority representation on the Board as well as the Chief Executive of the company/ partnership firm being resident Indians.
5. Full particulars of the Directors and the Chief Executives should be furnished along with the applications.
6. The Government reserves the right to verify the antecedents of the foreign collaborators and domestic promoters including their financial standing and credentials in the world market. Preference would be given to original equipment manufacturers or design establishments, and companies having a good track record of past supplies to Armed Forces, Space and Atomic energy sectors and having an established R&D base.
7. There would be no minimum capitalization for the FDI. A proper assessment, however, needs to be done by the management of the applicant company depending upon the product and the technology. The licensing authority would satisfy itself about the adequacy of the net worth of the foreign investor taking into account the category of weapons and equipment that are proposed to be manufactured.
8. There would be a three-year lock-in period for transfer of equity from one foreign investor to another foreign investor (including NRIs & OCBs with 60% or more NRI stake) and such transfer would be subject to prior approval of the FIPB and the Government.
9. The Ministry of Defence is not in a position to give purchase guarantee for products to be manufactured. However, the planned acquisition program for such equipment and overall requirements would be made available to the extent possible.
10. The capacity norms for production will be provided in the license based on the application as well as the recommendations of the Ministry of Defence, which will look into existing capacities of similar and allied products.
11. Import of equipment for pre-production activity including development of prototype by the applicant company would be permitted.

12. Adequate safety and security procedures would need to be put in place by the licensee once the license is granted and production commences. These would be subject to verification by authorized Government agencies.
13. The standards and testing procedures for equipment to be produced under license from foreign collaborators or from indigenous R&D will have to be provided by the licensee to the Government nominated quality assurance agency under appropriate confidentiality clause. The nominated quality assurance agency would inspect the finished product and would conduct surveillance and audit of the Quality Assurance Procedures of the licensee. Self-certification would be permitted by the Ministry of Defence on case to case basis, which may involve either individual items, or group of items manufactured by the licensee. Such permission would be for a fixed period and subject to renewals.
14. Purchase preference and price preference may be given to the Public Sector organizations as per guidelines of the Department of Public Enterprises.
15. Arms and ammunition produced by the private manufacturers will be primarily sold to the Ministry of Defence. These items may also be sold to other Government entities under the control of the Ministry of Home Affairs and State Governments with the prior approval of the Ministry of Defence. No such item should be sold within the country to any other person or entity. The export of manufactured items would be subject to policy and guidelines as applicable to Ordnance Factories and Defence Public Sector Undertakings. Non-lethal items would be permitted for sale to persons/entities other than the Central or State Governments with the prior approval of the Ministry of Defense. Licensee would also need to institute a verifiable system of removal of all goods out of their factories. Violation of these provisions may lead to cancellation of the license.
16. Government decision on applications to FIPB for FDI in defence industry sector will be normally communicated within a time frame of 10 weeks from the date of acknowledgment by the Secretariat for Industrial Assistance in the Department of Industrial Policy & Promotion.

APPENDIX - C

1. Guidelines for FDI in development of integrated township including housing and building material. Government vide Press Note No. 4 (2001 series) permitted FDI up to 100% for development of integrated townships, including housing, commercial premises, hotels, resorts, city and regional level urban infrastructure facilities such as roads and bridges, mass rapid transit systems and manufacture of building materials. Development of land and providing allied infrastructure will form an integrated part of township's development.

2. FDI in the development of integrated townships will be subject to the following guidelines:

(i) The foreign company intending to invest, shall be registered as an Indian Company under Companies Act 1956 and will henceforth be allowed to take up land assembly and its development as a part of Integrated Township Development. All such cases would be processed by FIPB on the recommendation of Ministry of Urban Development & Poverty Alleviation and other concerned Ministries/Departments. Ministry of Urban Development & Poverty Alleviation will develop an exclusive cell to deal with such cases.

(ii) The core business of the company seeking to make investment should be integrated township development with a record of successful execution of such projects elsewhere.

(iii) The minimum area to be developed by such a company should be 100 acres for which norms and standards are to be followed as per local by-laws/rules. In the absence of such by-laws/ rules, a minimum of two thousand dwelling units for about ten thousand populations will need to be developed by the investor.

(iv) The investing foreign company should achieve clear milestones once their proposal has been approved.

(a) The minimum capitalization form shall be US$ 10 million for a wholly owned subsidiary and US$ 5 million for joint ventures with Indian partner/s. The funds would have to be brought in upfront.

(b) A minimum lock-in period of three years from completion of minimum capitalization shall apply before repatriation of original investment is permitted.

(c) A minimum of 50% of the integrated project development must be completed within a period of five years from the date of possession of the first piece of land. However, if the investor intends to exit earlier due to reasons beyond his control, it shall be decided by FIPB on a case-to-case basis.

(v) Conditions regarding the use of land for commercial purposes, development charges, external development charges and other charges as laid down in Master Plan/By-laws, preparation of layout and building plan, development of internal and peripheral development, development of other infrastructure facilities including the trunk services, etc., will be the responsibility of the investor as per planning norms and standards on similar lines as those applicable to local investors. In the absence of such standards and norms, every State Government may decide their own conditions for which the Urban Development Plan Formulation and Implementation guidelines circulated by the Ministry of Urban Development & Poverty Alleviation may serve as a guiding principle.

(vi) Land with assembled area for peripheral services such as police stations, milk booths will be handed over free of cost to the Government/local authority/agency as the case may be.

(vii) The Developer will retain the lands for community services such as (i) schools (ii) shopping complex (iii) community centres (iv) ration shop (v) hospital/dispensary. These services will be developed by developer himself and shall be made operational before the houses are occupied.

(viii) The developer, after properly developing playgrounds, park, will make it available to the local authorities free of cost.

(ix) The developer will ensure the norms and standards as applicable under local laws / rules.

(x) For companies investing in Special Economic Zones, Foreign Investment Promotion Board may accord exemption to any of the above mentioned conditions on a case-to case basis. This will, however, be an interim measure till guidelines are evolved in due course in a need based manner.

ANNEXURE - V

List of cities with population of 10 lakhs (1 million) and above according to the provisional

RESULTS OF 1991 CENSUS

Name of the Cities

1. Greater Mumbai U.A.
2. Kolkata U.A.
3. Delhi U.A.
4. Chennai U.A.
5. Hyderabad U.A.
6. Bengaluru U.A.
7. Ahmedabad U.A.
8. Pune U.A.
9. Kanpur U.A.
10. Nagpur U.A.
11. Lucknow U.A.
12. Surat U.A.
13. Jaipur U.A.
14. Kochi U.A.
15. Coimbatore U.A.
16. Vadodara U.A.
17. Indore U.A.
18. Patna U.A.
19. Madurai U.A.
20. Bhopal M.C.
21. Visakhapatnam, U.A.
22. Varanasi U.A.
23. Ludhiana M.C.

Note: U.A. = Urban Area, M.C. = Municipal Corporation

SUMMARY

After the introduction of liberalization, privatization and globalization policies, the entire Indian economy have been changed drastically. The economy has been changed from traditional to digital economy or wired economy. There has been exponential growth in gross domestic product. The GDP is strongly built up by manufacturing sector, agriculture sector and service sector. In traditional economy the GDP was dominated by agriculture sector. After 1991, the entire situation had been changed in the components of GDP. In the digital economy, services sector dominate the components of GDP. Service sector is a highly intellectual component in human resource management. India has a vast pool of highly educated, talented and skilled resources. The increase in education levels of the community, a strong commitment made by the government towards education sector and an attitude towards a better education by the society enhanced the literacy levels. India is a reservoir of best talented human resource but lack of technical competency. The technical competency can be enhanced by giving proper training activities to the human resources. A strong and skilled man power can build the technical modern India. The GDP is a combination of "agriculture, manufacturing, service sectors". The agriculture sector can be re-built with the adaption of interlinking of rivers in India. It is a cost of estimated worth of more than ₹ 15 lakh crores. This project will give an intellectual process for the development of entire Indian economy within a period of 10 years. The mega project can be built with the help of financial markets and services. In the financial markets abundant supply of financial resources will be available, to convert them into the productive way of interlinking of rivers for modern India. The abundant supply of financial resources can be tapped by proper efficient financial resources. Financial services are a highly intellectual and innovative activity. It is not a just routine activity. It requires a proper and better understanding of investor's psychology and market trends. Investor psychology was dealt by behavioral finance.

Key Terms

1. **Financial Services:** It refers to services provided by the finance industry. The finance industry encompasses a broad range of organisations that deal with the management of money.
2. **Service:** A service is the intangible equivalent of an economic good. Service provision is often an economic where the buyer does generally, except by exclusive contract, obtains exclusive ownership of the thing purchased.
3. **Foreign Direct Investment:** It refers to long term participation by a country into another country. It usually involves participation in management, joint venture, transfer of technology, and expertise. There are two kinds of FDIs, inward FDI and outward FDI resulting in a net FDI inflow and stock of FDI, which is the cumulative number for a given period. Direct investment excludes investment through purchase of shares. Foreign investment can be a significant driver of development in poor nations.

Questions

1. What is financial services market?
2. Explain the main objectives of foreign direct investment.
3. What is policy? How a policy will effect a layman's life?
4. Explain the importance of gross domestic product in Indian economy.

10 Foreign Exchange Exposure

After the implementation of liberalization, privatization, globalization reforms by the government of India in 1991, a rapid industrialization, advancement in communications facilities and revolutionized means of transportation have increased the volume of trade across the globe. The business sector increased its activities exponentially and has no limits for their transactions. The globe is rotating on the flow of money. Money is always travelling for profit as a destination within a stipulated period of time. Profit is always chased by the corporate sector.

International financial management discipline became more popular after the introduction of globalization reform. It is an innovative and dynamic subject. It is always changing according to the global business environment. Funds are travelling from one nation to another, which is purely based on supply and demand factor. After the information technology revolution, it is very easy to make transactions through online and business has been increased and no geographical demarcation. Therefore the importance of international financial management had emerged as a specialized subject. Many business schools in India had introduced in their MBA program, International Business Management, International Financial Management as part of their curriculum. The international financial management deals with the financial decisions taken in the area of international business. The international financial management covers the study of "Foreign Exchange Market, Exchange Rate Determination, Exchange Rate Risk and its Management, Multinational Companies Investment Decisions, International Working Capital Decisions, Financing Decision of Global Companies, International Accounting, International Indebtedness".

The general agreement on trade and tariff was set up in order to cultivate the global business. The oldest mode of international business is foreign trade. Foreign trade is the most important factor for every nation. It is the part of their respected economies. The element of foreign trade occupies a dominant role in some of the countries exchequer.

FOREIGN EXCHANGE EXPOSURE AND RISK MANAGEMENT

In the global financial market, the currency exchange values are volatile and their values are based on demand and supply factor. Such changes influence the value of those firms that are involved in global transactions. The value of their assets and liabilities will reflect as per the fluctuated prices of various currencies they have. Such a situation is called as "foreign exchange exposure". It is an unanticipated change in the exchange rate. The exchange rate of various countries currency value depends upon several factors. Foreign exchange exposure can be categorized into two ways.

(A) Accounting or transaction exposure. (B) Economic exposure. Accounting exposure is related and reflected from the consolidated financial statement of the parent company and it does not influence the cash flow. Economic exposure is the result of the altered cash flow of a company. It is further categorized as transaction exposure and real operating exposure. Transaction exposure is concerned with the changes in the present cash flows. Real operating exposure transactions will be reflected in the future cash flows.

Transaction exposure is concerned with the impact of changes in exchange rate on present cash flows. It emerges in the following context.

(A) Open account

(B) Borrowing and lending of foreign currency

(C) Intra firm flow for MNCs.

Open account means if an Indian firm exports goods to the USA and the bill is invoiced in American dollars. It has to receive payments within two months, but within two months period, the dollar may depreciate, hence, the firm will lose its earning in rupee terms. If the dollar appreciates the firm will make export earnings bigger in terms of rupee. On the other hand if an importer imports goods from the USA and American dollar appreciates before payment is made in the form of dollars, it will have to pay more rupees. If the American dollar depreciates, the importer will be required to pay less amount of Indian rupee. This situation is beneficial to Indian importer. Therefore this environment is called as transaction exposure. It consists of three parts. (A) quotation exposure (B) backlog exposure. and (C) billing exposure. Quotation exposure is created when the exporter quotes a price in a foreign currency and exists till the importer places an order with the exporter at that price. This situation is called as quotation exposure. Backlog exposure means, it exists between the placement of order by the importer and the shipping and billing by the seller. Billing exposure exists between the billing of the shipment and the settlement of the trade payments.

The borrowing and lending in a foreign currency activity may create transaction exposure. The transaction exposure emerges when the foreign currency appreciates, there will be a lot of pressure in terms of domestic currency, and if the foreign currency depreciates, there will be less pressure on domestic currency. The same adverse conditions will be applied to the lender of the domestic currency.

The multinational companies are operating on the global basis. They are not restricted to a particular country. They are scattered throughout the world. The funds of multinational companies are rotating between their branches which are located at different countries on worldwide basis. Any change in exchange rate will show an impact on the cash flow of the company. For ex: the Indian subsidiary of an American company has declared a dividend and it has to send it to the parent company, in the mean time any fluctuation in foreign exchange will show impact on the company. If the rupee depreciates, it is beneficial to the subsidiary company and harmful to the parent company. If the exchange rate appreciates, it is harmful to the subsidiary company and beneficial to the parent company. This situation is the part of the transaction exposure.

The transaction exposure emerges in the following factors. They are —

- Operating environment
- Inflation

Operating environment means, the earning capacity of the company may also change the value of the firm due to volatile foreign exchange market prices. The changes in exchange rate will show an impact on the corporate sector, only when the companies are involved exporting goods to other nations, and the organisations which are importing the goods from other countries. If there is no relation to these activities of a particular company, it may not get impact on the operating environment of the commercial enterprise. But the company should face competition in the domestic market for price.

Inflation is another important factor in foreign exchange market. If the firm is involved in export business, it may be able to pass on the impact of inflation to the consumers when the demand for the product is price-inelastic, and the exporter enjoys a monopoly situation. If the firm is not in a position to enjoy the monopoly statues, the impact will be felt on its earnings of the company. The earning will diminish. If a firm which is concentrated only on domestic market and competition from abroad is present, imports will meet the domestic demand if it is highly price elastic. If there is no competition from abroad in the domestic market, the inflation will show an impact on the revenue of the company. Therefore it will reduce the profitability. But there will be larger revenue stream available in the post inflation period.

Translation exposure is also known as Accounting Exposure. It emerges on account of consolidation of financial statements of different units of a multinational firm. The multinational companies are operating their business activities through their subsidiary companies which are scattered throughout the globe. The parent company is interested in maximizing its overall profitability and to make it possible to ascertain overall profitability, it consolidates the financial statements of its subsidiaries with its own. They will make a comparative performance of their subsidiaries. There are different methods of translation or accounting exposure which they will depend upon their legal and accounting procedures of the different nations adopted in a particular country. They are —

- Current rate method/closing rate method
- Current/non current method
- Monetary/non monetary method

Temporal method.

EXCHANGE RATE DETERMINATION AND FORECASTING

Foreign exchange market is a highly complex environment and everyone may not be perfect in understanding the global markets. It requires a higher knowledge and a strong financial sense. A thorough understanding of the economic system only will enable to understand this concept very easily. Exchange rate determination is a crucial point in Forex market. It denotes the ratio between the values of two currencies. In a foreign exchange market, all currencies of different nations are bought and sold. In this market, every currency is available for a specified price. The globe is rotating on the flow of funds. The funds are travelling from content to another on the basis of supply and demand factor for a profit element. The various exchange rates of currencies are regularly quoted in news papers and television channels. The CNBC AND NDTV PROFIT, BLOOMBERG channels are showing live prices of different currencies of the world. The following are various quotations existing in the markets.

- Direct and indirect quote
- Buying and selling rates
- Forward market quotation
- Forward premium and discount
- Cross rates

Direct quotation in the foreign exchange market gives the home currency price of a certain amount of foreign currency. Generally it may be one or 100 units. For example a direct quote between India and USA will be written as ₹ 42/US $. Indirect quotation means, the value of one unit of home currency is presented in terms of foreign currency. For example India quote the exchange rate for dollars as "US $ 0.0356/Re."

Buying and Selling Rates are generally published in print media and journals. The news papers carrying a report on Forex market indicating different kinds of currencies which is available at buy price and sell price. The buying rate is also known as the bid rate. The selling rate is called as "ask rate or offer rate". The bid rate is always given at first and followed by the ask rate quotation. For example: if the rupee and pound rate is ₹ 75-75.50 /pounds. The first one is buy price and next one is sell price. Generally these rates are indicated by the banks and Forex brokers. In India, some banks are specialized in Forex markets, but all banks will not enter into this market. This market is operated by only the institutions and individuals who sought the permission from the reserve bank of India. The reserve bank of India will give permission to enter into this market. Hence only authorized bankers and brokers are allowed to carry the business activities in this market. For example if a bank indicates buy sell rate as follows ₹ 45.50 and ₹ 46.00, THEREFORE, the difference between sell price and buy price is known as SPREAD.

Spread = (ask price – bid price)/ask price X 100

Spread = (46.00 – 45.50)/46 X 100 = 1.08%

Forward Market Quotation

The quotations for forward market are published in print media. The rates maybe expressed as outright quotes or as swap quotes.

Outright quote quotation for US dollars in-terms of rupees for three month period\one month

Spot	One month	Three months
44.00-44.30	43.80-44.40	43.60-44.50
Swap rs. 44-30	₹ (20)-10	₹ (40)-20

The swap quotes expresses only the difference between the spot quotes and forward quotes. It may be noted that decimals are not written in swap quotes.

Forward Premium and Discount

In the above quotations, it is found that the larger the maturity, the greater is the change in forward rates. The forward premium (discount) can be computed by the following formula

= (n-day forward rate-spot rate)/spot rate*360/n.

If the forward rate is lower than spot rate, it will be called as forward discount on the other hand, if the forward rate is higher than the spot rate, it would be called as a forward premium.

Cross Rates

Cross rate means in some situations, the value of currency in-terms of other one is not known, in such case are currency is sold for a well recognized currency and again the recognized currency is exchanged for the desired currency. The rate established between two currencies is known as cross currency rate. For example: a newspaper quotes rupees 40.00 – 40.20/US $ and at the same time, it quotes Canadian $ 0.80-0.82/US $ but does not quote the exchange rate between rupees and Canadian dollar. Therefore the rate of exchange between the rupees and Canadian dollar will be found through the common currency the US $. The same technique will be applied for forward and spot cross rates.

Nominal, Real and Effective Exchange Rates

All the exchange rates discussed in the preceding sections are the nominal exchange rates/ bilateral exchange rates. The exchange rates represent the ratio between the two values of currencies at a particular point of time. The real exchange rate is the price adjusted nominal exchange rate. The relationship between nominal exchange rate and real exchange rate can be indicated by the following formula.

$e_r = eP/p^*$

e = nominal exchange rate

e_r = real exchange rate

p = domestic price indices

p^* = foreign price indices

Effective Exchange Rates

The foreign exchange market consists of various currencies and fluctuates from time to time. Therefore it is essential to develop an index in foreign exchange market. Such an index is known as "effective exchange market". For the construction of an effective exchange rate index, at first instance include all currencies of the world. The second step is to find out the weight of different currencies in the basket. The third step is to find out the exchange rate index.

The real exchange rate is based on real bilateral exchange rates, while the nominal effective exchange rate is based on nominal bilateral exchange rates. They are too important factors in effective exchange rates — (a) determination of exchange rate in spot market, (b) determination of exchange rate in forward market.

The spot market for foreign exchange is a complex environment. The exchange rate between two currencies in a free floating regime is determined by supply and demand forces. For example the exchange rate between the rupees and the US dollars depends upon the demand for the dollar and supply in the Forex market. The demand and supply for dollars demand upon the trade relationship between India and USA the following factors will influence exchange rates

(a) Inflation

(b) Interest rate

(c) Combined effect.

Forward market is not equal to the spot market. The forward market size depends on current expectation of future events. The determination of exchange rate in a forward market finds an important place in the theory of interest rate parity. The IRP theory states that equilibrium is achieved when the forward rate differential is approximately equal to the interest rate differential.

FOREIGN EXCHANGE MARKET

MARKET is a place where the buyer and seller meet at a place in a specified period of time to settle their transactions or make arrangement for buying and selling of goods or services. In the foreign exchange market, all foreign currencies are bought and sold. All nations' currencies are available for specified exchange rates to the customers/clients. They can buy and sell all nations' currencies according to their requirement. For ex., if an Indian exporter receives his proceeds for his transaction made with USA counterpart in the form dollars. He will approach the foreign exchange market for making conversion of dollars into Indian currency. This is the simplest transaction happening in the Forex market. But there are several transactions addition to the above said transaction. It is an over the counter market. It has no particular place or floor for making transactions by the clients or customers. It consists of trading desks at major agencies dealing in foreign exchange throughout the globe that are connected by powerful information channels such as telephone, telex, fax, internet and other instruments. Therefore the transactions in this market are based normally on oral followed by written communication. Even though the market is scattered throughout the globe but highly influenced by local regulatory authorities of the nations. The market in USA AND UK relies more on communication network. But in Paris and other European countries relies on physical meeting of participants at bourses. In India the foreign exchange operations are administered and controlled by reserve bank of India. The Forex brokers are spread all over the globe. The time of transaction differs from one place to another depending upon the longitude of the place. For ex; if a dealer in India transacts at 10 AM, it will just be at 4.30 AM in London. Therefore the foreign exchange market works around the clock. In the Forex market, there are several currencies, but normally the currencies which are strong, stable and convertible are in great demand.

The participants in the foreign exchange market are —

- Individuals
- Firms
- Governments
- International agencies
- Non-banking entities
- Non-banking entities (as traders)
- Banks (on behalf of their customers)

- Arbitrageurs
- Speculators.

The most crucial component of the foreign exchange market is Forex currency, which is bought and sold in this marketplace. The transaction of FX currency involves the exchange of currencies of various nations. Fluctuations in the value of a currency against that of other offer Forex traders opportunities to earn profits.

Although the currency of any nation can be exchanged in the Forex market, there are a few that are considered major currencies, as they dominate the world's foreign transactions. The value of other currencies is typically considered against these major currencies.

The most popular FX currency is the US dollar (USD). This currency is involved in over 80% of the Forex trades. With the collapse of the gold standard and the adoption of the Breton Woods system in 1944, the US dollar became the world's reserve currency. All currencies were valued in terms of the US dollar.

The Euro (EUR) is the currency of the Eurozone, which consists of 15 member states. With over €610 billion in circulation as of December 2006, the Euro has exceeded the US dollar in terms of total cash in circulation. The value of the Euro has been affected by factors such as unstable growth rates and unemployment.

The next most common FX currency is the Great British Pound (GBP), or Pound Sterling. Its popularity has been severely affected by the rising popularity of the US dollar. The Great British Pound is traded heavily against the Euro and the US dollar. This currency is also called "cable," as it was the first currency to be traded in the Forex market through trans- Atlantic cables.

The Japanese yen (JPY) is the third most-traded currency in the Forex market, next only to the US dollar and the Euro. The yen has featured prominently in the carry trade for years. However, yen carry trade started unwinding when the Financial Crisis of 2008 onwards caused all countries to reduce their interest rates. This has lead to the strengthening of the yen, despite Japan's economy being in dire straits.

The Swiss Franc (CHF) is considered as a safe currency due to the nation's neutral and independent economic policies and private banking system. The currency lacks liquidity, which has Forex currencies always traded in pairs. The rate at which a currency pair is traded is known as its exchange rate. While there could be countless currency pairs, the following account for about 70% of the total daily trade in the Forex market.

- Euro/US Dollar - EUR/USD
- Great Britain Pound/US Dollar - GBP/USD
- US Dollar/Confoederatio Helvetica Franc - USD/CHF
- US Dollar/Japanese Yen - USD/JPY

The first currency appearing in a currency pair is called the reference currency or the base currency. The second currency in the pair is known as the quote currency or the counter currency. When an exchange occurs, the amount of the transaction is quoted in the reference currency, while the result of the transaction (profit or loss) is expressed in the quoted currency.

Forex Broker

Forex, or foreign exchange, is the exchange of one currency for another. The Forex market has been in existence for more than thirty years. A Forex broker is a person or a firm that trades on behalf of investors in the Forex market. Choosing the right Forex broker is a complicated task, since the Forex market is loosely regulated and requires minimum qualifications to begin trading. The two types of brokers for beginners or slightly experienced traders are:

Retail Forex Brokers

They are small-scale brokers, with direct or intermediary access to the Forex market. Some of them charge a commission for their service.

Market Makers

The market makers are mainly large banks. They have direct access to the Forex market. They focus selling and buying Forex for their clients who are usually large corporations, financial institutions and high-net worth individuals. Both market makers and retail Forex brokers earn money through the spread between and ask prices on currencies, i.e., the difference between the price and the customer pays and the price they pay to buy the underlying currency.

Different brokers advertise different schemes and attractions to entice investors. There are some tips to find the right Forex broker:

- Check at the National Futures Association (NFA) website, which is considered a highly reliable source to find Forex brokers. This website maintains one of the strictest standards for its voluntary members.
- Consult your equity broker or other financial experts and ask for referrals. Inquire about the firm's or the person's reputation as a Forex broker. Use the NFA's Background Affiliation Status Information Centre (BASIC) to complete your research.
- Contact brokers over the phone or meet them in person. Ask questions and try to meet a client of theirs to directly inquire about their customer service and competency.
- Make a list of those brokers that you find suitable and then go into the details of their terms and conditions. Do inquire about their spread, trading tools and affiliations.
- Opt for Forex brokers who maintain low spreads. Spread is the difference between the buying cost and the selling cost of a currency pair. As Forex brokers do not charge a commission, they make their money through this difference.
- Check whether the Forex broker will feature real time data, news, technical analysis tools, real time charts and support for trading systems.
- Use online guides and reviews, such as those provided by EconomyWatch.com. These reviews give a good idea about the products, technologies and charges for the services provided by brokerage companies

The foreign exchange market can be categorized into two methods. (1) Spot market (2) Forward market.

Spot Market

In this market currencies are traded for immediate delivery at a rate existing on the day of transaction. The transactions will be made in the bank accounts of the seller and buyer through debit and credit entries. The market do the transfer of funds electronically thus saving time and energy. The arbitrageurs will take a price opportunity in the Forex market through powerful communication tools. He will buy the currency at low price where it is available in one market and sell the currency where the higher price is available in another market. He will take advantage of the inconsistency and garner profits by buying and selling of the currencies. This transaction will attract transaction cost. The arbitrageur will take into the consideration of transaction cost before making his buying and selling of currency at different market. He will show interest only where the transaction cost is low. Speculation in the spot market occurs when the speculator anticipates a change in the value of a particular currency especially an appreciation in the value of a foreign currency. He will buy at lower price and wait for higher price or his targeted price.

Forward Market

The forward market is a future market. They will make contract to buy and sell currencies for future delivery, i.e., after a fortnight, one month, two months etc. The forward rates with varying maturity are quoted in the newspapers and those rates form the basis of the contract. Both the parties have to abide by the rules and regulations.

EURO FOREX TRADING

The rate at which a country's currency is converted into Euros is known as the Euro exchange rate. In other words, it is the price at which a nation's currency is exchanged for Euros.

Factors affecting the Euro Exchange Rate

The final exchange rate is determined by several factors, including:

National banks: Exchange rates vary on the basis of the daily concertation process between the European Central Banks (ECB) and the national central banks (NCB) that are part of the European System of Central Banks (ESCB). This concertation process takes place around 2.15 pm. Furthermore, if the interest rate of a country's central bank is higher than that of the ECB; the currency of that country will appreciate *vis-à-vis* the Euro.

Inflation rate: The value of the Euro depreciates with respect to those currencies that belong to countries that have an inflation rate lower than that in the European Union (EU). A high inflation rate causes a currency to erode and, hence, investors shy away from such currencies.

Foreign trade: The Euro appreciates if the final value of exports from the EU is higher than that of imports. As the EU builds its monetary reserves, it spends on its trading partners, thereby strengthening the economies of member countries and consequently of the Euro.

Government intervention: Governments sometimes flood their domestic currency in the Forex market to lower its value *vis-à-vis* the Euro. However, such flooding alters the exchange value only for a short time span.

Economic variables: Economic variables that reflect the financial health of the EU member nations will also have an impact on the Euro exchange rate. These variables mainly include labor reports related to payrolls and the unemployment rate, producer price indices, gross domestic product figures, consumer price indices and industrial production.

Monitoring Euro Currency Exchange Rates

Keeping a track of fluctuating exchange rates can be a daunting task. Thus, investors can use a web-based currency converter to trade their national currencies for Euros. Most of the readily available currency converters perform currency conversions on the basis of live mid-term market rates.

The fact that the Euro is the official currency of some of the world's most developed nations makes it a tempting investment option. Traders from across the globe monitor the market and earn profits by capitalizing on any fluctuations in the Euro exchange rate.

Fundamental Analysis and Forex

Fundamental analysis is the method used by some of the most successful traders in history. Jim Rogers, George Soros, Warren Buffet are some of the many names that come to mind when we desire to recall a few of the great traders who owe their success to their proficiency in fundamental studies. George Soros is especially famous for his exploits in Forex trading which were always justified on fundamental grounds. Sadly, fundamental analysis is not that popular among traders partly because of a failure to comprehend what it is, and partly because of misunderstandings about how it should be applied. We'll take a look at this important topic in this article.

Fundamental analysis aims to make sense of market events in light of economic realities that drive human behavior. A trader can have all kinds of psychological reasons for why he is buying or selling a particular currency, or a stock, and many of them may not even make sense, but as long as he can obtain the funds to buy and sell, his opinion will count. Fundamental analysis can help us get to the root of this funding problem by characterizing the dynamism of an economy, the stages of the economic cycle, the social, and economic factors that influence people's decisions, and government policies, and finally condensing them all into a meaningful model which can be used to evaluate and predict market events. Unlike technical analysis, fundamental methods are not dependent on prices very much. Instead, from the point of view of the fundamental analyst, it may be reasonable to exclude the price action entirely from the analytical picture at times in order to get a purer evaluation of the economy.

That is not to say, of course, that fundamental studies are unaffected by market psychology, and irrationality. Fundamental studies do aim to tackle these subjects, but do so in the framework established by causality. A technical analyst does not know why something happens when it does happen, and indeed, we cannot say that he's very much concerned about causes. A fundamental analyst, on the other hand, always wants to get at the root of problems and reach at the causes that create trends in the market.

Fundamental analysis is the study of the causes of market events. Anything that can have an impact on prices will be considered by the analyst, but only as long as the weighting that each factor justifies the time and energy spent during analysis. These weightings change all the time. Politics, for example, does not have a dominant impact on stock prices during ordinary days of trading, but when there's government crisis, a war, or a scandal, it can become the dominant force behind market events. In addition, fundamental events take time to manifest their full effect. Trading the news, for example, can hardly be considered a fundamental strategy. In short, the fundamental school is effective, and reliable, but only if it is applied after a reasonable period of education, with a powerful commitment to analysis, and risk management.

FOREX MARGIN

Forex margin trading enables investors to trade in the Forex market with smaller capital investments. Forex margin accounts let traders use their leverage to acquire bigger purchasing power. This boosts profits in multiples but uncalculated risk may lead to financial disaster.

The term 'margin' was picked from Japanese. It means 'proof' in English. The idea is to deposit an amount which is usually 1% of the real value as proof to begin trading. Leverage is then expressed in margin terms. For example, if a trader opens an account with $1000 and leverage is 100:1, the person can trade with, up to $100,000.

Maintenance Margin versus Forex margin

For a beginner, these two terms may be confusing. Maintenance margin is the amount a trader needs to replenish his Forex account with so as to continue trading after incurring losses. In such cases, the account balance dips below the minimum amount that is required to carry on. Thus, the need for depositing the maintenance margin arises. Forex margin, however, is the least amount to kick start trading.

Advantages of Forex Margin Account

Forex margin accounts are useful as they help new investors become better informed about the Forex market and its tools.

Least investment: With investments as low as 1% of the real value, the Forex margin accounts let beginners and traders with less cash trade in the market and with equal competitive edge.

High leverage: As the Forex market deals in lots of minimum 10,000 units of a currency, leverage of just 100:1 for $1000 equips a trader with enough reserve to trade and multiply profits. For example in the above case, if the value of USD goes from 1.3256 to 1.3356, the profits becomes (100 pips * 100,000 units) $1000, whereas without leverage, it would have been only $10.

Disadvantage of Forex Market Margin Accounts

Leverage not only multiplies profits but also multiplies losses. This is a double edged sword. So, using leverage without caution or effective money management may require deposits of maintenance margin to continue trading.

Forex margin accounts are an effective way for traders to start trading with low investments. However, factors such as greed and gambling can negate the positives of this facility. Traders, who are new and experienced, are advised to exercise caution while availing such service.

The History of Currency Trading

The Forex online market was established in 1971, though it was only possible through a combination of technological, communicational and political advances. Understanding them and how they impact the trading of foreign currencies is a crucial element in becoming a successful, smart, trader. It is important to know that should there be a major event with any of these factors currencies will be affected on either side of the profit line. The goal of every trader should be to understand the market, to know what all the statistics mean and how major news can swing a countries currency by making it stronger or diluting its value.

The idea of a foreign currency exchange dates back to the middle Ages when the first paper money was introduced and represented a transferable payments for merchants and traders — like an I.O.U. — a promissory note. National governments, provinces and municipalities began storing gold, silver and other items of value and issued promissory notes against a set value. The problem was that on any given day that value could change based solely on the decisions of the kings and governors.

Up until the end of World War I (WWI), the Forex markets were relatively inactive and remained stable. However, after WWI the volatility of the Forex market greatly increased and investor speculation grew. From the mid 1870s, until shortly after WWI, the international currency systems ran off the principles of the gold exchange model. As a result of being supported by the hard value of gold, paper money, currencies as they became known as, experienced a healthy life under this gold standard. (The term commonly used to describe a value of currency in direct relationship to a the price of a fixed weight of gold). The gold standard helped put an end to the practice of monarchs and dictators of indiscriminately degrading money, which was and still is a major trigger of inflation.

However, as much of a step-up for currency stability as it was, the gold standard had many problems as the industrial revolution advanced. The primary problem was the patterns that would see the constant redistribution of wealth within the world's countries. The peaks and valleys that many of these countries experienced was due, in large part, to the economic instability caused by a lack of gold reserves and a devaluation of other commodities.

Recession was not kind to many of the early speculators; some believe that it was because of this high level of speculation and guesswork which ultimately brought about the Great Depression. And as a result of what was a very difficult period, people began learning the lessons needed to progress. Policymakers and politicians realized the weight of the currency markets on world finance and in 1931, a period of redefining the Forex and monetary policy began.

Breton Woods Agreement

The Breton Woods Agreement was designed to bring stability to the monetary system and restrict speculation in the world currencies.

As an economy strengthened, imports would increase. This action depleted the reserves of gold required to cover the valuation of its money. This caused the money supply to constrict, interest rates would rise and economic activity could slow to the extent of recession - (a period defined by 3 straight fiscal quarters of gross domestic product losses - in which unemployment and low consumer spending are high). Eventually, the prices of goods had to define a bottom and become palatable to other countries. These countries would start buying the currency *en masse,* injecting the economy with significant amounts of gold, enough to lead to an increase in the money supply. This drove interest rates down and helped to create wealth within the economy.

This was a pattern that was relived over and over again through history until the outbreak of World War I practically closed trading routes and the free exchange of gold and silver. This of course was followed by 'The Great Depression', which quite arguably was ended by World War II.

After the Second World War, the Breton Woods Agreement was established. Participating countries agreed to try and maintain the value of their currency with a small margin against the US dollar, economically, the largest country, and a corresponding rate of gold. Governments were not allowed, under the agreement, to devalue their currency in order to bring on an advantage in trade. If absolutely necessary, they were allowed to play with their valuations as long as it did not cause more than a 10% change. Throughout the 1950s, the increase in global trade brought on massive capital transfers created by post-WWII construction. This caused foreign exchange rates under the Breton Woods agreement to become unstable.

By 1971, the global situation had inevitably caused a move away from Breton Woods. US President, Richard Nixon had taken the dollar off the gold standard in order to be able to print more money to fund the Vietnam War. This marked a change in government policy in which a debit/credit system was born. By 1973, the currencies of major industrialized nations became free floating, and in part became more subject to the prices set for them in the Forex market. Prices fluctuated each day, with trading volumes and price volatility increasing throughout the 1970s. It was these drastic changes that gave rise to new financial instruments, market liberalization and deregulation.

With the growth in the telecommunication and computer industries in the early 1980's, the global financial markets surged and the world grew smaller. All markets became accessible to everyone, no matter what time zone, no matter what time of day.

Transactions in the Forex market increased from about $68 billion per day in the early 1980s, to over $3 trillion a day in 2006.

The Forex Market Today

There have been many factors that have led to the current structure of the Forex market. Since the early 1970s, the Forex market has grown in size, structure, and changed the way it operates.

The transformation resulted from changes in the global financial systems. A primary cause of the increase in foreign exchange trading was the rapid development of the Euro-Dollar market, where US dollars are deposited into central and local banks outside of the United States. Similarly, it is typical for countries within the European markets to have their assets deposited outside the currency of origin.

To contrast this concept, during the start of the Cold War in the mid 1950s, all the money made by Russia from the sale of oil (which came in the form of US Dollars) was deposited in banks that were outside of the US for fear that the US Government would freeze the funds. This helped bring about a large amount of dollars that were not in the control of the US authorities.

The US government tried to impose laws restricting the loaning of dollars internationally. The Euro markets were particularly attractive because they had far fewer regulations and offered a much higher yield. Towards the end of the 1980's, US companies began borrowing offshore and this is the norm today. Investors and savers find the Euro markets a lucrative and safe area to put their excess liquidity. In turn, these deposits provide short-term loans and finances import and export activities.

London was the principal offshore market, as it remains even now. In the 1980s, it became the key center in the Eurodollar market when British banks began lending dollars as an alternative to pounds. This allowed them to maintain their leading position in global finance. London's convenient geographical location allows it to operate during Asian, Pacific and American market hours as well.

As Forex trading has grown, several international cities have emerged as market leaders. Currently, London, England has the greatest share of transactions with over 32% of the total trade volume. Other leading trading centers listed in order of volume are New York, Tokyo, Zurich, Frankfurt, Hong Kong, Paris, and Sydney.

Currently, the Forex market has expanded from consisting of only banks to one where many other kinds of institutions participate. The evolution of the Forex — from a range of loosely connected national financial centers to a single integrated international market – brought about a system that offers means of trading to not only financial professionals but also individuals who began trading and investing, and one that also plays an important role in our economies — both individual and national.

Since the late 1970s the Forex has seen an influx of financial entities, such as banks, hedge funds, and broker trading houses, as well as individual traders enter the Forex arena. Today, instead of being controlled by national banks and governments, the main factor that drives today's Forex markets is supply and demand. The free-floating system is ideal for today's Forex markets as international trade and commerce are abundant in the 21st century. The tremendous growth and application of technology in the Forex market broke down all barriers between nations, as well as time zone barriers eventually resulting in a 24 hour market throughout the American, European, and Asian time zones. Through the popularization of the internet, the trading of Forex online has enabled the average investor to reach this vital and practical market.

Types of Forex Derivatives

Some of the financial instruments which have their values derived from Forex rates include the following derivatives:

- Currency Futures
- Currency Options, both Vanilla and Exotics
- Currency Exchange Traded Funds or ETFs
- Forex Contracts for Difference or CFDs
- Forwards
- Swaps
- Spot trades

These derivative instruments can be used to take Forex related positions on their own or in combinations.

Often, a strategic combination employing one or more of the above derivative instruments along with spot Forex positions can be used by Forex traders to maximize profits, minimize risks and generally adjust their overall risk profile.

Two of the Forex derivatives that are often traded on exchanges, and hence are also available to many individual Forex traders, include currency futures and options. They will be covered in greater detail in the sections below.

CURRENCY FUTURES TRADING

Currency futures used to be the main way that individual currency traders took positions before retail Forex brokers became widely available. They trade on the floor of exchanges like the Chicago International Monetary Market or IMM.

Each currency futures contract trades for a standardized forward delivery date, often maturing on a quarterly basis, and so have similar pricing to a forward outright contract delivering on those same value dates.

Currency futures can be actively traded by being either bought or sold via the exchange they trade on. Their values are directly related to the corresponding prices prevailing in the larger OTC spot and forward Forex market.

Watching currency futures trade on the floor of an exchange can be a confusing endeavor. The first thing that comes to mind is a pack of wild animals howling and making gestures at each other.

Nevertheless, the chaos is superficial at best, since almost everything happening in the trading pit is carefully orchestrated to provide instantaneous executions and fair prices for both the local traders and for off the floor traders.

Currency Option

American style currency options commonly trade on futures exchanges like the Chicago IMM, where they are options on futures. Other currency options trade on stock exchanges like the Philadelphia Stock Exchange where they are similar to the options traded in the OTC Interbank market which primarily tend to be European style options.

Furthermore, the OTC currency options market has recently expanded to include a wide range of exotic options like:

- Average rate and strike options,
- Knock out and knock in options,
- Basket options,
- Binary or digital options, and
- Look back options.

This area of exotic currency options has provided fertile ground for a growing list of new Forex related derivative products.

With respect to the factors that determine a European currency option's price, the first and most basic option contract specifications are the strike price, expiration date, style and whether it is a call or put on which currencies.

Furthermore, a currency option's value also depends on several market determined factors. Specifically, these additional parameters are:

- The prevailing spot rate
- Interbank deposit rates for each of the currencies
- The current implied volatility level for the expiration date

The implied volatility quantity is unique to option markets and is related to the annualized standard deviation of exchange rate movements expected by the market during the option's lifetime. Option market makers estimate this key pricing factor and usually express it in percentage terms.

SUMMARY

After the implementation of liberalization, privatization, globalization reforms by the government of India in 1991, a rapid industrialization, advancement in communications facilities, and revolutionized means of transportation have increased the volume of trade across the globe. The business sector increased its activities exponentially and has no limits for their transactions. The globe is rotating on the flow of money. Money is always travelling for profit as a destination within a stipulated period of time. Profit is always chased by the corporate sector.

International financial management discipline became more popular after the introduction of globalization reform. It is an innovative and dynamic subject. It is always changing according to the global business environment. Funds are travelling from one nation to another, which is purely based on supply and demand factor. After the information technology revolution, it is very easy to make transactions through online and business has been increased and no geographical demarcation. Therefore the importance of international financial management had emerged as a specialized subject. Many business schools in India had introduced in their MBA program International Business Management, International Financial Management as part of their curriculum. The international financial management deals with the financial decisions taken in the area of international business. The international financial management covers the study of "Foreign Exchange Market, Exchange Rate Determination, Exchange Rate Risk And Its Management, Multinational Companies Investment Decisions, International Working Capital Decisions, Financing Decision Of Global Companies, International Accounting, International Indebtedness".

Key Terms

1. **Appreciation:** Rise in the external value of currency in a floating exchange-rate regime.
2. **Arbitrage:** A risk-free trading in which the same currency/instrument is bought and sold simultaneously in two different markets in order to profit out of divergence between the two markets.
3. **Basis Risk:** Related primarily to financial companies, it arises when interest rate exposure on one instrument is not fully offset by the interest rate exposure on the other instrument.

4. **Benchmark Security**: The choice of a security that may serve as a guide for other securities especially from the viewpoint of return.
5. **Country Risk:** A trading risk emerging from a government's interference in the foreign exchange market

Questions

1. Distinguish between Current Account and Capital Account.
2. Explain Unilateral Transfer.
3. Is BoP in eqilibrium from accounting point of view?
4. Explain the monetary approach to BoP adjustment?
5. Distinguish between monetary and non-monetory movement of Gold.

11

Mergers, Acquisition and Restructuring

Survival in the market is a crucial point at present global scenario. The competition in the market reduces the growth of individual commercial enterprise. The growth is measured in terms of sales, profit and assets. Increase in the sales volume reveals that, the firm has been able to maintain its competitive edge in the market. Market is a combination of desires and dreams of crores of consumers. In order to survive an organization in the market, the firm, should increase its operational efficiency and realistic environment of the market composition. A commercial enterprise must grow internally or externally. A commercial enterprise must concentrate on increasing its operational efficiency. The external growth of the firm is possible through combining or joining with other firms or acquiring other firms. There are various forms of business combinations which can result in growth. The various combination programs had the objectives of business expansion. The usual objectives of the expansion are

A. Mergers

B. Amalgamations/Consolidation

C. Acquisition/Takeover

MERGERS

Merger means, a combination of one or two more companies into one company. One or more companies may merge with an existing company or they may merge to form a new company. It is a situation where one company acquires the net assets of other company and the latter is dissolved. There are three major types of mergers:

1. Horizontal Mergers
2. Vertical Merger
3. Conglomerate Merger

1. **Horizonal:** merger is a combination of two or more firms which are working in a similar type of production, distribution or area of business. For ex: combining of two companies which are producing two book publishers or two luggage manufacturing companies to capture dominant market share. It results in economies of scale, operating economies, and elimination of

duplication of facilities. It reduces competition and number of companies in an industry. It leads to creation of concentration of economic power.

2. **Vertical Merger:** Vertical merger means, it is a combination of two or more firms which are involved in different stages of production or distribution of a product. It may take the form of forward or backward merger. If a company combines with its suppliers of raw material is called BACKWARD MERGER. If it combines with the customer then it is known as FORWARD MERGER. The objective of the vertical merger is to ensure a guaranteed source of supply required for production of goods and services. It also leads to increased concentration of economic power in few hands. For ex: a coal mining company and thermal power project merge with each other in order to get more benefit from the market.

3. **Conglomerate Merger:** This is a situation where, joining of two or more companies whose businesses are not related with each other either vertically or horizontally. The two companies which are merged with each other are totally different and they are unrelated to the market. The main objective of the merger is to get the benefits of diversification aspects in the business. It may also lead to concentration of economic power in few hands.

   Mergers, acquisition and amalgamation and takeovers are important features of corporate structural changes. They have played an important role in external growth of a number of leading companies the world over.

Amalgamations

Amalgamation is also called as consolidation. It refers to a situation where two or more existing companies are combined into a new business company for the business purpose. The old company shareholders are to exist and the amount will be paid by the new company either in the form of cash or shares or debentures. In amalgamation, the new company will take over the business of existing two or more companies. There is a difference between merger and amalgamation. In case of merger, one existing company takeover the business of another existing company while in case of amalgamation, a new company takes over the business of two or more existing companies.

Acquisition/Takeover

An acquisition may be defined as an act of acquiring effective control by one company over assets or management of another company without any combination of companies. In acquisition, two or more companies may remain independent, separate legal entity, but there may be change in control of companies. A takeover may also be defined as obtaining of control over management of a company by another.

Causes for Mergers or Acquisitions or Amalgamations

The following factors are the important causes for mergers, amalgamations, acquisitions of business firms.

1. Fair value
2. Elimination of duplication
3. Large savings
4. Taxation

5. Competition reduction
6. Good financial planning
7. Expansion
8. Diversification
9. Integration
10. Government regulation

VALUATION RELATED TO MERGERS AND ACQUISITIONS

The methods of valuation related to mergers and acquisitions can be broadly categorized into three types, namely market based method, income based method, as well as asset based method. All these methods carry a significant degree of importance in the context of mergers and acquisitions. There are numerous elements, which ascertain whether a particular firm should be acquired or not.

The financial steadiness of the firm, which is to be taken over, is quite important to find out. In addition, the financial track record over the last few years and trends demonstrated in the macroeconomic ratio and indices require to be analyzed. Among the methods of valuation related to mergers and acquisitions, the market based method might be regarded as more appropriate, nevertheless, all the valuation methods are crucial, taking into account the condition that is prevalent at the time when a merger or acquisition is going to take place.

Methods of Valuation Related to Mergers and Acquisitions

The methods of valuation associated with mergers and acquisitions can be broadly classified into the following types:

1. Market-based Method
2. Income-based Method
3. Asset-based Method

(1) Market-based Method

In valuation of mergers and acquisitions with the help of market-based method, the different attributes of the firm which is going to be acquired are compared with the similar types of attributes of other firms in the market. These firms (not the firm in question) normally have a market value that has been set up earlier. Furthermore, some other factors are to be taken into consideration before the comparison of the different attributes is done. First of all, which elements need comparison is to be distinguished and secondly, which are the firms that are going to act as comparables. Public sector corporations involved in the same type of industry (of the target firm) can be chosen as comparables. Nevertheless, if the target firm is not registered with a stock exchange or is relatively small in its size than the public sector corporations, comparing it with the public sector corporations may not be useful. In these circumstances, public and private databases are there and these are basically commercial databases.

The other features that require to be compared are net earnings, gross revenue, and book value of assets. As soon as all the information has been gathered, a broad-based comparison is performed for obtaining the value of the target firm.

The market-based method can be further categorized into the following types:

- Market multiple (or price-earnings ratio) of comparable firms for firms that are not listed
- Market capitalization of listed firms

(2) Income-based Method

The income-based method of valuation associated with mergers and acquisitions takes into account the net present value. The net present value of earnings that is going to be received in the future is taken into consideration through the implementation of a mathematical formula.

The income-based method can be further classified into the following types:

- Cost to create technique
- Free cash flow/discounted cash flow method
- Capitalized earnings technique

(3) Asset-based Method

This method of valuation related to mergers and acquisitions is applied while the target firm is running at a loss. In this kind of a situation, the valuation of the assets of the firm at loss is estimated. Besides this procedure, the income and market-based method can also be applied. Valuation received with the help of these procedures may render small values. Nevertheless, there is a probability that these methods would produce the true condition of the assets of the target firm.

The asset based method can be further categorized into the following forms:

- Valuation of Intangible Assets
- Economic Book Value or Net Adjusted Asset Value
- Liquidation Value

Benefits of Mergers and Acquisitions

The following factors are benefits to the corporate sector for mergers and acquisition:

Merger refers to the process of combination of two companies, whereby a new company is formed. An acquisition refers to the process whereby a company simply purchases another company. In this case there is no new company being formed. Benefits of *mergers and acquisitions* are quite a handful.

Mergers and acquisitions generally succeed in generating cost efficiency through the implementation of economies of scale. It may also lead to tax gains and can even lead to a revenue enhancement through *market share* gain. The principal benefits from mergers and acquisitions can be listed as increased value generation, increase in cost efficiency and increase in market share. Mergers and acquisitions often lead to an increased value generation for the company. It is expected that the *shareholder value* of a firm after mergers or acquisitions would be greater than the sum of the shareholder values of the parent companies.

An increase in cost efficiency is affected through the procedure of mergers and acquisitions. This is because mergers and acquisitions lead to economies of scale. This in turn promotes cost efficiency. As the parent firms amalgamate to form a bigger new firm the scale of operations of the new firm increases. As output production rises there are chances that the cost per unit of production will come down.

An increase in market share is one of the plausible benefits of *mergers and acquisitions*. In case a financially strong company acquires a relatively distressed one, the resultant organization can experience a substantial increase in market share. The new firm is usually more cost-efficient and competitive as compared to its financially weak parent organization.

It can be noted that mergers and acquisitions prove to be useful in the following scenario: Firstly, when a business firm wishes to make its presence felt in a *new market*. Secondly, when a business organization wants to avail some administrative benefits. Thirdly, when a business firm is in the process of introduction of new products. New products are developed by the R&D wing of a company.

Employee Benefits under Mergers and Acquisitions in US

The 'Employee Retirement Income Security Act' was enacted in 1974. It is also known as ERISA. Since then programs for employee benefit have been a major component of the balance and income statements of US business organizations.

Current law promulgations have attached supreme importance to the presence of post retirement pension schemes and welfare benefit schemes as a part of corporate obligation. As a result employee benefit programs are affecting the viability of mergers and acquisitions in the USA.

MERGERS AND ACQUISITIONS LAWS: THE INDIAN SCENARIO

Indian competition law grants a maximum time period of 210 days for the determination of the combination, which comprises acquisitions, mergers, amalgamations and the like. One needs to take note of the fact that this stated time frame is clearly distinct from the minimum compulsory wait period for applicants.

As per the law, the compulsory period of waiting for applicants can either be 210 days starting from the day of notice filing or receipt of the Commission's order, whichever occurs earlier.

The threshold limits for firms entering business combinations are substantially high under the Indian law. The threshold limits are set either in terms of the asset value or in terms the firm's turnover. Indian threshold limits are greater than those for the EU. They are twice as high when compared with UK.

The Indian law also provides for the modern day phenomenon of merger and acquisitions, which are cross border in nature. As per the law domestic nexus is a pre-requisite for notification on this type of combinations.

It can be noted that Competition Act, 2002, has undergone a recent amendment. This has replaced the voluntary notification regime with a mandatory regime. Of the total number of 106 countries, which possess competition laws only 9 are thought to be credited with a voluntary notification regime. Voluntary notification regimes are generally associated with business uncertainties.

Post-combination, if firms are seen to be involved in anti-competitive practices de-merger shows the way out.

Indian Mergers and Acquisitions Laws

Indian Income Tax Act has provision for tax concessions for mergers/demergers between two Indian companies. These mergers/demergers need to satisfy the conditions pertaining to Section 2(19AA) and Section 2(1B) of the Indian Income Tax Act as per the applicable situation.

In case of an Indian merger when transfer of shares occurs for a company they are entitled to a specific exemption from the capital gains tax under the "Indian I-T Act". These companies can either be of Indian origin or foreign ones.

A different set of rules is however applicable for the 'foreign company mergers'. It is a situation where an Indian company owns the new company formed out of the merger of two foreign companies.

It can be noted that for foreign company mergers the share allotment in the merged foreign company in place of shares surrendered by the amalgamating foreign company would be termed as a transfer, which would be taxable under the Indian tax law.

Also as per conditions set under section 5(1), the 'Indian I-T Act' states that, global income accruing to an Indian company would also be included under the head of 'scope of income' for the Indian company.

History of Mergers and Acquisitions

Merger and acquisitions have evolved in five stages. The mergers and acquisitions are triggered by economic factors. The macroeconomic environment, which includes the growth in GDP, interest rates and monetary policies play a key role in designing the process of mergers or acquisitions between companies or organizations

First Stage Mergers

The first wave mergers commenced from 1897 to 1904. During this phase merger occurred between companies, which enjoyed monopoly over their lines of production like railroads, electricity etc. the first wave mergers that occurred during the aforesaid time period were mostly horizontal mergers that took place between heavy manufacturing industries.

End of 1st stage Merger

Majority of the mergers that were conceived during the 1st phase ended in failure since they could not achieve the desired efficiency. The failure was fuelled by the slowdown of the economy in 1903, followed by the stock market crash of 1904. The legal framework was not supportive either. The Supreme Court passed the mandate that the anticompetitive mergers could be halted using the Sherman Act.

Second Stage Mergers

The second wave mergers that took place from 1916 to 1929, focused on the mergers between oligopolies, rather than monopolies as in the previous phase. The economic boom that followed the post World War I gave rise to these mergers. Technological developments like the development of railroads and transportation by motor vehicles provided the necessary infrastructure for such mergers or acquisitions to take place. The government policy encouraged firms to work in unison. This policy was implemented in the 1920s.

The 2nd wave mergers that took place were mainly horizontal or conglomerate in nature. The industries that went for merger during this phase were producers of primary metals, food products, petroleum products, transportation equipments and chemicals. The investment banks played a pivotal role in facilitating the mergers and acquisitions.

End of 2nd Stage Mergers

The 2nd wave mergers ended with the stock market crash in 1929 and the great depression. The tax relief that was provided inspired mergers in the 1940s.

Third Stage Mergers

The mergers that took place during this period (1965-69) were mainly conglomerate mergers. Mergers were inspired by high stock prices, interest rates and strict enforcement of antitrust laws. The bidder firms in the 3rd wave merger were smaller than the Target Firm. Mergers were financed from equities; the investment banks no longer played an important role.

End of the 3rd Stage Merger

The 3rd wave merger ended with the plan of the Attorney General to split conglomerates in 1968. It was also due to the poor performance of the conglomerates. Some mergers in the 1970s, have set precedence. The most prominent ones were the INCO-ESB merger; United Technologies and OTIS Elevator Merger are the merger between Colt Industries and Garlock Industries

Fourth Stage Merger

The 4th wave merger that started from 1981 and ended by 1989, was characterized by acquisition targets that were much larger in size as compared to the 3rd wave mergers. Mergers took place between the oil and gas industries, pharmaceutical industries, banking and airline industries. Foreign takeovers became common with most of them being hostile takeovers. The 4th Wave mergers ended with anti takeover laws, Financial Institutions Reform and the Gulf War.

Fifth Stage Merger

The 5th Wave Merger (1992-2000) was inspired by globalization, stock market boom and deregulation. The 5th Wave Merger took place mainly in the banking and telecommunications industries. They were mostly equity financed rather than debt financed. The mergers were driven by long-term rather than short-term profit motives. The 5th Wave Merger ended with the burst in the stock market bubble.

Many economic factors have contributed to its development. There are several other factors that have impeded their growth. As long as economic units of production exist mergers and acquisitions would continue for an ever-expanding economy.

TERMS RELATING TO MERGERS AND ACQUISITIONS

The important terms that are used to explain the concepts of merger and acquisition.

Asset Stripping: When a company acquires another and sells it in parts expecting that the funds generated would match the costs of acquisition, it is known as asset stripping.

Black Knight: The company that makes a hostile takeover is known as the Black Knight.

Dawn Raid: It is a process of buying shares of the target company with the expectation that the market prices may fall till the acquisition is completed.

Demerger or Spin off: During the process of corporate restructuring, a part of the company may break up and set up as a new company and this is known as demerger. Zeneca and Argos are good examples in this regard that split from ICI and American Tobacco respectively.

Carve-out: This is a case of selling a small portion of the company as an Initial Public Offering.

Greenmail: Greenmail is a situation where the target company purchases back its own shares from the bidding company at a higher price.

Grey Knight: A grey knight is a company that takes over another company and its intentions are not clear.

Hostile Takeover: Hostile bids occur when acquisitions take place without the consent of the directors of the target company. This confrontation on the part of the directors of the target company may be short lived and the hostile takeover may end up being friendly. Most American and British companies like the phenomenon of hostile takeovers while there are some more which do not like such unfriendly takeovers.

Macaroni Defense: Macaroni Defense is a strategy that is taken up to prevent any hostile takeovers. The issue of bonds that can be redeemed at a higher price if the company is taken over does this.

Management Buy In: When a company is purchased and the investors bring in their managers to control the company, it is known as management buy-in.

Management Buy Out: In a management buyout, the managers of a company purchase it with support from venture capitalists.

Poison Pill or Suicide Pill Defense: This is a strategy that is taken by the target company to make itself less appealing for a hostile takeover. The bondholders are given the right to redeem their bonds at a premium should a takeover occur.

Mergers and Acquisitions in India

The process of mergers and acquisitions has gained substantial importance in today's corporate world. This process is extensively used for restructuring the business organizations. In India, the concept of mergers and acquisitions was initiated by the government bodies. Some well known financial organizations also took the necessary initiatives to restructure the corporate sector of India by adopting the mergers and acquisitions policies. The Indian economic reform since 1991, has opened up a whole lot of challenges both in the domestic and international spheres. The increased competition in the global market has prompted the Indian companies to go for mergers and acquisitions as an important strategic choice. The trends of mergers and acquisitions in India have changed over the years. The immediate effects of the mergers and acquisitions have also been diverse across the various sectors of the Indian economy.

Among the different Indian sectors that have resorted to mergers and acquisitions in recent times, telecom, finance, FMCG, construction materials, automobile industry and steel industry are worth mentioning. With the increasing number of Indian companies opting for mergers and acquisitions, India is now one of the leading nations in the world in terms of mergers and acquisitions.

The merger and acquisition business deals in India amounted to $ 40 billion during the initial 2 months in the year 2007. The total estimated value of mergers and acquisitions in India for 2007 was greater than $ 100 billion. It is twice the amount of mergers and acquisitions in 2006.

Latest Trends

Till recent past, the incidence of Indian entrepreneurs acquiring foreign enterprises was not so common. The situation has undergone a sea change in the last couple of years. Acquisition of foreign companies by the Indian businesses has been the latest trend in the Indian corporate sector.

There are different factors that played their parts in facilitating the mergers and acquisitions in India. Favorable government policies, buoyancy in economy, additional liquidity in the corporate sector, and dynamic attitudes of the Indian entrepreneurs are the key factors behind the changing trends of mergers and acquisitions in India.

The Indian IT and ITES sectors have already proved their potential in the global market. The other Indian sectors are also following the same trend. The increased participation of the Indian companies in the global corporate sector has further facilitated the merger and acquisition activities in India.

Recently the Indian companies have undertaken some important acquisitions. Some of those are as follows:

Hindalco acquired Canada based Novelis. The deal involved transaction of $ 5,982 million. Tata Steel acquired Corus Group plc. The acquisition deal amounted to $ 12,000 million. Dr. Reddy's Labs acquired Betapharm through a deal worth of $ 597 million. Ranbaxy Labs acquired Terapia SA. The deal amounted to $ 324 million. Suzlon Energy acquired Hansen Group through a deal of $ 565 million. The acquisition of Daewoo Electronics Corp. by Videocon involved transaction of $ 729 million. HPCL acquired Kenya Petroleum Refinery Ltd... The deal amounted to $500 million. VSNL acquired Teleglobe through a deal of $ 239 million.

When it comes to mergers and acquisitions deals in India, the total number was 287 from the month of January to May in 2007. It has involved monetary transaction of US $ 47.37 billion. Out of these 287 merger and acquisition deals, there have been 102 cross country deals with a total valuation of US $ 28.19 billion.

CASE STUDY: NTPC

National Thermal Power Corporation is India's largest power generation company. In Forbes Global 2000 list of companies NTPC is raked 411. This power generation company established in 1975 aims at becoming an integrated power commanding height with total power value chain. Total installed capacity of NTPC is 29,394 MW (mega watt), comprising 15 thermal power stations with installed capacity of 23,395 MW, 7 gas based power generating stations with capacity of 3955 MW and 4 joint venture power stations with capacity of 1794 MW. NTPC plans to have an installed capacity of 75,000 MW by 2017. During 2007-08, NTPC accounted for 28.5% of total power generated in India. Till March 2008 NTPC's installed capacity was slightly more than 19% of aggregate installed capacity of India.

NTPC had its inception in 1975 as a unit for developing electrical power for India. Initially set up as a public sector undertaking, National Thermal Power Corporation made its initial public offering in 2004 with 5.25% of its share. NTPC has 15 thermal power stations located in Badarpur (Delhi), Dadri (U.P.), Rihand (U.P.), Tanda (U.P.), Singrauli (U.P.), Unchahar (U.P.), Korba (Chattisgarh), Sipat (Chattisgarh), Simhadri (Andhra), Ramagundam (Andhra), Talcher Kaniha (Orissa), Talcher thermal (Orissa), Farakka (West Bengal), Kahalgaon (Bihar), and Vindhyachal (Madhya Pradesh). Total commissioned capacity of these thermal power stations is 23,895 MW Gas or liquid fuel based power plants of NTPC are located in Kawas (Gujarat), Jhanor – Gandhar (Gujarat), Auraiya (U.P.), Dadri (U.P.), Faridabad (Haryana), Anta (Rajasthan), Kayakulam (Kerala). These seven liquid/gas based power stations have a commissioned capacity of 3955 MW. NTPC has additional four power generating stations in Durgapur, Bhilai, Rourkela and Ratnagiri set up in joint collaboration. Products and services of NTPC Power generation is the main activity of NTPC which has an installed capacity of 27,850 MW shared by 22 generating stations. Four generating stations in joint venture have an additional capacity of 2044 MW. Consultancy in fields of water supply and treatment, fossil fuel based thermal power stations, environment engineering, and cogeneration plants. Consultancy service has got NTPC over 435 domestic and international orders. Power Management Institute in Noida provides classroom training in power plant operations and management. Full Scope Replica Training Simulator for coal and gas based power plants makes training meaningful and effective. Students from outside NTPC can also undergo these training schedules.

Finance

NTPC as on March 2008 achieved sales of US $7.84 billion and profit of US $1.6 billion. Total asset worth amounted to US $20.34 billion.

Awards

NTPC has won a number of awards for itself, some of them being:

- Great places to work' for 2008 awarded by Confederation of Indian Industries
- Customer excellence award' for 2007 conferred by SAP
- Golden peacock global award for excellence in corporate governance' for 2007

Source: www.economywatch.com

INTERNATIONAL MERGERS AND ACQUISITIONS

International mergers and acquisitions are growing day by day. These are taking place beyond the boundaries of a particular country. International mergers and acquisitions are also termed as global mergers and acquisitions or cross-border mergers and acquisitions.

Globalization and worldwide financial reforms have collectively contributed towards the development of international mergers and acquisitions to a substantial extent. International mergers and acquisitions are taking place in different forms, for example horizontal mergers, vertical mergers, conglomerate mergers, congeneric mergers, reverse mergers, dilutive mergers, accretive mergers and others.

International mergers and acquisitions are performed for the purpose of obtaining some strategic benefits in the markets of a particular country. With the help of international mergers and acquisitions, multinational corporations can enjoy a number of advantages, which include economies of scale and market dominance.

International mergers and acquisitions play an important role behind the growth of a company. These deals or transactions help a large number of companies penetrate into new markets fast and attain economies of scale. They also stimulate foreign direct investment or FDI.

The reputed international mergers and acquisitions agencies also provide educational programs and training in order to grow the expertise of the merger and acquisition professionals working in the global merger and acquisitions sector.

The rules and regulations regarding international mergers and acquisitions keep on changing constantly and it is mandatory that the parties to international mergers and acquisitions get themselves updated with the various amendments. Numerous investment bank professionals, consultants and attorneys are there to offer valuable and knowledgeable recommendations to the merger and acquisition clients.

Methods of Financing International Mergers and Acquisitions

Usually, the following methods are implemented for funding international mergers and acquisitions:

- Financing (or taking loans)
- Cash

- Factoring
- Hybrid Financing

Significant International Mergers and Acquisitions

Following are the instances of the major international mergers and acquisitions:

- The merger of British Petroleum (BP) with Amoco (erstwhile Standard Oil of Indiana)
- The acquisition of Mannesmann AG by Vodafone Airtouch PLC
- The merger of Exxon with Mobil (The name of the company formed as a result of the merger is ExxonMobil)
- The acquisition of Air Touch Communications by the Vodafone Group
- The acquisition of Compaq by Hewlett-Packard
- The acquisition of Shell Transport & Trading Company by Royal Dutch Petroleum Company
- The merger of Banc One Corporation with JPMorgan Chase & Company

FACTORS AFFECTING INTERNATIONAL MERGERS AND ACQUISITIONS

The following elements influence the international mergers and acquisitions from many aspects:

- Corporate governance
- Company Acts
- The capacity of average workers
- Expectation of the consumers
- Political features of a country
- Tradition and culture of a country

Global Trends for Merger and Acquisition

Trend essentially refers to the observed long-term movement in a time series data. Trend estimates are seasonally adjusted through an averaging process. Merger and acquisition trends provide an idea about the market movements. They are seen to affect an economy's product market, money market, and labor market. Global markets are also considerably influenced by the merger and acquisition trends.

Global Merger and Acquisition Trends for 2006 and 2007

In the year 2007 and 2006, were marked by a spate of mergers and acquisitions all over the globe in both developing and developed countries. The general trend was that, there was a decline in the number of public sector undertakings along with a hike in the number of private sector enterprises. This was due to the fact that many public sector organizations worldwide were either acquired by large private sector enterprises or merged with them.

The explanation to this merger and acquisition trend as observed in 2006 and 2007 lay in the robust growth recorded by the Private Equity Funds. The other factors propelling this trend were the emphasis on short term earnings growth and the strict regulatory structure of public sector enterprises.

This merger and acquisition trend towards increased privatization of public sector holdings was observed in Europe, Brazil, North America, and China. Europe in that period hosted a strong investment market, which catered to the public to private sector transition of companies. For China mergers and acquisitions from public to private business enterprises got government approval in 2006. Private equity transactions had been the buzzword for the world economy in 2007 and 2006. The real estate sector and the energy sector witnessed much of this type of activity. Private equity firms were working overnight for augmenting proprietary deal flows. China was a unique case in point. There the powerful trend towards mergers and acquisitions involving private equity dealings comprised a lot of policy and regional diversity. A great amount of equity capital flowed into China from US, Japan, Israel, and Europe as retail sector investments. This was primarily aimed at tapping China's heightened domestic consumer demand. Focus shifted to the northern and western regions of China as costs escalated for the commercial hubs alongside the eastern seacoast. In the US, private equity funds succeeded in raising more than $200 billion in this period for international merger and acquisition dealings.

As these types of funds usually possessed a time frame of 3 to 5 years for putting the new invested capital to work, they were expected by the analysts to power heightened merger and acquisition activities across major global markets for the coming decade.

For Europe the general prediction was that of a high transactional demand related to private equity. Analysts observed that certain European markets were characterized by different financial advantages and tax structures. Western European nations possessed well oiled legal machinery and conducive investment climates. In particular Britain exhibited a strong market for public to private investments.

After the accession of nations like Poland, Czech Republic and Hungary into the EU, a section of European funds for private equity were seen to be abstaining from applying the 'emerging market discount' for investment in those nations.

Equity investment in Brazil turned attractive with the program called Novo Mercado. Brazilian pension funds turned out to be a prime investment force. Their bankruptcy code got a revision. The elected government was supportive of a free market structure.

In North America domestic dealings in M&A executed by private equity investors of USA displayed a robust international component. The observed trend was that a majority of the funds wanted to secure offshore partners for distribution, contract manufacturing or joint ventures. This kind of cross-border transactions entailed a careful planning for tax obligations arising out of fund repatriation. Global leveraged buyouts figures for 2006 were above US$ 800 billion. This was more than twice the comparable figure for 2005. It constituted around 20 % of US international mergers and acquisitions. However, even then it was not a significant component of the world equity and debt market. In 2006 North America saw vigorous leveraged buyout activities, which amounted to half of the world activity in that field. Europe witnessed a fairly heightened activity in the arena of leveraged buyouts; while Asia had a relatively slow increase. France, Netherlands, and Germany were the biggest European buyout markets in 2006. The private equity has indeed become a major component of twenty-first century's capital market.

SUMMARY

Survival in the market is a crucial point at present global scenario. The competition in the market reduces the growth of individual commercial enterprise. The growth is measured in terms of sales, profit and assets. Increase in the sales volume reveals that, the firm has been able to maintain its competitive edge in the market. Market is a combination of desires and dreams of crores of consumers. In order to survive an organization in the market, the firm should increase its operational efficiency and realistic environment of the market composition. A commercial enterprise must grow internally or externally. A commercial enterprise must concentrate on increasing its operational efficiency. The external growth of the firm is possible through combining or joining with other firms or acquiring other firms. There are various forms of business combinations which can result in growth. The various combination programs had the objectives of business expansion.

Key Terms

1. **Monopoly:** A situation where a producer of particular goods or services controls the market, having eliminated all potential or real competitors, or is in possession of a patent to which no other producer has access. The elimination of competition can enable the producer to dictate prices and thereby earn excessive or monopoly profits.
2. **Acquisitions and Mergers:** Large stockholders in a closely held company want to convert their assets into marketable securities or cash, frequently in anticipation of high inheritance taxes. Poor health or old age makes them willing to merge at an attractive price.

   A rapidly growing company may absorb a declining firm because the latter has a large amount of cash that is much needed by the growing company. For tax reasons, the owners of the declining company prefer to hold stock rather than to receive a high cash dividend.

   A company may have suffered severe losses for several years and may have accumulated a large tax credit. If this company absorbs another firm with high profits, the past losses can be used to offset profits of the second firm and thereby to avoid paying about half of these profits to the government as income tax.

   The combined operation resulting from a merger should have clear economic advantages that were not available when the companies operated independently.

   Mergers involve more than identifying a major economic advantage and negotiating a deal. The two enterprises have to be fitted together into a new composite institute. Unless this true amalgamation is done effectively, many of the anticipated benefits may not materialize.

QUESTIONS

1. What is meant by Mergers?
2. Explain the concept of Acquisition.
3. Distinguish between Merger and Acquisition.